AN ECONOMIC HISTORY OF MODERN BRITAIN

MACHINES AND NATIONAL RIVALRIES (1887–1914)
WITH AN EPILOGUE (1914–1929)

AN ECONOMIC HISTORY OF MODERN BRITAIN

MACHINES AND NATIONAL RIVALRIES (1887–1914) WITH AN EPILOGUE (1914–1929)

By

SIR JOHN CLAPHAM

CAMBRIDGE
AT THE UNIVERSITY PRESS
1968

CAMBRIDGE UNIVERSITY PRESS
Cambridge, New York, Melbourne, Madrid, Cape Town, Singapore, São Paulo, Delhi

Cambridge University Press
The Edinburgh Building, Cambridge CB2 8RU, UK

Published in the United States of America by Cambridge University Press, New York

www.cambridge.org
Information on this title: www.cambridge.org/9780521046671

First published 1938
Reprinted 1951, 1963, 1968
This digitally printed version 2008

A catalogue record for this publication is available from the British Library

ISBN 978-0-521-04665-7 hardback (volume 1)
ISBN 978-0-521-10107-3 paperback (volume 1)
ISBN 978-0-521-04666-4 hardback (volume 2)
ISBN 978-0-521-10100-4 paperback (volume 2)
ISBN 978-0-521-04667-1 hardback (volume 3)
ISBN 978-0-521-10108-0 paperback (volume 3)
ISBN 978-0-521-75798-0 paperback (3 volume set)

PREFACE

In the Preface to the first volume of this book, published in 1926, I said that I hoped to bring the story down to 1914, "with at least an epilogue dealing with what I take to be the place of the decade 1914–24 in the economic history of Britain". This programme has now been carried out to the best of my ability, except that perhaps I might now say the years 1914–29 instead of the decade 1914–24. There was never any intention of writing a narrative history of the war years—aspects of that story have been admirably told by others—but only of suggesting some of the effects of the jolt then given to the British economy on its development. The epilogue has been written like an essay without the full apparatus of references and footnotes.

One has sometimes wondered whether 1914 has not slipped too far away to serve as a good stopping place for the narrative. In certain moods it seems far away beyond words; but these I think are either the moods of the poet—if an economic writer may link himself with anything so high—or, much oftener, those of one's common self that lives from day to day fancying problems and situations to be new that in deed are not. To the historical self which "von dreitausend Jahren sich weiss Rechenschaft zu geben" the war years are very near, and no later group of years is half so significant. And for the historical craftsman none is nearly so convenient. Besides, in British economic history—however it may be in German or Russian—they brought far fewer new things than accelerations. Changes that might have been anticipated within the next generation or two came in ten years. In some technical fields, invention and adjustment to fresh conditions meant not profit or loss but life or death: they were quickened. Underground forces whose existence was demonstrable, but whose power to break the crust was doubtful, broke it. There were new things, but the dominant impression is one of a rather surprising continuity. Therefore the year 1914 and the general scheme of the epilogue have been retained.

The changing importance and the more or less fluid nature of the different parts of the subject-matter have led to an arrangement of topics different at several points from that adopted in Vol. II. If it does not explain and justify itself nothing that can be said in a Preface will justify it; but I may mention that there was not, in my opinion, enough change in the British scene between 1886 and 1914 to carry a chapter corresponding to Ch. I of Vol. I or Ch. XII of Vol. II. Had the narrative come down to 1936, then a case might have been made out for a complete picture of the newly made-up "Face of the Country", instead of the scribbled suggestions that will be found in the epilogue.

Of the sources there is not much to be said. Periodical and technical literature becomes so voluminous in this period that a lifetime would not exhaust it. I have had to be satisfied with a selection, which I can only hope has been judiciously made. For general commercial history I have relied throughout principally on the annual *History and Review* of the *Economist*. Other journals began to do similar work at various dates during the period; but the continuity and uniform tradition of the *Economist* make it a particularly good source for the general historian who has not time to follow out the history of each trade thoroughly in its local and technical press. That is the function of the writers of trade monographs—of whom I could wish there were more.

I was recently in receipt of a letter from a student—I think an undergraduate student—of the earlier volumes, who begged me to give him with this one a bibliography and not so much *op. cit.* in the footnotes. I have tried to meet the second request, which seems to me reasonable. A bibliography I have not compiled. A complete bibliography of this subject for this period would be longer than the book. A bibliography of all the books, newspapers, articles and official publications which I have read at one time or another—many of which I have not utilised—would also be very long. Those that I have utilised effectively are all quoted and dated in the footnotes. Anyone interested in the study or criticism of my sources for any chapter or section will find them there. He will have no difficulty in finding others. I cannot see whom I should help by falling in with what in my heart I regard as the rather pedantic and ostentatious tradition of the formal bibliography in a book which contains footnotes. And if I did make a bibliography how should I insert my own memories, quite a useful little source for this volume? References to some of them also will be found in the footnotes.

Of my colleagues at King's I have to thank the late W. H. Macaulay for information about building, Dr H. McCombie for chemical, and Dr D. Stockdale for metallurgical, information; and Professor Pigou for loans, advice and encouragement. I have had advice, especially co-operative advice, from Mr C. R. Fay; advice about steel from Mr D. L. Burn; and a warning against one of his own early publications from Mr D. H. Robertson. I dissent from his view of it. I am indebted to Mr C. K. Hobson of the Board of Trade for important help in procuring information; to Mr A. M. Stephen, of Alexander Stephen and Son—who have been building ships without a break since 1750—for making inquiries for me in Glasgow; and to my son for checking what I have written about printing machinery. Domestic industry has also provided type-writing, the unavoidable Index, and a little helpful criticism of my less lucid passages.

And so a plan designed vaguely more than thirty years ago, and first drawn out in some detail more than twenty, is a plan no longer. *Laus Deo.*

J. H. CLAPHAM

Cambridge
13 *September*, 1937

CONTENTS

BOOK IV

MACHINES AND NATIONAL RIVALRIES

Chapter I. THE INDUSTRIAL STATE, ITS NEIGHBOURS AND VICISSITUDES, 1887–1914

Chapter II. AGRICULTURE IN THE INDUSTRIAL STATE

Chapter II. AGRICULTURE IN THE INDUSTRIAL STATE, *contd*

Chapter III. THE COURSE OF INDUSTRIAL CHANGE

Chapter IV. LIMITED LIABILITY, JOINT-STOCK AMALGAMATION AND CO-OPERATION

Chapter V. COMMERCIAL AND INDUSTRIAL ORGANISATION

Chapter V. COMMERCIAL AND INDUSTRIAL ORGANISATION, *contd*

Chapter VI. COMMUNICATIONS

Chapter VII. THE ECONOMIC ACTIVITIES OF THE STATE

Chapter VII. THE ECONOMIC ACTIVITIES OF THE STATE, *contd*

Chapter VIII. LIFE AND LABOUR IN INDUSTRIAL BRITAIN

Chapter VIII. LIFE AND LABOUR IN INDUSTRIAL BRITAIN, *contd*

EPILOGUE

DIAGRAMS

BOOK IV

MACHINES AND NATIONAL RIVALRIES

Every morning when the world woke up, some new machinery had started running. Every night while the world had supper, it was running still. WINSTON CHURCHILL

Romance, the season-tickets mourn,
He never ran to catch his train
. . . . and all unseen
Romance brought up the nine-fifteen
RUDYARD KIPLING

The superiority of the United States to England is ultimately as certain as the next eclipse.
Economist, March 8, 1851

Wenn wir noch hundert Jahre Frieden haben, werden wir England tot gemacht haben.
A GERMAN INDUSTRIALIST TO GENERAL VON STEIN, *c.* 1900

About this time he . . . gave a definition of Liberalism which would have stood as a very excellent statement of modern Socialism.
PHILIP SNOWDEN, OF H. H. ASQUITH

CHAPTER I

THE INDUSTRIAL STATE, ITS NEIGHBOURS AND VICISSITUDES, 1887–1914

In the late Victorian years and after them, pressmen, politicians, and rural economists said every now and then that agriculture was still England's greatest industry, trying, as it would seem, to convince the average urbanised Englishman of something which to him was not apparent. In a sense they were right, though there are so many ways of defining an industry and of measuring its size that such comparisons can seldom be exact. At least it was true, to the end of the nineteenth century, that "agricultural" was the label for the largest of the main social-economic groupings of the population of Britain. Even in 1911 the agricultural group was only exceeded by the equally wide group officially described as engaged in the "manufacture of metals".[1] But the saying of the rural economists had become more nearly false every year. In 1851, when Victoria was still a young wife, roughly a quarter of the grown men in Britain had been linked directly with agriculture; and of the males over ten years old one in six was an agricultural labourer. The latter figure had fallen by 1881 to less than one in ten. By 1911 it would be below one in twenty. There would then be many more British coal-miners than British agricultural labourers, although the whole miscellaneous agricultural group—farmers, market gardeners, crofters, fruit growers, labourers—would still be a good deal larger than the whole mining and quarrying group, in which wage-earners are so many, employers and independent workers so very few. But among the occupied people of the country, even the whole agricultural group, which had still amounted to more than 12 per cent. in 1881, and to nearly 11 per cent. in 1891, had fallen by 1911 to a bare 8 per cent.[2] It was criticised sometimes for failure to do more towards feeding the rest of the people; and some of the criticism was merited. Yet in view of its size,

[1] See e.g. the tables going back to 1881 in the *Survey of Industrial Relations* (*Committee on Industry and Trade*), 1926, pp. 416–17.

[2] *Survey of Industrial Relations*, as above and Census of 1851. *Ages and Occupations* (1852–3, LXXXVIII).

success in raising a fair proportion of all the essential foodstuffs except wheat and sugar was no mean achievement. The countries which fed, or nearly fed, themselves all had a much more even balance of agriculture with manufactures and commerce. A balance—a lack of balance—such as that in Britain had not been known before in the records of great nations.

Another commercial policy, in Peel's day or later—had it been politically workable—might have kept the agricultural group a great deal more prosperous and a little larger; but it is not easy to see how any change in policy or control could have affected the ultimate balance much, if other conditions had remained the same. In Peel's day there had been a race between life and food. As he watched it he had put over his helm. The crowds in the island had grown more dense ever since, in spite of opportunities for emigration unequalled in the world's history. Emigration from the United Kingdom and from Britain had reached a peak just before 1886. Something like 675,000 people had left Britain for good in five years (1881–5) compared with perhaps 2,250,000 during the previous twenty-seven years.[1] There was another, though lower, peak in 1887–8; after that a decade during which emigration was relatively small; a rise in the twentieth century to a peak in 1906–7; a very sharp drop in 1908; and the final rise to a plateau in 1910–13 when for four successive years well over 200,000 people, and in two of the four more than 260,000 people, most of them British, left the United Kingdom annually.[2] Yet the British population, which had been 29,709,000 in 1881, had grown to 37,000,000 by 1901 and by 1911 to 40,830,000. So powerfully worked that combination which had dominated social and economic history for over a century of a high birth-rate and a relatively low death-rate. The death-rate was becoming absolutely low. By 1911–14 it was slipping down towards 14 per thousand of the population.[3] The birth-rate, though it had been falling slowly but smoothly since the 'seventies, was still above 24 per thousand in 1913. With a population growth such as this, the crowds in streets, mines, factories and offices would in a few

[1] See the discussion in vol. II. 232 and in the *Survey*, pp. 65 *sqq.*, for the uncertainties in migration figures. The fact that nearly all statistics are for the United Kingdom, not Britain, increases the uncertainty.

[2] The "Excess of outward over inward British Passengers in the Traffic between the U.K. and Extra-European Countries" was: 1910, 233,709; 1911, 261,809; 1912, 268,485; 1913, 241,997. *Survey of Industrial Relations*, p. 66.

[3] It averaged 15·5 for 1901–10 and 14·0 in 1913.

years have been as dense as ever, even if the people on the land could have been doubled; and the most fervent agrarian reformer did not imagine that doubling was possible. No one now favoured Robert Owen's plan of cultivating the country altogether with the spade.

In the year of Victoria's jubilee, this crowded industrial country over which she presided probably shipped overseas—to supply its needs and add to its foreign investments—something like 20 or 25 per cent., by value, of everything that it produced. Twenty years later, in 1907, when such a calculation was first carefully made, the exports of United Kingdom produce and manufactures at the port of shipment were reckoned to be worth about 30 per cent. of the whole national output of goods of all sorts at their places of production—on farms, in mines, in factories; in both Britain and Ireland.[1] There had been no fundamental change in the character of British trade in the intervening years; but the exports in 1907, a year of very active international trade and foreign investment, were unusually high. The exports of 1887, whose total value was £221,000,000, included a little raw agricultural produce, mainly Irish, with some English wool; a few million pounds worth of crude metals—pig-iron, unwrought steel, pig-lead, copper ingots, unwrought tin; £10,000,000 worth of coal; £22,000,000 of manufactures of iron and steel, including cutlery and hardware but excluding machinery; of machinery £11,000,000 worth; of yarns and manufactures of wool, with ready-made clothing, £28,500,000 worth; and of cotton yarns and manufactures, £71,000,000 worth, or one-third of the whole export trade. The rest, worth about £70,000,000, was made up of manufactured and part-manufactured goods in endless variety. It was fortunate that this variety was increasing, though not so rapidly as could have been wished; for it was already obvious to men with vision that the great dependence on cotton exports which had marked the whole Victorian era had its dangers.[2] England could hardly equip the world with cotton machinery, as she did, and also supply it with finished cotton goods indefinitely.

The export of British produce and manufactures was associated with the huge re-export trade, the depot trade, in foreign

[1] *Final Report of the First Census of Production of the U.K.* (1907), 1912, Cd. 6320, p. 25.

[2] Cp. vol. II. 228–9.

and colonial merchandise, worth £59,000,000 in 1887. The list of merchandise was again bewilderingly varied, for there was no odd commodity on the face of the earth, from narwhal's tusks to divi-divi, which did not enter and leave some London warehouse; but raw wool and raw cotton were the main items —wool by far the most important—with coffee, tea, and latterly rubber as leading subsidiaries. In spite of an almost uninterrupted and precipitous fall in wholesale prices, the re-export trade was worth rather more in 1887 than it had been in 1877; and in years of active trade like 1882 and 1888 it was worth considerably more—a witness to its almost unimpaired vitality, based on the economic power of Britain overseas. If one article began to fall out of the list of re-exports there was usually another to replace it: at this very time rubber was thus replacing indigo.

Britain was a creditor not only for goods—grown, mined, made or warehoused—but also, as she had long been, for the services of her ships, her bankers, her insurance offices and her merchants; of her ships above all, for she owned about a third of the world's ocean-going tonnage, and of its ocean-going steamer tonnage nearly five-eighths.[1]

A country so placed was sensitive to the economic weather of the whole earth. A slight disturbance anywhere was registered on the delicate financial recording instruments of the City. Greater disturbances, such as might be caused by a failed monsoon in India or some drastic tariff change in the United States —the two countries which together took over a quarter of the British exports in the 'eighties—could bring trouble to whole industrial regions. What trouble, and what prosperity, wars among neighbours could bring had been shown in 1861–5 and 1871–3. Such uncontrollable accidents might accentuate that ebb and flow of economic activity, those alternations of good and bad times, to which the country had grown accustomed and about whose causes economists had argued, as yet not very profoundly. They had however at least suggested what is probably the truth, that their most general causes—or must one say antecedents?—had been the vicissitudes of the seasons and the rhythmic successions of confidence, over-confidence and discouragement in massed human investing, trading and in-

[1] Vol. II. 519, based on *Tables of Merchant Shipping*, 1902 (Cd. 329), pp. 48–51.

dustrial minds.[1] To these probable truths should be added the certain facts that the alternations might be intensified, or the spells of confidence and over-confidence actually initiated, by the equipping of nations in succession, and the re-equipping of those already once equipped, with durable, complicated, and expensive modern plant; or by an exciting event on the monetary plane such as a discovery of gold; and that both confidence and discouragement might be connected with war. Before 1887, one of the pauses between equipment and re-equipment in Britain, coinciding with the close of a fierce spell of first equipment in America, had given the trade union of the Boilermakers and Iron Shipbuilders three successive years (1884–6) in which on the average more than twenty per cent. of its members were out of work.[2]

For thirteen years before 1887 and for nine years after, fluctuations of good and bad trade, if viewed from the monetary side, showed as ripples on the surface of that great downward sweep of prices which brought with it, as was said in 1888, "a depression of interest...a depression of profits"[3] and a certain resultant discouragement and lack of initiative in the world of business. As moreover competition of foreign manufactures,

[1] This is not intended as a theory of the trade cycle, about which a library has been written. Before the 'eighties Mill (*Principles*, Bk. III, Ch. 12, § 3) had touched lightly on the rhythmic succession in his "analysis of the phenomena of a commercial crisis" and Jevons, in 1875 and 1878 (*Investigations in Currency and Finance*, ed. Foxwell, 1884, pp. 194 *sqq.*) had discussed various suggestions by others, including the 'mental' explanation of Mr John Mills (p. 203), and had formulated his own harvest-sun-spot theory. These, and all later, theories (up to 1927) are classified under (*a*) physical, (*b*) emotional, (*c*) institutional by Mitchell, Wesley C., *Business Cycles*. Keynes, J. M. (*The General Theory of Employment*, etc. 1936, p. 329), whose theory I will not attempt to classify, considers that Jevons' was "an extremely plausible approach to the problem", especially for the world of his day. Mr Keynes' own approach I have not mastered; nor am I sure how far he considers it appropriate to the world of 1886–1914.

[2] Cp. vol. II. 141, 453. The 'equipment' aspect of the trade cycle is developed in Robertson, D. H., *A Study of Industrial Fluctuation* (1915). That the 'seasonal' aspect became less important after 1880, with the reduced dependence on European and Northern Hemisphere harvests, is certain. Cp. vol. II. 385, Keynes, *op. cit.* p. 331 and p. 75 below. Pigou, A. C., *Industrial Fluctuations* (1927), p. 29, while fully recognising the importance of 'equipment' and other factors, "concludes definitely" that "the varying expectations of business men [affected of course by harvests, equipments, discoveries, wars, and the rest]... and not anything else, constitute the immediate and direct causes or antecedents of industrial fluctuations".

[3] Alfred Marshall, quoted in vol. II. 385.

both in overseas and home markets, was being felt from the 'eighties onwards in a way to which Englishmen had not been accustomed; while at the same time tariffs were closing doors into markets some of which had been wide, and some half, open hitherto, there was complaint whenever the ebb began, and in 1885–6 a full-dress inquiry into the Depression of Trade and Industry. It was the combination of the sustained price-fall with industrial ebb that brought the loud complaints; and so it was fortunate that the twenty-three years of price-fall were far from being one huge uncanny ebb.[1]

What employment statistics are available for the 'seventies certainly confirm all the other evidence which suggests a long dreary industrial ebb from 1874 to 1879, that black year both for manufactures and agriculture in which so far as we know there was more unemployment than in any year during the second half of the nineteenth century except 1858.[2] But after 1879 there was a definite flow. In 1882 the general trade union unemployment figure, which by this time is based on a fairly representative sample of picked men in skilled trades, was down to 2·3 per cent. and the Boilermakers had less than 1·0 per cent. of their members out of work.[3] (Which is not surprising: 769,000 tons of shipping were launched from British yards next year, most of it iron or steel.) That real depression in shipbuilding, engineering and the heavy metal trades which followed the completion of this new mercantile navy and the end of the American railway boom of 1880–3 lasted for four years. It had not lifted in 1887; but depression had not lain nearly so heavily on trades less connected with the making of durable plant.[4] For all trades 1886 was rather a bad year, even for the normally regular working printers and book-binders; but the employment position in the majority of the trade unions in 1887, though slightly worse than the average for the twenty years 1871–90, was still very tolerable—an unemployment per-

[1] There is normally a price-fall in the ebb, but in these years the fall always ended below the starting point of the previous rise. See the diagram on p. 12 below.

[2] Vol. II. 455.

[3] There is a full account of unemployment during the period, with figures and diagrams, in the *Second Series of Memoranda on British and Foreign Trade and Industrial Conditions* (1904, Cd. 2337), pp. 79–104, and a more exact discussion in Pigou, *op. cit.*

[4] E.g. in 1887 the unemployment percentage in the engineering, shipbuilding and metal trade unions, as a group, was 10·4; in all other trades making returns, as a group, 3·9; for building, 8·2; for printing and bookbinding, 2·6.

centage of no more than 3·9 for the non-metal trades against 10·4 for engineering, shipbuilding and the metals.

This jubilee year did in fact see the beginning of a brisk revival, accompanied by an upward ripple on the falling sweep of wholesale prices which, though shallow, was so broad that for a time it seemed to indicate the end of the long fall. There came a fresh outburst of shipbuilding—a "great forward leap"[1] in 1888—which cut unemployment among the Boilermakers, and the average of unemployment in all the heavy metal trades, down to 2·0 per cent. for 1889; provided foreign countries with more than 300,000 tons of new British-built shipping in two years; and raised the steamer tonnage on the register of the United Kingdom to 5,000,000 in 1890.[2] For those two years the general trade union unemployment figure stood at 2·1 per cent. The gloomy record of annual bankruptcies fell satisfactorily.[3] The value of the exports of United Kingdom produce in 1890 was nearly 25 per cent. higher than it had been in 1885–6; and although a small part of this rise was due to the upward ripple of prices, the figures of shipping cleared with cargoes from British ports showed that most of it came from a growth in the actual volume of the export trade. In the wool manufacturing districts in 1889 they were working day and night, and at the coal mines there was an excess of demand for coal over the capacity to supply it which recalled the coal famine of 1872–3.[4] The demand for capital in commerce and industry was so great that the Bank of England discount rate stood at 6 per cent. for the first two months of 1890, and averaged nearly 5 per cent. for the whole year.[5]

The average might have been lower had there not been trouble in the City towards the end of the year, when the indiscretions of one great firm in connection with company promotion at home and abroad led to the so called Baring Crisis.[6] The promotions had been on a gigantic scale; £446,000,000 of capital was called up in London during the three years 1888–

[1] *Economist, Commercial History and Review of* 1888.

[2] Shipbuilding figures are in the *Statistical Abstracts for the U.K.*

[3] They are given in the *Statistical Abstracts*; and cp. Tougan-Baronowsky, M., *Les crises commerciales en Angleterre* (1913), p. 139.

[4] *Economist, Comm. Hist.* 1889, 1890. For 1872–3, vol. II. 302.

[5] See the diagram on p. 17 below.

[6] "The liquidation of the Baring Crisis", *Economist*, Nov. 22, 1890. For some personal evidence O'Hagan, H. O., *Leaves from My Life* (1929), I. 378–81. And see p. 286 below.

90;[1] and Barings had underwritten a mass of South American and other securities which they were unable to dispose of to the public before their own liability fell due. The Bank, warned by Barings of their dangerous position, took steps to meet a monetary crisis. It bought gold in Russia and borrowed gold from the Bank of France; and, after securing a private guarantee from the associated bankers and financiers of London, it took over the whole burden and liquidated Barings, whose business —given time—was sound. In the end no guarantor paid a penny. Owing to this skilful handling there was no monetary crisis and no kind of panic. The "great mass of the country's business...was comparatively little affected".[2] Bank rate never went beyond 6 per cent.; and although in 1891 the investing public was said to have "lost all confidence",[3] this and the consequent contraction of investment was only what might have been expected after such an expansion, even if Barings had made no blunders. For the industry of the country, 1891 was not too bad a year; very unlike 1858 after the world crisis of 1857. Though profits were curtailed employment remained good. Engineering, locomotive building, bridge-making and shipbuilding firms had plenty of work, if not quite so much as in 1888–9. Cycle making was especially active.[4] The unemployment figure for the metal trades rose only to 4·1; the general figure only to 3·5.

This in spite of the fact that exporting interests had been scared in 1890 by a new United States tariff, McKinley's, the highest yet known. It did great harm to some particular industries, to that in worsted piece-goods from Bradford for example;[5] but ever since the Civil War the American tariff had been so high that British exports to the United States had rarely exceeded in value the level reached in 1866. In the 'eighties they had not grown at all. Tariffs and America's own masterful industrialism had already shouldered the British exporter towards other markets. The McKinley tariff only gave one more jostle; and even for the five years after it (1891–5) the average value of British exports to America was only £2,600,000 (that is 9·4 per cent.) less than during the five years before it. There

[1] According to the annual statistics compiled by the *Economist*.

[2] *Economist*, Nov. 22, 1890. In May, 1891, the City gave Mr Lidderdale, the Governor of the Bank, a well-deserved banquet.

[3] *Economist, Comm. Hist.* 1891.

[4] *Report of the Chief Inspector of Factories*, 1891 (1892, XX), p. 30.

[5] See e.g. *Report of the Chief Inspector of Factories*, 1892 (1893–4, XVII), p. 106.

was generally something which Americans could be induced to buy; though they were no longer Britain's best customers [1]

If the British industrial state was thus sensitive, because of its extended interests and its complete dependence on overseas trade for essential foodstuffs and raw materials, there were compensations. The very width of the interests made readjustment of exports comparatively easy. If the monsoon failed in India, and for the time crippled Indian purchasing power, there might be a good coffee crop in the Brazils or improved trade up the Yang-tse-kiang. The previous widening and opening up of markets for many of those things which the McKinley policy was meant to exclude made its application much more bearable. If America was registering her determination, and demonstrating her partial ability, to be no longer a young country, dependent on some older industrial state for rough capital goods like railway metal and for the finer manufactures, there had been plenty of railway building and fine manufacture buying during the 'eighties in India, South America, Australia and other lands still industrially young. In 1889, when the whole group of metal and engineering industries had been so uncommonly active, it was reported with satisfaction that the activity was due to orders from all over the earth and was not determined, as it had too often been in the past, simply by a freshening demand in the United States. Above all, it was said, South Africa was now providing for Britain "a new world of work".[2]

Further, the dependence on overseas trade for food and raw material illustrated that binding force of international commerce which was not the less real because individualist free-traders had exaggerated it. The higher the measure of dependence on some particular source of supply, the more likely was it that the producers there would themselves be dependent to a considerable degree on British consumption. American growers of middling uplands cotton needed the Lancashire market almost as much as the Lancashire market needed them. Where sources of supply were many, their distribution and variety had introduced a phase of low and stable

[1] See generally Taussig, F. W., *Tariff History of the United States* (1888 and later editions); Rabbeno, U., *American Commercial Policy* (1895). If the re-exports from the U.K. to the U.S.A. are included, the fall in value for the five years after the McKinley tariff was only 4·9 per cent.

[2] *Economist, Comm. Hist.* 1889.

prices, particularly of food prices, which was a new thing in history.[1] During the first three-quarters of the century, as in every previous century, the national harvest had been of outstanding, at times of overwhelming, importance. The ebbs and flows of economic activity, though never due exclusively to harvest failure or success, had always been intimately associated with them. For that reason, ebb following flow was not a new disease of a commercial and mechanical civilisation. If the disease had now some fresh provocatives, its symptoms were not more virulent than they had once been, but less. Agrarian civilisations, dependent on the weather and the crops of circumscribed areas—from Ruth's Moab to nineteenth-century Ireland or twentieth-century China—have always had to face the risk, or if population is dense the certainty, of recurrent famine; famine local or national. This risk had not been faced in Britain since 1812, a war year, and the only year of the French Wars in which, so an expert contemporary thought, there was "any prospect whatever of famine, of the people not being able to get sufficient" to eat.[2] But for sixty years after 1812 dependence mainly, though after 1846 decreasingly, on the national harvest had meant, if not famine risks, still periodic and sharp fluctuations in the price of bread. These in their turn, among a people who spent a much greater part of their income on bread than the late Victorians, had created fluctuations in the national demand for all other necessaries and minor luxuries; and had combined variously with the fluctuations due to intermittent jets of activity in the capital equipment industries, and to changes in the course and weight of international trade, to determine the succession of good and bad times. A generous harvest in the 'eighties might give the finishing touch to a good year—it did in 1889[3]—but it was not essential to any real measure of prosperity, as it had been fifty and even thirty years earlier.

Wheat now came into the country all the year round: there were no longer the conspicuously differing pre- and post-harvest prices. Supplies were stored more systematically and successfully in the countries of origin. The iron or steel ship

[1] Cp. Hooker, R. H., "The Course of Prices at Home and Abroad, 1890–1910", *S.J.* 1911–12, for the stability of food-prices.

[2] Joseph Sandars, Liverpool corn merchant, quoted in Tooke's *History of Prices*, I. 327n.

[3] *Economist, Comm. Hist.* 1889.

could carry them in bulk and yet dry: the wooden ship had carried its wheat in sacks in a hold that more often than not was wet. The produce of harvests in the Southern Hemisphere was now available between the seasons of the Northern temperate zone. So early as 1884, a tenth of the year's imported supply had come from the South—from Australia; from Chile; a very little from the Argentine Republic. Twenty years later the Southern Hemisphere, now dominated completely by the Argentine, sent nearly a third: in 1908 it sent its maximum of almost two-fifths. Light harvests in any country, it might almost be said on any continent, were sure to be balanced by abundant harvests somewhere else. When in 1904–5 the United States, which in 1887 and many times since had sent more than half the British imports of wheat,[1] was suddenly obliged to cut down her shipments hard, the Argentine, India, and Australia were able to increase theirs more than proportionately. Whereupon the average price of the 4 lb. loaf in London, instead of moving up as it certainly would have done, given a similar abrupt check to American wheat supplies twenty years earlier, fell a trifle from the level of 1903, and that at a time when prices in general were rising. After 1884 the price of the loaf, which in the previous thirty years had ranged between 6·8*d.* and 10·8*d.*, never got above 6·3*d.* or below 5*d.* When, after 1891, a general retail food price index for London was calculated, its fluctuations kept within almost precisely the same percentage limits; for in the free-importing industrial state the forces which tended to stabilise wheat and bread prices were working to keep the prices of most other foods almost equally steady.

Given peace, or only wars no more disturbing to the heart of the Empire than the colonial wars of those years, the society of late Victorian and Edwardian Britain was remarkably stable, whatever it may have thought. Its economic vicissitudes touched only the edges of things. Even its export industries, with the mighty exception of cotton and some minor exceptions, sold from two-thirds to three-quarters of their output at home, and had only the balance left vulnerable to tariffs and other uncontrollable outside circumstances. True, there was the competition of foreign manufactures in the home market; but so far as this was new it was not yet great, much as it had been talked about in 1884–6. The mass of imported manufactures

[1] See vol. II. 219.

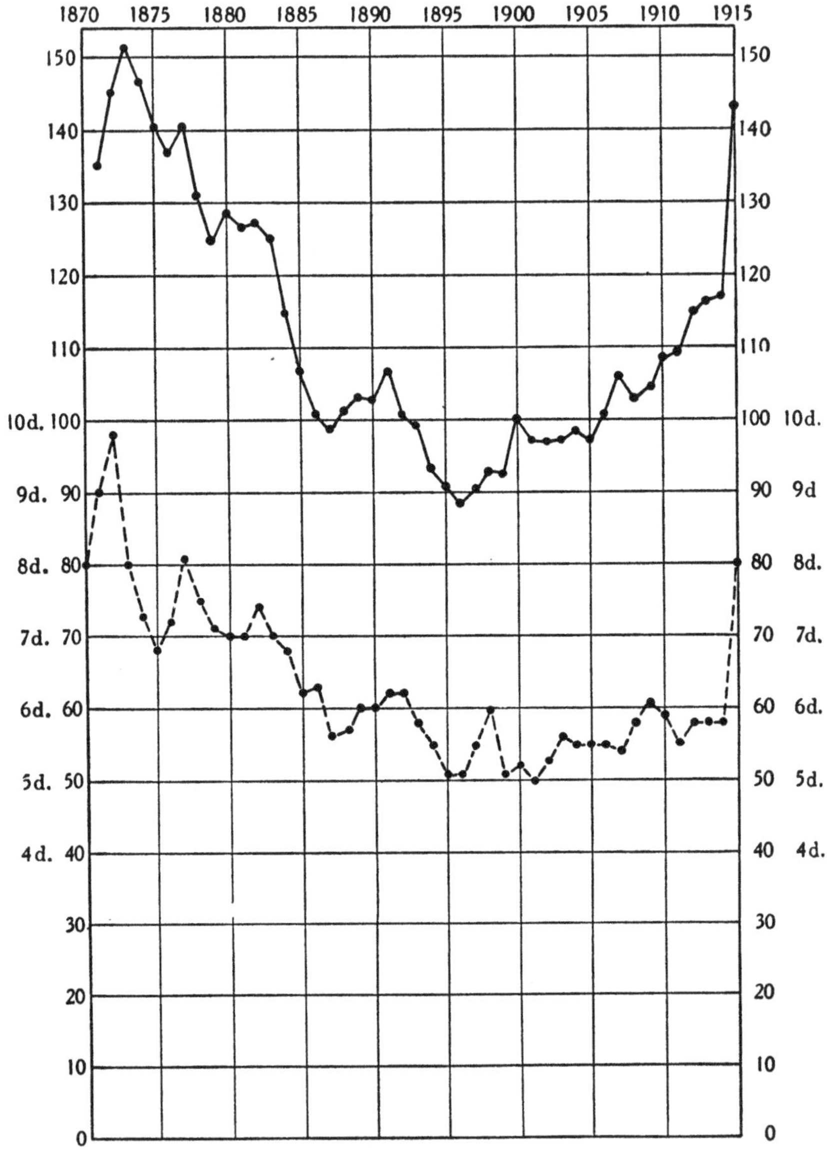

Board of Trade Index Number of wholesale prices (prices in 1900 = 100): ———
Price of 4 lb. loaf in London in pence: - - - - -

was still made up of the silks, the fine wool goods, and the glass; the gloves and toys and watches and musical instruments, which had been coming in, at varying speeds, since England first turned to free trade. In 1888, the imports of iron and steel 'wrought or manufactured' were not so much as a tenth of the corresponding exports; and although when the Merchandise Marks Act of 1887 (50 and 51 Vict. c. 28) ordered all foreign goods to be stamped with their country of origin the public was surprised to find how many, and what excellent, things were 'made in Germany', the aggregate value of those things was not great. Many of them were not directly competitive, being specialities which England did not make, although her native critics told her she should learn to make them; and all served some English user, the most criticised, such as cheap steel, being often the most serviceable. There was certainly no risk as yet of their arrival impairing Britain's productive forces or organisation. If they pricked the British producer that did no harm: he was sometimes sleepy.[1]

A fall in prices was to be expected when the manufacturing and investment activity of 1888–90 slackened during 1891. It came as scheduled in 1892. Coal, iron and steel fell of course, and sharply, with the slackening of rail, bridge and ship building.[2] Cleveland pig-iron, which had fetched 47*s*. 8*d*. per ton in 1890 stood at 34*s*. 6*d*. in 1893. Heavy steel rails fell from £5. 9*s*. 1*d*. to £3. 15*s*. 11*d*. over the same period. Cotton manufactures and other finished consumption goods fell, as always in such circumstances, much less but still perceptibly. Wheat, the price of which had been driven up less by trade activity—for that did not much affect consumption—than by a failure of French and Russian harvests from 29*s*. 9*d*. in 1889 to 37*s*. in 1891, resumed its fall towards the absolute nineteenth-century nadir of 22*s*. 10*d*. in 1894. The other grains and pulses went with it. Beans and peas also touched bottom in 1894; barley and oats in 1895, when wheat had only risen by a very few pence. For some other primary commodities—coal, and steel ingots, for example—the lowest point was reached in 1896,

[1] It is not necessary to give detailed references for the statements in this and similar paragraphs which are based on the annual *Trade Returns* and the *Statistical Abstracts*. The opinions on the nature of the goods imported are the author's.

[2] Specific prices quoted in this section are from the Board of Trade *Return of Wholesale and Retail Prices*, 1903, No. 321.

which ultimately proved to be the bottom year for wholesale prices in the aggregate as calculated by index numbers.[1] They then stood about 10 per cent. below the level of 1887, and about 15 per cent. below that of 1889–91.

Special forces had been at work, up and down the world, to reduce them—a perpetual extension of the wheat area in America, following another spawning of prairie railways in the late 'eighties: the same on the Argentine pampas: the same on the black soil of Russia. Over-development and the low prices then upset the young countries, making prices still lower. In 1890–1 political and economic unrest led to a default by the Argentine Government and the collapse of every bank in the country except one.[2] There was depression in Australia in 1891–3 culminating in a banking crisis; a railway collapse and a Wall Street crisis in America in 1893. The price of silver was falling with, but far beyond, other prices; and the silver-using East, while its own adjustments lagged, had been able to accept very low gold prices for its produce, and had been a poor buyer of things priced in gold. When silver fell in 1893 to what seemed the outrageously low figure of $36\frac{5}{16}$*d.* per ounce (it had been $50\frac{1}{2}$*d.* in 1884 and $60\frac{5}{16}$*d.* in 1872)[3] the Government of India, which received taxes in silver but had to meet many obligations in gold, shut its mints against the coinage of silver on private account and began the modern history of the managed rupee.[4] In the long run this might help British prices; but for the moment the desire of the Indian Government to improve its gold reserve in London meant a further demand for the fashionable metal; and the beginnings of such experiments are seldom favourable to business. America's long-drawn tariff and currency fights in 1893–4 were still less favourable. They were so deadening that for six months American demand for British wool and wool manufactures stopped all but completely.[5]

Although the broader special causes of falling prices—as in the case of wheat—and the narrower ones connected with the

[1] To be exact—as calculated by the Index Number here used. Index Numbers with different compositions or bases give slightly different results. See App. II to the *Return of...Prices.* Mr Fountain's *Memorandum on the construction of Index Numbers*, and n. 3, p. 18 below.

[2] The London and River Plate Bank: see Hobson, C. K., *The Export of Capital* (1914), p. 149.

[3] Cp. vol. II. 338.

[4] Keynes, J. M., *Indian Currency and Finance* (1913), p. 7 and *passim.*

[5] *Economist, Comm. Hist.* 1893.

ordinary waves of trade account adequately for very much of the fall, probably it would not have been so great if that pressure on the gold basis of the world's most important currencies which had been felt for twenty years had not continued. Certainly this was what all contemporary opinion believed.[1] Many thinkers and public men saw a way of escape in a revival of bimetallism[2]—the calling in of silver to redress the balance of the gold, and the fixing of a ratio between the metals which would smooth the financial relations of East and West. Other thinkers explained the merits of more refined solutions of a class which governments seldom adopt.[3] In America a silver party based on the silver-mining West had become politically powerful. Soon its leader would stir the mobile American electorate with his shouted protest against the "crucifying of humanity on a cross of gold".[4]

Meanwhile more gold was coming to make the appeal to silver superfluous; but at first this was not apparent. The discovery of the Kimberley diamond mines, following on that of gold in the Northern Transvaal during the late 'sixties and 'seventies, had filled South Africa with prospectors.[5] Mining for gold in its native quartz began near Barberton in 1882. Hunters told stories of King Solomon's Mines far away. In 1884 two of the prospectors had stumbled on the gold-in-pebble reef by Witwaters farm—the Rand. "There seems to be no doubt", a financial journalist wrote in September, 1886 —the first samples from the Rand had just been tested at Kimberley—"that gold fields of considerable productive capacity have been discovered in South Africa".[6] He warned

[1] The discussion of Hooker's paper of 1911 (*S.J.* 1911–12) at the Statistical Society illustrates the range of opinion some years later. The speaker who assigned least importance to gold was Mr J. M. Keynes: he said it was only one out of "at least" four or five important elements in determining prices.

[2] Among economic thinkers, Prof. Foxwell; among public men, A. J. Balfour. The most balanced contemporary discussion is Darwin, L., *Bimetallism* (1897).

[3] See Marshall's advocacy of what has been called symmetallism (what he called true bimetallism), i.e. a currency based on joint bars of gold and silver, before the Gold and Silver Commission of 1887–8. Marshall, A., *Official Papers* (1926), p. 29.

[4] W. J. Bryan in 1896.

[5] See *Cambs. Hist. of the Br. Empire*, vol. VIII, *South Africa* (1936), pp. 451, 781, etc. There were already over 1000 diggers on the Lydenburg field in 1872 when Kimberley was growing fast about Dutoitspan and the other mines. Curle, J. H., *The Goldmines of the World* (2 ed. 1902) was written by a man who has seen them nearly all and is very useful for the late nineteenth century.

[6] *Economist*, Sept. 25, 1886.

investors against rash action, emphasising the insignificance of African alluvial deposits, the certainty of slow returns. The new gold-mining was an engineer's—and a capitalist's—affair; and so must develop gradually. Both classes, however, were ready to take it up. The engineers' demand had created that "new world of work"[1] in Africa which cheered watchers of trade in 1889. That year the Rand produced £1,300,000 worth of gold.

By 1893 the output had risen to £5,200,000, this rather slow progress fully justifying the warning issued seven years before. But in spite of the warning there had been "rampant speculation" in London during 1889; and in 1892 nearly equal excitement in "that part of the Stock Exchange" which was now called the Kaffir Circus.[2] This was natural if unwise. Interest rates on secure investments had been falling steadily since 1890. 'Blind Capital' wanted more than 2½ to 3 per cent. In 1892 there was a longer spell of 2 per cent. at the Bank of England than there had been since that dead year 1879. The troubles overseas led to some short emergency raisings of the rate, to 4 and even 5 per cent., in 1893; but after that it settled down to the longest yet known unbroken spell of 2 per cent., from early in 1894 to late in 1896—the year wholesale prices reached bottom.[3]

There was a Royal Commission on Agricultural Depression sitting in 1894–6, very timely. They asked experts to forecast for them the future of prices. On April 20, 1894, Sir Robert Giffen suggested that we were "just about to see, in all probability, a turn" upwards. He argued from the position of gold; the increase in its output, not only from the Rand; and the "cessation of extraordinary demands for it", like the currency demand of the 'seventies when Germany changed over

[1] Above, p. 9.

[2] *Economist*, Nov. 12, 1892.

[3] Bank rate levels and changes were always significant, although they did not rule market rates or even signify the rates that the Bank itself charged. Since 1878 it had avowedly not adhered to its own rate "when discounting fine bills for its regular customers". In 1894–6 its 2 per cent. was "completely ineffective" (Sayers, R. S., *Bank of England Operations*, 1936, p. xi). "The rate is often through long periods a mere empty symbol", Hartley Withers, 1910, *The English Banking System* (*U.S.A. Monetary Commission*), p. 19. The average market rate of discount of good 3-months' bankers' bills in London was: for 1894, 1·18; for 1895, ·96; for 1896, 1·56. In active years Bank and market rates came nearer, e.g. in 1907 Bank rate averaged 4·92 and market rate 4·49. Williams, T. T., "The Rate of Discount and the Price of Consols," *S.J.* 1912.

to gold from silver.[1] On June 14, Professor Foxwell was "on the whole", though with reservations, inclined to expect a further price-fall, unless bimetallism were adopted. He had consulted "the best petrologists", he said, and he saw "no reason to apprehend any very considerable supply" of gold from South Africa.[2] Next year, in discussing the effects of increased gold supplies, the *Economist* pointed out that the effect

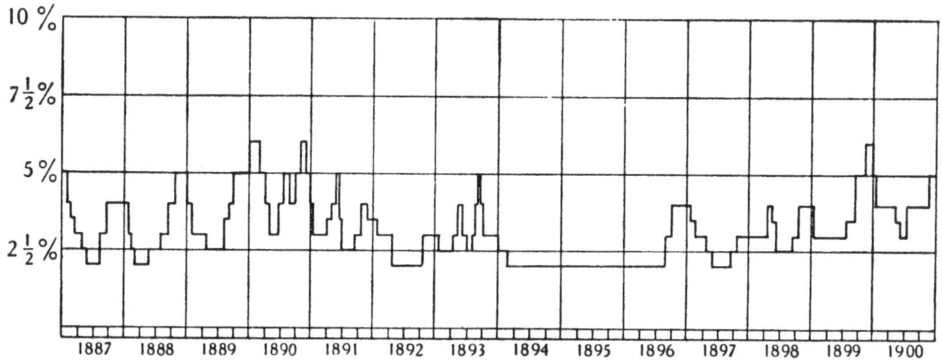

Bank of England official minimum Rate of Discount, 1887–1900.

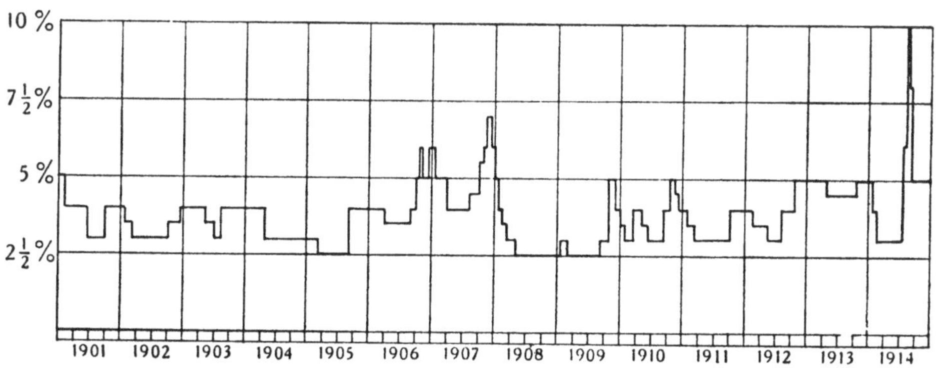

Bank of England official minimum Rate of Discount, 1901–1914.

on prices of the mid-nineteenth century increase had been much less than had at first been anticipated, and gave reasons, good reasons, for supposing that any effects of the new gold would probably be even more gradual and faint. Though France had not the capacity for absorbing gold into her currency which she had shown in the 'fifties and 'sixties, the writer

[1] *First R. of the R.C. on Ag. Depression*, 1894 (XVI), Q. 18,173 *sqq.*
[2] Q. 23,668; 23,678.

added, the United States could absorb a great deal, while Austria and Russia were preparing to adopt the gold standard and so to carry off some of the surplus.[1]

Giffen's was a brave forecast, in the spring of 1894; but in the next few years he was justified, even if only by accident; and so was the *Economist*'s prophet. The upward turn began, but it was very slight. Late in 1896 the Bank of England, where gold had been accumulating, woke from its two-and-a-half years' sleep on a level bed of 2 per cent.[2] By 1898 the Rand was yielding £15,000,000 worth of gold a year, in spite of the "best petrologists"; and by the time that the Transvaal was involved in war, when the grass had sprung on the veldt in 1899, the price tide was distinctly on the turn.[3] To what extent forces set in operation from the gold mines had brought this about is a delicate, and perhaps insoluble, problem. Influences from the side of bank money, and of those psychological changes which help to regulate its amount and the rate of its circulation, could easily have produced the 5 to 10 per cent. rise which was all that had yet come. The only really marked upward movement had been in the prices of metals and construction goods, a rise such as had occurred several times since the great price-fall first set in. For this the continuous expansion of gold-mining as an industry was no doubt partly responsible. And gold days, rationally or not, are always bright spots on the business calendar. But how far the gotten gold, working as bank treasure or coin, was responsible for the rise before 1899 is much less certain. The sharpest rise of all came between 1899 and 1900 when war drove up prices, as it always will, and stopped the flow of gold from the South African mines.

But at that moment the flow from South Africa could stop and the world still have enough gold and to spare. Johannesburg's £15,000,000 of 1898 had been not much more than a quarter of the recorded new supply in that year. The United States had nearly doubled their output (from £6,750,000 to

[1] *Economist*, Sept. 28, 1895.

[2] Gold was also accumulating in other European Banks and Treasuries; but most of these accumulations, being sterile, tended to delay rather than to encourage a price-rise.

[3] The best-known Index Number, Sauerbeck's, whose base (100) is the average prices of 1867–77, gives 61 for 1896 and 68 for 1899. The old Board of Trade number, used in the diagram on p. 12, whose base is prices in 1900, gives 88·2 for 1896 and 92·2 for 1899. The *Economist* number makes 1898 the bottom and only registers a rise in 1900.

£13,300,000) since 1890: the mines at Cripple Creek, Colorado, were in high activity, and there were many more.[1] Ten years later, when the rich days of alluvial mining at Klondyke had come and gone, the American output was still rising. There had been a revival during the 'nineties in Australia—mining not digging—which made the names of Coolgardie and Kalgoorlie nearly as familiar in England as Bendigo and Ballarat had once been; and this new Australian output was rising until 1903. So, even with the Transvaal closed by war, the world mined more gold in 1900 than it had mined in 1897. When work began again in the Transvaal, in 1903–4, the yield went up fast, reaching £30,000,000 in 1908, which was still only about a third of the world's huge output for the year. That single year added to the existing stock of gold more than two-thirds as much as had been added between 1801 and 1847. The eighteen years 1891–1908 had added as much as the forty-three years 1848–1890 and, so far as is known, nearly twice as much as the three centuries before 1848.

Hitherto it had been customary, and right, to argue that the world's gold stock was so great and so durable that additions made in any short period could have only a minute effect on the purchasing power of the mass. This argument was no longer valid. As prices moved up between the late 'nineties and 1914, with a slow powerful heave on the surface of which spells of good and bad times showed only as ripples just as they had shown on the surface of the earlier fall, there could be no doubt that the weight of the new gold was pushing down the purchasing power of the mass; though many other important forces were also tugging at the price level.[2] Those who had argued in the middle 'nineties that the operation of the gold would be very gradual turned out to be right, though they had not anticipated the amount of the pressure. It was eased because of the eagerness of all nations to join the group of gold users.[3]

[1] Figures from Lexis, W., Article, "Gold und Goldwährung" in *H. W. B. der Staatswissenschaften*, v (1910). See also the annual reports of the U.S. Director of the Mint, summarised in the *Final Report of the Industrial Commission* (1902), pp. 18 *sqq*.

[2] See generally Layton, W. T., *An Introduction to the Study of Prices*, and Pigou, A. C., *Industrial Fluctuations*, p. 95; where the small effect of variations in the annual output of gold is emphasised.

[3] See the short contemporary accounts by Pierson, N. G., a statesman-economist, *Principles of Economics* (1903), I. 403 *sqq*., "The principal monetary systems"; Dewey, D. R., *The Financial History of the United States* (1903); and vol. II. 337–8.

As prices rose bimetallism was forgotten, latest and least thoroughly as might have been expected in the gold and silver mining United States. Down to 1893, persuaded by the silver party, the Federal Government had been under obligation first to buy and coin, then to buy and store, large quantities of silver. The repeal of the Sherman silver buying law in 1893 led to the last great fight. Silver lost; but the victory of gold was insecure until prices measured in gold began to go up. Then, by an Act of March 14, 1900, the United States declared for the first time without reserve that gold only was standard money.

In Europe, Germany, Holland and the Scandinavian States had been on a gold basis since the early 'seventies; the richer franc-using nations, France, Switzerland and Belgium had been in effect on gold since 1878. Now all were glad to fill up their gold stocks. The Bank of France carried about twice as much gold (some £120,000,000) in 1907–8 as it had carried twenty years earlier. France's poorer Latin neighbours, Italy and Spain, whose currencies in the late nineteenth century were normally depreciated, used their opportunity to work back towards an effective gold standard. The Italian exchange came near the metallic par with Paris and London for the first time after 1900. Austria and Russia, who had only turned finally to gold in the 'nineties, became great accumulators of it.[1] By 1908, when the Bank of England was doing business with a gold reserve of less than £40,000,000, the Austro-Hungarian Bank usually carried nearly £50,000,000 and the Imperial Bank of Russia nearly £100,000,000, not counting balances in francs and sterling—potential gold—held abroad.[2]

Japan, to complete her western economic equipment, took gold for her standard in 1897. In India, where since the shutting of the mints to silver the rupee had been linked to the sovereign, sovereigns were made legal tender in 1899.[3] India sucked them in together with bar gold at an extraordinary rate. Neither ever came out in any quantity before 1931: gold was used for jewellery, sometimes it is said for medicine, or was just hoarded. In

[1] Austria adopted gold in principle in 1892, and more definitely in 1900. There was a considerable coinage of gold but not much circulation. The decisive Russian laws were of 1897 and 1899. Lexis in *H. W. B. der Staatswissenschaften*, as above.

[2] Central Bank figures were now regularly published in the *Economist*, *Statist*, *Times*, etc.

[3] At 1*s*. 4*d*. to the rupee.

the last years, 1906 to 1914, gold was being buried in India at the rate of nearly £15,000,000, or half the full annual output of the Transvaal, every year.[1]

Even Mexico, the Argentine and other silvery American Republics were turning towards gold between 1897 and 1907. Their demand was effective though their gold standards were not always secure. In the end, a few that had not turned were left alone with China as silver standard countries. Giffen had not anticipated this scurry to the side of gold, when he spoke in 1895 of the "cessation of extraordinary demands for it".[2] His forecast of a price-rise would probably have had a swingeing fulfilment if fewer nations had scurried across. The absorption of a large part of the world's yearly increment of gold into their currencies and their bank reserves, into war chests and Indian hoards, kept the rise within bounds. The social workings of a rapid and steep price-rise are usually so uncomfortable that this was all to the good.

So, in the twentieth century, Britain who in 1870 had still been the sole uncompromising gold standard country in the world stood among a crowd of imitators. All the great exchanges except those of China, with many of the less, were on a gold basis. Most of the countries which did not use gold, or used it imperfectly, would have preferred to be with the majority. London, much the greatest and freest gold market, was in easy monetary relations with all her neighbours. Every one knew the narrow limits within which a decent exchange could fluctuate. If international trade in goods was not so free as it had been thirty years earlier, international investment and finance were much freer and easier.

Perhaps Britain of the twentieth century overdid her foreign investment. If she did, the fact is not surprising; for investment could be worked very smoothly in this recently gilt world whose gilding looked so substantial and permanent. Investment both abroad and at home was very active at the last, from 1907 to 1914, partly no doubt because by that time the price-rise had become a thing on which people had learnt to count. The expectation of higher prices when an enterprise is concluded than when its initial expense is undertaken is always stimulating. By 1914 men could look back over eighteen years during which, at the close of any spell of specially active trade, prices had never fallen so low as they had been at its start.

[1] Keynes, *Indian Currency and Finance*, p. 76.

[2] Above, p. 16.

There had been a dragging spell during the later stages of the South African War and just after it. The price-level of 1900 was not passed until 1906; but the trough of 1901–5 though long was not deep. Its lowest point was well above that of the trough of 1894–8. War had been local and had not deeply marked the economy either of the world or of Britain. The United States and Canada escaped the post-war price trough altogether;[1] and when America has been bright Britain has seldom remained thoroughly gloomy.

Moreover the price-rise though persistent was never unwholesomely rapid, never fast enough to turn the heads of those who gained by it, or completely to ruin the patience of those who lost. Sufferers of course there were, people whose incomes could not be adjusted, or could be adjusted only with difficulty, to a slight increase in the cost of life; but the increase was so gentle, particularly in food prices, that for a long time it was barely felt.

Before the eighteen years of intermittent but persistent rise stood the nine years in which prices, after what from the long period point of view was the delusive rise of 1888–91, plunged lower than they had been even in 1886–7. It is against this background of the last years of the great price-fall and the eighteen years of succeeding rise that the external and commercial, and even much of the internal and social, history of Britain may best be viewed. The importance of the background must not be exaggerated. Whatever its tone, lights and shadows shift in the foreground. Some men make fortunes, many men live better, when prices are falling. But fortunes are mostly made during the spells in which the fall is interrupted; when it is resumed, good living is apt to be partially offset by more unemployment. Mere low prices do not mean unemployment, but the process of getting to a lower level often does. In this case it is not better to travel than to arrive. Employment was good in 1896, when prices were at their lowest; but it had been bad while they were getting there.[2]

Spells of rising prices have their shadows, often deep, as those of falling prices have their lights, often high; but these eighteen years were as a whole brighter than the nine, indeed than the twenty-three, which preceded them. To change the

[1] See Hooker's paper in *S.J.* 1911–12, quoted above, and the diagram on p. 12 above.

[2] See the diagram on p. 29 below.

metaphor, the pulse of the country beat stronger, with less intermission, in industry, in commerce, even in neglected agriculture. There was not a change from inanition to robust health. Statistically nothing is visible but small percentage movements, slight accelerations, slow rising curves. Yet very slight changes in the pulse may alter the outlook of the patient; and the Britain of 1896–1914, though liable to recurring accesses of pessimism and discontent, was more confident and adventurous than its former self. If it was also rather more pugnacious, that too is a natural accompaniment of a strong pulse.

The year 1890, in spite of the Baring crises, was in no sense a bad year. Employment generally remained good. Some young and growing trades, such as factory boot-making in the Midlands, were exceedingly active.[1] Some old and stable ones might have admitted, with the woollen industry of the Leeds district, that they had "little cause to complain".[2] (This is a significant admission from a Yorkshire source.) In iron and steel, though the output was satisfactory, prices and profits were described as disappointing; but in many branches of engineering the year was said to have been the most prosperous since 1873. This is not surprising. Exports of British and Irish produce and manufactures had never been so valuable (£263,500,000), in spite of fallen prices. The equipping of the world always brought business to the engineers. Heavy overseas lending and heavy export of capital goods had gone hand in hand, as they normally do.[3]

The trade revival since 1886 had in fact put overseas investment back into a position something like that which it had held fifteen years earlier. During the bad years 1876–80 the British trade-balance had been seriously deranged for the first time since 1847–8.[4] Abnormal imports of food had been needed to make good failed harvests: some channels of export had been blocked: discouraged investors and their advisers had been reluctant to force exports by free lending. Certainly for the first three of those years, and possibly for all five, the balance had been really adverse. Payments for exports, payments due

[1] The *Factory Inspector's Report* for 1890 (1890–1, XIX), p. 13.

[2] *Economist, Comm. Hist.* 1890.

[3] See the diagram of capital exports, p. 25 below.

[4] Vol. II. 233–5. Cp. Hobson, C. K., *The Export of Capital*, p. 219. Paish, G., "Great Britain's...investments in other Lands", *S.J.* 1909, p. 465; 1911, p. 167.

for services, and the yield of existing foreign investments had not—it is calculated—been quite sufficient to cover the cost of the imports. On the most favourable estimate, there was no net surplus for investment abroad for the whole quinquennium. In the next quinquennium (1881–5) things had improved. An estimated sum of about £30,000,000 a year was available for investment abroad.[1] Then, with that otherwise gloomy year 1886, began a remarkable rise in the investment surplus of the trade balance. The next quinquennium (1886–90) shows an average surplus of about £50,000,000 and for 1890, the culminating year, the surplus was over £82,000,000, nearly as great as that of the half-fabulous year 1872 when colliers, they say, drank champagne. In purchasing power, with the heavily fallen prices, it was very much greater. After that, for sixteen years this figure of 1890 was not passed; and for the first fourteen (1891–1904) the average surplus fell back almost exactly to the £30,000,000 of the early 'eighties. But three of those years were a time of expensive war in which surpluses for foreign investment are likely to be small.

Foreign investment fell off by more than a third in 1891, but it remained high if compared with this average; for the impetus gained during the years 1888–90 was not exhausted. Exports declined a little in value, partly no doubt as a direct result of the reduction in investment; but the clearances of ships with cargoes from British ports increased. There was no marked slackening of employment in the engineering, shipbuilding and metal trades; for more than 600,000 tons of shipping, of which over 100,000 tons were on foreign account, were launched from British yards. Though below the great outputs of 1889 and 1890, this was still good. Trades which had little or no connection with foreign markets, such as printing and building, remained really busy; and the impression of observers that, even if foreign trade was stagnant for the moment, internal trade had increased seems to have been correct.[2] Raw material prices had begun to fall; but the fall was masked, or more than masked, as an element in the general price-level by the rise in the prices of

[1] The estimates are those of C. K. Hobson on which the diagram on p. 25 is based. They have been criticised at various points—e.g. by Stamp, J. C., *British Incomes and Property*, pp. 227, 235, and by Cairncross, A. K., *Home and Foreign Investment in Great Britain* (unpublished Ph.D. Thesis in Cambridge U.L.), p. 225—but they are the only continuous series available.

[2] *Economist, Comm. Hist.* 1891.

foodstuff—especially wheat—which gave to farmers a much-needed increase of purchasing power without pressing harshly on the consumer.[1] "Vitality under most adverse conditions: more trade than could have been expected, if unprofitable" was the verdict on the year from the business man's angle.[2]

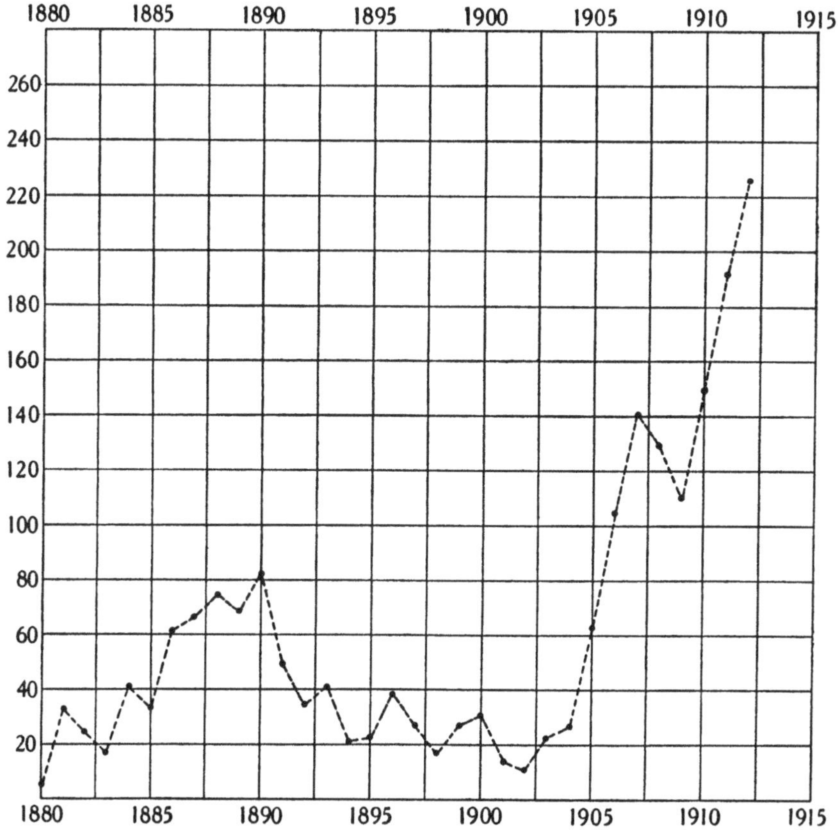

Exports of capital from the United Kingdom in millions sterling
(after C. K. Hobson)

Strength at the heart of the country's economic life was remarkable through the three difficult years which followed, and down to the first signs of a price-rise in 1896. The figures of employment among trade unionists stood up well in the period of ebb. They were much more satisfactory than they had been during the greater ebb of the 'eighties. For the four dull years, 1892–5, the metal constructional trades, invariably the chief sufferers at

[1] The price of the 4 lb. loaf in London rose only by a fraction of a penny.
[2] *Economist, Comm. Hist.* 1891.

such times, averaged only 9·6 per cent. of unemployment, and among them the boiler-makers and iron-shipbuilders, who always took the hardest knocks, had no more than 14·3 per cent. compared with 20·3 in 1884–7. All other unions of which records exist were better placed than these, with the result that on the average of the two worst unemployment years of the 'nineties, 1893 and 1894, not less than 92·3 per cent. of the membership of unions making returns was, it cannot be said in regular work, but at least not formally unemployed and drawing unemployment pay. The figures do not cover unemployment due to sickness, unpunctuality, or short-time working; and they take no account of time lost by industrial disputes. There were great disputes in 1892–3, by which in the first year 357,000 and in the second 636,000 wage-earners were directly affected. In 1893 they involved a loss of 31,000,000 working days; but even that is not so bad as it seems—little more than 1 per cent. of the potential working days of all wage-earners.[1]

Disputes were almost inevitable as things stood. Money wages had been rising satisfactorily if not notably since 1886 and the cost of living had remained about constant. After 1891 the wage-rise stopped. Indeed, there was a slight fall, taking industry in the mass. The cost of living was as before, a shade up in 1891–2, a shade down in 1893–5.[2] The discord between wages and living costs was very slight, but being accompanied by a sharp rise of unemployment in 1892 it was uncomfortable. Employers, their profits fallen, were trying to reduce wages. In various industries they succeeded. Where sliding scales governed the rates—as on several coal-fields—the reduction came automatically. These things need not make strikes, but they make resolute strikers, as the fifteen weeks' fight—to what was on the whole a losing finish—on the coal-fields from the Tees to the Severn in 1893 showed. It was remarkable that, in spite of this struggle, the trade union non-dispute unemployment figure for the year averaged only 7·5 per cent.

The more remarkable because, one after another, important fields for external investment had become temporarily unattractive and valuable markets had gone wrong. The troubles in the

[1] Cp. Webb, S. and B., *History of Trade Unionism*, 1902 ed., p. xv: "Strikes and lockouts [on the average of 1892–1900] account...for much less loss of working time in the year than our laudable custom of treating Good Friday and Christmas Day as Sundays."

[2] See Wood, G. H., "Real Wages and the Standard of Comfort since 1850", *S.J.* 1909. And compare the wage diagram on p. 468 below.

Argentine in 1890–1 led in a string of years during which little fresh capital ventured there and that already sunk gave the meanest returns.[1] Riot on the Kaffir Circus in 1892 was followed by well-deserved discomfort, and that by checked South African investment and purchasing. In America, the currency struggles were fought in 1893, like the strikes in England, on a falling market and, unlike those strikes, to the accompaniment of financial panic.[2] They caused the six months' block in American business which was so damaging to British exporters[3]—between March, when President Cleveland began his second term of office, and October, when the Senate agreed with reluctance to accept the law which stopped Federal purchases of silver. In the middle of the six months, in May and June, came the financial collapse and panic, a collapse made more shattering—since silver had touched the susceptible American nerves—by the closing of India's mints to silver in that same June. By the end of the year, the list of American failures included 158 national banks, 172 State banks, and 177 private banks.[4] Railway building had nearly ceased; and in 1894 a railway mileage approaching 39,000 was in the hands of receivers, including the Erie Road, the Union Pacific and the Northern Pacific.[4] There was much British capital in these half-bankrupt railways, though not much in the 507 banks which put up their shutters.

The American banking crisis had its parallel in Australia. Between 1886 and 1890 about £100,000,000 of British capital had been poured into the country. After the Baring troubles British investors became shy. Australian prices were tumbling: labour difficulties were continuous: land and finance companies and a bank or two, with plenty of British capital in them, came down in 1891–2. In January 1893, widespread bank suspensions began with the Federal Bank of Melbourne, which did government business. During the year all the Victorian banks but one needed reconstruction. Much fluid British capital had been withdrawn from them. With deficits on her various budgets Australia had little attraction for long-term investors. Both before and after the banking crisis came Australia's special curse of drought, worse after it than before. New agri-

[1] Hobson, C. K., *The Export of Capital*, p. 149; Paish, G. in *S.J.* 1909, p. 469.

[2] Dewey, *Financial History of the U.S.A.*, p. 444; Myers, M. G. in *The New York Money Market* (Columbia University, 1931), I, 414.

[3] Above, p. 14.

[4] Dewey, p. 446. Most of the banks opened again.

cultural resources were being tapped in the middle 'nineties, in spite of drought; but meanwhile Australia was neither a sanguine borrower nor a very good buyer.[1]

While the outer continents thus became indifferent markets, especially for construction goods, there were financial troubles in most of the Mediterranean lands and a recurrence of political trouble in South America. Fortunately, in spite of her currency difficulties, India was still buying both construction and consumption goods steadily, if not greedily. The users of Lancashire cotton, including India, took as much as ever; though owing to the fall in the price of the raw material they paid 10 to 15 per cent. less for it in 1893–4 than they had paid in 1890. As cotton goods seldom fell below 30 per cent. of the United Kingdom exports, and as no British industry was so utterly dependent on overseas markets as that of Lancashire, this made for national economic health. How little that health was really undermined, although the year 1893 appears most gloomy in many trade and market reports, is shown—amongst other signs—by the tolerable general unemployment figure and the decent activity of the building trades.[2] The country was evidently, as one penetrating report suggested, in "a state of suppressed energy".[3]

But the liberation of the energy was delayed while the last lap of the great price-fall was being run in 1894–6. Had it not been delayed, no doubt the lap would have been run faster. Business pioneers, promotors, investors, had not regained confidence after the shocks of the previous years. The United States, normally a quick recoverer, dallied over her tariff policy in '94 and bought less from the United Kingdom than she had bought since '78. Continents of the Southern Hemisphere, which were taking her place as buyers of British construction goods, remained under their various local clouds; and India had a budget deficit which led her to impose a tiny revenue tariff, the cotton clauses of which were vetoed by the India Office for Lancashire's importunate and important sake.[4]

[1] *C.H.B.E.*, vol. VII, Pt. I, *Australia*, pp. 369–78.

[2] The Carpenters' and Joiners' unemployment figure for the year was only 3·1.

[3] *Economist, Comm. Hist.* 1893. The *Factory Inspector's Report* for 1893 (1894, XXI) is very gloomy.

[4] By this time the Manchester Chamber of Commerce, which—it was alleged—had flirted with Fair Trade, advocated bimetallism to raise Indian costs of production, and then argued that bimetallism would save India, was being denounced for "selfish inconsistency" by the *Economist* of Nov. 10, 1894.

In public investment at home there was some stir during 1894, although in overseas investment very little. The money actually called up, not the nominal capital created, on the London market in 1889 had been no less that £168,000,000. In 1888 it had been £137,000,000: in 1891 it was £141,000,000. (Of these issues £41,000,000 in 1888 and £24,000,000 in 1889 had gone to railways overseas.) In 1891 calls fell below the half of the 1889 figure and by 1893 they were down to £42,000,000, lower than they had been even in 1878 and 1879.[1] And though there was said to be more confidence among investors in 1894 than there had been since the Baring crisis, there was not enough to prevent the Bank of England from settling down to that long spell of a 2 per cent. discount rate

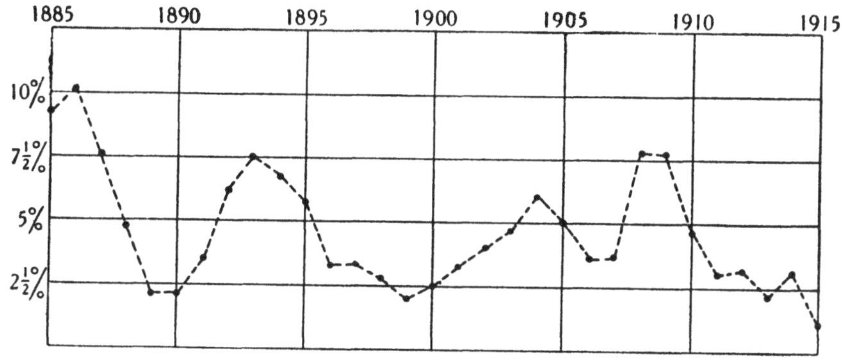

Annual percentage unemployed among members of certain trade unions

which showed that the accumulation of purchasing power was keeping ahead of its adventurous use. As a by-effect of this lack of adventure, employment in the metal-working trades, and indeed in industry generally, improved by only a trifling fraction. In some trades it even fell away.

There followed five years (1895–9) during which, although the public calls of capital kept markedly below the level of 1888–90; although exports of capital were inconsiderable and those of British produce barely climbed back to the level of 1890; yet the real wages of labour improved a little and employment improved quite steadily, until in 1899 of the half million trade union members upon whose fortunes the official figure was at that time based only 2 per cent. on the average were out

[1] From the *Economist*'s annual returns.

of work—the lowest figure of this series between the early 'seventies and the year 1915. Resources which might have gone abroad were being employed to advantage at home, and a quick expansion of foreign trade and investment was proving less necessary to the general welfare of the country than those interested in them had supposed.

The story of the building trades in the decade 1891–1901, during the whole of which foreign investment was comparatively low, illustrates this diversion of resources. Investment in building cannot be measured by public joint-stock-company and money market figures, for it was almost entirely private. But building activity can be gauged roughly by the number of men attracted into the trades. Judged by this standard the 'nineties show the greatest activity of any recorded decade. (They also show a greater increase of population and more movement from place to place than the 'eighties or the 'tens, which meant more demand for houses.[1]) Between the census of 1881 and that of 1891 the number of men and boys definitely returned as connected with the building trades in England and Wales had grown by only 2 per cent. The census of 1901 showed a growth of 35 per cent. How this growth was spread over the years of the 'nineties we do not know, but it must have been fairly continuous to yield so great a figure: the total increase is about a quarter of a million for England and Wales and 35–40,000 for Scotland. It is true that from about 1890 the efficiency of building labour began to decline: rather more men might be needed to produce a given amount of finished buildings. But this decline in efficiency persisted, may indeed have been accelerated, in the decade 1901–11; and in that decade the numbers in the building trades actually fell.[2] There can be no doubt therefore that the 'nineties really were a time of very great activity.

The unemployment figures bear this out. Although on the average something between 25,000 and 30,000 extra men came into the industries each year, in no single year of the decade had the carpenters and joiners an average unemployment figure of

[1] As is pointed out by Cairncross, A. K., *Home and Foreign Investment*, pp. 304–5. Cairncross also notes that heavy foreign investment and heavy emigration normally coincided and that this meant a certain amount of empty house property.

[2] See Jones, G. T., *Increasing Return* (1933), p. 90 and the whole section dealing with the London building industry, which suggested this line of thought. The decline of efficiency is also part of Jones's argument.

more than 4·4. In 1886 their figure had been 8·2 and in 1909 it would be 11·7.

The worst year of the 'nineties for the carpenters, worst though not really bad, was 1895. After that came for them, as for most wage-earners, the years of unusually good employment. There had been hopes, in the latter part of 1895 itself, that unusual prosperity might come at once to those export trades which, just because their vicissitudes were traceable in the customs returns, always received disproportionate attention from the public and the press. Much was hoped, especially by wool re-exporters and the wool-working industries, from an easier American tariff. But this favourable conjunction was short-lived. Bradford reports had been lyrical at the end of 1895: they were dejected by the end of 1896.[1] America was back in her silver quarrels and her aggregate purchases in Britain had dropped by £12,000,000. There was famine in India, and Dr Jameson's raid had gone far to spoil the year's business on the Rand. Yet in spite of all this, and in spite of apparently rather exaggerated stories of depression in the coal-mining industry, there was no question about the steady rise of the industrial tide at home. If America was not buying well, the building and associated trades were exceedingly busy, and so were the engineering trades, another excellent sign. The Indian famine and the African raid did not prevent a sharp drop in unemployment. In the latter part of the year the Bank of England, touched by the demands of trade and industry, at last abandoned its 2 per cent. Except during a few months in 1897, it was not to declare 2 per cent. again for more than thirty years.

Observers were disappointed during 1897–8 that these good signs were not followed by an improvement in foreign trade. In fact the foreign trade figures for the two years were worse than those of 1896, though rather better than those of 1892–5. Yet at home great activity continued in every branch of the engineering trades, accompanied at the turn of the year 1897–8 by a great strike. There was consequential activity in iron and steel, reaching almost to boom force in 1898 when shipbuilding, which had been reasonably vigorous and an underlying source of strength to the whole trade of the country ever since 1894, strode forward to an output of nearly 900,000 tons, a considerable part of which was on foreign account. The engineering and

[1] *Economist, Comm. Hist.* 1895 and 1896.

shipbuilding busyness was in part non-economic. The country had become dissatisfied with its fighting fleet and was rebuilding it at great cost.[1] Naval tonnage was additional to the huge output for the merchant services, and every ton for the navy had a vast deal more work behind it—on machinery, armour plate, guns—than any common mercantile ton. It is not surprising that unemployment was down to 2·1 per cent. in 1899 among the Boilermakers, and to 1·8 in the Amalgamated Society of Engineers. As for the Amalgamated Carpenters and Joiners, their 1899 figure was 1·2 per cent., itself a rise from what to minds of a later day is the almost incredible ·9 per cent. of 1898.

There were a few lamentations from small and decadent or temporarily ill-placed trades during 1898; but in 1899 even these ceased. Coal and metal prices rose sharply and so did the price of imported wool. Bradford, still a little sorry for herself in 1898 because America would not play her game, was now delighted to find that she could be busy without America: she had "one of the most prosperous...years in the history of the city". The cotton industry had made more profit than any time these twenty years. Coal was in "great prosperity". Iron and steel were "exceptionally prosperous", and the engineers could not get their raw material as fast as they wanted it.[2] Money-wages went up a little and real wages went with them, though the rise was not great in either.[3] The war in South Africa, into which England had just stumbled rather light-heartedly, was not expected to interfere much with all this; and indeed, though it proved not the sort of war to which most people had looked forward, and though it dragged on terribly, it remained to the end a colonial war of the nineteenth-century sort, the last and greatest of them. Its length and size did not dislocate, they barely marked or deranged, the economic life of Britain.

The value of the exports from the United Kingdom, climbing out of the trough of low prices, only got back in 1899 to the level of 1890. The excess of imports was always growing, and during the 'nineties it grew fast. The yield on the foreign investments so lavishly made during the late 'eighties was at first indifferent, as has been seen, and only began to rise a little from

[1] See Ensor, R. C. K., *England*, 1870–1914 (1936), pp. 288–9, and all the political Memoirs.

[2] *Economist*, *Comm. Hist.* 1898 and 1899.

[3] Wood, G. H. in *S.J.* 1909, as above.

1896. Every one was conscious of the arrival of new competitors for the world's markets. Naturally there began to be anxiety, often ignorant anxiety, about the balance of trade. It was suggested that Britain, like some ageing and incompetent man of business, must be living on her capital.[1] As a general proposition this was easily refuted, much more easily than it had been in 1876–8, when, in effect, she had sold a few of her foreign investments in order to pay her way.[2] Of this there was no evidence in 1894–9. But there were indications of what became demonstrable later, that most of the yield from old investments abroad was being brought home—where, incidentally, it was being used to very great advantage—while the share of this yield reinvested abroad was in some years very small, in 1898 not much more than a sixth. For the six years 1894–9 the share was nearer a quarter than a third. Now for 1889–90, the last years of very active export of capital, it is estimated that a sum equal to nearly nine-tenths of the then yield of all foreign investments was reinvested abroad. The balance for fresh investment in 1898 was cut so fine that, had it been cut only a trifle finer, the country would have been on the edge of living on capital as in 1876–8.[3] Not that this was very important, unless there were good reasons to expect that it would be permanent. A country with foreign investments, like an individual with savings, may properly realise a little in an emergency.

Critics of the trade balance whose eyes were fixed too much on exports and who saw those exports, as the average Englishman and average English politicians did, from the office stool of an exporting manufacturer, were very liable to ignore the extent to which during times of active export of capital the nation really gave some of its wealth away—gave purchasing power or capital goods to governments which repudiated, or to foreign companies which went bankrupt. The stagnation of the yield of foreign investments between 1890 and 1897 suggested much waste of this kind, or at best the existence of too many investments which for the time being had been made gratis. The growing excess of imports in the late 'nineties was in part

[1] The suggestion was not made at this time in very responsible circles. It is dealt with in the *Economist*, *Comm. Hist.* for 1898.

[2] Vol. II. 235, 240–1, and p. 23 above.

[3] The calculations are those of C. K. Hobson as used in the diagram on p. 25 above.

explained by the fact that some of these investments were at length beginning to pay. A wide review of the course of British trade showed that heavy foreign investment and the heavy exporting which goes with it, whether completely wholesome or not, had moved in long sweeping waves;[1] and that, provided industrial conditions at home were satisfactory—as in 1896–9 they certainly were—the next wave might be awaited without impatience or annoyance. In fact all exporting countries' statistics showed a certain stagnation.[2] It was in part real and in part only apparent, a mere reflection of the price-fall.

There was however the possibility that, apart from any accidents of war, the rhythmic wave-motion of export and investment might not be a permanent thing for Britain. The industrial balance of power was altering—had altered. Who could be sure that when the world's capacity for absorbing finished consumable manufactures revived, or expanded, British manufactures would be wanted? When large-scale equipment or re-equipment with capital goods again became urgent would the contracts go to England, or to Germany, or to America? Much depended on the class of goods; but for some—electrical equipment was a familiar class—the probability already was that the contract would go elsewhere.[3] This was how the problem of the future shaped itself for the industrialist or for the statesman trained, like Joseph Chamberlain, in industry; while some pessimistic man of letters might be wondering whether there was not a sinister forecast hidden in Rudyard Kipling's line of 1897—"Lo, all our pomp of yesterday is one with Nineveh and Tyre."[4]

More sanguine men argued, and with excellent sense, that there was room in the world for a number of industrial, or semi-industrial, nations. Such nations could, and did, exchange their specialities with one another and might compete with one

[1] See Bowley, A. L., *England's Foreign Trade in the Nineteenth Century*, first published in 1893.

[2] See a *Return of the Foreign Trade* of twelve countries made in 1898 (LXXXIV. 359).

[3] *The Trade of the British Empire and Foreign Competition*, 1897 (LX), being replies to a circular despatch from Joseph Chamberlain; Gastrell, W. S. H., *Our Trade in the World in relation to Foreign Competition* (1897); Flux, A. W., "The Commercial Supremacy of Great Britain", *E.J.* 1899.

[4] I cannot agree with Wingfield-Stratford, E., *The Victorian Sunset*, p. 369: "no one...felt the remotest shiver of apprehension at the words 'One with Nineveh and Tyre'." I know those who did.

another not unto death in the always expanding markets outside. But every one recognised the shift in the balance of power since the 'seventies and the need for internal and external adjustment to it. And it was agreed that the representative British merchant or manufacturer was not very quick in adjustment. Americans, in their calculations of the future, always counted—to their own prospective advantage—on "the conservatism of Great Britain".[1]

In America with the disappearance of the frontier of settlement during the 'eighties, a new period of industrial history had begun. It was marked by a more intensive development of natural resources; a completion of manufacturing equipment by the establishment of industries which had not previously been carried on; a diminishing dependence on sales of raw produce abroad and on imports of foreign capital; and, as corollaries, a growing export of American manufactures and the beginnings of the large scale export of American capital. By the opening year of the new century "American financiers for the first time" had come "to the aid of European governments in the purchase of nearly $100,000,000 in municipal and national loans".[2] During the 'nineties they had been buying back American securities held in Europe, especially railway securities; while American exporters had been acquiring the habit of letting part of the money owed to them lie for profitable use abroad.

In mere bulk of primary industrial production the United States got ahead of the United Kingdom easily and swiftly. By 1890 already they were producing over 1,000,000 more tons of pig-iron; by 1894–5 more coal. Their steel output increased more than eightfold between 1880 and 1899, when it was vastly greater than that of Britain; and in 1899–1900 they even consumed more cotton, though the quantity was to be explained mainly by the average coarseness of the yarns that they span. But not all their cottons were coarse: they were fast learning delicate textile manipulation. An effective modern linen in-

[1] *Report of the Industrial Commission* (1902), p. 519.

[2] *Ibid.* p. 41. The first important export of capital was naturally to Canada. A New York bank had helped to float a Canadian loan so far back as 1879. About $100,000,000 went to Canada in 1896–1900. Figures of investment in the British Boer War loan suggest that the $100,000,000 quoted in the text may be an understatement; Myers, M. G., in *The New York Money Market* (1931), I. 291–2.

dustry they had not developed; but by the end of the century they were consuming a greater weight of silk than any other Western nation, greater even than France; and, what was of much more direct importance to Britain, they had built up a thoroughly efficient manufacture of combed wool, both light worsted 'coatings' for men and 'dress-goods' for women. In 1876 they had not even made enough stout rough worsted 'lastings' to line all their shoes; and men dressed in broadcloth or other solid woollen materials. Twenty years later, helped by tariffs, by changes in women's fashions, and by the change in American domestic heating arrangements which favoured light clothing for indoor wear, they were making everything for average—if not for fashionable—men and women that Bradford or Huddersfield made; and Bradford was learning, for a time with great inconvenience, how to do without much of her American trade.[1]

A more deliberate and conspicuous instance of the creation of an industry intended to oust British imports is provided by the story of tin-plate. The McKinley tariff registered the determination of Congress to have an American tin-plate industry. The users protested: they must have their good cheap Welsh tin-plates. They were disregarded. Down to the end of June, 1891, there had been no American production on a commercial scale.[2] In 1892–3 the output was not one-sixth of the import, all Welsh.[3] By 1895–6 output and import were nearly level. By 1898–9 output was over seven times the import, and import a quarter of what it had been in 1891–2. For a time, after 1891–2, the huge growth of the American canning industry had allowed import and output to grow together; but that phase was short. In 1889 America had taken 327,000 tons of Welsh tin-plate: in 1899 she took 64,000 tons.[4] There, as it happened, the fall stopped; for of most British exports there was a remnant which even American tariffs could not keep out, sometimes because it was so cheap, more usually because it was so good.

Long before the 'nineties, exports of new American machinery, or of American mechanical notions, had affected the course and the pace of industrial change in Britain. Sometimes their influence had been dominant, as was that of the sewing-

[1] *Report of the Industrial Commission* (1902), pp. 218, 506–7, 495; Cole, A. H., *The American Wool Manufacture* (1926), II. 159; above, p. 32.

[2] Jones, J. H., *The Tinplate Industry* (1914), p. 76.

[3] *Report of the Industrial Commission* (1902), p. 509.

[4] Jones, *op. cit.* p. 275 (App. V).

machine. But, after a time, it had usually proved economical for those who controlled the invention to arrange for manufacture by a British firm. The total value of machinery and manufactured goods of all kinds sent from America to Britain had been trifling; and indeed the value of American manufactures exported to the whole world had averaged only £28,000,000 during the 'eighties, when it had been stagnant. (The British cotton exports alone were worth at that time more than twice as much.) It remained rather stagnant in the early 'nineties, that sluggish time in international trade; but in 1899 it was double what it had averaged from 1891 to 1895, and stood at £71,000,000. Next year it would be £90,000,000. Now the exports of British manufactures in 1899 were almost precisely what they had been in 1891, or £214,000,000: in 1900 they would grow by another £11,000,000, not more. This extraordinarily rapid American development was much discussed in Britain during the years 1897–8. No one there was the worse for it, since business was expanding; but in reviewing the year 1898 the *Economist* reminded its readers that American competition might prove uncomfortable in many markets when international trade again became slack.

The appearance on the world stage of America as a large-scale exporter of manufactures was to most Englishmen surprising; the improvement of Germany in the same role was not. But it was even more discussed, by Germans themselves and by Englishmen. A newspaper could hardly be opened that had not something to say about it. Germany was fast becoming urbanised and industrialised. She was acquiring an 'adverse' balance of trade, like that of the United Kingdom. This created popular alarm until her economists explained that it was normal and healthy for a rich commercial and manufacturing nation with foreign investments to receive more goods than it gave.[1] But her position in the world of trade, as compared with that of Britain, had not changed fundamentally since 1880; though since 1895 her exports of manufactures had grown faster. The statistical facts were that for fifteen years (1881–95) the average

[1] See e.g. von Halle, E., *Deutschland am Ende des 19ten Jahrhunderts*, in his volumes called *Volks- und Seewirtschaft* (1902), I. 69–70. This was part of the German stock-taking literature at the *Jahrhundertwende*, of which a popular sample is Huber, F. C., *Deutschland als Industriestaat* (1901), and the principal scientific products, Wagner, A., *Agrar- und Industriestaat* (1901), and Brentano, L., *Der Schrecken des überwiegenden Industriestaats* (1901).

value of the manufactured exports of both countries had been approximately stagnant, as a result of the price-fall. The United Kingdom figure had fluctuated violently about a level of £200,000,000. The violence was connected with her varying foreign investment. The figure for Germany, who invested less, had fluctuated less, about a level of £100,000,000. In the four years following 1895 the German figure rose fast—to £136,000,000. Germany was now doing more foreign investment. The British figure rose slowly—to £214,000,000.[1] She had not resumed active foreign investment.

The chatter of the newspapers about German competition was due less to these statistical facts, not perfectly known at the time, than to the steady arrival of German manufactured goods in Britain and her colonies, and to the growing realisation of the sound quality of most of them, the unique excellence of some. 'Made in Germany', in the 'eighties an ignorant popular phrase of contempt, became in the late 'nineties a not much less ignorant catchword of alarm. German sailors once had the humour to hang the words over the bows of a new Atlantic liner on her first entering Southampton Water. It was a fair retort, but it did not help to silence alarmists.

Though the French curve of manufactures exported had been almost identical in form with the German—fairly level for fifteen years and rising steeper than that of the United Kingdom for four—it was much less talked about because its component parts were older and more familiar. That France should send her luxury goods to England, America and the world at large was natural and proper. With some of them England had never really professed to compete. They were recognised specialities. And her plainer or cheaper commodities, shipped mainly to the reserved markets of her expanding tropical empire, did not often trip up the British merchant in places where their appearance would have seemed to him an intrusion. Moreover she was not yet a great exporter of capital goods.[2]

The widespread British anxiety about the export trade was reflected in an inquiry made during 1896 by order of Joseph Chamberlain into the progress of foreign competition within the Empire. The results were neither very encouraging nor

[1] From *British and Foreign Trade and Industry, Memoranda*, etc. (First Series), 1903 (Cd. 1761), pp. 6–7.

[2] *British and Foreign Trade and Industry* (First Series), p. 8 gives the figures.

very alarming.[1] Excluding India, whose manufactured imports were still overwhelmingly British,[2] it appeared that of the competitive imports into the colonies, the things which Britain really could or might supply, 26 per cent. had been foreign in 1884 and 32 per cent. in 1895. Part of this increase was more apparent than real, although it meant loss to British merchants; for the returns often mentioned that foreign goods formerly bought through London were now bought direct.[3] The rather ironical explanation given was the working of the Merchandise Marks Act which required goods to be labelled with the name of their country of manufacture. The colonial importer, having learnt that the best lead pencils were Bavarian, or the best cheap watches Swiss, sent to Switzerland or Bavaria for them and cut the profit of the London middleman. Even the India Office sent out only Faber's and Hardmuth's pencils—though *via* England.[4]

More significant than the small recorded percentage displacement of British manufactures in imperial markets generally were the lists of foreign goods which were said to be gaining ground in particular markets. In the West Indies and in Canada there was, as might have been expected, a very miscellaneous increase of American imports. At the Cape there was a specially heavy new import of American carriages and waggons, anticipating the later flood of American motor-cars; in Australia generally, of American tools and light machines; in Victoria of German tools, especially hammers; in Tasmania the same, with American agricultural implements. In New Zealand there was almost an American and German monopoly of musical instruments. Everywhere the best goods were said to be British, except some of the American machines and tools. But everywhere there was some influx of cheap things; and into Australia and Hong-Kong these were now beginning to come from Japan. Japan was selling "satisfactory" clothes brushes and was trying to sell "undershirts and pants" in South Australia. At Hong-Kong she had already "almost a monopoly of cotton waste, washing soda and sulphuric acid", and she was sending some cotton goods, paper, ships' lamps,

[1] Given in *The Trade of the British Empire and Foreign Competition*. And see Flux, A. W., "The Flag and Trade", *S.J.* 1899; "The Commercial Supremacy of Great Britain", *E.J.* 1899.

[2] Although there was a "very marked" displacement of British by Belgian iron and steel (p. 577) it did not leave a deep impression on the statistics.

[3] *The Trade of the British Empire etc.* p. 7.

[4] *Ibid.* p. 577.

and cheap substitutes for all sorts of things. Her cement, though inferior, was "cheaper than any European cement". This Japanese competition, the officials in Hong-Kong said, was only a small thing as yet, but it "promised to prove serious later on". They were very right, but it is not recorded that this little cloud in the Far East worried Joseph Chamberlain in London.[1]

Although the war in South Africa (1899–1902) did not dislocate Britain's economic life it diverted some of her national energy. The export of capital sank very low, as might have been expected: government was taking up the country's surplus resources. Contrary to what might perhaps have been expected, the export of men—the net emigration—increased a little in the two years of effective war, 1900 and 1901, although it was not absolutely great. For the six years 1893–9 it had sunk very low indeed. For the whole of the then United Kingdom it had averaged only 53,000 a year; had never risen above 76,000; and in one year (1894) was under 38,000.[2] Deducting the Irish—however many they may have been—this leaves only an inconsiderable figure for Britain. There had been so little activity in the outer continents during the last years of the price-fall that they had lost most of their attractive power; and when prices turned upwards and business became vigorous in Britain there was no reason to "seek employment out". On the average less than 2 per cent. of the Amalgamated Engineers or of the Associated Carpenters were unemployed in 1899, and most of these presumably were only changing their jobs or waiting for the weather to clear. It was when war was over, South Africa again open to immigration, and the economic pulse of the whole world beating stronger, that United Kingdom emigration climbed again to a peak of 235,000 in the boom year 1907. Of these, 218,000, more than four-fifths of them British, went to the United States and Canada; for the strongest pulses were in the New World, and the ports there were still wide open to immigrants.[3]

[1] *The Trade of the British Empire, etc.* pp. 4, 5; 472, 323 (Japanese competition).

[2] Figures as given in the *Survey of Industrial Relations* (1926), p. 66. Cp. p. 27 above.

[3] Johnson, S. C., *Emigration from the U.K. to North America* (1913), p. 347. The four-fifths is based on the assumption that the proportion of British and Irish among the permanent, or semi-permanent, emigrants was the same as among the passengers who sailed to N. America.

There was a slight fall in world-prices in the year 1901; the value of the manufactures exported by all the great industrial nations diminished. And though it was soon apparent that this fall was not the forerunner of a sustained decline like those of the 'eighties and 'nineties, prices remained stable at the 1901 level until 1905.[1] Up to 1904, British exports, and among them those of British manufactures, also remained stable or, if you will, stagnant. It was during these years (1903–5) that the country staged a full-dress discussion of its imperial and commercial policies. Even had there been no dominating political figure to provoke and direct the discussion, it might well have begun after the last and greatest of the nineteenth-century imperial wars and a subsequent spell of rather sluggish trade. There had been some critics of the existing policies for at least twenty years; and there were now more thinkers, voters and politicians prepared at least to consider change than there had been for a long time.

No word stronger than sluggish can fairly be used of the state of trade, though far stronger words were thrown about in political controversy.[2] The controversy itself, by introducing an extra dose of uncertainty into all commercial calculations, did nothing to purge out the sluggishness. A community whose business had been carried on for nearly half a century on a basis of what one party in the state called free trade, the other party free imports, was unavoidably hampered when making its long plans by even the chance of a radical change. Enemies of change probably exaggerated the bad effects of the uncertainty; but bad effects there undoubtedly were.[3] Some manufacturers waited in hope, some merchants and users of cheap manufactured or half-manufactured foreign goods in fear, of a possible remaking of the tariff; but they all waited a little. The year 1902, in which peace was at last made in South Africa, had been from the business point of view "fairly satisfactory".[4] There was no trace of a post-war boom, but unemployment among skilled men averaged only 4 per cent. The next year, the year in which the great discussion began, was definitely

[1] See the diagram on p. 12 above.

[2] And have been adopted since by historians: Mitchell, W. C., *Business Cycles*, p. 428 speaks of 'deep depression' in Britain in 1903. This is far too strong if intended to be of general application.

[3] The decidedly free-trade *Economist* in its *Comm. Hist.* of 1903 gave only part of the blame to Chamberlain.

[4] *Economist, Comm. Hist.* 1902.

disappointing. Investment was inactive; prices and exports were stagnant; the Bank rate of discount, which had been pushed up by the capital wastage of war, jogged about between three and four per cent.; and the unemployment figure slid up as the year went by. But though the tonnage of new shipping declined, the combined mercantile and naval tonnage launched was still over 900,000.[1] The pig-iron output showed a small increase. In engineering any contraction was "rather in prices and profits than in volume":[2] some trades and places admitted to having had a very fair year; and though unemployment increased it was never formidable. In 1904 however, if not exactly formidable, it certainly became grave. Among the 567,000 trade unionists, the monthly unemployment figures for the year averaged 6 per cent. In consequence there were a few reductions in wages. The average of unemployment had not been so high for ten years; though it was still below 1892–4 and well below the black figures of 1884–7. In 1884 Randolph Churchill had been moved to tell his countrymen that their iron industry was "dead, dead as mutton"; their coal industry "languishing"; their silk industry also dead, "assassinated by the foreigner"; their woollen industry "*in articulo mortis*"; and their cotton industry "seriously sick".[3] No irresponsible statesman went quite so far in 1904; but there was material for gloomy perorations and justification for some anxiety. If the iron industry was not dead—its output kept up reasonably well —iron prices were down; and in engineering there was said to be "not generally enough remunerative work to go round". The output of coal was stagnant and its prices gently "languishing". Silk, as it happened, reported "some revival".[4] In wool, although a few districts made no complaint and one at least was very busy,[5] the trade as a whole had to face the unpleasant and unusual combination of a rather poor demand with rising prices of the raw material. Cotton certainly did look a little sick: raw material prices were rising against a rather slack demand, with resultant market troubles and fluctuations. But

[1] It was part of what may not unfairly be called the official window-dressing policy of this period to publish statistics of naval tonnage and to include ships sold abroad in the exports. Both were legitimate, but as novelties they vitiated long-period comparisons.

[2] *Economist, Comm. Hist.* 1903.

[3] Vol. II. 250.

[4] *Economist, Comm. Hist.* 1904.

[5] The Colne Valley, home of the cheaper 'tweeds'.

cotton still made its immense standard contribution to the export values. Besides, before the year was over, there was a perceptible rise in the level of those values all along the line—the beginning of a movement which was to drive them from the £286,350,000 average for the years 1900–3, and the £300,700,000 of 1904 itself, to £426,000,000 in 1907. Already in 1903–4 the exports of capital had begun to climb a little from the trough of 1901–2, carrying up with them the exports of goods. The country was in fact starting its last and greatest campaign of capital export.[1] In 1907 alone, it would build nearly 300,000 tons of shipping for foreign owners and sell to them another 230,000 tons of old ships. In 1913 the tonnage of ships thus exported, new and old, would be 709,000. And these exports of whole navies would be only one item in the capital account.

It was while Britain was still pre-occupied with war, and while her capital export was at its lowest, that "American financiers for the first time" came "to the aid of European governments".[2] Some American circulating capital had been employed at the English end of Anglo-American trade for many years; but there is no means of determining how much. American citizens held British and other European securities, but no one knows how many. There had from time to time been repurchase on American account from British holders of United States government and railroad bonds and stock. But none of these things had been on a large scale. Even that adoption of American mechanical processes which had played so decisive a part in industry since the middle of the century had not led to any steady import of American machines, except some agricultural machinery, the sewing machines, and latterly the typewriters. The United States remained, and for another half-generation would remain, a debtor nation and an exporter mainly of food and raw, or only part-manufactured, materials. Already however she was seeking wider outlets for her surplus manufacturing, organising and financial power, not only on the American continent—that was no new thing—but in Britain. There some not very inventive person began to talk about "the American invasion".[3]

[1] Diagram, p. 25 above.

[2] Above, p. 35.

[3] See for instance, Sir Christopher Furness—who was not the first to use the phrase—in the *Pall Mall Magazine*, March, 1902, and his reprint and expansion, *The American Invasion* (1902).

Half a century back a competent judge had written that the economic "superiority of the United States to England" was "ultimately as certain as the next eclipse".[1] Now, as England crawled heavily out of South African barbed wire, America was apparently ready to supply the whole round world with iron and steel. In 1901 she produced twice as much steel as Germany and nearly three times as much as the United Kingdom; in 1902 fully three times as much. For ten years and more the Bethlehem Works and Andrew Carnegie had set the pace and the fashions in metallurgy and steelworks organisation.[2] By 1899 United States exports to the United Kingdom of iron and steel manufactures, including machinery, had risen from the £500,000 of 1890 to nearly £4,000,000. (Typewriters were an important fresh item in the account.) There seemed no special reason why they should not rise very much farther, and the relevant Americans were sure that they would. Until 1903 however press and public in Britain paid little attention to these after all rather trifling figures. When before that they discussed the American invasion, as they constantly did for it was a catchword easily spoken in war time, they were thinking perhaps of American typewriters, or boots, or watches, or soap, or of the many proposals for underground electric traction in London, the most important of which were inspired and directed from America.[3] They might be recalling the distinctive name of the American promoter Mr Yerkes, rhyming it sometimes with that of his ally, the Englishman who spoke with the roundest mouth about the merits of American electric traction, Mr Perks.[4] Or they might be considering the impressive creation in 1902 of the International Mercantile Marine Company of New Jersey, which through intricate financial controls, absorptions and alliances of American and English shipping lines was—in popular estimation—to make Mr J. Pierpont Morgan lord of the Atlantic. A year earlier, while the negotiations were proceeding, *Punch* had pictured little Jonathan, his arms full of toy ships, guessing that he would buy

[1] Vol. II. 10.

[2] See the *Journal of the Iron and Steel Institute, passim,* especially 1895, I. 71; 1897, I. 89; 1900, I. 33.

[3] See below, p. 137.

[4] The new chairman of the Metropolitan District Railway, described as the 'nominee' of the Yerkes-Speyer syndicate; "The Metropolitan District Railway", *Economist*, Aug. 2, 1902. And see Mr (afterwards Sir Robert) Perks' speech, as chairman, of Dec. 23, 1901, *The Times*, Dec. 24.

up not only more ships but the whole of old John Bull's store.[1] Most easily the thought of American invasion evoked, to a sound of flapping flags and of drums, the half-royal rhythm of the name of The Imperial Tobacco Company (of Great Britain and Ireland) Limited. The Company had been formed in 1901 for defence against brigaded American invaders of British markets. "Shoulder to shoulder and blade to blade", as a song of the late nineteenth century put it, the brigade of the tobacco merchants had stood facing the other tobacco merchants.[2] Peace came when it was clear that the embattled islanders would fight; and they were left free to send out the press-gang at home for recruits.[3]

The American invasion was well advertised on both sides of the water. Advertisement was warranted, for it did mark a turning point in the economic story of the world. But the captions were too strident. The President of the United States Shipbuilding Company, a combination which took final shape in 1902, had said that his concern would soon be exporting new ships to Europe. The ships did not come, and in 1903 the company was being indicted for mismanagement and fraud.[4] The International Mercantile Marine was hardly a financial success. In ten years it paid neither an ordinary nor a preferred dividend.[5] The American Tobacco Company came to terms, on a world-market-sharing basis, with the Imperial. America entered on another phase of such furious industrial activity that with all her metallurgical equipment she seldom had iron or steel to spare, except an occasional cargo, for the world outside: from time to time she was a buyer. And the familiar sequence under which many new types of American machines, after being imported for a time complete, were first assembled and then made throughout in Britain, was resumed.[6]

Although most people in Britain were at work in 1904, economic activity as a whole was certainly below par. The signs of revival which were visible before the end of the year were

[1] *Punch*, May 8, 1901.

[2] The song—"The Boys of the Old Brigade"—is, I believe, of 1881. It only acquired popularity gradually.

[3] For the treaty and policies see below, p. 269.

[4] "The American Shipbuilding Collapse", *Economist*, June 20, 1903.

[5] "The International Mercantile Marine", *Economist*, April 20, 1912, apropos of the sinking of the *Titanic* which was owned by the Oceanic Steam Navigation Coy, a subsidiary of the International. The 6 per cent. Preference of the International fluctuated in 1910–12 between 14½ and 26¾.

[6] See below, p. 177; and for the American boot 'invasion' p. 182.

not prominent. In a country so far from self-sufficing, and so sensitive to fluctuations even in comparatively small components of the world demand for its goods and services, an event such as the Russo-Japanese War, which began in February and only slackened with the beginning of negotiations in June of the following year, was bound to retard full recovery. It disturbed all the markets of the Far East. But meanwhile the road to recovery was being paved with savings. War borrowing was over, and by 1904 reduction of the national debt had already begun. In spite of the war in the East, which imposed financial caution, the general trend of the Bank rate was downward. Except for a panic 6 per cent. in the 'black week' of December, 1899, it had not been really high during the whole of the Boer War, which had only absorbed surpluses, had not strained the country's saving capacity. Now it dropped in jerks to a level of 2½ per cent. reached early in 1905 and held for several months. There had been no similar spell of 2½ per cent. for seven years.[1]

The spell was over before peace was concluded between Russia and Japan at the end of August, 1905. Peace removed the last obstacle to Britain's full sharing in a revival of world-trade already apparent. The United States, where the peace was signed, was also the world's greatest cauldron of economic activity.[2] Her war with Spain had given her, if not precisely a colonial empire, still immense economic opportunities in the Caribbean lands and in the Pacific. She was a pioneer in the electrical age. Motor-transport had begun but had not yet threatened her railways, whose extensions and renewals kept her steel industry busy. The steel-frame building technique had started its attack on the brown stone houses of New York and the wooden frame houses in hundreds of provincial cities. Soon San Francisco would be shaken down by an act of God,[3] and rebuilt with elastic steel. The United States had shown the world how to use steel pipe-lines for oil and had set it the pace, often a wicked pace, in the oil industries and in oil finance. Their grain and cotton, canned beef and hog products, with tobacco, timber, oil and other raw or only partially manufac-

[1] Diagram, p. 17.

[2] In this connection it is interesting to notice that in 1903–13 the employment cycle in Britain "followed from six months to a year behind the corresponding cycle in the United States"; Pigou, *Industrial Fluctuations*, p. 50, quoting Berridge in the *Rev. of Econ. Statistics*, Jan. 1922.

[3] In 1906.

tured produce, made up the bulk of those export values with which they settled accounts for imports, carrying services, and travelling expenses, and paid interest on their still heavy balance of indebtedness.[1] With all their recent industrial expansion, the increase of their agricultural exports had been much greater than the increase of population. And yet they were attracting immigrants of all types and races as never before. In the slack water of the late nineteenth century, the annual immigration figure had once fallen so low, by American standards, as 229,000 (in 1898); but from that point there was an almost uninterrupted rise through 648,000 in 1902 to the 1,026,000 of 1905. The peak was reached at 1,285,000 in 1907, with the result that in the three years 1905–7 the country had absorbed 3,412,000 people, not much less than half the number taken during the fifty years 1820–70, years which covered more than one of what had been reckoned great waves of immigration.[2]

North and South, Canada, Brazil and the Argentine were also sucking in men and, with Mexico, capital. Here there were opportunities for the exporting industrial countries of Europe which the United States no longer provided; although Canada, with strong industries of her own, a substantial tariff, and a close linkage with United States economy was not so easily accessible to European capital goods and manufactures as Mexico, the Argentine and Brazil.

South Africa and Australasia were not much less active than the Americas. From 1902 to 1907 the price of wool went steadily up and the flocks of Australasia went up with it. After a failed wheat harvest in 1903, Australia had fine export surpluses in 1904 and 1905, and good ones in 1906 and 1907. If the price of wheat was not so satisfactory as that of wool, it was at least better than it had recently been; and so, for the decade 1901 to 1911, the wheat area grew by nearly fifty per cent.[3] Railway building in Australasia was going on steadily, with capital raised for the most part in London. Meat exports increased; so did immigration; and so did the Australian towns in which so many of the immigrants stuck.

[1] Statistics in *Report of the Industrial Commission* (1902), pp. 550 *sqq.*

[2] *Annual Report of the Commissioners...for Immigration* (U.S.A.). Article "Auswanderung" in *H. W. B. der Staatswissenschaften*, II. 265 (1909), by von Philippovich.

[3] *C.H.B.E.* (*Australia*), VII. 519. Clapham, J. H., *The Woollen and Worsted Industries*, p. 276.

In South Africa the gold output of the Rand had got back to the pre-war level of 1898 by 1904. By 1908 it had very nearly doubled, with all that this implied in demand for men, goods and machines.[1] The work of reconstruction and renewal after war had made South Africa a good general market, and her gold made purchase and borrowing easy.

In Asia, Japan, fresh from that first modern Asiatic victory over a European power which was to prove vastly more important to the world than any local or general rises and falls of the economic barometer, was adding to her military and industrial equipment by buying and borrowing from the as yet undefeated European peoples, and from their offspring in America and Australia. It was the need for army cloth which first made Japanese buyers important in the Australian wool markets.[2] India, with better railways and more irrigation, was saved from famine between the widespread western famine, accompanied by plague, of 1899–1900, and a famine of 1908 localised in the United Provinces.[3] In 1904 she was able to send more wheat to Britain than any other country, and in 1905 more than any but the Argentine Republic. For those two years she supplied a fifth of the United Kingdom imports. Wheat surpluses are not the gauge of Indian prosperity, but the good general harvests they indicate are. A little more food in the peasant's belly, a little more ease in his home, make her merchants confident buyers, her governments more ready to incur debt. South of India, the new business of rubber-planting was drawing capital and equipment into the Malay States and the Dutch Indies.[4] Between the Indian Empire and Japan, China still had a single government, if an indifferent one, and about as much commercial security and buying power as was normal for her.

Britain's principal European competitor for a share in all this potential buying and borrowing, the other industrial state, against whose achievements she now habitually measured her own, Germany, had profited like America from British preoccupation with war in South Africa, and from her own diligence and vigour.[5] Though the agrarian protection to which

[1] Above, p. 19. [2] *C.H.B.E.* VII. 364, 602.

[3] Knowles, L. C. A., *Economic Development of the Overseas Empire* (1924), p. 411.

[4] Below, p. 143.

[5] Sartorius von Waltershausen, *Deutsche Wirtschaftsgeschichte*, 1815–1914 (1920), p. 590.

she had reverted certainly tended to drive up the cost of living, it was equally certain that her industrial protection, combined with high scientific and organising capacity, had kept her industries active and her people well employed. Her emigration had become negligible, very little greater than that of Sweden or Norway or Portugal, and she was drawing on neighbouring countries, in particular on what were then Russian and Austrian Poland, for a great deal of seasonal and some permanent settled labour. There was not much doubt that her industrial and commercial achievement during the two previous decades had been more remarkable that Britain's: her statesmen, business men and economists certainly thought so, and most sober and competent British observers agreed.[1] The only half-open question was: How far is it inevitable that a people young to modern industry will move faster in it, given equal capacity, than an older and so stiffer neighbour? If this is not inevitable, then the national capacities were for the time unequal, as many people in both nations were suggesting.

That Germany could do without emigration was the more remarkable because, although her birth-rate had begun to fall a little in the 'eighties, and fell sharply after 1900, a contemporary but greater fall in the death-rate gave a higher natural increase of population for the years 1901–10 than for any earlier decade. Lack of temperate colonies cannot be called in to explain this stay-at-home German habit; for the Germans had been great emigrants in their day. The United States were as open to them as to Englishmen, Canada little less open; and it was to North America that the bulk of the heavy British emigration of these years was directed. Nor, on the other hand, can that heavy British emigration be taken as evidence that Britain was in any general way less prosperous than Germany; for as British unemployment fell emigration rose, the latter reaching a short period maximum, the former a short period minimum, in the years 1906–7. Had there been less emigration there might no doubt have been more unemployment; but it is not at all certain that there would, for times were good and most of those who emigrated were not of the type which is idle in good times. They were reasonably comfortable people with

[1] Ashley, W. J., *The Progress of the German Working Classes during the last Quarter of a Century* (1904) contains much of the evidence and the references. See also Dawson, W. H., *The Evolution of Modern Germany* (1908); Sombart, W., *Die Deutsche Volkswirtschaft im Neunzehnten Jahrhundert* (1st ed. 1903).

initiative, who heard of something more than average British comfort in America and went to look for it. That so few Germans did the same is perhaps to be explained by the fact that, within living memory and thanks in part to deliberate state action, the level of comfort and security for the small man in Germany—peasant or wage-earner—whatever its absolute position, had risen faster than the British level. The peasant had a protected market, the wage-earner certain social insurances which he was presumably unwilling to give up. But this explanation is uncertain.[1]

Among all such uncertainties, it became evident during 1905 that, then and there, the world could carry a prosperous America receiving immigrants, a prosperous Britain supplying them, and a prosperous Germany whose people stayed at home—besides other great nations most of which were reasonably, and some excellently, prosperous according to their various standards. Her imperial connections, accumulated purchasing power, and ripe commercial and financial experience put Britain at least on a level with Germany and the United States in readiness and capacity for taking advantage of a prosperous world, even if she was now at certain points technically their inferior. But neither particular technical inferiorities nor the advantages of an imperial connection should be stressed. Following automatically the principles expounded in the classical theory of international trade, Britain was most active in those fields where she was technically not inferior;[2] she exchanged what she could most easily produce for the specialities of her rivals; and critics of Chamberlain's economic imperialism were quick to point out, as the facts were unrolled, that the greatest expansion of trade and investment between 1904 and 1907 was with foreign countries, not with other parts of the Empire.[3] In 1904 the value of the produce and manufactures of the United Kingdom consigned to British possessions was £112,000,000: in 1907 it was £138,000,000. The corresponding figures for foreign countries were £185,000,000 and £288,000,000. Imperial trade had grown in value by 23 against the 53 per cent. growth of foreign trade. The whole increase in exports to the Empire was actually less than the

[1] The working of social insurance in Britain since 1920 tells in favour of it.

[2] See Taussig, F. W., *International Trade* (1927) for a recent restatement and examination of the theory.

[3] See e.g. *Economist, Comm. Hist.* 1906.

increase in the exports to Britain's two great rivals, Germany and America. Free-traders, who at the end of 1905 took charge of the government of the country with a monstrous majority, were content almost to complacence. They had always said that one country's prosperity need not be another's adversity. And to the comment, "but in what does your increased trade with Germany consist? Largely of coal which we cannot afford to squander and of half-finished goods like cotton yarn and wool tops", they replied that plenty of finished cotton and wool manufactures were being sold elsewhere, and that the outward freights on coal helped to preserve for Britain her still unrivalled shipbuilding and carrying trades. The long future of our coal reserves grew longer at every inquiry:[1] our descendants in the ninth or tenth generation must see to themselves: coal-mining employed nearly a million of men. Why regret it?[2]

The argument from shipbuilding and shipping was apposite. A great output of new ships lay at the back of the prosperity of the years 1905–7, as was natural seeing that the roots of prosperity stretched far overseas. One million net tons of merchant shipping had never before been launched in a single year. Now, more than a million tons was launched in each of the three years, and in 1906 1,149,000 tons. It was partly replacement building, and it was accompanied by heavy selling of old-fashioned British ships to foreigners; but by 1908 the net tonnage on the United Kingdom register was a million tons greater than it had been in 1904. Such "unprecedented activity"[3] in shipbuilding meant prosperity for all the heavy trades and for the railways; and there were many other active trades. Cotton reports were sanguine in 1905, jubilant in 1906, and still satisfied and confident in 1907. Naturally, for the export of cotton goods was worth just over 50 per cent. more in 1907 than it had been on the average of the three years 1901–3. The rise was partly due to a 25 per cent. increase in the cost of raw cotton, but was still a fine achievement for an old, rather set, industry with a crowd of rising protected competitors.[4]

The general expansion of export trade values over the same

[1] Cp. vol. II. 100 and below, p. 167.

[2] These replies are summarised from the controversies of the day from memory. I made some of them myself. See e.g. Clapham, J. H., "Protection and the Wool Trade", *Independent Review* (now extinct), Jan. 1904.

[3] *Economist*, *Comm. Hist.* of 1905, when much of the 1906 tonnage was already on the stocks.

[4] Cp. p. 176 below.

period was just under 50 per cent., so cotton had done rather more than its share. Machinery and coal, iron and steel, had done considerably more, as might have been expected. No industry of importance had done much less: rises of under 40 per cent. in export values were rare. Even the flax and jute trades, the one faced with tariffs everywhere and with the waning interest of civilised man in fine linen, the other with the competition of Indian mills near the jute banks of the Brahmaputra, could register a 44 per cent. rise and were congratulating themselves, at the end of 1906, that they "had broken away from the low values which for a generation"[1] had overshadowed them.

That the roots of prosperity were overseas was fully recognised at the time. The only complaints during the three years came from trades mainly or entirely dependent on the home demand. There was some grumbling from Bradford in 1905–6; fashions were setting wrong; people would no longer buy all-wool serges; and what not. The carpet industry said it had been through "a cruel time"[2] in 1905. The coal traders were not satisfied with prices that year, and coal output had not felt the full effects of a rising demand. More important was the relative stagnation of the building trades. The carpenters had an average of 8 per cent. of their men out of work in 1905, compared with a national trade union average—including the carpenters—of 5; and although the carpenters' figure improved a little later, it stood at 7·3 for 1907, when the national average was only 3·7. That there was no accidental circumstance telling against the employment of carpenters, and that their figures were fairly representative for allied trades, the description of the state of building in contemporary trade reports show—"a great depression" in 1905; "still slack" in 1906; "almost everywhere dull" in 1907.[3] It would seem that the business and investing community, its eyes turned outward, was over-investing a little abroad and under-investing a little at home.[4] The troubles of the carpenters may perhaps have had some slight connection with progress in steel and concrete building,

[1] *Economist, Comm. Hist.* 1906.

[2] *Comm. Hist.* 1905.

[3] *Comm. Hists.* 1905–7. Cp. Dearle, N. B., *Problems of Unemployment in the London Building Trade* (1908) and Jones, G. T., *Increasing Return*, pp. 58, 76.

[4] There is also the fact referred to on p. 30, n. 1 above that capital and men are apt to be exported together, which affects demand for houses.

though as yet that was not rapid,[1] but the general flavour of stagnation in the reports must be explained otherwise.

A relatively small diversion of resources from foreign to home investment would soon have wiped out the few per cent. of extra unemployment in the building trades, if it had been directed towards them. For the sums invested abroad from 1905 onwards were immense. The 50 per cent. rise in exports between 1901–3 and 1907 was essentially an investment rise. Already in 1906 the two peak foreign investment years of the previous forty, 1872 and 1890, were overtopped. For 1907 the figure was £141,000,000, nearly 75 per cent. greater than that of 1890. Then there was a check. But even in the rather slack years 1908 and 1909 the curve kept well above the peak of 1890. After that it soared up again almost perpendicular to reach £226,000,000 in 1912.[2] Britain was accumulating claims on governments and enterprises of all sorts overseas faster than ever before. Manufacturers, and all who thought like manufacturers, gloried in the swollen exports, and every one welcomed the good employment which went with them. Hardly any one stopped to ask how much of the export might prove to be in effect a giving of goods away to governments which might repudiate and to enterprises not guaranteed to pay. A certain amount of both was taken for granted, and was allowed for in the rate of interest charged to Nicaragua or the dividend expected from an Ashanti gold mine. But it was assumed that the margins of risk were thus properly covered. Repudiations by great powers, bankruptcies of main trunk railway lines, were not normal and were not allowed for.

Resources were turned towards foreign investment rather than to the rebuilding of the dirty towns of Britain simply because foreign investment seemed more remunerative. Perhaps the gambling element in it attracted the investor, a 'bourgeois', as it would have attracted the average British 'proletarian', had he been a foreign investor. For home and foreign investment combined, the sum actually called up on the London money market in 1905 (£144,000,000) was greater than for any year since the boom of 1888–9. Surpluses waiting for remunerative use were absorbed. The Bank abandoned its

[1] See p. 199 below. "The use of steel in buildings is growing", *Comm. Hist.* 1904.

[2] Diagram, p. 25 above. Calculations on precisely the same basis (that adopted by C. K. Hobson) have not been published for 1913.

2½ per cent. rate. During the autumn it had difficulty in avoiding 5 per cent.[1] In 1906, although there was a seasonal fall of the rate early in the year, the general movement was decidedly upward. In October the rate was at 5, where it had not been since the winter of 1900–1, and then at 6, where it had not been since the black week of the Boer War.[2] The western wind had begun to blow and it was bringing up the rain clouds. For very many months Wall Street had been raising money in London for stock exchange operations by finance bills and by borrowing on American securities.[3] London, turned into a short period debtor by her complaisance towards New York, had sent nearly £5,000,000 of gold to America in September. As this helped to bring the Bank reserve below £19,000,000 (against a normal figure, at this time, of over £30,000,000) it was a formidable drain. Towards the turn of the year there was fear of 7 per cent., a level which might have been reached if the Bank of France had not agreed to help stabilisation by discounting a large amount of English bills.[4] As it was the year 1907 opened with 6 per cent.

At its close, observers could say with truth that cotton and wool, coal, iron and engineering, had been "remarkably prosperous". So had shipbuilding and railways. Nearly all statistics for the year were superficially excellent. But long before the year was over everyone knew that the tide had turned. Shipbuilders' order books were emptier than they had been for a decade. General unemployment, though not yet serious, had been crawling up since August. The international malaise of the later months of 1906 had never been completely relieved. Early in 1907, Japan, who had celebrated victory and an assured position among the great powers in the usual way, had seen a pricking of bubble companies and a vast depreciation of all security values. Then trouble was reported from the Mediterranean, difficulties and failures in Cairo and in Genoa.

[1] It had to resort to 'market operations'. "The B. of E. and the Money Market", *Economist*, Feb. 10, 1906; Sayers, R. S., *Bank of England Operations, 1890–1914* (1936), Ch. II and esp. pp. 34 *sqq*.

[2] Diagram, p. 17 above.

[3] "Two years ago it was plain to every one...that credit facilities were being granted too readily to the United States", "Competition in Lombard Street", *Economist*, Aug. 24, 1907; and *Comm. Hist.* 1906. The high bank rate in the autumn of 1906 was an attempt to check this. Sprague, O. M. V., "The American Crisis of 1907", *E.J.* 1908, p. 356. Myers, M. G., in *The New York Money Market*, I, 240, 242, 417 *sqq*.

[4] *Comm. Hist.* 1906.

Early in March there was a stock market collapse in New York, the ripples of which were easily traceable on the European stock markets; but it was hoped that they need have no considerable ill effects in industry. At the beginning of August, the United States Steel Corporation announced a 25 per cent. drop in demand for steel.[1] There was a contemporary contraction in the demand for copper, that other barometric metal of the modern world. Copper had a highly speculative international market, for which America was the main source of supply. On July 6 the London price was £104. 5*s.* On September 6 it was £73. 10*s.* In October it was jerking down to £60 and lower. A New York bank too much interested in copper had become involved in a futile attempt to corner the shares of a copper company.[2] Warned by the March trouble, the European lenders to Wall Street—they were mostly in Paris or London—became less generous with their credits: it was high time. Wall Street, nervous in July, lost its head in the sweltering American August. There were "rumours and rumours of rumours", and "hysterical emanations from the titular head of the great Standard Oil himself",[3] whose companies, with other monopolists and manipulators, had felt the lash of Theodore Roosevelt and of public opinion. The stage was set for a stock American drama of panic and crisis.[4] Many of the properties had appeared in 1873 and 1893 and were to appear again in 1933. But the curtain was not rung up for the main piece until late in October, though well-informed English members of the audience had expected it earlier, as they watched the curtain raisers.[5]

The English were cool while they waited, the Germans and the Dutch more restive. German banking was deeply involved with industry. The Amsterdam stock exchange was internationally minded, very sensitive. But as German heavy industry slackened off later than American, acute anxiety in

[1] "The American Crisis and a Comparison", *Economist*, Nov. 2, 1907. Cp. New York correspondence, *Economist*, Aug. 17, Oct. 26, 1907; the files for the year, *passim*; Sprague in *E.J.* as above; Foxwell, H. S., "The American Crisis of 1907" in *Papers on Current Finance* (1919).

[2] Sprague, *E.J.* p. 357.

[3] New York correspondence, *Economist*, Aug. 24, 1907.

[4] Although "contrasted with the previous year the financial position was vastly more satisfactory"—less speculation and fewer new issues. Sprague, *E.J.* p. 356.

[5] "The collapse in New York, so long apprehended has at last come to pass", *Economist*, Oct. 26, 1907.

Berlin was postponed until the big accidents began. That was only in October. During the second week there were Stock Exchange misfortunes in New York and in Amsterdam; and on October 17 a great century-old firm of Hamburg private bankers—Haller, Soehle and Co.—came to grief through having given too much credit to industrial concerns. Hamburg had not had such a shock since 1857. The same day news came that the Mercantile National Bank, New York, was in trouble.[1] It was the bank too much interested in copper, through its new copper-speculating president F. A. Heinze.

Much American money, whose owners wanted the barren stuff to breed fast, had gone into trust companies which took deposits for investment. Rumour had played about them for weeks: its malicious tongue often spoke the truth. On October 22 the ultimate panic began with a run on the Knickerbocker Trust Company of New York. The circle of the run widened fast. America had no central bank and no real branch banking—instead nearly 16,000 National and State Banks and over 3000 other banking institutions of various sorts. The trust company and the ordinary bank had been to some extent rivals.[2] Suspicion spread with horrid ease from the one to the other. From the very start of the panic, money withdrawn from either, while money was still withdrawable, was hidden in cellars or entrusted like jewels and title-deeds to safe deposit companies. Soon there was a currency famine. Trouble spread outwards from New York and had to be met by the proclamation of emergency bank holidays. At the centre, government funds were made available to stay the panic; gold was sought everywhere especially in London; various doubtful bank officials were dismissed; and on the last day of October the President of the Bankers' Clearing House Committee of New York was saying soothingly over the wires that, after the now inevitable "drastic and thorough reforms", his country would have "better banking and financing than for years past".[3]

[1] Amsterdam, Berlin and Hamburg correspondence, *Economist*, Oct. 26, 1907. Sprague as above. The Mercantile National Bank appealed to the bankers Clearing House, having failed to meet its clearing obligations, and was re-opened in a few days—but with a new president and directors.

[2] To meet their 'unfair' competition the Clearing House in 1903 had stiffened the conditions of admission for the trust companies. Rather than submit, most of them had given up clearing house privileges, but the Knickerbocker and some others retained them. Sprague, *E.J.* p. 360. Cp. Myers, *op. cit.* I. 244, 257.

[3] Mr Nash, "The Money Market", *Economist*, Nov. 2, 1907.

The same day the Bank of England rate was moved up to 5½ per cent. A week later the Bank took what financial journalists called "the extraordinary step"[1] of a move to 7 per cent. As the City had not known 7 per cent. since 1873, no wonder they used the long adjective. But as the metallic reserve in Threadneedle Street had fallen by £3,000,000 in a week, and by £10,000,000 since September 25, and as the amount of hoarding in America was described on November 5 as "almost incomprehensible",[2] the Bank's defensive measure can itself be defended. All European central banks were putting up their rates—Berlin to 7½ and Brussels to 6, though Amsterdam had not gone beyond 5, nor Paris beyond 4. In America the after effects of the crisis were not over. Lack of money curtailed railway facilities. It hindered the financing of the autumn crop movements. Mills and mines closed down at Pittsburg and elsewhere because alien miners when paid with cheques tore them up and asked for proper money; and there was not enough proper money. Outside New York, bank suspensions and business failures went on into December. Though quickly over, it was all very violent and primitive and annoying to Londoners, who also feared more bank failures in Germany, where the list of commercial stoppages was already unpleasantly long.[3]

Seven per cent. in London did its main work cleanly and reasonably soon. Gold reserves accumulated fast and the rate could be dropped at the end of the year. Three per cent. was reached by March 1908, and 2½ by May. Germany got through without any more first-class catastrophes. America, her productive powers somewhat impaired, licked her wounds, and had told the world at the end of 1907 that "business would be held in suspense for the next year by the possibilities of a Presidential election".[4] While the American political machine of eighteenth-century design swung round heavily the world must wait. This was hard on Britain, where there had been no kind

[1] *Economist*, Nov. 9, 1907. Note on the Discount and Loan Market.

[2] New York Correspondence of Nov. 5, *Economist*, Nov. 16, 1907.

[3] "The Money Market", *Economist*, Nov. 23, 1907; "The Sufferings of American Traders", *Economist*, Nov. 30, 1907; "Progress and Elucidation of the American Crisis", *Economist*, Dec. 14, 1907. There were few absolute failures of banks, and none in purely agricultural districts: the total number of American business failures was not excessive. Sprague, *E.J.* p. 355; Foxwell, *op. cit.* p. 172: "I maintain that this crisis was emphatically a banking [not a commercial] crisis": too simple a pronouncement.

[4] The Hon. A. B. Hepburn, president of the Chase National Bank, to the correspondent of the *Economist*, Dec. 23. *Economist*, Jan. 4, 1908.

of crisis or panic in 1907, no industrial collapse only a contraction, and fewer bankruptcies gazetted than in any year since 1902. The hesitation of adventurers and the industrial contraction were reflected in the 3 and 2½ per cent. Bank rates of 1908. When the rate got to 2½ there it stayed for nearly eight months, while the American machine did its work.

The absence of any organic disease in the British body economic was shown by the immediate healthy response to this cheap money. There was actually more investment, more capital paid up, on the London money market in 1908 than in 1907. If the United States were for the moment a barren field —well, investors had been looking elsewhere for some considerable time and could go on so doing. The British industrial state was much less dependent than it had once been on the winds from New York. Its citizens lent to South America and India and the Colonies and Japan, to governments and railways and municipalities.[1] There is a small contraction in the estimated exports of capital for 1908–9 as compared with 1907, but even so it remains above the level of 1906; and some of the decline is due to the temporary fall in world wholesale prices which occurred in 1907 and lowered the selling value of those exports on which the estimate is partly based.[2] It was recognised at the time that foreign trade contracted during 1908 more in value than in bulk. World prices, and with them the money value of British foreign trade, did not get back to the 1907 level until some way into 1910.

Though the body economic was tolerably healthy in 1908–9, some of its members were suffering from lack of use. The three fat years in shipbuilding were followed by three unusually lean ones. A lean spell was unavoidable, for ships wear out slowly; but so lean a spell was unexpected. There were similar, if much less damaging, spells in other constructional industries. As a result, the shipbuilding, engineering and metal trade unions had their worst taste of unemployment in twenty years. The percentage touched 13 for the whole group in 1909, and 21·4 for the Boilermakers. There was a consequent check in the demand for coal, and there were wage reductions with accompanying

[1] Cp. the diagrams on p. 12 and p. 25 above.

[2] The capital publicly subscribed in 1908 included £44,000,000 for colonial and foreign governments; £43,000,000 for foreign railways; £19,000,000 for Indian and colonial railways; and £10,500,000 for colonial and foreign municipalities.

strikes in mining and engineering and also in the cotton industry.[1] The reduction in wage rates did not amount to much. Already British wages, as compared with those of America for example, had become very inelastic, except in the few trades where they were based on sliding scales and so varied with the selling price of the product. But, combined with the unemployment—which for the whole body of trade unionists was double in 1908–9 what it had been in 1906–7—these reductions, and still more the friction which accompanied them, gave an impression of serious economic ill-health. Besides, although world wholesale prices fell in the aggregate during 1908, British retail prices of nearly all those things which the wage-earner chiefly consumes—except coal and sugar—went up a little.[2] Serious economic ill-health there was not; but this combination of slight declines in a number of wage-rates and a general decline in the amount of work paid for with a rise, although a tiny one, in the average cost of living led to widespread discomfort and some real distress.

The whole country, not simply the metal-working areas, was conscious of this discomfort because it was acute in the most evenly spread of all industries, building, with its heavy demand for unskilled or only half-skilled labour and its normally intermittent working which makes any unusual lengthening of the spells of idleness particularly troublesome. During the foreign trade expansion of 1904–7 building had been slack. Now it was much slacker. The carpenters and joiners had unemployment figures for 1908–9 not far below those of the metal workers.[3] Indeed it was the worst spell of unemployment which they and the other wood-working and furnishing trades had passed through since the 'seventies. The building of ships was slack as well as that of houses, and there may be a great deal of woodwork and furniture in a modern ship.

A slight rise of wholesale prices, a continuously satisfactory volume of exports, and an increase in recorded investment on

[1] See diagram, p. 468 below.

[2] These are London retail prices, as published in the *Labour Statistics*; but they are no doubt reasonably representative.

[3] The Carpenters' and Joiners' figures are 11·6 and 11·7 per cent. for 1908 and 1909. For the 1904–7 slackness see p. 52 above. A certain slackness when foreign trade and foreign investment were active was not unnatural (above, p. 30) and it is to be noted that such investment fell off very little in 1908–9. (See the diagram, p. 25 above.)

joint home and foreign account, during 1909, showed how successfully the country had come through the international rough weather of 1907–8. Very bad as unemployment still was in the constructional industries, it improved even there during the later months of the year; and, over the whole year and the whole recorded field of industry, there was a drop in unemployment of 24 per cent.[1] By February 1910 the figure was a trifle better than it had been in February 1908, and the general level of economic activity was approaching that of 1907. In the autumn of 1909 the Bank of England had abandoned the 2½ per cent. discount rate to which it had adhered, with one short interruption of 3 per cent., since the spring of 1908. For reasons partly of prosperity and partly of misfortune it was not to announce 2½ per cent. again for more than twenty years. In 1909, its reasons were of the prosperity, or at least of the activity, sort. The amount of money actually called up for public investment proved to have been greater during 1909 than in any year since that rather mad year 1889, when every one was investing and hardly any trade unionists were out of work.

The money calls of 1909 did not mark an upward limit: 1910 as an investment year was well above 1889. Its foreign investment was greater than that of 1907, and far greater than that of 1889, or of any earlier year.[2] And although the money called up in London by governments and companies did not again touch the level of 1910 until 1914—when it was called up avowedly to be destroyed—the exports of capital during those last double-faced years of peace and gathering war went on climbing from height to height. "Wonderful tales of trade activity come from all parts", the Chief Inspector of Factories wrote in his report on 1912.[3] With demand so insistent abroad and the greatest economic activity at home, it is not surprising that there were longer spells of a 5 per cent. Bank rate during 1912–13 than at any time since 1907. But, as there was no act of major business folly or crime, either in Europe or America,

[1] I.e. between Jan. and Dec. For the whole year unemployment averaged little less than for 1908; but in 1908 it was rising, in 1909 falling. Cp. diagram, p. 29 above.

[2] The figures are: 1889, £168,000; 1909, £153,000; 1910, £190,000. For capital exported for foreign investment in 1910 (estimated at £150,000,000) see diagram, p. 25 above.

[3] *Report* (1913, XXIII), p. xiii. Cp. *Economist, Comm. Hist.*—"trade and commerce in 1912 have eclipsed all records".

the Bank was never moved to go above 5, the rate which, if not exceeded, implied profit and prosperity without troublesome risk.

It is estimated that, during the two years 1911 and 1912, upwards of 30 per cent. more capital was exported than during the whole decade between 1890 and 1901, and in each of the two years vastly more than in any peak year of capital export during the 'eighties or the 'seventies. When Britain at war, in order to pay her way, had to sell some of her claims to receive money from overseas she had a long list from which to choose. When she had made her selection and sold, there were still claims enough—not all of which would be honoured in the long run. Such are the gains and the risks of capital export, and indeed of all investment, by individuals or by the State, for a future which can never be more than dimly seen.

Through much political tension, national and international; at a time when what statesmen of the eighteenth century used to call 'the general war' drew very near but just did not come; when there was fighting in the Balkans and in Tripoli though not in the West; while at home the usual lag of wages behind prices led to justifiable grumbling, much industrial diplomacy, and some stubborn industrial war; through all this and much else—Parliament Acts; Home Rule Bills; processions and outrages of women demanding the suffrage—the economic pulse of the country beat briskly and strong right to the end of 1913. Then it slowed a little, a very little. The Bank dropped its rate to 3 per cent. in the spring of 1914. Some such drop was usual, except in times of quite abnormal activity. There had been a spell of 3 per cent., or less, in every year since 1907 except 1913. But this spell was a rather long one. It extended into the last week of July. It was accompanied by a slow widening of trade union unemployment. For the three years since 1910 employment had been abnormally good, in spite of the reactions of some big trade disputes. For 1913, when disputes were few, the mean monthly unemployment figure as reported was 2·1; and in April of that year it was 1·7, a figure which had not been reported since April 1899, and before that only two or three times in the boom of 1889–90. Now, in 1914, the figure crept up to 2·8 in July; but this was still well below the July average for the previous decade. The pulse was not yet weak. With August came war, and a department of the Board of Trade was set up to study that anticipated wartime unemployment which within a few unbelievable months was turned into a wartime shortage of men.

All the old industries of the country took part in the rush of 1910–14: for the time-honoured wool-industries, 1910 was a year of exceptional prosperity. New ones were coming up beside them—from 1906–7 even general surveys of national trade gave a column to motor-cars—but it was on the old favourites that Britain relied. They were still full of running. The constructional trades had been the last to get into their stride. They were lying behind in 1910, when house building was rather slack and less than 700,000 tons of shipping were launched. But the world's harvests were splendid that year. They provided freights, a demand for more ships, and favourable terms of real exchange between British manufactures and the imported food. Shipbuilding and ship-selling responded at once: 1911 was a fine shipbuilding year; so was 1912; and in 1913 an absolute maximum output of 1,200,000 net tons was reached.[1] It was in 1913 that 225,000 tons of new and 448,000 tons of old British shipping were sold abroad. The figures for 1912 and 1911 had not been much lower. In 1910–11 a whole fleet, 256,000 tons, of the sailing ships which Britain no longer wanted and had almost ceased to build had been sold to foreigners who still saw profit in running them. The narrow seas were crowded with ships in 1913–14—ready for the torpedo and the floating mine—and there was a minimum of unemployment among the Boilermakers and Iron Shipbuilders.

Unemployment figures for the building trades were a shade worse than the national average in 1912–13; and the evidence provided by the 1911 Census that the trades had not been expanding suggests that, even during these last busy years, they were not quite so active as they might properly have been in a country whose population was still growing fast and was on the average ill-housed.[2] There had been no sudden displacement of hand-labour in building by the machine. What competition from machinery there was had been there already in the 'nineties, when the trades were expanding. The London bricklayer laid his sixty bricks an hour, as he had for thirty years.[3] If he was not working slower, as newspaper correspondents often

[1] Of this all but 30,000 tons was steam: there were also 193,000 tons of naval launchings.

[2] Cp. p. 52 above.

[3] Jones, *Increasing Returns*, p. 92.

suggested, he was certainly not displacing other bricklayers by working faster. The physical efficiency of the industry—the return in bricks and mortar for a given amount of labour time and capital use—was in fact falling a little. But building was not really slack at the close, only leisurely. Its wage-rates, like its brick-laying habits, shifted hardly at all from 1900 to 1911. A rise of 7 per cent. in the rates between 1911 and July 1914 suggests a certain briskness in the demand for labour; but even so, wage-rates had not risen so fast as the cost of food, though a rather greater regularity of employment may possibly have made up the difference. However, in this matter of wage-rise and price-rise the position of the building trades was not unique.[1]

No industry was more active than coal-mining at the last, though the price-wage problem—with some others—twice led to important coal wars. Unlike building, coal-mining was extraordinarily, dangerously, greedy of men. Like building, its physical efficiency was declining.[2] In 1881 the coal output of 382,000 miners had averaged 403 tons per man; and up to that time this average output had grown. By 1901 a working force of 644,000 averaged only 340 tons per man; and in 1911 a force of 877,000 only 309 tons. In other words, at the end of that decade 36 per cent. more miners were working to get 19 per cent. more coal. But a rising output, and an export of coal which was rising fast, masked the weakness of this position. By 1913, more than a quarter of all the coal raised, and there had never been so much, was being shipped abroad, exclusive of the bunker coal. Ten years earlier the proportion had been a fifth and thirty years earlier a seventh. In value, the coal exports of 1913—it was a year of high prices—came to rather more than a tenth of all the exports of United Kingdom produce: in 1883 they had not been one twenty-third. This rise in their relative importance was the most marked alteration in the export trade of the age. They filled the tramp steamers outward bound and so kept the return freights on British imports low. They brought English miners in thousands into South Wales, and helped to find work for all the sons of all the miners' big families in Northumberland, Durham and Yorkshire. But this very great army of workers had been drawn into an industry which was using up faster than was necessary, if not so fast as Stanley Jevons had once feared, a national capital asset that

[1] See p. 469 below.

[2] Cp. vol. II. 103–4 and Jevons, H. S., *The British Coal Trade* (1915), p. 117.

might have been conserved.[1] And, although Britain's unusual geological and geographical advantages as a coal producer made at least a partial continuance of the exports reasonably certain, much of the trade lay open to damaging competition. It was unlikely, for instance, that England would always supply a fifth of the coal burnt in Berlin, as in the early years of the twentieth century she sometimes did.[2] The relative inefficiency of the industry was all against full maintenance of the exports, apart from that rivalry of other fuels which was already present and was sure to increase.

Coal exports had for years been treated by foreign critics of the British industrial state, and by some domestic critics of British policy, as an item of at least questionable value, if the long future were taken into account.[3] With the coal exports it had been usual to link the exports of machinery, which had grown almost equally fast.[4] For the decade 1881–90 machinery exported had been worth on the average £12,200,000; for the five years 1909–13 it averaged £32,300,000; in 1913 itself it was worth £37,000,000. Some of the critics would probably have sympathised with the arguments which had led parliament in the early years of the industrial revolution to prohibit the export of machinery altogether—we must keep our inventions to ourselves.[5] Only in the difficult 'eighties had such arguments come back to mind. Revived in the slack years after the Boer War, in the prosperous 'tens they were once more forgotten. Britain, they stated in their modern form, was equipping her rivals, or potential rivals; undermining her own foundations; digging her own grave. Obviously it was in years of active capital export that this alleged undermining went on fastest: 1889–90 had been peak years in the export both of machinery and of capital generally. But for these machinery exports the average exports of the 'eighties would have been several points lower. Now, in the furious producing, exporting and investing of the last years, the peak of 1913 rose above its predecessor of 1907 by more than five millions.

[1] The free-trade argument against this view is suggested on p. 51 above.

[2] *Consular Report on Germany for* 1906 (F.O. Annual Reports, 3796).

[3] This is e.g. part of the theme of Wagner, A., *Agrar- und Industriestaat*, and a subject of discussion in the *Memoranda on British and Foreign Trade and Industry* of 1903. And cp. Jevons, H. S., *op. cit.* p. 752.

[4] Also dealt with by Wagner and in the *Memoranda*.

[5] The various Acts are set out in Held, A., *Soziale Geschichte Englands* (1881), p. 519.

In a vague, general, but in practice unimportant way the whole argument was correct—the more machines of any sort any people has the nearer they are likely to be to a machine age in which they can make their own. There were however degrees of nearness. The wisest of the machine buyers, those who worked below the slopes of Fujiyama and prayed "to Buddha at Kamakura", were brilliant craftsmen following a thought-out policy. They were very near. But it could not be said that there was any danger worth considering for Britain in the export of gold-crushing machinery to South Africa, of tin dredges to Malaya, or of boilers and steam engines and turbines to a score of countries short both of coal and of steel and behind her in mechanical capacity. Even had the danger been greater, there was nothing to be gained by refusing to do to-day work which you could do well merely because your children might have to do work of another kind to-morrow. The farsighted policy for an industrial nation and its business leaders was to concentrate on the most elaborate and ingenious work of which it was capable.

It remained true that, with those exports of textile machinery which came to about a quarter of the total machinery exports, British engineering firms, helped by makers of flax machines in Belfast, were systematically equipping textile industries abroad to compete with those of the United Kingdom. And Britain's textile exports were still the main element in her export trade, as England's had been for five hundred years. If the world could increase its consumption of textiles at the rate assumed to be normal during the nineteenth century, there might be work for more than all the mills of Britain, the Continent and America; of India and China and Japan—otherwise not. Even if the world's demand expanded at the old rate, mills could easily be sucked, so to speak, out of Britain by appropriate tariff appliances, or by cheap labour. Already there were British-owned sewing-cotton mills inside the tariff bounds of a dozen foreign countries; there was British capital in other Indian and Chinese cotton mills, and in Indian jute mills. The general arguments for the continuance of the export of machinery were as applicable in this as in other spheres, only in this the consequences were nearer and more certain. The thing was not new: the export of textile machinery had not grown excessively of late years. That was one reason why the consequences were so certain. Recently some countries had been equipped, and as markets for British textiles had declined. Others, which at one time or another had bought British equipment, were competing in third markets, or even in the British market. But in the British market there had always been a good deal of textile competition, especially from France, helped more by special aptitudes and good taste than by purchases of British machinery.

Dominant as the textile yarns and fabrics still were in the export trade, their relative importance had been declining steadily for two generations. In 1850 they had furnished 60 per cent. of the export values of the United Kingdom. By the early 'eighties (1880–4) their share had fallen to 46 per cent.[1] A generation later (1909–13), the fall continuing almost uniformly, the share was 34 per cent. Those who, in the politico-economic discussions of 1903–6, worked to defend Peelite and Gladstonian tradition, and the leaving of trades to find their natural level, pointed with a justifiable satisfaction to the growing diversity of the manufactured exports. Though Britain, they argued, had equipped textile mills overseas, other exports —electric cables, boots, 'apparel'; yes, and machinery—had gradually replaced some of the cottons and woollens, without producing any crisis. Lancashire was unusually busy in 1911–12, and the Yorkshire wool-manufacturing cities had led the revival of trade in 1910. For the absolute quantities of textiles exported were in the aggregate as large as ever, in some important groups much larger than ever; and there was an expanding market at home, in spite of foreign competition. The yardage of cotton piece-goods shipped annually during the quinquennium 1909–13 was 40 per cent. greater than it had been in 1880–4. Here was nothing to complain about. In fact cotton, the industry in which rivals had been most obviously helped by exports of British machinery, was holding its own in the export markets, absolutely and relatively, rather better than the others. Wool and silk were more harassed by foreign tariffs; flax more by changes in world fashions and the competition of cotton itself; jute, a rough trade, more by the competition of rough native labour in India. As a result, during the period (1880–4 to 1909–13) in which textile exports as a whole had fallen from 46 to 34 per cent. of total exports, cotton exports had fallen from 32·5 per cent. of total exports only to 25 per cent., while in quantity and value they had increased con-

[1] Cp. vol. II. 229.

siderably. If the world's demand and Lancashire's efficiency were such as to yield these results, the raising up of competitors and the profits from the export of machinery could be pursued with equanimity. The slow relative contraction of an industry hurts no one: it only means that, if the families of those engaged in it are large, not all of them can follow their parents. Absolutely the industry was not contracting: new factories were growing up, "trade was good, labour was well employed, new spindles and looms were erected in large numbers, profits were well maintained".[1]

This was satisfactory, for of all British industries, textile or non-textile, cotton was the one most completely dependent on the export market. It always had been. Now, if, *per impossibile*, exporting were to cease, the industry would have to contract to less than a third of its size, perhaps to much less. The coarser sections of the trade would certainly have to contract to much less; for of all the piece-goods manufactured nearly 90 per cent. —by yards, not by value—were exported.[2] And it was precisely this coarser end of the trade—in spinning the lower counts; in manufacturing the grey cloth and the dhooties—which was most threatened by newly risen competitors. Threatened but, as has been seen, not yet hurt.

The wool industries were in the safer position of producing from two-thirds to three-fifths for the home market and from a third to two-fifths for export. That is to say, they were near the centre line of the whole British economy, which was selling overseas something like a third of all the values that it produced.[3] They were never fully occupied when foreign trade was slack; but they could bear a very great reduction in it without catastrophe. Of great reduction there was no prospect in 1909–13. There was contraction on one side of the trade, the worsteds, after the exceptionally busy year 1910; but there was expansion on the other, the woollens. Such changes of emphasis were normal.

[1] *Report of the Dep. Comm. on the Textile Trades after the War* (1918, Cd. 9070), p. 45. The account of the cotton trade in this report is specially valuable. And cp. p. 126 below.

[2] The figure for 1907 was 88·9. *Final Report of the first Census of Production*, p. 290. It was approximately representative for that decade.

[3] Above, p. 3; *Census of Production*, p. 295; *Report on Textile Trades after the War*, p. 71. The Census gave an estimated export of one-third, which the *Report* estimated to have risen to two-fifths by 1913.

A national industrial economy which habitually shipped abroad one-third of all that it produced was not on that account in a state of dangerously unstable equilibrium—given peace and the freedom of the seas. If it was bound to sell heavily and continuously to provide itself with food and raw material, there were plenty of food and raw material producing lands who also were obliged to sell, if they wanted to preserve their economic health; and who in effect gave a great deal of produce annually as interest on old borrowings. There was no prospect of a sudden change in the economic organisation of these predominantly agrarian countries, and no one supposed that they would all repudiate their debts. Even if they did, they would still have to get rid of their produce. The possibility that they might plough it in or burn it had not yet been considered.

But if there was no prospect of any sudden interference with Britain's essential selling and buying, analysis of the statistical evidence does suggest that the terms of interchange of British exports—mainly manufactures and coal—for the foodstuffs and raw materials which made up the bulk of her imports had taken a slight turn for the worse in the new century. In that barter of goods for goods which lies behind the money façade of foreign trade, Britain was swapping rather more of her exports for a given quantity of imports. She was not so much of an exporting monopolist manufacturer who can get his own prices as she had once been. Those who like pictures may think, without serious error, of John Bull offering a rather better bit of steel-work or another few yards of unbleached cotton for each quarter of wheat or load of timber.[1]

The change had set in about the year 1900. During the two previous decades the terms of the barter had been increasingly favourable to Britain—more and more wheat or timber for the same bit of steel-work or bale of cottons. But, during the first decade of the twentieth century, the statistical evidence suggests that they had become definitely, though not ruinously, less favourable. From 1910 they began to improve again, and in 1913 were nearly back to the level of 1900.[2] There are diffi-

[1] See Taussig, F. W., "Great Britain's Foreign Trade Terms after 1900", *E.J.* March, 1925; Taussig, *International Trade*, p. 253 and *passim*. The statistics used are of course those of the U.K. but it is fair to assume that strictly British statistics would not yield appreciably different results.

[2] In the *Comm. Hist.* for 1910 the *Economist* pointed out that abundant world harvests had affected the exchange of agricultural for manufactured goods in Britain's favour.

culties in the handling of the evidence; but it is at least reasonably certain that between 1900 and 1913 the terms of the international barter had not become more favourable to Britain, whereas in earlier decades they had.

Was there then a stagnation, a relative inefficiency, in British industry after 1900? Foreign critics certainly believed it to be stagnant, relatively inefficient, rather idle. Frenchmen made jokes about English business men's long week-ends and about the English wage-earners' short working week. Americans expected to profit by English conservatism. "Wenn wir noch hundert Jahre Frieden haben," an eminent German business man said to a German general, "werden wir England tot gemacht haben."[1] Many English critics of England said much the same thing. But these opinions are hardly evidence, certainly not proof. Satisfactory evidence is not easy to get; but those exact tests of efficiency which can be, and have been, applied to a few leading British industries bear out the Americans' expectations, if not the German's remote forecast. Some of the older British primary industries were almost certainly stagnant, or worse, at this particular time.

Coal, as the rough test already applied shows, had been worse than stagnant in efficiency since before 1900. Not only the money costs but the real costs, the expenditure in labour and material and organisation, of bringing a ton of coal to bank had been rising since some date subsequent to 1891.[2] Whatever the explanation, the fact was patent that an increase in the number of miners, accompanied by heavy investments of capital, produced a less than proportionate increase in the output of coal. And not only was coal now third on the list of export values, coming between the iron and steel manufactures and the wool manufactures, but it was the only raw material which every industry was bound to use.

More refined statistical tests have been applied to the Lancashire cotton and the Cleveland pig-iron industries.[3] They

[1] von Stein, *Erlebnisse* (1919), p. 122. Stein said that he asked his business friend "ob er denn glaube, dass England diese hundert Jahre geduldig abwarten werde?" And adds—"die Antwort ist jetzt in deutlichster Form gegeben." For America, above, p. 35.

[2] Above, p. 63 and vol. II. 103; Jones, *Increasing Return*, p. 51, and his whole discussion of the coal industry.

[3] By Jones, *op. cit.* pp. 100–45. It is not possible to discuss the tests here. For iron, cp. *Report on the Iron and Steel Trades after the War* (1918, Cd. 9071), p. 25, and below, p. 122.

yield results which might have been anticipated from a non-statistical study of those two industries at the close of the nineteenth and the beginning of the twentieth centuries. Most of the economies of machinery had been attained in cotton long since. There was no fundamental improvement in the blast furnace and its accessories between 1886 and 1913. In neither industry was there any reorganisation which might have made labour and capital on the average much more productive. In both the week's work tended to become shorter or less intense. In both, with the fall and rise of general prices, there was first a fall, then a rise, in the money costs of production. The start of the rise in money costs came a little earlier for iron than for cotton, though for both it came just where it would be expected, between 1895 and 1897. But, behind these monetary fluctuations, the real costs of producing cotton goods and pig-iron, the expenditures of labour and capital to produce a given quantity of either, were in 1910–13 much what they had been in the 'eighties. There had been slight ups and downs in the interval. After a rise in the 'nineties, for example, there was a slight fall in the real costs of producing pig-iron in Cleveland due to technical economies, after 1900. The real costs of cotton manufacture, on the other hand, fell a little in the 'nineties and subsequently rose. But, looking from the beginning to the end, "there was little, if any, net change in the efficiency of the British cotton and pig-iron industries...during the period 1885–1910; whereas"[1]—similar tests applied to these industries in America indicate a definite, in pig-iron a very marked, increase of efficiency over the same period.[2] It is most probable that the German iron industry, if similarly tested, would also have shown increased efficiency.

The analysis certainly points at least to stagnation at the primary stages of cotton and iron manufacture. It has not been applied, probably cannot be applied, to the complex finishing processes in the cotton industry or to the working up of the pig-iron into iron and steel goods. Here efficiency may have been increasing, as it almost certainly was in young and adaptable industries such as machine boot-making and the making of motor-cars.[3] Had British industry as a whole been yielding

[1] Jones, p. 50.

[2] Jones, pp. 146–244. The conclusions for cotton apply only to Massachusetts, which is unfortunate as the cotton industry was growing so fast at this time in the south.

[3] For boot-making see p. 182 below.

an increasing return to human effort, the fact that rather more of its produce had to be bartered for a given quantity of imports would have involved no real loss. Perhaps as a whole it was yielding an increasing return; but we do not know. If it was, the small estimated deterioration in the terms of barter over the years 1900–13 is of no account. (It is of no very great account in any event.) And the improvement in those terms between 1910 and 1913 should have been an encouraging sign, if any contemporaries were aware of it. There can have been very few who were. Economists had not then completed their analysis, and few other people thought in economists' terms, terms of real not money prices, terms of efforts and sacrifices. Had many contemporaries been so thinking, and had they been masters of all the facts, they might have been confirmed in a common opinion that Britain, though as fully occupied with work in 1910–13 as any country can hope to be, was yet not so stirring industrially as America or Germany, nor so stirring as she had herself once been; but that her conservatism had been shaken and that she was preparing, at her own pace, in those last years, to prove that she was not decadent, though both enemies and desponding friends often said that she was.

For it is to a reading no more new and curious than this that the delicate and ingeniously mounted pointer on the economist's statistical dial approximately swings.

CHAPTER II

AGRICULTURE IN THE INDUSTRIAL STATE

BEFORE Victoria's jubilee far-sighted people knew that the British farmer was fast losing, for one thing after another, that natural protection of distance on which the free-traders of the early nineteenth century had naturally reckoned, and upon which James Caird was still reckoning, though now without warrant, in 1878.[1] For things not perishable and of high value in proportion to their bulk there was not a great deal to lose. It had long been possible to ship a pound of greasy New Zealand wool, usually worth more than a shilling on the London market, half-way round the world for 1*d.* or less. The cost during the twenty-seven years after 1886 never fell appreciably below ½*d.*; so that the fall of 26 per cent. in the average cost of imported wool, from the decade of 1877–86 to the decade 1887–96, cannot be explained by the lowering of the distance barrier.[2] But wheat, which on the average of the twelve years 1868–79 had cost 11*s.* a quarter in carriage from Chicago to Liverpool, and still cost 9*s.* 1½*d.* in 1880, could be brought for 6*s.* 2½*d.* in 1886. By 1892 the figure would be 4*s.* 3*d.*, and by 1902, 2*s.* 10½*d.*[3] The carriage costs of all grains, on equally well organised trade routes, had fallen, and would fall, similarly. Fresh meat which would always have been in the same class as wool, had it been able to stand transport, now could stand transport and was in the same class; though the imports of frozen and chilled meats grew rather slowly during the 'eighties, while the processes for handling them were being worked out. So pigs' meat, which came cured, dominated the meat imports down to 1886, when the stock of it imported was still more valuable than those of beef and mutton together.[4] Twenty

[1] Cp. vol. II. 281–2.

[2] For prices see the Return of *Wholesale and Retail Prices*, 1903 (321), p. xxxix; for wool freights, *Second Series of Memoranda* [on]... *British and Foreign Trade*, 1904 (Cd. 2337), p. 261.

[3] First series of *Memoranda* [on]... *British and Foreign Trade*, 1903 (Cd. 1761), p. 130; cp. *Decline and Recovery of Wheat Prices in the 'Nineties* (*Stanford University Wheat Studies*, June–July, 1934), pp. 293–4; Crawford, R. F., "An Inquiry into Wheat Prices", *S.J.* 1895, pp. 75 *sqq.*

[4] Craigie, P. G., "Twenty Years' Changes in our Foreign Meat Supply", *J.R.A.S.* 1887, pp. 465 *sqq.* Hooker, R. H., "The Meat Supplies of the U.K.", *S.J.* 1909, pp. 304 *sqq.*

years later—the processes having been perfected, and the Argentine having been added to America and Australasia as an important source of fresh meat supply—the pigs' meat was only one-third of the total.

With transport costs little heavier between continents than they once had been between counties, only the bulkiest and most perishable agricultural produce was left outside the range of international competition—roots, mostly consumed on the farms; main-crop potatoes;[1] fresh milk, hay, and a few other things of less importance. Even these were subject to any price-reducing forces which might be at work, other than those connected with transport, especially to the effect of the steady change over from unsheltered corn growing to partially sheltered dairy farming. Happily for the farmers, the demand of a growing population, whose consuming power per head was also growing, almost completely counteracted any such forces in the milk trade. St Thomas' Hospital made its milk contracts at an average price of 10·2*d.* a gallon in the decade 1871–80; at 9·0*d.* a gallon in 1881–90; and at 8·6*d.* a gallon in 1891–1900. The average for the 'seventies would have been rather less but for the very high prices of the bad seasons at their close.[2] Hay prices appear not to have fallen on the average at all.[3] This is what might be expected. In the 'eighties there was no import of hay worth recording and, except during the Boer War, there was never an import really considerable. Until well into the twentieth century, demand from the town stables was expanding; and even on the land the number of horses, as well as that of cattle, was going up. The supplies of hay were always uncertain; and although the area used for hay growing was extended considerably in course of time, extension was not everywhere easy.[4]

Potato growing, though reasonably well protected by circumstance, was in a somewhat less favourable price situation than dairy or hay farming. Though population grew, the demand for

[1] The import of potatoes was negligible: Crawford, R. F., "Notes on the Food Supplies of the U.K., Belgium, France and Germany", *S.J.* 1899, p. 600.

[2] Retail prices in London followed the same course as these contract prices. *Wholesale and Retail Prices*, as above, pp. 136–7, 279.

[3] Figures are defective, but the result suggested is as given. *Wholesale and Retail Prices*, pp. 202–3, and the Annual Trade Returns as summarised in the *Statistical Abstracts for the U.K.*

[4] The hay statistics in the Board of Agriculture's annual *Acreage and Live Stock Returns* are naturally not the best series, but they justify this statement.

potatoes per head of the population did not. Almost certainly it declined, though there are no satisfactory statistics to prove this; for as modern populations become more comfortable the potato invariably takes a less important place in their dietaries. Meanwhile the acreage under potatoes in Britain changed very little. It was slightly less for the five years 1906–10 than it had been for the years 1886–90—a reflection of the price history which itself reflects, among other things, the sluggishness of demand.[1] Taking again the St Thomas' contracts, which no doubt indicate the curve though not necessarily the precise level of urban prices, the decade average per cwt. is 6*s*. 8½*d*. for the 'sixties, 7*s*. 11*d*. for the 'seventies, 6*s*. 1*d*. for the 'eighties and 5*s*. 1½*d*. for the 'nineties. In the late 'nineties the price of potatoes was still falling.[2]

Intercontinental competition hardly affected meat prices before the 'eighties. Great as the potential productive power of the Americas and Australasia was, it was not developed so rapidly as that for wheat had been, and continued to be. The improvement in dietaries which worked against the potato grower worked for the cattle trader and the grazier. In 1883 mutton prices had been higher than ever before, and beef prices only a shade below the maximum of 1873. Both fell sharply from 1883 to 1887, mutton prices by nearly 28 per cent., beef prices by rather less; though beef in 1887 was cheaper than it had been since 1851. However, the 1883 prices were abnormal and so were those of 1887. Those of 1871, a good year both for agriculture and industry, and of 1888, another good year, are more representative. Between these the fall was trifling; 8·5 per cent. for beef; 1·4 per cent. for mutton. There were worse years ahead. So late as 1898, beef prices were just over 20 per cent. below the level of 1871; and in 1893 and again in 1896 mutton prices were 8·5 per cent. below it; but for the ten years 1887–96—the most difficult decade for agriculture—average beef prices were not quite 13 per cent., those of hides 20 per cent., and average mutton prices not quite 3 per cent. below the level of 1871.[3] Contrast this with the corresponding fall of

[1] The average for 1886–90 was 561,000: the maximum was 608,000 acres in 1905: the average for 1906–10 was 558,000.

[2] *Wholesale and Retail Prices*, pp. xxiv *sqq*.

[3] *Wholesale and Retail Prices*, p. xliii, figures, xxvi, diagrams; hides, p. xlv. And see Hooker, R. H., "The Course of Prices at Home and Abroad, 1890–1910", *S.J.* 1911–12, pp. 1 *sqq*.

29 per cent. for barley, 30·8 per cent. for oats and 48·6 per cent. for wheat.

All the price curves of important home grown foodstuffs, except that of potatoes, turned slightly upwards at some point between 1895 and 1899. For wheat and corn generally the turn began in 1896. The upward turn of wool prices was delayed until 1903; but when it came it was decided:[1] ten years later a level had been reached equal to that of the early 'fifties, of 1870, or of 1881–2, if still well below the peaks of the cotton famine or of the trade boom in the 'seventies. The index number for animal food—meat of all kinds and butter—which had never fallen far, had about recovered all that it had ever lost by 1913.[2] Wheat prices, which had suffered most, recovered least. They never touched again—in this age—the devastating low level of 22*s.* 10*d.* a quarter registered for 1894. There was a false recovery in 1897–8, to 30*s.* 2*d.* and then to 34*s.*, at the time of a notorious cornering enterprise—itself based on American crop shortages—on the Chicago wheat market; but a slide back to levels between 25*s.* and 30*s.* followed.[3] From 1907 however the level kept constantly above 30*s.* In 1909 wheat growers were even cheered by prices above 40*s.* in the months preceding harvest, and by an average of 36*s.* 11*d.* for the year, the highest since 1891 (37*s.*) and before that since 1883 (41*s.* 7*d.*). But although, at the time of the false recovery of 1897–8, the President of the British Association for the Advancement of Science had set tongues and pens loose to discuss his proposition that "under present conditions of heedless culture, a scarcity of wheat is within appreciable distance",[4] his distance drew out into more and more remote perspectives. If United States and Indian surpluses for export slackened a little, those of Canada and the Argentine increased. By 1912–13 Canada was reckoned "our most trustworthy" purveyor.[5] So even in the last seven years of peace, when wheat growers got what

[1] For the period to 1903 see Turner, J. W., "The Position of the Wool Trade", *J.R.A.S.* 1896, pp. 67 *sqq.*; Thompson, R. J., "Wool Prices in Great Britain", *J.R.A.S.* 1902, pp. 395 *sqq.* And cp. Clapham, J. H., *The Woollen and Worsted Industries* (1907), p. 276.

[2] See Paish, G., continuation of Sauerbeck's Index Number for animal food in *S.J.* 1913–14, p. 556.

[3] Layton, W. T., "Wheat Prices and the World's Production", *J.R.A.S.* 1909, pp. 99 *sqq.* and *Decline and Recovery of Wheat Prices in the Nineties*, p. 334, discuss the wheat price peak of 1897 and the Leiter corner.

[4] Crookes, Sir Wm., *The Wheat Problem* (1899), p. vi.

[5] Rew, R. H., "The Nation's Food Supply", *S.J.* 1912–13, p. 98.

pleasure they could from prices above 30*s*., the average price of wheat was still 40 per cent. lower than it had been in 1871, and the 4 lb. loaf in London 35 per cent. cheaper.[1]

To these different and successive price-changes British agriculture, like the agriculture of all Europe, had been obliged to adjust itself during nearly twenty difficult years, before the stabler and more favourable conditions of the period after 1895–9 set in.[2] Alone among the great countries of Europe, Britain made no use of protective tariffs to ease the adjustment, though from time to time some faintly protective flavour was detected by critical taste in one or other of her agricultural policies. In 1892, for example, the import of foreign live stock was prohibited, to save from disease those British flocks and herds which included the finest pedigree animals of the world, and from which those of the new continents were regularly replenished. Initiated for excellent reasons, the prohibition was maintained until the reasons were at least less urgent, maintained, some of its critics argued, as a measure of general agricultural protection, or, others argued, in the sole interest of Irish breeders whose store cattle thus had sheltered access to the British market.[3] There was a tiny measure of protection in the so-called 1*s*. registration duty on corn imposed in 1902 and abolished in the following year.[4] But the occasional slight deviations from the strait way of Gladstonian finance, and the sharp controversies to which they led, serve only to emphasise how conscientiously, on the whole, it was followed. Various kinds of state relief or assistance for agriculture were suggested at different times, and some of them were tried;[5] but crude

[1] This is a rough conclusion based on the figures for 1871–1911 now used by the Ministry of Labour. The 4 lb. loaf had many prices at the same time. Rew, R. H., "The Middleman in Agriculture", *J.R.A.S.* 1893, p. 63; Bear, W. E., "The Food Supply of Manchester", *J.R.A.S.* 1897, p. 207. See the diagram p. 12 above.

[2] A general reference may be made here to Lord Ernle's classic, *English Farming Past and Present* (1912), which touches on most of the topics here discussed in its last two chapters, and to Flavigny, *Le régime agraire en Angleterre* (1933).

[3] There is a detached discussion in Besse, P., *La crise et l'évolution de l'agriculture en Angleterre de 1875 à nos jours* (1910), p. 134. Cp. Hall, Sir Daniel, *A Pilgrimage of British Farming* (1913), p. 383.

[4] See below, p. 407.

[5] The Agricultural Rates Act of 1896 (59 and 60 Vic. c. 16) relieved occupiers of agricultural land of half the local rates. Introduced at a time of real depression and enacted for five years only, it was continuously renewed. There were also easings of the Land Tax. See Malet, B., *British Budgets*, 1887–1913 (1913), pp. 107 *sqq*., 283 *sqq*.

tariff protection, though often advocated a little draped and occasionally advocated naked, was not tried. There were plenty of elderly men of affairs in the 'eighties and 'nineties to whom corn law repeal was a vivid and blessed memory; many younger men for whom it had been canonised. So, just because agricultural depression first presented itself as a problem in wheat and wheaten bread, the political chance of its being handled by way of tariffs was almost infinitely small.

The depression into which a Royal Commission had been set to inquire in 1881 was connected with more things than corn—the price-fall in wool down to 1883 was swifter and deeper than that in wheat—but the inquiries showed to those who read them carefully that, apart from an Act of God—the dripping seasons of the late 'seventies—to which the commissioners themselves attached too much importance in their diagnosis, the deepest and most permanent depression was likely to be in the prices of corn.[1] Stock breeding and fattening, milk-farming and dairying, had suffered like other branches of agriculture from the malice of the rains; but districts—sometimes whole counties—in which they were prominent were in no real way depressed. As kindlier seasons set in, some part of the damage was made good everywhere. Sanguine people fell to hoping that the trouble would pass as the clouds rolled by, and that adjustment might wait. The evidence suggests that, on the whole, farmers' losses were not met soon enough or generously enough by abatements of rent, either at this or at a later stage of the depression.[2] That was natural: everyone always hoped that the long corner would soon be turned. The yield of Schedule A of the Income Tax (Lands) had not fallen by 18 per cent. from its recorded maximum of £59,810,000 for 1879–80 until 1888–9; and it did not settle down at what was to be its almost stationary level for the first fourteen years of the twentieth century, a level of about 30 per cent. below the maximum of 1879–80, until the very end of the nineteenth.[3]

The hopes of the late 'eighties, which tended to postpone

[1] See vol. II. 281–2.

[2] Levy, H., *Entstehung und Rückgang des landwirtschaftlichen Grossbetriebes in England* (1904), p. 95. (The English version, *Large and Small Holdings*, 1911, is modified and brought up to date.)

[3] Stamp, Sir J. C., *British Incomes and Property* (1927); and Thompson, R. J., "An inquiry into the rent of agricultural land in England and Wales during the nineteenth century", *S.J.* 1907, where groups of estates are discussed in detail and a fall in average rental for these groups, between 1878–9 and the late 'nineties, of from 25*s*. 6*d*. to 16*s*. 9*d*. is established.

drastic adjustment to new conditions, had some justification in the course of prices. The sharp fall in all meat prices, which had come since 1883 on top of the earlier and continuous fall in corn prices, was recovered for a time from 1887. So was the fall in corn prices itself. Even wool prices were at least steadying. Milk prices had never fallen far. By 1889–90 a brisk demand for vacant farms was reported, and a cautious optimism about the prospects of agriculture found its way into surveys of the economic life of the country. In 1891 the Bursar of an Oxford College, speaking from first-hand knowledge of agricultural land in nine counties, reported his good hopes to the Royal Statistical Society.[1] Three years later he confessed to the Society that these hopes had been an "amiable delusion".[2] They had been declared at exactly the wrong moment. From 1891 British corn prices took their final plunge to the absolute minimum of 1895. Despairing of wheat, which touched its minimum the year before, farmers had put more land under oats and barley—to produce this discouraging result. Meat prices also had turned downwards from 1891, and there was little help from wool. By 1894 the first reports of a new Royal Commission on Agricultural Depression were beginning to set out the facts.

There was a weather fact, an act of God, as there had been fifteen years earlier. Witnesses straight from the land talked almost as much about the drought of 1894 as their predecessors had talked about the rain of 1879.[3] But no one now made the mistake of supposing that this was the dominating cause. Nor was there excessive complaint of the landlords. Tenant farmers in Suffolk, for example, a county very hard hit, "usually considered that landlords had met them fairly".[4] "Why talk about rents," one English farming witness said. "It is a matter of prices not of rents. My prices are down £3. 10*s*. an acre. How can I ask my landlord for that off my rent?"[5] By this time most landlords had given a great deal, though none could give so much. In Hertfordshire they were said to have 20 per cent. of their farms in hand; these were now the economist's no-rent

[1] Price, L. L., "The recent depression in agriculture as shown in the accounts of an Oxford College, 1876–90", *S.J.* 1892, pp. 2 *sqq*.

[2] Price, L. L., "The Colleges of Oxford and the agricultural depression", *S.J.* 1895, p. 49. And cp. Venn, J. A., *Foundations of Agricultural Economics* (1933 ed.), pp. 378–9.

[3] See e.g. Report of J. Turner, Assistant Commissioner, in *First Rep. of the R.C. on Agric. Depression*, 1894, XVI.

[4] Report of A. Wilson-Fox on Suffolk, p. 43 (1895, XVI).

[5] R. Dickie, Q. 52,404 (1896, XVII).

land.[1] In Essex, eight large estates showed a net reduction in rental of 52·6 per cent. in thirteen years; and a terrible map, dotted thick with black patches, showed the land gone to "coarse, weedy pasture", between the Blackwater and Maplin Sands.[2] Eleven great Lincolnshire properties showed an average fall in rental of 48 per cent. Among them the Ancaster rentals had fallen by 67½ per cent.[3] In Suffolk six similar properties showed a fall of 55 per cent.[4] No wonder Suffolk tenants agreed that landlords had done their share.

Where there were no landlords to help the position might be desperate. The small owners in the open fields of Axholme, whose "selions" scattered over their fields puzzled the non-historically minded experts of the 'nineties, had banked too much on wheat and potatoes, though the wiser among them were growing celery and other special crops. They had mortgages of course; and "most of them were in utter despair", as a needlessly gloomy reporter put it. Despair was in fact not so general.[5] Farther south—about Spalding and elsewhere—many small men who had bought, "not infrequently" with "family money", were in a wretched plight. It was thought that nineteen out of twenty of them would be better off as farmers' foremen. Admitting this, some of these sturdy fellows added, "but we are our own masters", or "the position is better".[6] They deserved to survive and did.

These all, owners and farmers, were in the arable East, the counties whose terrific rent reductions were to bring the "income from lands" in the country down by about 30 per cent. A little westward things were better—tenants on the fine Northampton grass lands were upright, though bruised[7]—but even far to the West counties and districts which had escaped depression in the early 'eighties were now depressed, though not to the ground. Almost everywhere there had been some fall in rents; and wherever there had been a fall there had been tenant's losses first which justified the appeal to the landlord.

[1] Report of A. Spencer, p. 22 (1895, XVI).

[2] Report of R. H. Pringle, p. 51 (1894, XVI) and map.

[3] But the Yarborough rentals 'only' by 28. Report of A. Wilson-Fox on Lincoln, p. 55 (1895, XVI).

[4] Report of A. Wilson-Fox on Suffolk, p. 41 (1895, XVI).

[5] Report of Pringle on Axholme, pp. 6, 12, 15 (1894, XVI). For criticism of Pringle's Report, Haggard, H. Rider, *Rural England* (1902), II. 191. It is described as "incorrect as a whole" and proved to have been too gloomy.

[6] Wilson-Fox on Lincoln, pp. 59, 75.

[7] Report of Pringle on Bedford, Huntingdon and Northampton, p. 12 (1895, XVII).

In the Cheddar and "blue Dosset" cheese country, over more than 8000 acres the maximum reduction in rental reported was under 21 per cent. There had been no abnormal rate of change among the tenants and few bankruptcies; though it was added in explanation that the Dorset farmer was seldom driven into court. There was usually a composition with creditors when he "came to grief".[1] Things were much the same in the "eminently cattle rearing" parts of North Devon. Losses, abatements, reductions had been common, but bankruptcies and unlet farms were few.[2] In the six westernmost counties of Wales an unlet farm was hardly known and rents—judged by the Income Tax returns—had only fallen by rather more than 2 per cent. between 1878–9 and 1893–4.[3] Those were counties in which much of the farming was not for the market.

North of the Humber, even on the East side of the island, there was not so much wreckage as farther South. The arable farmers of the East Riding wolds were said to have pulled through so far without collapse, though they had made huge losses. With the North Riding and Durham came less corn, more stock, and less depression. An Assistant Commissioner had never seen such a fine average of cattle and horses as he found in that country.[4] Northumberland had carried on stiffly until the fall in prices of stock had followed the fall in corn. Now it was reckoned that in one representative district there had been a reduction in rents of about 25 per cent.[5] In Cumberland there was little outward and visible sign of depression. No farms were unlet, few rents unpaid, though farmers had lost on their stock. They and their landlords were economising at points where economy was hardly in the national interest. They and their families were working and living rather harder. Up there every one worked, the largest farmers like foremen among their hands. So the expert reported, and drew conclusions not too gloomy.[6]

[1] Report of R. H. Rew on Dorset, pp. 13, 19 (1895, XVII).

[2] Rew on N. Devon, *passim* (1895, XVI); the phrase is from Haggard, *op. cit.* I. 113.

[3] See evidence quoted in vol. II. 282.

[4] Pringle on South Durham and parts of North and East Ridings (1895, XVI).

[5] The Glendale Union; Wilson-Fox on Garstang and Glendale, p. 82 (1894, XVI).

[6] Wilson-Fox on Cumberland (1895, XVII). There is the usual discussion of the decline of the "statesmen", here attributed to sales when high prices of land tempted them; wild living and burdening their land with jointures; and letting it to tenants. Not all of these things connote genuine decay.

Moving South, the same expert found Lancashire also in half light. It was turning more and more to milk farming—milk instead of corn, milk instead of cheese. The towns seemed ready to take an "unlimited supply". The milkmen had been the least "bitten in pocket" of all and their numbers were naturally growing. "Rents are very fairly paid...no farms are unlet".[1] As for Cheshire, with its old established cattle and dairy farming, its potato growing, its market gardening, and its almost unbroken ring-fence of commercial and industrial consumers—from Birkenhead by Liverpool, to Manchester, Stockport and Macclesfield, and so to the Five Towns—it had suffered less than any county and was still paying what would have seemed to an East Anglian landlord impossible rents.[2]

Scotland grew so little wheat that she was insured against one source of loss and spared one need for adjustment; but her oats and barley fell into the price trough of 1895, and wool prices in Teviotdale did not touch bottom until 1901.[3] She had been helped by the intelligence of farmers and of landlords. In the South-East, the Border counties and the Lothians, there was depression but no rout. Landlords had had the sense to accept five-yearly breaks in the "almost universal"[4] nineteen-year farming leases to make abatements on the rentals. The 'overall' shrinkage of rental was estimated at from 25 to 30 per cent. and at this level the demand for farms was keen. Farther North, in Perth, Fife, Forfar and Aberdeen, depression was said to be very acute, yet there had been no abnormal changes of tenancy. Although there were many complaints of the impossibility of complying with the strict farming covenants usual in Scotland, there had been much relaxation of them. More important still; in making abatements landlords had acted quickly, before the tenant had wasted his capital in an attempt to pay at the old, now impossible, rate. The abatements varied greatly from district to district. They were less necessary in the cattle country of Aberdeen than in the more arable southern Perthshire and Fife. Sometimes they were not more than 10 per cent.; but 30 per cent. was the estimated average for the decade 1883–93.[5]

[1] Wilson-Fox on Garstang, pp. 7, 14.

[2] See in the *Report of Agric. Depression*, Q. 26,114 (T. Parton) and Bear, "The Food Supply of Manchester", *J.R.A.S.* 1897, p. 190.

[3] *Return of...Prices*, 1903, p. 53.

[4] Report of J. Hope on these counties (1895, XVII), p. 19.

[5] Hope on Perth, Fife, Forfar and Aberdeen (1894, XVI).

The agrarian problem of the true Highlands was a thing apart, for they were so much concerned with subsistence farming. In the far North and the Isles, as a result of an inquiry made in 1884 into the causes of discontent often leading to "open lawlessness" among the crofters, a Commission had been at work since 1887, fixing 'fair' rents, cancelling arrears, establishing security of tenure, enlarging holdings and regulating the common use of peat-mosses, 'seaware', and grazing land. Here the State was doing for one class of tenants what had to be done otherwise for all classes in the rest of Scotland.[1] The South-West, from Ayr to Galloway, a country of dairying, breeding, grazing and mountain flocks, with some patches of intensive cultivation, showed "no signs of collapse" in 1894–6, as might have been anticipated; but bankers gave grim accounts of the financial position of tenants "farming under long leases where the rent has not been adjusted", which suggests that landlords, relying on the relatively prosperous condition of their estates, had not been so prompt in action as those of the East. Some adjustment of rents was needed, though usually a small adjustment sufficed; and the tenants, for the most part, were still fond of their traditional fifteen- or nineteen-year leases.[2]

The Commissioners of 1894–6, well informed by witnesses and by their assistants about the technical defects of British farming, and much occupied with plans for easing its burdens and improving agrarian law, did not make the mistake of supposing that either faulty technique, or the incidence of those burdens, or the state of the law, or the course of the weather was a chief cause of its distress. Through the usual tangle of a majority and a minority report, and of signed reservations to each, ran a clear recognition that the trouble was one of prices, of world prices. Sir Robert Giffen, a member of the Commission, encouraged his colleagues by forecasting the near arrival of an upward turn in world gold prices. They were probably sceptical; for other experts demurred and prices had

[1] *R.C. on the condition of the Crofters and Cottars in the Highlands and Isles*, 1884 (XXXII). Annual *Reports of the Crofters' Commission*, e.g. *Seventh Report*, 1894 (LXIX). *Twenty-Fifth and Final Report*, 1913 (XIX. 213). Annual *Reports of the Congested District Board* (*Scotland*) closing with the *Fourteenth*, for 1911–12 (1912–13, XVII. 489).

[2] Report of J. Speir on Ayr, etc. (1895, XIII), pp. 4, 5.

been falling so long. In two years however the turn of the tide came, but so quietly—as is the way with tides—that it was at first hardly perceptible.[1]

The faint rise in prices brought no rise in rents. Indeed a slow fall continued. Landlords were broken in to remission and abatement. There were still arrears of reduction due in some places. Old tenants who survived had their lost capital to replace: new ones would take no risks. 'Income from lands' was nearly 5 per cent. less in 1901–2 than in 1896–7. In 1911–12 it was a shade lower than in 1901–2. Farmers were regaining confidence by the turn of the century and farms were letting more readily everywhere; but the Oxford bursar, who had ventured to hope untimely in 1891, would not admit to the Statistical Society that the "tide of agricultural depression" had turned by 1903. He allowed only "a sensible retardation in a continuing movement".[2] A well-known romantic writer, who was also a farming Norfolk squire, touring England in 1900–1, could see little hope anywhere; and when Scotsmen or Yorkshiremen kept their heads unbowed wondered how they did it. He recorded various gloomy forecasts about England reverting to rough grass and forest.[3] But a foreign student of English agriculture in 1903–4 noticed that people no longer talked of a crisis. "Every sign indicated", he thought, that "a betterment of agricultural affairs was setting in."[4] His opinion does not necessarily contradict that of the Oxford bursar; but it comes rather nearer to the historical truth as revealed later. It was in 1903, as has been seen,[5] that the most sluggish of the important agricultural price-curves, that of wool, took its decided upward turn.

Throughout the country the first, most obvious, and often most undesirable, response to the great price-fall had been economy. Landlords stopped building and draining. Farmers worked and cleaned their land less thoroughly. Hedging and ditching and thistle spudding fell into arrears, and there was saving on fertilisers. All this, if not universal, was very general. Where land did not 'tumble down' to third-rate pasture, as on

[1] Above, p. 18.
[2] Price, L. L. in *S.J.* 1905, p. 585.
[3] Haggard, H. Rider, *Rural England*, *passim* and, in particular, II. 282.
[4] Levy, *op. cit.* p. 109: his word is "eine Gesundung".
[5] Above, p. 75.

the Essex 'three-horse' clays[1]—a thing less common, taking the country as a whole, than the outcry about it might suggest—it usually suffered in some other way. In Suffolk, for example, every one agreed in 1894–5 that the land had deteriorated during the previous fifteen years.[2] The men who came through the depression most successfully were those who knew either how to adapt the whole system of farming to the new conditions, or how to 'farm light', to get all they could from the land for a minimum of giving. "The high scientific costly farming of 25 years since will not answer."[3] Light farming methods were not always anti-social. Sometimes there was only economy of old-fashioned extravagant practices. But there was always a risk of the land being 'let down', of some overdraft on the economists' "natural and indestructible properties of the soil", properties which may be natural but are not indestructible.

The story of the considerable migration of Scottish farmers into Essex, Hertfordshire and Suffolk illustrates these, and other, points in the history of the depression. A Wigtown man seems to have been the first to arrive in Essex, in 1880.[4] But most of his successors came from dairying districts in Ayrshire. They came because at home competition for farms was so keen—a significant fact—and because the conditions imposed on tenants were still so strict. In Essex a landlord was only too glad to get a tenant on any terms. The Scots brought their Ayrshire milch-cows, and kept them. In Essex they found an irregular four-course husbandry with much bare fallowing, and abandoned it. They also found some antiquated implements and much wasteful working of men and horses. These also they abandoned. Rootcrops were cut out because they were so expensive in labour. In place of them the Scots used short spells of temporary grass, usually perennial rye-grass. They learnt that the Essex clays were no place for good permanent pasture. Their rotation was one of seven or eight years, of which three to five was the spell of 'seeds'. Their chief cereal was oats, not wheat. The best of them used London gas-lime on their land.[5] Working hard themselves, they brought working wives and children—

[1] Pringle's Report, as above, pp. 36–7.

[2] Wilson-Fox's Report, as above, p. 30. Cp. Haggard, *op. cit.* I. 63 (Hants), II. 59 (Hunts).

[3] Bruce, R., "Some typical Farms in East Anglia", *J.R.A.S.* 1894, p. 529.

[4] Pringle's Report, as above, p. 43.

[5] "Experiences of a Scotsman on the Essex Clays", *J.R.A.S.* 1891, pp. 311 *sqq.*

whom possibly they exploited; for everywhere that was the working farmer's easiest economy. "The labourers' wives and daughters" in Suffolk had "for some years withdrawn from farm work"; but a Scotch woman would "muck out a pig-stye". "They eat porridge and brown bread which Suffolk men won't touch."[1] It was in short the competition of two standards of living.

Scots and East Anglians agreed that the dairy was the making of the Scot. Suffolk knew nothing about dairying, the incomers said. Of the incomers Suffolk said that they were bad arable farmers; that they seldom stayed more than five years, and that a Scot would not follow a Scot: he was too certain of finding the land let down. No doubt there was some malice here, as there was in the kinder saying of a Suffolk farmer of the old school—"well, they are occupying the land, but they're not farming it".[2] But every one agreed that some of the immigrants were "mere adventurers", and that the best of them had to 'learn the clay'. Still, in Essex few had been complete failures, and all who had not were satisfied in 1894–5 that the move South had been worth it, in spite of the clay.[3] No doubt it had been; but some of them may have been letting the land down to make it so, as their critics said.

Scots farmers came into many other parts of England, but nowhere in such numbers as into Essex, with the possible exception of Hertfordshire.[4] A parallel movement in the West was that of working farmers with knowledge of dairying from Cornwall and Devon into East Somerset, Gloucester and Warwick. They were reported to hold their own in districts where the current opinion was that a Scot could not manage stiff land —nor a Welshman any land.[5]

The Scots' abandonment of wheat in Essex was only a special case of what was happening all over the country. It was not that wheat prices had merely fallen like the rest. Since the 'seventies they had fallen out of, and below, the whole scale of prices, agricultural and industrial. Almost any crop paid better. So whereas in 1874 there had been 3,630,000 acres under wheat in Great Britain, and still 2,317,000 in 1887, by 1900 there

[1] Wilson-Fox's Report, as above, pp. 66, 70.
[2] *Ibid.* p. 70.
[3] Pringle's Report, pp. 44–5.
[4] For Scots in Hertford, Haggard, I. 511.
[5] Report of J. Turner on Frome and Stratford, 1894 (XVI), p. 29.

were only 1,845,000. The maximum and minimum for the years 1901–14 were 1,926,000 in 1912 and 1,375,000 in 1904. The recovery at the end shows how ready farmers were to plant the old staple crop, given the slightest encouragement by its price. But encouragement had been so scanty that in those last years less than one-fifth of the wheat consumed in the country was home grown; and the British consumer was accustomed to a kind of bread which unmixed home-grown wheat would not produce.[1]

Decline in the wheat area was responsible for nearly the whole decline in the aggregate corn-growing area, from 9,431,000 acres in 1874 to 8,146,000 in 1887, 6,953,000 in 1904 or the 7,152,000 in 1912. In the 'seventies that area had not fallen below a round 9,000,000 acres: in the ten years 1904–13 it averaged exactly 7,000,000. The prices of barley and oats were not out of step with other prices: some of the wheat-lands whose surpluses kept wheat prices out of step did not export the other grains largely. Besides, no barley was better than the best English for malting, and inferior barley, with a great deal of the oats, could be consumed on the land.

Down to 1888–90 the acreage under green crops—roots, potatoes, cabbages, lucerne and the like—had fluctuated round about 3,500,000. In 1904–13 it remained almost absolutely steady at 3,000,000. The fall was almost all due to a reduction in those crops of turnips or swedes, the cultivation of which the Scots had found too costly for their programme in Essex. When conditions had become approximately stabilised, in 1901–3, the increase in the acreage under those more economical crops which the Scots preferred—clover, sainfoin and 'grasses under rotation', whether cut for hay or eaten off by cattle and sheep—corresponded very nearly with the fall in the acreage under roots.

These changes, if the national statistics can be trusted—and there is nothing else to trust—were smaller in size, when the country is viewed as a whole, than contemporary accounts would suggest. Almost everywhere the cheap expedient of a longer spell of 'seeds' in the rotation is referred to as a principal adjustment to new conditions.[2] But apparently what

[1] Layton, W. T., *J.R.A.S.* 1909, p. 99 and Wood, T. B., "The Composition and Food Value of Bread", *J.R.A.S.* 1911.

[2] See e.g. Murray, G., "Variations of the four-course system", *J.R.A.S.* 1892, pp. 291 *sqq.*: the four-course has generally become a six-course, with two

happened was that a method already old merely spread somewhat and got talked about, especially in a few conservative districts like Essex where it had not hitherto been often tried. Even in the 'fifties Léonce de Lavergne had noted that "of late" the "practice had been to add another year to the [Norfolk] course, by allowing the artificial grasses to retain possession of the land for two years, thus making the rotation quinquennial";[1] and in the greater elasticity of rotation which came with the depression, an extension of this practice was only one way out of the difficulty. Another, and a very common one, was to take two 'white crops' running, the second—probably oats—being used on the farm for feed just as the 'artificial grasses' might have been.[2]

Even the really important change, an increase of permanent pasture in Britain, was only the dragging conclusion of a very ancient story. The actual area affected was again much less than many contemporary accounts might suggest. So it has always been. So it was at the time of the enclosures for sheep-farming in the sixteenth century. In the late 'sixties and early 'seventies of the nineteenth, the percentage of the cultivated land of Britain in permanent pasture was about 42; it was 42·1 in 1874. After a smooth almost uninterrupted rise, it was 52·9 in 1904 and 55·2 in 1914, the rate of increase having slowed down at the close. True, there had never been so great a change in forty years before, apart perhaps from the enclosures of 1775–1815. Yet this new change affected only some 13 per cent. of the cultivated area. In the early 'fifties Léonce de Lavergne had supposed that "nearly half the cultivated soil"[3] was in permanent grass. If permitted to revisit after sixty years, and supplied with more precise facts, he would only have had to write "rather more than half".

Nor had there been much dramatic change: whole stretches of land once arable had not become mainly pastoral. In the arable East soil and climate usually forbade any such wholesale

years' 'seeds' and only one root-crop in the six; Malden, W. J., "Recent changes in farm practices", *J.R.A.S.* 1896, pp. 30 *sqq.* McConnell, P., "Rotations", *J.R.A.S.* 1908, pp. 17 *sqq.*; with samples of new rotations, in which the longer spells of 'seeds' are very prominent.

[1] Lavergne, *The rural economy of Great Britain and Ireland* (1855), p. 51.

[2] Dugdale, J. H., "Select farms in the Darlington district", *J.R.A.S.* 1895, p. 488 and sample rotations in McConnell's article, as above.

[3] *Op. cit.* p. 51. The percentages are drawn from the Annual Statistics of *Crops and Live Stock.*

conversions. In the green West there was no place for them. It merely became greener. Devon had only 30 and Cornwall only 31 per cent. of its cultivated area under corn in the early 'seventies, compared with about 58 per cent. for all Britain. Already in 1890 the corn area in Devon had contracted to 21 and that in Cornwall to 22 per cent. of the whole, by slight transferences more or less everywhere. By 1910 the corn percentage was 19 in Cornwall and only 17 in Devon.[1] In Cumberland it was easy to drop corn in the same way: rainfall and soil enabled the farmer to make good permanent pasture in seven years, or less.[2] Sometimes, near the wavering line which divides East from West, an estate had changed character; but such things were rare. For they involved a re-equipping, and perhaps a subdividing of farms, for which only the more fortunate landlords of the depression were prepared.[3]

Though no one tale can be fully representative of Britain's geological and climatic variety, that of the Salisbury Plain country is typical. Farms there lay—and lie—in long strips, from the precious water-meadows by the chalk stream, up slopes of land that gets lighter as it rises, to the crests of the down broken up from sheep walk in the Crimean or the French Wars. There only a few inches of soil cover the chalk rock, and the manure cart had seldom gone so far. These 'tops' of the farms, true margins of cultivation, were going back to their old use and to nature. The more resolute and solvent farmers had sown them down and put black-faced sheep on them. Others left them, as the phrase was at Salisbury, to "lie in lark leaze". (The larks sing well there, and "up on the hill the wind blows strong".) Below, arable farming went on as before; though the dairy herd had often been increased.[4]

During the years of enforced and often unwise economy the mechanisation of agriculture went forward slowly. Here and there it went back: a decline is reported in the steam cultivation, particularly of the Essex clays, in 1894.[5] Perhaps it was out of kindness to his men that in the same year a representative East

[1] *Crops and Live Stock* and Punchard, F., "Farming in Devon and Cornwall", *J.R.A.S.* 1890, pp. 511 *sqq.*

[2] Wilson-Fox on Cumberland, 1895, as above, p. 6.

[3] The landlord of which the author is a small part (King's College, Cambridge) did a heavy job of this kind in Wiltshire.

[4] Report of R. H. Rew on Salisbury Plain, pp. 4, 15, *R.C. on Agric. Depression* (1895, XVI).

[5] Report of Pringle on Essex, p. 57 and evidence of H. H. Scott, Q. 30,034–5.

Anglian farmer, Mr Parsons of Horseheath, Cambridgeshire, still threshed "a considerable quantity of his corn with flails";[1] but it seems hardly the way to meet a price-fall connected with the world's mechanical progress in a district in which steam threshing had long been well established. Was it local wisdom or local stupidity that kept in action until 1899, and very much later, in Mid-Kent and the Sussex Weald, the old wooden Kentish turn-wrest plough, whose share "is merely a somewhat flattened point...which tears up the soil, leaving a crumbly bed"?[2] That there should be "in ploughs a wonderful variety" in an isolated county such as Pembroke, in 1887, is not surprising; but to read that what corn there was there, with a great deal of the hay, was still scythed is a reminder of the broad fringe of slow-moving areas which lay around and among those on whose practice generalisations about British agriculture were usually based.[3]

Into these latter the reaper-and-binder had followed the mere reaper from America, the faster since, in 1878–80, binders had begun to come on the market which used twine instead of the wire that British farmers had never liked. By 1895 full two-thirds of the efficient farms about the lower course of the Tees were using binders; but the not very confident pronouncement of an agricultural writer in 1900—"we are...all well aware that any one who has corn to cut should use a binder if possible"[4]—suggests that there was still a good deal of old-fashioned reaping at the close of the century. No doubt an era in which farmers were everywhere turning away from corn growing was not likely to see much enterprise in the mechanics of corn-production. If you did get a binder before your old reaper was worn out, was there any guarantee that your corn crop would pay? Yet binders had reduced the demand for harvest labour appreciably since the 'eighties, and would reduce

[1] Bruce, "Some typical farms in East Anglia", *J.R.A.S.* 1894, p. 506.

[2] Whitehead, C., "A sketch of the agriculture of Kent", *J.R.A.S.* 1899, p. 456. It is defended, and said to do "its work extremely well", by Hennell, T., *Change in the Farm* (1934), p. 74. It is possible that Hennell's love of the old ways has influenced his judgment. He also notes (p. 24) the "dozen or more" Sussex bullock-teams of 1914 (since extinct) and the widespread survival in the West and North (p. 87) of that broadcast sowing, which many agricultural writers, their eyes fixed on the arable East, are apt to treat as extinct.

[3] Wall, W. B., "The agriculture of Pembrokeshire", *J.R.A.S.* 1887, pp. 83, 86.

[4] Edwards, J., "Reaping machines, past and present", *J.R.A.S.* 1900, p. 299. For the Tees farm, Dugdale, J. H., "Select farms in the Darlington district", *J.R.A.S.* 1895, p. 494.

it further in the new century. For whereas, in the 'eighties, "labour-saving machinery"—of all kinds; not binders only—"was fully employed by comparatively few", by 1906 it was "almost universal on all holdings of sufficient size to make its use practicable".[1]

Before the depression, steam cultivation of the older sort had reached limits beyond which it was never likely to spread far.[2] Formal trials of "the capability of the tractor for field work" were not made until 1910. The machine which best fulfilled the conditions laid down for the trial was a steam tractor of road type but with special wheels. However the judges prophesied that "the oil-engine will ultimately best suit the farmer's requirements" as a general purposes motor.[3]

The dairy had not been a mechanical place when the depression began. It was in the rank wet year 1879 that a cream separator was first exhibited at the Royal Agricultural Show. The machine was Swedish, a Laval.[4] No British make was shown for another nine years. Adopted first by milk distributors, the separator gradually made its way into some well-equipped farms which could find a use for it from about 1890. But the average milk farmer, whether he distributed himself or sold to a distributor, had no use for it. It remained a specialist's tool.[5] As for milking machinery, inventors were at work in the twentieth century but the first trial at the Royal Show came only in 1913. Eleven machines competed and the prize again went to a Swede.[6] So the age closed, with discussion in Britain.

"The fruit industry", an official committee reported in June, 1905, after eighteen months' inquiry, "appears to be a most progressive industry; in fact, it is the only form of agriculture which has exhibited any sign of progress in recent years."[7] The extreme negative clause of this verdict might be disputed: the

[1] Rew, R. H., *Rep. on the decline in the Ag. Population of G.B.* 1906 (XCVI. 583), p. 14.

[2] Cp. vol. II. 268.

[3] Report on Trials of Agricultural Motors, *J.R.A.S.* 1910.

[4] Reports on Trials of Cream Separators, *J.R.A.S.* 1879, 1891.

[5] "During the last six years or so [1895–1901] several of the farmers [on a Wharfedale estate] have purchased hand separators." Haggard, *op. cit.* II. 305.

[6] Report on Trials of Milking Machines, *J.R.A.S.* 1913.

[7] *Report of the Departmental Committee on the Fruit Industry* (1905, Cd. 2589), p. 2.

positive clause is indisputable. The orchard area had increased by nearly 100,000 acres, or 63·9 per cent., since 1873, and the area under small fruit—not accurately known for the years before 1897—had increased by 11·7 per cent. in the short period since that date. About half the orchard growth had been before, and about half of it since, the year 1886. The acreage reached in 1904 remained almost steady for the next decade. So far as mere area is a test, a change which began before depression became acute ceased with the acute phase.[1]

Area is not however a complete test; for there was progress in quality and method both before and after 1904, and great progress in that type of fruit growing for which area is least important—the glass-house industry. The most unsatisfactory story is that of the cider orchards of the West. Many of them had been planted in the seventeenth century and were worn out. In 1890 they were said to be often in a shocking condition in Devon;[2] in 1905 to have been "terribly neglected" in many parts, "notably in Devonshire". There had been a revival of interest and a good deal of fresh planting, mainly in Hereford, in the years 1895–1905; and by the latter year progress and neglect were perhaps about balanced. The chief stimulus to improvement had come from the growing factory cider industry.[3]

In Kent, on the other hand, progress had been most satisfactory. By 1904–5 fears were being expressed that planting there had been overdone, as there was still a considerable planted area which had not yet come into bearing. The subsequent stagnation in the area of British orchards suggests that, for the time, this may have been true. "Every class of grower, and of plantation" was to be found in Kent, "from the ordinary farmer with the old grass orchard, to the highly specialised... grower, having possibly 500 to 1000 acres of fruit, in mixed plantations".[4] The specialists were naturally progressive, but —in contrast to the West Country—"very great improvement" had been reported some years earlier in the management of the classical Kentish cherry orchards.[5] It is true that the men of Kent had London at their door, and the continental fruit imports passing by to keep them awake, whereas in the nineteenth

[1] Figures in the *Crops and Live Stock* annual reports.
[2] Punchard, F. in *J.R.A.S.* 1890, p. 524.
[3] *Report* of 1905, pp. 2, 5, 6.
[4] *Ibid.* p. 6.
[5] Whitehead in *J.R.A.S.* 1899, p. 440.

century the market for cider had been dwindling and no one ever imported it from Normandy.

Kent had important glass-house centres, such as Erith and Bexley Heath, and there were others West of London; but the greatest were on the North side. Peter Kay of Finchley had started business in 1874: by 1899 he had 19½ acres under glass, growing grapes and tomatoes. All up the valley of the Lea, from Ponder's End in Middlesex to Chesham in Hertfordshire, the glass roofs had been rising. There had been a single house at Chesham in 1869: in 1899 there were 125 acres of houses. It was supposed that, in the whole country, the land under strictly commercial glass houses had grown from a negligible area to 1100 or 1200 acres by that time. The growth continued, though profits were narrow, depreciation heavy, and continental competition threatening and incessant.[1]

Among old fruit-growing areas other than Kent, most vitality had been shown about Evesham, the country of the Pershore plum, where an area "of many thousand acres stretching in every direction from the town" was "devoted to the cultivation of fruit, flowers and vegetables, and mostly divided into small holdings, varying from two to twenty acres".[2] Most of the Evesham holders were tenants. In the new fruit and flower district of Wisbech they were often owners. Here, and elsewhere in Cambridgeshire, as at Tiptree in Essex and in many parts of Kent, the stimulus to an agricultural industry which employed more men per acre than any other except the allied business of market gardening came chiefly from the jam factories which, helped by absurdly cheap sugar and a change in consumers' habits, had been growing fast since the 'eighties.[3]

Forestry had remained stagnant as always, though not acutely depressed. True, timber prices fell with the rest, but the greater part of the British wood lands were not managed with an eye to the market. "The sylvicultural details", to adopt the style of Whitehall, had "to be accommodated to the hunting and shoot-

[1] Bear, W. E., "Fruit and Flowers under Glass", *J.R.A.S.* 1899, p. 267 *sqq.* For other local history of fruit growing and glass-houses see *V.C.H. Bedford*, II. 139; *Cornwall*, II. 578–82; *Kent*, II. 460.

[2] *Report* of 1905, p. 6.

[3] See e.g. Wilson-Fox's Report on Cambridgeshire to *R.C. on Agric. Depression* in 1895 (XVII). The Tiptree jam industry grew out of Mr Wilkin's fruit farm in 1885. *V.C.H. Essex*, II. 478.

ing", "even on an estate that is considered to possess some of the best managed woods in England."[1] An inquiry in 1884–5 had produced information but none of that State action without which serious progress in afforestation, if desirable, was impossible.[2] Private landlords in the 'eighties and 'nineties could hardly be expected to plan extensively at a present loss for a generation or two ahead, though a few of them actually did. In its little Forest of Dean the Crown also did some good work. A serious attempt was made to manage it as a timber producing property and in 1897 a twenty-year plan was drawn up. At that time—and this is characteristic of the casual earlier management even of the best forest in England—the whole was immature except eighty acres of fine straight oak.[3] A few years later (in 1902) there was inquiry into the education of foresters,[4] but no suggestion as to where—in Britain—more of them might best be employed. Then, in 1906–9, a Royal Commission repeated what all previous Commissions and Committees had said—that Britain compared with other countries really had no forests; that "speaking generally" what timber she did produce was "not of the highest quality"; that nevertheless, when properly managed, both hard and soft woods could be grown here to great perfection; that there was plenty of land at present unused or lightly used, which might carry new forests; that a world timber famine, if not inevitable, was at least reasonably probable, though at an uncertain date: and that afforestation was a task for the State.[5]

Next year the new Development Commission made provision for regional advisers in forestry and offered to make grants to assist landowners in afforestation.[6] This was not what the Commission of inquiry had suggested; but the revived interest in forestry set people dreaming of woods once more covering the hills and waste places, and of a future Britain with at least as much forest in proportion to her area as Holland or Denmark. At the moment she had rather more than half as much. That

[1] *Second Report of the R.C. on Coast Erosion and Afforestation*, 1909 (XIV. 125), p. 4.

[2] See vol. II. 501.

[3] *V.C.H. Gloucester*, II. 278. (The straight oak was felled in 1914–18. It had probably been planted about the time of Trafalgar.)

[4] By a Committee of the Board of Agriculture. See Venn, *op. cit.* p. 410.

[5] *Second Report of the R.C.* pp. 3, 41 *sqq.*

[6] Venn, *op. cit.* p. 410. For the Development Commission, below, pp. 373, 389.

she would ever have so much as France was hardly within the range of dreams.[1]

These stirrings of new policies came at a time when, by general agreement, agriculture was in no proper sense depressed. Landlords' incomes had recovered very little, but they had performed their function of shock-absorbers and now there were prospects of recovery. The taxable income from lands in England and Wales in the year the Great War began (£37,000,000) was, as it happened, precisely the same as it had been in the year of Waterloo: at the worst, it had been a few hundred thousand pounds less: at the best (1879–80) £15,000,000 more.[2] But rents were well paid. Competition for farms was brisk. The columns for arrears in the estate books were emptying, and every now and then, since about 1907–8, when "in no part of Great Britain had there been any difficulty in letting farms"[3] at the low rents then current, it had been possible to relet at an advance. Yet on the whole the rents of 1900–13 were about stabilised at the level to which they had fallen by 1900, while prices were not. In general price history 1900 was a short period peak year.[4] But there was no appreciable decline from the level of agricultural prices then reached: and from 1906 the rise was resumed. By 1913 certain dominant prices had risen since 1900 as follows:

Imported cereals (wheat, oats and barley together)	by	20	per cent.
" fresh meat (beef, mutton and pork)	"	3·5	"
" butter and cheese together	"	15	"
" hides	"	65	"
Exported British wool[5]	"	100	"

Or to use different groupings, which include some other important articles of produce, wholesale prices of cereals, potatoes and hops, grouped together, had risen by 18·6 per cent., and

[1] Percentage of surface under forest: England, 5·3; Scotland, 4·6; Wales, 3·9; Denmark, 7·2; Holland, 7·9; France, 17·0; Germany, 25·9. *Second Report of the R.C.* p. 3n.

[2] Stamp, *British Incomes and Property*, p. 49: 1814–15, £37,063,000; 1913–14, £37,071,000. The income in Scotland had grown from £5,075,000 to £5,713,000.

[3] Eversley, Lord, "The decline in numbers of the agricultural labourers in Great Britain", *S.J.* 1907, p. 293. This is confirmed by the experience of King's College, Cambridge, which held land in thirteen counties, most of which had been hard hit by the depression. Cp. vol. II. 283.

[4] See the diagram on p. 12.

[5] For wool, 1913 was a year of unusually high prices: the rise from 1900 to the average of 1910–13 was 73 per cent.

of meat, eggs and dairy produce together by rather more.[1] Within these bounds the luck of farmers varied; but he was a weak or very unfortunate man who was not taking 20 per cent. more on a given yield from his farm in 1913 than he, or his now bankrupt predecessor, had taken in 1900. And, if he were a sitting tenant, it was most unlikely that his landlord would have raised his rent.

The situation was reviewed during 1910–12 in one of those personal surveys, a successor to Caird's and Lavergne's and Arthur Young's, which break up the general into its particulars and put flesh on to the bones of statistics. Sir Daniel Hall "saw no longer the derelict Essex which was once the type example of ruined English agriculture". The land "was cheaply worked and...not so clean as formerly", but it was yielding a living.[2] And if Essex, then certainly the rest of the arable East. The big modern arable farms on Lincoln Heath, for example, were all let and vacant ones were quickly taken.[3] The Isle of Axholme, so miserable in the 'nineties, was "reasonably prosperous", the mortgagees, local men mostly, having had the good sense to "act the part of landlords" (a deserved compliment to the landlord class) and not press too heavily on the small owners while times were bad.[4] About Evesham asparagus was the latest of many successful orchard and market-garden crops, and the whole industry "had been extending rapidly".[5] Towards the other end of the island, the Aberdeen manufacturers of Scotch beef for the London market, largely out of fattened Irish store cattle, were quietly comfortable; though by neglecting to lime fields which needed it they "were living on the stock...with which their forbears endowed the soil".[6] The Welsh too were exporting the phosphoric acid of their country—in the form of young stock and milk—and had done so "for centuries...until within very recent years the practice of using basic slag has become more general".[7]

[1] These are the old (pre-1920) Board of Trade Index Numbers of Wholesale Prices. Paish's continuation of Sauerbeck's Index Numbers (*S.J.* 1913–14, p. 556) shows a rise between 1899 and 1913 in animal food (meat and butter) of from 79 to 99, and in vegetable food (all grains, plus potatoes and flour) of from 60 to 69.

[2] *A Pilgrimage of British Farming*, p. 69. Extensive use is made of Sir Daniel Hall's book here, for the reason given. It is based on letters to *The Times*. Haggard's book of a decade earlier is not in the same select class.

[3] Hall, p. 98. [4] Hall, p. 106. And cp. Venn, *op. cit.* p. 42.

[5] Hall, p. 176. [6] Hall, pp. 377–8. [7] Hall, p. 316.

But in many districts increased use of artificial manures and feeding stuffs had helped good arable farmers to do what would otherwise have been bad farming—grow three crops in five which might be sold off the farm, using "what is now the usual English variant of the Norfolk rotation, a five-course shift of roots, barley, seeds, wheat, and oats or other spring corn".[1]

There was some wasting of soil resources. There were plenty of wasted opportunities—Britain which bred pedigree stock for the world was still full of farms whose stock had no quality: North Wales, with an annual influx of summer visitors, with South Lancashire at its door, and admirable soil and climate, was too proud to grow fruit, vegetables, and early potatoes for market—"we were informed that the Welsh farmer would scorn to grow a cabbage lest he should derogate from his social status as a farmer".[2] There were memories everywhere of the wreckage of the storm—very few left of the farmers who had made "East Lothian farming a model to the...world"; some of the small holders of South Lincolnshire ruined and sold up, and new men in their places.[3] But the conclusion was clear and definite. Under stress, men had learnt "to cheapen production, in some cases by improved machinery...in others by a change of objective". Before 1900 "a new race of farmers had grown up capable of making a living under the existing conditions". From that time, advancing prices had been "so much clear gain". Particularly since 1909, the industry had become "sound and prosperous", and "in all parts of the country" able men were "obtaining very large returns indeed on the capital they embarked" in it.[4]

The owners of rural land had lost, since their richest days, £15,000,000 a year or thereabouts. What farmers as a class had lost no one knows. Until the last good years, it may well have been as much in annual values, besides the capital swept away in the storm; but as the ascertainment of "the average income of farmers is...a task which has always proved beyond the power of statisticians", no more can be said.[5] And the third group of partners in the venture of British agriculture, the

[1] Hall, p. 415.
[2] Hall, p. 317.
[3] Hall, pp. 132, 92.
[4] Hall, p. 431: the summary.
[5] The quotation is from Bowley, A. L. in *S.J.* 1910, p. 58. It is discussed in Stamp, *op. cit.* p. 96, where the discussion leads to the provisional conclusion that the statutory estimate of farmers' income at one-third of his rent is far too low and that, in 1912–14, it may have been on the average equal to the rent (p. 103).

labourers? The first phase of the depression had brought a sharp fall in their cash wages. But when the second phase had set in, after meat prices had followed corn prices down hill in the late 'eighties, wages began to move up. The movement at first was slight and indeterminate, not everywhere perceptible. By the early 'nineties it was most perceptible in the Eastern Counties, where the fall had been greatest, but was not important for the country as a whole: *6d.* a week would probably cover it, though calculations differ.

By 1900–2 there was no question about it. On the most unfavourable estimate average English weekly wages had risen by about 1*s.* 8*d.* and wages in the Eastern Counties by about 2*s.* 4*d.*,[1] from their lowest point in 1887–8. As the point to which they had risen was between 14*s.* and 15*s.* for the country, and just over 13*s.* for the Eastern Counties, these additions are far from negligible, grotesquely small as all the figures may appear. The weekly wage was well below the average weekly earnings, as it always had been. Extra pay for harvest and other special work, together with the estimated money value of the various and varying allowances in kind, brought the East Anglian figure, for example, up to nearly 16*s.* Variations in earnings from county to county remained astonishingly great. The broad divisions corresponded roughly with differences in labour efficiency. Scots farmers when they came South into Essex had found the labour very inferior, and only "perhaps" cheaper than in Ayrshire, though the difference between Ayrshire and Essex earnings was about 4*s.* a week.[2] Yet differences in efficiency can hardly explain such gaps as those between the 14*s.* 6*d.* of Oxfordshire—the lowest figure in England—the 16*s.* 4*d.* of Buckingham, the 16*s.* 11*d.* of Essex and the 20*s.* of Surrey. Surrey no doubt runs into London; but so does Essex, and the Buckingham and Oxford boundaries are not very far away. Some explanation connected with mobility is more probable—the men of Surrey may be pictured moving easily over their suburban sands; those of Essex, stuck beyond East London

[1] In 1915 Index Numbers for agricultural wages 1880–1914 were published in the annual *Abstract of Labour Statistics*. These suggest a smaller rise between 1886 and 1892 than that indicated in the diagram in vol. II. 286 (based on Bowley's estimates of total earnings, i.e. wages plus harvest pay, allowances, etc.). Cash wages to 1903 are in Wilson-Fox, *Report on Wages, Earnings, etc. of Agric. Labourers in the U.K.* (1905, Cd. 2376), p. 68.

[2] Pringle's Report on Essex as above, p. 46. The other figures in this section are from Wilson-Fox's Report of 1905, from which the map on p. 99 is taken.

in deep clays or hidden in the folds of their north-western chalk; Buckingham men immobile in vale and beechwood, and Oxfordshire men tied, by affection surely not by inertia, to the valleys of the Windrush and the Evenlode.[1]

Generally speaking, in 1900–2, earnings exceeded 19*s*. North of Trent, with a maximum of over 22*s*. in Durham. In Lincoln, Nottingham and the North-West Midlands they exceeded 18*s*.: in Cornwall, Devon and Somerset they averaged just over 17*s*.: in Kent, with all its advantages of situation, soil and varied agriculture, they rose to 19*s*. 7*d*.; to 20*s*. 4*d*. in Middlesex. Above Oxford came Norfolk, Gloucester, Dorset and Suffolk, all at or below 15*s*. 6*d*. The remaining counties fell between Suffolk and Somerset. In Wales, the range of earnings was between 15*s*. 8*d*. in Cardigan, where the railway hardly runs, to 21*s*. 3*d*. among the coal-valleys of Glamorgan.

In Scotland, where the fall in the depression had been less, the range was also less, if the far North, the true Highlands and the Isles be excluded. It was only from 17*s*. 8*d*. in Wigtown and 17*s*. 10*d*. in Elgin to 22*s*. in Stirling and 22*s*. 2*d*. in Lanark.

This was the earnings position at the opening of the new century. Wages continued to improve, though slowly, until 1912. In 1913 there was a sharp rise, which brought the general level to about 11 per cent. above that of 1900. The rise continued into 1914, reaching some 14 per cent. above the 1900 level by July.[2] This final rise coincided with, and almost exactly balanced, the contemporary rise in the retail prices of food and clothing in Britain. It is of course not possible to show that in every rural district prices exactly followed this general movement, the detailed evidence for which comes from urban sources. There can in fact be no doubt that, thanks to rural immobility, they did not. But as by this time even the countryman was a large consumer of imported foodstuffs, the prices that he paid were getting every year closer to those paid by the

[1] See, in general, Ashby, A. W., *Allotments and Small Holdings in Oxfordshire* (1917). Haggard, *Rural England*, I. 437, noted the immobility of the Essex men. He thought they knew London too well to go there.

[2] These are the Board of Trade (Ministry of Labour) Index Numbers quoted above. They contain a few Irish figures and Scottish figures which include earnings and allowances. The predominant figures are English cash wage-rates. There are no earnings calculations for 1912–14 quite so elaborate as those of Wilson-Fox for 1902; but the general movement either of wage-rates or of total earnings was no doubt very nearly that here given. See the estimates for 1914 in Bowley, A. L., *Prices and Wages in the U.K.* 1914–20 (1921), p. 169.

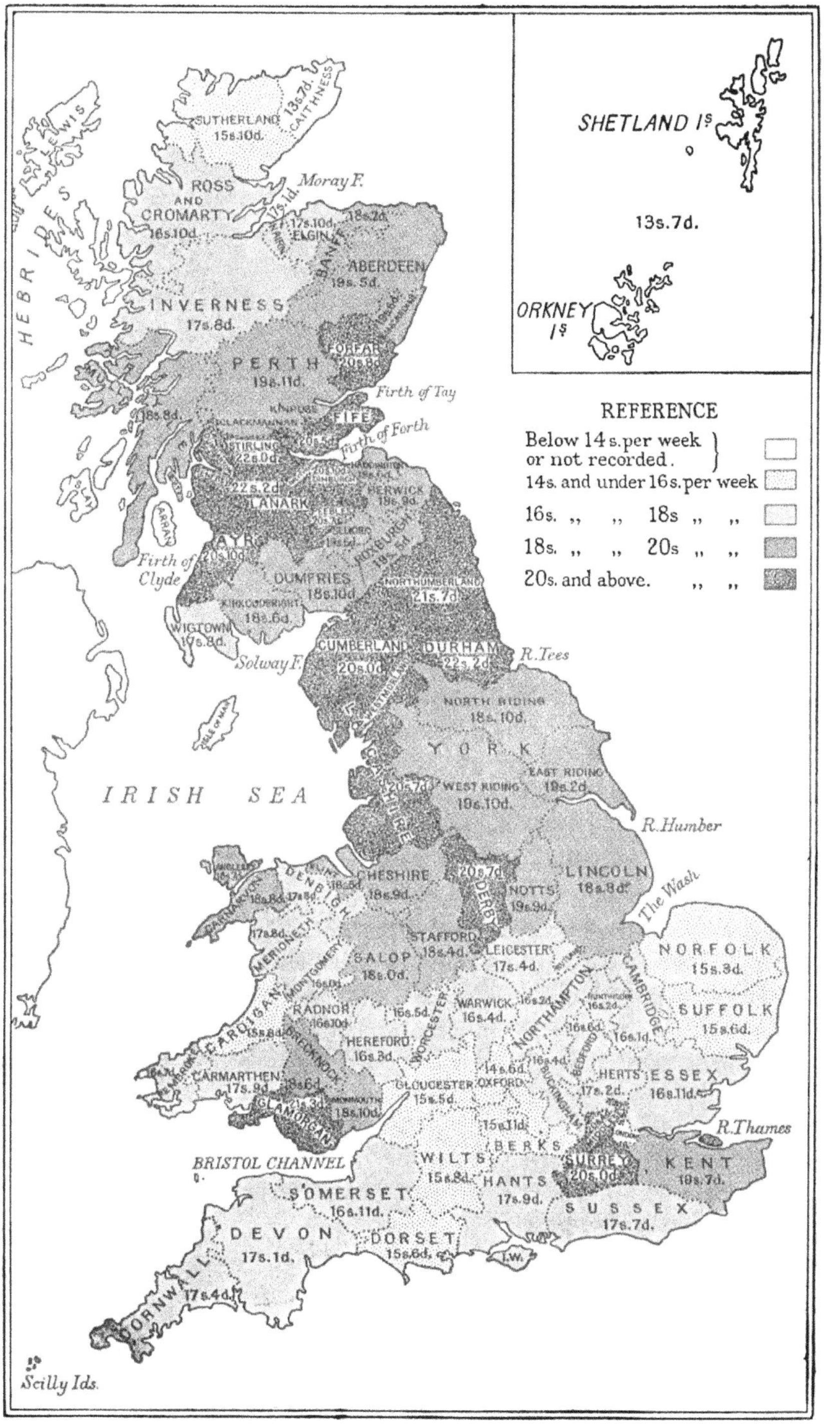

Average total weekly earnings of ordinary agricultural labourers, by counties, 1902

townsman; and it is likely that the percentage changes were much the same. The definite gain in real wages registered for the country labourer in 1892,[1] due largely to the depression of landlord and farmer, had not been lost: in the middle and late 'nineties, when food prices were at their minimum and wages slowly rising, it had been slightly increased. But since 1900 the farmer, the man nearest the market, had been the first to profit by rising prices, as he had been first loser when they fell. The evidence suggests, however, that—thanks to a relative shortage of agricultural labour—wages lagged surprisingly little behind the rise in the cost of living; though they did not get ahead of it, so that there was a certain stagnation in rural well-being after the sharp upward motion of the late Victorian age.

The statistical skeleton of the narrative is of this shape, 1900 being the base year for the index numbers:[2]

	Food (retail prices)	Clothes (retail prices)	Agricultural wages
1892	103·9	101·0	93·9
1897	95·5	98·2	95·0
1900	*100*	*100*	*100*
1907	105·0	106·2	102·9
1913	114·8	115·9	111·1
1914 (Jan.–Aug.)	111·6	117·4	114·2

The clothes column is of secondary importance because so much of an agricultural wage goes in food.

The ease with which farm labourers, when demand for their services slackened, could get work under, or could even become, gardeners, market-gardeners and fruit growers; could turn their knowledge of horses to account in the towns; could put their boys, now educated, into trades or themselves into emigrant ships, goes far to explain the comparatively favourable course of their wage history. The whole body of people engaged in British agriculture—in the widest sense—was only 6 per cent. less in 1911 than it had been in 1881; though in Scotland alone it was 17 per cent. less. Meanwhile the number of agricultural wage-earners in the narrow sense—bailiffs, foremen, shepherds,

[1] See vol. II. 285, 296.

[2] Board of Trade I.N. of Retail Prices and Wages. It is worth noting that in agriculture "wages, including payments in kind, etc. appear to amount to about one-third of the product", the whole product, of the industry. Bowley, A. L., *The Division of the Product of Industry, An Analysis of National Increase before the War* (1919), p. 24.

labourers and farm servants—had fallen by nearly 25 per cent. The farmers and graziers had remained perfectly steady at 279,000, falling a little in Scotland, rising a little in England and Wales; but the gardeners, nurserymen, seedsmen, florists and 'others' had increased by 139,000, or nearly 77 per cent. in the thirty years.[1]

The growth in 'gardeners' was mainly English, a fact which explains the disproportionate decline of the Scottish agricultural population. In 1881 English labourers and farm servants had outnumbered the 'gardeners' group by nearly 8 to 1: by 1911 the figure was less than $2\frac{1}{2}$ to 1. This is uncommonly significant.

Except for some woman farmers, widows mostly no doubt, the women in the 1911 figures are negligible—13,000 'labourers and farm servants' with 4700 'gardeners' and 'others' in England and Wales: 15,000 'labourers and farm servants' with 700 'gardeners and others' in Scotland. Thirty years earlier there had been nearly three times as many. Farmers' wives in 1911 did comparatively light jobs in farmhouse and dairy in England, and heavier jobs sometimes in Scotland. Other women lent a hand in harvest; did dairy work; or joined gangs of hop-pickers, fruit-pickers, and potato-lifters; but the regular hired general woman farm worker was almost extinct. Even in Northumberland, where field-work by women was traditional, and even for dairying in other parts of the country, women were said to be "more difficult to obtain every year", so early as 1895.[2] It will be recalled that no Englishwoman at that time would "muck out a pigstye", and that in Suffolk labourers' wives and daughters had "for some years withdrawn from farm work". Some people deplored this. Whether deplorable or not, it reflected the stronger economic position of the labourer and his family.

Until the very last years, this strength had not been reflected in any revival of trade union organisation. Unless a fear of revival made some employers more ready to make wage concessions, which is unlikely, before these final years trade unionism

[1] The movement of occupation groups in the United Kingdom for the thirty years is summarised in Appendix C, Table 9, of the *General Report of the Census of England and Wales*, 1911 (1917, Cd. 8491). Cp. Venn, *op. cit.* p. 238. Rew's 1906 *Report on the decline in the Agric. Population of Great Britain* omits the transfer into the 'gardeners' group, which is discussed by Lord Eversley, "The decline in numbers of the agricultural labourers", *S.J.* 1907.

[2] Wilson-Fox's Report on Suffolk, p. 66.

can claim no credit for any improvements that there may have been since the Unions of the 'seventies had collapsed. In the early 'nineties, not one district in six of those reported on by the agents of the Royal Commission on Labour had any unions at all; and in those which had, the membership was insignificant.[1] While the number of unions and unionists in the whole country grew fast in the late 'nineties, the agricultural unions dwindled further. In 1900 the Labour Department of the Board of Trade could find only two, with a membership of a few scores; though there were some agricultural workers in the General Labourers' unions.[2] After that there was a revival, slow at first, then rapid, a revival which the price-rise and wage-lag of the new century stimulated. There is no doubt a connection, at least locally, between the rise in membership of agricultural unions proper from 7000 in 1911 to 32,000 in 1914 and the final wage-rise of 1912–14 which disposed of the lag; though these 32,000 were not 5 per cent. of the labourers, and though in most districts direct union influence was negligible.[3]

The influence of the labourers' stronger economic and social position was, on the contrary, not negligible. No longer illiterate, and because literate more alert and mobile; a voter with a place in county and national politics, courted by all political parties; usually a Friendly Society member if seldom a Member of Parliament; an allotment holder if he wanted to be in perhaps nine parishes out of ten;[4] now insured against sickness and freed from his grandfather's prospect of a workhouse death by the institution of Old Age Pensions; familiar in many villages since the depression with farmers who had started as labourers or were at least labourers' sons[5]—he was able to stand up for himself against an employer who was now seldom in a position to pick and choose, and was always glad to give a good man as high a wage as the finance of the farm would bear.

[1] Vol. II. 296, n. 4.

[2] *Report on Trade Unions*, 1902–4 (1906, Cd. 2838), p. 64.

[3] Figures from the Board of Trade (Ministry of Labour) *Abstracts of Labour Statistics*.

[4] "So far as Allotments are concerned...requirements are as a rule well satisfied. In not more than some half-a-dozen counties...is a scarcity of available allotments mentioned." Rew, *Decline in the Agric. Population*, p. 16.

[5] For this see Haggard, *op. cit.* II. 412 (a Suffolk parish). Many such cases are to be found in Cambridgeshire. On the other hand inquiries by R. V. Lennard in 24 counties showed that 71 per cent. of the 597 farmers reported on were farmers' sons, and very few labourers' sons: *English Agricultural Wages in 1914* (1915), pp. 57–9.

That slow widening of the gap between labourer and farmer which had been in progress for the greater part of the nineteenth century, as a result of the slowly growing size of the average farm, had ceased. Indeed the gap had narrowed a little. The holding of 300 acres and upwards was no longer so obviously advantageous, from the landlord's and capitalist farmer's point of view, as it once had been. So, far from more small holdings being thrown together, some large ones had been subdivided. If the agricultural returns may be taken at their face value, the holdings above 300 acres in Britain had declined by 9 per cent. in the quarter of a century between 1885 and 1910.[1] These returns need cautious handling, though they cannot be neglected. The fact that the number of persons who thought of themselves at census time as 'farmers or graziers' did not increase must be taken into account. There can be no talk of a general retreat of large-scale farming in Britain. Yet its advance had certainly been checked: in a time when farmers were losing capital it was hard to relet the biggest farms. Further, the stationary group of census 'farmers' was associated with the fast-growing group of census 'gardeners'. Although the hundreds of thousands of small 'holdings' of between 1 and 50 acres which the national agricultural statistics continued to record were largely residential properties, or lands "held by village tradespeople by way of occupation land, sometimes by the village publican and people of that class",[2] they also included the holdings of the 'gardeners' of Evesham and Wisbech, and of the vegetable growers of Cornwall and Bedfordshire and all suburban areas—a wholesomely expanding agricultural class.

Since the 'holdings' figures had first been collected and discussed, between 1885 and 1890, they had sometimes been turned against those many social and agrarian reformers who wanted to set townsmen "back on the land", or somehow to give countrymen a bigger share in it. Were there not small holdings enough already, it was suggested, for any reasonable require-

[1] See the discussion in vol. II. 262–7. The subject is the theme of Levy's *Large and Small Holdings* (1911), which however relies rather too much on the *Agricultural Statistics* and the annual (from 1903) *Returns of the Agric. Holdings in each County of Great Britain.* So does Adams, W. G. S., "The position of the Small Holder in the U.K.", *S.J.* 1907, pp. 411 *sqq.*

[2] Lord Eversley, in *S.J.* 1907, p. 438, criticising Adams. There is an important criticism of the statistics, and of conclusions based too implicitly on them, in Craigie, P. G., "The place of the Small Holder in English Agriculture", *J.R.A.S.* 1906.

ment or policy? The argument, always misleading because of the very mixed and largely non-agricultural character of the small holdings of the statistics, left most reformers cold, especially those of the 'eighties and 'nineties. Generally bred in the radical tradition; diligent readers in Mill's eloquent and unusually well documented chapters *Of Peasant Proprietors*; dreaming about "the magic of property"; familiar with the land hunger of Ireland; aware that whatever the British small holders of the statistics might be they were not a class of owner-cultivators; and perhaps not fully aware that there really was a sprinkling of such people among them, these reformers felt that a beginning had not yet been made.[1] Their more expert critics asked them to consider the natural decline of the Cumberland statesmen, or the hardships of small owners during the depression in South Lincolnshire or Axholme or Wales—the mortgage burdens of the East or the little broken Welsh proprietors who had begged Lord Penrhyn to buy them out.[2] If you somehow manage to create more peasant owners, except in a few specialised branches of agriculture—so the argument or implication ran—you will merely be setting up uneconomic agricultural units, preparing for their owners wretchedness, and for their holdings reabsorption into larger units, at the next vicissitude of prices.[3] As no British radical reformer of the 'eighties or 'nineties contemplated what was already happening on the continent, preservation of a peasantry by a tariff fence, the argument bit; or should have bitten.

Setting ownership on one side, there was much debate in the course of the depression about whether the small working farmer or the big managing farmer was coming best through the storm.[4] There had certainly been most ruin where the land had been asked to provide a living for two gentlemen, farmer and landlord. But that was not an economic necessity of large-scale agriculture. There were more small working farmers in

[1] Of this class Jesse Collings was a representative figure. See his evidence before the *S.C. on Small Holdings*, 1889 (XII), Q. 553 *sqq.* He refused to sign the Report of a *Departmental Committee on Small Holdings* of 1906 (LV. 411) because its proposals tended to "create a distinct barrier to the restoration of a peasant proprietary" (p. 59).

[2] Above, p. 79, and vol. II. 260.

[3] See e.g. evidence of Craigie, P. G., and especially that of Squarey, E. P., an experienced land agent, before the *S.C. on Small Holdings*, 1889.

[4] See e.g. Read, C. S., "Large and small holdings", *J.R.A.S.* 1887, pp. 1 *sqq.* and Venn, *op. cit.* p. 79.

the West than in the East, and the circumstances of the depression had favoured the West: rentals in Wales and Cheshire had fallen comparatively little. Whether the small dairy farm was essentially a more economic unit than some factory dairy farm, of the type which developed subsequently in America, may be doubted; but it had special advantages for survival at that time. One was an opportunity which the working farmer shared with the continental peasant—of abusing the unpaid labour of his family. It was the Cumberland statesmen and small farmers of the 'sixties who had been most reluctant to let their children go to school: it was from a part of Lancashire held exclusively by small working farmers that an Assistant Commissioner reported in 1894 how the farmers' sons and daughters had suffered more than his land.[1]

In discussing arable and general mixed farming, the friends of small holdings never went so far as to argue that they were certainly more productive, acre for acre, than large ones; only that they were economically possible and socially most desirable. This was the view of a Select Committee of the Commons appointed in 1888 to inquire into "the facilities which exist for the creation of small holdings...in Great Britain". Though the whole report was conservative in tone, no one—witness or Committee member—questioned the desirability of an increase in small holdings; and no one proved that they were economically more efficient than large ones. Many types of holding were discussed together in the Report—the allotment; the cottage garden; the few acres which a picked labourer might work in conjunction with his wage work; the small farm proper of from 10 to 50 acres. Above that level it was assumed, accurately enough, that there were plenty of holdings already available in the country, if not in every parish.[2]

The gradual ascent of a labourer into the position of a proprietor, "however qualified",[3] was the Committee's ideal; and they would only admit tenancy as a transitional phase, though a majority of the witnesses had in fact favoured it. The resulting

[1] *R.C. on Employment of Children...in Agriculture*, 1868–9 (XIII), vol. II. 142. Tremenheere's Report on Cumberland and Westmorland; Wilson-Fox's Report on Garstang, p. 14.

[2] The evidence and Report are in *Accounts and Papers*, 1889, XII and 1890, XVII. 183. See also Jebb, L., *The Small Holdings of England* (1907), pp. 317 *sqq.*, a summary and criticism of the Report.

[3] *Report*, 1890, p. xvii.

Act (55 and 56 Vict. c. 31), which came into force in October 1892 empowered the new County Councils to buy land and adapt it for small holdings. These were to be resold on a hire-purchase system with an initial deposit by the purchaser; but, to men who could not find a deposit, the Council might let areas not exceeding fifteen acres.

The Act was a blank failure. Critics often argued that it might have been more successful if the Councils had been given compulsory powers of purchase.[1] This may be true, but more important causes of failure were the nature of the law itself, with its proprietorship bias; the apathy, or even the hostility, of the Councils towards it; and the absence of any central machinery to stir them up. Whatever the explanation, fourteen years after the Act the County Councils in Great Britain had acquired 812 acres, of which less than 300 had been sold as peasant properties. The Council of Holland had done most, in the flat country about Spalding where there had always been plenty of small holders and owners; but even the Holland Council had acquired less than 200 acres, and had sold no land whatever.[2]

Meanwhile, in the Evesham district alone, far more had been done by unplanned development than by the official action of all the County Councils put together. "There are more than 10,000 acres in the district under garden cultivation in holdings from 1 to 8 acres", an observer wrote in 1907, "and the breaking up of farm lands for this purpose has been steadily on the increase since 1865." What was more, it was believed that 75 per cent. of the Evesham gardeners had "started life as labourers".[3]

About Sandy and Biggleswade, land had also become fluid without plan though, there and elsewhere, the recent action of Parish Councils in supplementing the existing supply of allotments had sometimes given the eager man his opportunity. These Bedfordshire men started with an acre or two of their light sandy land, and worked for their neighbours until they could get land enough to live on, which in that country of cabbages, carrots, runner-beans and Brussels sprouts was from

[1] As local authorities already had under the Allotments Act of 1887 (50 and 51 Vict. c. 48).

[2] Jebb, *op. cit.* pp. 331–3. Levy, *op. cit.* (1911 ed.), p. 126. For the small holders of the Spalding district, see vol. II. 261.

[3] Jebb, p. 57.

7 to 10 acres. And when they had so much they usually wanted more.[1]

In these districts of unplanned development, all of which had special qualities of soil or site or climate favourable to small-scale and non-arable agriculture, rents—or where, as at Wisbech, there was much ownership, land values—were high compared with the average of the country. Rents in the good Evesham orchard-gardens ran from £4 to £10 an acre: a freehold acre at Wisbech would not fetch less than £40 or £50.[2] At these rates, when once development had begun, land was sure to become available. Reformers complained that, where large landowners ruled, the start was, or might be, the difficulty; but it was not easy to find a district well adapted to the gardeners' agriculture in which gardening communities had not sprung up. Evesham had no doubt benefited by the "Evesham custom", under which the tenant who had planted and wished to quit made his own bargain with his successor, whom the landlord had to accept or himself pay for the 'ingoing' at the bargain price. Thus safeguarded, Evesham men, though mostly "fierce Individualists",[3] had no interest whatever in ownership. Wisbech and Spalding men had. Such interest was native to the fen soils. Yet gardening communities had grown up without the Evesham custom or the Wisbech ownership. And they continued to grow, even though an attempt to generalise that custom under a Market Gardeners' Compensation Act of 1895[4] was foiled by certain landlords in other districts who, to avoid dual ownership and the choice of tenants by tenants, put clauses into their agreements declaring that the land let was not to be regarded as a market garden under the Act.[5]

This is an instance of that landlord power—still real, and still a possible drag on change—against which reformers were turning the law. The power was no doubt a stouter hindrance to experiments with small arable and mixed holdings than to the local beginnings of gardening or other specialised agriculture. To block the latter was mere stupidity; but, to the end,

[1] Jebb, pp. 85, 387; Stirton, T., "Small Holdings", *J.R.A.S.* 1894, pp. 84 *sqq.* Venn, *op. cit.* p. 120.

[2] Jebb, pp. 72, 105.

[3] Hall, *op. cit.* p. 178.

[4] Incorporated in the Agricultural Holdings Act, 1900 (63 and 64 Vict. c. 50).

[5] *Report on the Fruit Industry in Great Britain*, 1905, pp. 13–14. Hall, *op. cit.* p. 179.

not only intelligent landlords but most disinterested experts doubted the wisdom of the former. There had been experiments already, philanthropic and economic, and they had seldom been encouraging. It was most doubtful whether, not a living, but such a living as many Englishmen would accept, could be wrung year in year out from an arable or mixed holding of some 30 to 50 acres, either by an owner or a tenant, under a private landlord or a County Council or the State.[1] Where farming was sufficiently specialised already for some such acreage to yield an English living, the really large farm had never become dominant. Farms, sometimes owned by the farmer, with 40–60 acres of hay and grazing land, plus some sheep run on the moor, were common in the Yorkshire Dales. The average acreage of a holding in the West Riding, Lancashire, Cheshire, Derbyshire, North Wales and Cornwall was about two-thirds of the national average. In all these counties the reformers' ideal holding, one which a family could work with little or no outside help, was known. It had never died out.

There were always stern partisans of the allotment and the small holding who held that landlords should be compelled to sell. For allotments, the new Parish Councils had been given, in modified form, the compulsory power granted to local authorities in 1887, now extended to the provision of allotments up to four acres in size. But very little use was made of these powers. The demand from agricultural labourers for small allotments, fractions of an acre used mainly for potatoes, was nearly satiated; and for the purposes of the labourer a holding of three or four acres was either too large or too small.

The application of these Acts of the 'eighties and 'nineties had depended on the initiative of petitioners and the response of County Councils and Parishes. Neither was very vigorous at the time. In 1907 (under 7 Ed. VII, c. 56) there came a new and most significant procedure. County Councils were given compulsory powers to acquire land for small holdings. But this was the lesser change: in the event these powers were comparatively little used. The greater was that the Board of Agriculture, now grown into a powerful department of the central government, was instructed to appoint special commissioners who were to ascertain local needs and facilities for

[1] See the incisive remarks in this sense, with criticism of Levy's *Large and Small Holdings*, by Orwin, C. S., in his Preface to Thomas, E., *The Economics of Small Holdings* (1927).

the development of small holdings, to provoke reluctant Councils to action, and if necessary set them an example. The Councils responded to provocation. Observers a few years later were struck "by the loyal way in which the...Act had been carried out by...Councils composed to a large extent of men who disagree with its principles".[1] The statistical result was impressive. By the end of 1914, 14,000 small holdings, of an average size of about 14 acres, had come into existence under the Act.[2] As there were 292,000 holdings in England and Wales of the class (1–50 acres) into which the new ones fell, and as many of the 292,000 were not really agricultural holdings, this was a considerable administrative achievement for seven years.

Yet an achievement not to be overrated as an episode in agrarian history. Firstly, because while the planned holdings had increased, the total of holdings of 1–50 acres in the country had actually declined; though the important group from 20 to 50 acres, into which some of the planned holdings fell, had grown. Secondly, because the chief successes had been in parts of the country—the Fens, Bedfordshire, Worcestershire[3]—and in classes of specialised farming or gardening—fruit, vegetables, milk and poultry—for which the small holding was already a proved success, and was already developing steadily. No doubt there would have been fewer holdings set up had there been no Act and no provocative commissioners. But although some landowners had to be cajoled or forced to sell, without the Act a good part of the acreage of about 200,000 handled under it—if not necessarily the very same acres—would certainly have followed the other acres at Evesham and Sandy, Wisbech and Spalding which had gone to make small holdings before 1907. The machinery of the Councils and the Board did however work quickly, efficiently, and even economically. With the help of cheap money from the Public Works Loan Commissioner the scheme "was always solvent".[4]

[1] Hall, *op. cit.* p. 25.

[2] Venn, *op. cit.* pp. 132–3. Of the some 200,000 acres bought or leased by County Councils under the Act, compulsion had been applied to only 35,000.

[3] Ashby, *Allotments and Small Holdings in Oxfordshire*, p. 98, points out that in only four counties were small holdings under the Act of 1907 enough to provide for more than 4 per cent. of the labouring population. The four are Cambridge, Huntingdon, Bedford and Worcester.

[4] Venn, *op. cit.* p. 133. The point that the Act succeeded where small holdings were already a success is, of course, made by Venn.

But was the work likely to be enduring? Where, as in many western counties, small holdings were not a creation but a survival, their competitive efficiency was often low, and the standard of living of the holder and his family low with it. Years later it was possible to say of the small holdings of Carmarthenshire that their cultivation was still "too often merely a copy on a small scale of large farming practice, whereas the real interest of the small holder lies in a certain degree of specialisation".[1] The criticism would have been true far beyond Carmarthen, and beyond Wales, in 1907–14. There was plenty of small third-rate milk farming near the industrial towns; and even the new and specialised holdings might not be able to maintain themselves in competition where there was free trade in land. At Sandy, by 1907, a start for the small man was getting difficult, because good land easy of access was "taken up by the successful growers to add to their holdings".[2] Evesham, that country of "fierce Individualists", was described in 1911 "as not strictly a small holding district; the plantations are of all sizes, and the man with five acres does not think of himself as a member of a community of equals, but as having made a first step towards the position of one of his bigger neighbours".[3] That way of thinking was not confined to the Vale of Evesham. The black soil of the Fens, easily worked and in some danger of being worked out, was ideal for the small holding: "nothing else in this country will yield so much for so little expenditure, either in manure or labour".[4] It carried a big head of men, and its potatoes, carrots, celery and asparagus could still yield a living for them from few acres. But all wanted more acres, for larger holders could also raise these crops. Some of the most successful growers were big men. Some of the small men had replaced other small men ruined in the great depression. There are limits to the demand for celery and asparagus. "More crops suited to small holders are wanted",[5] it was said, if the story of those ruined in the depression was not to be repeated—too many small people farming in the same way and cutting down one another's living margins. Fortunately the fen men were tough and adaptable, and the specialisation of demand seems to be a law of economic progress. So, given progress, their outlook was not dark.

[1] Thomas, *op. cit.* (1927), pp. 97–8.
[2] Jebb, *op. cit.* p. 85.
[3] Hall, *op. cit.* p. 178.
[4] Hall, p. 76.
[5] Hall, p. 77.

When it came to marketing, the really small holder was normally at a disadvantage, unless he were working for an uncritical local market, like the milkman of Lancashire, or for a local market not yet satiated. "In some districts", the expert criticism of the Act of 1907 ran, "small holders have been set too thickly in one place, so that they must swamp the strictly local demand" for poultry and vegetables and other special produce. "Of course," the critic continued, "supporters of the movement look to see each small-holding community become co-operative, pooling the produce of its members, and selling it in bulk"—"but such a system has not yet been seen at work in England."[1]

Certainly such a system was not indigenous here. It is not anywhere. Wherever it had sprung up—and by 1900 it had sprung up more or less in most European countries—it had been deliberately sown. Only in England the sower had gone out late, and the ground was more unkindly than most. In Ireland, since 1889, Horace Plunkett had been an untiring sower. By 1902 he had a crop of several hundred co-operative societies of various sorts, principally dairies and banks, with a membership of from 60,000 to 70,000. At that time the Board of Trade could trace less than 4000 agricultural co-operators of every sort in Great Britain: most of them were recent converts.[2] For the Agricultural Organisation Society had been founded in England in 1901, in frank and admiring imitation of Plunkett's Irish Society, to do propaganda and advisory work. A Scottish Society followed in 1905. Before 1901, although there had been plenty of co-operative discussion and a few experiments, there had been no real co-operative movement in any section of British agriculture.[3]

The general explanations are simple. Since Robert Owen no prophet had arisen, and Owen's gospel had not succeeded with farmers; nor had it deserved to succeed with them. Even the small farmer now usually had his banking account; so that, although he was often indebted to a dealer, there was not that

[1] Hall, p. 25.

[2] *Report on Industrial and Agricultural Co-operative Societies*, 1912 (Cd. 6045). There is a large literature on Plunkett. See his *Ireland in the New Century* (popular edition, with Epilogue, 1905); Pratt, E. A., *The Organization of Agriculture* (1904); and for the literature Fay, C. R., *Co-operation at Home and Abroad* (1908 and subsequent editions).

[3] For the years after 1901 there are *Annual Reports* of the *A.O.S.* besides official publications.

complete dependence on the Jewish village usurer, or the "gombeen man", or the "kulak" on which advocates of co-operative banking in other countries had preached such telling sermons. Co-operative propaganda always succeeds best in societies of small cultivators approximately equal: the face of British agricultural society was almost everywhere unequal, with hollows above the peaks of most peasant countries. The land of an average German *Grossbauer* would make only a small English farm. Propaganda is easiest where cultivators are mostly doing the same thing—cows and dairy: pigs and poultry—for a common market; and in Britain this was rare.[1] It is noticeable that, when the propaganda started, some of its first successes were among Welsh farmers not far removed in type from continental peasants, or were connected with simple wants common to all farmers—the purchase of pure fertilisers and feeding stuffs and seeds and good wire netting, and so forth.[2]

No doubt the individualist English temper and English tradition counted for much—including the snob tradition of the girl in the ballad who left her father mowing the barley, married the lawyer, and lived "in a happy content of life in a station well above her". The type of small holder who thought of himself as "having made the first step towards the position of one of his bigger neighbours", the man with eyes fixed on a "station well above him", was not likely to be a good member of a co-operative society. Nor did he in fact often join one. Of the small holders of Axholme it was written in 1913 that, if they furnished any indication of the future, "the men who are going to teach the English farmers to co-operate have got an uphill task before them".[3] In 1911 the majority of the Vale of Evesham growers were "keenly on the look out for some special private market, or content to do business through some friend who has taken to dealing";[4] though the ordinary distributive co-operative society at Pershore was well supported. The Evesham men were so narrowly individualist at that time that they had not got beyond the rudiments of joint action even in their relations with the railway companies, who were always com-

[1] In Denmark common. Venn, *op. cit.* p. 338.

[2] Pratt, *op. cit.* p. 307. Besse, *La crise...de l'agriculture en Angleterre*, pp. 219 *sqq.* Thomas, *op. cit.*, points out that failure to co-operate, as well as failure to make a decent living, among the small farmers of Carmarthenshire was due to their neglect of specialisation and their slavish imitation of large farming practice.

[3] Hall, *op. cit.* p. 107.

[4] Hall, p. 178.

plaining, in response to the growers' attacks on high transport charges, that they could seldom induce small holders, or large, at Evesham or anywhere else, to co-operate enough to secure the low rates offered for truckload consignments.[1] In Oxfordshire, in 1914–16, though there were several small holders' colonies—including Charterville at Minster Lovell, the remnant of Feargus O'Connor's back to the land enterprise[2]—there was in all of them a "complete lack of that co-operation which forms such a strong argument for the group system".[3]

Not that the seed of the Agricultural Organisation Society and the Board of Agriculture, which was behind it, had all fallen by the wayside. In 1914 there were in Great Britain 274 'requirement societies', for the purchase of farmers' supplies and utensils, with a membership of 30,000, and £1,800,000 worth of business: some of them sold produce for their members besides buying supplies. There were 129 'produce societies', whose main business was the selling of members' stuff, though they too might buy supplies. They had a membership of 10,000 and £900,000 worth of business. In the group classed officially as 'service societies' there were again 30,000 members.[4] More than half of these (17,000) belonged to new Small Holdings and Allotment Societies founded under Acts of 1907 and 1908.[5] They were mostly groups of intending small holders who negotiated collectively with their County Council and, when the holdings had been secured, collectively prepared the site, bought the supplies, and perhaps marketed the produce. In 1914 they were at every stage of development. The remaining 13,000 'service society' members were a miscellaneous body of co-operative threshers, co-operative cattle insurers, horticultural society members, and what not.

Probably there was some overlap in this aggregate membership of about 70,000. It contains many people who would not think of themselves as farmers. But it must contain not less than 40,000, though probably not so many as 50,000, who would so think. All told, 279,000 people in Britain had returned themselves, or had been grouped, as 'farmers or graziers' at the Census of 1911. Apparently co-operation in some form, a form no doubt often rather feeble and dilute, involving very

[1] Pratt, *op. cit.* p. 335 *sqq.*; from the point of view of the companies.

[2] See vol. II. 485.

[3] Ashby, *op. cit.* p. 139.

[4] These statistics are in the annual *Abstract of Labour Statistics*, e.g. 1926, p. 194 for the years 1912–24.

[5] *Report* of 1912, p. xxxix.

little sacrifice of individual marketing, as the low figure of the produce society membership attests, had touched one British farmer in every six or seven. No doubt it had touched only a vastly smaller proportion of the farmed acres or of the agricultural output of the country, which were dominated by large farmers who mostly had no use for co-operation. It was this fact which inclined some agricultural experts, their eyes turned naturally towards quantity and high efficiency, to underrate the progress actually made. After all, to have touched, even lightly, in less than half a generation one farmer in six or seven, and a higher proportion of the small farmers who most needed touching, was an achievement and a proof of increasing adaptability in the farming mind. Coke of Norfolk had drilled his corn for sixteen years before any neighbour began to imitate him. But the modern world could not afford delays which were inevitable, if already dangerous, in Coke's time. The average farmer by 1910–14 had abandoned "those denunciations of technical education" that had been "common enough among farmers twenty years ago",[1] without becoming an educated man. That persistence side by side of the best and the worst farming which Caird had noted in 1851,[2] and others before and since, showed less an absence of set technical instruction than a lack of trained common sense. "Men mostly learn by example, by looking over the hedge";[3] but too many British farmers had not imagination enough to look for their lessons over the hedge. Agricultural colleges and instruction under the County Councils had been multiplied everywhere since 1890, and some of the best young farmers were either college-bred or college-inspired. But the farmer's well-wishers expected more from "the general tuning up of the country grammar schools"[4] than from specialised training, however necessary and excellent that might be. In the flexibility and resource of a disciplined and curious mind, the English farmer—it is always of averages that one speaks—was certainly inferior to his Danish, and probably to his Dutch and German, fellow. So, although his well-wishers were glad that motion in the right way was faster than had seemed likely twenty years before, they were not sanguine about the needed acceleration. "The appalling obstinacy of the British farmer"[5] oppressed them.

[1] Hall, *op. cit.* p. 355. [2] Vol. I. 457. [3] Hall, p. 441. [4] Hall, p. 152.
[5] Haggard, *op. cit.* II. 470. Cp. Haggard's *Rural Denmark and its Lessons* (1911).

Education, small holdings, action against cattle diseases, and other matters of rural interest were now being watched over by the new Board of Agriculture. The way in which this organ of the State specialised out, grew, and extended its functions is very characteristic of late Victorian and early post-Victorian Britain. It sprang, one might say, from a mid-nineteenth-century Benthamite proposal for the collection of badly needed statistical information. There had been the usual complaints of national ignorance and backwardness; the usual experiments by private statisticians and societies; the usual suspicion of suggested 'interference' among farmers who might have to supply the facts, before the first statistics of crops and live stock were collected in 1866.[1] In that year the Board of Trade did the work, through the local Customs and Excise officials. Later, various supervisory agricultural duties, created by Parliament from time to time, were entrusted to a Committee of the Privy Council. This was turned into a Board of Agriculture in 1889; took over the statistical work from the Board of Trade; and entered on twenty-five years of the typical life of a modern British Government Department—first collecting information useful to the State; then spreading information meant to be useful to the agricultural community; administering government grants for this or that; acting as the agent of new policies, such as the Small Holdings policy of 1907; building up a body of inspectors and experts of various sorts; and serving as a factory of agrarian law. By 1914 the President of the Board of Agriculture was no longer merely "a compiler of labour statistics, an officer for the enforcement of regulations as to diseased cattle, a disseminator of useful information about beetles, and a peripatetic utterer of speeches at Agricultural Shows".[2]

Of agrarian law there was a vast deal between the Agricul-

[1] Cp. Venn, *op. cit.* p. 427. James Caird, from the 'fifties to the 'seventies, complained of the miserable state of British agrarian statistics: he was not alone.

[2] Haggard, *op. cit.* II. 553. His disseminating activities twenty years earlier, not all connected with beetles, may be illustrated by the titles of the Board of Agriculture leaflets issued in 1893 (1894, LXIX. 671): The Black Currant Mite—Farmers and the Income Tax—Cultivation of Osiers—Insects on Fruit Trees—The Mangel Wurzel Fly—The Field Vole and its...Enemies—Autumn Catch Crops and Fodder Supply—Farmers and Assessment to Local Rates—Ensilage—The Ribbon-footed Corn Fly—Anthrax—The Gooseberry Saw Fly—Acorn Poisoning—The Raspberry Moth—The Apple Blossom Weevil—The Apple Sucker—Preservation of Commons—Fertilisers and Feeding Stuffs Act, 1893. From 1895 the Minister was normally given cabinet rank. Jennings, W. J., *Cabinet Government* (1936), p. 175.

tural Holdings Acts of 1883 (English and Scottish) and that of 1914 (4 and 5 Geo. V, c. 7)—Holdings Acts, Small Holdings Acts, Market Gardeners' Acts and others. Of these the most generally important were the Holdings Act of 1900 (63 and 64 Vict. c. 50) and that of 1906 (6 Ed. VII, c. 56) which came into force on 1st January, 1909.[1] The former improved the law of compensation for tenants' improvements as laid down in the Acts of 1883, and was to be read with those Acts: it regulated claim and counter claim and made provision for arbitration. The latter, like its predecessors more of a tenure Act than a holdings Act, carried further the law of arbitration; provided for compensation for tenants' repairs, for unreasonable disturbance of a tenant by his landlord, and for damage inflicted on the tenant by game. It amended the Market Gardeners' Compensation Act of 1895 (58 and 59 Vict. c. 27); and—most important of all—established freedom of cropping by law (§3) "notwithstanding any custom...or the provisions of any contract" to the contrary. The qualification that cropping was free only so long as the land was kept clean and "in good heart" gave the landlord an opportunity, if he cared to take it, of dealing with a farmer who was working his fields out. It also gave an opening for plenty of litigation.

The farmer was thus abundantly protected, but protected rather against what the grandfather of a twentieth-century landlord had been in a position to do than against what that landlord himself was likely to try. There was little wish to dictate cropping practice absolutely, and the equity of compensation for unexhausted tenants' improvements, a disputable innovation in the 'seventies,[2] was now generally allowed.

So protected, the English farmer of the new era was even more firmly attached to the system of year to year tenancy than his father or grandfather had been. If a good farmer, he knew that he was perfectly secure: even if bad, he was seldom given notice. In the unstable agricultural world of 1879–1906 the certainty of being able to get out at the year's end, if necessary, was increasingly attractive to farmers good and bad. The tenure for lives, copyhold or simple leasehold, common at one time in Devon and Cornwall, was almost extinct by 1890, except for copyhold cottages and bits of land enclosed from the moors in

[1] For the Acts of 1883 and their predecessors see vol. II. 256–7. For the Act of 1906 see Poley, A. P., *J.R.A.S.* 1907.

[2] Vol. II. 256.

Cornwall.[1] In Essex leases for 7 or 14 years had been common before the 'eighties: by the middle 'nineties very few survived.[2] It was the same in Lincolnshire, where also there had been some long leases in the old days.[3] The Scot, it is true, clung to his lease, and sometimes even stood out for it when he came down into Essex. But even he, when at home, had found opportunities for breaking it a convenience in the difficult years.[4] English farmers seem seldom to have shown the least interest in it.[5]

Nor were they interested in land purchase or eager to become owners. Some had bought at the swollen prices of the 'sixties and 'seventies, too often with resultant mortgage or bankruptcy in the 'eighties and 'nineties. Their successors were not likely to imitate them; and when the State tried to tempt other men, ex-labourers and such, to buy in small parcels, they generally declined. The proportion of holdings 'owned or mainly owned' by the men who cultivated them changed very little. In the 'nineties and the 'tens—before the 'nineties figures were not published[6]—it fluctuated about 12 per cent. for all Britain, being highest in England and lowest in Scotland. There was no tendency to rise and in the last years, 1909–13, it fell a little.[7] Ownership was rarest in the great central group of holdings of from 50 to 300 acres, the normal British farms; commonest, though still not common, in the group below five acres which contained no true farms. The old pockets of small proprietors survived in the Fens, and there were a few cultivating owners scattered over the whole country, some of them cultivating squires. But there was no change of importance in the unequal balance of owned and rented land

Ever since depression began, prophets had been crying that British agriculture had declined and would go on declining, not merely in its power of yielding farmer's profit and landlord's rent, but in sheer efficiency, unless Britain turned with her whole heart to their gospel—peasant property, education, co-operation, small holdings, tariffs, as the case might be. Though

[1] Punchard, F., in *J.R.A.S.* 1890, p. 516.

[2] Pringle's Report on Essex of 1894, as above, p. 46.

[3] Wilson-Fox on Lincolnshire, p. 49: "not many leases are now in existence."

[4] Pringle's Report, p. 44, and above, p. 81.

[5] By 1901–2 there were said to be no leases in Herts. Haggard, I. 541.

[6] "How many of our holdings are worked by their owners we do not know." Craigie, P. G., "Ag. holdings in England and abroad", *S.J.* 1887, p. 87.

[7] Venn, *op. cit.* p. 113, referring to England and Wales only.

generalisation about the whole island was always hard, down to the quiet revival of the twentieth century there was enough evidence of decline to fill prophets' note-books. And it was generally agreed that there was a lack, though not a decline, of efficiency in agricultural marketing. Even when the revival had begun, one melancholy fact was certain: though Britain still bred much pedigree stock for the world, pilgrims no longer came to her to study agricultural practice, as they had come in early Victorian times.[1] True, the yield of wheat per acre was going up and was higher in 1905–14 than it had ever been in good Victoria's most golden days; but wheat was now only grown on the best acres. The head of cattle had increased by about 1,000,000, or 16 per cent. since the early 'eighties;[2] but this was most certainly not more than the decline in corn-growing demanded. *Per contra*, the yield of milk from the average cow, and the weight of the average ox's carcase, were both going up.[3] The sheep, a fluctuating population, had certainly not increased, though Britain had maintained her flocks in a way that no other European country had—a thing which her critics often overlooked.[4] As for the pigs, another fluctuating race, they had increased a little, but very little. There was only one pig to every fifteen Britons, a poor showing.

The appropriate comparison in those last years was with Germany; though comparisons were in fact more often made with Denmark. Germany had education, small holders, peasant properties, co-operation—and a tariff. In the thirty years from 1883 to 1912, the period of the greatest fall and the partial recovery of world agricultural prices, her acreage under all the grain crops had been well maintained, for some of them decidedly increased. The potato acreage had also been increased. In all, she had added about 4,000,000 acres to the land under potatoes and the four chief grains. (Unlike Britain, she had a huge acreage of rye.) Her sheep it is true had fallen by over 13,000,000, from 19,200,000 to 5,800,000, and nothing so

[1] Besse, who discusses the matter, *op. cit.* pp. 290–1, was perhaps too gloomy, as he relied overmuch on the not completely impartial reports of Joseph Chamberlain's Tariff Commission; but there is no doubt of the fact.

[2] Roughly from 6,000,000 to 7,000,000.

[3] Venn, *op. cit.* p. 475; wheat yields are fully discussed, pp. 450 *sqq.*

[4] Cp. Clapham, J. H., *The Economic Development of France and Germany* (1921), p. 220. Besse's suggestion (p. 290) that the maintenance of the sheep was somehow a symptom of decadence shows ignorance of the place of the sheep in British farm practice.

catastrophic had happened in Britain; but she had 1,000,000, or nearly 30 per cent., more horses; 4,400,000, or nearly 22 per cent., more and better cattle; nearly 1,000,000 more goats, creatures not found in British schedules; 12,700,000, or 138 per cent., more pigs, and more fat per pig. There was a pig to every three Germans, and nearly one of what French statisticians call the *espèce bovine* to every three; whereas in Britain the people were to the cattle nearly as six to one. Besides all that, Germany had her vineyards, her fruits, her hops, her forests, some flax and a magnificent sugar-beet industry.

Germans had more space in which to operate, and the cultivable parts of Britain had been more thoroughly utilised than those of Germany in 1883. It would hardly have been possible to add 4,000,000 acres to Britain's cropped area, however skilful and diligent her farming; or to make British vineyards by any means; or great British forests without some sacrifice of sheep. Germany had protected her agriculture systematically, and paid for it in prices higher than the world prices. But when all had been said, the working of tariffs fully discounted, and Britain's success in sheep-farming fully appreciated, it was impossible not to believe that—given more thought and work and adaptability—she might have done better, if not with her grain crops under her system of free imports, at least with her cattle and pigs and fruit and poultry. There were no poultry statistics; but it was calculated that 35 per cent. of the eggs eaten in Britain were imported, with 60 per cent. of the butter, 80 per cent. of the cheese and 44 per cent. of the pigs' meat.[1] No reasonable person supposed that, with tariffs or without them, the country could ever again feed itself, unless its population declined; but even without tariffs it might have come nearer to doing so. After all, critics said,[2] the Danes—many eyes were now turned towards Denmark—the Danes work without a tariff and yet send us all that butter and bacon and all those eggs. Encourage the small man, co-operate, educate, grade your produce,[3] begin to organise your marketing and you will

[1] Venn, *op. cit.* average figures "prior to the war". Others are, wheat and flour 21 per cent.; barley, 58; oats, 79; beans, 72; peas, 56; beef and veal, 61; mutton and lamb, 54; milk, 95.

[2] E.g. Haggard, *op. cit.* II. 570.

[3] See e.g. Harris, J. N., agent of the A.O.S., "The organisation of the Wool Industry", *J.R.A.S.* 1913, with an account of the first co-operative grading of wool by farmers in Flint. Two other groups—Carnarvon, Brandsley and Morton —were following in 1913.

see wonderful things. Even if the critics' visions were not all veridical, their arguments were sound.

Meanwhile, profitable knowledge was accumulating against the time when the countryside should be willing to make use of it. In the *Journal of Agriculture* for 1904—how many farmers read it?—a Cambridge lecturer pointed out that Mendel's rediscovered principles had "opened up lines of research that bid fair to give us more command over nature than breeders some five years back dared to dream of". Already experiments with wheat pointed towards "the certainty of valuable discoveries in the near future".[1] The discoveries were made as promised. New bred and admirable wheats, Yeoman and Little Joss, were put on the market and found their way slowly into the fields. That however was only a beginning. British agriculture, with its less than 1,900,000 acres of wheat on a cultivated area of nearly 32,000,000 acres, would not be saved by calling on Little Joss. But this efficient college-bred small deity was a symbol of what had been and what might be done —with wheat, oats or beetroot, chickens, cattle, or perhaps even men—in a society prepared to worship at new shrines.

[1] Biffen, R. H., *J.R.A.S.* 1904, p. 337.

CHAPTER III

THE COURSE OF INDUSTRIAL CHANGE

THAT Britain in the early years of the twentieth century was less stirring industrially than some of her neighbours, and less stirring than she had formerly been herself, was an opinion commonly held at the time, probable on broad historical grounds, and supported—as has been seen—by a certain amount of statistical evidence.[1] During the course of a national stock-taking, carried out in the years 1916 and 1917, when plans were being laid for an always coming peace, alleged British inferiorities in technique, equipment or organisation were underlined. Some comparatively recent and, as it might be said, discreditable industrial inferiorities or neglects were demonstrated. They were most numerous, perhaps because most easily demonstrated, in the primary metallurgical industries. Beyond these, a few important gaps in the national equipment were noted, sometimes with pained surprise. Several were of old standing and should not have excited surprise; but there has always been a sort of Englishman who, while quite prepared to say that they manage these things better in France (or in Holland or in America or in Germany, according to the century) is at bottom hurt to think that they should manage anything better anywhere. Besides, war had inevitably provoked a half irrational wish for a maximum of self-sufficiency. On the whole, the result of the stock-taking was reasonably satisfactory. It showed that there was a rigidity, a slowness in starting and a stiffness in working, which might have been anticipated in the oldest of national industrial machines. It also showed, among those who controlled the machine, a certain indifference towards the attainment of maximum technical efficiency at the expense of other values, values sometimes doubtful sometimes high. This was the indifference which French and German and American men of business mocked when they spoke in caricature of the English week-end; which French wage-earners envied when they pressed for the Saturday half-holiday, *la semaine anglaise*; and which some American wage-earners should have envied, had they been in a position to

[1] Above, p. 70.

compare English with American ways of settling industrial disputes.

British industries certainly did not lead the world's advance all along the line. Their critics sometimes forgot that in fact they never had so led it; though at one time they had held many more leading places. The critics were also needlessly apt to judge by size rather than by quality. Half a continent is likely in course of time to raise more coal and make more steel than a small island, though the fact still surprised people between 1890 and 1910.[1] But there was no permanent lack of leading qualities in a nation which had of late years made the steam-turbine a working success, and could still, when it had long since lost the advantages while retaining many of the drawbacks of early industrialisation, turn out what were for it the most essential products of the machine age—a complete textile plant, a fully equipped battleship—faster, perhaps better, than any of its neighbours, and at least as cheaply.[2]

The auditors for the metallurgical stock-taking of 1916–17 gave it as their considered opinion that the efficiency of British iron and steel plants was "very far behind that of their competitors in the United States and Germany",[3] to whom they might have added some competitors in Belgium, Bohemia, Austrian Silesia and France. The opinion was loosely framed, but it had a heavy core of truth. Britain, they pointed out, had invented and then neglected basic steel.[4] This also was true, though there were partial explanations and justifications of the neglect. Britain had been the first to turn out solid-drawn weldless steel tubes; but had been so passed in this line of work by Germany, that "even British railway companies and boiler makers"[5] in 1913 were buying German tubes. In the rolling of steel joists the record was worse. Belgium and

[1] The fact that Germany was making more steel by 1900 was, from the British point of view, more serious. The steel figures for 1901 were: U.S.A., 13,500,000 tons; Germany, 6,400,000; the United Kingdom [which for this figure = Britain], 4,900,000. *Iron and Steel Returns*, 1903 (LXVIII. 565).

[2] 'Better' for the battleship is disputed. See for the (unfavourable) opinion of a recent critic (inferiority in design, shells and fuses), Corbino, E., *La battaglia dello Jutland* (1935).

[3] *Report*...[on] *the Iron and Steel Trades after the War*, 1918 (Cd. 9071), p. 19. And see Appendix D with figures of pig-iron output per furnace in Britain, Germany and the U.S.A.

[4] *Iron and Steel*, p. 5 and *Report*...[on] *Shipping and Shipbuilding Industries after the War*, 1918 (Cd. 9092), pp. 25, 27. The reports are all by Departmental Committees.

[5] *Iron and Steel*, p. 13.

Germany had been the pioneers, so it was perhaps not surprising that Germany had sold inside the British Empire in 1913 nearly 50 per cent. more joists than Britain had sold to the world.[1]

The account of the engineering industries was less critical.[2] Exports vastly exceeded imports at the last; and in so varied a group, with so much specialisation, a good deal of purchase from abroad was not in itself a sign of decadence, every manufacturing country having its specialities. For more than half a century, since the first despatch of reaping-machines, revolvers and sewing-machines, America had been sending specialities into Britain. She still sent plenty of agricultural machinery; but by 1913 the typewriters were as important as the agricultural machines; the engineers' machine tools nearly as important as either; and the motor-cars as important as all three put together. These were the years when Henry Ford alone turned out a cheap car. They were also the years in which, for the first time, England was heavily in debt to France on engineering account—for the better sorts of cars, their chassis, and their parts. Indeed the state of the motor-car trade was one of the foundations for the suggestion of an elderly rigidity in the British body economic; imports of cars still exceeded the exports in 1913. The reply to the charge, a reasonably good reply, was that the adverse balance on motor-car account was very nearly offset by the favourable balance on account of motor-cycles and cycles, of which Britain exported enough to pay for the whole of her retained engineering imports from France, including the near £2,000,000 worth of cars and car parts. The import of cycles was negligible, though Germany sent cycle parts.[3]

The machine tools were actually in the same category as the cycles and the cars. Specialities were bought abroad—almost exclusively in the United States and Germany. British specialities to a much greater value were sold abroad, and that to no one country or group of countries, but distributed very evenly over the machine-using world.[4]

[1] *Iron and Steel*, p. 8. And see the complaints of Belgian competition in rails and girders so early as 1867, vol. II. 248–9.

[2] *Report*...[on] *the Engineering Trades after the War*, 1918 (Cd. 9073), e.g. p. 23: "we are not impressed with the seriousness of German competition in engineering products in this country."

[3] *Engineering*, pp. 22, 43. For the familiar slow start of the British motor-car industry, see p. 140 below.

[4] *Engineering*, p. 44 and the *Annual Trade Returns*. Machine tools were not entered separately before 1910.

The position of the electrical industries was much less satisfactory—with one exception, that of the oldest branch, the manufacture of electric cables, which had been "consistently successful in maintaining its lead, both in the quality of its manufactures and in financial results".[1] Britain's late and slow start in the large-scale manufacture of other kinds of electrical equipment was shown by the great amount of foreign, mainly American, capital and control to be met with in the industry. In spite of this it had not been particularly prosperous. Much capital invested in it had failed to earn well, much had failed to earn at all.[2] The total output of the whole group of industries, including the cables, was supposed to have been worth little more than a third of the German output in 1912–13; and the value of the exports was barely half that of the German exports.[3] Yet even so the industry was far from negligible. Its exports, half of them cables, were in 1913 almost as valuable as those of Britain's unrivalled textile machinery industry. They had been growing fast in the previous decade, much faster than those of older industries, as it was indeed proper that they should. And in spite of the acknowledged efficiency of America and Germany, of the wide British market both for cheap and high-quality electrical specialities, and of the absence of any kind of British tariff, the import of electrical goods of all kinds was not much more than a third of the export.

The great coal industry was powerful and sanguine, though its leaders admitted and deplored that decline in the output of coal per worker on which the charge of relative inefficiency mainly rested.[4] War had interrupted important fresh developments, especially on the South Yorkshire and Kentish coalfields, developments which had shown that there was vigour and imagination in the industry. "No lack of private enterprise need be feared", said its spokesmen with confidence.[5] The position of their coalfields on the map of Britain and on the map of the world, with the quality of the stuff which God had given them, explain this confidence. True, Pocohontas coal in Pennsylvania could be put on rail at a third of the cost of Welsh

[1] *Report*...[on] *the Electrical Trades after the War*, 1918 (Cd. 9072), p. 6.
[2] *Electrical Trades*, pp. 3, 5, 6, 7.
[3] *Electrical Trades*, pp. 6, 7 and *Report of the First Census of Production*, 1912, p. 126.
[4] Above, p. 63 and *Report*...[on] *the Coal Trade after the War*, 1918 (Cd. 9093), p. 9.
[5] *Coal Trade*, p. 7.

coal:[1] it was far nearer the surface and far easier to get: its mechanical working was more developed and the miners were harder driven. But it was so distant from the sea that Welsh owners were not much afraid of it, even in South American markets; and in other markets not at all. There was much to be learnt technically and commercially from Westphalia, whose methods had long been under observation. The future of German competition in Northern, Eastern and Central Europe was a matter for consideration; but that the most competent German coal-owner could compete effectively in Britain no one supposed. Before 1914 such competition had been negligible.[2] And if negligible in Britain, then not, under normal conditions, likely to be serious in the outer seas. Indeed, Britain is so favoured geologically and geographically that in 1913 she had still exported 11,000,000 tons of coal to Holland and Germany jointly. Of all countries Holland was the one most easily and most predominantly supplied from Westphalia; but the North Sea is not much harder to navigate than the Lower Rhine.

In shipbuilding no inferiority was suggested. It would indeed have been singularly to the discredit of British industrial enterprise had an inferiority been even suggestible. All that could be said in criticism of the industry was that in 1910–14 it had produced only 61·9 per cent. of the world's mercantile tonnage, against 81·6 per cent. in 1892–4.[3] But the fall to a percentage round about 60 had happened in the nineteenth century, since when the British share had been well maintained. Not the most critical patriot was disposed to argue that the much faster growth of German than of British shipbuilding in the previous generation was in any way to Britain's industrial dishonour; though the speed with which Germany had reached both quantity and excellence of output was greatly to her credit. But it was suggested that in the provision and handling of the steel requirements of the shipbuilding industry Germany, and surprisingly enough also Denmark and Bohemia, had established some partial superiorities, or at least offered some very attractive bargains[4]—once again a case against the primary metallurgical industries. The things imported were, first, castings of steel for stems and stern-posts and so forth, but these were of no great account; then forgings of steel and iron for

[1] *Coal Trade*, p. 8.
[2] *Ibid.* p. 19.
[3] *Shipping and Shipbuilding*, p. 22.
[4] *Ibid.* p. 42.

similar purposes; last and much more important, forgings for crank, propeller and other shafts. These imported forgings had been worth £600,000 in 1912 and again in 1913. As British shipyards were exceedingly busy in 1912–13[1] they were welcome, and they probably helped to equip some ships built for sale abroad. The charge made against British iron-masters was that they had not all been so quick as Essen and Skoda to replace the steam hammers, with which the old light iron shafts had been forged, by the powerful hydraulic presses needed in the making of heavy shafts out of steel ingots. It is however possible that, at a time of intense shipbuilding activity, orders went abroad simply because the British iron-masters could not guarantee quick delivery.

In the textile industries there had been no marked recent and demonstrable increase of efficiency. In the economist's sense of the term efficiency—the material return to a given amount of effort and sacrifice—there may even have been some slight decline.[2] But there was no suggestion of decay or newly acquired inferiority. Cotton had been so active at the last that its representatives in 1916–17 looked to the near future of peace with an excessive confidence: "the machinery and plant are on the whole highly efficient": "the strength of the British cotton trade...in the competitive markets of the world is practically unimpaired". Yet they did "sound" one "serious note of warning", by setting out the convincing reasons which made them believe "that Japan is destined to become Lancashire's principal competitor in years to come".[3] In how many years they did not say.

The import of cotton goods compared with the export was negligible, except for laces, trimmings, gloves and some other articles all manufactured largely from English fine yarn, and so not altogether foreign. With wool goods the position was different, as it had been ever since import duties were abolished.[4] The imported yarns and fabrics of wool came to more than a quarter of the exports in 1910–13. But as they had been considerably more than that during the whole twenty years from 1886 to 1906, no charge of recent incompetence could be

[1] Above, p. 62.

[2] Above, p. 70.

[3] *Report*...[on] *the Textile Trades after the War*, 1918 (Cd. 9070), pp. 51, 53, 61.

[4] Vol. II. 17.

brought against the native industry on their account.[1] The main articles imported were what they always had been, light 'dress goods' from France, and yarns suitable for the manufacture of such goods and of light hosiery, from France and Belgium. The English industry, having adjusted itself to fashion changes since the 'eighties, was stronger for competition in this trade than it had once, or ever, been. In other trades, especially that in cloth for men's wear, not British competence but only foreign tariffs limited the overseas business, and the unprotected home market was all but a British monopoly area.[2]

Silk was now a very small industry. Its newest section, the manufacture of artificial silk, was most efficient but still young.[3] The next oldest, spun silk, was efficient. Its yarns and thread were said to be the best in the world and were shipped in large quantities into the United States over the tariff.[4] For the rest —"it cannot be said that all branches are equipped with anything like up-to-date machinery".[5] Made by protection and undone by free trade, not strictly incompetent but always in difficulties, the silk industry proper could not supply one-quarter of the home demand, and had no great national significance. It looked enviously at the vast new industry of the United States, made out of nothing—as it had once been itself —by tariffs.

Linen and jute were competent but, for reasons which no amount of competence could control, now stationary. Linen had all but ceased to be an English industry. In Scotland it was declining or fading into jute. In Ireland it had grown, but not fast; and it was dangerously dependent on an uncertain and capricious foreign demand. Of jute the Dundee district used in 1914 almost precisely the quantity that it had used thirty years before. The continent used four times as much. India, where it was all grown, used nearly six times as much, or half the total crop. Dundee had wisely shifted more and more from its original business, the manufacture of common sacking, to the making of specialities. A third of its output was now the

[1] See Clapham, J. H., *The Woollen and Worsted Industries* (1907), p. 296 for the years 1886–1906. The fall after 1906, in a time of rising prices, is remarkable. The maximum import of 'yarns and textile fabrics of wool' was just over £13,000,000 in 1895. The import was just under £13,000,000 in 1905. From 1908 to 1913, both inclusive, it averaged under £10,000,000. And in 1908–13 the raw material was rather dearer than it had been in 1895.

[2] *Textile Industries*, pp. 65–6.

[3] Below, p. 180.

[4] *Textile Industries*, p. 77.

[5] *Ibid.* p. 80.

better floorcloths and mattings. It was holding its own by efficiency, but its industry could hardly hope to expand.[1]

Lace and hosiery, unlike the textile industries proper, but like many other light industries, used a good deal of foreign machinery. The older staple lace machines, the Leavers type used in the main Nottingham trade, were not only a British manufacture but a British export. So were the machines used in curtain-making and the making of plain nets, mosquito nets for instance. But for the specialities of foreign origin—Barmen trimmings, Plauen lace, St Gallen embroideries—foreign machines were naturally used to make the small quantities turned out in England. The bulk of the British consumption in these lines was imported. In hosiery, though most of the early inventions had been English, machinery had been perfected and made more automatic in the United States. There had also been German improvements, with the rather unsatisfactory result that about half the machines in use were imported.[2] The satisfactory side of the shield was that the American connection encouraged "ruthless scrapping" of old-fashioned equipment and helped to keep the whole industry up to date.[3] The industry was certainly efficient, if not conspicuous. Taking all knitted goods together—cotton, wool and silk hosiery and the gloves of cotton fabric, a German speciality—the imports exceeded the exports, though not by very much. This was a normal and perhaps wholesome balance, for a free-trade country, and in a group of industries which fashion dominated, and for certain sections of which—particularly the glove-making—diligent and not too highly paid continental domestic workers had trained themselves.[4]

Some of the gaps discovered in British industrial equipment by the anxious eye of a nation at war had significance only for war time. Such was the once-famous discovery that all the machines which made one particular part of the British service rifle were in Belgium. Others were of wider significance. Those which were watched in time of war with the greatest anxiety were, for the most part, only widenings of gaps which had

[1] Above, p. 66 and *Textile Industries*, pp. 85, 89.
[2] *Textile Industries*, pp. 94, 98, 102. And below, p. 179.
[3] *Textile Industries*, p. 102.
[4] *Textile Industries*, p. 103 where domestic wages at Chemnitz are 'stated' to be about 25 per cent. below the English level. They were certainly below it.

existed for many years, but which might no doubt have been closed long since by a proper combination of enterprise and education. That Germany was superior to Britain "in chemical knowledge in its various branches" had been known when German industrialism was still young and weak.[1] Upon this superiority, and with the aid of chemical discoveries made in Britain, Germans had built up the great industry in synthetic dyestuffs which supplied most of the world's needs in the early twentieth century. So powerful and efficient were the German factories that nine-tenths of the synthetic dyestuffs consumed in Britain were of their make.[2] Here was a definite and faintly discreditable British inferiority; although in that world of peaceful exchange which British economists had been no doubt too ready to postulate, where the military value of a highly developed chemical industry had little significance, it was no more discreditable that Britain should get from Germany nine-tenths of the dyestuffs, at a cost of less than £2,000,000, than that Germany should—as in fact she did—depend on Lancashire for more than £5,000,000 worth of her finest cotton yarns for weaving and knitting. Germany had always been more fully equipped than Britain for work in fine chemistry, the laboratory chemistry; and it was upon this foundation that the dyestuffs industry had been raised.

The British weakness in glass was older than that in chemicals. When thrown open to foreign competition by Peel and Gladstone, the British glass industry was inferior to some continental industry at nearly every point—to the Venetian perhaps for this, to the Bohemian certainly for that, to the French or the German for something else.[3] This leeway had never been completely made up. All the best chimneys for paraffin lamps in Edward VII's England were Bohemian. The best laboratory glass, and what most people believed to be the best optical glass, was German. French and Bohemian optical glasses were also of high quality. And latterly, as might almost have been anticipated, British and continental glass-makers had been engaged in feverish negotiations about the terms on which they might use an American-invented machine which turned out common glass bottles extremely fast and cheap.[4] The net result,

[1] Vol. II. 111.

[2] For a rather hysterical summary of the dyestuffs business see *Textile Industries*, p. 107; and cp. vol. II. 106.

[3] See vol. II. 16–17.

[4] The Owens Machine: see e.g. *Report of Committee on Trusts* (Ministry of Reconstruction), 1919 (Cd. 9236), p. 41 and below, p. 312.

in terms of trade output and values, was that the imports of glass of all sorts came to about three-fifths of the value of the British output, but that the exports of British glass were worth rather more than half these imports.[1] To set against the long list of foreign specialities there were British specialities of some importance, though they were perhaps not the most difficult things to make cheaply and well. Plate glass and certain kinds of bottles were at the head of the list. But in spite of the weak patches, the British industry was not negligible. And it had been left like every other industry in Britain, feeble or healthy, essential by some reasonable standard or relatively superfluous by any standard, to sink or swim, to prove its own survival value by surviving. Under this bracing regime, peculiar to Britain among all the great industrial nations, it was rather remarkable how few old industries had in fact failed to survive, and how many odd infants had struggled into the world without any governmental midwifery. In the 'eighties nearly all the lead soldiers of the nurseries had been German made; by 1914 they were mostly British.[2]

But, ever since the 'eighties, that lag in the use of electric current and in the growth of electrical industries of which critics spoke in 1916–17 had worried those who thought ahead; for the world was in the sign of electricity. "In the age of steam", a factory inspector wrote sadly in 1901, "this country led the way, whereas in the age of electricity we seem to follow America and other countries".[3] He was not very precise, but he was repeating what well-informed people had been saying for more than a dozen years. Britain, it was claimed in 1918, "was and should have continued, first in electrical enterprise".[4] She had certainly not lacked discoverers and inventors nor enterprising individuals to experiment with their processes. A Scottish coal-pit had been lit and an English pit pumped by electricity as early as any in the world, perhaps earlier. Lord Salisbury, that experimental conservative, had trailed electric

[1] The estimate of the value of the British output is that of the 1907 *Census of Production*, p. 758—£5,000,000. The import was £3,000,000 in 1907 and £3,400,000 in 1913; the export £1,600,000 in 1907 and £1,800,000 in 1913. Probably the output was rather more valuable in 1913.

[2] For the 'eighties see vol. II. 249 and the memories of persons born in the 'seventies. For 1914 I am relying on memory and unprinted evidence given before the Industries Committee of the War Cabinet on which I served in 1918.

[3] *Factory Report*, 1901 (1902, XII), p. 3. Cp. vol. II. 109.

[4] *Electrical Trades*, p. 3.

wires about Hatfield House, and for a time had forced his guests to dine by arc-light.[1] So reputedly conservative a place as a Cambridge College had been lit with electricity, by Lord Kelvin, in 1882.[2] The delay had been not in this kind of thing but in wholesale production and distribution. In 1886–8, when electricity companies were still rare in Britain, although in connection with pioneer London companies some critical experiments were being made, there was "hardly a city or town of 20,000 inhabitants in the United States which had not a central station".[3] It was generally held by electrical enthusiasts and promoters and by many more detached people, at that time and later, that the chief causes of the lag were the state of the law and the apathy or hostility of local authorities.[4] The necessary private Bill for an electricity company was costly, and was apt to have inserted in it expensive conditions about laying the mains underground and supplying the peak load at any time.[5] There was also the natural hostility of strong gas companies. Where the municipality owned gas-works, as at Manchester, either tolerance or rapid creation of a rival lighting plant was hardly to be expected.[6] Electricity, in spite of the pump in Trafalgar pit, was thought of as light.[7] The first two Acts of Parliament dealing with it, those of 1882 and 1888, were quoted as the Electric Lighting Acts. In the year that the first was passed William Siemens had prophesied the sure victory of electricity, but only as "the light of luxury".[8] The introduction of the competing incandescent gas-burner in the late 'eighties was a

[1] Cecil, Lady Gwendolen, *Life of Robert, Marquis of Salisbury*, III. 3 (1931).

[2] His College, Peterhouse. The Bank of England had its first electric lights in 1886. Acres, W. M., *The Bank of England from Within* (1931), II. 588.

[3] See vol. II. 109; Ziani di Ferranti, G. and Ince, R., *Sebastian Ziani di Ferranti* (1934), pp. 50–7, and the obituary notice of Ferranti, *The Times*, Jan. 14, 1930, for the experiments.

[4] See e.g. the discussion at the Institution of Mechanical Engineers following a paper by P. Dawson on "Mechanical Features of Electric Traction", *Trans. Inst. Mech. Eng.* 1898, especially the speech of Col. R. E. Crompton. Cp. Hirst, Sir Hugo, in *The Times* (*Faraday Number*, Sept. 21, 1931). "To this cause [hampering legislation] and to this cause alone, we owe the reproach of backwardness", etc.

[5] See Harbord, F. W. and Hall, J. W., *The Metallurgy of Steel* (6th ed. 1918), I. 736 with references to the *Journ. of the Iron and Steel Inst.* 1910, II. 217.

[6] Manchester however started its own electric plant in the early 'nineties. Hopkinson, J., "Manchester's new Electric Lighting Works", *Trans. Inst. Mech. Eng.* 1894.

[7] The first small pump was used in Trafalgar pit in 1882. *Dep. Com. on Electricity in Mines*, 1904 (XXIV), Q. 5002. Cp. vol. II. 109.

[8] Vol. II. 108. The Acts are 45 and 46 Vict. c. 56 and 51 and 52 Vict. c. 12.

strong and, so long as electricity remained dear, a sufficient reminder that it was not yet to be the light of the people.[1]

Both these Acts contemplated the early municipalisation of electric enterprise, or at least gave every facility for it. Under that of 1882 the local authority might enforce sale by an electric company at the end of twenty-one years. If agreement was not reached there was to be arbitration, but the arbitrator was to aim at the then market value "without any addition in respect of compulsory purchase or goodwill" (§ 27). The period of twenty-one years was doubled in the Act of 1888, Parliament clearly regarding it as unduly discouraging to those whom the law still called undertakers. Forty-two years, even without any final compensation for compulsory sale, was no doubt enough for the average investor; so discouragement was over by 1889. Most of the twelve important metropolitan companies of the twentieth century secured their provisional orders from the Board of Trade either in 1889 or 1890.[2] Both Acts gave local authorities opportunity to oppose any electric project, and full control over the transmission of electricity—the breaking up of streets and the laying of wires—in the public interest. One reason why America had gone ahead so fast was that in America such controls were more lax.[3] They were probably not excessive for urbanised Britain, but they lent themselves to delay; and in the early 'nineties it was already obvious that the existing units of local government, the powers with rights to delay, were not necessarily the proper units for the generation of electricity.

With their abundance of excellent steam-coal and gas-coal, and their fully developed system of urban gas distribution, the British people, 'town-bred', did not turn naturally to electricity as people did in countries short of coal and rich in water power. The travelling Briton of the 'nineties came with surprise, and perhaps some dim feeling that he had been unfairly outdistanced, on the handy village electric light of Switzerland or Norway. Yet with the knowledge of electrical generation and transmission then available, it was doubtful whether it was economically worth while to desert steam and coal-gas; though

[1] Welsbach's patent was of 1885. Vol. II. 107.

[2] "London Electric Lighting Companies", *Economist*, March 7, 1903: "to, possibly, the majority of investors a period of twenty-seven years is an eternity."

[3] See the 1898 discussion at the Institution of Mechanical Engineers quoted above.

electricity was winning as the "light of luxury", and for certain selected purposes as power. Even so late as 1901 however, before the Society of Chemical Industry, J. W. Swan of the Ediswan lamp was wondering whether in countries short of water power electricity could be produced cheaply enough for success in the heavier industrial processes, such as the isolation of aluminium. So far, he said, water ruled these processes. At fifty European sites known to him where they were in use barely 11 per cent. of the power was generated by steam.[1]

While Britain had hesitated, Sir Charles Parsons had invented, for her and the world, what was to become the link mechanism—and in time the economical link mechanism—between coal and electricity, the steam turbine. When he was first working at it, in the early 'eighties, there was just a suspicion among English engineers that steam might have had its day. Everyone knew how wasteful of the power in the coal the best steam engines were. Internal combustion was attractive *a priori*, and had proved very successful, though hitherto on a rather small scale, in the various types of gas engines. Leaders among the engineers were prophesying the end of the age of steam. Sir Frederick Bramwell had told the British Association in 1881 that in fifty years very probably the steam engine would be no more than "a curiosity...in a museum". To Fleeming Jenkin in 1884 the conclusion seemed "irresistible that gas engines will ultimately supplant the steam engine".[2] It was internal combustion that was to win, one notes, not transmitted electrical power; for the technique of transmission was as yet only rudimentary. But before any gas engine had been built of more than 220 h.p., that is before 1898,[3] Parsons had perfected his turbine and driven the *Turbinia* with it, and Daimler and Diesel had utilised the combustion, Daimler of light and Diesel of heavy oils, for quick running engines, in place of the gas or later the paraffin of the

[1] Presidential Address to the Society of Chemical Industry quoted in the *Alkali Report* for 1901 (1902, XI), p. 47. "Electricity has revolutionised copper refining, made aluminium one of the common metals, and so far reduced the cost of sodium that new and large uses have been found for it. Electricity... now threatens to encroach on the province of the blast-furnace and the Bessemer converter", etc. Could these things be done in Britain?

[2] Ewing, Sir J. A., "Power", *Presidential Address B.A. Section G*, 1931, pp. 6, 7. Bramwell repeated his prophecy in 1901 in a discussion, *Trans. Inst. Mech. Eng.* 1901, p. 128.

[3] Ewing, as above, p. 8, quoting Sir Dugald Clerk.

early internal combustion engines, which were all both heavy and slow.[1]

When he put his turbine into a ship, Parsons gave renewed and self-contained life to the steam engine with its new form. But he had first worked out the steam turbine to generate electricity, "for the express purpose of driving a dynamo".[2] He patented his high-speed turbine and a high-speed dynamo fitted to it on the same day in April, 1884. Four years later, he told the Institution of Mechanical Engineers that his first turbo-electric generator "had been in almost constant use since".[3] Most of his early installations were for generating electricity on ship-board: the second was on a tramp, the *Earl Percy*, the fourth or fifth on a liner of repute, the *City of Berlin*. In 1888 every part of the installations was still experimental; but the Mechanical Engineers were naturally excited about this machine which had already touched 18,000 revolutions a minute, and was comfortable at 12,000, compared with a maximum of 300 revolutions for any engine "twenty years ago", as a Past President said.[4]

The steam turbine of the 'eighties was relatively wasteful of power; but in 1891 Parsons patented his condensing turbine, which in its fully developed and largest forms could get "more work out of coal than can be got in any other way".[5] Full development, and still more general adoption, took time. Numerous modifications and adjustments were made in the machine by its inventor, and the world of users had to be convinced. Parsons patented the exhaust steam turbine in 1894. It takes its power from steam that has already done some work, usually in a marine reciprocating engine, and would otherwise be wasted. But the first of these economical machines was not built for use, it is said, until 1902.[6] The marine turbine was more fortunate. It had a well-planned dramatic entry and a fighting use. At Victoria's second jubilee, in 1897, Parsons' little *Turbinia* twisted about at unheard of speeds among the great ships gathered for the naval review at Spithead. The Ad-

[1] "In 1897...after four years of difficult experiments, the author...put the first engine into working order in the factory of the Augsburg works"; Diesel, R., *Trans. Inst. Mech. Eng.* 1912, p. 179. For Daimler see below, p. 139.

[2] Ewing, "Power", p. 13.

[3] *Trans. Inst. Mech. Eng.* 1888, p. 480.

[4] Jeremiah Head, in the discussion of Parsons' paper.

[5] Ewing, "Power", p. 13.

[6] So Harbord and Hall, *The Metallurgy of Steel*, p. 682.

miralty soon began experiments with the new engine in destroyers. When the tests were finished the Admiralty, and soon all admiralties, recognised the new age. From 1904 no reciprocating engines were ordered for any ship of the Royal Navy.[1]

Meanwhile the turbine was doing its most important and most universally recognised work in the field for which it had been first designed; although, with the slow progress of large scale electrical generation in Britain, the field was for years much narrower than it might have been. The fuel economy, the high speeds, the wide range of efficient working with varying loads, the compactness which enabled immense power to be generated in small space, all commended the turbine to engineers in charge of large central generating plants, where such existed. But private plants, at pits, in factories, in houses, were exceedingly common in the electrical development of the 'nineties; and they survived for years. These mostly used reciprocating engines. So late as 1907 not 6 per cent. of the dynamo capacity privately owned in the engineering trades was actuated by turbines.[2]

To those whose business it was to report on technical change in Britain, the progress of electricity during the later 'nineties seemed reasonably satisfactory, although everyone saw that there had been undue delay in its adoption as power. As power it is "still in its infancy", the Chief Factory Inspector reported in 1896.[3] The Manchester Corporation, which had opened its first generating station in 1894, was something of a pioneer. It sold power at 1½*d.* a unit, and in 1896 it had 72 power consumers, all small.[4] Four years later, a South Country Inspector, while admitting that "we are somewhat behindhand", remarks that the "extended use of electricity both for lighting and power" is what most "strikes an Inspector in going through factories now-a-days".[5] His experience was mainly in the light

[1] Ewing, J. A., *The steam-engine and other heat-engines* (4th ed. 1926), pp. 30–2, 301–2. The original direct-coupled turbines had the defect that the screw produced 'cavitation', i.e. failed to grip, at high speeds. Parsons developed the geared turbine from 1910. See Appleyard, R., *Charles Parsons* (1933) and Parsons, *Scientific Papers*, ed. Lord Rayleigh (1934).

[2] *Census of Production*, p. 132.

[3] *Factory Report*, 1896 (1897, XVII), p. 35.

[4] *Ibid.*, p. 36. For the use of electric power abroad ten years earlier, see vol. II. 109.

[5] *Factory Report*, 1900 (1901, X), p. 156.

industries. But in the heavier trades of the North-West and the North-East a good deal had been accomplished before the Chief Inspector, at the turn of the century, recorded his sad opinion that, in the whole movement of electrification, Britain had been a follower not a leader.[1] The new engineering works of the Manchester district were all adopting the electric drive—the heavy machine tools each with its own motor, the light grouped about a common motor. On the North-East coast its adoption was "the most outstanding feature" of the last years of the nineteenth century. Nearly all the great engineering firms on Tyneside had their own generating plant: the steam driven "line and counter-shafting was being rapidly superseded".[2] In the shipyards, where electricity had been introduced more than a dozen years back, it was now in general use.[3]

But at that time, and later, large scale manufacture of electrical plant was hampered by the slow development of the demand for it and the existence of full grown rival suppliers abroad. In anticipation of demand some ambitious enterprises had been started at the end of the nineteenth century. The inspiration was often American, as in the British Westinghouse Company of 1898. In that particular business there was a great deal of miscalculation and no doubt also of mismanagement; but the history of its first eight years is significant. At the start its most important orders were executed in the parent business at Pittsburg. By 1902 the chairman was able to announce that "all further orders for electrical machinery, steam turbines, and gas engines" were to be executed at the company's Manchester works.[4] Four years later however he was tracing a wretched financial and manufacturing record—how truly who shall say?—to the failure of the British market to expand as had been anticipated. An experienced shareholder alleged that for the most important contracts this and other British companies were constantly underbid by Germany. The German export, it was alleged, was dumped below cost price—which it may

[1] Above, p. 130.

[2] *Factory Report*, 1901 (1902, XII), p. 87; and see 1900, p. 156.

[3] Electromagnetic riveters were tried by Denny's of Dumbarton in 1886–7, vol. II. 109.

[4] Chairman's speech, Dec. 12, 1902, reported in *Economist*, Dec. 13, 1902. In the original Westinghouse brake works at King's Cross, when Tom Mann started work in 1880, "most of the machinery" was American. *Tom Mann's Memoirs* (1923), p. 22.

well have been—and the remedy suggested was protection.[1] From such reports as this, and from those of the British Electric Traction Company—a company interested both in traction and electrical production—in the early years of the twentieth century, it is evident that the British industry was at best only third in efficiency; and that a claim made in 1903 that Britain could "now compete with Germany and America",[2] if grammatically true, was hardly true in the business sense of competing with good prospect of success. When, in 1905, the electrification of the London underground railways was in hand, much of the rolling stock was said to be "of special construction and to be built abroad".[3]

One cause of the delayed expansion of the British market had been the conflict between private and municipal enterprise for the control of urban electric traction; and the traction demand was potentially the largest power demand of that day.[4] Private enterprise was personified in the British Electric Traction Company with its various sub-companies, public in such huge enterprises as the Leeds or Manchester City Tramways. Delay in discussion and decision had been two- or three-fold. Was electric traction desirable? If it was, who was to undertake it? If the municipality, what were to be its relations—if any—with neighbouring municipalities? If a company, what latitude should the local authority allow to it? When, as in South Yorkshire or the Potteries, a company ran across the territory of several local authorities, the amount of time spent in preliminary diplomacy might be excessive. There were also intermunicipal delays and discords. To the outsider it was not obvious where Manchester stopped and Salford began; but in the end, after much negotiation between the high contracting parties, they had distinct tramway systems. Midway in the nine miles between Bradford and Leeds, on territory belonging to neither, the new trams of the one met those of the other head on—but on different gauges.[5] One result of all these negotia-

[1] Report of annual meeting, *Economist*, Jan. 19, 1907. The shareholder was Sir Joseph Lawrence.

[2] *Economist*, *Comm. Hist.* of 1903, p. 26.

[3] *Comm. Hist.* 1905, p. 29.

[4] See Siemens, A., "Electric Transmission of Power", *Trans. Inst. Mining Eng.* VIII. 247 (1894–5). It is "only lately that...power has been taken up in earnest", tramway plans giving the stimulus.

[5] Bradford had decided that a narrower gauge suited her precipitous gradients and ugly corners.

tions and delays had been that electric trams were clanging interminably round and round Milan cathedral some years before their noise became familiar in English streets.[1]

When the first, and as it was to prove the last, spell of active electric tramway construction came to an end in Britain, in 1906–7, about 1000 miles had been added to the tramway system of the country, and the horse and the steam-tram were nearly extinct. There had been 799 miles of the old sorts of tramway in 1887, and only 1040 miles, still mostly of the old sorts, in 1900.[2] By 1907 the mileage was 2232: it had risen to only 2530 seven years later, almost entirely by extensions of existing municipal systems. For the municipalities, with the law and the rates on their side, had won. They owned more than 60 per cent. of the mileage and most of the densest traffic areas. As for the British Electric Traction Company, it ceased to pay a dividend on its ordinary shares after 1905–6, and a few years later fell into arrears with its preference shares and then into a reconstruction.[3] The municipalities had no call to reconstruct; but that did not mean that their enterprises had all shown genuine profits.

In 1907, when the first Census of Production was taken, electrical engineering was still a very subordinate part of the general engineering business of the country. It produced only about 14 per cent. of the whole national engineering output by value.[4] A comparison with some ancient industry is however more instructive. Electrical industry then, this thing of yesterday, in spite of its admitted backwardness, had a product worth nearly one-fifth of the whole product of the woollen and worsted mills. It is fair to add that one part of the industry, and that the most efficient, was of the day before yesterday. This was the making of electric cables, which had grown from, and still included, the manufacture of the submarine telegraph cables.

[1] The clang was heard by the author at Milan in 1900. As he was domiciled partly in Manchester and partly in Leeds during these years and was a (small) shareholder in the British and the Potteries E.T.C.'s he may claim to be a contemporary authority.

[2] The U.S.A. had 2500 miles of electric tramway in 1890, Germany 618 miles in 1896: Dawson, P., in *Trans. Inst. Mech. Eng.* 1898, p. 44.

[3] Memories of a shareholder and "British Electric Traction", *Economist*, June 6, 1910. And cp. p. 141 below.

[4] *Census of Production*, p. 126.

Before the electric trams were fully at work, and before electricity had been applied seriously to any other type of rail traction above ground, electric traction was challenged for street and road work by the internal combustion engine. In 1905–6 a Select Committee of the Commons was inquiring into various matters connected with cabs and omnibuses—cab licensing; the nuisance of the slow-moving empty cabs looking out for a fare, the 'crawlers'; the railway companies' habit of allowing only certain privileged cabs to wait on their premises; and so forth.[1] It was also instructed to pay attention to the "structural requirements of mechanically propelled vehicles"; for motor hackney carriages already existed, though when the Committee's report was signed, on July 31, 1906, there were only 52 of them on the London streets. This was manageable. What worried the Committee was the sudden "advent and rapid increase of public motor carriages"—the coming of the motor-bus. *Et complebat omne forum copia motorum borum*, as the Oxford poet sang. "Practically within the brief period of one year", their mileage, reckoned annually, had risen from something trifling to 17,000,000. There had been 31 motor buses on December 31, 1904: there were 521 by July, 1906, and the number, the Committee reported, was growing every week.[2]

Goldsworthy Gurney's English steam road carriage had been nearly forgotten when in 1887 Daimler first put his petrol engine into a "four wheeled, wood-built, light waggonette".[3] No one had interfered with Gurney, but since his day, to protect horses against monstrous traction engines dragging threshing machines and steam-plough tackle, an Act of 1865 (28 and 29 Vict. c. 89) had required all horseless vehicles to carry a crew of two, not to run at more than four miles an hour, and to send ahead a third man with a red flag. An Act of 1878 (41 and 42 Vict. c. 58) had omitted the flag but not the man, who usually in practice still carried the flag—before traction engines. Motorists usually broke the law, until it was repealed in 1896 (by 59 and 60 Vict. c. 36).[4] Under the new Act "light locomotives" might run on the roads at a legal maximum speed

[1] *S.C. on Cabs and Omnibuses in the Metropolis*, 1906 (VII. 581).

[2] P. x. The Oxford poet was A. D. Godley.

[3] Hooper, W. E., *The Motor Car* (1908), a useful survey and picture-book.

[4] The popular belief that the red flag was abolished in 1896 was pricked in a letter to *The Times*, Nov. 18, 1936. But Mr Herbert Austin, as he then was, told the R.C. of 1906 that he had a red flag in front of him in 1895. *R.C. on Motor Cars*, 1906 (XLVIII), Q. 6781.

of fourteen miles an hour. A Local Government Board regulation made the administrative maximum twelve. The years of experiment and of races to Brighton followed, in which the twelve mile limit was not always observed. Many of the cars which exceeded it had been imported from the continent, where Daimler was born and where there had been no red-flag acts, only the rational notices at the entry to so many villages ordering all vehicles to pass through at a walking pace. Petrol cars, steam cars, electric cars were all tried. Gradually the petrol car prevailed, although in 1905–6 there were a score or two of steam omnibuses in the London area and about a hundred in the whole country. They were mainly English built, by Clarkson, though there were a few of Serpollet's from France.[1]

When the first experimental years were over, when motor-car law had been overhauled and licensing regularised, it appeared that there were 23,340 licensed cars in Britain.[2] This was at the close of 1904. There were then no 'motor hackney carriages' and, as has been seen, only 31 motor omnibuses in London. But 8000 of these rich men's cars were registered in London and the suburban counties. As about £4,750,000 had been spent, in that and the two preceding years, on foreign cars, besides another £750,000 on foreign chassis, the proportion of imported cars on the roads was high. It may well have been a quarter or more, even if a rather high figure of average cost is taken. Among imported parts were the Daimler chassis, made at this time in Berlin; although there had been an English Daimler Company, "the first...in this country...for horseless carriages or autocars",[3] since 1896. Several English cycle companies and a sheep-shearing machine company—Wolseley's[4]—had turned to motor-car making. A crowd of inventors and resolute engineering adventurers had thrown themselves and their notions into the trade. Already a few English names were acquiring an international repute.[5] Chassis and taxi however

[1] Hele-Shaw, H. S., "Road Locomotion"; Longridge, C. C., "Oil Motor Cars of 1902"; Clarkson, T., "Steam Omnibuses", in *Trans. Inst. Mech. Eng.* 1900, 1902, 1906.

[2] And 24,201 in the U.K. Appendix A 1. to the *Report* of 1906. The law had been overhauled by an Act to amend the Locomotives on Highways Act (Motor Cars), 3 Ed. VII, c. 36.

[3] Ormond, F. J., "Some points on Cycle Construction", *Trans. Inst. Mech. Eng.* 1897, p. 419. For the chassis made in Berlin, *R.C. on Motor Cars*, Q. 1112.

[4] Lord Nuffield in *The Book of British Industries* (1933), p. 251.

[5] Rolls-Royce was floated as a public company in 1906.

are not English words. They indicate where much of the best early work was done. But Gottlieb Daimler holds his leading place in the record.

England can perhaps claim that if she did not invent the car, though being rich she was quick to buy it, she taught the world how to use the motor-bus. So far at least the memory of Goldsworthy Gurney was honoured. The early experimental buses of 1903–4—Thomas Tilling and Co. ran the first—were all, or nearly all, built and engined abroad. Three years later there were de Dions, Daimlers, Ackermanns, Durkopps and Brilliés. But there were also Leylands, Crossleys, Maudslays and Morcoms; for by 1907 rather more than a third of the nine hundred London buses had English engines and chassis.[1] The countries where the early building was done had so far made no mass-use of what they built. That costly and at first not too popular experiment was made in England, in London. Put together in a hurry, many of the early buses were ill-made and noisy. "Give us a little time", the engineers and bus-company promoters were saying to their critics: "we do not like noise any more than you do: we know that some of our machines are overworked and that they rattle: we appreciate the wise elasticity of the police licensing methods."[2] "No standardisation can be expected for some time."[3] All was experiment and rush. Drivers were trained in a month, provided they were recruited among horse-busmen who did not fear the traffic.[4] "They're all busmen, with their whiskers shaved off because of the oil", an unshaved bus-driver said to a member of the public who sat by his side.[5] After 1907 the bus-running and bus-building industries were moving towards standardisation, but they did not reach it in six years. Local authorities who owned electric trams usually declined to license buses as regular competitors, though they might permit them as traffic feeders. Authorities who had only given concession to tramway companies were freer with their bus licences. The private companies lamented; and the British Electric Traction Company, their parent or guardian, had to reconstruct. Where, as in London, there was

[1] Beaumont, W. W., "Petrol Motor Omnibuses", *Trans. Inst. Mech. Eng.* 1907: an excellent paper, with a discussion led by A. A. Campbell Swinton and Col. R. E. Crompton.

[2] The general tone of witnesses before the *S.C.* of 1906.

[3] Beaumont, p. 436.

[4] Tibbs, P. W., *S.C.* of 1906, Q. 2434.

[5] The author.

neither a complete municipal nor a complete private electric traction system, the new thing won easily, the great bus companies turning from horses to engines; and the motor-bus began to appear in unlikely rural districts to compete with the fly, the carrier's cart, and the horse charabanc.[1] British industry took firm hold of bus-building. Even by 1906, British chassis had been said to be "almost if not quite as reliable as the best machines of continental manufacture".[2] The more experimental imports ceased, and the Daimler Company now did nearly everything at its English works.

The motor-car industry in general, entirely without the tariff protection which all its rivals had, and often grumbling on that account, was making steady progress, acquiring more control of the home market and building up an export trade of some importance, though in no way comparable with that of the United States. In 1904 the import of cars and car parts had been nearly eight times the export. In 1907 it was less than four times the export, although the motor-cabs, in great demand that year, were nearly all "of foreign manufacture".[3] In 1913 it was not twice the export. The proportion of parts to finished cars imported grew steadily, in spite of the absence of the familiar fiscal device of an extra duty on a completed article. Although the import of cars and their parts in 1913 was three times what it had been in 1904, that of finished cars was actually less. More and more assembling was being done in Britain. Besides, the excess export of cycles, motor-cycles and cycle parts balanced within a few hundred thousand pounds the excess import of cars and car parts. In the associated industries, that is, Britain was about on a level with the world. She and her neighbours had their superiorities; but could the statistical curves have followed the trend of 1904–13 in a time of peace, her superiorities might well have been the more numerous by 1917, without any state-applied stimulants. But that is a most debatable and no doubt a vain speculation.

The car, following the cycle, had made the rubber industry in its modern form. If the United Kingdom was slow with the car she was first with the pneumatic-tyre, invented—strictly speaking re-invented—for cycles by J. B. Dunlop, a veterinary

[1] Below, p. 380.

[2] *Economist*, Oct. 27, 1906. Speech of the Chairman of the London Motor Omnibus Company.

[3] *Comm. Hist.* 1907, p. 34.

surgeon of Belfast, in 1888 and perfected by other British workers.[1] In the late 'fifties the rubber imports had fluctuated between 1000 and 2000 tons. In the late 'seventies (1876–80) they averaged 7500 tons, of which more than half was re-exported. In the year that Daimler put his petrol engine into a waggonette, the bicycle being now common, nearly 12,000 tons were imported and 6000 tons were retained. The customs officials still called it caoutchouc. In 1901–5 the average amount retained was nearly 9000 tons: in 1913 it was 21,000 tons. In the late 'seventies, the average price of all the rubber imported was 1*s.* 1*d.* a lb.: in 1901–5 it was 2*s.* 6*d.*: in 1909–13 it was 3*s.* 8¾*d.*: in 1913 alone it was 2*s.* 7*d.* Wild rubber fairly cheap when the demand was limited; wild rubber getting dear as the demand stiffened; Congo atrocities and Putumayo atrocities as tropical natives were exploited for the demand's sake; lastly, the coming of plantation rubber to drive down prices and save the people of the Congo and the Amazon—all can be read into the price-curve.

Back in the 'seventies, before caoutchouc became dear, an Englishman had smuggled the seeds of *hevea braziliensis* out of its native country. It is not a quick-growing tree, and many years had gone before the seeds of the seeds were sent to Ceylon and to Malaya for experiment. Thirty years had gone before plantation rubber came to market in any quantity. In 1900 the world's rubber supply was estimated at 57,500 tons. Nearly half of it went to British ports, and of this two-thirds was re-exported. Once again London became the world market for a 'colonial ware', even though this time little of it came from British territory—as yet. It was all wild rubber, from the various rubber trees and rubber vines, but mainly from the original tree of Brazil.[2] The Amazon basin supplied 25,000 tons and neighbouring areas 6000. From Africa, and chiefly from the Congo, came 24,000 tons. This was the new supply. The small balance came from Java and the Malay islands. But shortly after 1900 people began to distinguish plantation rubber from proper rubber. "This 'plantation rubber' is much liked for special work and for solution"[3] in 1904. It was so much

[1] R. W. Thomson of Stonehaven had patented "elastic bearings round the wheels of carriages...inflated with air" in 1845: Dawson, T. R. in *The Book of British Industries*, p. 354.

[2] "None compete seriously with *hevea braziliensis*"; Good, R., *Plants and Human Economics* (1933), p. 128.

[3] *Economist, Comm. Hist.* 1904, p. 14.

liked that it fetched very high prices. The highest that year was 6*s.* 1*d.* a lb. against a top price of 5*s.* 5½*d.* for the best South American—'Para fine hard' is the market term.

Between 1905 and 1909 plantation rubber slowly began to tell. In 1905 the British import was 205 tons. In 1909 it was just over 4000 tons. But that was a very small contribution to the world's gluttonous demand in 1909–10. Brazilian finance was in one of its periodical states of disease, after the American crisis of 1907. Rubber stocks had been slaughtered, and the more costly methods of forest collection interrupted. So, in September 1909, Para rubber touched 8*s.* 8½*d.* a lb. and 'best plantation', retaining its lead, 9*s.* 7*d.* British plantation finance had been sound. Even if the price dropped by a half, it was said, this "would leave most plantations a handsome profit".[1] As prices went up further in 1910 and the average price of all rubber imported, good and bad, waste, reclaimed, plantation and Para, was 5*s.* 3¾*d.* for the year they got their profit with a margin.[2]

After that the market pressure eased, although the plantation supplies were not yet growing fast enough for the demand, and serious extension of the world supplies for the near future was impossible. Indeed, it was not certain that they could be maintained.[3] But the planted trees were growing and the tappings in Kuala Lumpur or Selangor could be dated ahead. Prices dropped sharply in 1913, though trade was active all the world over. The fall continued in 1914. On July 27, when the armies were gathering, 'Para fine hard' was at 2*s.* 9¾*d.*—and rubber was one of the very few commodities whose price war did not drive up. It was precisely the same in 1919 as it had been in 1914.

The rubber manufacturing industry, in spite of its critical importance, could never in the nature of things reach a great size. A very few thousand work-people had done it all in the nineteenth century, even if rubber is followed into its many secondary uses. Between 1901 and 1911 the number certainly

1 *Economist, Comm. Hist.* 1909. In 1936 a price of "6*d.* or thereabouts... would give some profits to European estates", Rowe, J. W. F., *Markets and Men* (1936), p. 149.

2 This is the figure in the *Statistical Abstract*'s average prices of imports. Rowe, *Markets and Men*, p. 182, says: "rubber averaged nearly 9*s.* for the whole of 1910." This, if correct, must apply to best new rubber only.

3 So late as 1908 "almost the whole" supply came "from non-cultivated sources"; "The World's Rubber Trade", *Economist*, Sept. 19, 1908. All Asia at that time only supplied 3 per cent. of the supply, including a little wild rubber.

doubled, standing at the latter date somewhere between 20,000 and 30,000, according to the trades included. There had been steady progress in handling and in the size of the business units, but the essentials of preparation and vulcanisation had not changed much since the days of Goodyear and Hancock.[1]

That criticism of the primary iron and steel industries which became loud in 1916–17 was not at all new. Twenty years earlier, Windsor Richards, the man who had backed Thomas and Gilchrist in 1878–9, was repudiating before the Institute of Mechanical Engineers, of which he was President, what had been "persistently said and written" about the alleged "decadence of our metallurgical...industries".[2] He had no difficulty in disproving that vague indictment of decadence: he would have found it harder to dismiss a charge of dilatoriness. And his defence betrayed a rather dangerous complacency.

It was no fault of the British industry that because of tariff developments in America, and the inestimable value of the basic process to continental producers, its era of swift expansion was over. The average British output of pig-iron for the years 1880–5 had been 7,800,000 tons. In 1896, the year of Richards' apology, and a busy year, it was 8,600,000. In the five years 1908–13, also busy, it averaged 9,600,000 tons. Here was growth, but quiet growth—very unlike the upward rush in America and Germany.[3] Nor was it a fault, nor need it have been a defect, that the British industry had been approximately stabilised geographically. The years 1830–50 had seen the sudden rise of the West of Scotland; 1850–70 the rise of the North-East Coast and of the North Lancashire and Cumberland hematite district.[4] Between 1885 and 1913 there was no comparable change of site. The North-East Coast raised its share of the whole make of pig-iron from 33 to 37 per cent. Scotland in 1913 made rather more than in 1885, the Lancashire and Cumberland district rather less. South Wales and Monmouth, fourth in 1885, was still fourth in 1913. These four

[1] Vol. II. 42–4 and for 1908, *Economist*, as above.

[2] Richards, E. Windsor, "Blast Furnace Practice", *Trans. Inst. Mech. Eng.* 1896, p. 107. Cp. vol. II. 60. Richards referred to the alleged decadence of engineering as well as that of metallurgy.

[3] Between 1880–5 and 1908–13 (quinquennial averages) the British output grew by 23 per cent., the German nearly fivefold, the American more than sixfold.

[4] Vol. II. 47–9.

districts together had made 77 per cent. of the iron of 1885: they made 70 per cent. of the iron of 1913.[1] The slight relative decline was due to stagnation in the three areas other than Cleveland and to increased smelting on the lias ironstone workings of Lincolnshire, Leicestershire and Northampton. Having allowed its "many old-fashioned furnaces"[2] to go cold, South Staffordshire, with the black bits of the three adjacent counties, was holding its own as a primary producer in 1908–13 better than might perhaps have been expected, thanks to its vigorous secondary trades; but with the shift of heavy work towards tidewater more could not be asked of it.

Geographical stabilisation was not necessarily a defect; but among a people conservative by temperament, and in an industry whose equipment is not easily remodelled, a new district occupied by pioneers, or an old one in which production is rapidly expanding and new works springing up, has undoubted advantages.[3] Cleveland had been new once. Now it was dominant. With the dismantling of the last of the older works in the district, about 1892, and the bringing of average smelting practice up to the level of the best practice of the 'seventies and 'eighties, its industry got on to a limited plateau whose upward slope was gentle.[4] The capacity of furnaces was increased, in the next twenty years, by enlarging the hearth. So, though the external size of the major furnaces changed hardly at all, the output per furnace in blast went up steadily—from 27,200 tons in 1885–90 to 33,800 tons in 1895–1900 and 43,300 tons in 1905–10.[5] Improvements were made in the preheating of fuel gases blown into the hearth and in the pressures at which they were injected. Waste heat and blast-furnace gas were utilised in various new ways—boilers were fired with the gas; exhaust steam went into low-pressure turbines to generate electricity; and so on. But before 1900 change had been slow, as the blast-furnace output figures suggest. And after 1900 it was not rapid.

[1] From the annual *Mineral Returns*; and see *Statistics of the Iron and Steel Industries* (1926, with retrospective figures), published by the Nat. Fed. of Iron and Steel Manufacturers.

[2] *Factory Report*, 1894 (1895, XIX), p. 211.

[3] It has been suggested to me by Mr D. L. Burn of Christ's College that a more thorough examination and use of those Northamptonshire ores which now (1937) supply the Corby ironworks might have been made long before 1913 with great advantage to the industry and the country. If this is so there was too much geographical stabilisation.

[4] Vol. II. 50 and Jones, G. T., *Increasing Return*, p. 144.

[5] Jones, App. IV, p. 282.

Very rapid it probably could not have been, as things then lay. But the constant criticism, and the constant appeal to American or German practice, suggest that the pace should have been bettered.

Some of the criticism was no doubt captious, or at least exaggerated; but most of it had foundation. Take the charge commonly made about the year 1900 that, at the second stage of the industry, the country in which the basic process of steel-making was invented had hitherto neglected it, in spite of her great reserves of phosphoric, non-Bessemer, ores and her very limited reserves of the non-phosphoric hematite. Statistically the charge was valid. The greatly increased output of basic steel in the next twelve or thirteen years, still more in the next twenty-four or twenty-five, indicates the possibilities. The figures (in tons) are:[1]

	Total steel output	Made by converter		Made on open-hearth	
		Acid	Basic	Acid	Basic
1901	4,904,000	1,116,000	491,000	2,947,000	351,000
1913	7,664,000	1,049,000	552,000	3,811,000	2,252,000
1925	7,385,000	447,000	28,000	1,969,000	4,744,000

The reply usually made to the charge of neglect in Windsor Richards' day was that, with her unrivalled position for importing non-phosphoric ores from Spain and Scandinavia, Britain—and in particular Cleveland and South Wales—did well to concentrate on the process which they understood best, so long as the demand for acid steel remained good. It was usually added that America had also neglected the basic process, because she had such abundance of Bessemer ores; and that as the non-Bessemer ores of Cleveland were not inexhaustible[2] there was sound sense behind the import trade. The arguments are all valid. Besides, critics of Britain were often only railing at an ineluctable fact—the basic process had robbed her of a

[1] According to the 1926 *Stat. of the Iron and Steel Industries*, p. 10. Statistics with all these details are not available before 1901, the acid and basic open-hearth steels being lumped together. The maximum aggregate output was 9,717,000 in 1917.

[2] See Hawdon, W., "The Iron and Steel Industries of the Cleveland district during the last quarter of a century", *J. Iron and Steel Inst.* 1908, I. 28. Jones, *op. cit.* p. 145n., speaks of their being "within measurable distance of exhaustion". The *Statistics* of 1926 (following the *Report of the Imperial Resources Bureau*) give an 'actual' Cleveland reserve of 190,000,000 tons. South Wales reserves are now negligible.

differential competitive advantage. Yet it is hard to believe that a process employed so extensively in 1925 and 1913 might not have been employed to advantage rather more than it was in 1901 and earlier.[1]

Dependence on imported ore had increased greatly since the early 'eighties (1880–5), when the import was just over a sixth of the home production by weight, though by value nearly a half of it, because so much richer in iron. In 1908–13 the import was worth 45 per cent. more than the home-raised ore, and even in mere bulk was not much less than a half of it. Technically, this was no sign of weakness; but it was a geological misfortune and a political risk that the country should be so short of the richer and the non-phosphoric ores, and yet so wedded to their use.

Even in backward districts, those old-fashioned blast-furnaces at which in the 'seventies the gases flared to waste had disappeared, or at least gone out of blast, by the end of the century. But the adoption of similar, and more vital, economies at the coke ovens had been a dragging business. Lowthian Bell had complained in 1884 that "until very recently no kind of progress had been made for fifty years" in coke-making.[2] At that time, his firm was one of the very few which even attempted to economise the waste heat of the ovens, and save the invaluable by-products of the process. The so-called beehive oven, the type in general use, did neither. Various already existing foreign-invented types did both, though as yet not perfectly. From the 'eighties, invention went on steadily abroad, and adoption very slowly in England. With a few insignificant exceptions, all the types of by-product oven adopted in England during the thirty years after Lowthian Bell made his complaint had foreign names. After twenty-nine years, in 1913, though there were nearly 2000 Coppées, nearly 1500 Otto Hilgenstocks, and 1400 Simon Carvès, with various other continental types, among the 21,000 coke-ovens in Britain, there were still 13,200 beehives, at which if the waste gases were sometimes utilised the by-products were never conserved. The only conspicuously English type whose name appears on the 1913 list is the Collins;

[1] Basic steel made by the original process (in a converter) though useful for many purposes was unreliable for such things as ship-plates, and the open-hearth process is slow; but the rapid introduction of basic open-hearth steel after 1901 suggests what might have been done earlier.

[2] Vol. II. 51.

and there were only 45 Collinses.[1] This is an indictment of British invention and British adaptability, in the vital borderland between metallurgy and chemistry, which only the most special pleading could hope to refute. Though the conservation of coal by-products may not have been the business of the metallurgist as such, the widespread retention of a wasteful and unscientific method of preparing fuel for the blast-furnaces was not creditable even to the iron firms which bought coke, still less to those who controlled their own supplies of fuel.[2]

Nor was the slow advent of electrical metallurgy entirely creditable to the steel-makers; although the heaviest blame, if terms of praise and blame are to be used, should not fall on them. So early as 1879 William Siemens had designed a laboratory electric furnace in which he could melt a few pounds of steel: the method was direct radiation from the electric arc and reflection of heat from the furnace walls. But the British lag in electrical development combined with the abundance and excellence of British coal to leave the commercial pioneering of electrical metallurgy to others. Americans were soon experimenting with electric welding. Elihu Thomson was their leader, and the Thomson-Houston welding dynamo was used occasionally in England from about 1891.[3] Other processes followed, all foreign. So it was to the end; although by 1907, in the greater iron and steel works, "almost all the auxiliary items and outlying machines" were electrically driven.[4] Two accounts of electric welding, one written in 1895 the other in 1914, give a catena of foreign names and little else.[5] With the electric furnace there was experimentation from Siemens' time onwards. It was being used, on a limited scale, to make the most valuable of the special steels, early in the twentieth cen-

[1] There were 275 Simplex, not obviously foreign; 814 Koppers; 1107 Semet-Solvay; 374 Huessner, and 299 'other kinds'. *Stat. of the Iron and Steel Industries*, p. 24.

[2] In 1902 only 10 per cent. of British coke was produced from by-product recovery plants. *R.C. on Coal Supplies*, 1905 (XVI), pp. 9, 10. And see the strictures on ironmasters and others of Hooghwinkel, G. H. J., "The generation of electricity by the waste gases of modern coke-ovens", *Trans. Inst. Mining Eng.* 1905–6. There was considerable progress in the next decade as the oven statistics of 1913 show.

[3] Dobson, B. A., "Electric Welding", *Trans. Inst. Mech. Eng.* 1894.

[4] Bigge, D. Selby, "Electricity in the Iron and Steel Industries", *J. Iron and Steel Inst.* 1907, I. 57.

[5] Scott-Anderson, T., "Electric Welding", *Trans. Inst. Mining Eng.* 1895–6, and Heaton, T. T., "Welding", *Trans. Inst. Mech. Eng.* 1914.

tury. But the discussion was all of foreign types—the Kjellin from Sweden, the Héroult, the Stassano, the Frick, the Röchling-Rodenhauser—and of what might be done in Britain if electricity were cheap enough.[1]

Apart from its relative neglect of the basic process during the last years of the nineteenth century, the iron and steel industry developed along lines which might have been anticipated in the 'eighties—except for the suddenly acquired importance of the new steel alloys, those special steels which were the peculiar contribution of the age. Wrought iron, the product of the puddler and his under-hand, continued to decline before steel until its make, which had been 2,800,000 tons in 1882, settled down at an average of a million tons a year for the first decade of the twentieth century.[2] The output of steel of all kinds increased very steadily, with only occasional setbacks in years of depression, from an average of 1,920,000 tons in 1880–5 to a maximum of 7,664,000 tons in 1913, thus:

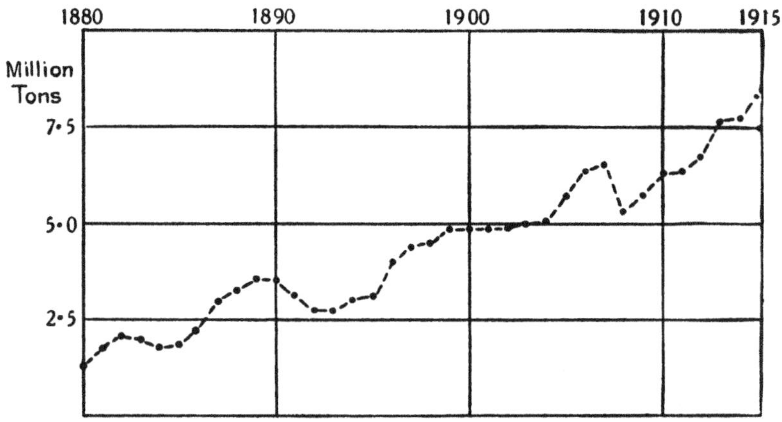

Steel output of the United Kingdom

Wrought iron, in its 'crown' and 'common' bars, from the puddling furnaces of the Midlands, no longer wanted for

[1] Keller, A., "The application of the electric furnace in metallurgy", *J. Iron and Steel Inst.* 1903, I. Harbord and Hall, *The Metallurgy of Steel* (3rd ed. 1907), p. 717, based on *R. of the Canadian Commission on Electric Smelting* of 1905; Rodenhauser, W., "The electric...process of steel-making", *J. Iron and Steel Inst.* 1909, I. Naturally enough, Italy, being short of coal, was an early experimenter with electricity—Stassano got results in 1898.

[2] Cp. vol. II. 53, where the concentration of puddling into the Midlands is described. The process continued.

chemins de fer or ironclads or even tramp steamers, was working back to its original uses, by the blacksmith, the chainmaker, the anchor-smith, and their like.

Among the steels, British makers concentrated for many years on the acid, the Bessemer; though as time went on less and less was made in Bessemer converters, more and more on improved variants of the Siemens open-hearth. In 1889 nearly half the steel made came out of Bessemer converters; in 1898, the year of Bessemer's death, little more than a quarter; in 1908 barely a sixth; in 1913 not a seventh, although nearly two-thirds of the make of steel in that year was still acid.[1]

The dream of Bessemer and Siemens of steel made absolutely direct from the ore was never realised. Steel can be so made, but it has always proved spongy, not fluid, and so not good for casting.[2] Even Bessemer's semi-direct method, by which molten metal from the blast-furnace goes to the converter, has serious limitations. The resulting steel is apt to lack steel's most essential quality, homogeneity. This can be overcome by the use of a mixer in which the flow from several furnaces is blended. The method had first been used successfully at Carnegie's works in America. It was adopted at Barrow in 1889 and by the North-Eastern Steel Company in 1892. By 1908 it was "practically universal" at the great works which owned blast-furnaces. Others perforce did what Bessemer had originally done at Sheffield—melted pig-iron of the right quality for their converter or in their open-hearth.[3] However the steel was made, it was never wise to run it direct into moulds for the finished article. It was made into billets, ingots or slabs, which were heated and worked to ensure that uniformity which steel tends to acquire under the hammer, or between the rolls, or in the press. The finest and most homogeneous steels had always been those blended and melted in the crucible, and then forged. In all the processes, over-economy of time or of working was likely to vitiate the result.[4]

Whitworth's method for obtaining a homogeneous steel by compression while it is in the fluid state fell into the background after his death in 1887.[5] It had been devised as an alternative

[1] Cp. the table from 1901 on p. 147 above.

[2] Harbord and Hall, p. 291.

[3] Cooper, A., "Metal mixers", *J. Iron and Steel Inst.* 1895, I; Pratt, A. G., "The future development of the metal mixer", *J. Iron and Steel Inst.* 1908, I. 156, the phrase quoted.

[4] Harbord and Hall, *passim.*

[5] Cp. vol. II. 78–9.

to hammering—it is said, because a big hammer was a nuisance to Whitworth's neighbours. A second alternative method also used by Whitworth and for which Bessemer had taken patents as far back as the 'fifties, but which had not beaten the hammer while ingots were small, was the exertion of hydraulic pressure on the heated ingot. Big ingots as cast are loose in texture at the core. Hammer-blows which would solidify a small ingot are not enough. Steady continuous pressure is better. Pressure does not make a different steel but it does make more of each ingot available for use. The repute of Whitworth steel, an ex-member of his firm argued within a few years of Whitworth's death, was due to its quality, not to the fluid pressure as such, or to pressure of any kind: that had "absolutely nothing to do with its quality"[1]—that is with the quality of the best parts of the ingot. Fluid compression was a difficult process, so the tendency was to use the alternative method, the forging press, to reduce the waste in great ingots.

Meanwhile the centre of gravity both of scientific and practical interest, for those interested in the finest steel, was shifting towards the chemical problems of the alloys and what came to be known as the special steels. Steel had seldom been merely that combination of pure iron with some percentage of carbon which it is by elementary definition. Many famous steels of history have been impure, and may have owed their fame to their impurity. Meteoric iron, possibly the first iron known to man, was always prized for its excellence and its resistance to rust: it normally contains nickel. Early in the nineteenth century, Faraday had experimented with nickel steel and chromium steel, his interest being mainly in this problem of non-rusting. That a small amount of manganese improved steel was a bit of old empirical German knowledge, patented in England by Heath in 1840, and used when the patent was out by both Bessemer and Siemens. The manganese, usually introduced in the form of spiegeleisen, made the steel more forgeable at all temperatures, and gave it other useful properties.[2]

[1] Col. Dyer in a discussion of a paper on "The treatment of steel by hydraulic pressure", *Proc. Inst. Civ. Eng.* XCVIII (1889), p. 162. Cp. Capron, A. J., "Compression of steel ingots in the mould", *J. Iron and Steel Inst.* 1906, I, and Hadfield, Sir R. A., "A method of producing sound ingots" [without compression], *J. Iron and Steel Inst.* 1912, I.

[2] Harbord and Hall, p. 394 *sqq.*; Bessemer, *Autobiography* (1905), ch. XVIII; Becker, O. M., *High Speed Steel* (New York, 1910), and information from Dr D. Stockdale of the Cambridge Metallurgical Department. Spiegeleisen is

It was while experimenting with manganese steel—about which he had a lifelong quarrel with Bessemer—that R. F. Mushet, a metallurgist of the second generation, hit on a steel which proved to have unusual qualities because it contained, besides carbon, manganese and some silicon, a small proportion of tungsten.[1] That was in the late 'sixties. He took out his patent in 1870. But he had the usual business failures of an inventor, and it was not for a number of years, and through other hands, that Mushet 'special' or 'self-hardening' steel came effectively on to the market as a material for engineers' tools. Meanwhile, from the early 'eighties through some thirty years, Hadfield and Arnold at Sheffield made systematic investigations into the natures of the innumerable possible steel mixtures and alloys.[2] A dose of aluminium was already known to be a great help in casting. It gets rid of oxygen and produces ingots with fewer blowholes. A little chromium increases the tensile strength of the steel. So does nickel, which also both checks rusting and raises the elastic limit. Further experiments with tungsten, both at Sheffield and elsewhere, confirmed Mushet's opinion that it was specially important in tool steels. When his special steel had been improved on, and the practical difficulties incidental to its use overcome, there were created—during the 'nineties—tools which could cut mild steel at 150 feet a minute without lubricant and without collapse.

"Those engineers", an Englishman wrote in 1910, "who saw at the Paris Exhibition of 1900 a lathe running at a high speed, with a tool with its point red-hot removing a dark blue chip, felt that they were witnessing the beginning of a revolution in tool steel and in machines fitted for its use."[3] It was hardly a beginning, but the date is a convenient one. The exhibit at Paris was that of the Bethlehem Steel Corporation of Pittsburg; it was a product of experiments by F. W. Taylor and Maunsel White; and the tool which ran red-hot was made

defined as a "crystalline white cast iron containing carbon and manganese". Bessemer maintained that all the old famous steel areas (Solingen, etc.) had iron ores containing manganese.

[1] Besides the above, see the article on Mushet in the *D.N.B.* Mushet died in 1891.

[2] See Hadfield's many papers, e.g. in the *J. Iron and Steel Inst.* 1888, II; 1889, II; 1892, II; 1903, II; in the *Trans. Inst. Civ. Eng.* 1887; also the reports of the Alloys Research Committee of the Inst. in *Trans. Inst. Mech. Eng.* 1891, 1893, etc.

[3] Brackenbury, H. I., *Trans. Inst. Mech. Eng.* 1910, p. 929.

of chromium-tungsten steel subjected, in the making, to "a heat treatment which would utterly ruin ordinary steels".[1] The leading American firms had been quick to see the merit of these incredibly resistant steels, and to plan powerful tools—lathes, planes, drills, milling-cutters—in which they might be utilised. At first the high-speed steels were used only for rough-cutting, but they were improved, and gradually all sorts of tools were speeded up so as to use them. Very gradually indeed, it must be added, in the more backward provinces of the engineering world. "The revolution has now taken place", the English writer of 1910 continued, "and we are slowly accommodating ourselves to the new regime."[2] "In comparatively few shops", an American wrote in the same year, "is high-speed steel largely used; in most, to a very moderate extent only; while in a great many it is quite unknown."[3] There was still a good deal of both British and American accommodation needed when quick and accurate engineering became a matter of life and death in 1914–18.

It was natural that America, with its well-established tradition of time-saving, labour-saving and automatism, should blaze the trail for the entry of more and more quick-running and 'fool-proof' machinery into engineering shops and shipyards. Besides her lead with the high-speed steels, she was well ahead of Britain in the nineteenth century in the use of portable pneumatic tools—hammers, riveters, drills, road-breakers.[4] For certain purposes, especially in the mines, use was at least as old in Britain as in America; but America generalised it earlier, Britain only following in the late 'nineties, and then slowly. In 1899 machine-riveting, whether pneumatic or electric, was not yet an established practice in British shipyards; though the experiments with both types were by that time an old story.[5] A few years later however, in 1902 and 1903, the familiar complaint against automatism is heard from Clydeside yards—with a pneumatic chisel "one lad in a few hours" can do the day's task of a grown man: the 'prentice is supplanting the journeyman.[6]

[1] Gledhill, J. M., "On the development and use of high-speed steel", *J. Iron and Steel Inst.* 1904, II; Becker, *op. cit.* pp. 14–17, from which the quotation comes.

[2] Brackenbury, as above.

[3] Becker, p. 64.

[4] Amos, E. C., "Portable pneumatic tools", *Trans. Inst. Mech. Eng.* 1900.

[5] White, Sir Wm., "The connection between Mechanical Engineering and Shipbuilding", *Trans. Inst. Mech. Eng.* 1899, p. 161, and cp. vol. II. 109.

[6] *Factory Reports*, 1903 (XII), p. 126; 1904 (X), p. 101.

America, the evidence suggests, also led in the development and use of the milling-cutter. Most of the older machine-tools —planes, shapers, slotters—were reciprocating: they made their stroke and drew back for the next. The milling-cutter is rotary. It may resemble a circular saw or a drill, or a wheel set with planing blades, or the working part of a mowing-machine. There are things that it cannot do, though they are few; but whatever it does it does continuously. It was an old, because an obvious, notion; but there had always been trouble with its teeth or its blades. They needed constant filing in early days, even when made of the best temper steel. This trouble had been partially got over before 1890, by the use of emery-wheel grinders. Side by side with that improvement, the cutter itself in its various forms was much improved—"in America and on the continent, where it is now successfully used to a far greater extent than in England." "Now" is the year 1890.[1] After that, the milling-cutter came into its own in England, greatly helped from about 1900 by the improved high-speed steels.[2] The steels were being made at Sheffield as well as at any place in the world; perhaps better. And, in view of the early history of their invention, that was appropriate.

A good deal of such delayed, but then efficient, adoption of methods and devices utilised with success, if not initiated, abroad runs through the records of British metallurgy and engineering at this time. In following the story, it is not to be forgotten that foreign countries were adopting British devices and methods, just as in the early years of the machine age, though not nearly so often. Still, a worried, if perhaps an exaggerated, consciousness of loss of leadership is evident in much of the official and technical literature of the day. No doubt an engineer with faith in electric trams for cities, or in milling-cutters for all sorts of metal work, is apt to overdo the backwardness of his countrymen and the deadly universal efficiency of someone else. That is an old trick. But when the process advocated has a foreign name, there is not much risk of error as to its place of origin or earliest efficient commercial application. There is a rather naïve satisfaction, with a touch of conscious inferiority which can hardly mislead, running through the reports of the Factory Inspectors about how some foreign skilled firm has immigrated or how, in this, that or the other,

[1] Addy, G., "On Milling Cutters", *Trans. Inst. Mech. Eng.* 1890, p. 528.
[2] See Brackenbury's address of 1910 in *Trans. Inst. Mech. Eng.* quoted above.

England is abreast of America, Germany or France. Now and again they refer by the way to some acknowledged British supremacy or invention which is taken for granted, and this must not be ignored; but their reports leave a continuous and deep impression of how many things they think are done better elsewhere, or very recently have been.

By 1888 works for grinding basic slag are reported: "our neighbours the Germans were the first to recognise its value." The same year a new metallurgical industry for South Wales is observed, the making of seamless steel tubes—by the Mannesman Company. By 1896, in the lock-making country, there has been a "marvellous improvement...in...English iron-foundry, which now compares favourably with the best American productions". From America also has come the quickly extending use of stamped steel. Six years later, the first machine ever installed at Cradley Heath for making chain-cables is American. In 1904 an iron works on Tyneside has been completely replanned: it is "as advanced as anything America can show". Next year is Germany's turn again, "German methods and machinery" have been introduced to a "large extent" into the file and cutlery trades at Sheffield. "The machinery is highly ingenious."[1] Such simple records and opinions could easily be multiplied. Britain had always done some industrial borrowing, but never nearly so much in these vital fields of metal work as during the two decades 1885–1905. By about 1905–10 however her most deadly lag, that in electrical development, was being wiped out. Though the electricity producing and distributing organisation of the country was still exceedingly ragged and defective, so were those of other industrial countries with which it was now becoming at least comparable in efficiency.

The electrical lag was responsible, among other things, for the late development of a British aluminium industry; though in this case the lag was due less to lack of enterprise than to Britain's relative shortage of water power and suitable aluminium ores. Whatever the cause, it remained true that well into the twentieth century an Englishman could get aluminium wares better in almost any country than in his own.

[1] *Factory Reports*, 1889 (XVIII), pp. 63, 141; 1897 (XVII), p. 37; 1903 (XII), p. 39; 1905 (X), p. 106; 1906 (XV), p. 111.

Free aluminium occurs nowhere in nature and even its oxide generally in awkward combinations. The isolation of the pure metal had taken the laboratory chemists nearly forty years. Humphry Davy was first in the attack, in 1809, and Wöhler of Göttingen drove it home in the 'forties. In the 'fifties Deville at the *École Normale* in Paris had worked out a method of production which, under his guidance, was used later by Lowthian Bell to provide the small quantities of aluminium employed experimentally in the metallurgy of iron and steel.[1] Bell Brothers, it is said, made nearly 2 cwt. a year. Large-scale production by electrolysis waited on the dynamo; and the first commercial electrolytic process, which was operated both in England and America in 1885–6, yielded only an alloy. Then, in 1886–7, came the joint patenting, by Hall for America and by Héroult for France and England, of the electrolytic method which subsequently became universal. Hall started at Pittsburg; but in 1894 he moved to Niagara. From 1888 Héroult had been among the alps and waterfalls of Dauphiné and Savoy. The development of other Alpine sites followed. In England nothing happened except a fall in the price of aluminium from anything between 10*s.* and 20*s.* a lb. to 4*s.*, and the ruin of a small company which, with the steam-made electricity of 1890, had tried to compete with the great waterfalls. In 1895 however came the British Aluminium Company. It was to dig 'alum clay' (bauxite) at Larne in Antrim, the only place in the British Isles where it occurs in quantity; to reduce it by the Héroult process at the Falls of Foyers by Loch Ness; and to refine the ingots at Milton in Staffordshire. This is a big triangle; but it was supposed that aluminium was valuable enough to stand some carriage, and the rough ingots from Foyers served for foundry work.[2]

Eleven years later, Foyers was still the only British producing centre of the Company. But late in 1907 production began in temporary works at Leven, while the Company's great Kinlochleven enterprise was in progress. In 1908 production began at a Norwegian site, Stangfjord, and negotiations were in hand for an Alpine site. By 1912 alumina (the oxide) was being made at Larne and shipped to Kinlochleven, Foyers and Stangfjord, and arrangements had been made for additional foreign supplies

[1] Above, p. 153.

[2] Ristori, E., "Aluminium Manufacture", *Trans. Inst. Mech. Eng.* 1898 and the article Aluminium in *Encyc. Brit.* (11th ed. 1910), also by Ristori.

of bauxite.[1] Yet, all told, the British industry took a very humble place in the mineral returns of 1913. A fair amount of home-reduced aluminium went to the foundries; but the British mountaineer, buying his excellent light aluminium equipment at Bern, was disposed to criticise his own country.

Aluminium pots are small and cheap. The total value of them, with that of all the crude aluminium imported into the United Kingdom, was trifling.[2] Britain had no special natural facilities for carrying on the industry; was in fact deficient in them. Canada, among other places, was not. From the standpoint of a sane world economy therefore, or even of a sane imperial economy, there was no reason why all the aluminium should not have been imported, while Britain concentrated on the things which she could make supremely well—ships for instance, of which she sold £11,000,000 worth new in 1913, besides 488,000 tons of second-hand shipping, value unknown.

In the early 'eighties steel had not yet finally beaten wrought-iron out of the shipyards. Even a few boilers were still built of iron in 1885. For frames and plates, steel "of the quality required by Lloyds" was more than 40 per cent. dearer.[3] During the next few years however this margin was cut down. Steel was made of a texture more suitable for shipyard work. Already in 1887 this mild (low carbon) steel was coming into use fast;[4] and soon the merits of steel-construction, even when a little dearer than construction in iron, were generally admitted. By 1895, as the aged Bessemer noted with satisfaction in his autobiography, 98·8 per cent. of the ships launched were of steel[5]—though not of Bessemer steel—including the last of the high-seas sailing ships. For working purposes, the transition to steel was finished. Indeed, ever since 1890, the number of iron ships built had been negligible.

With the coming of steel and the sad exit of the sailing ship vessels of all kinds grew in bulk. With the specialisation of

[1] Reports of the Company's meeting, *Economist*, April 25, 1908 and March 30, 1912.

[2] There was no special heading in the monthly trade returns: aluminium came under "other metals".

[3] Vol. II. 63.

[4] See e.g. a reference in the *Economist's* trade notes, Nov. 22, 1887.

[5] *Autobiography*, p. 254; White, Sir Wm., in *Trans. Inst. Mech. Eng.* 1899, as above, pp. 162–3; *Factory Report*, 1890 (xx), p. 8: ships are now "almost exclusively...steel".

trade and travel the number of types also grew—refrigerator ships, tankers, the more elaborate and specialised passenger liners, Aquitanias, Mauretanias, Titanics. In one Clydeside yard, which did a miscellaneous representative business in ocean-going ships, the average vessel launched in the 'seventies had been of 1260 tons: many of these were composite or all-iron sailing ships. The average in the 'eighties was 2000 tons: there were still a few barques among them. In 1892 the firm launched its last ocean-going steel clipper, the *Afon Cefni* of 2066 tons. Its average ship of the 'nineties was of 3500 tons.[1]

While the transition to steel and the growth of the average ship were in progress, there were no really fundamental changes in design either of the ship or of its engines. Paddle-steamers were no longer built for ordinary uses. Screw-propellers were multiplied and improved. Boiler pressures increased and fuel economy was pursued, though it was economy of the old fuel, steam-coal. The water-tube boiler was coming into use. Electricity on board ship, an exciting novelty in the early 'eighties, had become standard practice twenty years later. All Parsons' early turbo-generators had been tried out at sea, and his exhaust steam turbine of 1894 was specially useful there. But from invention to general use is often a long step, though with Parsons' inventions it was probably shorter than it had ever been before. When he gave the world the marine turbine at the close of the century, there was no lack of interest in the shipyards; but there was inevitably a series of experimental years during which destroyers, yachts, and the light channel steamers in which turbines were tried out were carefully watched, and the performances of their engines contrasted with those of the ordinary reciprocating sort.[2]

About the beginning of the new century, there was great activity in the re-equipment of the leading shipyards. Pneumatic or electric drilling, riveting, and other processes were now coming into general use. By 1901, nearly all the great firms of the North-East Coast and Tyneside generated their own electric power[3]—Parsons worked among them—and utilised it in a great variety of ways; for the first-grade shipyard could

[1] *A Shipbuilding History* (1932): Alexander Stephen and Sons, pp. 80, 86, and Appendix, with list of all ships built.

[2] Messrs Stephen e.g. put turbine machinery, built at Parsons' works, into a yacht in 1903 and into an Atlantic liner in 1905. They began to build turbines themselves in 1912; *A Shipbuilding History*, pp. 165, 208.

[3] *Factory Report*, 1902 (XII), p. 87, and cp. p. 136 above.

carry an electric plant big enough to be economical. It was from Clydeside yards that complaints about automatism and 'technological unemployment' came in 1902–3.[1] "As soon as electrical power production became a practical proposition", that is to say shortly after 1900, the historian of one of them writes,[2] "the Firm installed a large plant to produce its own electricity, and gradually changed over from a complete steam-driven plant to a completely electric one." That a firm of such importance, though not one of the very greatest—it finished 34,000 tons of shipping in 1903—should be turning over in this complete way to electricity was rightly entered by the Factory Inspectors as a symptom of the new phase in industrial history.[3]

By that time the marine turbine was well beyond the experimental stage and was coming into use both for warships of all sizes and for the most important liners. The years 1903–6, which saw the first crossing of the Atlantic by a turbine steam yacht (1903), the launch of the first two Atlantic turbine liners (1905), and the building of the Dreadnought, mark the transition.[4] They also mark the effective start of the use of oil-fuel by the world's warships and liners. For many years oil burning had been confined to the Caspian Sea. There were woodcuts of it in the old illustrated papers—this semi-oriental oddity from the lands where once there had been fire worshippers. In the 'nineties serious experiment began on the high seas. By 1901, the Shell Company, naturally and appropriately, had a whole fleet of oil-burning boats.[5] There were obvious advantages in oil, quite apart from those special advantages which recommended its use very early to Admiralties. Its action was steady. The furnace could be fired while shut. There was economy of two of the most desperate sorts of human labour, trimming and stoking. The sweat and grime of coaling vanished. But there remained the problem of supply—technical and strategic—for a country which produced steam-coal easily and in abundance, but had neither an oil production worth mentioning nor any immediate prospect of creating one.

[1] Above, p. 154.

[2] *A Shipbuilding History*, p. 164.

[3] *Factory Report*, 1903 (1904, x. 133) does not name the firm, speaking only of "one Clyde yard"; but the reference is obvious.

[4] Sir Ch. Furness' *Emerald*, referred to above, was the yacht: *A Shipbuilding History*, p. 182 and p. 142 (the liners).

[5] Orde, E. L., "Liquid fuel for steamships", *Trans. Inst. Mech. Eng.* 1902; Ewing, *The Steam Engine* (4th ed. 1926), p. 546.

Except however for the naval problem, a thing apart, the real conflict between oil and coal in Britain was hardly begun before 1909, as the imports of fuel-oils show. The imports are not a complete test, because oil-burning ships naturally filled their tanks so far as possible in oil-producing countries, and because ships are not the only consumers of fuel-oil. But comparison between the 15,000,000 gallons of fuel-oil imported in 1908, which was the highest then recorded, the average of 48,000,000 gallons of 1909–13, the 228,000,000 war gallons of 1914, and the 383,000,000 peace gallons of 1924 tells a clear enough tale. In 1908 an oil-burning ship in the mercantile marine was still an oddity or a luxury. Even in 1913 only 2·65 per cent. of the world's sea-going tonnage burnt oil, including all the ships whose trade with oil-producing countries or in oil products made it a specially obvious thing for them to do.[1]

At the same date, less than half of 1 per cent. of the world's tonnage was driven by internal combustion engines. Most of these were auxiliary paraffin engines in fishing boats and other small craft; and they were commoner outside than inside British waters. There the steam-trawler was well established and efficient. Scandinavian fishermen and seamen, in their coalless countries whose narrow fjords and channels a sailing-boat cannot easily leave when the wind is wrong, had for some years found the auxiliary motor a great convenience.[2] Meanwhile the Diesel type of heavy-oil engine was being adapted for marine use. It was a comparatively new thing for any use. Only in 1897, "after four years of difficult experiments", had Diesel got his first engine "into working order in the factory of the Augsburg works".[3] Thousands of them, much improved, had been delivered in the next fourteen years for all sorts of purposes, particularly, as might have been expected, in Germany; but it was not until 1912 that the first marine Diesel engine was put into a big ship, the *Selandia*. Appropriately enough, considering the interest which the Northern nations had shown in internal combustion at sea, it was built by Burmeister and Wain of Copenhagen.[4]

[1] *Lloyd's List.*

[2] In the fjords their number surprised and impressed a visiting Englishman in 1908.

[3] Above, p. 134, n. 1. Cp. the discussion of coal economy in the *R.C. on Coal Supplies*, 1905, pp. 11 *sqq.* The internal-combustion engine generally, and "the still more recent invention of Mr Diesel", may result in economy.

[4] Ewing, *The Steam Engine*, p. 635.

The relatively stagnant trade of the years of falling prices had interfered with the geographical expansion of coal-mining and discouraged mechanical enterprise about the mines. An average annual output for the United Kingdom of 130,000,000 tons in 1874–6 had risen to only 163,000,000 by 1886–8; and the output per head of the population had increased hardly at all. "Very few pits have been sunk during the last twelve years", an experienced owner and financier of collieries told the Institute of Mechanical Engineers in 1890.[1] Improvement at the existing pits there had of course been—speedings up of machinery and a general adoption of the safety and ventilating methods worked out during the previous generation. In coal-cutting machinery there had been "very little progress" in twenty years. Electricity had however arrived and, though still "in its infancy", had in a few places got beyond the lighting and pumping of the first experiments. It was "already...successfully applied" for underground haulage in some South Yorkshire pits before 1890; but this was a very exceptional novelty.[2]

There were other novelties, rather obvious ones to the outside lay mind, which mining engineers were being asked to consider at that time. One was the use of steel underground for purposes which had been served hitherto by timber, with a little help occasionally from cast iron—for girders in the roofs of the underground ways and for the props which support them. Steel is said to have been first tried in a Warwickshire thick-coal colliery in 1885. Eleven years later there was very little wood left in the main roads or return airways there. At first steel had only been employed for the girders, in this and in other collieries. By 1895, mining engineers in conference were agreeing that one of their number had "made out a strong case in favour of...more general use"[3] of the steel girder. It was evidently still regarded as a bit of an experiment. The steel prop was much more experimental. The pioneering Warwickshire colliery had only tried it in 1894. Two or three years later, the men were said to prefer it to the timber prop, an essential fact, if true;[4] for the conservatism of the pit-man was often the

[1] *Trans. Inst. Mech. Eng.* 1890, p. 361: Emerson Bainbridge.

[2] *Ibid.* pp. 383, 384. And see the *D.C. on Electricity in Mines*, 1904 (XXIV), Q. 189: "by 1888 it was moving very rapidly", L. B. Atkinson, a pioneer.

[3] From the discussion of a paper by Thompson, E., "The Use of Steel Girders in Mines", *Trans. Inst. Mining Eng.* 1895–6.

[4] Melly, F. E., "The Use of Steel Girders and Props in Coal Mines", *Trans. Inst. Mining Eng.* 1896–7.

main obstacle to change in his immediate working environment. In the introduction of a new hauling or lighting or ventilating system he had little say: if it was efficient he probably welcomed it. But about the lamp or the pick or the prop he had a great deal to say. If he did not like them they might not work.

Steel gained ground slowly for the more obvious and permanent uses in the main highways underground; but the huge and growing import of pit-wood and pit-props shows that it had not won the vote of the average miner or mining engineer, in many, perhaps most, cases no doubt for sound reasons of economy or efficiency. Besides the home supplies which were always considerable, for British woodlands do yield pit-props, these imports grew from an average of 2,100,000 loads in 1901–3 to one of 3,100,000 loads in 1911–13. As the output of coal had not grown nearly so fast, there cannot have been much replacement of timber by steel.

British mining was in fact a little backward in that general adoption of steel for structural purposes which was characteristic of the time. It seems to have been backward also in the adventurous use of cement and concrete. There were records of cement blocks being employed for the walling of pit-shafts in the 'sixties; but in 1892 mining engineers were still having their attention directed to the "noticeable increase in the boldness of the application of Portland cement to engineering works"; to its recent ingenious use "for consolidating shifting sand in water-bearing strata"; and to the "tubbing of cement blocks for stopping back water"—on the continent.[1] They may have reflected with satisfaction that they were less troubled with shifting water-bearing sands than some continentals. Besides, they had not been asked to sink many new pits lately. When more active sinking was resumed, they did not often find it necessary to resort to Poetsch's continental system of freezing the ground before sinking. It had only been used six times down to 1911.[2] At one of its uses, an early one, Messrs Gebhardt and Koenig had brought all the plant from Nordhausen. But the fact that there was then no English plant was more England's good fortune than her disgrace. You do not need to freeze magnesian limestone or chalk when you sink through them.

[1] Brough, D. H., "The Use of Cement in Shaft Sinking", *Trans. Inst. Mining Eng.* 1892–3.

[2] Wilson, W. B., "The Advantages of Freezing as a Method of Sinking", *Trans. Inst. Mining Eng.* 1910–11. Cp. vol. II. 90, 111.

Whether the engineers ought to have 'Poetsched' more or not, and very likely they ought not, it seems clear that they were slow to adopt reinforced concrete for general purposes. So late as 1912, a Professor came before their gathering as "a special pleader" for its "more extended use".[1] One of his audience admitted that mining engineers really were rather ignorant about concrete, just, he added, as civil engineers were ignorant about mines. Next year, when one of the mining engineers described his experiments with reinforced concrete underground since 1908, he was congratulated and thanked especially for his costing figures "of this new work".[2]

Electricity, as might have been anticipated, made only sluggish progress in the mines. A departmental committee appointed in 1902 to discuss the safeguards which should accompany its use, was writing, in 1904, about the very large part that it was "likely to play"; was asking why there was no electric winding in England such as was to be found on the continent; and was proclaiming, perhaps a little superfluously, that "this new agent ought to be welcomed". They stated that no witness was hostile to its use, provided it were properly regulated. That it could even be called a "new agent" twenty years after it was first tried is significant.[3] On the other hand, not a great deal had been known about long distance electrical transmission in the earlier of these years, and in the absence of such knowledge progress in some of the uses of electricity had necessarily been rather slow.

Among the committee's first witnesses were engineers who had themselves designed electrical installations. "Hundreds" of collieries use electricity one of these eager pioneers said.[4] He was reminded that the number of possible users was three thousand. Trade Union witnesses were properly solicitous about safeguards, but had no objection of principle. They knew of one electric coal-cutter in Northumberland and of twenty in Durham.[5] There were also a few compressed-air cutters. In Lanark there were forty or fifty machines, by no means all electric.[6] In South Wales there was no coal-cutting machinery

[1] Prof. Dixon, "Reinforced Concrete in Mines", *Trans. Inst. Mining Eng.* 1912–13.

[2] Gregory, J., "Examples of the use of Concrete at Collieries", *Trans. Inst. Mining Eng.* 1913–14.

[3] *D.C. on Electricity in Mines*, pp. 6, 7, 8.

[4] L. B. Atkinson, Q. 191.

[5] H. Boyle, Q. 2997; J. Johnson, Q. 3361.

[6] R. Smillie, Q. 3181.

of any kind, though there was a little electric haulage underground. In the Rhondda, electricity was used only for signalling, shot-firing, and other minor purposes.[1] In South Yorkshire and Nottingham a few of the leading collieries used it extensively—for pumping, hauling, lighting, cutting, ventilation; in fact for everything except winding in the main shafts.[2] Their enterprise was mainly responsible for the 231 electric coal-cutters at work in the whole country in 1903.[3] But the coalowners agreed with Robert Smillie, speaking for the men, that electric cutters were dangerous in a fiery mine. Indeed, one of them would have had the use of electricity prohibited altogether in such mines.[4]

It was while the committee was sitting that one mining engineer told his colleagues how when he wanted an electrical 'heading' machine—to break a strike of 'headers' for more pay—he had to fetch it from America.[5] A year after the committee reported, another described the great strides made "of late" in Westphalia, where electricity was used for almost every conceivable purpose. He had only found one or two really high-power electrical winding engines there, but a great number of small ones.[6] After that, electric power made its way quietly into British coalfields and British pits, though there was nothing that could be called a revolution and many districts lagged. When the Cannock Chase Colliery was electrified in 1912, the man who was responsible said that hitherto electricity had not been used so much on the Cannock Chase field as on some others; which is English for had been used there very little, if at all.[7]

The technical change which might most fairly be called

[1] A. Onions, Q. 3904; D. W. Morgan, Q. 4026.

[2] Evidence of A. B. Markham, M.P., Q. 4269 *sqq.*

[3] *R.C. on Coal Supplies*, p. 7. There were also 412 pneumatic machines. For the types and uses of machines see vol. II. 102–3. As in 1914 only 7 per cent. of the coal raised in Britain was cut by machinery (*Statistical Tables Relating to British and Foreign Trade and Industry*, Cd. 3849, 1931, II. 10), progress was evidently slow.

[4] Markham, Q. 4273; Smillie, Q. 3184.

[5] Greaves, P. C., "An electrical Heading Machine", *Trans. Inst. Mining Eng.* 1903–4. A header "drives narrow roads in coal...to open new work", etc. —*Dic. of Occupational Terms.*

[6] Brown, E. O. F., "Notes on the Applications of Electric Power at Mines in Germany", *Trans. Inst. Mining Eng.* 1904–5.

[7] Sopwith, S. F., "The Electrification of Cannock Chase Colliery", *Trans. Inst. Mining Eng.* 1912–13.

revolutionary was probably that which had taken place in the handling of coal at the pit-head. Before the great price-fall, when Britain had no rivals in the world's markets and economy and grading did not matter, the methods had been most crude and primitive—tipping, shovelling and carting, with plenty of dust and waste and dirt, though there was always a certain amount of hand picking—picking out the stone—and hand sorting. By the twentieth century every colliery of any repute had its mechanical installations for screening, sizing, sorting and washing the coal before it was delivered in its various sizes and grades into railway trucks. Even in this field, however, it was being suggested in 1905 that the Germans were ahead, at least in the marketing of the sorted coal: they were said to be selling on guaranteed chemical analyses and guaranteed percentages of error in the sizes of the coals supplied.[1] And in 1914 Britain was still said to be "far behind the continental countries" in preparing coal for market.[2] But as the British collieries had no difficulty in increasing their exports by more than 40 per cent. between 1905, itself a peak year, and the average of 1911–13, while over the same period the price per ton of coal exported went up by 20 per cent., there was no great stimulus to a reform in their selling practice; and at home there was no fear of any real competition by foreigners.

Anxiety, or at least curiosity, about the future of the national coal supplies, never quite dormant since Jevons formulated his brilliant prophecy in 1865,[3] had led to the appointment of a Royal Commission of inquiry in 1903. After Jevons' day, there had been a good many sinkings through overlying geological formations to the coal measures proper; and in 1890 Boyd-Dawkins, when testing a geological hypothesis of Godwin-Austen, had struck coal at Dover.[4] This was the first time that it had been reached in England through the chalk. There had been further boring in 1897–9; and while the Commission was sitting the Kent Coal Concessions Company got to work.

[1] *R.C. on Coal Supplies*, p. 8. The report says that these pit-head improvements had been made "since 1870"; but most were in fact made after 1880.

[2] Jevons, H. S., *The British Coal Trade* (1915), p. 230.

[3] See e.g. Courtney, Rt. Hon. L., "Jevons' 'Coal Question' thirty years after", *S.J.* 1897, and vol. II, 99–100.

[4] Boyd-Dawkins, W., "The South-Eastern Coalfield", *Trans. Inst. Mining Eng.* 1912–13, and references there. Godwin-Austen in the *D.N.B.* His essay "On the possible extension of the coal-measures beneath the south-eastern parts of England" was published in 1854. He died in 1884.

Before that, borings and pit sinkings had carried the effective South Yorkshire coalfield nearer and nearer to the Humber. There had been no sinking before 1905 East of Cadeby; but bore-holes had struck the 'Barnsley bed' at a depth of 1848 feet just North of Doncaster, and at 3186 feet South-East by East of the town. There was also boring in progress in 1904 North-East of Doncaster, and very near tide-water, at Thorne.[1] Some geologists were convinced that concealed coal lay under most of Lincolnshire, though whether at workable depths or not only experiment could determine.[2]

So, seeing that the coal consumption of more than 234,000,000 tons which Jevons had forecast for 1891 was only passed in 1905; that the concealed coal was turning out much better than had once been anticipated; and that there was still a wide margin for economy in consumption, the Commissioners made no alarmist report. They did print in an Appendix an estimate of trouble about the year A.D. 2100; but this estimate assumed a British population of 130,000,000 in A.D. 2091, and an export of coal growing in the interval as fast as it had grown in the years 1890–1905. The estimator added that if by any chance coal consumption could be kept down to 250,000,000 tons a year, which was almost precisely the figure for 1906, there was certainly enough for four more centuries. Stabilisation at such a figure seemed at the time most unlikely; but economies in consumption which would give the British coal era at least another three centuries were certainly attainable. The Commissioners scheduled these economies.[3] If all engines were as good as the best, they could run on 50 per cent. less fuel. There were the admitted wastes of heat at collieries and ironworks, by small power users, and in domestic fire-grates. There was the turbine; there was powdered fuel; and there were gases or oil for internal combustion engines.

Fuel economy made no great progress in the eight years following the Report of 1905; but time was on its side. The output of British coal touched what will no doubt prove to have been its absolute historical maximum, 287,000,000 tons, in 1913.[4] By that time the Kent coalfield was on the edge of

[1] *R.C. on Coal Supplies*, p. 115, with a map, based on the evidence of A. Currer-Briggs, coalowner.

[2] The strongly held opinion of Prof. P. F. Kendall of Leeds, a colleague of the author, 1902–8.

[3] *R.C. on Coal Supplies*, p. 12.

[4] It now (1937) seems likely that stabilisation may occur round about 225,000,000 tons or less, instead of the 250,000,000 of the first hypothesis.

production, and so were some of the great new well-laid-out collieries in the Doncaster area. There had been important fresh sinkings through the magnesian limestone to the coal-measures on the Durham coast, and into the coal-measures direct in Glamorgan. The whole industry, though full of conflict, was active and expanding, both commercially and geographically. Its best units were admirably equipped; though its very nature implied the existence of backward marginal pits, and even marginal districts, whose future was in no circumstance assured. The national need for economy in coal consumption, for the distant future's sake, clashed with the miners' and coal-owners' wish for an ever-rising output. A future of possible coal-shortage was however now so distant that to leave it to take care of itself, while at the same time discouraging all forms of waste, was not only the easy obvious course but also the way of good sense.

The mining and quarrying of ironstone had been altered in no important way since the 'eighties. No entirely fresh fields had been opened out, though the deposits on the curving sweep of the lias and oolite formations, from Cleveland through Lincolnshire into Northampton and Oxford, had been more fully utilised as the coal-measure ironstones of the older producing districts gave out. The changes had been thus:

	1885	Average 1909–13
Staffordshire (coal-measure)	1·8 million tons	0·9 million tons
Scotland (coal-measure)	1·8 "	0·6 "
Cumberland and Lancashire (hematite)	2·4 "	1·7 "
Cleveland (lias)	6·0 "	5·9 "
Lincoln and Northampton (lias and oolite)	2·3 "	5·0 "
Other districts—Wales, West Riding, Shropshire, Derby (coal-measure); Leicester, Rutland, Oxford (lias and oolite)	0·4 "	0·9 "
Foreign ore used	3·3 "	6·7 "

Of the 'other districts', all but Leicester, Rutland and Oxford were negligible as ore-raisers by 1909–13. The hematite supply from Cumberland and Furness could not be increased, and was terminable. The demand for Bessemer ore was met by increasing imports, of which 67 per cent. came from Spain in 1909–13, 10 per cent. from Scandinavia, and 10 per cent. from Algeria. As the imported ores were rich in iron, and all native ores except the hematite relatively poor, half the iron made came out of foreign ore. The British make in 1913 was 10,260,000 tons. Three-eighths of it was made on the North-East coast; more than an eighth in Scotland; and a ninth on the North-West coast. South Wales and Monmouth made a twelfth and the Black Country an eleventh.[1]

Of other metallic mining there is little to be said because it was so uniformly decadent. Eight figures tell the story:

	1885	Average 1909–13
Copper from British ores	2,800 tons	400 tons
Lead ,,	37,700 ,,	19,900 ,,
Tin ,,	9,300 ,,	5,100 ,,
Zinc ,,	9,800 ,,	5,200 ,,

In every case the decline had been almost continuous, though tin had recovered a little at the last from its absolute minimum of 4132 tons in 1904. These are not industries in which technical changes of importance are to be looked for. Cornish mining enterprise was gone to the Rand or Malaya, to Canada or the United States; and the lead miners had drifted from their Welsh or Pennine valleys down to the coalfields.[2]

How the strongly entrenched position and inherent strength of the gas industry delayed the advance of electricity has already been seen. There was gas and there were gas-engines everywhere in the middle 'eighties, and the incandescent burner had just been invented. For the first time new qualities were demanded in the gas, instead of the high illuminating power when used with an open burner which had satisfied almost everyone for more than half a century.[3] The threat of electrical competition put the 700 or so statutory gas undertakings on the defensive. The best of them decided that attack was the right defence. They began to experiment, to advertise, to push, to listen more readily to what chemists told them about the value of their by-products. Within ten or twelve years of the invention of the incandescent burner, in 1885, the old-style gas was not much made, and consumers who had not adopted the incandescent were complaining. Gas-fires, gas-cookers more complex than the primitive ring, and various types of gas water-heaters were invented or improved. Electricity, when introduced as the "light of luxury" into private houses, was usually generated by

[1] *Statistical Tables*, 1931, II. 55–8 based on the *Mineral Returns*.
[2] Cp. vol. II. 104.
[3] Vol. II. 107.

a gas-engine. Gas had many and increasing direct uses in industry. It held its own for street-lighting, at first no doubt because it was there, but later because its use had been made both effective and economical.[1]

In primitive gas-making the 'ammonia-water' had been a waste product: the coke and the tar had been sold off cheap: too much sulphur had gone into the gas. By the end of the 'eighties, sulphate of ammonia was a standard product of the gas-works, or of chemical works which bought 'ammonia water' from them. The 'water' which at the Sunderland gas-works had been disposed of at 3*s*. per 1000 gallons in 1850 fetched 40*s*. by 1899–1900. The coke had risen rather faster in value than the coal from which it was made. Tar alone had fallen, but then the tar of 1850 contained neglected benzol, toluol, and what not, which by 1900 were fractionated out in all well-managed gas-works. It may be assumed that the tar was not the same tar, and that the company was getting good prices for fractions.[2]

The statistical story of sulphate of ammonia illustrates the gradual way in which various industrial users of coal, of which the gas-works were the most important, were provoked into saving—for the ultimate benefit of agriculture—what had once been a waste product. In the middle 'eighties there were already three sources of supply besides the gas-works; the works in the Scottish Lowlands which distilled oil-shale; a few blast-furnaces, nearly all Scottish, which smelted with coal and had begun to save and utilise the waste gases; and the very few English coke-ovens which had been equipped for the same purpose. (The ordinary coke-burning blast-furnace was not a possible contributor; for the coke had lost its ammonia.)[3] In the late 'eighties came the makers of 'Mond gas' or 'producer gas', who extracted the ammonia before turning the rest of the coal into a gaseous fuel.[4] The amount of their contribution was not however known exactly for some years.

[1] See generally Bone, W. A., *Coal and its Scientific Uses* (1918), and Thorpe, Sir T. E., in *Dic. of Applied Chemistry* (ed. 1922), s.v. Coal Gas.

[2] The figures from Sunderland are in the *Report of the Alkali Inspector*, 1900 (x), p. 27. And cp. the *Reports* of 1892 (xx) and 1894 (xix). The probable explanation of the tar prices was suggested by Dr H. McCombie of King's College. The figures are: coal, 3*s*. to 12*s*. a ton; coke, 2*s*. 6*d*. to 10*s*. 6*d*. a ton; tar, 2*d*. to 1¼*d*. a gallon; ammonia liquid, as above.

[3] See the analysis of the position in the *Alkali Report* of 1892.

[4] See the account of this "novelty" in the *Alkali Report* of 1888 (xxvi), p. 14.

The subsequent course of the output of sulphate of ammonia, in tons, was:[1]

	1891	1897	1904	1909	1911	1913
From gas-works	108,000	134,000	150,000	164,000	169,000	182,000
„ shale-works	28,000	37,000	42,000	57,000	60,000	63,000
„ ironworks	6,000	18,000	20,000	20,000	20,000	20,000
„ coke-ovens	3,000 }	11,000	{ 21,000	83,000	105,000	134,000
„ producer gas	? }		{ 13,000	25,000	30,000	34,000

The gas-works and the shale-works are established industries from the start, expanding normally with the growth of demand, especially of the overseas demand; for three-quarters of the whole production was exported. Output from ironworks was limited rigidly because so few of them burnt coal in the blast-furnace.[2] Producer gas was a novelty with a limited appeal. The figure for coke-ovens is the most significant. It registers the rapid, if delayed and still only partial, adoption of one or other of the various methods of by-product-recovery coking after 1904. The speed with which the output was raised at the finish is some measure of the previous quantity of destructive waste. The 45,000 tons of sulphur which Durham coke-ovens had belched up into the air in the 'eighties are only an item in the discreditable account.[3]

That the chemical trades proper, with such allied trades as paints, soap and explosives, should have expanded in this more scientific generation was natural. As employers of labour they grew slowly from 1881 to 1891; after 1891 fast. Whether the whole group be taken, or any of the principal subdivisions, the numbers employed approximately doubled between 1891 and 1911. The amount of labour required corresponded more nearly with the economic and social significance of the industries than it had thirty years earlier;[4] and their net output as estimated in the Census of Production of 1907 was comparable in value with that of all the wood-working trades, and was twice the value of

[1] Compiled from the *Alkali Reports*.

[2] Those that did were in Scotland. In 1901 all but two firms worked "with raw coal". The recovery of tar and ammonia from the furnaces only began in 1884–5. Burnby, H., "The iron and steel industries of the West of Scotland", *J. Iron and Steel Inst.* 1901, II.

[3] Vol. II. 51.

[4] The whole chemical group grew from 47,000 to 96,000, 1881–1911; chemicals (not dyes) from 22,000 to 44,000; soap, candles, glycerine, 7000 to 14,000. *Survey of Industrial Relations* (1926), p. 418.

that of all the metal-working trades other than iron and steel.[1]

These facts were insufficient to console contemporaries for the notorious British failure to develop an adequate coal-tar dyestuffs industry. The Census of Production of 1907 valued the output of coal-tar products of all sorts at about £3,860,000; but of this nearly two-thirds were the common stuff, pitch, tar-oil and creosote. Dyes from coal-tar were put at only £373,000.[2] The imports of these dyes had been worth nearly 50 per cent. more than that on an average even in 1886–8. In 1907 they were worth £1,700,000, and for the next six years the average was rather more. In 1913 the import was three and a half times the home production by weight, and probably more by value. There were a score of explanations but the fundamental one was that given by John Bowring two generations earlier: "chemical knowledge in its various branches" was more widespread, better appreciated, and better exploited in Germany than in Britain.[3] Having secured their lead by knowledge and application, the Germans had used various unpleasant but familiar commercial devices to retain it—underselling, restrictive contracts with customers, and so forth.[4] But great scientific industries are not built on such tricky foundations which, for the rest, were not a German monopoly. Besides, three of the most familiar names in the world of British chemical industry at this time rang German, if not all Aryan.[5]

The heavy chemical industry, originally based on the salt deposits of Cheshire, and occupied mainly in the production of soda and chlorine by the Leblanc process, had lost its control of the world's markets before 1887, but was too well placed and too well endowed to lose strength, unless by grave technical incompetence.[6] Its situation in the early and middle 'eighties had however been most difficult. A new and more adaptable salt industry was growing up in the Middlesborough area, and

[1] *Census of Production*, p. 21. The net output represents the value added to materials in the course of the process of manufacture; the gross output the selling value of the goods. Because chemical materials are cheap and non-ferrous metals dear the gross output of the non-ferrous trades was above that of the chemical trades. For commercial aspects of the soap industry see p. 264 below.

[2] *Census of Production*, p. 547.

[3] Vol. II. III. For the 1913 imports see *Statistical Tables* (1931), II. 371.

[4] *Report on the Textile Trades after the War*, p. 107—no doubt biassed.

[5] Brunner, Mond, Levinstein.

[6] Cp. vol. II. 106–7.

the so-called ammonia process, which made soda purer and more cheaply than the Leblanc, was competing with it—first from Belgium and in the world's markets; then, from 1883, at home.[1] There were said to be £3,000,000 invested in Leblanc plant, and many firms had to face the possibility of shutting down. In 1887, the "uncertain result" of the conflict of processes was being watched with the "keenest interest" by that detached expert the Alkali Inspector.[2] So far the ammonia process had not been successful in producing chlorine: the Leblanc people were therefore recouping losses on soda by putting up the price of what Lancashire called 'bleach' (chloride of lime). In this way, and by direct sale as a liquid, the hydrochloric acid which many soda-makers had sent into the air as 'acid mist' twenty years before, came to their help. The Inspector, who had conducted a long war against the acid mist, was interested.[3]

By 1889 the struggle between the processes was said to be "no longer doubtful";[4] but it was far from done. The development of a sub-process, by which sulphur could be recovered from 'tank waste', gave the users of the Leblanc another marketable joint-product. (It also kept the tank-waste from going into dumps or made ground in which sulphuretted hydrogen was generated.) There were other sub-processes and hybrid processes which delayed a complete change over. By 1893 the ammonia process had outstripped the Leblanc for the production of the various kinds of soda; but the older method, living on what had been its chlorine by-products, decomposed more salt than its rival.[5] It still remained decidedly active in 1899–1900; but in 1901 it passed again under a cloud. Electrolysis had just "invaded the domain of the alkali and chlorine manufacture"; and once more there was a British electrical lag, though there were sound British electrolytic patents.[6] By 1904 all the chlorine produced in America and 65 per cent. of that produced in Germany was electrolytic: in France the proportion was 19 and in England 18 per cent.[7] After that, electrolysis gained ground in England steadily but did not in any way displace alternative processes—the Weldon and the Deacon—

[1] Cp. vol. II. 515.

[2] *Alkali Report*, 1888 (XXVI), p. 8.

[3] Cp. vol. II. 105.

[4] *Alkali Report*, 1890 (XX), p. 13.

[5] *Alkali Report*, 1894 (XIX), p. 9; for the sub-processes see 1890–1 (XIX), p. 9.

[6] *Alkali Reports*, 1900 (X) and 1902 (XI), p. 47.

[7] *Alkali Report*, 1905 (IX), p. 11.

which had developed out of the original Leblanc.[1] It is noticeable that in this last electrolytic period the export of British bleaching materials remained stagnant in quantity and fell a little in value.

But this did not mean that either the heavy chemical industry or the chemical industries generally had decayed or stood still. It was merely a local weakness. The industries were exceedingly varied and, in spite of this weakness and of the comparative failure with synthetic dyestuffs, were at most points not less efficient than their competitors, as the course of the import and export trades in the twentieth century shows. It is true that the rougher and heavier chemicals—sulphate of ammonia, copper sulphate, the various forms of soda, cyanide of potassium, with tar and creosote made up a great part of the exports; but there were important trades in drugs and medicines and in paints and colours, with a great range of smaller miscellaneous trades. The figures under the customs classification 'Chemicals, Drugs, Dyes and Colours', which excludes soap and explosives, were as follows:

	Average of 1901–3	Average of 1911–13
Exports	£12,800,000	£21,000,000
Imports	£9,000,000	£12,300,000

While the exports had grown much faster than the imports, about a third of the imports were not competing manufactures at all, but raw drugs and vegetable dyewares, from opium to indigo. As a mere matter of value, the sulphate of ammonia from the gas-works and coke-ovens exported in 1911–13 was worth more than twice as much as all the imported synthetic dyes.[2] That there should be a long list of competing manufactures, in so varied a group of trades and in the open British market, was to be expected. It was to the credit of the British industries that the value of these imported manufactures in 1911–13, including the synthetic dyestuffs, was not nearly half that of the exports. How much of this credit should be transferred to the account of those geological forces which had arranged the British Isles and their mineral deposits, who shall say?

The textile industries had got beyond the era of rapid expansion as employers of labour. Between 1881 and 1901 the

[1] *Alkali Report*, 1912–13 (XIII), p. 59: and see the *Dic. of Applied Chemistry*.

[2] Sulphate of ammonia exported, annual average, £4,000,000; dyestuffs from coal-tar imported, £1,800,000.

numbers in the whole group were almost stationary. An expansion came in the next decade, especially in cotton, which increased its working staff by 14 per cent.[1] But the wool industries, excluding hosiery, employed a few thousand less in 1911 than in 1881.[2] The rougher miscellaneous group—hemp, jute, cocoa-fibre and so on—had grown steadily all the time, and so had hosiery; but flax and silk had as steadily declined. The net employment expansion for the whole group over a space of thirty years was 10·5 per cent. It was well that it was not more. The employment of the British people had been, and was, unduly dependent on the fortunes of these industries, fortunes over which it had inadequate control.

In some of the lesser industries of the group there may have been an absolute decline in production accompanying decline in employment; but in the greater, above all in cotton, the greatest and the best known, there was no question of this; though even in cotton there had been a certain stagnation in equipment and output from the late 'eighties to the late 'nineties. Typical figures for that stagnation and for the motion which followed it are these:[3]

	Average 1886–90	Average 1896–1900	Average 1906–10	Average 1910–13
Cotton spindles in the Lancashire district, millions	41·2	42·2	54·1	58·2
Yarn produced in Great Britain, million lb.	1458	1576	1707	1964

The rapid increase in spindles began precisely in 1905–6, with the boom which culminated in 1907: 95 new spinning mills with 8,500,000 spindles went up in two years.[4] It was accompanied by a corresponding increase in looms. For the whole country, spinning spindles increased by 40 per cent. and looms by 39 per cent. between 1885 and 1913.[5] They also became faster and more efficient. And about half the spindles and half

[1] And cp. Jones, *Increasing Return*, p. 277, for the increase in the number of firms in the Lancashire district. It remained steady between a minimum of 1735 and a maximum of 1818 from 1887–8 to 1905. By 1908 it was 1976 and in 1914 it touched 2011.

[2] 248,000 and 252,000.

[3] Jones, *Increasing Return*, pp. 275, 277.

[4] *Factory Report*, 1907 (x), p. 113. There were now too many mills; *Factory Report*, 1910 (XXVIII), p. 83.

[5] *Factory Return* of 1885 (1884–5, LXXI. 1087) and *Statistical Tables*, 1931, II. 191, 195.

the power looms in the world outside the United States of America were in Britain.[1]

The twentieth-century spinning mills, steel-framed, light and almost beautiful, were very different from their older neighbours, and were on the average much bigger. As small old-fashioned places went out of commission, the typical spinning mill more than doubled, from a place of 25,000 spindles in 1884 to one of 60,000 spindles in 1911. But the typical size of a weaving firm—spinning and weaving were normally distinct businesses, and long had been—grew much more slowly, from 325 only to 475 looms.[2] Nothing revolutionary happened inside either kind of mill. Everything was better and quicker—if the machinery was new: a good deal of it was not. There were all sorts of small adjustments and improvements. Ring spinning, very little used in 1885, was a well-recognised process by the twentieth century.[3] But the ring-frame was only a variant of the old throstle; it had been well established in the United States for half a century; and in 1913 certainly more than three-quarters of the spindles still moved in and out on the carriage of a self-acting mule, a mule much improved since Roberts' day and as nearly perfect for its task as a machine can be, but modified only in detail since the 'eighties.[4]

There had been a long controversy over the loom, with no great resulting change. America (again America) had worked out the most completely independent loom yet devised, so automatic that it was commonly called just 'an automatic'. It did not have to be stopped at intervals and fed with a fresh shuttleful of yarn; either it was 'self-shuttling', the empty shuttle being mechanically replaced, or its shuttle fed itself with fresh 'cops' of yarn.[5] As perfected in later years, two or three score of these robots can be supervised by a single person. Even in the years round 1900, Lancashire, where four looms per weaver was a maximum, heard with scepticism and dis-

[1] *Economic Advisory Council; Report on the Cotton Industry*, 1930 (Cd. 3615), p. 5.

[2] Chapman, S. J. and Ashton, T., "Sizes of businesses mainly in the Textile Industries", *S.J.* 1914.

[3] Chapman, S. J., *The Lancashire Cotton Industry* (1904), p. 71. See vol. II. 13, 80, for its earlier history.

[4] There are no complete statistics of mule and ring spindles for 1913; but in 1924 the ring spindles were not quite a quarter of the total number of spinning spindles in the U.K. and the total was very near what it had been in 1913. *Statistical Tables* of 1931, II. 191.

[5] The Northrop, the best-known 'automatic', is of the second sort.

approval of ten, fifteen, and twenty.[1] She "made great argument about it and about". For her best and better work 'automatics' were certainly not suited. Their field was the plain, rather coarse, standardised cotton sheeting. If she wanted to keep her old share of this end of the trade, it was unfortunate that, although Northrop automatics were made on her own territory at the finish, she was using not more than 15,000 of any pattern against a reputed 400,000 in America.[2]

Besides the 'automatic' loom and the ring-frame, also made in England, America had contributed and actually shipped some deft machines for minor processes, winding, knotting, drawing-in; but all essential machines were British made.[3]

Early in the twentieth century, isolated experiments with the electric drive were made both in the cotton and in the wool industries. An electrically driven cotton weaving factory is reported from Burnley in 1904, a new spinning-mill with 75,000 electrically driven spindles from Pendlebury in the following year.[4] About the same time electricity was first tried to drive woollen carding machinery near Leeds.[5] But no great progress was made in either industry; and though the electric drive for looms was used in several of "the most up-to-date concerns" in the wool industries by 1914, the reporters of 1918 noted "that electric power is very little used in Lancashire for driving textile machinery".[6] How far this neglect of electricity was a defect is an open question. From the social standpoint it certainly was. Cleanliness, quiet, and the absence of shafting and belting all tell in favour of electricity. But electric power was still relatively dear, in the absence of great central power stations. The best mill steam engines are remarkably efficient. Coal was cheap. The proportion of the price of a pound of yarn which represents the cost of motive power is singularly small; so that to make a change in the power economically attractive there must be a large demonstrable saving. And the advantages of electricity, even in new mills, were still in the balance during

[1] Chapman, *op. cit.* pp. 32–3 and the files of the *Manchester Guardian* and the *Textile Recorder* for 1900–3.

[2] *Report on Textile Trades after the War*, p. 51.

[3] *Ibid.* p. 51.

[4] *Factory Reports*, 1905, p. 136; 1906, p. 147.

[5] The statement in the *Factory Report*, 1912–13 (xxv), p. 62 that the electric drive for carding was new is incorrect. I saw it in a mill owned by a pioneer of electric power distribution in Yorkshire in 1905 or 1906, and it was then not quite new.

[6] *The Wool Year Book*, 1916, p. 303, and *Report on Textile Trades after the War*, p. 51.

the last spell of very active—of over active—cotton-mill building between 1905 and 1908.[1]

In the wool industries there was no similar spell of activity, only the ordinary enlarging, improving and occasional building of mills in times of good trade. The Yorkshire stone mill is durable. So is its machinery; and there was a great deal of old machinery in every branch of the industries, especially in the smaller mills.[2] In the bigger and more progressive, there were improvements of many kinds and a good deal of speeding up, but no fundamental change. Experiments with automatic looms are heard of about the same time as in Lancashire.[3] A considerable number were adopted for plain woollen or worsted weaving during the next ten or twelve years;[4] but the field in which they might be used to advantage was more limited for wool than for cotton. The ring spindle gained ground in worsted as in cotton spinning; but it was only an alternative to the perhaps more widely used 'cap' and 'flyer' spindles. The three main types of combs had not changed in any essential; and, apart from the automatics, there was nothing which could be called a fresh principle in weaving. The total number of machinery units—spindles, looms, combs and so forth—probably changed very little; but there was a constant shifting between their various types, as the products first of one and then of another came into fashion. The principal shift was from woollen to worsted, from spindles on mules to spindles on frames. The units did such different things and worked at such different paces—or stood idle for such varying times—that broad numerical statements about them would not be useful, even if they were available. In fact, for the years after 1904 they are not.[5]

Cotton and wool factory spinning and weaving were industries already formed and rather set in the 'eighties. Hosiery was in transition and growth. There were still a reputed 5000

[1] Wilson, H. W., "The electric operation of Textile Factories", and the resulting discussions in *Trans. Inst. Mech. Eng.* 1909.

[2] See *Factory Report*, 1903, p. 79 on old weaving machinery in Yorkshire. About that time I saw a swivel-loom in a Lancashire small-ware mill which was reputed to be a hundred years old. It was weaving red tape.

[3] Self-shuttling looms, in the Huddersfield district; *Factory Report* for 1903, as above.

[4] *The Wool Year Book*, 1916, p. 329, says they were "extensively" adopted.

[5] Machinery statistics were not collected. There are none whatever in the *Statistical Tables* of 1931.

hand-driven knitting frames in 1892,[1] not, like most of the surviving woollen hand-looms, in remote Scottish islands or Welsh valleys, but in the Midland hosiery district itself—in Lancashire as it were. Even eleven years later a factory inspector was pointing out that, as "the new automatic knitting machine can only be worked by power",[2] the surviving hand-driven machines in cottages and workshops would certainly die out. The factory system was still only in the making, or the finishing. Factories were of all sizes; for the simpler plant was light, and so the little knitting factory with a gas-engine as prime mover was common. Demand was so good that in spite of labour-saving machines the working staff of the industry was expanding every year.[3] It was 56 per cent. greater in 1911 than in 1881—but the number of men in it was 19 per cent. less. Hosiery machinery, the factory inspectors reported in 1905, was ousting adult male labour "slowly but surely".[4] There was a change such as there had been in the primary textile industries a century before, when they "took the children". Only now children were taken not so young, and without the "bitter weeping", taken perhaps from insanitary cottages and frame shops into factories under a tested and efficient law of inspection. As for the men, their numbers declined no faster than men naturally die, indeed not so fast; so they were not driven out of the trade but only had to put some of their lads into another.

The original hosiery machinery had been all British, but that of the late nineteenth and early twentieth century was not. The new automatic machine of which the inspector wrote in 1903 was probably American. Cotton's English machine, a patent of 1864, was always widely used; but more completely automatic types, and machines for the making of 'fashioned' and 'seamless' hosiery, were worked out, as might have been anticipated, in the United States.[5] Americans excelled with such light nimble mechanisms. Germans made almost all the needles of

[1] Vol. II. 96. [2] *Factory Report*, 1904, p. 42.

[3] It was estimated that between the 1907 *Census of Production* and that of 1912 the gross value of the product went up from £8,726,000 to £12,040,000 (*Statistical Tables*, 1931, II. 308), raw material prices not varying much meanwhile, what variation there was being downward. As the census of 1912 was never finished owing to the War its results cannot be used generally: for hosiery they happen to be available.

[4] *Factory Report*, 1906, p. 65; and see vol. II. 86.

[5] *Report on Textile Trades after the War*, p. 102.

one important type—the German cotton hosiery industry was supreme—together with some machinery. All told, about a half of the machinery used in 1913–14 was imported. "The competition among machine builders both at home and abroad, combined with co-operation between manufacturer and machinist" had led to continuous mechanical improvement. It was only "by ruthless scrapping" that firms had been able "to keep thoroughly up to date".[1] In this harsh but stimulating international atmosphere, the industry maintained and increased its vigour and adaptability.

While the pure silk and the linen industries declined, and hosiery with the rougher textile industries grew, England made a rather late but a quick and successful start in the new industry of artificial silk. That there was no chemical difficulty about 'making' silk had been known for many years; but the problem of commercial production had called for much ingenuity and patience. It had naturally attracted Frenchmen. By about 1880, Chardonnet, dissolving nitro-cellulose in alcohol and ether, pumping the jelly through fine holes, drying it into a fibre, and converting the spun fibre back into cellulose, produced a marketable silk—so marketable that in the early days it fetched 10*s*. a pound. Other processes followed, less roundabout and expensive chemically, the *glanzstoff* process in which purified cellulose is dissolved in ammoniacal copper hydrate, and the viscose process in which it is treated with caustic soda and carbon bisulphide. In each the resulting jelly is handled much as it had been handled by Chardonnet.[2]

So long as the price remained high, that is in the nineteenth century, there was a good deal of experimental production in France, Germany and Switzerland; but the aggregate output appears to have been inconsiderable. A price-fall broke many of the producers. The course of events was being watched from England, where experiment was in progress.[3] There were what had now become the usual international manœuvrings for position over patents, and the usual buyings of patent rights. The strong silk firm of Courtaulds took up the experiments, a rare

[1] *Report on Textile Trades after the War*, p. 102 as above.

[2] *Dictionary of Applied Chemistry* (ed. 1926), *s.v.* "Silk". There is a clear non-technical account of the Chardonnet processes in the *Factory Report*, 1901, p. 249.

[3] In which C. F. Cross was a pioneer about 1890. "C. F. Cross, An Appreciation", Armstrong, H. E., *The Times*, April 22, 1935. Cross became a consultant to the paper trade.

case in industrial history of an old and honourably established business anticipating competition from a revolutionary innovation by itself becoming the innovator. By 1900 the first important English factory was working, at Wolston near Coventry.[1] Nine years later there were 2000 artificial silk factory workers in the Coventry district.[2] In Courtaulds' hands, the viscose process, based on the work of Cross, Bevan and Beadle became the dominant, almost the sole, English method of production. There was an excellent market in the Bradford dress-goods industry and elsewhere, even before artificial silk became perfectly respectable.[3] As a result, by 1913 the British output was twice the French, and only slightly below the German. The United States, Italy and Japan were as yet negligible, the British output being a full quarter of the known output of the world, which was however, if judged by later standards, still insignificant.[4]

The making of boots and clothes, like the making of hosiery, was passing under the control of the machine and into the factory continuously, though never completely. The handicraft and outworking bespoke tailors and bootmakers with the cobblers remained, but in diminishing numbers. So did scores, perhaps hundreds, of thousands of handicraft, if generally machine-using, dressmakers and seamstresses; but rather fewer women were reported under each of these descriptions at the census of 1911 than at that of 1901, although population had grown by several millions in the decade. The most conspicuous decline over the whole period was in continuation of that started in the 'sixties among bootmakers working 'out' for large employers. So late as 1892 and in Leeds, a machine-using town if ever one was, "nearly half the work" of finishing "heavy medium strong" boots was still done at home.[5] About that time bootmaking villages in Northamptonshire were full of outworkers. By 1904 these people or their successors had been mostly gathered into fine new factories.[6] At first, in that district as indeed generally, only the uppers had been turned out

[1] *Factory Report*, 1901, p. 249. [2] *Factory Report*, 1910, p. 38.

[3] See *The Wool Year Book* which soon began to pay attention to 'Artificial Silk'.

[4] *Statistical Tables*, 1931, II. 296. [5] Vol. II. 94–6.

[6] *Factory Report*, 1905, p. 6. The villages were full of outworkers "ten or fifteen years ago".

in factories, the 'making' being done by master bootmakers at home. But by 1887 places which retained this system, like Wellingborough, were losing trade to places where the whole boot was made 'in', like Kettering.[1] Yet in 1889 in the little town of Raunds, with a population of 3000, work was being done on army boots at 260 places, of which less than 100 were even workshops as defined by the Factory and Workshop Acts; although all over that area 'workshops' were being fast turned into 'factories' by the installation of gas-engines.[2] Factory conditions came as a boon to many workers; but whispers were heard of nervous diseases due to factory noise, among people accustomed to "the quietness of the workshop".[3]

America had led the way in machine bootmaking.[4] She kept ahead in mechanisation and automatism—and towards the end of the century had worked out that system of many sizes, half-sizes, and 'fittings' upon which modern factory bootmaking relies. An import of American boots for men began to swell the existing British imports, which were mainly of French and Austrian women's boots. Between 1890 and 1900, the import of boots and shoes made of leather rose from just over a sixth of the export to nearly a half. By 1903 it was full half. The course of foreign trade after that was as follows:

	Leather boots and shoes					
	1900	1903	1906	1909	1912	1913
Imports, million £	0·69	0·94	0·84	0·74	0·84	0·84
Exports, million £	1·48	1·84	1·96	2·29	3·97	4·19

Free traders who congratulated their country and themselves on this outstanding instance of the stimulating effect of free competition on a resolute industry were entirely in order.[5] In a time of rising prices, the value of imports had declined over a decade (1903–13) during which that of the exports had more than doubled. The factory system had been generalised. American methods and machinery had been adopted and adjusted to British conditions, with results satisfactory in nearly every way. Probably not one pair of foot-wear in a hundred in the United Kingdom was American-made in 1913.

But America had a grip on the British industry nevertheless —through its machinery—a grip which dated from about 1900.

[1] *Factory Report*, 1888, p. 58.
[2] *Factory Report*, 1890–1, p. 15.
[3] *Factory Report*, 1897, p. 38.
[4] Vol. II. 96.
[5] "The Victory of British Boots", *Economist*, May 3, 1913.

By 1913 some 80 per cent. of the manufacturing firms, it is said,[1] were clients for many important machines of American origin to a company which, though half English in capital and management, had its centre of will-power—the voting which goes with the control of ordinary stock—in the United States. This company did not sell its more indispensable machines. It leased them, on terms so ingeniously stringent that the lessee had difficulty in dealing elsewhere. Critics allowed that it had apparently not made inordinate profits and that its despotism appeared to have been benevolent, had in fact "contributed in no small degree to the development of the boot trade of the Midlands".[2] A small man could easily make a start with leased machines. But even benevolent half-foreign despotisms are not fully appreciated in free countries.

In the clothing trades, as in bootmaking, factories and workshops multiplied year by year. Leeds, a pioneering town, had seven or eight clothing factories in 1881. By 1891 it had fifty-four, of which the greater employed up to 1250 people on the premises, besides a hundred and fifty workshops and a crowd of outworkers.[3] Indeed there was in many towns a steady increase of outworkers, as the rising factories attached to themselves those who would otherwise have been little dressmakers, tailoresses, or sewing women. Such people might be attached to a single factory or might work for several in turn. The great factory which thus had its fringe of dependent outworkers for one class of job—finishing waistcoats perhaps—might find it convenient to deal with the head of a client workshop for another. In London, Leeds and Manchester, the principal headquarters of wholesale clothing, the head of the workshop was often a Jew.[4]

The earlier factories had generally made 'clothes', men's clothes, or at any rate tailored things. They were followed by millinery and dressmaking factories. The 'nineties were the

[1] *Engineering Trades after the War* (1918), p. 32; *Committee on Trusts* (1919), p. 28, presumably quoting the former and so not an independent source for the percentage. Both accounts are critical of the system, which is still (1937) in operation.

[2] *Engineering Trades*, p. 33. I have had a similar account from a gentleman connected with the firm, who will naturally not be regarded as a quite impartial witness. The statement about not inordinate profits comes from the *Committee on Trusts*, p. 28.

[3] Vol. II. 92–3. *Factory Report*, 1892, p. 16.

[4] *Factory Report*, 1895, p. 185. Personal observation in Leeds, 1902 *sqq.*

great days of the blouse and skirt, and these brought out a crop of them.[1] In tailoring, more and more of the nominally bespoke shops—though not those of the West Ends—had their goods made up at factories in Leeds or Manchester.[2] All the time, the terrible ease of sewing made it economical for clothing factories and workshops of all sorts to keep their outworkers—lone women, the wives of men sick or out of work, with the women-folk of regular workers who "usually selected pleasant work", but did it cheap for dress-money.[3] Meanwhile the quality of factory machinery and factory workmanship went up steadily. At first the goods had been very rough, in direct succession from the old slop clothing. Gradually "ready made" lost its Victorian connotation of both cheap and ill-fitting. By 1909–10, a woman factory inspector, who should have been a good judge and who evidently started with the old rather hostile prepossessions, was "surprised to find what skilled and really beautiful work the workers in these factories are capable of".[4]

This same inspector hazarded the opinion that laundry work might "rank in the future as one of the best and most skilled of women's industries".[5] No one would have ventured such a forecast thirty years earlier, when the washerwoman still bent over her universal tub; but power, factory organisation, and factory law, with a little help from organised education—by 1909 the London County Council had a laundry school—were raising the status of this steamy trade: raising the status and lowering the numbers engaged in it. There had been 145,000 British washerwomen at the census of 1851.[6] The population of Britain had doubled by 1911, and there were then only 180,000 women "laundry workers". (Census officials had abandoned the plain old "washerwoman".) Up to 1881, the washerwomen had kept pace with the population; had indeed increased rather faster than the population, as was fitting. There were many large hand laundries in 1881, but few if any labour-saving machine laundries. A small group of men, 3600 in all Britain, worked in or for these larger concerns. The arrival of the factory laundry, during the next thirty years, is registered by a

[1] *Factory Report*, 1903, p. 148: the trade "no longer solely, as it was, of the 'tailoring' class of goods, originally so characteristically English".

[2] *Factory Report*, 1905, p. 136.

[3] *S.C. on Home Work*, 1908 (VIII), pp. iv, v.

[4] *Factory Report*, 1910, p. 124 (Miss Paterson).

[5] Miss Paterson, *loc. cit.*

[6] See their position on the list of selected occupations, 1851, vol. II. 24.

rise in male laundry workers from 3600 to 13,000 and a fall in women laundry workers and washerwomen from 189,000 to 180,000. But it was only after 1901 that the number of women ceased to grow, a direct result of the active creation of large steam laundries from the late 'nineties onwards.[1] The machinery, or the ideas for the machinery, in these laundries had come "almost entirely from the United States".[2]

In the food industries there had been no revolutionary innovation, only the perfecting and swift application of principles and methods known and used in the 'eighties. Corn-milling, after some preliminary shakings, had been turned inside out between 1881 and 1889.[3] In 1885 a Yorkshireman, who had started life in a wind-mill, had put the first triple-expansion engine into a steam-mill fitted with the new roller grinders, "centrifugal dressers", and other automatic machinery, at Hull.[4] This machinery was improved and added to and concentrated more and more into other great port mills, which both by their equipment and their location were driving the up-country mills, whether wind or water, out of commission. The process was gradual but very sure. At some inland points, a timely adoption of the steam drive, the new machinery, and a site by the rail instead of by the river, saved a local milling industry. Cambridge was such a point. There the King's Mill and Newnham Mill ceased grinding corn; Station Mill began to grind in the new way in 1900. As a rule however, at any serious distance from tide-water or from the most accessible rivers and canals, mills of considerable size were scarce. Canal Flour Mills, Manchester, and waterside mills of the new fashion at Doncaster, Selby and York—to name some of the favourable sites—retained their importance; but in the twentieth century all the greatest mills were about the ports, at Glasgow and Birkenhead, Cardiff and Barry Dock, Bristol, London and Hull.[5] If a firm controlled both an inland and a tide-water mill,

[1] *Census of* 1911. *General Report*, p. 270: occupations, 1881–1911. For the growth of the steam laundries, *Factory Report*, 1901, p. 187.

[2] Tebbutt, S., "Steam Laundry Machinery", *Trans. Inst. Mech. Eng.* 1898, p. 268.

[3] Vol. II. 89.

[4] See a "History of the House of Rank" (Ad.); *The Times*, Nov. 23, 1933. Cp. p. 219 below.

[5] See *Factory Reports*, 1910, p. 104; 1911, p. 22.

the second was sure to be the more important.[1] On their Domesday sites, thousands of village mills did a little corn-milling for a time. Then perhaps they ground some feeding stuffs for the local cattle. Last, more often than not, the wheel stopped and rotted, unless it had the rare good fortune of that wheel in romance which talked in Domesday Latin and was set for a time to generate electricity.[2] The sails of most of the windmills stopped also. Many fell off and many of the older mills fell down, until preservative people began to shore them up as museum pieces. A few mills of both sorts still turned in 1914, and indeed twenty years later, but the country was mainly fed from the port mills with their hourly output capacities of 30, 50, 80, 100 sacks of flour, or even more.

In the middle 'eighties there was an established import trade in frozen mutton and frozen or chilled beef; but it was small and very new and the facilities for its conduct were far from satisfactory. In 1886 nearly 30,000 tons of frozen mutton, almost two-thirds of it from New Zealand, was landed at British ports: the first landing had only been in 1880, from Australia.[3] Nearly 40,000 tons of frozen or chilled beef also came, 97 per cent. of it from the United States which had begun to ship in 1874–5. A little was already coming from the River Plate; but for this rather long South American and the very long Australasian transit the trades waited for further installations of refrigerated space on shipboard, and for the development of uniform temperature in them. The problem of temperature was easier for things frozen than for things only chilled, so the Australasian mutton trade grew without any check except those set by Australian climate and British demand. But for a number of years it was believed that the voyage from the River Plate or Australia was too long for chilled meats, as with imperfect refrigeration it was.[4] Experiments with chilled beef began from Australia in 1894 and from the Argentine in 1901. But there were mishaps and mouldy cargoes, so that it was not until well into the twentieth century that shipments could be made regularly and with no more than an

[1] Rank's mill at Bootle became more than twice the size of that at Blackburn, for example.

[2] Kipling, R., *Below the Mill Dam.* In the end it became a water-turbine.

[3] Vol. II. 90–1.

[4] Critchell and Raymond, *A History of the Frozen Meat Trade* (1912), ch. XVII, "The Chilled Beef Trade".

average risk of loss. Then South America easily outstripped the United States, who had her own fast-growing population to feed. United States shipments of beef, frozen or chilled, after remaining fairly steady from 1896 to 1907, fell away suddenly from 1908 and never recovered. By 1910, five-sevenths of the imported beef—there were now 350,000 tons of it—came from South America, and more than half of what South America sent was the more valuable chilled. Refrigerated shipping space was by this time abundant and entirely efficient. Mutton had never been chilled successfully: for one thing its fat always became discoloured.[1] Happily it froze and thawed out well. From the 30,000 tons of 1886 the import had risen to 250,000 in 1910–13, two-fifths of it from New Zealand.[2]

The more intricate problems of fruit refrigeration, more intricate because while a leg of mutton is dead an apple is alive and breathing, were also being studied; but about these there was still a great deal to be learnt.

While milling was being set on new foundations and the preservation of food by science and machinery perfected, man's earliest craft, pottery, was moving slowly towards something that might be called its modern machine age. Potters had long been collected on to their employers' premises, so that even in 1870 the average pottery employed more people than the average woollen mill.[3] Even before Wedgwood's day flints and other raw materials had been ground in water-mills or wind-mills. Wedgwood had been the very first factory-owner to install one of Watt's engines, which he used—or proposed to use—for grinding, crushing and clay-mixing.[4] Mill-grinding became universal; but far down the nineteenth century most raw materials were "blunged", that is mixed by hand, and were laboriously "wedged", clay lumps combined and recombined to secure uniformity of texture in the mass, also by hand. The first machine capable of displacing labour in the actual shaping of things only arrived in 1844–5;[5] it was not important. Steam was gradually applied to drive the potter's wheel, as might have

[1] *Ibid.* p. 247.

[2] The statistics from the *Annual Trade Returns* are summarised, down to 1910, in Critchell and Raymond, App. IX and XI.

[3] Vol. II. 117–19.

[4] Thomas, J., "The Pottery Industry and the Industrial Revolution", *E.J. (Hist.)*, 1937.

[5] It made "paste-boxes"; Owen, H., *The Staffordshire Potter* (1901), p. 63.

been expected.[1] A mechanical blunger and the "pugmill", to facilitate or supersede wedging, came in the 'sixties and 'seventies.[2] A new machine age—the mill and the wheel were not new—cannot be said to have begun before the 'seventies. By 1875–80 wheels were power-driven in all large establishments. A few classes of simple round pots—"chambers" is the illustration given—were actually machine-made.[3] The labour-saving, though not mechanical, device of "casting"—pouring liquid clay into a mould of plaster which absorbs the water, instead of pressing the clay into place—was known but not widely used. It did not begin to spread fast until the end of the century.[4] Several years later the pressers were fighting against it; and it has never become universal. Some baths were still built up with lumps of clay by hand, "with or without the use of moulds", in the nineteen 'twenties.[5]

The mechanical device which made most progress was that first used for the simple round hollow-ware—a revolving vertical spindle with a mould on it. The "jollier" pressed a "bat" of clay into a hollow mould which formed the outside of the "chamber" or what not, and fixed a "profile tool" in a clamp to form the inside. After that, he stood by to regulate the speed, until a runner came to carry mould and pot to the stove. Later, and mainly after 1900,[6] the "jigger" or "jiggerer" made shallow flat ware—plates, saucers, and suchlike—by a slight modification of the same device, which involved rather more use of the hand: he smoothed the top surface with it in the true potter's way.[7] Neither process was very far from that way: the jollier was vastly nearer to the Old Testament potter than the mule-spinner was to a spinster of Queen Anne's day. Besides, jolleying and jiggering and all other mechanical methods spread very slowly. There was never any "catastrophic displacement

[1] Thomas, *op. cit.* p. 408, who argues in favour of an earlier "industrial revolution" in pottery than has usually been allowed gives no dates after 1816. He has however made clear the early and widespread use of power for grinding; and his note that "once inside the factory gate, steam-power was applied to the ...wheels" indicates, though without dating, the course of events.

[2] Warburton, W. H., *The History of Trade Union Organisation in the... Potteries* (1931), p. 196. Hand-wedging was still used for ware of "the highest class" in 1927, *Dictionary of Occupational Terms*, s.v. wedge.

[3] Warburton, p. 191.

[4] Warburton, pp. 195, 207.

[5] *Dictionary of Occupational Terms*, s.v. bathmaker, sanitary-ware maker.

[6] Warburton, p. 195.

[7] *Dictionary of Occupational Terms*, s.v. jigger, jiggerer.

of labour",[1] partly because the sanitary ware industry was growing fast in the new century, although the typical domestic bath of 1912–14 was still of iron—enamelled internally however, not painted as its predecessor had been. To the last, many pottery workers retained that control of their times and movements which the historian associates with work in the pre-factory age. "To an observer accustomed to the atmosphere of the Lancashire cotton industry it seemed" that they "started work and stopped work much as they pleased."[2]

In pottery the wheel had satisfied mankind for thousands of years. In printing the inventions of the fifteenth century served almost unimproved until well into the nineteenth—some of them into the twentieth. Type was cast by hand and set by hand and the press was worked by hand. The stimulus to change had come from the modern newspapers' desire for speed. When on November 29, 1814 *The Times* announced "the greatest improvement connected with printing since the discovery of the art itself",[3] it referred to Koenig and Bauer's steam press, the first, which could strike off copies of the paper more than four times as fast as they had hitherto been struck. Before 1830, Applegarth and Cowper, *The Times'* engineers, working on Koenig's machine, had multiplied this speed by five. The speed of 1830 was again doubled on Applegarth's rotary machine of 1848, in which for the first time the type was not laid flat but fixed to a cylinder. The Hoe machine, an American development of the rotary principle, was tried by *The Times* in 1857. Forty years later, a different creature in almost everything but name, it had displaced not only the Applegarth but the Applegarth's successor, the once famous Walter rotary press, *The Times'* own invention, for which the patent had been taken out in 1866.[4]

In all these developments for rapid machining other papers

[1] Warburton, p. 198.

[2] Tawney, R. H., *Introduction* to Warburton, *op. cit.* p. 12.

[3] *The Times Book of Printing* (1930), p. 15. Koenig only came to England because he could not get financial backing in Germany. He and Bauer returned to Germany in 1817 and founded the firm which still bears their name at Oberzell near Würzburg. Schnabel, F., *Deut. Gesch. im Neunzehnten Jahrhundert* (1934), III. 283–4.

[4] *The Times Book of Printing, passim.* And see Legros, L. A. and Grant, J. C., *Typographical Printing Surfaces* (1916), and Article "Typography" in *Encyc. Brit.* by Hessels, J. H. and Southward, J.

followed *The Times* at suitable distances in the early years. Later, some of them had at least kept pace with Printing House Square by purchase from America. Meanwhile book printing changed hardly at all, although power was gradually, very gradually applied to presses during the second half of the century.

The problem of mechanical type-casting had attracted inventive minds of the first rank in England, among them Brunel the elder and Bessemer;[1] but it was in America that simple casting machines first came into fairly general use, even before 1850. It is at least curious that one of the earliest English type-casting patents was taken out in 1822 by a man, Dr William Church, who patented in the same year the first composing machine, and who was a native of Boston, Mass.[2] For an American combination of mechanical composition with mechanical type-casting is the basis of the most modern practice in typography. Church's composing machine had a keyboard. So had James Young's machine, invented independently eighteen years later. It greatly interested Bessemer, was successfully shown off to Walter of *The Times*, and "died a natural death"[3]—from neglect—though it was used on the *Family Herald* in 1842.[4] After that, keyboard "machines of this class appeared at intervals of from two to three years";[5] but little use was made of them until Carl Kastenbein, a German working for *The Times*, by a series of patents beginning in 1869, developed a machine which his patrons used regularly from the later 'seventies. The Kastenbein delivered a line of type, as the operator struck the keys, from a magazine filled with the various 'sorts' in the upper part of the machine; but each line had to be "justified"—spaced to exactly the right length—by hand. To supply the Kastenbein's greedy consumption, Wicks was perfecting for *The Times* during the 'eighties and 'nineties a rotary type-casting machine of uncommon efficiency.[6]

To gain maximum speed and efficiency, however, keyboard, type-casting and line-justifying had to be combined. At this

[1] Bessemer's father, Anthony, cut faces for Caslon; Legros, L. A., "Type-casting and Composing Machinery", *Trans. Inst. Mech. Eng.* 1908.

[2] Legros and Grant, p. 321.

[3] Bessemer, quoted in Legros and Grant, p. 325.

[4] *Encyc. Brit.* Women could use it and so men disliked it.

[5] Legros and Grant, p. 325.

[6] See Legros in *Trans. Inst. Mech. Eng.* as above, and the discussion in which Wicks took part.

problem Ottmar Mergenthaler in New York and Tolbert Lanston in Washington were working during the 'eighties. Mergenthaler's earliest patents are of 1884–6; Lanston's patents came all in a bunch in 1887. The upshots were the Linotype and Monotype Machines and American companies to push and sell them. A link between keyboard and casting was found by Lanston for the Monotype in a device which goes back to Jacquard's loom, and indeed further—the perforated card or paper strip whose perforations dictate subsequent mechanical action.[1] It had already been used on a composing machine by Mackie of Warrington in 1868. The keyboard operator taps out the perforations. The perforated strip, transferred to the casting machine, in which molten type-metal is waiting to be pumped into all the various matrices, determines those into which it shall go, their sizes and spaces; and a justified line of separate type is duly cast. In the Linotype—a single machine whereas "the" Monotype is two—the keyboard calls matrices into position direct from a matrix magazine similar to the type magazine of the Kastenbein machine; they are automatically justified into a line; metal is pumped in automatically to fill them and a "slug" for a whole line is cast.

The Linotype was essentially for the newspaper, the Monotype, whose distinct letter-types facilitate correction in proof, for the printed book.

Linotype machines of the earliest sort came to England in 1889. But, outside the offices of the daily newspapers, printers were "very slow in taking up the idea"[2] of mechanical type-setting of any kind. Twenty-five years later, not only books but the better weekly periodicals and magazines were still mostly set by hand; although hand type-casting was dead and the hand press for commercial printing was moribund. It was estimated in 1915–16 that there were perhaps 5000 Monotype machines in the world, against nearly 40,000 Linotype and other line-casting machines.[3] What the British proportion was is not known; but as the world includes America the number of Monotypes working in Britain must have been rather small.[4]

So in a country in which every one could now read there was no question of displacement of printers by the machine—no

[1] Legros and Grant, p. 327.
[2] *The Times Book of Printing*, p. 12.
[3] Legros and Grant, p. 572.
[4] The conservative Cambridge University Press got its first in Oct. 1913.

general question. In the thirty years from 1881 to 1911 the number of printers grew by 131 per cent. That of the paper makers did not grow nearly so fast, but yet as fast as the population of the country. The output of paper of course grew very much faster, from about 290,000 tons in 1880 to about 900,000 tons in 1907—the nearest comparable dates for which estimates exist.[1] The increase was not due to any technical revolution. There had been only the normal improvement, enlargement and speeding up of existing types of machinery.[2] The great change had been in the raw materials. After something like a rag-famine in the 'fifties, relief had come through the import of esparto grass (*Stipa tenacissima*) from Spain and North Africa in the 'sixties.[3] Its use became a British speciality. Wood fibre, whose use had often been discussed, is said to have arrived first as 'mechanical' pulp—chewed up wood as it were—in 1871. At that time chemical processes which should preserve the wood fibre unbroken, and so make a better paper, were being worked out. Tilghman an American and Eskman a Swede did the best work. Eskman's process was in use at Ilford by 1879; but most of the pulp was imported.[4] At first the imports were not recorded. The 229,000 tons of "esparto and other materials for paper making", excluding rags, imported in 1880, was no doubt mainly esparto; but at least half of the 428,000 tons of 1888 must have been pulp. By 1900 "esparto and other vegetable fibres" stood at 200,000 and pulp, now recorded, at 488,000 tons. The esparto was still about 200,000 tons in 1913; the pulp nearly 1,000,000. Thus modern Britain got its great drums of bad perishable mechanical news-print and cheap book paper, with better chemical wood, esparto and blended papers, to supplement the two or three thousand tons of the now aristocratic 'pure rag'.

The typewriter was an older and far simpler thing than the linotype or monotype. As in printing, the final success of the machine came by way of American invention, exploited with American business zest and organising power for a market in which copying clerks could not be bought for a pittance.

[1] Spicer, A. D., *The Paper Trade* (1907), App. IX and *Census of Production*, p. 599.

[2] Spicer, pp. 66–7. The output of hand-made paper in 1900–3 was almost exactly what it had been in 1860, and was about 5 per cent. of the total output.

[3] Spicer, p. 14.

[4] Spicer, pp. 17–22.

Sholes and Gliden the inventors of the 'seventies had many predecessors, English, American and French. There was a French writing machine at the Great Exhibition of 1851. Between 1855 and 1860, Sir Charles Wheatstone made several. But in 1875 Sholes and Gliden's patents were put into the hands of Remington and Sons, gunmakers, of Ilion, N.Y. who knew what to do next in the factory and in salesmanship.[1] It was their name that England began to learn in the 'eighties, as she had learnt Singer's and Colt's names before. The other familiar names of the next twenty years, Yost and Blickensderfer and so forth, were also American. Following what had now become standard precedent, factories were in due course erected in England; but the import of typewriters and their parts, to be assembled here, grew from £383,000 in 1908, the first year of separate record, to £551,000 in 1913. By that time they were much more valuable than the imported American sewing-machines, and their value was two-thirds that of the imported agricultural machinery.[2]

The light intermittently working machines of a press or a pottery were well suited to electric power, and when it was made available in the twentieth century a few of them came to be driven by it. But the new power was taken up sooner and more readily, as the gas-engine had been before it, by all sorts of miscellaneous light or new industries and occupations which, because they had hitherto made little or no use of power, had not much fixed capital to scrap. Although even in 1894 the President of the Institute of Mechanical Engineers—a conservative no doubt—had been saying that the chief business of public electric generating plants "was, and probably always would be, to supply energy for lighting purposes",[3] two years later the new plant at Manchester supplied a few score of small power users;[4] and by 1900 a South Country factory inspector was commenting on the "extended use of electricity" as power.[5] By 1902 electric motors are reported from "boot and cycle repairing shops, small coach repairing works and (even) grocery stores".[6] In Sheffield tenement factories scrapping begins: the elderly steam engines, whose power tenants had

[1] Article "Typewriter" in *Encyc. Brit.* [2] Above, p. 43.

[3] Kennedy, A. W. in *Trans. Inst. Mech. Eng.* 1894, p. 181.

[4] *Factory Report*, 1897, p. 36; and above, p. 135.

[5] *Factory Report*, 1901, p. 156, quoted above, p. 135.

[6] *Factory Report*, 1903, p. 3.

hired in doses, begin to be replaced by motors for each tenant. So one "factory" becomes several, in the eye of the law, a multiplication which helps the placing of legal liability and the enforcement of factory regulations.[1] By 1905 the electric motor is replacing the small man's gas-engine in London and elsewhere, besides being adopted by crowds of men who had never installed a gas-engine.[2] Birmingham City pushes its power supply among all the light trades of its territory. So do Glasgow and other Scottish towns, with the result that, by 1912–13 "many small joiners, tailors, watchmakers, bootmakers" and the like used electric power in urban Scotland, even when they employed only two or three men.[3] In the metropolitan borough of Islington 48 per cent., in that of St Pancras 63 per cent., and in that of Holborn 69 per cent. of the factories were electrically driven.[4] Many of them were no doubt only factories by definition, because they used this power. If larger on the average than the two or three man Scottish type, they still suggested that electricity was a diffusive force in industry. The majority were only fair-sized workshops or non-manufacturing businesses which, like the grocery stores, wanted power units for work of some sort subsidiary to their ordinary trading. St Pancras and Holborn were not dominated by "black satanic mills"; though they had more true factories than many of those who hurried through their main streets may have supposed.

The inclusion of all power-using businesses in the category of factories had led to an increase in that category considerably in excess of the increase in the population, as the figures show.[5]

Factories and Workshops under Inspection in Britain

	Population, enumerated or estimated	Factories	Workshops
1895	34,660,000	74,000	99,000
1901	37,000,000	90,000	131,000
1913	41,334,000	113,000	148,000

[1] *Factory Report*, 1905, p. 105.

[2] *Factory Report*, 1906, p. 4. In that year, however, and again in the *Report* of 1911 (p. 2) an increase of large gas-engines, using power gas, is noted. The *Report* of 1907 (p. 2) considers this development a serious rival to electricity.

[3] Birmingham, *Factory Report*, 1908, p. 34; Scotland, *Report*, 1914, p. 3.

[4] *Factory Report*, 1913, p. 2.

[5] Many of the *Factory Reports* summarise the statistics, e.g. those for 1913 are in 1914, XXIX and those for 1901 in 1902, XII. Full annual returns were made from 1895; but laundries were not under inspection until 1896, when 1100 'factory' laundries and 5000 'workshop' laundries were brought in (Table 25 of the 1902 *Report*).

In eighteen years, the years which cover the effective introduction of electric driving, the number of factories inspected grew by 53 per cent. That of workshops had grown almost equally fast; but at the very end this growth stopped, while that of factories continued. In 1913 there were nearly 3000 more factories and 2000 fewer workshops than in 1912.[1] In spite of the inclusion of so many small establishments, the average factory of the early twentieth century, an unsubstantial but interesting entity, contained from 40 to 50 workpeople, whereas the average workshop contained only between 4 and 5. The factory population was about seven times the workshop population.[2] And a very large part of the factory population, though exactly how large a part cannot be calculated from the statistics available, was concentrated into a comparatively small number of great establishments, the factories and works as these terms are popularly understood. In the London of 1898, for example, there were 8500 factories; but 56 per cent. of the factory workers were in 750 of them.[3] The diffusive force of electricity kept up the supply of small factories during the next fifteen years, but did not lessen the attractive force of the great ones.

Of all great industries, building—and it was among the greatest—had been least affected by invention, by metallurgy, or by the machine during the first half of the nineteenth century; nor was it much affected during the second half. As to invention, some heavy preparatory work for the carpenter had been taken over by saw-mills at an early date; but even the hand sawyer was not nearly extinct in 1850.[4] The actual course of building was untouched in all essentials. The use of iron had made no progress in ordinary work. When, in 1849, John Ruskin was arguing in support of his conviction that "true architecture does not admit iron as a constructive material", he took his illustrations from "the iron roofs and pillars of our railway stations and some of our churches", and from that architectural monstrosity "the cast-iron spire of Rouen cathedral".[5] These, with the pillars and girders in some mills and

[1] *Report*, 1914, p. vi.

[2] In 1913, 4,489,000 to 638,000. In all these statistics the term factory excludes many places liable to inspection—docks, wharves, warehouses, building enterprises, railways, mines—and so has very nearly its popular meaning, except for the smaller units, shops and workshops where a little power was used.

[3] *Factory Report*, 1902, Table 24.

[4] Vol. II. 24.

[5] *The Seven Lamps of Architecture*, p. 72.

warehouses and the various sorts of iron bridges, about complete the list of the structural uses of iron in 1849. Eighteen years earlier Dionysius Lardner had welcomed the replacement of "cumbrous unsightly columns" in churches by light slender shafts of iron.[1] No cultivated writer would have dared to repeat Lardner's welcome eighteen years later. Ruskin and the Oxford Movement had seen to that. Iron gallery pillars were by that time only put into Nonconformist chapels—for sound functional reasons. They ceased to be put in when the chapels began to speak of themselves as churches, in the 'eighties.

During the second half of the century there was a little change. Machinery, confined up to this time to the saw-mills, found its way into the joiners' shops during the 'seventies and 'eighties.[2] Small builders began to buy some of their woodwork ready joined. By the end of the century there was even an import of such stuff. For masonry, more machinery was used at the quarries and more stone was bought by the builder quarry-dressed, or even quarry-finished. With the new century, the pneumatic chisel was coming into use for stone-dressing.[3] But in mason's work on the building, as in bricklaying and painting and plastering and plumbing, there was no change of importance; though the plumber installed more varied fittings and the painter had a greater range of paints.

There was however concrete. The only real structural innovation which a conservative British architect of a fine building would allow himself in the late 'eighties was a plain concrete foundation.[4] With cement and concrete—in their proper places—Ruskin had no quarrel. He greatly admired old Roman concrete. It was also part of his doctrine that iron might be used as a binder and strengthener, though not as a support. Had he been aware of the experimental combinations of concrete and iron which were being tried during his later life he would, presumably, have approved of some but condemned most, according to their use. Perhaps he would have eased his

[1] Vol. I. 71. [2] Jones, *Increasing Return*, pp. 94–5.

[3] *Factory Report*, 1904, p. 134.

[4] As used by Bodley for a building at King's College, Cambridge, finished in 1892. There was no reinforcement, the author was informed by the late Mr W. H. Macaulay who, as Bursar, superintended the work. The use of steel in foundations was regular at Chicago long before 1888: steel beams were laid close on a two-foot bed of concrete: iron plates as bases for columns were laid on them, and both were then "enveloped in concrete". Note in *J. Iron and Steel Inst.* 1888, II. 293.

doctrine of support so as to cover concrete and iron in foundations. The idea of such a combination must have occurred to many architects, engineers and public works contractors. The principle of reinforcement had been adopted by William Wilkins so early as 1826–7 when he constructed the pendants in the roof of the Hall of King's College, Cambridge, of plaster reinforced by wires. They have stood well. In the sixty years following what is believed to be the first patent—an English patent of 1831[1]—scores of ferro-concrete systems were patented and tried in different countries; but it is customary to give credit for the decisive impulse to Joseph Monier, a French market-gardener, who patented in 1865 a method he had worked out of making concrete tubs for trees and water-basins, with a network of iron in the concrete.[2] Germany gave him full credit by calling this method of construction for many years *Monierbau*. But before *Monierbau* had been much used in anything that could properly be called building work, the principle was adopted, precisely for such work, by François Hennebique of Paris, who began to construct ferro-concrete beams and floors in 1879.[3] Hennebique was only one among many continental and American engineers who worked at the theory and practice of ferro-concrete during the 'eighties. Whether or not he was their intellectual leader, he certainly led in enterprise. Probably his greatest feat was to demonstrate, in the 'nineties, to a world at first pretty sceptical, that piles made of his material would not shiver under impact but could really be driven. Pile-making and driving was still being described as "perhaps the most astonishing feature of the invention" in 1911.[4] To the ordinary observer it remains astonishing still.

It was in works of construction—docks, harbours and so forth—where concrete had long been used that the new fortified concrete was most sure of a trial. From 1892, Hennebique and his associates were pushing the "système Hennebique" all over the world. His firm and its sub-firms are said to have undertaken three thousand important contracts between 1892 and 1899, including some on British harbours and docks.[5] The

[1] Auden, C. A., "Reinforced Concrete", *Trans. Inst. Mech. Eng.* 1909.

[2] Article "Ferro-concrete" in *Encyc. Brit.* And see Marsh, C. F., *Reinforced Concrete* (1904); Buel, A. W. and Hill, C. S., *Reinforced Concrete Construction* (1905).

[3] See the monthly journal *Ferro-concrete* which began to appear in 1909, p. 24.

[4] *Encyc. Brit.*

[5] Article on Ferro-concrete in *The Times*, Jan. 5, 1934.

experiments in actual building, as opposed to foundation and floor or basement structure, mostly came rather later. By 1909 there was nearing completion in England what was claimed to be "the most imposing example of ferro-concrete work hitherto undertaken in any part of the world",[1] the Royal Liver building at Liverpool. It was built to the design of one of Hennebique's men, L. G. Mouchel. Some Englishmen had by that time overcome the appropriate insular inhibition. The construction, rather earlier, of the King Edward Building of the General Post Office with reinforced concrete had been a remarkable public experiment and a turning point. England had certainly been slow to turn, although in the end she swung about briskly, if without abandon. The ferro-concrete bridge over the Neckar at Esslingen, one of the first, if not the very first, to be attempted, dates from 1895.[2] Ten years later, when a Belgian described to the Institute of Mechanical Engineers the various methods employed in his country, and the "phenomenal rapidity" with which they had recently penetrated "into all branches of constructional work", quoting such a remarkable ferro-concrete erection as the dome of the Antwerp Railway Station, his English hosts admitted in discussion that in their country there had been "no such advance" as on the continent or in the United States.[3] Still, said they, the thing was "coming to the front"; and they gave the impression that they knew all about it, and would use it in their own way and at their own pace. Naturally they had faith in the judgment of British contractors and engineers at a time when what an American journal called "the greatest engineering undertaking in this country", the Hudson Tunnel of the Pennsylvania Rail Road, was in the hands of an English firm, Pearson's.[4] How far ferro-concrete, in any of its forms, was economical and desirable as the main substance of ordinary building superstructures was then, and perhaps is still, an open question. Its place in works of construction the British engineers thought that they understood sufficiently for their purposes; and there is no proof that they were wrong.

Whatever John Ruskin might have thought of ferro-concrete

[1] *Ferro-concrete*, 1909, p. 91. [2] Auden in *Trans. Inst. Mech. Eng.* as above.

[3] Noaillon, E., "Ferro-concrete", *Trans. Inst. Mech. Eng.* 1905, and the discussion.

[4] Spender, J. A., *Weetman Pearson, First Viscount Cowdray* (1930), p. 83. The tunnel was finished in 1908.

as a building material, the steel-frame building, had he perceived its coming in his extreme old age—he died in 1900—must to his eyes have dimmed the very Lamp of Truth. And not to his eyes only. In its early sophisticated forms it was usually one great lie, with its pasted-on columns supporting nothing and its deliberate concealment of the sources of its strength.

The steel-frame building was never invented or patented. It was a natural growth, in all countries, from the regular use of cast-iron pillars and wrought-iron girders in railway and industrial buildings during the first three-quarters of the nineteenth century; and it came with the cheapening, more suitable quality and better rolling of steel joists and girders during the fourth quarter. Engineers who had seen the girders of Siemens-Martin steel of the Forth Bridge rise between 1882 and 1890, on the site for which a suspension bridge of iron in the Telford tradition had been designed in 1873, were not likely to stop at bridges.[1] They waited only for architects to call them in. So far as is known, the first British call came in 1895–6 from an architect in Durham to a firm in Edinburgh. They were to design the steel framework for a furniture warehouse.[2] The name of that Edinburgh firm has appeared on very many steel building frames since. But for nearly ten years the method made slow progress. "The use of steel in buildings is growing", is an entry in a trade review of the year 1904;[3] but there might be, and was, a greatly increased use of steel girders without the adoption of the complete steel skeleton and later the concrete muscle, skinned over with brickwork or masonry, of the new technique. But in the next two years the full change is registered. By 1906, not only are more ironworks, factories, and wharf-sheds being built of steel, but "new hotels and theatres are being more than ever made of steel-framings".[4] All the early steel-frame buildings were architecturally false, except gaunt ironworks and the like, openly and honourably func-

[1] The Forth Bridge was opened on April 4, 1890. The original plan was abandoned after the 1879 disaster to the Tay Bridge, designed by the engineer who had advised the Forth Bridge Company from its start in 1873. Work on the new design, of Fowler and Baker, began in 1882. The story is summarised in the press of 1890. And see Cooper, F. E., "The Forth Bridge", *J. Iron and Steel Inst.* 1888, II. For Siemens-Martin steel, vol. II. 58–9.

[2] See a letter from W. Basil Scott of Redpath, Brown and Co. of Edinburgh, who designed the steelwork; *Observer*, Feb. 10, 1929.

[3] *Economist, Comm. Hist.* of 1904.

[4] *Comm. Hist.* 1906.

tional. "We have seen hitherto no difference in appearance between a building really carried on an iron framework and one built in the old way", a great architect was writing in 1915, by which time "huge examples" of steel skeleton and ferro-concrete construction were "rising all around" him.[1]

As an honest artist he deplored this, for he had always taught that construction should be expressed in design. But it was not all sheer dishonesty. Iron, "the strongest but also the weakest of building materials"—the time of rustless steel was not yet—must be hidden from damp lest it rot. You should conceal yet reveal the ferrous skeleton. "The problem seems almost insoluble." Yet it must be solved. For this crisis meant "either the beginning or the end of architecture". That it might not mean the end "the rectangle must be recognised as the ruling figure and not the curve". With our power to fabricate monoliths, we must look for inspiration to Egypt. Things should be done "in the way of open spans that would be impossible in the old way of building". There must be no weakness. "Let us away with all features proper to the older styles and for the present be content with plain, bald, undesigned effects arising purely from constructional necessities. Something good may come of it." The man who wrote this in 1915 had just put into his book drawings of his own made in 1859–61 and had heard of the shelling of the cathedrals which he had drawn. The trace of despondency mixed with his magnificent resolve is easy to understand. So is his hope that "this way of building" might not endure; that the iron might betray those who leaned on it; and that the architecture which he had known and practised might survive in churches and private houses "till perhaps it comes by its own again elsewhere". He was shaken by the knowledge that, in his old age, changes had come into the art greater than any building craftsman had known since man first put brick to brick or stone to stone. And by their accomplishment in this art of his whole civilisations have been weighed.

[1] Jackson, T. G., *Gothic Architecture*, II. 319, Appendix.

CHAPTER IV

LIMITED LIABILITY, JOINT-STOCK AMALGAMATION AND CO-OPERATION

OBSERVERS in the early 'eighties had spoken with even too much emphasis of the changes in commercial and industrial life which had followed the eighteen years of joint-stock and limited-liability legislation from 1844 to 1862.[1] The final codifying Act of 1862, 25 and 26 Vict. c. 89, now presided over every stock and share certificate. Certainly the change was great from the 348 limited companies registered in the boom year 1857, just after the Act of 1856 had established "effective general limited liability",[2] or the 276 of the succeeding year of slump, to the average of over 1600 for the three active years 1881–3. Even the 691 registrations of that very stirring year 1863 had been far outstripped by the 1034 of 1879, a year as dark and lifeless economically as any that the century had known.[3]

But a glance at the annual registrations, and at the estimates made by the Registrar of Joint-Stock Companies of the companies believed by him to be still carrying on business at the end of April in the same year, shows how long a road had still to be travelled before the joint-stock company became the dominant, or even the representative, form of business organisation. The ten thousand odd companies "believed to be carrying on business" in 1887 included a great many whose weight of business was small, and no doubt some about which the Registrar's belief was ill-founded.[4] The very roughest com-

[1] Vol. II. 297.

[2] Shannon, H. A., "The Coming of General Limited Liability", *E. J.* (*Econ. Hist.*), 1931, and "The First Five Thousand Limited Companies", *E. J.* (*Econ. Hist.*), 1932, has emphasised the merely codifying character of the Act of 1862: all essentials were in the Act of 1856 (19 and 20 Vict. c. 47). The quotation is from the later article, p. 399.

[3] These are U.K. figures. Shannon's work is based on the London registrations, which were always the vast majority. There are naturally statistical difficulties, which cannot be discussed here. Cf. Shannon, as above; Macgregor, D. H., "Joint-Stock Companies and the Risk Factor", *E.J.* Dec. 1929; Todd, G., "Some Aspects of Joint-Stock Companies, 1844–1900", *Econ. Hist. Rev.* Oct. 1932.

[4] Macgregor, D. H., *Enterprise, Purpose and Profit* (1934), pp. 89 *sqq.*

parisons of registrations and survivals show how short-lived most companies have always been. During the decade which closed in 1887 there were 15,165 registrations. On April 30, 1888, only 11,001 companies were even believed to be carrying on business, including the numerous and important survivors from the registrations of earlier decades. It is known that, of all companies registered down to 1883, roughly a third were either abortive, that is were filed on the register but never came to anything, or were so small as to be negligible. A great many more—for the years 1875–83 something like 20 per cent. of the registrations—became insolvent within five years, as a result of mismanagement or blank fraud.[1] The crash of the City of Glasgow Bank in 1878, and its consequences, had both revealed the possibilities of company fraud on a large scale and swelled the figure of insolvencies through misfortune, or through mismanagement not necessarily amounting to fraud. But ever since 1856, the proportion of insolvencies in the first five years had been high;[2] and so, unhappily, had been the percentage of fraud.

No doubt there were even in 1879 a fair proportion of small and abortive registrations. But there was not much fantastic or wild-cat company promotion in that trough of depression. The high number of registrations in spite of the depression shows how the limited liability habit was gaining strength with time.

Among the industries, before 1886–7, it had shown itself strongest, and probably also most wholesome in coal, iron and heavy engineering. A considerable number of the greater firms, from Ebbw Vale and Bolckow Vaughan to Whitworths and Tangyes, had 'been limited'; and the proportion of small, abortive and fraudulent registrations in these industries was low.[3] (The questionable promoter could not easily fasten on such conspicuous enterprises, as yet.) Besides coal, iron and

[1] Shannon, H. A., "The Limited Companies of 1866–83", *Econ. Hist. Rev.* Oct. 1933. Again based on the London registrations, which are a more than adequate sample. The discussion is very elaborate and thorough. Cf. *Fourth Ann. Rep. of the Board of Trade under* §9 *of the Companies* (*Winding-Up*) *Act of* 1890 (1895, LXXXVIII. 371), Annex No. I, where it is estimated that only about a third of the registrations effectively survived.

[2] In 1875–83 it was not in fact much above normal; Shannon, as above, p. 295.

[3] Vol. II. 138–9 and Shannon, p. 310, Table B, in which the fates of different groups of companies are analysed.

engineering, there was hardly an industry, large or small, in connection with which companies had not been at least registered; but the vast majority of the manufacturing firms of the country were family businesses in 1886–7[1]—all, or nearly all, the wool firms; outside Oldham, nearly all the cotton firms; and the same in linen, silk, jute, lace and hosiery. Most of the smaller, and some of the largest, engineering firms, and nearly all the cutlery and pottery firms, were still private. Brewing was generally a family affair. So, with certain outstanding exceptions, were the Birmingham trades and a great, perhaps the major, part of the shipbuilding industry. In housebuilding and the associated trades there were very few limited companies; few in the clothing trades; few in the food trades. Although the joint-stock banks were many and strong, merchants of all kinds had rarely 'limited' their existing firms, and the flotation of a brand new mercantile company was not easy. Add the many scores of thousands of retail businesses, 'unlimited' almost to a shop.[2]

There are no satisfactory statistics of firms to compare with those of the limited companies; but the factory statistics furnish an interesting comparison. In April 1885, 9344 companies of all kinds were believed to be carrying on business in the United Kingdom. Many hundreds of these had only London offices: their real business was overseas. Many hundreds more were insignificant, smaller by far than any textile factory. In the same year there were 7465 textile factories. There may have been as many companies working effectively in the United Kingdom as there were textile factories, and comparable with them in importance; but it is very unlikely. There were certainly some hundreds of thousands of distinct firms, each of them a potential company, in the whole range of British industry and commerce, even excluding the retail businesses.

None of these figures includes the railway companies. Being founded by Act of Parliament, they fell into a different official category. Their total paid-up capital for the United Kingdom in 1885 was £816,000,000. That of all the other companies on

[1] Vol. II. 140.

[2] Of 9551 registrations in London from 1857 to 1883, the largest group (812, of which nearly half were abortive or small) was Hotels and Restaurants; the next (682) Shipping; then Food and Provisions (544); Land and Buildings (539); Mines and Lands, Foreign (476); Local Halls and Clubs (373); Lead, etc. Mines (366); Coal and Iron Mines (310), etc. Of the 9551 companies 779 still existed in 1929. Shannon in *Econ. Hist. Rev.*, Table B, as above.

the Registrar's list was £495,000,000.[1] By 1912 the railway capital had increased to £1,335,000,000; that on the Registrar's list to £2,335,000,000. For close statistical or economic use, these figures would need a great deal of criticism and comment; but their broad significance is clear enough. Railway capital grows by 63 per cent. non-railway capital nearly fivefold.[2]

The distinction here drawn between private firms and companies on the Registrar's list is much less sharp than it appears at first sight, because of a development which, so far as is known, was hardly anticipated by the statesmen who were responsible for the early Company Acts—that of the private company.[3] The thing occurred early and the term was soon in common use; but the law of England did not recognise it until 1907. The more conspicuous 'limitations' of private firms in the early years often involved the creation of a really public company and the regular marketing of shares—of Palmer's Shipbuilding Company or Bolckow Vaughan and Co.—but the smaller ones were normally private. There was no appeal to the public for subscription. The number of shareholders was small, and might be limited in the articles of association. The power of transferring shares might also be limited. Even without these formal restrictions, which however became usual, there might be effective privacy, or a spell of privacy, because the inner group had enough capital to render a public appeal superfluous.[4] The Cunard Line became a limited company in 1878. It did not offer shares to the public until 1880. Even after that, the greater part of the capital, and with it the control, remained in the hands of only three families.[5] Well into the twentieth century, Harland and Wolff, Huntley and Palmer, Crosse and Blackwell and J. and J. Colman were all private companies.[6]

As the private company had no legal definition before 1907, the term may be used in ways which vary a little; but in all

[1] U.K. figures; but the omission of Ireland would not make much difference. Irish paid-up railway capital in 1885 was £36,000,000; the paid-up capital of all the joint-stock companies registered in Dublin was £13,000,000.

[2] The year 1912 is taken and not 1913 or 1914 because, as from Jan. 1, 1913, the railway returns of accounts were made in a form which vitiates comparison a trifle.

[3] Cf. vol. II. 138–9, 360–1, and Shannon in *Econ. Hist. Rev.* pp. 290, 302.

[4] See *Report of Company Law Amendment Committee*, 1906 (XCVII. 199), p. 17.

[5] Vol. II. 139.

[6] *Report* of 1906, as above.

uses its essence is the absence of any appeal to the general investing public. On a rather wide definition, private companies had come to be about one in five of the companies actually formed, as opposed to those merely registered, during the years 1875–83. For the year 1890, the Registrar calculated, on a stricter definition, that they made up about a third of the registrations, which means about half the actual formations.[1] By that time the habit of limitation was spreading fast, as the 2711 companies registered that year show. A private registration, unlike a promoter's registration, was pretty certain to yield a real company, because as a rule the business was already there.[2] It was not certain to yield a sound or a permanent company, because although it might be the reasonable act of a fine old family business, like Cunard or Huntley and Palmer, it might also be the questionable dodge of a falling firm with debts in excess of its assets. Still, so far as the facts are known, the private companies of the 'eighties had longer lives than the public ones. That is what might have been expected.

The normal private company had very few shareholders. To oblige the law it was necessary to get seven men to form an association. But four, five or even six of those who signed the memorandum might be dummies. An analysis of 415 registrations of 'private or family' companies, made during the first six months of 1890, is no doubt fairly representative of the position round about that year. (One of them was Lever Bros. an infant with a future.) The biggest had 20 shareholders. The huge majority (82 per cent.) had less than 10; and more than a third (35 per cent.) had a body of shareholders varying from three to one.[3]

The branches of business in which private companies were most freely formed varied from time to time. In the 'seventies it had been in iron, engineering and the associated industries. In these there was a steady flow of formations, both private and public, at all times. Probably the most numerous, certainly the most discussed, type of private company of the 'eighties was the single-ship company. There was an outburst of these at the

[1] Shannon, as above, p. 302.

[2] "As a rule", but not invariably: the private company came to be used freely for putting inventions on the market and 'adventuring' of various sorts. *Report* of 1906, p. 17.

[3] *Report of Departmental Committee of the Board of Trade on the Company Acts*, 1895 (LXXXVIII. 151), p. 56.

beginning of the decade, when "whole fleets of vessels belonging to the same company were registered in as many separate companies as there were ships".[1] They were discussed rather fully before the Commission on Trade Depression of 1885–6; and they were still being registered, either by companies with many ships or by those with only one, in 1890.[2] They were much criticised at the time and have been criticised since; but there is more capital invested in an average modern ship than in many small businesses which secure registration, and the sharing of the risks of the sea is a very old and respectable habit. Ships had been owned in fractions time out of mind. You called them 'sixty-fourthers', for that was the standard fraction—based on a dividing and subdividing of halves, quarters and eighths—both for ships and for coal mines, a fraction specially familiar to the people of the North-East Coast.[3] Liability for sixty-fourths had of course been unlimited. A ship so owned was the first steam command of a master mariner named Walter Runciman in the 'seventies. This master mariner later became a shipowner, helped by the system which allowed him to start with one or two old vessels, and sell off some sixty-fourths of them. He kept separate interests in a number of sixty-fourthers—"these unlimited boats"—long after he had started the South Shields Shipping Company, with £10 shares, in 1889; although by 1889–90 the system of sixty-fourths was "thought to be out of date".[4] Seafaring people and their neighbours, accustomed to the sixty-fourths, had naturally accepted the offer of the law to curtail the liability on their shares, when it was put before them. There was nothing novel to them about shares in a single ship; though the new technique of it gave openings for sharp practice to shipping clerks turned company promoters and other venturesome young men.

This technique of company promotion and flotation had developed considerably in the decade 1877–87. The most respectable method practised when an existing business was limited, before 1877, was described to the Committee of that

[1] *First Rep. of R.C. on the Depression of Trade*, Q. 670; J. S. Purcell, Registrar of Joint-Stock Companies.

[2] *Report* of 1895, as above, p. 56.

[3] For mines see vol. I. 434, and for early ownership in fractions (though not sixty-fourths) Nef, J. U., *The Rise of the British Coal Industry* (1932), II. 44–60.

[4] Runciman, Sir Walter (Lord Runciman), *Before the Mast—and After* (1924), pp. 250–6.

year by David Chadwick, an experienced and responsible investing agent, who specialised in coal and iron flotations and had become a Member of Parliament. The initiative, he said, always came from the seller of the business. The agent found capitalists who were willing to put up money and sign the memorandum of association, and he also circularised other likely investors. "We should feel quite certain before we registered", he said, "that the whole of the remainder [i.e. beyond what vendors and signatories were prepared to find] would be subscribed." On this basis, either a public or a private company might be floated.[1] Whether the initiative always really came from the seller, even in Chadwick's time, may be doubted. An agent of a rather younger generation explained that in his experience the investing agent, or financier, "tried to persuade the owner...to allow him to form a company".[2] No doubt things happened both ways, but increasingly in the second as time went on and more agents looked out for more business. When a company was being promoted for some really new enterprise, not an owner but local people who might be of use had to be persuaded, and beyond them the investing public at large. The younger agent, H. O. O'Hagan, tells how, about the year 1880, he gave a champagne luncheon to the Corporation of a Lancashire town to convince them of the utility of a steam tramway company for their district. It is a lively story.[3] Having persuaded the owner or the interested parties, the agent had to make his appeal to the public. If the public did not bite the venture miscarried: the tramway was not built, or the man who had been persuaded to sell had to take back his business. Now "few owners of profitable and substantial undertakings"[4] who were ready to sell were also ready to run this risk. To meet the difficulty, the system of insuring, of underwriting, the flotation was devised; that is to say of paying a fee to some person or company who promises, in the event of the public not taking up all the shares, to accept some agreed-upon proportion of them.

When this was done absolutely for the first time does not greatly matter. Syndicates to place foreign loans, or guarantee the taking up of some part of them, appeared in the late

[1] Vol. II. 360, and Shannon in *Econ. Hist. Rev.* p. 296.
[2] O'Hagan, H. O., *Leaves from my Life* (1929), I. 149.
[3] *Leaves*, I. 68.
[4] *Leaves*, I. 149.

'sixties.[1] The first share underwriting case came before the Courts in 1888. Two investing agents, called in as experts on that occasion, explained that the practice had been known "for many years".[2] As one of them was O'Hagan, who claimed later that he was "one of the originators"[3] of underwriting, and as he started business, a very young man, in 1873, the emergence of underwriting as at all a general practice may be dated from the decade 1877–87. By 1895 it was thoroughly established: a witness from the Stock Exchange was defending before a Committee of the Board of Trade the still newer practice of paying for underwriting out of capital. "I would not like to forbid it. Many most profitable and useful undertakings have been established which without underwriting would not have been in existence."[4] By 1900, the payment of underwriting fees was being regulated by Act of Parliament.[5]

Underwriting was applied from the first to both shares and debentures. Though the leading authority on Company Law was still writing in 1909 that "no one seems to know exactly what 'debenture' means",[6] railway companies had their debentures before the Acts which generalised Limited Liability; and the power of creating those various kinds of mortgage charges on their assets which came to be classed as debentures was inherent in the corporate character of the later companies. This had been recognised in the legislation of the 'fifties and 'sixties;[7] though the subsequent bewildering intricacy of debenture practice, and of the case and statute law arising out of it, can hardly have been anticipated.

The man who claimed that he was "one of the originators" of underwriting claimed also that he went about his work with great circumspection. He would induce investment companies and "persons of means" to agree to take some debentures or shares in his enterprises unconditionally; and he would pay

[1] An Egyptian loan of 1868 and a Turkish loan of 1869 were so dealt with. Cairncross, A. K., *Home and Foreign Investment in Great Britain* 1870–1913 (unpublished Cambridge Thesis), p. 146.

[2] *Re Licensed Victuallers Mutual Trading Association* (L.R. 42 Ch.D. p. 1). I am indebted for this reference to Prof. H. C. Gutteridge.

[3] *Loc. cit.* The other expert was Harry Marks.

[4] H. R. Price before the 1895 *Committee on the Company Acts*, p. 83. In 1890, at the time of the Baring crisis the *Economist* wrote (Nov. 23): "finance institutions, underwriters and others, have become loaded up with...securities."

[5] By §8 of the Companies Act of that year (63 and 64 Vict. c. 48). See Buckley, *On the Companies and Limited Partnership Acts* (9th ed.), p. 216.

[6] Buckley, p. 242. [7] See e.g. §43 of 25 and 26 Vict. c. 89 (1862).

them a fee for the promise to take more in an emergency. But he always did some of the underwriting himself, as proof of his good faith. With the success of his flotations, he got a fine list of underwriters, who saw the prospect of earning their fees easily, although—it is still his account—the bankers and the greater financial houses were at first rather shy of the business. His practice was to pay the prospective vendor for an option to make a company out of his business; and he was prepared to lose his option fee if, even with the aid of the underwriting system, he failed to bring off the flotation.[1]

When first O'Hagan began to make use of investment companies they were not very numerous nor all very successful.[2] But the trade and company creating activity of the late 'eighties, with company registrations rising from the 1446 of 1885 to 2661 in 1889, brought them out with a rush. Financial journalists were writing about an investment company boom in 1888–9. "Quite an important market"[3] in these shares had grown up. There had been 15 of them with a nominal capital of £9,500,000 early in 1888: there were 19 with a capital of £25,000,000 by April, 1889; and there were more to come. Goschen's conversion of consols from 3 to 2½ per cent. had set money free, and investors were seeking higher rates. The companies both did the investment and helped to create securities in which they might invest their clients' money—an anomalous arrangement. They were eager about this creation, because the supply of attractive securities was relatively so limited that they were uncommonly dear. Investment companies could not get much of a yield for their clients by buying London and North Western ordinary at 188 when 6 per cent. was the standard dividend. So they looked about in South Africa and South America, especially in South America; and at home they were helpful to the individual promoter—promising in advance to

[1] O'Hagan, *Leaves*, I. 150–1. So far as I know O'Hagan is the only man of his class and of this period who has written Memoirs. He wrote from memory but, where it can be checked, his memory was, as he claimed, very accurate. On questions of method and policy he would be likely to remember quite well if somewhat rosily.

[2] For their early history see vol. II. 358–9. Ripley, P., *A Short History of Investment* (1934), adds little for the early period. The success of the Scottish American Investment Company of 1873, and the prominent part taken by its founder Mr Robert Fleming in the later movement, has led to some exaggeration of its historical importance.

[3] *Economist*, July 21, 1888. And see "The boom in Trust Companies". *Economist*, April 6, 1889, and the files of the *Economist* generally for 1889–91: there is a reference in nearly every number.

take shares in his flotations and underwriting for him. Underwriting brought in fees whatever happened. If you were well informed and the public was not, it was also a way of getting good stock on easy terms, as a defender of the investment companies explained.[1] But the thing went so far that investment companies were even found underwriting one another, a very odd affair if they had been doing only their proper work; for your competitive business firm does not help the struggling steps of infant rivals. It was conjectured that they did it to get profits which would not come otherwise—and left the competition of the future to take care of itself.[2]

Much of the promotion and investment of those furious investing years 1888–90 was on capital export account.[3] Among new creations at home, the investment companies themselves, and among 'limitations' of existing firms those of breweries, were the most conspicuous and probably the most important. The turning of Guinness' into Guinness Ltd. set the fashion, in 1886. The work was done by Barings, and was "the first attempt of bankers to enter the field of promotion".[4] It was a great success and it sharpened the public appetite. That was when Barings were beginning the rather high play which ended in October, 1890. In 1887 the Westminster Bank sponsored Allsopps Ltd.; and after that brewery companies came to the birth fast, all over the country and even outside it, with maximum birth-rates in 1888–9.[5]

The "unprecedented activity"[6] in the launching of new financial and industrial companies of the year 1889 continued into 1890—until Barings broke. Barings had helped to float the Manchester Ship Canal at home, and abroad the Burmah ruby mines; but it was their operations in South America which dragged them down at the finish and for a time tarnished the reputation of the whole business of underwriting. Yet it was a reasonable business, like all other forms of insurance; and when the crisis and its after-effects had brought flotations for companies and governments abroad, and with them the export of capital, down abruptly, underwriting emerged more necessary than ever, if more cautious than of late.

[1] A correspondent of the *Economist*, Nov. 29, 1890.

[2] *Economist*, Aug. 9, 1890.

[3] See diagram, p. 25 and p. 23 above.

[4] So O'Hagan says: *Leaves*, I. 240. It was at least a very early attempt.

[5] Below, p. 257.

[6] *Economist*, *Comm. Hist.* of 1889.

Tested simply by the number of companies registered, the "unprecedented activity in flotation" of 1889–90 hardly slackened during 1891–3.[1] The fall taken at its maximum, between the figure of registrations for 1890 and that for 1892, was under 8 per cent. What did decline precipitately was the figure of the nominal share capital of the new companies. It had averaged £278,000,000 for the three years 1888–90: the average was only £111,000,000 for the three following years.[2] Here the sharp interruption of overseas flotation, and of the more ambitious projects at home, made itself felt. From £106,000 per company registered the figure shrinks to £43,000. Nominal capital 'created' is more a test of vendors' and promoters' hopes than of investors' cash payments. At the end of the three years 1888–90, during which £838,000,000 of capital was nominally created, the Registrar of Joint-Stock Companies reported that the really paid-up capital of all the live companies on his list, new and old, was not much more than that, in fact £891,500,000.[3] Yet the shrinkage of nominal capital annually created remains significant—of promoters' and vendors' hopes disappointed. Grandiose projects have become rare, although the limited company habit is so well established that a Baring crisis may check the registration figures but will not reverse them. Nor will it stop the growth in the Registrar's annual figure of paid-up capital in live companies within his purview. After April, 1892, when the last calls of the boom years had been paid, the growth slackens; but it never quite stops, and after April, 1895, it begins to quicken very perceptibly.[4] In which connection it is to be remembered that the trouble in 1890 was in no sense a crisis of production.[5] Nothing happened to check the normal creation of companies for necessary work at home, or to weaken the motives which led traders and manufacturers to 'limit' their businesses. And the company form had already proved its utility when businesses came to amalgamate.

[1] See diagram, p. 222 below.

[2] From the *Economist*'s annual estimates.

[3] Some, perhaps a great deal, had been paid into companies no longer alive. Unfortunately Mr Shannon's detailed studies of company history have not yet been carried beyond 1883.

[4] The Registrar's figures, given in the *Statistical Abstracts*, are—in £1,000,000—1892, 989·3; 1893, 1013·1; 1899, 1035·0; 1895, 1062·7; 1896, 1145·4; 1897, 1285·0.

[5] *Economist, Comm. Hist.* of 1892, and above, p. 23.

Joint-Stock railway capital had been uncommonly malleable and weldable. While the railway companies were still raw and plastic, in the 'forties and 'fifties, before the growth of internal vested interests and the corporate sentiment of directors and shareholders had given them the rigidity of age, dominant personalities had been able to arrange easily for the hammering together of their great masses of anonymous capital. The national economic case for amalgamation, indeed for more amalgamation than the State finally allowed, was strong:[1] the prospective gains to shareholders could always be stated plausibly, and nearly always rationally: there was not, as there might have been in the 'eighties or 'nineties, any strong emotional reluctance to blend the white and black of the London and North Western with the Midland's warm red; to put Euston above St Pancras, or King's Cross above Liverpool Street.[2] Indeed Gilbert Scott's St Pancras did not exist, and Liverpool Street was an ugly shed.

In commerce and industry, amalgamation of family businesses and private partnerships, though not unknown, had been rare before the 'eighties and remained rare into the 'nineties. The big fellow might buy up the little fellow, but it was simpler to crush him in free and open competition. Critics of competition had often pointed out that monopoly was its logical and inevitable result. But, in the era of private manufacturing firms, things had seldom, if ever, gone quite so far: things were not quite so logical. A rather near approach to this logical perfection had however been made in the sewing-thread trade, where, after three able and laborious generations, J. and P. Coats of Paisley were amazingly strong and efficient.[3] Yet, when their business was floated as a public limited company in 1890, with a capital of £5,750,000, though it was selling thread all round the world it still had several important British competitors. There is not much doubt that the public corporate organisation then acquired, and the resultant hold on the investing public, helped its later progress towards monopoly.

So long as a company remained effectively private, if its

[1] Cp. vol. II. 186.

[2] These colour bars may have been forgotten by a generation which thinks not of the L.N.W. and the M.R. but of the L.M.S. and of a Euston which is getting above St Pancras; but they were real in their day.

[3] Most of the facts of the company amalgamations of this period are given in Macrosty, H. W., *The Trust Movement in British Industry* (1907), and Levy, H., *Monopole, Kartelle und Trusts* (1909). For Coats see Macrosty, p. 126.

directors contemplated amalgamation with some other private company or partnership, the position would be essentially what it would have been if both firms had been partnerships. The families or the small stockholding groups would have to be convinced; the loss of identity faced. Perhaps only those somewhat familiar in memory with the Victorian world of business, or with its survivals in the quieter walks of a later world, can appreciate the extreme reluctance of John Smith junior, while still active, to merge the firm, honourably built up by Smith senior or by generations of Smiths, in that of Robinson. Still, it can be done; and if both firms are limited companies—though private ones—the mechanism of shares and boards of directors eases appreciably the financial, family, and personal problems of the amalgamation.

In some industries and areas, private firms had been reluctant not only to amalgamate but to co-operate. A little informal and intermittent co-operation among them there had been everywhere and always, especially in times of trouble; but they were more likely to act together as sellers of goods or employers of labour than as producers. They had petitioned against the Orders in Council, or had supported free trade; they had complained jointly about the policies of railway and shipping lines; above all they had dealt collectively with emergent and combative trade unions. The prosperity and the economic outlook of the third quarter of the century had reduced the occasions for such co-operation; and there is some reason to think that there was less of it in the middle 'seventies than there had been before 1850. Since the beginning of the great price-fall there had certainly been more.[1] Yet it was possible in 1890 to say that in one important industry, the woollen manufacture of the West Riding, there was "not a particle"[2] of organisation amongst employers. Yorkshire, and the textiles, were rather specially individualistic; but there were other important industries which might have been described in nearly the same way, although by the middle 'eighties a network of trade associations, more or less formal, more or less efficient, covered a good part of the industrial field.[3] And, besides the public

[1] Vol. II. 144 *sqq.*

[2] *R.C. on Labour* (1892, xxxv), Section C, Q. 5705; evidence of (Sir) B. Turner.

[3] Vol. II. 152–3.

associations, there existed in the files of inconspicuous offices, or perhaps only in the memories of groups of business men, arrangements and understandings and gentlemen's agreements not meant for publicity. "We have had a working arrangement [about prices] in the [soap] trade for the past thirty years", the man who would be Lord Leverhulme wrote in 1906; but it might not be easy to find satisfactory records of this arrangement dating from the 'seventies.[1]

Association and attempted price control were probably oldest, were certainly most suspected and most observed, in the extractive industries, with their geographically determined potential monopolies, and in metallurgy. The coal-owners of the Tyne and the Wear had in their time 'limited the vend' of coal. But for the competition of rail-borne coal after 1850, they might have gone on limiting it.[2] A committee of the Cheshire salt-mine owners had thought it "highly prudential to make an addition to the price" in the 'twenties; and there had been intermittent attempts to regulate the make of salt, or the prices, or both, ever since.[3] The makers of the new steel rails had formed, and dissolved, the first international rail pool in 1882–6. It had tried to share up markets and ration producers, to plan the world's rail-making and rail-selling economy. But the world was not ready for it.[4]

Falling prices were its prime cause. The price of salt had been falling like the rest since 1873; and just as the older British metallurgical industry had felt the growing power of Belgium, Germany and France, and had bowed to it for a time, so the Cheshire and Worcestershire salt firms, in districts where salt had been won before Domesday Book was compiled, had been touched, since 1882, by the competition of new salt works on the Tees estuary.[5] In 1885 one more selling agreement had pushed prices up a little, but they were slipping back again in 1887–8. Then a promoting syndicate from London took hold; easily persuaded many discouraged producers to sell out to it;

[1] The quotation is in Macrosty, p. 203. In *Factors in Industrial and Commercial Efficiency* (Committee on Industry and Trade, 1927), p. 86, it is stated that "an association regulating the price of household soap had been established so long ago as 1867". It was no doubt this to which Mr Lever referred.

[2] Vol. II. 151.

[3] Vol. I. 200, II. 147–8 and Calvert, A. F., *A History of the Salt Union* (1913), p. 15. The earliest known German *Kartelle* were also in the salt industry; Liefmann, R., *Die Unternehmerverbände* (1897), p. 139.

[4] Vol. II. 150–1.

[5] Vol. II. 515.

offered "extravagant prices"[1] to the more obdurate, and floated the Salt Union, the first British joint-stock industrial combination—"the great Salt Trust" as *The Times* called it.[2] How well prepared the ground was for some such experiment is shown by the history of the two generations of abortive combination among firms which had retained their individuality.

The Salt Union of 1888 included all the Cheshire firms, one Middlesbrough firm, and a few from Ireland. It claimed to control 91 per cent. of the salt output of the United Kingdom. The constituent firms were bought for £3,704,519, a price well above their value, and turned into one monster company with a nominal capital of £4,000,000.[3] The investing public came in open-mouthed. There were some 4000 original shareholders and in the financial hothouse of 1888 the shares were at a premium before allotment.[4] (This is what promoters liked and like: they work up a premium by 'stag' dealings and it makes the public hungry.) In 1889 the Union bought up other important works. Its position seemed very strong, both to its management—who declared a first dividend of 10 per cent.—and to critical observers. The management ostentatiously repudiated all thought of monopoly; but the critics, misusing the word Trust, told the public to look West and observe John D. Rockefeller and his Standard Oil.[5] The *Economist* advised Parliament to watch vigilantly this attempt to monopolise "what is really national property".[6] A strong saying for the *Economist*, but not a novel attitude; it was in the direct tradition of Mill and Bagehot.[7]

However, the Union was not efficient enough to be dangerous; was indeed incompetent enough to discredit industrial combination for a time, even with those who had no scruples about

[1] The words of a later chairman of the company, whose speech of March 15, 1905, is given in Calvert, p. 228.

[2] *The Times*, Sept. 15, 1888.

[3] Seven properties valued at £703,500 were sold to the promoters for £1,085,400; Calvert, p. xi. See also Carter, G. R., *The Tendency towards Industrial Combination* (1913), p. 250.

[4] *Economist*, Oct. 13, 1888.

[5] The Trust properly so called, in which a board of trustees was given, in various ways, "absolute control of the management of the separate properties", each a company, was the invention of S. C. T. Dodd and had been used by the Rockefeller group in 1882. *Final Report of the Industrial Commission* [of the U.S.A.], 1902, p. 598. And cp. Tarbell, I. M., *The History of the Standard Oil Trust* (1905).

[6] *Comm. Hist.* of 1888, p. 3.

[7] Vol. II. 189–90, 390–1.

monopoly. For 1890, salt prices were pushed nearly 70 per cent. above the level of 1888, and very near to the boom level of 1873.[1] This, in relation to the course of general prices, was absurd. It called up rivals at home and spoilt some of the export markets. In 1891 the chairman of the Union was deploring the shipments of German rock-salt to Calcutta, and explaining that prices must be cut.[2] Cut they were, again and again, nearly to the starting level. From 1894 to the end of the century, prices at the works kept pretty steady at 8 or 9 per cent. above the average price for 1888. Consequently, after 1896, an ordinary dividend was only paid once. From 1898 there were repeated failures of the preference dividend; and in 1901 the *Economist* was describing with austere satisfaction the pitiful state of this 'derelict combine', which had just proposed to write down its capital by one-half.[3] By 1905, a member of a cleaning-up board of the Salt Union's own directors was summarising its early history as harshly as any outside critic could have wished—there had been greedy competition among the salt firms when independent: "to save themselves they formed the Union": "they strove to make a complete monopoly": the Union was "vastly overcapitalised": it entered into "extremely onerous leasehold agreements" with owners of salt lands: "to crown all their directors raised prices enormously."[4]

Before the Salt Union had quite lost its savour for the investing public, a greater combination had been floated in an allied trade—United Alkali; forty-nine salt-using firms turned into one with a capital of £8,500,000.[5] The plan had been formed and the company registered before the Baring crisis; but neither the crisis nor solemn warnings from *The Times*[6] stopped flotation, in the spring of 1891. As in the salt industry, there had been reckless competition among the alkali firms, especially in the sale of bleaching powder. Most of the firms concerned used the Le Blanc process. That process was not so

[1] Declared values at works and average export values; *Return of Wholesale and Retail Prices* (1902), pp. 189–90. Prices in 1888 were abnormally low. A rise of 20 to 30 per cent. could be defended.

[2] Calvert, p. 47: Calvert gives chairmen's speeches nearly *in extenso*.

[3] *Economist*, Nov. 18, 1901.

[4] Speech of March 15, 1905, in Calvert, p. 228.

[5] There is a convenient list of numbers of firms and capitalisation in Carter, *The Tendency towards Industrial Combination*, p. 25. And see Macrosty, pp. 187 *sqq*.

[6] Feb. 5, 1891.

efficient for the making of soda as its rival, the Solvay (ammonia) process but it preserved the chlorine which the ammonia process wasted. Le Blanc firms therefore lived on the 'bleach', and this their process yielded in quantities exceeding the average demand.[1] Hence bitter competition; ineffective agreements to 'limit the vend'; and persuasive arguments ready to the hand of the financial promoters of combination.

Though the Baring crisis did not ruin the flotation it damaged it, and the outside investing public put up less than £1,500,000 of the total capital. The rest the vendor firms had to subscribe. But excessive valuations were not made, and there appears to have been no serious overcapitalisation. Yet the very awkward technical position of the constituent works was a formidable drag on prosperity from the start; and after 1896 no ordinary dividend was paid for ten years, though net profits usually covered both debenture interest and the dividend on £3,000,000 of 7 per cent. preferred shares. Seeing that the home demand for chlorine was falling, with the growing use in the paper industry of wood pulp bleached with sulphurous acid; that American and continental chemical tariffs were rising; and that by the end of the decade electrolytic methods of producing 'bleach' were coming in, the financial record of the company is not discreditable. Nor, on the whole, was its technical record; though all contemporaries would probably have agreed that it was well behind its German competitors. By various adaptations, the Le Blanc process was kept in being, 82 per cent. of British chlorine being produced by it in 1904.[2] The many other 'lines' of a great association of chemical firms were worked with reasonable efficiency; and experiments, not too successful, were made in international price regulation.[3] But it is not surprising that, in the middle 'nineties, joint-stock industrial combination as a cure for industrial ills was a little fly-blown.

Yet combination and the joint-stock company, separately or in association, were striding over the industrial world. In the United States, in the early 'eighties, when Rockefeller was completing the Standard Oil, manufacturing corporations had

[1] Above, p. 173. The great firm of Brunner, Mond and Co. used the Solvay process. In 1890 the Alkali Inspector (*Report*, 1890, XVIII. 13) had thought "the struggle no longer doubtful", i.e. that the Solvay process would win.

[2] *Alkali Report* for 1905 (IX), p. 11. Cp. pp. 173–4, above. The *Alkali Reports* are full of the processes and their competition.

[3] Liefmann, *Die Unternehmerverbände*, pp. 141–2; Macrosty, p. 192.

not been very common. Railways and transport of other kinds, with such public utilities as water, gas and electricity, were the main fields for corporate action. Oil refining was an exception; but Rockefeller's success was based more on his control of oil transport, first by rail and then by the pipe lines, than on control of refineries. By the middle 'nineties the manufacturing corporation was common, even general; and although that particular device which Rockefeller had employed for centralising control of a group of corporations, the Trust properly so called, was declared illegal in the State of New York in 1890, and was thereafter generally abandoned, corporation lawyers had no difficulty in meeting the situation. Usually the Trust—Rockefeller had been imitated by various manufacturing groups, sugar refiners, whiskey distillers, and others—simply became a single, more or less monopolistic, corporation, a 'trust' in the popular usage of the word.[1]

Meanwhile English promoters had crossed the Atlantic to lend a hand in joint-stock combination and even to help make it international. One of them, after uniting (in 1883) the two Havana cigar firms of Alvarez Gonzalez and Bock with money raised in London, had gone on to build the international meat company of Eastmans Ltd. out of the firms of Eastmans, dealers in cattle and meat of New York, and Bells of London and Glasgow, their agents for storage and distribution on this side.[2] But the most interesting international concern which made use of British capital during the 'eighties was the Nobel Dynamite Trust Company of 1886; for it was the first important instance, if not absolutely the first instance, of a true holding company.[3] It was planned as its chairman said thirteen years later, "on lines which, although perfectly familiar now, were then of a novel character".[4] That central control which Rockefeller had established by means of Trustees in 1882 Nobel's secured by the new device. For some years there had been "a strong

[1] *Report of the Industrial Commission*, vols. I, II, and *Final Report*, pp. 595 *sqq.* Jenks, J. W., *The Trust Problem* (2nd ed.), 1901.

[2] O'Hagan, *Leaves*, I. 157, 329. O'Hagan was the promoter. Cp. p. 240 below.

[3] Liefmann, R., *Kartelle, Konzerne und Trusts* (1930: the revised 8th ed. of his *Die Unternehmerverbände*), p. 352, refers generally to a few earlier American cases, but adds: "erst in den neunziger Jahren wurde dieses Mittel häufiger angewendet." The term does not occur in the *Dic. Pol. Econ.* of 1890. Even in 1923 Garnsey, Sir Gilbert, *Holding Companies and their Published Accounts*, p. I, wrote of them as "little known in this country until recent years".

[4] Chairman's speech, June 3, 1899, quoted in Macrosty, p. 200.

competition" between the British and the German companies working Nobel's patents. This competition the Swedish inventor had tried to regulate. But he had not had much success until the new constitution was adopted. Under it, the manufacturing companies retained their technical autonomy, but the Trust Company owned shares in them all. Its directors were elected by those of the now subordinate companies, and were in a position to control their commercial policies and tactics, though in speaking to the public they were apt to minimise this control. "It was a fundamental part of the arrangement", they said, "that each...was to retain its autonomy, and the business carried on by it was in every respect to be as if no trust company was in existence."[1] If "in every respect", why all this trouble in creating an otiose company? And if the company really was otiose, how did businesses which had suffered from "a strong competition" before 1886 provide it with an average dividend of nearly 10 per cent. per annum for the next twenty years?

Besides the establishment of the Salt Union and the planning of United Alkali, the boom years preceding the Baring crisis saw several minor joint-stock amalgamations and at least one curious and ambitious scheme which came to nothing. This was a project of 1888 for the fusion into a North-Eastern Milling Company of all the corn mills between Humber and Tweed.[2] But though millers were familiar with trade associations for the defence of milling interests, and for such things as the regulation of conditions of sale, they were not ready for this, at a time when the concentration of milling had not yet gone far. There may well have been a thousand mills in the area, so failure was predestined. That an equally ambitious but more promising scheme in a different industry should have come to nothing three years after the Baring crisis is just as easily understood. Prices were still falling. There was an Australian bank crisis, an American currency crisis, and a peak of unemployment in 1893.[3] Much less money went into public investment in that year than in any year between 1880 and 1914; and this second scheme required a great deal of money.

[1] The speech of 1899, as above.

[2] Macrosty, p. 225, and the whole chapter on "Grain Milling". Among the minor amalgamations were the combination of seven firms in the Bath Stone industry and the analogous Leeds Fireclay Company. See lists in Macrosty and Carter.

[3] Above, pp. 27, 29.

It was Sir George Elliot's once famous and still instructive plan for a gigantic amalgamation in coal-mining; and its occasion was a big coal strike that had been preceded by savage competitive price-cutting. Those technical and economic defects in the structure of British coal-mining which have filled a library of reports during the last forty years Elliot knew by heart. He had started life as a coal-miner and had become one of the greatest of coal-owners. Wasteful lay-out of coal workings underground due to the divisions of property at the surface; wasteful methods of extraction; wasteful and stupid customs of competitive sale; waste of the labour and goodwill of the miners—all were set out in his letter to *The Times* of September 20, 1893. There should be a semi-public giant coal company, he argued. Under it the collieries should be grouped according to areas and qualities of coal. It should pay good wages everywhere. It should set up a miners' welfare fund—though that was not Elliot's term—for aged and broken men. And if dividends passed a certain level, the excess should be divided between the shareholder, the miner, and the consumer, under the supervision of the Board of Trade.[1]

But as that library of reports has demonstrated in volume after volume, the British coal industry of 1893, with its thousands of distinct stiff-necked and often suspicious units and its stubborn geographical diversities, was not nearly ready for a grand scheme of public utility national organisation. Besides, the money could not have been raised.

While America had developed the Trust and Britain had made her first large-scale experiments with joint-stock industrial combination, Germany of the 'eighties had been covered at an amazing rate with a network of *Kartelle*, agreements of the most various kinds for the limiting of competition.[2] The only difference between them and many contemporary, or older, British agreements to the same end was a greater formality, precision, and detailed accuracy of definition of the objects to be attained and the methods of procedure, such as

[1] All books on 'trusts' refer to the letter. For the strike see p. 486 below.

[2] There is a formidable *Kartell* literature. Besides the official *Bericht über Kartellwesen* (1905) the best books for the nineteenth century are Liefmann, as above (1897), Pohle, L., *Die Kartelle der Gewerblichen Unternehmer* (1898), and Grunzel, J., *Ueber Kartelle* (1902). There is a full discussion in Marshall, A., *Industry and Trade* (1919), pp. 544–76.

might be expected from Germans. A *Kartell* could be made among joint-stock companies, and was so made more and more as time went on; but the company form and limited liability had nothing to do with its essence. It was just an agreement among firms hitherto competitive to compete less at some point, or at several. The older British coal and salt and iron agreements, for fixing prices and regulating output, were pure *Kartelle*, if—as a German might have argued—untidy and unscientific ones. The international rail pool of 1882, into which Britain had dipped, was a typical *Kartell* both in its precision and in its weaknesses. The British free-trader of the 'eighties often argued that the crowd of German anti-competitive associations was a mere by-product of protection. Certainly they had grown very fast since the return of Germany to a protective policy in 1879; but the principal link between them and the tariff was the realisation by the German world of business that a tariff alone was a poor safeguard against the consequences of too much competition, though evidently if a *Kartell* put up internal prices the tariff assured it a longer life than it could have looked for in a free-trade world.[1] The British trade agreements and combinations themselves were sufficient proof that a tariff was not, as was said of the American Trusts, "the father and mother of them all". But, however the rapid propagation of western Trusts and eastern *Kartelle* is to be explained, there is no doubt that it influenced the British Isles between. There must be value in these things, a generation of business men who had lost some of their old individualistic confidence began to argue as they learnt about them.

Early in 1894 started that two years' spell of very cheap money in which the great price-fall ended.[2] With it there started also a very sharp rise in the annual registrations of new limited companies, which carried the figure from 2515 in 1893 to 5148 in 1897. Promoters could raise funds easily. Investors were recovering confidence; and as the export of capital continued to decline, though with fluctuations, right into the twentieth century, and the central government did not borrow much before 1899, the bulk of the now growing amount of savings available yearly for public investment went into joint-stock or municipal enterprise at home. Some was taken by railways and other existing companies which were extending

[1] Liefmann, *Die Unternehmerverbände*, p. 67.

[2] Above, p. 16, and diagrams, p. 12 and p. 17.

their equipment, but most by the new flotations. The 'limitation' of private firms went on steadily, though without official record. And the leading firms in many industries, having themselves adopted limited liability either public or private, continued to find the limited company form most convenient for purposes of extension, trade war, and amalgamation. Thus, by two stages in 1890 and in 1894, four Coatbridge firms of tube-makers stopped competition locally, and strengthened

Limited Companies in the United Kingdom

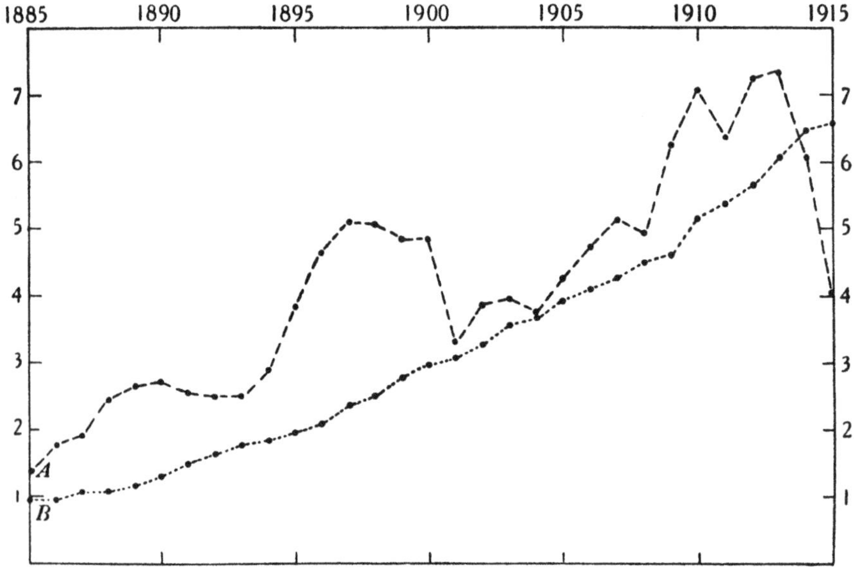

A, Number of new limited company registrations in the U.K. in thousands.

B, Number of registered companies carrying on business in the U.K. on April 30 in tens of thousands.

themselves for it outside, by welding their businesses together into A. J. Stewart and Menzies. (Eight years later the process was repeated with their chief English rivals, Lloyd and Lloyd of Birmingham; and there emerged Stewarts and Lloyds.)[1] In 1895, Brunner, Mond and Co. of Cheshire, efficient makers of soda by the Solvay process, and of many other things—a firm whose business methods and dividends always contrasted to their advantage with those of the Salt Union and United Alkali—began a long series of absorptions, as successful as

[1] Macrosty, pp. 46 *sqq.*

their manufacturing processes, by the purchase of Murgatroyd's Ammonia Soda and Salt Syndicate.[1]

In the autumn of 1896 eight London firms of coal merchants, coal factors, lightermen and owners of steam colliers, were grouped around and under the name of the largest and oldest of them, William Cory and Son, who had been one of the first to bring coal into the Thames by steamer. In 1893–5 the associated firms had handled about a third of London's coal; so that although not a monopoly they formed an uncommonly strong trading unit. They united their home merchanting businesses only: those of them who, like the original Cory firm, had colliery and coal export interests retained control of these.[2]

Such efficiency combinations as they have been called—Stewarts, Lloyds, Brunner-Monds and Corys were all unquestionably efficient—were merely extensions, but under convenient limited liability forms, of that buying up by the strong man of useful neighbours or possible competitors, that industrial and commercial laying of field to field, which had always been known in competitive society. Where conditions were savagely competitive, the strong man had usually weakened his neighbours in fight before deciding to buy them up. When he was not too strong, he may have had agreements with them, *Kartelle*, about prices or what not, which paved the way for closer union. But however strong he was, he could not now be insensitive to the strains of competition. Prices had fallen; tariffs had risen; foreign commercial and industrial efficiency had increased.[3] Some fairly strong people had tried to solve export difficulties as a Preston cotton manufacturer did before 1885; he found his business was "so exceedingly bare" that he was forced "to leave the merchant out and go beyond him".[4] Neighbours of his, the old firm of Horrocks, had tried amalgamation as well: in 1885 they took over another Preston firm; in 1887, Crewdsons of Bolton, a firm limited ten years earlier; and about the same time they began to sell their longcloths and calicoes direct to the draper. Like Brunner-Monds and Corys they did exceedingly well.[5]

[1] Macrosty, p. 193.

[2] In 1899 the retailing part of the business was amalgamated with Rickett, Smith and Co. in which William Cory and Son became holders of £163,000 of fully paid up shares. *Stock Exchange Year Book*, 1901.

[3] For an American treatment, see Jerome, H., *Mechanisation in Industry* (1934), and review by Burn, D. L., in *Econ. Hist. Rev.* Oct. 1935.

[4] Vol. II. 30.

[5] Macrosty, p. 125, and *Stock Exchange Year Book*.

So, then and always, did that outstanding instance of efficiency combination, J. and P. Coats of Paisley. After flotation as a public limited company in 1890, it paid its new shareholders very satisfactory dividends. It had a thread-mill inside the United States tariff fence, and it arranged a *Kartell* for joint-marketing, the Central Thread Agency, with its strongest home competitors, English and Scottish. One of the Scottish firms was bought up in 1895. The remaining three, one Scottish and two English, came into the great combination of 1896. It now had a capital of £7,500,000, and controlled sixteen of the best factories in the trade, including that in the United States, one in Canada, and one in Russia. The old Coats firm had just paid 20 per cent. on its ordinary shares, and the new firm went on paying that and more. At the end of ten years, it was making a net profit (for 1906) of nearly £3,000,000, mainly however from the mills which it owned or controlled outside the United Kingdom, the number of which was always increasing.[1] Its selling agency dealt direct with retailers and large consumers, eliminating middlemen everywhere; and at so high a level was efficiency maintained that, although there were always competitors, they were never able to threaten the position of Coats. Whether its strength kept prices higher than they might conceivably have been no one can say. The company had the fortune to supply an article whose price forms only a tiny part of that of the goods into which it goes, and which has a wide household use. Provided the quality of such an article is kept up—no one questioned Coats' quality—and its selling-price kept steady, consumers are not likely to be too critical of some possible small element of extra profit in that price. Coats always argued that their economies in production and distribution meant both cheapness to the consumer and a defensible profit to themselves.[2] The profit was very large. Naturally some self-appointed consumer's advocate, if not the consumer herself, was often tempted to question the argument. But, not having access to the Coats' books, he could never disprove the Coats' claim that all was due to sheer efficiency and quality, and that the profit was a rent of

[1] By 1907 there were mills in Germany, Austria, Hungary, with interests in mills elsewhere, besides those mentioned above. See a study of the firm in the *Economist*, Nov. 14, 1908. Its history is also dealt with in Macrosty, pp. 13, 121 *sqq.*

[2] See what reads like an inspired article on "The Trade in Sewing Cotton", *Times Financial Supp.* Dec. 31, 1906, which is used by Macrosty.

organising ability. As their chairman once pointed out, there were a hundred and eighty other makers of sewing cotton up and down the world, who would gladly have undersold or made better thread than Coats, had they been able.[1] His argument was sound; although the hundred and eighty were perhaps rather a ragged and badly drilled regiment.

Before the Coats broadening out of 1896, there had been a trade association of English sewing-cotton makers but no combine. In December of the following year, eleven of them, with a few silk and linen thread firms, united defensively and imitatively as the English Sewing-Cotton Company, capital £2,250,000. Even the prospectus allowed that "the average profits of the past years had been comparatively small".[2] The prices paid for the constituent businesses were certainly too high, the goodwill of these poor earning concerns being reckoned at about a quarter of their assets. All were allowed to retain their individualities as sub-companies, usually with one of the old partners or directors in charge.[3] It is not therefore surprising that after two years of specious success the main company was in trouble. By 1901–2 it was losing heavily. Not an efficiency combine, it had not hacked away its dead wood. From the first, its relations with Coats had been close and unusual. Coats held what was for them a small block (£200,000) of its ordinary shares, to know what was going on, one supposes. There was a working arrangement about the sharing of markets, which did not work very well. The English Company made some use of the central selling agency which Coats had organised. Before long there was a proposal that Coats should finally absorb the English; but the men of Paisley were too public-spirited, or too wise, to do that.

"The admitted want of efficient management", Archibald Coats explained some years later, brought the English Company to "the verge of liquidation. We were repeatedly urged to take over the business, but declined, as we did not wish to profit by the misfortunes of the 10,000 or more shareholders."[4] Instead, they gave advice and even financial assistance in a complete

[1] Speech at the annual meeting for 1906, *Economist*, Dec. 1, 1906. The strong family element in the firm is shown by the composition of the board of directors in 1901: 11 Coats, 4 Clarks, and five others including O. E. Philippi (see p. 231 below).

[2] Quoted in Macrosty, p. 129.

[3] *Economist*, March 14, 1900.

[4] The speech of Dec. 1906, quoted above.

administrative reorganisation undertaken in 1902.[1] Later, some of the dead wood of the English Company was lopped off, by closings down and cancellations of debentures issued at the start to vendor firms; and by 1906, when Archibald Coats spoke, the company had paid off its preference arrears and declared a satisfactory ordinary dividend. The £100,000 of ordinary shares which Coats still held—they had sold £100,000 at a time when they were not too well pleased with the English Company—were worth £175,000. This was satisfactory, for in the autumn of 1902 they might not have fetched £40,000.[2]

The deceptive excellence of the first two balance sheets of the English Company (1898–9) had been due to a little manipulation and the great business activity of those years, especially of 1899, when trade-union unemployment was at 2 per cent. and the cotton industry had its best year in five and twenty.[3] It was in this season of clear weather, not under any pressure of storm, that some of the textile industries of the North turned towards joint-stock industrial combination as a reputed means of keeping the barometer at set fair. The cheap money of 1894–6 had done its work. Prices were rising. Convincing promoters were at hand. Firms of accountants were ready to play the midwife.[4] The outside investing public had regained its nerve and not lost its credulity. The better business heads of the various industries appreciated the real economies and advantages of well-designed and wisely directed combinations. The worse heads were fascinated by what they heard from the promoters and the accountants, and thought they saw in combination a way of capitalising the prosperity of 1899, when wool did as well for Bradford as cotton did for Manchester.[5] There were Yorkshire stories of men with oil-cans standing behind the over-driven machines, upon whose output was to be based the valuation of their mill for sale to "t'combine".

Those machines were combs: the combine was the Yorkshire Woolcombers Association of 1899, nominal capital £2,500,000. It comprised thirty-eight firms, or combing sections of firms,

[1] *U.S. Industrial Commission*, vol. XVIII. 1901; *Industrial Combinations in Europe*, p. 31. This report (by J. W. Jenks) contains the best short account of English combinations to that date. Its compilers were given some information not easily accessible to financial journalists and economic writers.

[2] Judging by the market prices of 1902. [3] Above, p. 32.

[4] The accountants who did the most important work were Jones, Crewdson and Youatt of Manchester. The most prominent promoter was Mr Scott Lings.

[5] *Economist, Comm. Hist.* of 1899.

and within five years it had gone to pieces. The other textile amalgamations of 1899 were two small ones in the dyeing business, the Yorkshire Indigo Dyers and the Velvet and Cord Dyers, and the great Calico Printers Association, fifty-nine firms with a capital of £9,200,000. In 1898 the textile flotations had been the small and secretly managed Turkey Red Company of only three firms; the Linen Thread Company, an international amalgamation of nine Irish, Scottish, and American firms, which had points of contact with the cotton thread combinations and in consequence had a Coats on its board of directors; the powerful Bradford Dyers Association, twenty-two piece-dyeing firms in Yorkshire and Lancashire, with a capital of £4,750,000; and the still more powerful Fine Cotton Spinners and Doublers Association, with an initial capital of £6,750,000, made up of forty firms which spun the best Egyptian cotton and fed the most exacting users of cotton yarn, including the makers of sewing thread.

The last of the great textile amalgamations of this group were the British Cotton and Wool Dyers of 1900, forty-six firms with a capital of £2,750,000, usually known as the slubbers because they dyed not pieces but yarn, or part made yarn ('slubbings'), or even rawer material than that; and the Bleachers Association also of 1900. The Bleachers had more constituent firms than any, fifty-three, and a greater nominal capital, £8,250,000; though within a few years the capital of J. and P. Coats was greater, and so far as is known there was no water in Coats' capital. In the Bleachers there was some; but as the vendor firms themselves took all the ordinary stock, and as it averaged only a 2 per cent. dividend for the first six years, no great number of innocent outside investing persons can have got the water.[1]

The firms which came together into these textile combinations of 1897–1900 were nearly all family businesses, ordinary partnerships, or private limited companies.[2] Some few, even of

[1] Dates, firms and capitalisations are in the Prospectuses of the various combinations, the *Stock Exchange Year Book* and Carter, G. B., *The Tendency towards Industrial Combination*; dividends in the financial press; chairmen's speeches in the *Manchester Guardian*, *Bradford Observer*, *Yorkshire Post*, *The Times*, *Economist*, etc. Four typical Prospectuses are printed in *Industrial Combinations in Europe*, pp. 39 *sqq*. Most of the important episodes are discussed in the *Economist*. It has not seemed necessary to give references for all these easily verified facts.

[2] For instance the Calico Printers contained 28 limited companies and 31 other firms; the Bradford Dyers, 11 limited and 11 other. The limited companies were nearly all of the private type.

the combinations, retained a semi-private character: there was no public subscription, and no regular reports or records of the dividends paid were published.[1] But all the greatest of them were very public indeed. Their doings filled long columns of the Yorkshire and Lancashire daily papers and of the London weekly financial reviews. Examination and criticism brought out no single compelling motive for their creation, and no exact likeness in their economic positions; though there was of course a universal desire to limit the discomforts of a too free competition. If, in some instances, the declining vigour and interest of the second or third generation of an industrial family saw in the promoters' schemes the attractions which had long been associated with simple limitation of a family business,[2] in a great many the families or directors in control at the time of fusion were eager to retain control, and even an independence incompatible with the efficient working of large combinations which must have a compact headquarters staff whose orders are obeyed. It was this desire to check competition and yet preserve independence, to eat the cake and have it, which more than anything else led to the difficulties of the English Sewing Cotton, the Bleachers, the Calico Printers and the British Cotton and Wool Dyers. In all of them cumbersome boards of directors, excessive local autonomies, and the reluctance of inefficient units to accept amputation or extinction, had to be overcome by reorganisations before a tolerable level of prosperity was reached.[3]

Whilst all trying to limit competition, the textile combines were careful to repudiate any idea of harmful monopoly. In fact not one of them had a strict monopoly, and some nothing approaching it; but several started with a control of 80 to 90 per cent. of the existing productive power in their class of business.[4] The Bleachers suggested in their prospectus that as most of the best bleaching sites were in their hands, and as laws against fresh water pollution were strict, there was not much risk of new competitors growing up. Nor was that risk great in several of the other trades. Industrial and urban conditions were set and

[1] See the list in Macrosty, p. 124, with the entry "Reports not available" against five textile combinations.

[2] There is some discussion of this important factor in the combination movement in Allen, G. C., *The Industrial Development of Birmingham and the Black Country* (1929), p. 355. For its influence in 'limitation', cp. vol. II. 360.

[3] Cp. "The Textile 'Combine' Collapse", *Economist*, Aug. 31, 1901. I knew the chairmen of two of the textile 'combines' and took a small-holding in a third in order to keep in touch with the movement.

[4] *Ind. Comb. in Europe*, pp. 34–5.

stiff on both sides of the Pennines, and the creation of an important new dyeworks, printworks, or fine cotton spinning mill in the face of a decently run combination would not have been easy. Serious difficulties from outside seldom arose, except when the combination had failed to bring in strong existing businesses. The Yorkshire Woolcombers failed hopelessly in this and other ways, and were wrecked.[1] The Calico Printers, though they claimed to have secured 85 per cent. of the British printing capacity, had a powerful outside rival in Steiner and Co. This was probably good for them and may have hastened the complete reorganisation carried through in 1902, by which a mob of seventy or eighty directors was replaced by a Board of six and an Executive of three, with a group of advisory committees, and plans were laid for statistical and research departments and for the proper selection, training and encouragement of future staff officers.[2] Next year the Printers paid their first ordinary dividend. Six years later, a critic with no love for industrial combinations allowed that the new management had "certainly been a great success",[3] as it deserved to be. It was planned by the best business brains in the country, and conducted by men of high ability and integrity.

An adequate organisation of this type had been introduced at the outset by the two strongest and most consistently successful of the textile combines, the Fine Spinners and the Bradford Dyers.[4] Both were made up of efficient units: very little closing down was needed. Neither appears to have been seriously over-capitalised. The Spinners valued goodwill only at three years' ascertained profits;[5] and although the Dyers told the world that about a quarter of their capital valuation represented goodwill,[6] the reality of this goodwill in patents, processes and trade connections was shown by their sustained ability to pay 5 per cent. on their ordinary shares even in bad years, though they failed to keep up the 8 and 9 per cent. of 1899–1900.[7] The Fine Spinners'

[1] "The Yorkshire Woolcombers' Collapse", *Economist*, Nov. 29, 1902, and the files of the *Bradford* (later *Yorkshire Daily*) *Observer*.

[2] The Report of the Committee of Inquiry which preceded the reorganisation, a document of first-rate importance, is given in Macrosty, App. IV.

[3] *Economist*, Sept. 18, 1909.

[4] Unfortunately for the historian, the more successful a combine was the less the public learnt about it. Cp. Macrosty, p. 140.

[5] Macrosty, p. 137.

[6] In their Prospectus, reprinted in *Ind. Comb. in Europe*, p. 48.

[7] See the comments of the *Economist*, Feb. 22, 1913. The Dyers paid 7 per cent., 1903–7; 5 per cent., 1908–10; 6 per cent., 1911–12.

record was even better: dividends averaged over 8 per cent. for the fifteen years 1899 to 1913.[1] Both concerns worked largely, if sometimes indirectly, for the export markets of a free-trade country, and so were not in a position to make abnormal gain at the consumer's expense. Any monopoly they may have had was in essence one of efficiency. The Fine Spinners did not explain in public the exact balance of power between the directors who were only managers of branches and the central executive directors; but the balance was evidently appropriate to their circumstances. They are known to have arranged for the training of future staff officers from the start.[2] The Dyers' methods were made quite public in their prospectus, and in the remarkable annual speeches of their managing director, and subsequent chairman, Milton Sheridan Sharp.[3] Managing directors were to retire from their firms and concentrate on central direction. Their remuneration was to be entirely dependent on profits. Branch managers were to be given bonuses on results. The purchase of dye-wares and other supplies was centralised. All quotations to customers were passed through the central office, to insure uniformity of policy. Special pains were taken to establish common and generous wage and working conditions, and to co-operate with the trade unions.[4]

Most of the textile combines benefited by being what might be called process combinations. Their members were concerned with only one stage in production. Combers, Bleachers, Dyers, Calico Printers were precisely of this type. Nearly all their work was done on commission. Their market, that is to say, was relatively an easy one. They did not carry stocks and their risks were limited. In a few cases, the course of combination had accentuated process specialisation, firms which conducted more than one process having sold, it might be, their combing or piece-dyeing department to the appropriate combine, and possibly the rest to another. Trade-union history shows that producers of any sort who are concerned only with a single essential process, and whose earnings do not form an important

[1] *Economist*, Feb. 22, 1913.

[2] Mentioned in a speech by Mr Scott Lings, Macrosty, p. 140.

[3] Whose echoing name merits record.

[4] *Ind. Comb. in Europe*, p. 50 (Prospectus), pp. 30, 32 (points of policy) and Mr Sharp's speeches. Cf. Clapham, J. H., *The Woollen and Worsted Industries* (1907), pp. 151 *sqq*.

part of the selling price of the finished goods, have special opportunities for securing by combination what appears to them a reasonable reward. One of the most masterful trade unions of Sheffield was that of the men who fitted knife-blades into knife-handles.[1]

The Fine Spinners however were in a different, and the sewing-cotton combinations in a very different, position. Spinning is only a process, though a complex one of many stages. But the spinners were not commission workers. They bore the risks incidental to buying cotton and selling yarn; and although their yarn came into the ultimate consumers' hands as muslin, or fine calico, or lace, or sewing thread, it also entered into commerce, particularly into international commerce, as a distinct commodity with its own highly organised and sensitive market. (When trouble fell on Lancashire thirty years later, bleachers, printers and dyers held their ground longer than spinners, even than fine spinners: their strategic position was stronger.)[2] Sewing thread, though its producers profited like the others by its tiny share in the price of finished goods, has a specially intricate and tiresome market among retailers. That market its producers should understand. Coats' did. "It is commonly believed", an American enquirer wrote in 1901, "that the very great success of the J. and P. Coats' Thread Company has been largely due to the very great skill shown by Mr Philippi, their chief salesman."[3] (Now Mr Philippi was not a Scot.) If a combine with an equally difficult market could find out a Mr Philippi, and trust him, all might be well; but there was nothing in combination itself to guarantee the discovery, or the trust. The English Sewing Cotton Company might have gone to pieces unless it had been able to get advice from Mr Philippi,[4] and later to make use of that sales organisation with which he was associated, an organisation which was used also by another self-contained textile concern, the huge spun-silk mill at Manningham which Samuel Cunliffe Lister sold to a limited company in 1889 for a sum greater than the whole capital value

[1] A member of this union once explained their position concisely to the author and how it was that he could go fishing at some distance from Sheffield every week-end.

[2] *Report of the Committee of the Economic Advisory Council on the Cotton Industry* (1930), p. 15.

[3] *Ind. Comb. in Europe*, p. 31.

[4] He was chairman of a committee on reorganisation of 1902; Macrosty, p. 135.

of several of the smaller textile combines.[1] Coats' had always known how to harvest the advantages both of selective combination and of individual enterprise.

That localisation and long experience with an identical and limited group of manufacturing problems helped combination is certain. Though most of the textile combines had outlying units—Scottish and even Irish—all had a local dominant group; and the most effective were the most strictly localised, like the Bradford Dyers. On the other hand, localisation did away with one strong argument for combination, an argument which Sir George Elliot had used to the coal-owners, and which was commonly used in the spacious United States[2]—the saving of long cross-carriage charges, the economy of giving each manufacturing unit its own locality as a preserved market. Half a day's carting at most would usually take the worsted pieces from the weaving shed to any suitable works of the Bradford Dyers. Their next journey was the merchant's affair. The Dyers even quoted this localisation as a reason for believing that no one at a distance was likely to be a dangerous rival.[3]

Again, several of the combines had been preceded, like the Salt Union, by associations of the *Kartell* type. The English Sewing Cotton Company had, for one. There had been voluntary associations in the Manchester bleaching trade, "for a great number of years for the regulation of prices...and for other purposes".[4] The Master Dyers Association of the West Riding had been a strong body in the 'eighties, and had attempted to co-operate with the trade unions in a novel wage policy expected to be advantageous to both, in 1894. No doubt the failure to bring a minority of masters into line influenced those who during the next four years worked for closer union with its disciplinary possibilities. The failure may indeed help to explain the early and effective centralisation of authority in the Bradford Dyers. But associations were not bound to produce joint-stock amalgamations. A whole generation later, bleachers, dyers and printers had their strong price-fixing associations, inside which it is true the combines of 1898–1900 "exercised a dominating influence";[5] but in all that time the combines had not monopolised the trades;

[1] Vol. II. 88, and information from a director of Listers given to the author in 1903.

[2] *Ind. Comb. in Europe*, p. 17.

[3] In their Prospectus, as above.

[4] The Bleachers' Prospectus, quoted in Macrosty, p. 141.

[5] *Report* of 1930, p. 15.

and effective associations might well have been built up had they never existed.

There was, in short, plenty of raw material for the manufacture of joint-stock textile amalgamations in the late 'nineties; but in the actual manufacturing of them there was a good deal of accident, of fashion, of imitation, of the will power and persuasive diplomacy of promoters who, in the textile districts at least, were often well-informed chartered accountants. "When the manufacturers themselves would probably not have taken the initiative", it was reported to the Congress of the United States, "the promoter, seeing the opportunity, has entered the field, and through his persuasive power, has succeeded in convincing the manufacturers that combination would be to their advantage." It was added that, "as far as the evidence went", promoting charges had been relatively much less than in America, but still sufficient to yield the promoters "very substantial fees", and so to serve as a true and important cause of combination.[1]

There was little to complain of in the financial methods of flotation. The capital contained some water; but Americans were on the whole surprised at its dryness.[2] As has been seen, the vendors sometimes took the ordinary stock with its risks, leaving to the general investor only the safer preference stock and debentures. There was not much outside underwriting and underwriters' fees. The vendors often agreed to accept extra quantities of stock if the amount offered to the public were not all taken up. These heavy holdings of the new stock by the vendors both helped the flotation and bound the experienced proprietors of the associating firms to the new company. They were hardly in a position to sell out and buy places in good sporting country, leaving untried or merely financial people to superintend the works. (That some old hands of doubtful skill were so retained, and that all those retained were sometimes left too free,[3] does not discredit the method.) Nor did the better textile promoters secure options personally and privately on each of the firms which they hoped to combine, and then float a new company with the highest capitalisation which they thought the public would stand. That was a method common in England, still commoner in America.[4] It was employed by that notorious

[1] *Ind. Comb. in Europe*, pp. 17, 29.
[2] *Ibid.* p. 29.
[3] Above, p. 228.
[4] *Ind. Comb. in Europe*, p. 23, and cp. O'Hagan, *Leaves*, I. 149–50.

contemporary of the textile promoters Ernest Terah Hooley, whose refloating of the Dunlop Tyre Company in 1896—"a most extraordinary venture", as a sharer in it wrote admiringly[1]—consisted in purchase for three millions sterling and a sale to the public within six weeks for five.[2] The textile firms were usually either sold as going concerns, at a valuation made by selected appraisers, or on the basis of their profits over a term of years, as certified by accountants. There were risks in these methods, as there are in all. Those legendary men with the oil-cans might be at work during valuation to help the over-driven machines whose output was to serve as basis.[3] Accountants, as their habit is, might accept the books without too close inquiry into how the profits declared had been arrived at.[4] But there was at least some effort to ascertain a just price. Once ascertained, it was seldom much diluted at the next stage—at least not as average promoters and Americans measured dilution.[5]

Two important industrial joint-stock combinations of the prolific year 1900, outside the textile trades, illustrate the varied forces at work in the combination movement. They show also how a lingering memory of low prices bred combination, as a means of preventing their recurrence, when prices had in fact risen. And they cover the nearest approach to actual monopoly made by any of the combines. They are the Associated Portland Cement Manufacturers and the Wallpaper Manufacturers.

In cement there was an element of natural monopoly, but it proved much weaker than those interested had hoped. Nearly all the great works were on the Thames and Medway.[6] There they had huge reserves of good cheap raw material and proximity to the London market. It was believed that they produced more than 80 per cent. of the entire British output of cement. Projects for limiting the output were under discussion in 1895–6, when cement prices were in the trough with the rest—17 per cent.

[1] Weston-Webb, W. F. M., *The Autobiography of a British Yarn Merchant* (1929), p. 167.

[2] O'Hagan, *Leaves*, I. 410; *Economist*, *Comm. Hist.* of 1896, p. 6; "The Lawson group of companies", Oct. 2, 1897; "Results of the Hooley system of finance", Aug. 20, 1898.

[3] Above, p. 226.

[4] "The accountant...does not feel called upon to go back of the books." *Ind. Comb. in Europe*, p. 27.

[5] The making of common stock out of a capitalisation of profits only anticipated has been common in America.

[6] Vol. II. 45.

below the average of 1886–90, and 14 per cent. below the level reached in 1898–1900. After years of coming and going, in 1900 twenty-four Thames and Medway firms with three others entered the Association, which was given a nominal capital of £8,000,000, including a stiff price for goodwill based on the rather better run of profits which higher prices had brought.[1]

The Association did badly from the start. Some firms, after promising to sell, had backed out. Floated in war time, it lacked public support, and the vendors had to take more of its capital than they had wished. Prices held in 1901, but then began to fall again. The building trades were slack; the Thames and Medway were found to have no effective monopoly of mud and chalk; and the ports were open to cheap German and Belgian cements.[2] By 1905 prices were below the level of 1895–6, and 1905 was not the bottom. So the ordinary shares rose above rubbish values for the first time in 1910, and the first ordinary dividend was paid in the boom of 1913.[3]

Associated Portland Cement might almost be called a process combine; for cement-using is only one, and normally a subordinate, process in any work of construction. Compared with dyeing or spinning, cement-making is a single, and a simple, process. Combination could not do much to help firms to specialise. Wallpaper-making, on the other hand, is a whole manufacture full of specialities, only at its simplest comparable with calico printing. It was not much localised, although about half of the thirty-one firms in the original combination were Lancastrian. The objects sought and attained were monopoly, though that of course was denied, and a set of very reasonable economies. After combination, less was spent on competitive commercial travelling. Specialisation was pushed further. Bad debts were much reduced, as in most of the combines. This one, with its associates, covered 98 per cent. of the trade.[4] A bad payer could not well take his custom elsewhere; for payers, both bad and good, might be refused the papers of the combine if they bought any others. Even before it issued its prospectus, it had "entered into agreements for a fixed period of years for the distribution of its goods". It was strong enough to put up a few

[1] O'Hagan, *Leaves*, II. 39–59. Macrosty, p. 109.

[2] O'Hagan, *Leaves*, II. 58; "Another combine in difficulties", *Economist*, Oct. 18, 1902.

[3] *Economist*, Sept. 18, 1909; Sept. 27, 1913.

[4] The Prospectus is in *Ind. Comb. in Europe*, pp. 53 *sqq*. The combine had working arrangements with some firms not formally absorbed; Macrosty, p. 309.

prices;[1] but it always claimed in later years that the general level had, if anything, fallen.[2]

Its ordinary and deferred and some of its preferred shares went to the vendors. An agreement that these should not be sold for five years bound vendors' interests to those of the company. Valuations had been scientifically conducted. No promoters' or underwriting fees were paid, and the vendors bore all expenses of promotion.[3] The dividend policy in early years was cautious. Thanks to this restrained businesslike management, and its near approach to monopoly, the company was a complete financial success.[4] Among the combinations of the 'nineties it ranks with the Fine Spinners and the Bradford Dyers.

The industrial-combination movement proper was only an episode, or aspect, of that marked spread of joint-stock company organisation which began in the cheap-money atmosphere of 1894–6. The curve of limited-company registrations turns up sharply in 1894, climbs fast to 1897, and keeps near the level thus reached until interrupted by war and the war demand for the nation's savings, in 1899.[5] At first, in 1894–5, the applications for new capital advertised were spread pretty evenly over the commercial and industrial fields—banks, theatres, "companies to acquire patents", railways, electricity, gas and water—with a rather heavy concentration (£5,600,000) on a plot much favoured in 1888–90, the breweries and distilleries, and another (£5,100,000) on a new plot, the "stores and trading companies".[6] The new plot was heavily fertilised again in 1896; but the principal events in that year of avid promotion, besides the start of the textile-combination movement with the great extension of J. and P. Coats, were the huge revival in the relatively old business of brewery and distillery limitation, and a very new business in cycle and cycle-accessory companies, of which Hooley's inflation of Dunlop Tyres formed a part. More than £18,000,000 was demanded for beer and spirits and more than

[1] *Ind. Comb. in Europe*, pp. 34, 36, 53.

[2] Chairman's speeches, quoted in Macrosty, p. 311.

[3] The Prospectus.

[4] It paid 8 per cent. yearly for its first seven years, in good trade and bad. Thirty-five years after its formation (Jan. 22, 1935) its £1 share was quoted at 45*s*.

[5] Diagram, p. 222 above.

[6] From the analyses in the *Economist's* annual reviews. Applications from overseas are omitted here. For a fuller account of the Breweries, pp. 257–9 below.

£17,000,000 for the companies grouped under "cycles and appliances". If to the cycle group be added that of the "horseless or motor cars", a suitable addition, it becomes larger than the beer and spirits group. Significantly enough, it was also larger than the whole railway group—Home, Indian, Colonial and Foreign—though it would be many years before locomotion without rails would again take more feeding than what Victorians liked to call the iron horse. "Company manufacturers who are nothing if not fertile", the *Economist's* censor wrote severely, had shifted from gold mines in West Australia to cycle and car companies in the Midlands.[1] Investors were warned not to forget "the very modified success achieved by the motor-cars themselves in the historic tour from London to Brighton",[2] and were reminded of how company capital was puffed out, and the progress of the associated locomotive industries delayed, by the "preposterous sums" demanded for concessions and licences by holders of so-called "master patents".

Five years later, this severe but informed critic saw some prospect, "at length", of the survivors from the cycle and motor companies floated in the boom "being placed upon a sound and profitable basis and giving a fair return upon the capital employed".[3]

Such warnings and sombre retrospects were not issued to holders of brewery capital. But then breweries were normally old going concerns, newly limited, with experienced brewers and, it might be, rings of tied houses. Brewery flotations had mostly been carried out by promoters of the more responsible sort.[4] There was little risk of fashion and whim in the trade. The bicycle, like the car, was still a machine for recreation; and there had been a high level of irresponsibility in the cycle and car flotations—Humber, Daimler, Beeston Tyre, Beeston Rim, New Beeston Cycle, and the rest. Among them moved with astonishing rapidity of calculation and decision the two best-known promoters of the day, Hooley and Harry J. Lawson. In less than three years Hooley promoted twenty-six companies—by no means all for cycles—with a nominal capital of £18,600,000, of

[1] *Economist*, Feb. 20, 1897.

[2] The tour of 1896, to celebrate the freedom of the car from traction-engine rules. Above, p. 139.

[3] *Economist*, Nov. 8, 1902; by Nov. 16, 1907 the tone has changed.

[4] O'Hagan, *Leaves*, I. 240, and the flotations by strong banks and financial houses referred to above, p. 210.

which £5,000,000 was his gross profit. He made "large gifts to obtain the names of titled and other persons as directors", and he was an expert tuner of the press.[1] It was all brief. By 1898 Hooley, a teetotaller and non-smoker, was also a bankrupt for £491,000, and his companies were left in pretty deep water. His bankruptcy, said the officials of the Board of Trade in their cool language, was in many ways the most noteworthy since the Act of 1883. He went under, as he had sailed, well in the public eye.[2]

The heavy capitalisation of "stores and trading companies" in 1895–6 (£14,400,000) marked a wave in the flooding of the joint-stock tide across the broad flats of distributive and retail business. It was not the first wave, but it was one of the biggest. The 'sixties had seen the start of the middle-class supply stores with the Civil Service Supply, organised under co-operative law.[3] This society and its successors, whether legally co-operative or joint-stock, were directed—like their wage-earners' prototypes—against the high prices and doubtful quality in at least some retail shops. In the 'sixties was founded also the firm which became the first London multiple-shop joint-stock business, the Aerated Bread Company. Its start was slow and its capital at first small;[4] but in the 'eighties and 'nineties, when competition was not yet sharp, it was doing very well under a chairman-managing-director who seems to have been something of a dictator.[5] In the company spawning time of 1888–9, attempts were made to imitate it by the formation of the Yorkshire A.B.C., the Midland Counties A.B.C., and so on; but business and social conditions in the industrial districts were not favourable, and the projects miscarried.[6]

The A.B.C. had started as a company. What the original 'aeration' of its bread was does not now matter. It was a project become a permanency. But most multiple shops and most department stores started otherwise: they were the emanation

[1] *Annual Report on Bankruptcy of the Board of Trade*, 1899 (LXXXVIII. 105), p. 5. "The Lawson group of Companies", *Economist*, Oct. 2, 1897. For Hooley and the Press, *Economist*, June 11, 1898, and the *Report*, as above. "Results of the Hooley system of Finance", *Economist*, Aug. 20, 1898.

[2] For personal characteristics, Weston-Webb, *Autobiography*, as above, p. 162.

[3] Vol. II. 311.

[4] Registered in 1862, it was one of the few companies which took advantage of facilities offered by law in 1867 to reduce its capital. *S.C. on Companies Acts*, 1877 (VIII. 419), App. p. 175.

[5] See the interesting retrospective accounts in the *Economist*, Dec. 25, 1909; June 4, 1910.

[6] *Economist*, Oct. 23, 1890.

of some patient, dominant, and expansive personality or group. With the wave of 1894 came, for example, a company with the comparatively modest share capital of £120,000, to take over what the 'nineties called a bunshop and a refreshment contracting business belonging to Joseph Lyons. The personality remaining, and being associated with other like personalities,[1] in six or seven years the company was far beyond bunshops; and the net profit for 1902 just exceeded the original share capital.[2] The A.B.C. carried on and paid well, but it was overshadowed. It had kept so closely to bread and buns.

In 1895 another multiple food shop business, Lipton's, was still a private firm. Thomas Lipton started as a Glasgow grocer without assistant in 1876. Fourteen years later he had 70 London shops. Flotation as a public limited company was however delayed until 1898. There were then 245 shops, of which a mere 27 were in Scotland; and 3800 agencies for the sale of Lipton's teas. Among the original shareholders were H. H. Asquith, Lord Rothschild and the Duke of Fife—an oddly symbolic group—and the capital stood, a little later, at £2,500,000.[3] Another pair of grocers of the 'eighties, Kearley and Tonge, marking Lipton's footsteps but deviating a little to their own advantage, had made a great success of the sale of tea in packets —wholesale to other grocers and retail through a chain of shops. Kearley had started business at twenty. He was his own tea-buyer, blender and traveller. He and Tonge took the wave of 1894–5, or perhaps the wave took them; and their International Tea Co. became the International Tea Company Stores Ltd. Fifteen years later the company owned 340–350 shops. The experienced promoter who arranged the flotation found Kearley unusually difficult to handle—men of his group are seldom easy —but he succeeded in the second year.[4]

Some of the grocery personalities still preferred to carry on

[1] Lyons was the first managing-director: the directorate of 1901 contained a Salmon, two Gluckseins, and a Marks. The Salmon and Gluckstein families had previous experience of the multiple shop in the tobacco business. Their tobacco firm only became a limited company in 1895. *Stock Exchange Year Book.*

[2] Chairman's speech of Mr Joseph Lyons, with a full financial retrospect, June 6, 1905 (*Economist*, June 10, 1905); "The Progress of J. Lyons and Co. Ltd.", *Economist*, June 2, 1906.

[3] Rees, J. A., *The Grocery Trade, its History and Romance* (1910), II. 245–9.

[4] *Stock Exchange Year Book*; O'Hagan, *Leaves*, I. 397; *The Times*, Obituary of Lord Devonport (H. E. Kearley), Sept. 6, 1934.

multiple-shop business privately, at a much later date. In 1910 there were in the country at least four firms of this class, whose shops were counted in scores. One of them had as many as 78; but the very greatest were at that time limited without exception.[1]

Among them, one or two had done all their growth, or nearly all, in the anonymous stage; though this does not mean that there was no individual driving power in the background. The extreme case, after the A.B.C., is the Home and Colonial Trading Association. Its career suggests a succession of such powers, a crescendo. It started as a company for "a co-operative store in all its branches"[2] in 1885. Its initial capital of £3000 shows what sort of a store it was. In the boom of 1888, a new company took over the assets, now 14 shops, and fixed the capital at £200,000. The process was repeated twice in the 'nineties; and on the crest of the wave of 1895 the fourth Home and Colonial floated with a capital of £1,000,000. It specialised in small shops, uniform in design and lay-out, each with a short identical list of goods. This was economical. Its diagnosis of the standardised mental make-up of one type of consumer was evidently exact; for within fifteen years it had nearly 600 of these standardised shops. The history of the Maypole Dairy Company is rather similar, though it had not the repeated fresh starts.[3] Established as a small affair in 1893, it utilised the successive waves of cheap money or confidence—and the advantages which the huge increase of imported dairy produce gave to large-scale centralised buying—to expand capital and operations continuously, until it also, at the end of sixteen or seventeen years, had its £1,000,000 of capital and full 600 shops.

The case of Eastmans, the multiple meat-shop business, stands apart. Originally an 1889 amalgamation of New York exporters and British distributors, it took over the chain of shops which J. Bell and Sons, the distributors, had been building up since 1879. They were the "multiple frozen meat shop pioneers".[4] Successful for a time, the amalgamation made heavy losses on the shipment of American cattle and beef during 1891–4, from which it did not recover in years. For thirteen the ordinary shareholder had no dividend, and the preference shareholder sometimes had to wait. The United States at this

[1] Rees, *op. cit.* II. 255. [2] *Ibid.* II. 251. [3] *Ibid.* II. 253.

[4] Raymond and Critchell, *History of the Frozen Meat Trade*, p. 209; O'Hagan, *Leaves*, I. 329.

time were losing to the Argentine the trade in meat and cattle shipment. In the end, the company abandoned the wholesale shipping business altogether, concentrated on cold storage and retailing, and extended its chain of shops. Then, in 1904, it began to pay a little; but an ordinary share in Eastmans was never a treasure.[1] Nor, for that matter, were ordinary shares in many of the other food shop companies; though in 1912–14 a £1 share in the A.B.C. was still usually worth more than £3; and £5 or £6 had to be paid for a £1 share in Lyons.

Until 1908–9, when Gordon Selfridge made "the experiment of starting a big store at full speed",[2] on a site which the man who had floated Harrods twenty years earlier thought quite unsuitable,[3] the department stores had all added department to department gradually, as the multiple shops had added shop to shop, at the will of the expansive personalities who owned or controlled them. Departments to meet novel needs were added constantly. There was a store in the 'eighties which was credited by humourists with a department for supplying hostesses with stop-gap diners-out.[4] But there was nothing new in the department system. Before the first Reform Bill, there had been "eight or ten" places in London "where a person wanting the articles which a shopkeeper sells" could "be accommodated with every article at once"; in Glasgow, J. and W. Campbell's sixty-four shopmen, if not quite so omnicompetent as that, could at least show their customers "every kind of soft goods";[5] and in scores of other towns drapers and mercers were taking up fresh 'lines'. Starting usually as some sort of drapery, grocery, or furnishing shop, the developing store of the later nineteenth century might pass from the supply of dress materials to that of dresses, or from the supply of furnishing materials to that of furniture, and vice versa. Sometimes it imposed restrictions on itself and never became a quite universal provider. Sometimes, following its impersonal competitors the Civil Service and the Army and Navy Stores, it recognised no limits; passed perhaps from 'soft goods' to harder goods and so to food; became florist, poulterer, wine-merchant, what you will. Or contrariwise it might go from food to dishes and so on to softer things. Although

[1] "Eastman's Recuperation", *Economist*, March 12, 1904.
[2] *Economist*, June 4, 1910.
[3] O'Hagan, *Leaves*, II. 7, 15.
[4] Anstey, F., *The Man from Blankley's* (1893); first published in *Punch*.
[5] Vol. I. 224.

a few businesses of this class in London, and many in the provinces, remained ordinary partnerships far into the twentieth century, most found at least the private joint-stock organisation more convenient for their work; and the leading London businesses went their almost predestined way to the public joint stock, with its appeal to investors already very familiar with their names.

Promotion and flotation began in the boom of 1889. On the grocery side, Harrods went down the slipways from a promoter's yard that year.[1] On the furniture side, Maples followed in 1891. The capitals were not at first absolutely large, but gigantic if judged by older standards of what even a great single shop might be expected to employ. At the end of twenty years, Harrods' nominal capital was about equal to, and Maples' two and a half times greater than, that of the Maypole Dairies. As compared with the Maypole, on a basis of capitalisation, one might be called a 600-shop, the other a 1500-shop, unit. Harrods was in fact far more than that; for, with an ordinary dividend which soon got above 10 per cent. touched 20 per cent. by 1897, and averaged all but 23 per cent. for the first decade of the twentieth century, its sales power and goodwill were vastly greater than its nominal capital of just under £1,000,000 in 1909–10 would suggest.[2] The day seemed far off on which some one had told the original Mr Harrod, who could expand but had difficulty in delegating, and who having started life as a working shopman retained the trick of serving in his shirt sleeves, that "if he could not learn to keep his coat on he would soon find himself in bankruptcy".[3] Bankruptcy was far from any founder of Harrods in 1909–10. Mr Maple had died some years before—a baronet with his racing colours.

Bankruptcy was far because Harrods had adopted an invention of the late nineteenth-century promoter known as founders' shares. It was in fact "one of the classical examples" of the use of the invention.[4] Though founders' shares were never a con-

[1] O'Hagan's yard; *Leaves*, II. 7.

[2] *Stock Exchange Year Book*; Chairman's speeches in the *Economist*; "The Finance of the Big Shop", *Economist*, March 20, 1909.

[3] "The Growth of Harrods", *Economist*, Feb. 25, 1911.

[4] *Ibid.* At the annual meetings (e.g. 1904, *Economist*, March 5, 1904) it was usual to mention a sum, not a rate, assigned to founders' shares. Founders' shares were perfectly legal (Buckley, *Companies* (9th ed.), p. 175). In another great store, Whiteleys, they took the form of 'management' shares, of which half were assigned to directors and half to heads of departments.

siderable part of the total mass of shares in the country, they are of some importance in the general history of the joint-stock system. There were £1400 of them in Harrods, allotted to the inner circle of those connected with the foundation. These were registered as a separate but associated company, with a nominal capital of £140,000 and an arrangement by which, as profits in the main company grew, the founders' proportion of them should grow also. It was in effect a separate capitalisation of the good-will, present and future. What weight of dividends went to ordinary shareholders, after the initial years, has been seen. As a result, founders' shares became almost impossibly precious. In 1911 their aggregate value was put at £1,470,000. Yet it could not fairly be said that the ordinary shareholder, who had been assigned 29 per cent. for 1910, had been robbed. The prestige and efficiency of the stores had made him fat, the holder of founders' shares very much fatter. And the comfortable consumer seemed to like consuming through Harrods.

In 1909, while Gordon Selfridge was building his new store on its unlikely site in Oxford Street, the great event in the worlds of bourgeois and joint-stock shopkeeping during the last years of the peace; while the *Economist*, always conservative and sceptical, was doubting "the future of a huge shop which has not been built up by degrees";[1] the Royal Arsenal Co-operative Society, Woolwich, was ending a quinquennium in which its annual sales had averaged £509,000 and its membership more than 26,000. That was good for the Royal Arsenal. Just outside political London, the Stratford society in West Ham was doing even better: its sales rose from £358,000 in 1904 to £526,000 in 1909. But, within the County of London, the Labour Department of the Board of Trade in 1910–11 could procure statistics from only nineteen societies besides the Arsenal, with an aggregate membership of just under 11,000, and sales under £175,000.[2] Including Stratford and a few other places which were economically part of London, the sales of all the London co-operative stores in 1909 were under £1,400,000, of which sum Stratford and the Arsenal accounted for over £1,000,000. Now the net profits of Harrods alone were £210,000 that year.

Many of the customers at Harrods were rich; few, if any, were

[1] March 20, 1909.

[2] *Report on...Co-operative Societies*, 1912 (Cd. 6045) in succession to the similar *Report* of 1901 (Cd. 698).

wage-earners. The wage-earning membership of the Arsenal and of Stratford was growing fast. By 1913 their sales were up by nearly 50 per cent. on 1909.[1] But even so, the hold of the co-operative movement on metropolitan wage-earners remained weak.[2] Except in the spheres of influence of the two great societies, the vast majority of them did their shopping either at the thousands of branches of the different multiple shops or at the scores of thousands of private shops. Contrast the little half-rural, if dirty, woollen town of Birstall in the West Riding, whose 'co-op.' had more members than the place had families; or the Leeds 'co-op.', fully organised on the multiple-shop system, which had a member for every two families in a city with widespread bourgeois suburbs and a great and efficient non-co-operative public market.[3] The Leeds society was the biggest single unit in the North, that is in the country, in 1909–10. Its capital was comparable with Harrods, though the comparison is loose. Its membership was over 70 per cent. of the aggregate membership, and its sales 16 per cent. greater than the aggregate sales, of all the co-operative societies in greater London. Only in 1912–13 did the London sales overtake it.

Barnsley, essentially a wage-earners' town and what is more largely a mining town, gives a more remarkable result. The exact figures for 1911, the census year, are—population, 50,614; families, 10,620; co-operative membership, 34,266; co-operative sales, £1,064,227. Even assuming, as one must, that not all the members were domiciled in the census borough, this was a much better showing even than that of Rochdale of the Pioneers, which in a population of 91,428 had a total membership, in its two great societies and their tiny neighbour the Rochdale Potato Chippers, of only 31,309, and total sales of £630,370. Whilst the average Barnsley member spent £31 a year at the stores, £20 was the Rochdale figure. Perhaps the schism between Pioneers and Provident had told a little on Rochdale's co-operative faith and practice;[4] and perhaps the private enterprise shop windows were better in Rochdale than in Barnsley. This is very likely.

[1] *Report of the Chief Registrar of Friendly Societies* for 1914 (1914–16, LIX), p. xxiv.

[2] Cp. vol. I. 599; vol. II. 308.

[3] These are the 'families or separate occupancies' in private dwellings of the tenement statistics of the 1911 *Census*.

[4] For the schism see vol. II. 310. The Provident was founded in 1870.

The Barnsley standard of co-operative saturation had not been reached by any other town of equal size; but it was passed in smaller and purer mining communities, from Durham to Glamorgan. In some of them the sales per member were astonishingly high, when the average income of the members is taken into account. Compared with Barnsley's £31, the figure for Bishop Auckland, one stage nearer the pure mining community, was £37, and for the pure mining communities of Cwmbach and Ferndale in South Wales, it was £67 in the first, and no less than £79 in the second. In Barnsley, though many families must have done nearly all their buying at the stores, there was plenty of room for the private shopkeeper. In these pit-head communities there was little. Co-operation had often "almost monopolised the trade of the district".[1]

From its main centres of expansion in South Lancasnire, the West Riding and Central Scotland, the co-operative store had spread steadily over industrial Britain; but in districts of highly diversified and what might be called individualistic industry, as in all predominantly commercial neighbourhoods, the spread had tended to be slow and patchy. London is a case in point; but there are others in the centres of expansion themselves.[2] The store was weak in Liverpool, rather weak even in Manchester proper, although the headquarters of the Co-operative Wholesale Society are there; but very strong where the coal-measures are worked on the edges of greater Manchester and Salford.[3] Colliers and textile workers had become good co-operators almost everywhere. The stores can be traced, thick sown and full of business, on all the coalfields, even on such tiny detached ones as that of the Forest of Dean. Among the innumerable trades and manufactures of the Birmingham region, which in the pioneering days of the co-operative movement had been highly individualistic, the stores, although present almost everywhere, had never acquired the same mastery as in places of a single industry, or of few and large-scale industries. There were only five co-operative societies in Warwickshire that had been founded before 1870, though one of them, Lockhurst Lane, was older than the Rochdale Pioneers; the Birmingham society of the twentieth century only dated from 1881; the sales of the

[1] *Report* of 1912, p. xviii.

[2] But Edinburgh was an exception. By 1913 the great St Cuthbert's society, founded in 1859, did more business than the Leeds society.

[3] At Pendleton and Eccles.

Birmingham and Coventry societies together in 1909 were little over half those of the Barnsley society; and the sales of all the Warwickshire societies little over half those of Leeds. That it was no mere case of the Yorkshireman against the Warwickshire man, the one co-operative by temperament the other not, is shown by the conspicuous weakness of co-operation in Sheffield, the home of the little master—a very representative Yorkshire-man. The Sheffield society, founded in 1865, was going down-hill in the 'eighties. Never large, by 1899 its membership had fallen to 1080. A few years afterwards it went out. Meanwhile, a society founded in 1874 at Ecclesall, on the south-west side of the city, was growing. By 1909 it had collected 12,651 members—a poor recruitment compared with Barnsley, twelve miles North over the hill. It is curious to read in the later lists of societies "Sheffield (see Ecclesall)".[1]

The birth and growth of a successful co-operative store was no more determined by brazen economic law than was the growth of an eminent private retail firm. For one, the dominant personality, for the other the group of a few earnest men was essential.[2] These essentials are not quite evenly distributed among the towns and the trades. Few towns had lacked their earnest groups, but the number and the earnestness had varied. And the evidence suggests that, however numerous and however earnest, these group-seeds had found the continuous uniform communal soil of coal-pit or textile-mill more favourable to germination and growth than the broken-up patches in little workshops and tenement factories at Sheffield, in small and varied businesses about Birmingham, or in the shifting industries of Coventry.

Slow co-operative growth in the deep country needs no explanation. A single society in Herefordshire, small and in the county town; a single one in Rutland, smaller; three in Dorset; three in Huntingdon; few if any in the Highlands—these things are not surprising. The result of this, and of the relative weakness of co-operation in the English industrial Midlands, in all so-called residential districts, and in London, was a strong concentration of co-operative activity in the English North and the Scottish Midlands, the central valley of Scotland and its adjacent coasts. Of the British sales in 1913 precisely a half were in the

[1] As in the *Report* of 1912.

[2] The phrase about 'earnest men' comes from an official Report, but the reference has been mislaid.

English North, nearly a fifth in the Scottish Midlands. The English North also had half the membership.

Co-operative stores were not immortal, but they were on the average vastly more long-lived than joint-stock companies; and

Co-operative Stores in Great Britain

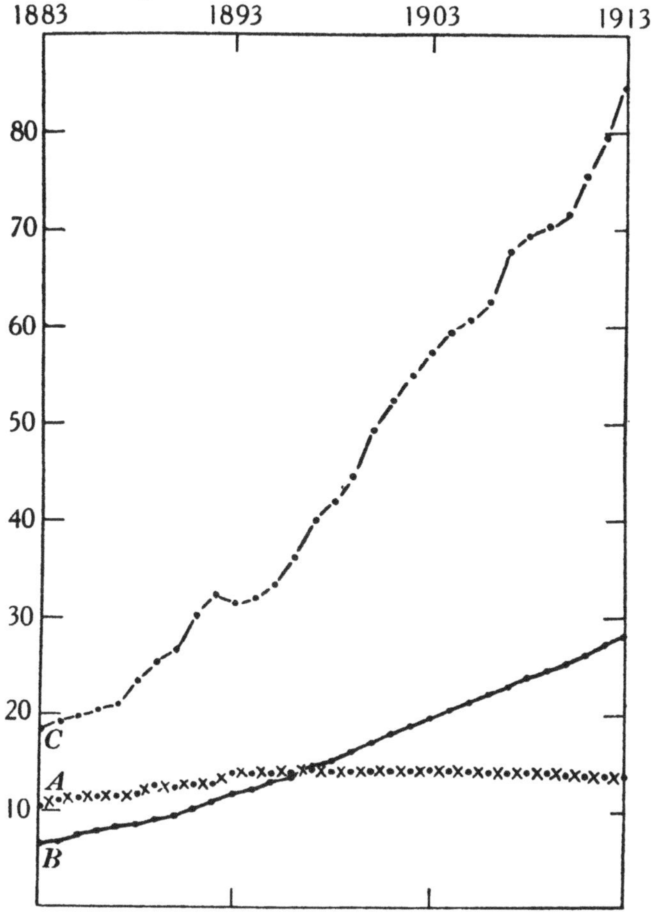

A, Number of Societies making returns, in hundreds.

B, Aggregate membership of these societies, in hundreds of thousands.

C, Aggregate sales of these societies, in millions of pounds. N.B. The curve would not rise quite so steeply after 1896 had prices not been rising.

by the end of the nineteenth century the composite co-operative organism had become exceedingly stable. There had naturally been most stillbirths and most deaths in the early years. Subsequently there were few of either, though even in the twentieth century the Registrar of Friendly Societies reported year by year a few windings-up, and—more interesting—a few amalgamations. Some small local society might find its interest in absorption into a stronger neighbouring one, which was feeling outwards like any other growing organism. As every place of importance, and in Scotland and the North many most insignificant places, already had its Society by 1887–90, the natural development of the next twenty years—in co-operative as in private shopkeeping—was the opening of branches. The creation of brand-new societies had nearly ceased. After 1909, there was not even quite enough of it to balance the few annual windings-up and amalgamations. So the total of distinct British societies, after fluctuating slightly for many years round about 1400, declined a little at the last—while the membership climbed steadily and the sales rushed up.

A record of the foundation dates of the societies existing in Lancashire in 1910 illustrates both the continuous slowing up in the work of foundation, after the 'sixties, and the very respectable antiquity of the average Lancastrian 'co-op.'

Lancashire Co-operative Societies, 1910

Founded, up to 1850	5	Founded 1870–79	35
Founded 1850–9	40	Founded 1880–9	18
Founded 1860–9	61	Founded after 1889	15

Counties which came rather late into the movement would naturally show larger groups of late foundations; but all would illustrate the tenacity of life in the average co-operative society.

There had been no important change, legal or administrative, in the principles of co-operative organisation since the 'eighties; but a great increase of co-operative prosperity.[1] All capital was still found by the members, and old societies had now often accumulated far more than they could use in their ordinary business.[2] Much of this went into the two Wholesale Societies, English and Scottish, and into various Productive Societies; much of the balance into house property, either let to members, or held on mortgage as security for advances made to enable members to become house owners; some was invested latterly

[1] Cp. vol. II. 309–11.

[2] *Report* of 1912, pp. xiv–xvii. And cp. the valuable new survey of the most recent co-operative history and policy in Hough, J. A., *Dividend on Co-operative Purchases* (1936).

outside 'the Movement'—in government securities, in railways, or in Lancashire cotton mills.[1] By law, no one could hold more than £200 worth of shares. By society regulation, the limit was often put lower, at £100, £50 or even £10. The last figure was rare, and as a general thing would have been impracticable; for the average holding per member in the whole co-operative movement had risen to £12–14 by 1910–13. Since members had constantly used their shares as a means of automatic saving, leaving the interest and perhaps also the 'divis' on their purchases to accumulate in their share account, there were many small co-operative capitalists of the second or third generation at the statutory or local limit. The limit reached, further accumulations might be left with the society on loan. To a member's holding of loan capital there was by law no limit, but the societies might impose one. A prosperous member was able to keep his capital in both categories at the maximum, withdrawing further profit as it accrued. Such people were however a small minority; for in the country as a whole the average member's holding of loan capital was less than £2.[2]

The practice of leaving capital to accumulate had been encouraged by the way in which one became a shareholder. Shares were normally of £1,[3] but membership was secured as a rule by a payment on account, frequently as low as 1*s*. After that, the member might pay up by instalments, usually of 3*d*. a week; or he might leave the balance to be deducted from his share of the profits on purchases, his 'divis', as they accrued.[4]

The 'divi', the consumer's surplus proportional to purchases made, had always been the core of co-operative finance and faith. On shares and loans the interest was kept low, 5 per cent., 4 per cent. or even less. In societies whose co-operative conviction

[1] Hough, *op. cit.* p. 43, referring to the present day; but the policy of outside investment is older.

[2] In 1912 the aggregate share capital of retail societies was nearly seven times the loan capital (£34,745,000 *versus* £5,072,000).

[3] Though other and smaller denominations were possible: "societies can and have been registered with 1*d*. shares". Fay, C. R., *Co-operation at Home and Abroad* (1908), p. 363 n.

[4] *Report* of 1912, as above. See in general for this period *Industrial Co-operation, the Story of a Peaceful Revolution*, ed. C. Webb (1904); Aves, E., *Co-operative Industry* (1907); Fay, C. R., *Co-operation at Home and Abroad* (1908). The bones of the story are in the *Reports* of 1901 and 1912 and the annual *Returns of the Registrar of Friendly Societies*. See also the *Co-operative News* (weekly), the *Co-operative Wholesale Society's Annual* and the *Reports of the Co-operative Congress.*

was strong, members who did not buy enough might be refused interest altogether, or even be asked to resign their membership. The society was not to become a mere savings bank. In the same spirit, men of faith demanded low prices to bring in the poor consumer, instead of such prices as would leave the established co-operator a nice sum to accumulate, or to be drawn out for his summer trip to Blackpool, Bridlington or the Isle of Man.[1] 'Divis' had reached their maximum in 1896, when they averaged 2*s*. 8½*d*. in the pound of purchases. After that they fell slowly, but only to 2*s*. 5¾*d*. in 1909 and 1910. And the main group of dividend receivers, 32·8 per cent. of the whole body, were still drawing at rates between 2*s*. 6*d*. and 3*s*. It was the less successful and younger societies which kept the average down. The critics, with some of the best friends, of the movement believed that there was too much 'divi-hunting', and not enough care for the really poor, most of whom everywhere remained outside the co-operative store, finding the little credit-giving private shop more to their, perhaps vitiated, taste. They could not afford to pay a round price for a sound article, and then wait six months for a 'divi', like the substantial wage-earners and small salaried people who determined co-operative policy and managed the societies without stipend.[2]

There were salaried people in the movement, and others who bought some articles at the stores without being members, but the rank and file were the substantial wage-earners, and the purchasing non-members were a tiny minority.[3] In the middle 'eighties, the share of the national wage bill spent at co-operative stores was still insignificant, £20,000,000 out of some £480,000,000.[4] By 1911–13, the wage bill of Britain was well above £700,000,000; but the stores sales were climbing above £80,000,000.[5] They still did not sell many important things on

[1] Or the corresponding Scottish resorts. It is here assumed, it is believed correctly, that the mass of 'established co-operators' were clients of the places mentioned in the text.

[2] The problem of co-operative and non-co-operative prices is most difficult, because of the variations of quality and credit. To-day co-operative prices for staple food commodities are never, so far as is known, below those in competitive trade, and are sometimes rather higher, "There is sufficient available evidence to show that in co-operative trade there is, in a broad sense, a relationship between high prices and high dividend." Hough, *op. cit.* p. 178; and cp. p. 111.

[3] This is still true to-day: Hough, *op. cit.* pp. 80–1.

[4] Vol. II. 309.

[5] For wages see Bowley, A. L., *The Division of the Product of Industry* (1919), pp. 14, 30.

which wages are spent—house-rent, newspapers, beer, racing tips, football-match tickets, holidays, doctors' bills, subscriptions to trade unions, friendly societies, churches and chapels; though no doubt 'divis' supplied some of the expenditure on these things. Probably they were potential competitors for something like £500,000,000 worth of wage-spending. If so, they had made a notable advance in the occupation of that territory which the pioneers had set out to conquer.

Although the stores were primarily distributive organisations, nearly four-fifths of them also did some production.[1] It generally took obvious forms, of which the bakery was the most obvious. To this might be added a boot-repairing, then a boot-making, department; and so on. Very occasionally production had been the original aim: the great Leeds society started as a co-operative flour-mill; but the normal growth was the other way. Although the value put upon this store production sounds impressive, measured by employment it was a little thing—22,300 workers in all Britain in 1909, of whom 20,400 were butchers, bakers, boot-makers, dress-makers and tailors.

Behind the stores stood the two great Wholesale Societies, now very strong.[2] In 1880 not half the English stores were affiliated to the English Wholesale. By 1910 six-sevenths of them were; and the ratio of Wholesale sales to stores sales in Great Britain suggests that between two-thirds and three-quarters of the goods that the Stores disposed of had been handled first by the Wholesales. There was least dependence on the Wholesales for fresh meat, milk and other foodstuffs produced locally; most for the groceries and overseas butter which they now imported direct—currants from Greece; some of the tea from their own plantations in Ceylon; butter from Ireland, France and Denmark, and latterly from Siberia. In manufactures, it was a point of honour for an active and zealous store to sell so far as possible goods handled or made by the Wholesale Societies. These added steadily to their productive enterprises, so that by 1913 the English Society had between forty and fifty of them—flour-mills; textile, boot and shoe, and clothing factories; biscuit, tobacco, hardware, corset, brush factories; printing-works, soapworks, ironworks, fruit farms. They were scattered over the country; but one in three was in a ten-mile

[1] *Report* of 1912, p. xxi.

[2] Sources as above, with Redfern, P., *The Story of the Co-operative Wholesale Society* (1913) written from the Societys' records.

radius from the Manchester headquarters of the C.W.S. As they employed on an average about 300 people, they were considerable industrial units; but their 13–14,000 employees, together with the 5500–6000 people similarly employed by the Scottish Wholesale, were only a small fraction of 1 per cent. of the wage-earners of Britain.[1]

Their employees—they were that without any qualification; and in 1911 the Amalgamated Union of Co-operative Employees started a strike fund. Strikes had been rare, for the C.W.S. was a good employer and always paid Trade Union rates; but they were known.[2] The wage-earner in a C.W.S. factory, if a member of a store, had open to him, like other wage-earners, the co-operator's whole career. The baton was in his knapsack and he might in time help to direct the brigade in which he had earned his wage. But, in spite of protests from among the old co-operative guard, the C.W.S. had broken very deliberately with the conception of self-employment by co-operating productive groups. Several of their manufacturing concerns—flour-mills, a boot-factory, a brush-factory, a hosiery-mill—had been taken over from productive societies,[3] but were run in the twentieth century on what hostile critics called capitalist lines with ordinary wage labour. "June 20, 1891. Profit sharing finally rejected", the entry runs in the chronological summary of the official history of the C.W.S.[4] That was when the issue raised in 1887 by Tom Hughes of the old guard had been decided against him. Hughes had demanded that the C.W.S. should aim at co-partnership in its factories. Operatives were to find some of the capital, to share in profits and losses, and to choose their own managers. In life, the scheme broke against the rocks of this election and loss-sharing. In thought and word, its opponents stressed the primacy of consumption both in society and in co-operative history; the justice of returning to stores which found the capital and took the risks some profits when they

[1] Redfern, p. 313, gives 13,370 at the end of 1912, the *Registrar of Friendly Societies Report* for 1914, 14,000 for the C.W.S. and 6000 for the S.W.S. These are the 'productive' workers, not all the employees.

[2] Speaking of the stores, not the C.W.S. Factories, Webb (*op. cit.* p. 100) wrote in 1904 that the position of their employees was "distinctly a weak spot in co-operative organisation" and quoted a Congress speech of 1893: "you will rarely find interest or enthusiasm for co-operation" among storemen. This may not be a fair generalisation, but must have some facts behind it.

[3] *Report* of 1912, p. xxix.

[4] Redfern, p. 427.

accrued; the great moderation of the stores in being content with an uncommonly low average 'divi' from the Wholesale—3½*d.* in the pound of purchases during the 'nineties, and thereafter 4*d.*—over and above the fixed 5 per cent. on any capital which they had subscribed.[1] In the competitive world, among the joint-stock companies, these would certainly have been reckoned meagre returns.

The working case for the English Wholesale's policy was strong. Completely proof it could not be, because the Scottish Wholesale had always managed successfully, if not the full co-partnership of Hughes' scheme, at least a wage-bonus system.[2] Defenders of the English policy might however fairly ask whether the almost fixed 8*d.* in the pound of wages, at which the Scottish bonus settled down during the 'nineties, was a sufficient mark of co-operative grace, its absence, as critics had sometimes implied, an indication of competitive greed. They were impatient of praise spent on "the rather sterile idea"[3] of the mere wage bonus, a thing very far from the co-operation of dreams. They may have reflected that the crystallised Scottish 8*d.* in the pound cannot have been real profit sharing, and that its smallness and its crystallisation were probably due to a wise reluctance to face the worries and disappointments of loss sharing.

Unquestionably the comfortable success of the Wholesales and the greater stores left flanks open to critical attack. It was so hard to distinguish a co-operative buyer, salesman, or manager from others of his kind. "We fear that the homely Pioneers... would be ill at ease beside the flowing banks of millinery or amidst the riches of silks and furs at a C.W.S. drapery show", the historian of 1913 writes.[4] It is certainly to be feared; but as co-operation set out to make men comfortable, it must not be blamed for success. If there are to be furs and silks for any, silks and furs for all, or for more, is no abandonment of co-operative doctrine, provided that the supplying of them does not interfere with a supply of plainer goods for co-operators below the silk horizon. There is no reason to think that it did. About an earlier entry in the annals doubt is more permissible. It refers to the modest payments made to C.W.S. committee men, and how in 1897 they were raised a little. "First class railway tickets

[1] The case is stated, or suggested, in Redfern, p. 317 and *passim.*
[2] See *Report* of 1912, p. xxv, and Webb, *op. cit.* p. 133.
[3] Redfern, p. 183. [4] Redfern, p. 259.

were at last allowed."[1] No great harm in that perhaps; yet thirds were already comfortable; and it is the most consciously competitive sort of trader who says that he travels first for the credit of the firm. To which again a slightly cynical co-operative apologist might reply—but co-operation is competitive: it competes with competition.

The course of time, and the policy of stores and Wholesales, had left that form of co-operative production for which Christian Socialists had pleaded weak and insignificant. There were in 1910–13 some scores of societies, with six to seven thousand work-people, run ostensibly in the interests not of consumers but of the six to seven thousand. They were strongest and most effectively self-governing in the boot and shoe country. But they had grown hardly at all in a decade; in two-thirds of them work-people had not a majority on the managing Committee; and some forty per cent. of the work-people were not even members of the society which employed them. Good or bad, this was evidently a type of organism unsuited to either the co-operative or the competitive environment in early twentieth-century Britain.[2]

As compared with that of joint-stock companies, the finance of co-operative societies was stable and smoothly continuous. Failures and losses there were, especially when societies were young and struggling. But the initial stage once overcome, they were apt to move and act very steadily. If the start was often hard, it was not complicated by the chance of extravagance or abuse in promotion. It resembled not the floating of a company by a daring pioneer but the setting up of a little private business by a thrifty man. The perpetual openness of the capital account, and the adherence to the low fixed return, comparable with that on the debentures of joint-stock companies, kept the value of the shares almost perfectly steady.[3] Wage-earners who put savings into them did not see the savings melt away. This openness and attractiveness of the capital account tended, in an old society, to make it over-full, as has been seen. One use for the overflow was deposit with the banking department of the

[1] Redfern, p. 206.

[2] *Report* of 1912, pp. xxxi–ii; *Report* of 1901, pp. xxviii–xxx; *Report on Contracts given out by Public Authorities to Associations of Workmen*, 1896 (LXXX). For the limited progress of Agricultural Co-operation in Britain, see p. 111 above.

[3] Cp. vol. II. 310.

Wholesale. This had been started, with difficulty and over opposition, in 1872. In early days it had made some losses.[1] But by 1887 it had attracted the accounts of 210 societies; by 1912 those of 987. It was the natural banker for a society with a substantial surplus. In standard co-operative fashion, it paid a low rate of interest on deposits, and returned surplus profits to customers in proportion to their business done with it. It increased the already great stability of the whole co-operative movement by its policy of making advances for heavy Wholesale purchases, and also to individual stores, at rates more uniform, if not on the average lower, than those of the London money market. That a tiny store could thus borrow about as cheaply as some great municipality was a notable thing. Co-operators argued, though not quite convincingly, that in fact it could borrow a shade cheaper.[2]

In the early 'eighties, proposals that this banking department of the Wholesale should hold investments like an ordinary bank had been rejected by the delegates from the depositing stores. They felt, or fancied, that there was something not co-operative about it. But in 1885 the ban on consols had been lifted.[3] As a result, the investments stood at £195,000 in 1892, and twenty years later at £2,911,000, a figure rather higher than that of the investments held in the same year by a joint-stock neighbour of the C.W.S., the Lancashire and Yorkshire Bank, with its 129 branches.[4] The Lancashire and Yorkshire was important, but it was not one of the greater English banks.

There was nothing inconsistent with co-operative principle in this adoption of standard banking methods, any more than there was in the adoption of the multiple shop. In the latter co-operators had been pioneers, the branches of a central store having often been opened in outlying parts of some town or area, to compete with the private shops, before branches of any

[1] There was a strong minority of co-operators opposed to the policy of 1872. Shortly after its inception an independent 'Industrial Bank' was started. This was a failure and it disappeared in the depression of the 'seventies; when the Wholesale's Bank was also making losses. *Report* of 1912, p. xli; Redfern, *passim*; Webb, *op. cit.* pp. 166–70.

[2] Redfern, p. 326. The play which Redfern makes with the Wholesale Bank's 3½ against the Bank of England's 7 per cent. in Nov. 1907 is of course not evidence. Cp. diagram, p. 17, above. But a steady 3½ or less was an excellently favourable rate for a small borrower. In Nov. 1907 most municipal 3½'s stood a little above par.

[3] Redfern, p. 158, and banking statistics, p. 417.

[4] Figures in the *Banking Number* of the *Economist*, Oct. 12, 1912.

non-co-operative multiple shop had appeared there. But likenesses of organisation inevitably produced some like results, of which the most important socially was the emergence of the retail manager. Here again the co-operators, with a few such firms as the A.B.C., had been pioneers. Very early in their history they had paid men to serve in the stores;[1] and the co-operative manager had been a distinct social type at a time when most shopmen, even of the first rank, managed individual businesses without branches, the time when Lipton had no assistant and Harrod still took his coat off. Now, under his boss or his board in competitive trade, in co-operative trade under his committee, the manager was to be found almost everywhere. In co-operative trade, he was given the pay of a skilled artisan.[2] For the other sort there are not good statistics; but where the work was comparable pay was no doubt of the same order. The departmental manager in a big department store was a functionary of quite another class.

The healthy continuity of co-operative development, and the stabilisation of the number of distinct co-operative societies at about the level reached early in the 'nineties, rule a sharp line between the co-operative and the joint-stock stories. That is why the former has been told here all in one piece, in the middle of the more feverish story of the joint stock. Cycles of trade touched the co-operators, but not vitally.[3] The Stores, in spite of their silks and their furs, lived by supplying those primary human needs which are continuous. The demands which they served were inelastic. Wars and money-market fluctuations affected them very little; new inventions, new social and business fashions, and economic vicissitudes overseas hardly at all. These were precisely the things which did affect the curve of joint-stock company creation, and the lives of joint-stock companies; though beneath the jagged mounting line of the creation curve

[1] Though even in 1910–11 it was "not unknown in small Societies when first established" for the committeemen to serve in rotation in the evenings without pay: *Report* of 1912, p. xx.

[2] *Report* of 1912, p. xx. Central Managers in 1909–10 averaged 38*s.* 2¼*d.*; the minimum for a Branch Manager (in 220 societies) was 31*s.* 10¾*d.* The standard rate for an engineer in Manchester was 38*s.* On "the creation of a race of managers" in the multiple-shop grocery trade, see Rees, *The Grocery Trade*, II. 256.

[3] They are just traceable on the curve of co-operative sales, e.g. round about 1893 and 1907–9. Diagram, p. 247 above.

runs the line which indicates the steady secular shifting of business of all kinds on to a joint-stock and limited-liability basis.[1]

It has been seen how in the middle 'nineties, with their cheap money, the curve of company creations turned steeply upwards, registering activity in the promotion of brand new projects, in the remodelling of businesses already limited and powerful, in amalgamations of business units more or less equal, and above all in the organisation on a joint-stock basis of considerable firms hitherto private.[2] The change over to a joint stock had been commonest since the middle 'eighties among the breweries. It began, on a large scale, with the flotations of Guinness and Ind Coope in 1886.[3] Before that, there had not been a score of 'limiteds' among the thousands of firms in the Trade.[4] In 1887 Allsopps had followed Guinness' lead; in 1888 Meux; in the same year Bass, limited in 1880, had been reregistered and enlarged; Whitbread and Truman Hanbury Buxton had become limited companies in 1889. These are only samples, taken from the greater names.[5]

Slackening a little in the ebb of the early 'nineties, the change from partnership to limited liability, accompanied by amalgamations, went on furiously afterwards. Only one or two lean years between 1893 and 1901 saw so little as £5,000,000 of capital subscribed for the breweries. In the years 1896–8 the registrations averaged over £18,000,000.[6] This covers distilleries, but they were quite subordinate. The figure for 1896 includes Barclay, Perkins and Co.; that for 1898 one huge amalgamation —of Watneys with Combes and Reids—on a capital, in shares and debentures, of nearly £15,000,000. There were a number of other amalgamations in these three years; but they were all local, not of many units, and not of the sort to facilitate even a local monopoly. The Bristol United Breweries, of four units, had to face the Bristol Brewery and six other firms. The Manchester Breweries, again of four units, had more than thirty Manchester competitors. The Newcastle Breweries, eight units, were nearer

[1] Diagram, p. 222 above.

[2] Above, p. 221.

[3] Above, p. 210.

[4] Among them were the City of London, 1860; the Alton Court, the Birkenhead and the Lion, opposite Charing Cross, 1865; the Albion, 1872; Ilkley, 1873; Browns, Preston, 1875; Devonport and Tiverton, 1876; and a few more.

[5] And from the *Stock Exchange Year Book*.

[6] From the 'capital applications' analyses of the *Economist*.

monopoly; but there were nine other brewers in Newcastle; and a Newcastle man might call for Bass.[1]

Price agreements there were of course, and a very formidable organisation of the brewing interest against teetotallers and threatenings of legislation. But this did not prevent a fierce, and a stupid, competition among the breweries, which showed itself mainly during the beer boom of the late 'nineties in the swollen competitive prices which were being given by breweries for licensed houses.[2] "Nothing approaching the prices paid... could possibly be obtained for the same houses, if again offered for sale",[3] five or six years later. This stupid game of beggar-my-neighbour was being played both by the giant joint-stock breweries with national reputations, by the local amalgamations, and by what was still the representative, and numerically the dominant, type of company, that of a single brewery. In spite of the national power of the giants and the reasonable territorial strength of the amalgamations, more than a quarter of the capital known to be invested in brewery companies at the opening of the twentieth century was in these single unit firms.

Between 1885 and 1901 the joint-stock breweries had grown from less than a score to upwards of 300. More than that had been registered, but there had been absorptions, amalgamations, and a few—a very few—failures.[4] The 300 or so of 1901 includes a number of firms which, though limited, would have been officially labelled private, had the law permitted it. They published no regular reports and were reticent about their finance. But as the public had an appetite for brewery shares, all or nearly all the enterprises of any size had let the public in, if not always on what is called the ground-floor. There had been no trouble about raising the money. A good deal was raised even in 1901. What the precise total came to by that time is not easy to determine; probably to not less than £175,000,000.[5]

[1] *Brewer's Almanac*, 1906 and *Stock Exchange Year Book* as above. There are some brewery facts and figures in Macrosty, *Trust Movement*, pp. 241–3.

[2] *R.C. on Liquor Licensing Laws*, 1897–9; three-quarters of the houses were by that time more or less tied: the movement had been very rapid in the previous 20 years: but there was no evidence that more 'tying' meant more drinking; *Final Report* (1899, XXXIV–V), Ch. 7.

[3] *The Statist*, June 13, 1903.

[4] The number given in the *Stock Exchange Year Book* for 1901 is, if correctly counted, 325. For 1906, Burdett's *Official Intelligence* (quoted in Macrosty, p. 241) gives 307.

[5] *The Statist* of Oct. 20, 1894 put the capital at £104,000,000: the *Brewer's*

It may be safely assumed that much the greater part of brewing capital was in the limited companies by the beginning of the twentieth century; but numerous and powerful as they were, they were still vastly outnumbered by the private breweries. And although every few months—perhaps every few weeks—a private brewing firm somewhere was learning to appreciate the advantages of limitation and publicity or semi-publicity, not half as much capital went into joint-stock breweries during the decade which began in 1902 as in the single year 1896.[1] The position in 1901, at the end of the joint-stock beer boom, is therefore worth recording, the more so as brewing—with distilling—is the solitary British industry for which complete continuous statistics of firms exist.[2] The number of "common brewers not retailing on the premises *or* with a victuallers' licence subsidiary to the main business of a brewer",[3] in England and Wales, had now fallen from the 2470 of 1853 and the 2242 of 1886 to 1688, of whom 99 were in London. (There were still 2638 victuallers with brewing licences; but this once important class had lost all national significance.)[4] There were plenty of private firms in some large towns—15 out of the 37 Manchester breweries were private—but it was the hundreds of private breweries in the lesser towns and the big villages of rural England which swelled the total figure to nearly 1400. In Cambridgeshire and the Isle of Ely, including the two towns, there were 23 'common brewers'. Of these only 2 were limited companies. Of the 34 Warwickshire breweries, 15 were limited; of the 10 in Cornwall, 2; of the 16 in Dorset, 6; and of the 34 in Hertfordshire, so near to London, 13 only. A Bass or a Whitbread could no doubt outbrew whole counties full of these minor businesses, but they were still there—waiting, most of them, to be limited or bought up by limited companies in the course of the next generation, though not of the next decade.

It was in iron, steel, and heavy engineering that the joint-stock limited company—adopted there earlier than anywhere

Almanac for 1906 (p. 131) thought that by that time it was "at least" £185,000,000. Not much fresh capital was subscribed between 1901 and 1906—£6,300,000 according to the analyses of capital applications in the *Economist*.

[1] Capital application, breweries; 1896, £18,200,000; 1902–11, £7,600,000.

[2] Cp. vol. I. 170; vol. II. 122.

[3] *Return of Brewers' Licenses* for 1901 (1902, XCIII. 87).

[4] There were 121 brewers in Scotland, but only 2 victuallers with brewing licences.

else in industry—was used most freely for the establishment, or the expansion, of that so-called vertical combination, from raw material to finished goods, which so far from being a new thing was indigenous to the trades. Iron-ware had always been made where the iron was smelted. The ownership of coal and iron ore by iron firms was an old story in the Black Country and the West Riding, in Scotland and in South Wales. In Cleveland the stronger firms had controlled their ore supplies almost from the start. If local ores ran short, or were unsuitable, mines might be bought elsewhere, though that could not always be done. Partly as a result of this difficulty, the integrated business had lost ground in the Black Country since the depression of the 'seventies, the rise of steel, and the shift of iron-working towards tide-water.[1] Puddling, once its mainstay, was in continuous decline.[2] The replacement of wrought iron by rolled steel might turn an iron-maker into a 're-roller'; and the steel billets for re-rolling might, usually did, come from outside the old Black Country, often from Belgium or Germany. This all tended to disintegration. Only a few South Staffordshire firms held their own by becoming steel makers.[3] Some just died, as the Gospel Oak Works did in the 'nineties. Some migrated to South Wales and tide-water, using there foreign or Cumbrian ore, as those older Welsh firms now did who had once quarried their ore and mined their coal near Merthyr.

Meanwhile in Cleveland expansion and the joint stock went forward. Bolckow Vaughan and Co., pioneers in the use of Cleveland ore and a limited company since 1865,[4] simply expanded where it stood. For its Bessemer steel it bought iron-mines in Spain. The purchase out of profits of a comparatively small adjacent iron company, in 1899, was its only nineteenth-century absorption. On the Tyne, Palmer's Shipbuilding Company, as a company of the same generation as Bolckow Vaughan, "by the progressive development of its own force without alliances" had "covered the whole field of production from pig iron to battleships".[5] But, in that field, alliances of old companies had become commoner than this sort of expansion in situ, partly because not many companies had so favourable a

[1] Allen, G. C., *The Industrial Development of Birmingham and the Black Country*, p. 286.

[2] Vol. II. 52–4.

[3] Among them, the Earl of Dudley's works; Allen, p. 287.

[4] Vol. II. 138.

[5] Macrosty, p. 40.

site as Palmer's then was. John Brown and Co. of the Atlas Works, the first Sheffield firm to trust Bessemer's process and early makers of armour plate, had bought coal and iron mines in the 'seventies. In 1899 they joined Palmer's class by the purchase of the Clydebank Engineering and Shipbuilding Company.[1] Cammells of Sheffield—like Browns and Palmers, a limited company of the 'sixties—moved on parallel lines. As they controlled hematite mines in Cumberland, they had shifted their steel-rail business to Workington in the early 'eighties. There and elsewherc they absorbed various complementary businesses; but the alliance which finally put them in the same class as Browns and Palmers only came in 1903, when they joined up with Lairds, the pioneer iron shipbuilding firm of Birkenhead.

The stories of the other great firms of what came to be known as the armaments group are similar. Both Armstrongs and Whitworths had made guns, among scores of other things, from early days. As the ship of war became each year a more complex mass of interrelated mechanisms, either there must be an elaborate fitting together of the products of many specialised firms, or single many-sided firms must do most of the essential work themselves, as government dockyards had always done. A firm which supplied guns and plate should know all about their steel; and one which could speak for the whole ship was at an advantage in dealing with admiralties at home and abroad. (Since the days of armour-plate and steel the warship had become an article of British export.) These considerations encouraged extensive vertical combination in armaments. Only a few of the firms kept their own blast-furnaces however. At one time Armstrongs did; but in their greatest days their work began at the steel-making. They had absorbed a shipyard in 1882, when the modern warship was just taking its terrible form.[2] Fifteen years later came the amalgamation with Whitworths. In 1899, by a purchase of shares, control was secured over graving docks on the Tyne belonging to Robert Stephenson and Co.; and in 1900 armour-plate shops were set up in connection with the Whitworth works at Manchester.

[1] From the firm of W. G. Thomson; "More Iron and Steel Combines", *Economist*, Nov. 1, 1902; a summary of the amalgamations to date; Macrosty, ch. II, "The Iron and Steel Industries, Amalgamations", *passim*; and the *Stock Exchange Year Book* for dates and capitalisations.

[2] Vol. II. 82

Vickers, like Browns, came into the group along the steel route: they were originally a firm of Sheffield steel-makers turned into a joint-stock company in the 'sixties. From steel to castings and forgings, to guns and armour-plate, was a natural progression. Once more, the final stride was taken during the joint-stock and combination boom of the late 'nineties. In 1897, the year Armstrongs joined Whitworths, Vickers bought the Naval Construction and Armaments Company, Barrow, and the Maxim-Nordenfelt Gun Company, Erith. By 1902 they had absorbed Robert Napier's classic shipbuilding and marine engineering business,[1] and had a half share in Beardmores of Glasgow, who were also steel-makers and shipbuilders. And there were other smaller acquisitions about that time.

Iron and steel firms which did not cater directly for the admiralties were attracted less strongly to the complete vertical combination; though there was every degree of joint-stock combination short of it. Bell Brothers, a private limited company since 1873, reconstructed in 1895, became a public company in 1899. So far it had only made iron with its own ore, coal, and limestone. Latterly it had been experimenting with steel; and now part of its publicly raised capital was to go into a works for the production of finished steel—works erected in conjunction with Dorman, Long and Co. a firm limited so recently as 1889. Dorman's speciality had been girders and structural steel; but in the year of the joint arrangement with Bells they had absorbed a steel sheet-works and a wire-works. The arrangement gave them access to Bell's reserves of raw material. In the past they had made their steel from pig-iron bought in open market, with its market fluctuations. Like many other firms, in Durham and elsewhere, they were pushing back towards that control of the raw material which before the age of steel ironmasters using coal-measure iron ore on the coal-measures had enjoyed automatically. The flexibility of joint-stock organisation allowed the composite enterprise of 1899 to be supervised by a board of directors representing the Bell and the Dorman interests.

By that time the limited company had almost completed its conquest of the business of iron-making. In the year 1900 there were 604 blast-furnaces in Britain—by no means all in blast. Of these 506 were owned by limited companies, public or private.[2] In the now dominant iron-making areas—Scotland,

[1] Vol. II. 64.

[2] *Mineral Returns*, 1902 (CXVI. 2).

Cumberland and Furness, Durham and the North Riding, Monmouth and South Wales—only 31 furnaces out of 383 were owned by old style partnerships. (In 1901 the figure fell to 21.) The proportion was much higher, as might have been expected, in Stafford, Shropshire and Worcester—35 out of 90—where an unusually large number of both the partnership and the company furnaces were out of blast. In Durham, Furness and Monmouth there was not a single partnership furnace left.

In coal-mining the situation was entirely different. There were far more coal mines than blast furnaces. Hundreds of them were small workings near the outcrop, of little importance. These swelled the official count of British mines to something like 3000.[1] But of fairly important mines there were about 2000; that is the number of the circulars which Sir George Elliot is said to have sent out when he planned his national coal company in 1893.[2] Yet in 1901 there were only between 70 and 80 pure coal-mining limited companies known to the London Stock Exchange. There were nearly as many distinct 'unlimited' collieries on the little anthracite field of South-West Wales. The companies, it is true, did a big share of the total production. A few of them were, as companies, both old and strong, and controlled several distinct collieries and many actual pits. In Wales, the Powell Duffryn Company went back to 1864; in Yorkshire, Henry Briggs Son and Co. to 1865; in Lancashire, Andrew Knowles and Co. to 1873; in the Forest of Dean, the Trafalgar Co. to 1883. But the great majority, as in so many other industries, were limitations of private firms arranged during the late 'eighties and the 'nineties. More often than not, the company retained the private firm's name, and had a great measure of privacy in its management and finance. The whole of the capital had frequently been found by the vendors. When, in 1899, Lord Londonderry's Durham collieries were made into a company under his name, the Stock Exchange was unable to get any information about it.[3] It was the greatest surviving aristocratic colliery enterprise. The Earl of Dudley's collieries were subordinate to his iron and steel works; and Lord Durham had sold all his, three years earlier, to Sir James Joicey, already a coal-

[1] Even in 1925 there were "about 1400 colliery undertakings owning about 2500 mines", *R. C. on the Coal Industry*, 1926 (Cmd. 2600), p. 45.

[2] Macrosty, p. 87.

[3] See the notices of the various companies in the *Stock Exchange Year Book*. Cp. Williams, D. J., *Capitalistic Combination in the Coal Industry* (1924).

owner in a large way, who by this purchase came to control an output of over 4,000,000 tons.[1]

Lord Durham's collieries formed a big unit. And there were others. Most of the South Wales steam coal was raised by about twenty companies, including the Cambrian Collieries, a creation of 1895 with a capital of £400,000 controlled by D. A. Thomas. Sometimes a company had been floated for the amalgamation of adjacent collieries, or having been floated had bought out a neighbour or two. A few of the greater figures in the world of coal had interests in more than one coal-field. Sir George Elliot had: hence his critical knowledge of the condition of the industry.[2] But there was no approach even to local monopoly, even on the smallest field. Prices were competitive. There had been no serious attempt to control output since the relatively remote breakdown of the Vend.[3] The complete failure of Elliot's project was both natural and significant. Things were not ripe for such a masterful application of joint stock and public utility principles. The private firm, the fighting trade, capitalism according to Karl Marx, were still the notes of the coal industry as the nineteenth century ran out.

Other considerations apart, geology itself had made coal-mining intractable even to dominating personalities like Elliot and D. A. Thomas.[4] New trades and fresh phases of old ones gave such men more scope. The outstanding examples of the late 'eighties and the 'nineties were the handling of soap-making by W. H. Lever, at a time when the vegetable oils were just coming into common use in the soap industry, and of drug-making and distribution as part of the new multiple-shop system by Jesse Boot. Both men died in the Peerage. An acquired knowledge of the average consumer, great determination, and a genius for advertisement carried Lever, a wholesale grocer from Wigan turned soap-maker at Warrington, to the headship of a private company in 1890, and to that of a great international public company with capital paid up to over £1,000,000 by 1901.[5] In 1901 its expansion had barely begun.

[1] And just before a coal boom. He repeated this coup when he bought the Hetton collieries in 1911, at the start of the trade boom of 1911–12. As Lord Joicey he died in 1936. See Jevons, H. S., *The British Coal Trade* (1915), p. 318.

[2] Above, p. 220.

[3] Vol. I. 202–3; vol. II. 301.

[4] The future Lord Rhondda; see p. 271 below.

[5] Rees, *The Grocery Trade*, II. 283.

But it had already built Port Sunlight, started a copra-crushing mill at Sydney and a cotton-seed mill at Vicksburg, a soap works in Germany and another in Switzerland. It had also absorbed, in 1899, a singularly well-chosen firm, not rival but complementary. Lever's principal soap was meant for washing day. "As the aspirations of working housewives rose above the wash-tub ...the want became felt of...soaps which would make the washing day shorter." Lever "saw the chance, produced a soap to meet the need, advertised it in terms appealing to every busy woman, and captured the demand".[1] The terms were very familiar in the 'nineties—'WHY does A WOMAN look old sooner than A MAN'? Levers advertised in season and out but they also produced the soap. The well chosen absorption of 1899 gave their 'Sunlight' a consort, the 'Monkey Brand' of the American firm Brooke and Co. which had won its place by an advertisement campaign that allowed no one to forget that the only thing it would not wash was the clothes for which Lever's 'Sunlight' had been designed.

Levers had no monopoly in 1901. There was another firm in the trade, old and famous, with almost as much paid-up capital;[2] and the aggregate capital of the five greatest firms, which had all become joint-stock companies since 1888, was two and a half times that of Levers. There were besides many smaller firms. But Levers, after a short life, stood head if not shoulders above them all. It worked with them in their trade association to regulate prices, and was acquiring an intimacy with them which might at any time lead to closer relations. But as yet it was only the young King of the soap-makers.

Soap-making had been organised occasionally on a large scale since the seventeenth century. The joint-stock company was very appropriate to it. Drug-making had grown with the nineteenth century, and several firms of manufacturing chemists had been limited rather early. But drug retailing had remained a business of single shops, qualified dispensers, high prices and long credits. That some of this individualised organisation should survive was to be desired. For the growing mass of drugs which were not compounded to prescription, but standardised and sold by name, it was superfluous. Boots began as the cash chemists, selling below old-fashioned chemists' prices. Their shops were pushing out from headquarters at Nottingham

[1] Redfern, P., *The Consumer's Place in Society* (1920), p. 41.

[2] A and F. Pears.

during the 'eighties. In 1888 had been registered the private manufacturing company which was to supply the shops, Boots Pure Drug Company. In 1892, the shops having already spread some way, preceded by the announcement that "Boots is coming", the distributive company was registered in its turn. Nine years later, for the convenience of its widespread operations, it had been split up into four, beginning with Boots Western of 1897, and ending with Boots Southern of 1901, a section which included the Boots shops of the South and what had been a rival concern, Day's Metropolitan Drug Company and Day's Southern Drug Company. Control lay with the parent Pure Drug Company of Nottingham, which held—for example—all the capital of the Southern. By this time the actual shops had got beyond drugs. They were assuming their later character of stores, with lending libraries and other adjuncts. Like all multiple shops, and like the co-operative movement, they were hastening the replacement of the shopkeeper type in society by the manager type.[1]

The years of the South African War (October 1899—March 1902) encouraged that slackening of company promotion which must, in any event, have followed the fierce activity of 1896–9.[2] But the slackening was delayed, in spite of war demands for capital, by an Act of Parliament of 1900—63 and 64 Vict. c. 48: *An Act to amend the Companies Acts*. Some amendment of the law might have been expected after Hooley's years. By this Act it was made stricter towards both promoters and directors. The issue of prospectuses, the allotment of shares, the starting of business, the creation of mortgages on company property, were all more narrowly regulated. Though payments for underwriting were legalised, they were so hedged about that the underwriter's work became more onerous.[3] A year earlier, the company registration duty had been raised. These new and heavy liabilities on company makers and managers increased the difficulty of promotion, especially when it involved a public appeal. Very naturally, promoters hurried to put jobs through

[1] The sources of this paragraph are the *Stock Exchange Year Book*, the financial press, and the author's memory. Information about the position and policy of the central Pure Drug Company for this period is not accessible; only the external facts are known.

[2] Diagram, p. 222 above.

[3] *Report of the Company Law Amendment Committee*, 1906 (XCVII. 199), p. 5.

before the new law came into force with the new century, on January 1, 1901.[1] Hence the 4859 new limited companies of 1900, with their nominal share capital of over £221,000,000. Next year the registrations fell by nearly a third; and by 1904, though the number had recovered a little, the amount of capital nominally created had shrunk to £92,000,000. It rose above £200,000,000 only once again during the next decade,[2] whereas for the two years 1896–7 it had averaged £300,000,000. For this the law was only in part responsible. The activity of the late 'nineties left less to do—in limitation, expansion, amalgamation. That activity had come at the end of a period of more than two years of a 2 per cent. Bank rate. During the years 1904–14 there was never 2 per cent. and rarely 2½. After an eight months' spell of 2½ per cent. in 1908–9, the number of flotations leapt up at once.[3]

The number of flotations; but not the size of the average company floated. In 1896, the year in which the aggregate nominal capital of new companies was at its maximum, the average per company was £65,000. For 1909–10 it was only £26,500. This decline in the average size of projects told in time on the average amount of paid-up capital in those companies which really came into being and endured. In 1885 the figure for such companies had been £54,000. In 1896 it was still £54,000. In 1906 it was £49,000. By 1914 it was just under £40,000.[4] A curve of the companies in existence multiplied by their effective size would be as smooth as the curve of their mere numbers, but not so steep.

This apparent paradox of declining size is to be explained by the spread of limitation to enterprises of smaller and smaller type, which in the nineteenth century would have remained ordinary partnerships, as well as by the new, and for the most part desirable, obstacles put in the way of careless public flotation by the law of 1900. Promoters found that the company "in common parlance"[5] private could be made to serve their turn. Even in 1890, about a half of the companies actually formed had made no appeal to the public.[6] In 1906, some of the greatest businesses in the country were still private companies; and this

[1] *Ibid.*

[2] In 1910, £213,000,000.

[3] Compare the diagrams on p. 17 and p. 222 above.

[4] The Table in *Factors in Industrial and Commercial Efficiency*, 1927, p. 125 gives some of these figures.

[5] *Report* of 1906, p. 17.

[6] Above, p. 205.

mode of association—the "readiest and safest"[1]—was much used for the essential work of putting inventions on the market and starting new business ventures. At length, in 1907, it was recognised and defined by § 37 of the Companies Act of that year (7 Edw. VII, c. 50) which came into force on July 1, 1908.[2] By the end of the year 18,554 companies in Great Britain were registered as legally private.[3] These were in part new formations and in part existing companies whose articles of association already agreed with the new legal definition.[4] After that, thousands of companies nominally public, but in essence private, changed their articles in order to comply with the law; and the private company became the normal organisation for businesses of moderate size which wished to gain the advantage of limited liability. Of the 7321 new limited companies registered in the United Kingdom in 1913 no less than 6328 were private; and of all companies on the Registrar's list for 1914 three-quarters were private. Nearly all the curiosities were now in that class—the American Cockroach Company of Paris and the Tocsin Syndicate, the Universal Ox Yoke Syndicate and Zalo Foods.[5]

While small companies multiplied big ones grew bigger and public limitations and amalgamations did not cease. But there was not again any general amalgamation movement like that of the late 'nineties. In the early years of the new century, the industrial amalgamations were learning their business, and some of them were correcting their mistakes. There had been added to them as a result of that American Invasion, whose name, though it contained a truth, became a cant phrase in 1900 and 1901, the Imperial Tobacco Company and its half-breed child the British-American Tobacco Company.[6] In 1900 and 1901

[1] *Report* of 1906, p. 17. And see p. 205, n. 2 above.

[2] There was a great consolidating Companies Act in the following year, 8 Edw. VII, c. 69. See *Report of Joint S.C. of Lords and Commons on the Companies Consolidation Bill*, 1908 (VII. 1).

[3] *Factors in Ind. and Comm. Efficiency*, p. 126.

[4] A private company henceforward was one which by its articles (*a*) restricts the right to transfer its shares; and (*b*) limits the number of its members...to fifty; and (*c*) prohibits any invitation to the public to subscribe for any shares or debentures....

[5] *Ann. Rep. of the Board of Trade on Companies*, 1914 (LXXIX. 5). A short new Companies Act had been made necessary in 1913 (3 and 4 Geo. V, c. 25) because of the decision in *Park* v. *Royalties Syndicate Ltd.* that a company was private if it had the above restrictions in its articles even though it broke them.

[6] Above, p. 45.

John B. Duke's American Tobacco Company and its allies had set out to conquer the world. The United States Steel Corporation, the Great Billion Dollar Trust, set out also, but with not nearly such good prospects.[1] To meet John B. Duke, a dangerous opponent, nearly all the exceedingly well-known names of the British tobacco world came together into the Imperial in 1901—Wills and Player and Mitchell and Hignett and Butler and Smith of the Glasgow Mixture, with others. Next year Ogden and Churchman and some more joined. There was "no longer any serious competitor".[2] Appreciating the strength of this organisation, and the hold that its brands had on the British tobacco smoker, the Americans came to terms and left the British market in peace; the Imperial left the American market. The British-American of 1902 took over the export business, to all places except the United Kingdom and the United States, of the Imperial and the American and of the American's associates, the Continental Tobacco Company, the American Cigar Company, and the Consolidated Tobacco Company, all of New Jersey. Duke was in the British-American chair, and the board had its Hignetts, Ogdens and Churchmans.

With their assured markets and immense power, the Imperial and the British-American were thoroughly successful. By 1914 the Imperial had an authorised capital of £18,000,000; the British-American a capital of £14,500,000; and even the deferred ordinary shares of the Imperial stood at a premium of nearly 100 per cent. It was the nearest thing in Britain to a true monopoly.

In the heavy industries, and especially among the armament firms, the process of joint-stock integration went on during and after the South African War. After Vickers had joined Beardmores of the Clyde (1902) and Cammells Lairds of Birkenhead (1903) there was a pause, during the slack trade of 1904–5. Motion was resumed with the activity of 1906–7, and continued when cheap money made the raising of fresh capital easy in 1908–9. In 1907, John Brown and Co., already shipbuilders at Clydebank, took over part of the capital of Harland and Wolff of Belfast. They added to their raw material resources some iron

[1] *Economist*, Oct. 11, 1902; "Our Foreign Trade." And see the *Comm. Hist.* of 1901, p. 1.

[2] *Economist*, Dec. 12, 1902: "Is the Trust System a Restraint on Trade?"

land and a couple of blast furnaces in North Lincolnshire. They already had iron-ore interests in Spain. In 1909 they made a further important colliery purchase[1] and bought a half interest in the Coventry Ordnance Works. That same year, Cammells organised the Workington Iron and Steel Company, with a capital of £2,200,000, to amalgamate their Cumberland properties with three other iron companies of those parts. After that the great armament firms, now fairly complete and set, surrounded by dependent projectile, gun-mounting and ammunition companies, and busy with the affairs of a world drawing through armament towards war, made only minor additions or acquisitions, as when Vickers took all the shares of Electric and Ordnance Accessories Ltd.[2]

Outside the circle of the armaments firms, the chief events in the heavy industries during the early years of the century were the creation of Baldwins Ltd. and the amalgamation of Nettlefolds, the screw firm, with Guest, Keen and Co. Both happened in 1902. Baldwins was an association of hard-ware and galvanised-sheet-making firms from the Black Country and Monmouthshire with colliery, iron-mine and blast-furnace-owning firms in Glamorgan. All its chief constituents were already limited. As heavy combinations went, the new company which absorbed them was small, with a capital of barely £1,000,000. Guest, Keen and Nettlefold, on the other hand, was bigger than Browns or Cammell Lairds, and not far behind Armstrong-Whitworth or even Vickers. In 1900, two ancient Dowlais and Cardiff firms, Guests and the Dowlais Iron Company, had joined the Patent Nut and Bolt Company of Birmingham, West Bromwich and Cwm Bran in Monmouth, to form Guest, Keen and Co.[3] The Bolt Company had collieries and blast-furnaces and made many kinds of railway material. The Dowlais Companies also had collieries and interests in Spanish ore-mines. Nettlefolds made and sold steel, and some of their screws were bolts. So there was competition at several points. Hence the amalgamation of 1902. It was followed by the absorption of another famous old coal, iron and steel firm, Crawshays

[1] Most of the capital of the Dalton Main Colliery.

[2] There is a full tabular statement of the company-grouping which enabled John Brown and Co. in 1913 to turn out complete warships in Carter, *The Tendency towards Industrial Combination*, p. 81. And see Macrosty, *Trust Movement*, ch. II.

[3] The Patent Nut and Bolt was one of the oldest iron-working joint-stock companies, dating from the 'fifties.

of Merthyr; after which the capital of the absorbing company stood at upwards of £4,000,000.[1]

These various amalgamations had been made at all points on the trade curve—in 1902 when money was not very cheap and employment was getting worse; in the eager national and international activity of 1907; and in the dead months of cheap money and much unemployment in 1909. Forces were at work below, stronger than those which whipped the surface into ripples. And during the final spell of good trade, in 1910–13, when unemployment was almost negligible, money not cheap because it was in such demand, and capital pouring abroad, amalgamation projects naturally revived with the rest. In the South Wales coal trade, D. A. Thomas (Lord Rhondda) had been working for years, first towards a *Kartell* of steam-coal-owners with assigned quotas for the various firms and, failing the necessary agreement, then towards amalgamations—always towards rationalisation of some kind. Strongly established in the Cambrian Collieries, with interests spread wide over the coal valleys of Glamorganshire, he turned the Cambrian into the Consolidated Cambrian early in 1913 by the absorption of three other important colliery companies. The authorised capital was £2,000,000.[2]

A year earlier, the last of a series of attempts to consolidate iron-working and steel-making in Scotland, in the face of English and foreign competition, had produced the Scottish Iron and Steel Company. It was "to acquire as from 1 Jan. 1912 the businesses of thirteen malleable iron and steel manufacturing companies and firms".[3] The very word 'firms', and the relatively small capital of the new company (£750,000 and £300,000 in debentures), indicate the situation. An industry rather backward in organisation as compared, for example, with the North-

[1] Macrosty, pp. 37–53.

[2] For the *Kartell* plan see Thomas, D. A., *Some Notes on the Present Situation of the Coal Trade...with a Plan for the Prevention of Undue Competition and for maintaining Prices at a Remunerative Level* (1896). There is a general account of the position up to 1913 in Carter, *The Tendency towards Industrial Combination*, p. 288. Cp. Jevons, H. S., *The British Coal Trade*, p. 322, and Neuman, C., *The Economic Organisation of the British Coal Industry* (1934), pp. 145 *sqq*.

[3] *Stock Exchange Year Book*. Ten years earlier an attempt to secure the price-controlling advantages of combination by means of a Scottish steel-makers *Kartell* had collapsed: "A combine that failed", *Economist*, April 25, 1903. The arrangement was made in 1902. Early in 1903 it no longer functioned. For previous attempts, going back to 1885, see Macrosty, pp. 66–72, and the files of the *Iron and Coal Trades Review*.

East Coast or with the Ruhr, and for the prosecution of which Scotland had lost some of the geographical and geological advantages which she had once possessed, was trying to strengthen itself by the recognised method of amalgamation. The efficiency of that method in this instance had not time to be tested thoroughly before 1914 deranged the whole environment of the metallurgical industries.

Somewhat earlier again, in 1911, an attempt had been made to reapply the principles of joint-stock amalgamation and price control on a heavy field where they had not so far worked well—that of cement. Associated Portland Cement, the Thames and Medway amalgamation, had paid no dividend on its ordinary shares since its foundation in 1900.[1] True, the ordinary shares were less than a quarter of its total capital; for it was loaded with first and second debentures. The situation called for treatment. In 1910–11 the company was presided over by a financial chairman not bred in cement.[2] Now he also took the chair of a new company, the British—authorised capital £2,800,000—formed to amalgamate a number of firms which had worked hitherto in competition with the Associated. There was not only a common chairman: the Associated had "a very considerable interest" in the British.[3] The establishment of these cross relations no doubt explains in part the rise of the ordinary shares of the Associated above "rubbish prices" for the first time, in 1910, and the payment of its first ordinary dividend in 1913. Help came also from the slowly growing use of reinforced concrete. One of the troubles of the industry had been a demand which did not widen so fast as had been hoped at the time of the first amalgamation, and which in dull years, such as 1908–9, was liable to contract. Now a new prospect was opening out on the demand side.[4]

In the textiles there was no important development in joint-stock organisation after the remodelling of the Calico Printers in 1902, except the taking over of the wreckage of the Yorkshire Woolcombers' Association by a salvaging company, called Woolcombers Limited, in 1904. The combines learnt, or prac-

[1] Above, p. 234. [2] Lord St David's.

[3] *Stock Exchange Year Book.*

[4] Notes on the Company, *Economist*, Sept. 18, 1909, where it is called "this unsuccessful combine" and demand is discussed; and Sept. 27, 1913, where the recovery from "rubbish prices" is described.

tised, their business; sometimes they brought in fresh firms, or groups of firms. From time to time, but rarely, other textile firms were limited. In Lancashire, new joint-stock spinning-mills, of the brood of the 'Oldham Limiteds', were hatched regularly when trade was good;[1] but apart from cotton spinning, "the proportion of privately owned firms to public companies in the textile trades" was "probably higher than in any other large group of trades".[2] The great joint-stock concerns and efficiency combinations—Coats, Manningham Mills, and the like—expanded and grew in strength. To them was added, in the twentieth century, the firm which had known how to blend an inherited experience of the pure silk manufacture with an appreciation of the future of artificial silk, Courtaulds.[3] First appearing before the public under the personal description of Samuel Courtauld and Co. in 1904, it depersonalised itself a little in 1913 into Courtaulds Ltd. makers of "crape and dress fabrics and artificial silk yarns", with an authorised capital of £2,500,000. As the love of silk, or what looks like it, seems stronger than death, the years of death were to do its prospects no kind of harm.

Courtauld's £2,500,000, and the capitals of some of the textile and steel combines, appeared modest beside the always expanding capital of the most expansive company of the early twentieth century—Lever Brothers.[4] Levers habitually gave itself financial elbow-room. In 1901, two years after it had taken over Brookes of the Monkey Brand, its authorised capital was £4,000,000; its issued capital was £1,985,000; and of this only £1,077,000 was paid up. It had something of a set-back, a rebuff at least, in 1906, when it made a working arrangement with ten other soap-makers. Soap prices were to be raised to the retailing grocer. The consumer's bar of soap was to be lightened. Money spent on competitive newspaper advertising was, very properly, to be saved. But these three proposals raised a consolidated opposition too strong even for Lever and his *Kartell.* Besides, its members controlled not more than two-thirds of the trade; and there were potential competitors who could easily

[1] Vol. II. 140 *sqq.* Chapman, S. J., *The Lancashire Cotton Industry* (1904), pp. 171 *sqq.*

[2] *Report* [*on*]...*the Textile Trades after the War* (1918), p. 113.

[3] Above, p. 180. Chapman, S. J. and Ashton, T., "Sizes of businesses mainly in the textile industries", *S. J.* 1914.

[4] Above, p. 265.

come into it. So the working arrangement was dropped, after a three weeks' trial.[1]

Without neglecting opportunities for less public and less provocative arrangements, Levers then reverted to absorption. Between 1907 and 1913 they bought up the Vinolia Company; Hudsons of the 'Matchless Cleanser'; the soap-making department of United Alkali; and some others. During the slack trade of 1908–9, their progress was "really wonderful";[2] advertisement had been resumed and people would wash. In 1911 they organised a subsidiary for the working of palm forests in the Congo. Every few years the authorised capital was raised, finally by a £10,000,000 leap in 1913 to £30,000,000. Following their usual method, they were working in 1913 on less than a third of that figure, issued and paid up; but they had not then made use of any of the latest authorisation. It was twenty-three years since the firm had first been registered as a private company.[3]

Levers, like many of the greater industrial companies, had become international. Coats were everywhere. Armstrongs had a yard of their own at Pozzuoli and, from 1904, a share in the Ansaldo works at Genoa. These are only two prominent samples from the limited-company age of an arrangement well known before it. Wilkinson, the pioneering ironmaster of the eighteenth century, had works in France, and so had Holdens the machine woolcombers of the mid-nineteenth century. For a company to be domiciled financially in England but to have all its main activities elsewhere, from making a railway to working a tin-mine or a plantation, was a very old and familiar story. Had it not been, the export of British capital would have been very much less. But there was a definite increase in international company activity of all kinds from about the time of the great American economic expansion around the turn of the century. Oil had much to do with it; for the transport, storage and distribution of oil—unlike that of coal—is a business which requires huge capitals, and in which the advantages and the gains of unified control by those who manage the refining and perhaps also the wells, are at a maximum. John D. Rockefeller had been teaching the world some of these things since the 'eighties.

[1] Largely owing to the "disgraceful newspaper attacks", whose motive needs no explanation, *Economist*, Feb. 26, 1910, a retrospective reference; Macrosty, pp. 203 *sqq*, an excellent account written at the time of the episode.

[2] *Economist*, as above.

[3] Above, p. 205.

Ocean transport however was not his affair; and in the 'eighties the ocean transport of oil was only just beginning to take its modern form. It was in 1886 that Armstrongs launched a vessel with tanks formed by the hull, which was "the direct forerunner of the present oil tanker";[1] and it was another ten years or so before companies began to own regular tanker fleets. Among those which did, between 1896 and 1902, were the Anglo-American Oil Company, closely associated with the Standard Oil, and the Shell Transport and Trading Company of 1897, an amalgamation of firms engaged in the transport, storage and sale of oil—illuminating oil it then was—in the Eastern Seas.[2] The Shell early acquired oil concessions in Dutch Borneo, and was a rival of the Royal Dutch Company, which also produced and distributed in the East. As the Shell also shipped Russian oil from the Black Sea, and Texas oil from the Caribbean, it was in touch, which for an oil company meant in conflict, with all the great powers in the world of oil.[3] There was much British and French capital in the Russian oil-fields, and firms originally only producers there had become refiners and exporters.[4]

By 1902, after a long spell of fighting trade—"a war of prices extending over a period of almost ten years"[5]—a treaty was signed between the Shell, the Royal Dutch, and the Paris house of Rothschild representing Caucasian interests, which led in 1903 to the joint establishment by these three groups of the Asiatic Petroleum Company, to carry out the marketing arrangements of the treaty. Four years later, Royal Dutch and the Shell came even closer together, and the Royal Dutch got "practical control of the business".[6] The old companies remained: two new ones were created; and a period of complex arrangements and rearrangements, share exchanges and holding companies set in. Essentially, a small powerful Anglo-Dutch group domiciled in England had acquired influence over a great part of the oil-using world—influence which was strongest in the

[1] Hardy, A. C., *Bulk Cargoes* (1926), p. 36.

[2] Hardy, A. C., *Oil Ships and Sea Transport* (1931), p. 37 and *passim*. The Shell Company had steam tankers in 1897; but the Anglo-American was still ordering sailing 'oilers' in 1902, and did not begin to sell them till 1911.

[3] See the speech of Sir Marcus Samuel at the 1903 meeting of the Company, *Economist*, Dec. 26, 1903.

[4] Such as the Russian Petroleum and Liquid Fuel Company and the Baku Russian Petroleum Company.

[5] Sir Marcus Samuel, as above.

[6] From the account of the Shell Company in *Stock Exchange Year Book*, 1914.

Near and Far East, though by no means limited to those quarters.

In 1901 an accident had brought Weetman Pearson, last in succession of the great nineteenth-century English contractors, into touch with the oil-fields of Mexico, where his firm was building a railway. It also brought him into conflict with an American Company which had monopolised the retailing of oil in Mexico for thirty years. There was a ten years' fight with the gloves off and, it is said, much hitting below the belt. In order to win, Pearson found it necessary to produce, refine, and distribute oil himself. He bore the pioneering costs: his Mexican Eagle Oil Company only came before the public in 1910. The Eagle Oil Transport, and the Anglo-Mexican Petroleum for distribution, followed in 1912. Next year he was pressing his enterprise on the Admiralty, asking £5,000,000 for it; and the Admiralty was refusing.[1] Considerations of price apart, there were serious strategical and more serious political objections to a Mexican oil base for the British Navy. And a safer alternative base, much more attractive politically, was in sight.

After the long negotiations and the formation of preliminary companies usual when a concession is being sought from a foreign, and in this case an oriental, power, the Anglo-Persian Oil Company had been launched in 1909. By an audacious Admiralty decision, the Government of England became a shareholder in the Company under 4 & 5 Geo. V, c. 37, the *Anglo-Persian Oil Company (Acquisition of Capital) Act* of 1914.[2] The Admiralty got its oil base far from the naval base of any great power, and also some control of oil prices. It was only the second or third time that the British Crown had acquired shares in a joint-stock company since Queen Elizabeth put money into Drake's privateering voyages and other enterprises of her subjects, or King Charles I put money into a trading venture to the China Seas.[3] Appropriately enough, world-wide oil power, embodied in world-wide companies, came into intimate contact with an imperial government.

[1] Spender, J. A., *Weetman Pearson, First Viscount Cowdray* (1930), pp. 149–204; Hendrick, B. J., *The Life and Letters of Walter H. Page*, I. 175 *sqq.*; Halévy, E., *Hist. du peuple anglais, Epilogue* (1932), II. 583.

[2] Churchill, Winston S., *The World Crisis*, I. 132–4, 172 (1923); Halévy, as above.

[3] For Queen Elizabeth, Scott, W. R., *Joint-Stock Companies to 1720*, I. 30, 67, 70, 74 *sqq.*; for Charles I, Morse, H. B., *The East India Company trading to China*, I. 15.

Besides the precedent of Disraeli's purchase of shares in the Suez Canal, there was a more recent half-precedent. When the International Mercantile Marine Company of New Jersey in 1902 was buying up British and American shipping lines[1]—all by that time joint-stock companies—the announcement made in April of the coming transfer of the White Star to American control, though not to the American flag, alarmed both the public and the Government. It was known that the Cunard Line was also being approached; though it may not have been known at the time that an offer 80 per cent. above the market value of their shares had been made to them. The Government determined to stop the sale; and the result was a famous loan of £2,600,000 to the Cunard, for the building of two fast mail ships, and the promise of a subsidy of £150,000 a year. This subsidy was additional to the ordinary mail subsidies, and was given in return for promises by the company which safeguarded its British character, secured British subjects against excessive freight rates or unfavourable preferences, and put the whole Cunard fleet at the disposal of the State in an emergency.[2] Thus the glare of a war concluded, and another glare of war on the horizon, made it hard to see the line where companies ended and the State began.

International companies which handled essential foodstuffs had not yet attracted the public attention of Government, probably because most of the food-handling trades—above all the grain trade—had been markedly individualistic down to the end of the nineteenth century. But, when food had to be processed, there was an obvious field for operations on a great scale, as the Chicago meat-packing houses had shown. The development of cold storage, and the emancipation of the British meat market from the dominant influence of the United States, since the 'eighties, had coincided with the rise of powerful British meat-handling companies, of which the Union Cold Storage may be taken as representative.[3] Founded in 1897, with

[1] Above, p. 44.

[2] O'Hagan, *Leaves*, I. 386, says he was "asked to endeavour to purchase the Cunard" at the price quoted. He failed and found out later that the Government had beaten him. The rest of the story is told, among other places, in Douglas, O., *Ocean Trade and Shipping* (1914), pp. 57 *sqq.* and in Macrosty, *op. cit.* p. 307. As the capital of the Company was increased by £20, the new share being assigned to the Government, this may perhaps be regarded as a full, not merely as a half, precedent for government shareholding. The transaction was given legal force by the Cunard Agreement Act of 1904 (4 Ed. VII, c. 22).

[3] Cp. p. 186 above and vol. II. 90.

a quite modest capital, as the Union Cold Storage of Liverpool, to acquire the business of Vestey Bros., by 1903 it had dropped Liverpool from its title. Absorptions and extensions in 1906, 1911 and 1913, had left it in 1914 with an authorised capital of £1,600,000 and with cold-storage establishments, or cold-storage plans, which ranged from the Argentine, its home ground, to Astrakhan and Hankow.[1]

In only one type of business besides brewing can the progress of joint-stock organisation be traced with absolute accuracy—and to a finish. It is the historically allied business of banking. Here the State had given early encouragement to the joint stock; so much so that, within a few years of the codification of limited liability law in 1862, far-sighted people had been inclined to think that the amalgamation of all existing private banks with powerful joint-stock banks had become "a mere question of time".[2] The forecast was reasonable, for when it was made private banks had long been extinct in Scotland;[3] and in the forty years since joint-stock banks had been legalised in England and Wales they had absorbed 129 private banks.[4] As it happened, in the next twenty years (1865–85), the rate of absorption slackened to an average of only two and a quarter a year; and in the two years 1885–6 only one private bank was swallowed by a joint-stock bank. But all the while private had been joining private and joint-stock joint-stock. Amalgamations of all sorts for the twenty years to 1885 had averaged nearly five a year. Yet the banking system of England and Wales, in the middle 'eighties, still contained about 120 distinct joint-stock banks, and about 250 private banks of different kinds, of which between 80 and 90 held note issuing rights under Peel's banking legislation.

These 370 or so separate firms had all told between 2500 and 2700 bank offices, including the head offices and the smallest agencies, in 1886–7.[5] Two of them had more than 150 branches,

[1] The authorised capital of 1897 was £100,000. The cold-storage works at Hankow were bought with the International Export Company; those at Astrakhan were still only a project in 1914. Facts from the *Stock Exchange Year Book.*

[2] Martin, F. (1865), p. 186 quoted in Sykes, J., *The Amalgamation Movement in British Banking*, 1825–1924 (1926), p. 32.

[3] Vol. I. 267; vol. II. 341.

[4] Statistics of absorptions are in Sykes, *op. cit.* App. I.

[5] I make the figure 2533 for 1887 (vol. II. 342 n. 1); Sykes makes it 2716 for 1886; the *Economist* gives lower figures, presumably by omitting the agencies. But as the number varied from month to month absolute accuracy is not important.

and seven had between 50 and 100. At the time these figures seemed high. Twenty-eight years later there were a round 7000 banking offices. There were 20 joint-stock banks each with more than 100 offices; and of these three had more than 500 each. The biggest, the London City and Midland, had more than 700. A dozen lesser strictly local joint-stock banks, working on the branch system, survived—and that, with the Bank of England, really completed the list of English joint-stock banks; although there were also eight or nine firms classed as joint-stock banks without branches. These last were a miscellaneous collection, ranging from Baring Bros., the firm created to salve the wreckage of 1890; through Coutts and Co. and Glyn, Mills Currie and Co., old-style private banks turned into unlimited companies; to a few weak or questionable concerns of no importance.[1]

The 250 private banks of the 'eighties, of which at least four-fifths had been ordinary banks of deposit, had dwindled to little more than a dozen. For the country as a whole, private deposit banking was extinct; and these few ancient and honourable remnants of the London private banking system were only waiting for that near euthanasia which was now certain. It came to nearly every one of them within the next ten years.

In Scotland there had been nothing of all this, except a growth in the number of bank offices slightly faster than the growth of the population which they served, and a very little amalgamation. Back in 1872, when England had only one bank office for every 12,800 people, Scotland had one for every 4137. She had one for every 4088 in 1901, and for every 3880 in 1911. England never quite got to that figure; but her assimilation to Scottish practice had provided an office for every 5150 of her population by 1914. As for the Scottish banks, there had been thirteen in 1864, all joint-stock, and ten in 1886. In 1914 there were nine. All that had happened had been the absorption by neighbours of two banks on the 1886 list, the two weakest—the Town and County, with £252,000 capital paid-up, and the Caledonian with £150,000. Besides, one institution of straw had come into existence. The ten effective banks of 1886 had averaged just under 100 branches each, the eight of 1914 averaged just under 150. They were broadly speaking a society of equals, whether tested by the number of branches, by paid-up capital, or by total assets; and they had worked in exceedingly

[1] Figures from the *Banker's Almanac*, the *Economist's* annual banking number, and Sykes.

close association for many years. "Happy is that banking system that hath no annals", their historian had written in 1902 of the previous eighteen years. He could have written in the same strain in 1914.[1]

To a Scottish eye, and it may be to the eye of history, England had merely been carrying a stage nearer completion an inevitable and wholesome development, which had been delayed down to the 'eighties by her incorrigible conservatism. If the development was inevitable however, and there are few absolute inevitables even in economic history, its precise date was not. For one thing, it was certainly affected by the Baring crisis, and there was nothing inevitable about that. Barings were not ordinary bankers, but there was no banking name better known. If they were rotten who was sound? G. J. Goschen, statesman and city man combined, told the public that the private banks were working on insufficient reserves.[2] As many of them still did not publish their accounts, it was open to their clients to believe the worst. There were no runs, no panic—the clients did not desert them; but the private bankers were losing faith in themselves. "The public criticism of all banking institutions has become much more intense", the President of their Institute said to them in 1891. The business "has greatly changed from its old, easy, comfortable character: the private banker has the feeling that his day is past. His great joint-stock neighbour overshadows and disturbs him...": "the desire created in the public mind for large reserves and published balance sheets will drive some to adopt the habits of joint-stock banks, and others with less courage into the haven of amalgamation."[3]

A great number seem to have lacked the courage. There were twenty-four amalgamations of private banks that year, either with one another or with joint-stock banks. So many have never been arranged in a single year before or since.

There were also three amalgamations of joint-stock with joint-stock; for evening was setting in for the small local bank,

[1] Kerr, A. W., *History of Banking in Scotland* (2nd ed. 1902), p. 321. For the statistics see the *Banker's Almanac*; the *Economist*, banking numbers; Sykes, *op. cit.* p. 113 (England and Wales); Jaffé, *Die Englischen Bankwesen* (Schmoller's *Forschungen*, 1904), p. 235. The Town and County Bank and the Caledonian were absorbed after 1902.

[2] Goschen, *Essays and Addresses*, p. 106. And cp. Jaffé, *op. cit.* pp. 44–5, 196.

[3] Thomas Salt, M.P., in *J. of the Inst. of Bankers*, Dec. 1891; quoted also in Sykes, *op. cit.* p. 51. Jaffé's "Von nun an war das Vertrauen des Publikums in die Privatbanken völlig geschwunden" (p. 192) is too Teutonic-emphatic.

whatever its organisation, and London banks, joint-stock or private, were being absorbed by the greater ambitions and more active creations of the provinces.[1] It was precisely in 1891 that the Birmingham and Midland Bank, which already covered with its branches a good deal more than the Midlands, took over the Central Bank of London, to become the London and Midland.[2] Seven years later it added the City Bank to its acquisitions, and the word City, after London, to its name. A year earlier, in 1897, its general management had been taken over by E. H. Holden, who more than any single man was responsible for the pace, and sometimes the recklessness, of banking competition and amalgamation in the next five and twenty years.

Lloyds, another bank from the Midlands, expansive and controlling many branches, was in London already: it had absorbed Bosanquet, Salt and Co. and Barnett, Hoares and Co., fine old London names, in 1884. Lloyds had only followed an example set as much as twenty years earlier by the National Provincial, when it sacrificed its rights of issue to secure a London office, and by the National Bank of Scotland. As all the important Scottish banks had London offices by 1883, the provincials had precedent enough.[3]

Apart from any lack of nerve among private bankers or greed of size among ambitious general managers, there were decisive economic arguments against the continuance of the small banking unit, when in commerce and industry the unit and its needs were expanding with the progress of joint-stock organisation. "We have had to refuse business which was too much for our limit", the chairman of one small bank said, in justifying an amalgamation to his shareholders in 1901.[4] It was a sufficient justification. The bank of the late nineteenth century needed size and a varied body of clients—agricultural and industrial; long period depositors and clients with chronic, but approved, overdrafts; people from various trades and occupations and places, not likely to be affected financially all in the same way at

[1] See Gregory, T. E., *The Westminster Bank through a Century* (1936), I. 235; Withers, H., *The National Provincial Bank*, 1833–1933 (1933), pp. 79–80; Crick, W. F. and Wadsworth, J. E., *A Hundred Years of Joint-Stock Banking* (1936), pp. 313 *sqq.*; *Lloyds Bank Limited, its History and Progress* (1914); and Sykes, *op. cit. passim.*

[2] So keen was the Midland to get into London, that it was the—much smaller—Central "that imposed conditions". Crick and Wadsworth, *op. cit.* p. 312.

[3] Vol. II. 243–4. The Scots did not absorb any London banks however.

[4] Chairman of the Bucks and Oxon Bank quoted in Sykes, *op. cit.* p. 59.

the same time. A Scot might have observed that sound banking had required these things long before and that Scottish banking had secured them.

In the eleven years from 1891 to 1902 there were a hundred and fourteen banking amalgamations, contemporary with the great amalgamations in industry. The banks had shown the way. Now they were in the fashion. London joint-stock institutions spread outwards to balance, as it were, the in-spreading of the provincial firms. These contended with one another for influence and territory; and no doubt considerations of mere prestige and the crude joy in size began to tell.

Meanwhile the most enterprising of the private bankers did both those things which Thomas Salt had anticipated in 1891; they "adopted the habits of joint-stock banks" and also entered "the haven of amalgamation". One comparatively small group of them took action that very year. Seven bankers of London, the South, and the South-West came together—remaining private—and proceeded at once to publish balance sheets.[1] But the outstanding episodes in the story are the creation of Barclays Bank, in 1896, and of the Union of London and Smiths, in 1902. Barclays gathered into itself in time nearly the whole honourable inheritance of a century of Quaker banking.[2] Its fifteen original constituent firms, all private, stretched along the Eastern side of England from Brighton, through the City, into East Anglia—where they were specially strong, on a foundation of Gurney banks—and up to Scarborough and Darlington, where they came into contact with pure nineteenth-century industrialism of which elsewhere they were rather short. But perhaps a wish to protect their native rural districts from invasion by those "octopus-like"[3] joint-stock concerns which had been bred amid industrialism carried more weight with the organisers of Barclays than any eagerness to profit by the financing of industry. Unlike their predecessors of 1891, they registered as a joint-stock company; and as most of their constituent banks had adopted the branch system, some of them long since,[4] they made a start with no less than 180 branches. The amalgamation had no doubt been helped by the long list of intermarriages among the Barclays,

[1] Sykes, *op. cit.* p. 51.

[2] Matthews, P. W. and Tuke, A. W., *A History of Barclays Bank* (1926).

[3] The term applied to the National Provincial by Phillips, M., *A History of Banks...in Northumberland, Durham and North Yorkshire* (1894), p. 117.

[4] Cp. vol. II. 341.

Bevans, Goslings, Gurneys and Tukes, whose names recur so often in the titles of the fifteen associates.

By 1902 several more sound Quaker names, and a number of local joint-stock banks, had come into Barclays. Their branches had risen to 311, a figure below only the 432 of the London City and Midland and the 392 of Lloyds, both of which had been expanding and amalgamating furiously.

The Union of London and Smiths was not so widespread at the start. It had only 53 branches. But its units were very strong. Messrs Smith, Payne and Smith of Lombard Street owned the site of the bankers' Clearing House next door.[1] The Union had started as an unlimited bank in 1839, but like others had re-registered as a limited company in 1882 after the catastrophe to the unlimited City of Glasgow Bank.[2] The Smith banks of Nottingham, Derby, Newark, Lincoln and Hull had a fine mixed agricultural, commercial and industrial sphere of influence. All these, with their 25 branches, the Union—hitherto "a purely London institution"[3]—now bought. "The initiative", a foreign observer noted, "which lay at first with the provincial banks" had passed in part to those of London. In the whole country, the process of amalgamation and 'limitation' had gone so far that he could speak in 1902–3 of the basis of the English banking system having been "completely changed".[4] There would be a fight, he said, among the big banks in the next few years and then some sort of equilibrium, or territorial division, between a few institutions of approximately equal strength as in Scotland.

He was right; and the fighting led to a good deal of rather wasteful duplication of facilities, when banks amalgamated whose areas overlapped one another, or when one of the great conquerors felt bound as a matter of prestige to open in Coaltown or Cottonborough, where there were plenty of banks already, merely because another had.[5]

It was only in the Cottonboroughs however—in Manchester and Liverpool—that there was any active and successful opposition. None of the banks which came to be known, in later years,

[1] See Easton, H. T., *The History of a Banking House*, Smith, Payne and Smiths (1903), and vol. I. 283; *National Monetary Commission* (U.S.A.); *Banking Interviews* (1910); interview with Sir Felix Schuster of the Union of London and Smiths. (The Union amalgamated with the National Provincial in 1918.)

[2] Vol. II. 383. [3] *Banking Interviews*, p. 35. [4] Jaffé, *op. cit.* p. 191.

[5] See *Report of the Treasury Committee on Bank Amalgamations*, 1918 (VI. 333), p. 3, for the extent of this competitive waste.

as the Big Five sprang from South Lancashire. Therefore they were outsiders. Worse; they were now all Londoners. They could not possibly comprehend cotton. (Yet they seemed to be learning wool and steel.) When, in 1904, two Lancashire joint-stock banks amalgamated, the directors assured their public that the control would be all local, that is knowledgeable. And when a third made arrangements to join Lloyds, in the same year, opposition was so fierce that after a time the plan had to be dropped. Six years later a similar scheme had a yet shorter life. The private bank in Lancashire was already extinct; but a group of specifically Lancastrian joint-stock banks with Yorkshire and other connections survived, five of which were very strong and well equipped with branches.[1] One of them had been the pioneer of branch banking in England.[2] Perhaps Lancashire was right; but there was something a little ominous in her thinking about banks to-day what England had thought yesterday.[3]

Lancashire opposition was due not only to fear of management from London, which knew not cotton, but also—and perhaps more—to fear of a management which might be too bureaucratic and too rigid, and to fear of a banking system which might become ultimately non-competitive in its terms of business as in Scotland. There, a disinterested English observer wrote, "the banks are few and stand together like a close corporation; they agree absolutely and arbitrarily...as to the rates they will allow to depositors, the rates at which they will advance or discount, and the terms and commissions for which they will do business for customers". He found this uniformity "almost incredible from the English point of view".[4] Lancashire wanted to have it both ways. Disliking the Scottish standardisation of the selling prices of banking facilities, she greatly liked Scottish bankers' readiness "to take into consideration the personal standing of the applicant rather than the stuff or paper which he brings to it as security for an advance".[5] This habit had survived in Scotland

[1] Among them Parrs, originally a Warrington private bank, turned into a limited company in 1865, joined the Westminster in 1918: Gregory, *The Westminster Bank*, II. 24 *sqq.*

[2] The Manchester and Liverpool District. See vol. I. 278–9; vol. II. 341.

[3] The Lancashire story is summarised in Sykes, *op. cit.* pp. 65–6. And see the files of the *Manchester Guardian.*

[4] Withers, Hartley, *The English Banking System* (*National Monetary Commission*), p. 49; and cp. Tait, Adam, of the Royal Bank of Scotland in *Banking Interviews*, p. 137.

[5] Withers on Scotland, *The English Banking System*, p. 43.

from the old days of personal advances against a formal bond; and it had prevailed also in North-English banking practice, and "particularly in Manchester",[1] in the form of the overdraft on personal security.

The amalgamation movement had not yet produced uniformity or a "close corporation", as the Englishman's "incredible" and the English banks' fights for business show. A few years earlier, a foreigner had been struck by the survival of local banking idiosyncrasies after amalgamation.[2] In 1909–10 local practices still varied "very much indeed".[3] But there was certainly a tendency for what might be called London practice to spread—no interest on balances of current account and advances only against carefully considered collateral security. "It has become much more the practice in the country to ask and to get security against advances", the chairman of the Union of London and Smiths said in 1909.[4] And, as main reasons for this, he gave not only the "more rigid rules" of the great banks, the thing Lancashire so much disliked, but "the conversion of... unlimited partnerships...into limited liability companies often with debentures out". "The position of the banker or any other creditor", he added, "becomes quite different." It was an expert summary of the new situation in banking and industry which the spread of the joint-stock limited company with debenture-issuing powers had brought about.

From their London head offices the great banks were extending their functions. Joint-stock banks had done some accepting business for many years, the Scots having led the way in this as in most other innovations.[5] The banks now did much more; for their "high standing...and their big reserve resource in the shape of their uncalled capital" made "their acceptances an exceedingly fine credit instrument".[6] Their power in this field of bill acceptance was further increased, somewhat anomalously, because by acting as bankers for the private accepting houses, with whom they competed, they helped to determine the amount of these competitors' business.

[1] Sir Felix Schuster in *Banking Interviews*, p. 43. Any curtailment of these regular overdrafts was apt to be resented by Manchester business men known to the author. Cp. vol. II. 350.

[2] Jaffé, *op. cit.* p. 41.

[3] Sir Felix Schuster, as above, p. 43.

[4] *Ibid.*

[5] Vol. II. 348.

[6] Withers, p. 40; and see vol. II. 352.

A strictly new function, that of dealing in foreign exchange, began with the opening of the foreign department of the London City and Midland in 1905. The London and County followed in 1907. In 1913 Lloyds went further and opened a branch in Paris.[1] Exchange dealings had been left hitherto to the finance houses and to the sixty or seventy London offices of foreign banks, from those of the Crédit Lyonnais and the Deutsche Bank downwards. Competition by the English joint-stock banks with the foreigners for a share of this business was an obvious, indeed an overdue, sign of vitality; but there was some head shaking over it among financial conservatives. The cobbler, it was suggested, should stick to his old English last.[2]

All the while, very slowly, the British joint-stock banking system was becoming more coherent. The action of the Governor of the Bank of England in calling the whole high financial world into council over the Baring crisis had pointed the way.[3] It could no longer be said, as it had been said in 1879, that in time of panic no one in Lombard Street "would fortify his neighbour with ready money or help him with information."[4] Late in the 'nineties, the problem of banking reserves, which had worried Bagehot twenty-five years before, again came to the front. Were these new giant banks—national institutions now—in a way to overshadow even The Bank; were they to rely for ever on a tenuous single reserve of cash and gold?[5] The response was slow but it came, though only, so far as is known, after the American crisis of 1907, when in sixty days America had drawn over £17,000,000 of gold from London and the Bank had put up its rate from 4½ to 7 per cent. within a fortnight.[6] By 1911 the chairman of one of the great banks was reminding his shareholders that in the previous year the Bank of England had held more gold than in any year since 1896. When he spoke, the holding had dropped by £2,000,000. So he added—"it ought to be known that all the large Banks have been greatly increasing

[1] Sykes, *op. cit.* p. 170; Crick and Wadsworth, *A Hundred Years of Joint-Stock Banking*, p. 338.

[2] Withers, p. 40.

[3] Above, p. 7; diagram, p. 17; and cp. Powell, E. T., *The evolution of the London Money Market* (1915), p. 637. King, W. T. C., *History of the London Discount Market* (1936), pp. 310 *sqq.*

[4] Ellis, A., *The rationale of market fluctuations*, quoted, vol. II. 345.

[5] See e.g. Pownall, G. H., "Bank Reserves", *E. J.* 1899.

[6] Above, p. 57.

their stock of gold...so that...we hold many millions of gold and notes in excess of till requirements, and in case of any great emergency these millions of gold held by the Joint-Stock Banks would be available in addition to the gold held by the Bank of England."[1] Most of the banks were too cautious to state the number of millions, but Edward Holden of the Midland Bank let it be known that there were eight in his tills and strong-rooms in 1914.[2]

A few years earlier, in December 1905, the Bank of England had taken an unusual step. When a drain of gold to the Continent was threatening in connection with a fall in the French exchange, the directors "approached the principal clearing bankers and asked them to co-operate...to take the surplus money off the market and place it on deposit with the Bank at a low rate of interest".[3] This they did and easy borrowing was checked. The Bank then put up its rate for advances, "and the effect was electrical". In January, 1906, the process was repeated. "The more the Bank co-operates with the leading bankers the better for everybody", the chairman who explained these measures added. Following up this act of co-operation, on July 21, 1911, the Governor of the Bank of England, speaking in the presence of the Chancellor of the Exchequer—who had just made his 'Agadir' speech—announced that arrangements had been completed for quarterly meetings of his directors with representatives of the Clearing Banks. He thought this would be very useful, though "it will probably only be on rare occasions that important matters will come up for discussion".[4] Three years later to a month, a number of important matters came up for discussion among bankers. It was well that their relations had become more intimate and the British banking systems more coherent.

By occupying nearly the whole field of banking, the joint stock had about completed its conquest of the economic territory

[1] The chairman of Barclays Bank, at the meeting held July 20, 1911 (*Report of the Meeting*).

[2] Crick and Wadsworth, *A Hundred Years of Joint-Stock Banking*, p. 442. The Bank of England, in the years 1910–14, carried from £30,000,000 to £40,000,000. In July, 1914, it had £38–9,000,000.

[3] Phillips, J. G., address to the shareholders of Lloyds Bank, Jan. 26, 1906, quoted in Powell, *op. cit.* pp. 651–2; cp. Sayers, R. S., *Bank of England Operations*, 1890–1913 (1936), p. 37, and p. 54 above.

[4] *The Times*, July 22; and cp. Churchill, Winston S., *The World Crisis*, I. 47.

necessary for the day-to-day working of British industry and commerce—except the land itself and those streets and other things which public authorities owned. The canals and the railways and many of the tramways; the docks and harbours—except in so far as they, like some of the tramways, were now public or semi-public property—much of the shipping that frequented them, and all the greatest shipping lines; the ocean cables and Marconi's new wireless stations; that very important group of gasworks, waterworks and electric-supply works which did not belong to the local authorities, and until 1911 the whole telephone system; with banking and insurance in every form, except the private underwriting at Lloyds; a good deal even of the social insurance with which the State had just begun to experiment[1]—all these essential capital goods and public services were owned or managed on the joint-stock and limited-liability pattern. Without it, or some system of universal state enterprise unthinkable under British eighteenth- and nineteenth-century conditions, the greater part of them could never have existed. It had been devised and developed that they might exist and grow; and it had served its purpose well.

Meanwhile this system which now dominated the whole background of day-to-day commercial and industrial activity had been applied more extensively every year to the units of that activity itself. Most of the greater industrial units, and very many of the smaller, were limited companies by 1914. The large mercantile firms, and in particular the export firms, the shippers, had more often retained the old partnership organisation. But the relative importance of the mere merchant was not what it had once been, partly because of the rise of the huge industrial companies and combines and of the multiple shops. The multiple shops went straight to the producer. Some producers, like Coats and Listers, went straight even to small shops; and in some trades or sections of trades production and distribution were regularly combined. For export even, Coats or Listers or Armstrongs or the Imperial Tobacco Company did not make much use of shippers; though the Fine Cotton Spinners and the Bradford Dyers did.

Precisely how far the British had become a nation of shareholders cannot be determined. If co-operative shareholders are included, as they well may be, small and specialised in type as

[1] By way of the approved societies some of which were joint-stock companies; p. 424 below.

their average holding was, the thing had gone far; since there were about 3,000,000 members of co-operative societies. There were probably some 900,000 distinct railway shareholdings, and perhaps 300,000 shareholdings in the banks.[1] Twelve years later, seven of the greatest industrial and commercial companies, all of which existed in 1914, had an aggregate of 385,500 shareholders. They ranged from the Imperial Tobacco, with 107,000; through Vickers, with 70,000; to the Cunard, with 14,000.[2] Between the co-operative and the true joint-stock shareholders there was not much overlap; although in the South Lancashire home country of both Co-ops and Oldham Limiteds there was no doubt a little. Among joint-stock shareholders there was abundance of overlap: the number of people who were Barclays Bank or Midland Railway shareholders and nothing else must have been negligible. Perhaps the number who were shareholders worth the name may not have been greater than the 1,000,000 or more of the Income Tax payers of 1913–14;[3] though the railway figures, in spite of the duplication which they contain —for many people held shares in both the Midland and the Great Western—suggest that the aggregate of those who held any shares whatsoever, or were beneficiaries from dividends in any way, may have been considerably greater. All is very speculative and uncertain.[4] The most that can be said with some confidence is that the shareholding group was smaller, probably much smaller, than the group of co-operative members.

Everyone noted, and most people deplored, the widening gap between the legal ownership of absentee shareholders and the effective control of industry by directors, managers, and other salaried persons. Occasionally the men of administrative genius who had built up great businesses, even great combines, were able to make their personalities felt throughout. That was of necessity exceptional. The giant business of the general limited liability age, like the railway company before it, normally developed a bureaucratic organisation; and if it were not to set in

[1] The figures suggested here are based on those collected in 1926–7 by the Committee on Industry and Trade, *Factors in Industrial and Commercial Efficiency* (1927), pp. 127 *sqq.* There were then 895,000 railway shareholdings and 275,000 holdings in the five greatest banks.

[2] *Factors*, p. 128.

[3] An estimate of 1,190,000 for the U.K. in 1913–14 was given in Parliament. Stamp, J. C., *British Incomes and Property*, p. 449. Some, unknown, deduction must be made for Ireland.

[4] Some shares were held abroad.

bureaucratic rigidity, it had to learn, from the example of the State or by a skilled avoidance of the State's blunders, how to recruit and train its managing staff. Some learnt and some failed to learn.

This was all so true, and is so obvious, that there is some risk of exaggerating in retrospect the economic and social significance of the shift over from private to joint-stock organisation during the half century since limited liability had been made perfectly accessible to all. The emergence and the persistence of the private company until it was at last recognised by the law in 1907, and its very widespread use after recognition, shows how well adapted it was to British business habits and conditions;[1] and in the private company the divorce between ownership and management, and the need for an impersonal and bureaucratic administration, though not entirely absent, were at their minima. In essentials the private company resembled closely the old private partnership, which had often used money lent by members or friends of the partners' families, not themselves connected with the management. To regularise and improve this type of organisation, legal reformers for nearly a hundred years had been praising the continental partnership *en commandite*, with its liability unlimited for the active partners, limited for the dormant;[2] and in 1907 it had at last found its way on to the Statute Book by the Limited Partnerships Act (7 Ed. VII, c. 24). But the private company, though only recognised legally in that same year, had long been in use. It was familiar. It had the advantages of the limited partnership for dormant shareholders, if any, and it attracted the central active shareholders, who meant to go on directing the business, by its limitation of liability for all. By the end of 1909 there were 24,000, and by the middle of 1914 some 50,000, private companies in the country.[3] If there were any body of limited partnerships worth mentioning, no one had troubled to publish statistics of them. The private company might, and often did, pass into a public company, should it expand beyond the resources of the original small, and at least potentially coherent and informed, body of shareholders. But in the 50,000 private companies of 1914 there were still possibilities of coherence, knowledge, com-

[1] Above, p. 205.

[2] Vol. II. 136–7.

[3] By April 30, 1914, 48,492: the number was growing at the rate of several thousands a year: *Factors in Industrial and Commercial Efficiency*, p. 125.

bination of ownership with management, and a management that was not impersonal. What their average paid-up capital was is not known; but as the average for all companies, including the public giants, had dropped, with the multiplication of the private type, to below £40,000, it may well have been less, and cannot possibly have been much greater, than the £21,700 of the average British co-operative society in that year.

CHAPTER V

COMMERCIAL AND INDUSTRIAL ORGANISATION

CHANGES in basic commercial or financial organisation, other than those which the spread of the joint stock and limited liability brought, were so slight between 1886 and 1914 that, in any general survey, many can be treated as imperceptible and ignored. By the 'eighties railway, cable, and steamship had done their main work of speeding up and elimination; telephones, more and better steamships, and the beginnings of wireless telegraphy merely extended that work. Future dealings in cotton and grain were well established. The sphere for such dealings did not widen greatly, and commodities such as timber and wool which had proved intractable to them so remained.[1] The concentration and the growing coherence of British banking had increased its efficiency, and with it the efficiency of that central ganglion of national economic life the London money market; but there had been few important modifications in the essence or working of either. Things were bigger; movements were quicker and more precise; but they were much the same things and the same sort of movements. It was a modest novelty for a joint-stock bank to do foreign exchange business. It was no novelty for that business to be done from London. Money, in the narrow sense, was unaltered. Englishmen said every now and then that they favoured £1 notes: no one introduced them: Scotsmen went on using them. The issue of bank-notes for England fell nearly all into the hands of the Bank. That was only what Peel had designed seventy years back[2] and it made no real difference to any one. More and more people had banking accounts; the Bank of England was little safer than most other banks had now become; and the English bank-note had never been much used for wage payment. No doubt the percentage of transactions settled in cash and the proportion of cash paid into the banks declined, but they were so low already, in active places, by the 'eighties that there was little room for a general declension. The mechanism of deposit banks with correspondents or head offices in London, by which surplus capital was sucked into the metropolitan money market, was no doubt

[1] Cp. vol. II. 297, 320. [2] Vol. I. 522.

made more effective by the great amalgamations in banking;[1] but it had seemed wonderfully effective already to Walter Bagehot when he wrote *Lombard Street* in 1873. Probably the most important change at the centre of things in London was the steadily increasing amount of money put on deposit there or claimable there by foreigners.[2] In the last years of peace, the deposits came to exceed the advances made on foreign account by the English banks, and in the end left a balance "used in advances to home trade—home customers"—a delicate situation should international trouble come.[3]

The Bank of England was certainly more conscious of its position and responsibilities as a bank of central reserve, and better able to fulfil them, than it had been in the 'seventies and early 'eighties.[4] This the Directors' action in 1890, 1906–7 and 1910 showed. The repeated reissues of *Lombard Street* had not been wasted. Free lending, but at high rates, in times of financial trouble—Bagehot's policy though not his invention—had become a working rule. The "enormous growth in the importance of the Treasury in the market",[5] especially after 1902 when the use of Treasury Bills was greatly extended, indirectly strengthened the Bank's control of credit; for whereas the old Treasury habit of borrowing from the Bank by Ways and Means put money on to the market, the issue of Treasury Bills—which the banks took up—put it into Treasury account at the Bank, from which it only leaked out slowly as the various disbursements were made. The Bank had also been developing the technique of open-market operations—borrowing the market's surplus funds, or drawing them in by selling securities—so as to increase its control over market rates and over the international movements of gold. From time to time it had given direct assistance to importers of gold, or in other ways guided its flow.[6] These facts and policies, combined with the greatly increased

[1] Which also led to further decline of the domestic bill of exchange. See vol. II. 336 and King, W. T. C., *History of the London Discount Market* (1936), p. 274.

[2] Cp. King, *op. cit.* p. 278.

[3] The quotation is from evidence on behalf of the Midland Bank given in 1929 (*Committee on Finance and Industry*, 1931, Cd. 3897, p. 42), but the facts were there in 1914.

[4] Largely due to the force and insight of William Lidderdale, Governor in 1890. See p. 8 above and King, *op. cit.* pp. 301 *sqq.*

[5] King, *op. cit.* p. 277. The Treasury Bill dates from 1877 and was created on Bagehot's advice.

[6] Sayers, R. S., *Bank of England Operations*, 1890–1914 (1936), *passim*.

gold stocks available in banks and treasuries abroad for attraction to London, when good rates offered there, help to explain England's easy passage through the international crisis of 1907. While banks put up their shutters and business stood still in America, just a touch of 7 per cent. was enough in London. And after that well-navigated passage, the leading joint-stock banks, as has been seen, recognised their duty to help in the maintenance of the British gold reserve. So the central mechanism of the money market ran more smoothly. Some useful additions and some gadgets had been added. But the principal working parts were the same.

About that time the banks were said to be taking "an increasingly large and important part in the creation of bills of exchange by placing their acceptances at the disposal of their customers". It was "a grievance...resented rather keenly" by the merchant bankers, the accepting houses.[1] But it was a grievance that had not been new in 1875;[2] and the merchant bankers were still powerful forty years later—very rich, very respectable; accepting trade bills, 'fine' and less fine, and finance bills of agreed-on amount; often even giving a blank credit to a client "well-known and financially strong";[3] acting as agents for foreign governments and issuing their bonds; dealing in foreign exchange; incidentally supplying the Bank of England with many of its directors and governors, as they always had.

There had been no great change in the position and work of the bill-brokers or discount houses. Only their sphere of action had been further curtailed by that steady decline in the use of home-trade bills which had been going on for many years, and by the competition of the telegraphic transfer with the bill, and of banks for the remaining bills in the foreign trade. The discount group after 1911 comprised three strong public joint-stock companies and the score or so of private firms who, with money borrowed from the banks or deposited by the public, bought bills either to hold until mature or to sell again.[4] Below them were the remnants of the mere bill-brokers, long distinguished as the running brokers, intermediaries who brought together buyers and sellers of bills and took a broker's commission.[5]

[1] Withers, H., *The English Banking System* (U.S.A. Monetary Commission, 1910), p. 39. [2] Vol. II. 348.

[3] *Committee on Finance and Industry*, p. 41: see Withers, *op. cit.* p. 57, for twenty years earlier.

[4] Vol. II. 355 n. 2: a much fuller account in King, *op. cit.* p. 262.

[5] Withers, *op. cit.* p. 62.

The "money brokers" of the mid-nineteenth century, intermediaries in the short money market, were as a class quite extinct. The name however was applied sometimes round about 1900 to a different group—substantial firms connected with the Stock Exchange who could borrow on good terms from the banks, and derived "much profit by lending...to smaller brokers".[1] They were middlemen, that is to say, not true brokers.

This financing of the Stock Exchange had occupied a greater part of the bankers' attention every year. That was inevitable, for growing bank resources and the vast growth of stock dealing accompanied the "gradual diminution in the number of bills seeking discount". "Nearly the whole of the 'professional' speculation" was carried on with bank money;[2] and the banks lay wide open to criticism in the speculative 'nineties. With Chartered Companies and gold-mines, breweries, rubber, industrial combinations and electric traction; in the days of Rhodes and Barnato and Yerkes, of Lawson and Hooley, the Exchange got bigger and bigger, busier and busier. Finally, it got too big and began to contract. The maximum was reached in 1905, when membership stood at 5567. At the time of the Commission of 1877 it had been only a little over 2000; and most of the growth had come since 1886.[3] In the year before the maximum was reached, during that spell of slack water for company promotion and speculative dealings which followed the Boer War, the Committee had arranged to close the doors a little, and at the same time give something to those already inside, by making a rule that a candidate for admission who had no previous connection with the Exchange must not merely pay a fee and find sureties but acquire a nomination from a member retiring, or recently retired, or from the representatives of one recently dead.[4] The nomination had a market value—and no doubt the average member of the House was critical of the restrictive policies of Trade Unions.

[1] Gellender, E. B., "The relation between banks and stock exchanges", *J. Inst. Bankers*, 1899, p. 462. For the older money brokers, see vol. II. 353–4.

[2] Cole, W. A., "The relation between banks and stock exchanges", *J. Inst. Bankers*, 1899, p. 409. And cp. Jackson, F. Huth, "The draft on London and tariff reform" *E. J.* 1904, for the bills.

[3] Armstrong, F. E., *The Book of the Stock Exchange* (1934), p. 39; and vol. II. 325.

[4] See the admirable account of the Exchange in ch. IV of Withers' *English Banking System*. There were certain privileged admissions of clerks allowed.

The new rule and the sluggish flow of the speculative tide during the next few years first stopped the growth in membership and then brought about a decline. The figure was down to 4855 by 1914.

During the years of maximum activity there had been a certain blurring of the old sharp line of division between the groups of brokers and jobbers in their jostling race for business.[1] Some brokers, instead of merely buying and selling for clients, began to specialise in particular classes of securities and to 'make prices' in them like jobbers. Other brokers bought from outside firms—South African and American firms in particular—instead of from the jobbers, when they could do so to their own advantage. Jobbers retaliated by doing business not through brokers but with outsiders direct, especially arbitrage business with Wall Street, or the similar 'shunting' business with members of the provincial exchanges. But the conservatism of the Exchange as a whole was against these innovations, and its rules were revised in 1908 so as to check both sorts of poaching, although "most of the leading firms", successful poachers it is to be assumed, were said to be in the minority.[2] Direct foreign arbitrage business either by brokers or jobbers was not interfered with, though a special permit to carry it on was instituted; but the new rules did what they could to preserve the inherited organisation and division of functions.

The number and weight of the provincial exchanges had increased considerably as was to be expected. Hence the importance of their relations with London. At the time of the Stock Exchange Commission of 1877 only Liverpool, Manchester and Glasgow had been significant;[3] though Edinburgh was as old as Glasgow and there were small groups of dealers in several other towns. Except Edinburgh, none of these exchanges of the second rank had so many as 30 members even in the early 'nineties, when Manchester had about 75, Glasgow about 140 and Liverpool about 160.[4] But, Liverpool leading, there had already been organised, in 1890, a Council of Associated [provincial] Stock Exchanges. Its aim was to harmonise their trading rules and practices, to give them weight as against London, and

[1] Cp. vol. II. 324.

[2] Withers, *op. cit.* p. 119. Cp. Armstrong, *op. cit.* pp. 139, 165–7.

[3] *R.C. on the London Stock Exchange*, 1878 (XIX. 265), p. 9.

[4] *Dic. Pol. Econ.* (1892–3) *s.v.* For the provincial exchanges generally, Armstrong, *op. cit.* ch. VIII, and the 1899 articles in the *J. Inst. Bankers* quoted above.

generally to take care of the interests of stock dealers and their clients. It had won prestige immediately by pressing for and securing, when London had held back, an important legal reform, the Forged Transfers Act of 1891 (54 and 55 Vict. c. 43). "The benefits resulting from" the Act, a contemporary wrote, "will always be associated with the provincial exchanges, and more especially with that of Liverpool."[1]

At Liverpool there had been plenty of business for years, English and American, with a specially active market in insurance shares. Glasgow had its ships and iron and Paisley thread; Manchester its railways, its Ship Canal and, from the later 'nineties, its textile combines. All three did a great deal of general investment business. With the cycle and rubber and motor developments, the Birmingham exchange came to the front. By 1914 it ranked, in numbers, above Edinburgh but still below Manchester. The others—Leeds, Sheffield, Bristol, Cardiff and so on; some fourteen in all—remained small, with an average membership of from 20 to 30.

There was however in all an active business in local shares, many of which were hardly known to Throgmorton Street, besides the general business for the transaction of which latterly there were often private wires from provincial exchanges to the offices of London jobbers. If a provincial broker could get what his client wanted on the home exchange naturally he got it; but as groups of jobbers who specialised in particular markets had never developed outside London, "the majority of the business collected by the Provinces"[2] flowed through to them, although, besides the professional arbitrage business, London found it convenient at times to buy or sell in the provinces for clients. Scales of commissions and dates of settlements there had been adjusted to the London practice, so that in essentials there was a single stock-dealing community for the whole country. But the London part of that community was four or five times the size of all the others put together.

Of stock-exchange customers there was probably no group so important as the Insurance Companies, whose business though unchanged in its essentials was becoming every year more necessary to the daily life and death of the people. This demand was naturally very conservative, concerned only with investment

[1] *Dic. Pol. Econ.* I. 770.

[2] Armstrong, *op. cit.* p. 138, describing the position as it still is.

from a point on the security scale marked by railway and the best industrial debentures upwards. They were both conservative and well conserved. An old company was sometimes absorbed, though not very often: fortunately for the country such a company was never wound up. There was a great increase in the number of companies prepared to do fire insurance business, from 66 in 1875 to 147 in 1913;[1] but in fact at the close "practically all the premiums received and losses paid were shared by 31 companies",[2] and the number carrying on successful fire business had not grown perceptibly since 1875–80. Of six with the largest fire insurance funds in 1913, the youngest—the Commercial Union—was more than fifty years old; no other was less than ninety; and the oldest—the Sun—was more than two hundred.[3] These cautious, experienced and very stable elders had not lost their vitality or their power to attract and handle fresh business. The new and experimental it was that died; though even among them mortality was remarkably low.

Having already by the 'eighties insured most things of importance exposed to risks of fire at home, the great companies now carried—and had long carried—very heavy overseas and foreign liabilities. Many of them had subsidiary companies abroad, chiefly in America. They stood up to their losses at the time of the San Francisco earthquake of 1906—that earthquake which it was correct to describe subsequently in San Francisco not as an earthquake but as a fire; and indeed there was a very great fire—paying with admirable punctuality and fortitude, though the strain on the younger companies was severe. The State Assurance of 1891, a relatively small Liverpool concern with the American connections usual in all Liverpool business, was specially hard hit; but it came through. Greater companies took the strain almost with ease. One chairman, it is true, said at the time that the "fire insurance business of the world had been shaken to its foundation";[4] but as he also declared that half his reserves were intact, although the losses of his company

[1] Walford, *The Insurance Cyclopaedia*, II. 515, and the *Stock Exchange Year Book*, 1914.

[2] Art. "Insurance", *Encyc. Brit.* 11th ed. 1910–11.

[3] There are *Annual Returns* from 1909 under the Assurance Companies Act (9 Ed. VII. c. 49) of that year. Those for 1913 are in *Parl. Papers*, 1914, LXXIV and LXXV.

[4] "British Fire Offices and the San Francisco Disaster", *Economist*, April 28, 1906. See also a note with the same title of April 21, and another of August 11.

approached £1,000,000, the foundations in fact stood. Reserves are meant for emergencies and an emergency so great was not likely to recur soon. Two or three other companies lost about as much as his, one considerably more. The total British losses were estimated within a week of the disaster at not less than £10,000,000. A year later more than £5,000,000 of claims had been settled and reported.[1] Four years later, when all had been dealt with, the preliminary estimate was confirmed: British (including some colonial) companies had paid out over £10,000,000 net.[2] Not one had failed, though many American companies had. This was the most noticeable event in the fire-insurance history of the time.

Marine insurance was set and standardised, and for the British mercantile marine all but universal, by the 'eighties.[3] Some more companies opened marine departments. The companies and the private underwriters at Lloyds did a growing amount of work for all marines on all seas; and the underwriters continued their experiments with the new sorts of non-marine insurance for which occasion was given by the cycle, the motor-car, by all the other risk-creators in nature and human society, and by the new and uncertainly spaced liabilities imposed upon individuals and groups by a more paternal and detailed body of legislation.

Although the bulk of the business, and all the best business both in fire and life insurance, was concentrated in the hands of a comparatively small group of companies, there were 240–50 insurance companies of all sorts existing in 1913, of which more than 50 had been registered since 1886.[4] Many of these were specialised. Specialisation had begun long before. The Huddersfield Mutual Plate Glass Insurance Society went back to 1854. The Employers Liability Assurance Corporation of London was founded in 1880 to deal with a new-made risk. But the years after 1886 were the most prolific in such experiments. There were founded, for example, the Iron Trade Employers Liability in 1898; the Liverpool Grain Contract Insurance in 1902; the National Live Stock in 1907; the United Scottish Herring Drifters in 1909; the Letters Patent Insurance in 1912. Yet, taking insurance as a whole, not specialisation but a growing

[1] "The effects of San Francisco", *Economist*, April 27, 1907.
[2] *Encyc. Brit.* as above.
[3] Vol. II. 328.
[4] *Stock Exchange Year Book*, 1914.

variety of activities was the mark of the representative company, new or old. The names of many of the new companies show that they realised from the start that, even if they took up some particular brand of insurance, they were not likely to be satisfied with it. Such are the Fine Art and General (1890), the Vulcan Boiler and General (1896), the Car and General (1906), the Printing Trades and General (1907). A representative new company is the British Law Fire of 1888 which twenty-five years later would insure its clients against fire, accident, sickness, burglary, glass breakage, workmen's compensation—the Workmen's Compensation Act of 1906 had greatly extended the classes of employers liable—and a few other things. Fresh insurable risks were always being realised or devised; usually experimented in first at Lloyds;[1] taken up next by young companies hunting for business; taken over later by older ones anxious not to lose it.

The great fire companies all did business of other sorts, though their range of activity varied. Of the 240–50 companies of every kind, about 100 did not even offer to carry fire risks. Forty-two of these were the specialised Life Insurance Companies, including the so-called Industrial Companies, whose 'industrial' business—they also did some so-called 'ordinary' business—was based on contributions from wage-earners collected weekly, and paid for the most part to provide for funeral expenses. At the head of the Industrial Companies stood the now gigantic Prudential. It did more than half of all the industrial business, carrying more than 19,000,000 policies with an average value of just over £10; and besides that a large 'ordinary' business among people who could not afford heavy insurances but did not need to pay out weekly. There were 900,000 of these on its books in 1913, with an average value of just over £100—the policies of small traders, clerks, and perhaps some substantial wage earners.[2]

Including those issued by the Industrial Companies, there were 3,036,000 'ordinary' policies in force in 1913, with an aggregate guaranteed value of £836,000,000 and an actual value considerably greater. There were some 1,100,000 income-tax payers in the United Kingdom at that time; so that, neglecting the small folk—upwards of 1,000,000—insured to the amount of about £100 each by the Industrial Companies, there were far

[1] Vol. II. 327.
[2] The *Annual Returns* and the *Encyc. Brit.* as above.

more individuals carrying life insurance policies of several hundred pounds than there were payers of income tax. However, the main significance of these remarkable figures is neither industrial nor commercial, but social.[1]

In the commercial and industrial spheres, the great expansion and diversification of insurance registers a growing desire for that maximum of security and peace of mind which a provision against well-calculated risks can give. A desire most rational, though its growth might perhaps be associated with a state of society in which risk and adventure have lost something of their charm. The English business man, a German critic may be imagined saying, was not *kampflustig* enough. Some such opinion was in fact often expressed in Germany. Yet however much a man enjoys battle there is no sense in going into it unprotected. The adoption of the insurance shield, of a whole series of insurance shields, in itself proves nothing. But it may still be true, probably is true, that the average attitude of British business about the turn of the century was rather too defensive. There was certainly some decline in the love of fighting for fighting's sake; a decline which showed itself in the rapid growth of trade associations of all sorts and in the adoption of new, more rational, and more restrictive policies by many of them. It was in an extended framework of association that many of the great joint-stock amalgamations, many of the recently registered private limited companies, and many of the still exceedingly numerous private partnerships and family businesses did their work in the last decade of the peace.

Contemporary inquiries reported in 1919 that "by far the greater part" of the trade associations 'appeared' to have come into existence "since the end of the nineteenth century"[2]—that is since the amalgamation movement of the late 'nineties had lost its first impetus. No doubt very many had; even if some which 'appeared' to have come so late into existence had in fact only come late into the light of day. Association was an alternative to amalgamation; it appealed to the lesser firms; and in the years of rather slack trade and hesitating company promotion

[1] The figures necessarily refer to the U.K. not to Britain only. See Bowley, A. L., *The Division of the Product of Industry* (1919), p. 47.

[2] *Report of Committee on Trusts* (1919, Cd. 9236), p. 2. And cp. p. 213 above. Piotrowski, R., *Cartels and Trusts* (1933), adds nothing of importance for this period.

which followed the South African War grandiose schemes of amalgamation were out of fashion. But the trade association to deal with organised labour; with legal, technical, and commercial problems common to a whole industry; even with the prices to be charged in that industry, was no new thing in 1900 or in 1886.[1] Very far from it. There had been in various industries a good deal of quiet price fixing without formal association all through the nineteenth century. 'Free and open competition' had never been perfectly attained, or even universally and sincerely desired. Some of the joint-stock amalgamations of the late 'nineties had developed out of formal associations, as has been seen. But before 1900, and even after 1914, there was a strong and ancient tradition of secrecy. At one of the inquests of the war period, when the secrets of so many business hearts were being revealed, the very free-spoken chairman of the Steel Sheet Makers Conference (of 1904) and of the Steel Nail Association preferred not to lay the written constitutions of these groups before the committee, "as that would be a departure from their established practice, which had been determined upon originally simply because in the past associations had always been looked on askance by the government".[2] And another experienced chairman, of groups dealing with wire in its various forms, who had mentioned incidentally that "the most generally known forms of association in this country" were price associations, explained that their unpopularity had led to their "being conducted in a sort of clandestine manner as if there was something that ought to be kept dark about them".[3] In the wire trades—and this is a very typical evolution—there had been what he called a 'political association' ever since 1884. Price associations had apparently developed from it in the early years of the new century; and at first they did not recruit anything like all the wire-making and wire-working firms.

For the most part, those associations which were concerned mainly with prices or the regulation of output were based rather on the commodity, or group of closely related commodities, than

[1] Cp. vol. II. 145 *sqq.* The R.C. on Labour of the 'nineties collected 70 sets of rules of such associations (1892, XXXVI. part 5, p. xxii).

[2] From the Papers of the Committee on Trusts (unpublished), upon which the 1919 *Report on Trusts* was based. The MSS. to which I was given access, are not catalogued and so cannot be specified. The two sources are quoted below as *Papers* and *Report.*

[3] *Papers.*

on the firm. The same firm might perhaps make wire, wire netting, and woven wire; but the associations were distinct. A firm with many activities might be connected with several associations, as Guest, Keen and Nettlefold said they were in 1918.[1] The North-East Coast Steel Plate Makers of 1897 were not a group of firms apart from those in the North-East Coast Steel Angle Makers of 1905. It was merely that the setting up of agreed price minima for plates had been easier, and so had come earlier, than the setting up of minima for angles and the various forms of rolled steel for shipbuilding which were grouped with them. Similarly the Glazed Brick Manufacturers Association, the Stock Brick Manufacturers Association, and the Pressed Brick Manufacturers Association were not necessarily exclusive, though as the processes of making Stocks and 'Flettons' (Pressed Bricks) are different, and were carried on in different districts, in this case the average firm did in fact only belong to one of the Associations.[2]

The iron and steel trades, and the trades which worked up steel and iron, were the chief nursing ground for associations, as illustrations already given suggest. In no trades, with the possible exceptions of coal and salt, had price fixing and output regulation a longer and more interesting history;[3] and it was most natural that manufacturers in touch with the South Staffordshire Ironmasters Association should adopt and develop policies employed by that Association, with more or less success, almost time out of mind. By 1914 there must have been something like fourscore associations of one kind or another in the trades;[4] and though some of these, such as the Bridge and Constructional Ironwork Association (of 1908–10), fulfilled only the elementary, what critics of an old school might have called the legitimate, functions of an association—regularising specifications, standardising designs, watching the law grow, and so forth—most of them were there to regulate prices or output or both. Some, when asked later about aims and methods were perfectly explicit; others, retaining the traditional defensive secrecy, would say no more than that they had done what they could "to prevent prices being forced down to unremunerative

[1] *Papers.*

[2] *Papers* and *S.C. on the Investigation of Prices under the Profiteering Acts*, 1919 and 1920 (1920, XXIII. 409), p. 4.

[3] Cp. vol. I. 204; vol. II. 148.

[4] There were 87 on the revised list of 1918; *Papers.*

levels".[1] Some never told anybody anything, and "were purposely carried on as secretly as possible".[2]

Among the most explicit and the most interesting was the Bedstead Makers Association. Its rules were only dated February, 1912; but it seems to have existed before that, and it was drawing on experience gained by the trade between 1893 and 1900.[3] At that time the so-called Birmingham Alliances, of which the Bedstead Makers Alliance was the pioneer, were much to the front in economic and political discussion. Employers and employees had come together and had drawn up a scheme of devices to safeguard their joint interest against the public and against potential competitors. In return for good wages and good working rules the men had promised not to serve any new firm which might try to invade the monopoly of those in possession. The promoter of the Alliances supposed that he had found the key of the social problem. Therefore he undertook a good deal of propaganda work. He had not found the key; but he had done something to make Englishmen sleep again in wooden, or part wooden, bedsteads. The great furniture retailers, faced by undesirable monopoly policies, "directed and developed"[4] the new public taste for wood; and after a time the Alliance broke down.

Its successor avoided the risky agreement with the men. Beginning as a price *Kartell*, to use the German classification, it proceeded to pooled production. Each constituent firm was assigned a share of the year's demand proportional to its output and sales in the year before federation—a quota method which has since become very familiar in the industrial world and was not new, but only rather rare, in British industry at the time. To secure control over distributors, the Bedstead Makers adopted another device, which also was not new, the offer of a deferred rebate to those who agreed to buy only from their members.[5] It was this sort of policy which set distributors against them and encouraged powerful distributors to defy them. They were compared to their great disadvantage with the much more powerful and comprehensive Wallpaper Manufacturers—a

[1] *Papers.*

[2] Hilton, J., *A Study of Trade Organisation and Combination* (in the *Report on Trusts*), p. 20.

[3] Ashley, P., *Memo. on Industrial Combinations* (in *Report on Trusts*), p. 39. And see Webb, S. and B., *Industrial Democracy* (1897), II. 578, for an early appreciation.

[4] *Papers.* [5] *Ibid.*

combination, not an association—who were said, by one great distributing firm, to have benefited consumers through the intelligent and efficient specialisation of their various plants, and to have shown all proper consideration for the retailer.[1]

The bedstead people went about as far in organisation and compulsion as any of the associations of the time. The central selling agency, a common piece of mechanism in contemporary German *Kartelle*, had not been adopted by any of them.[2] True, J. and P. Coats had a splendidly managed sales department to which the English Sewing Cotton Company and also Listers' Manningham silk-mills had been admitted;[3] but this was not an association of the ordinary sort, rather an alliance. The goods of the three firms were hardly competitive, Coats' and Listers' not at all, Coats' and the English only in part. Coats' speciality was the reel of domestic sewing cotton. The English specialised in fancier sorts. It was a great economy, especially in the export markets on which all three largely depended, to have a combined agency for dealing with the innumerable retailers of the different kinds of thread.[4]

Some associations, in the metal trades and outside them, concentrated on the regulation of output, leaving the prices of the regulated outputs to take care of themselves. The Steel Sheet Makers Association was of this type. They assigned to each constituent firm its quota. This quota it was "perfectly free to expand or contract".[5] But if it expanded it paid a fine; if it contracted it received a compensatory payment. Asked whether this method of subsidising the unenterprising and presumably inefficient firm was not wasteful and inexpedient, the spokesman of the association made a reasoned reply. He knew, he said, "that it was a law of progress that the inefficient should go, but in practice progress was impeded because he would not go, so instead of trying to kill him they had decided it was better to pension him off, since that cost far less...the more efficient man...working more economically, can well afford to pay into the pool from which the inefficient man can draw compensation".[6]

[1] *Papers.*

[2] *Report*, pp. 22, 38.

[3] Above, p. 231; and evidence from Coats' in *Papers.*

[4] *S.C. on...Prices*, 1920, p. 5. The Committee was disposed to acquit Coats' of the vague sin of 'profiteering'.

[5] *Papers.*

[6] *Report*, p. 3.

That is the case, well stated but not entirely convincing. Several of the great amalgamations of 1896–1900 had suffered at first from undue consideration of the relatively inefficient man, and from reluctance to scrap antiquated plants.[1] It was natural that the associations, which often took credit for not being amalgamations and for the way in which they protected small industrial lives, should thus advertise their rather contemptuous tolerance of lives which were both small and feeble; but how far this was either in the national interest or permanently possible is another question. The tendency of the pooling system, as a critic put it, was "to stereotype what may be called the ground-plan of the industry".[2] It should be added that the Steel Sheet witness evidently saw his association's policy not as a permanent endowment of the inefficient but as their euthanasia. Something kinder than the Devil was to take the hindmost.

The year before the Bedstead Makers drew up their final set of rules, that is to say in 1911, a much greater and more important organisation had been completed among firms supplying the ordinary cast metal goods used in the building trade—rainwater pipes, boilers, baths, stoves and the like. This was the National Light Castings Association. It was formed, as its representatives explained, "after a long period of severe depression".[3] Depression in such explanations—it occurs there almost invariably—must as a rule be translated by competition; but the building trades had in fact been almost continuously slack from 1904 to 1910.[4] There was considerably more unemployment in them in 1908–9 than there had been in any of the previous twenty-seven years. In 1911 there was a marked improvement, and after that employment and demand were continuously good.[5] The Association had the luck to start its operations on a rising market. Its programme and much of its work were excellent. Besides doing the ordinary political and labour business of an employers' association, it proposed to encourage standardisation, specialisation, and research, and to establish a central clearing house for information. All these things it began to do before 1914. Also it offered deferred rebates to builders' merchants who dealt with its members only. It did not pool production, but naturally it had something to say about prices. There was no risk of abuse here,

[1] Above, p. 228.
[2] Hilton's *Study of Trade Organisations*, p. 18.
[3] *Papers*.
[4] Above, p. 59. [5] Above, p. 62.

its representatives explained in 1918, because foreign competition would always be there to keep the prices reasonable.[1]

Other associations and combinations, either of makers or dealers, had grown up to control, with varying degrees of thoroughness, most building materials except timber, carpentry, gravel and sand.[2] There were the great combinations in wall-paper and cement. Tiles and bricks and lead pipes and sanitary earthenware had their associations. Though some were only local others were general, and several of them employed the deferred rebate. (However inclusive the association, outsiders were never eliminated.) "There was understood to be a price agreement between the only two makers"[3] of sheet glass in the United Kingdom, Pilkingtons and Chances. The National Federation of Paint, Colour and Varnish Manufacturers did not formally control either prices or output; but at least it gave opportunities for collaboration, and as Adam Smith once said, though in more stinging words, it is always hard for manufacturers to meet and never mention prices. The British Electrical and Allied Manufacturers Association was interested primarily in standardisation and research. It did not regulate prices or output, "consideration of such matters being left to groups of individual manufacturers in each section of the industry"; but it had encouraged co-operative action "with regard to distribution and marketing of products".[4] The results it claimed were beneficial and no doubt the claim was just.

Altogether about a quarter, by value, of the materials used in ordinary cottage building were thoroughly controlled, and considerably more than a second quarter partially or lightly.[5] Thorough control does not mean damaging control, only the possibility of it—especially if foreign competition is cut off, as it was in 1914. And even so the conclusion is less impressive than it sounds; for so much of the cost of a cottage is site-value and that labour value which was also pretty thoroughly controlled. The completely controlled materials can hardly have claimed more than 10 per cent. of the total cost; and as no

[1] *Papers.* Later foreign competition was curbed by duties.

[2] See the special *Report...on Combinations in Building Material Trades* in the *Report on Trusts*, pp. 35–7.

[3] Ashley, P., *Memo.* as above, p. 39. The author has been assured by a member of one of the firms that they have always been "good friends". See the *S.C. on...Prices, Final Report* (1921, XVI), p. 6.

[4] *Papers.*

[5] *Report on...Building Material Trades.*

association would have been foolish enough to try to drive up its prices artificially by 20 per cent., the risk of appreciable addition to the cost of housing due to association policies was small. What is most impressive is the rapid growth of organisations bearing on this ancient nation-wide business of home building.

In house furnishing, beside the bedstead and wallpaper people, there was, among some others, the Linoleum and Floorcloth Manufacturers Association. It "is for the purpose of agreeing on prices and has been the means of preventing cutting"[1] was the account that it gave of itself, concise and representative of many associations not connected with house building or house furnishing.

Nearly all had their political function, that of keeping an eye on the law as it affected trade interests, or might be changed so as to affect them. Nearly all would on occasion, and some very systematically, do the work for which many had been first established—negotiation with organised or discontented wage-earners.[2] A great number of associations did these things and not much else. Care for the quality of the goods, as practised by the Electrical Manufacturers, was a recent and far from universal aim. It is found however in the Cable Makers Association of 1899, an early instance. The quality of British insulated cables, it was alleged, was suffering under the strain of competition. The Association was "to regulate...standards and maintain...qualities";[3] and it got to work on its special problems before the general, and infinitely valuable, Engineering Standards Committee was created. It also standardised forms of tender and contract, and may be assumed to have standardised prices on the higher, the high quality, level for a range of goods whose excellence no one denied.[4]

It was with the merchant or the retailer that most associations of producers had to reckon immediately. The consumer was normally distant by at least one remove. Merchants fought to keep open alternative sources of supply, buying abroad—as the Light Castings Association said that they always would—when home association prices seemed to them unreasonable.[5] In a free-trade country this was in fact the safety valve. Sometimes the bringing of the merchant to heel for what producers reckoned misdemeanours was an association's first concern. The Fine

[1] *Papers*. [2] Cp. vol. II. 146. [3] *Papers*.
[4] Cp. p. 138 above. [5] *Papers*.

Cloth Manufacturers, dealing with the merchants who deal with the bespoke tailors, had made rules limiting the supply by manufacturers of cheap and repeat samples, stopping the uneconomic supply of short lengths from which only one or two 'exclusive' suits could be made, stopping certain claims of the merchants for extra carriage payments, standardising terms of credit—a thing very necessary in this luxury trade—and so forth. They had also, they reported euphemistically, occupied themselves in "stabilising...the price of cloths when changes have been necessary owing to the change in the cost of raw material".[1] To that it generally came at the last, if not in the professed creed of an association yet somewhere in its weekday practice. And, it should be added, stabilisation might be honourably defensive and thoroughly defensible. In such a trade as that in fine cloth certainly, and in many others probably, the normal merchant's economic position is stronger than that of a manufacturer acting alone in free and open competition.

When associations were based on districts, as they often were in the iron and steel trades, there might be treaties between them on the lines of the great international market-sharing treaty between the Imperial and the American tobacco companies. Thus the North-East Coast Steel Makers, in their two associations for plates and angles, had an agreement with the Scottish Steel Makers to respect one another's "home districts". When in 1910–11 the Germans "made a determined onslaught" on the British plate and angle markets, the North-Easterners began to operate the system of rebates to those merchants or users—for these things are often sold direct—who would undertake to deal with them only. But some of the merchants put up a fight and "beat us", buying the foreign stuff, as the representatives of the associations admitted.[2] Experiences of this sort had led, especially in the heavy trades, to a renewal of those international industrial treaties of which the steel-rail pool of 1883–6 had been the pioneer, and the tobacco treaties the most permanently successful.

Price control among British rail-makers had never altogether died out. It revived in spells of low prices but tended to fade when demand was brisk. After three years (1893–5) during which the average price of heavy rails was only £3. 15*s*. 7*d*. a ton the trade journals were complaining of it. When the price rose to £5. 15*s*. 10*d*. for 1899 and to £7. 2*s*. 6*d*. for 1900 it lapsed for

[1] *Papers*. [2] *Papers*.

a time, only to be renewed when the fall started again in 1901.[1] Prices were then falling everywhere. Germany began dumping: the working of her protective tariff, and eventually of her *Stahlwerksverband*, enabled her to sell in Britain at 30*s*. a ton[2] below her home price, it was said. The import of rails rose sharply in 1903, though even so it was not an eighth of the export. All through 1904 therefore negotiations went on between the rail-makers of Britain, Germany, France and Belgium; and in November a three years' treaty was signed, to which the United States makers subsequently acceded.[3] By this treaty the British got 53·50 per cent. of the export trade with a prior claim to the sales in British possessions; but the Americans demanded, and won, admission to the markets of Canada and Newfoundland, which in the end they nearly monopolised. The treaty was twice renewed before 1914. At the renewal in 1912 the British share had fallen to 33·63 per cent. Its general effect had been "gradually to restrict the activity of the British makers to British Colonial markets".[4] The average annual export for the ten years 1904–13 was rather less than it had been in the four years 1900–3. On the other hand the treaty guarded the home market against dumping. The average annual imports for those ten years were barely a third of what they had been in the peak year 1903, were indeed almost negligible though sometimes complained of.

These simple, relatively well-known, and easily estimated rail treaties are units in a group which was always growing, but about most sections of which much less is known. The treaty makers did not file their treaties in any generally accessible place. Germans often opened the negotiations. In 1903 they tried to come to terms with the British steel-tube makers, but failed.[5] After a struggle for the world's screw markets, in which the fighting firm of Guest Keen and Nettlefolds attacked the German home front resolutely, makers in Germany and Britain promised one another, in September, 1905, to accept no more orders from the other country.[6] That same year cement-makers in the two countries came to an arrangement with those of France and Belgium about the supply of the Dutch market.[7] The makers of wire netting, who used little but German wire,

[1] *Report on Wholesale and Retail Prices*, 1903, p. 28.
[2] Macrosty, *The Trust Movement in British Industry*, p. 65.
[3] Ashley, P., *Memo. on Industrial Combinations*, pp. 40–1.
[4] *Ibid.* p. 41.
[5] Macrosty, p. 78.
[6] *Ibid.* p. 79.
[7] *Ibid.* p. 116.

had a treaty with the Germans for several years before 1914.[1] Its terms have not become known and probably it is now forgotten. Steel-sheet makers had some kind of "gentleman's agreement" with the makers in the United States, containing presumably promises to "respect one another's territories".[2] The wallpaper combination in its early years was not troubled with foreign competition: only a few specialities were imported. When competition began, it bought up one works in France and another in Germany, "to compete from the inside".[3] There is no record of a treaty before 1914, and it seems unlikely that there was one, as the circumstances do not suggest the necessity. But there may have been. In 1909, international Lead and Spelter Conventions were signed, for the regulation of selling prices and ultimately of output.[4] German interests dominated both. And in 1912 a similar arrangement was made among the chief European aluminium producers, French, English and Swiss, who were also in touch with the Canadians and the Americans.[5]

It was known, an official of the Board of Trade wrote, "that other international agreements existed for price regulations, the restriction of output, or delimitation of marketing areas...but for obvious reasons it was almost impossible to obtain definite information as to their precise nature and extent".[6] Governments had not yet begun to take a hand in them. Most of them had not existed long enough to furnish evidence of their own fragility; but both national and international economic history show that private commercial treaties are at least as liable to breach, neglect, and denunciation as the treaties concluded by High Contracting Parties for the maintenance of the world's peace.

The international treaty between associations, *Kartelle* and less formal groups was a far weaker and more ephemeral thing than the treaties between great consolidated powers like the tobacco, oil or dynamite companies; though even these might be rather short-lived. Strongest of all were arrangements made by firms such as Coats' and Levers', themselves domiciled in many countries; able to exercise in them that internal competition which the wallpaper makers had judiciously initiated; so powerful that they had little need to defend the home market, and could often apportion other markets by domestic arrangements

[1] *Papers*.
[2] *Ibid.*
[3] *Ibid.*
[4] Ashley, p. 41.
[5] Plummer, A., *International Combinations in Modern Industry* (1934), p. 68.
[6] Ashley, p. 42.

between the head office in Britain and the subsidiaries overseas. Such arrangements were naturally not made public; nor were the treaties, if such existed, between the giant company domiciled in Britain and competitors in the places where its subsidiaries were domiciled. All these matters were of the greatest importance for Coats', whose home trade was only about 10 per cent. of the whole.[1]

A type of treaty which was acquiring considerable importance during the last years of the peace was that designed to regulate the use of decisive patents internationally.[2] Patenting in several countries at once was an old inventor's device. The patent expert and the patent lawyer were well-established types. Where local law was not an impediment, the taking out of a patent in country *A*, not to be used there, was a useful weapon for a manufacturer in country *B* where he was using it. Britain suffered from this abuse and did not change her law to prevent it until 1907:[3] a patent taken out in this country but not worked here within three years now lapsed. But no law could prevent a revolutionary patent made and worked abroad from damaging home producers who had not access to it. Hence the bargains and treaties to secure access. Such a situation arose in the glass-bottle trade after 1906.[4] An American invention, the Owens machine, turned out bottles with unheard of ease. The American company which held the patent meant to make all it could out of it. It offered the rights for £600,000 to the British Association of Glass Bottle Makers, formed in 1907. The Association could not find the money. Then bottle-makers in seven European countries, including Britain, came together in 1908 as the *Verband der Flaschenfabriken*, which raised the £600,000. They then proceeded to share up markets and regulate prices in Europe to their mutual advantage. Extra-European markets were divided between the *Verband* and the Americans, who reserved for themselves Canada, Mexico and of course the United States. The lumbering machine of the *Verband* got to work very slowly, partly because of a laudable wish not to displace too much labour, and it was not working very well when 1914 upset it.

In the aluminium industry, young, struggling and as yet

[1] *Papers*

[2] Liefmann, R., *Kartelle, Konzerne und Trusts* (8th ed., 1930, of his original *Unternehmerverbände*), pp. 183 *sqq.* gives a general account.

[3] See p. 435 below.

[4] Ashley, p. 41; *S.C. on...Prices*, p. 7; and cp. p. 129 above.

relatively inefficient in Britain, international agreements and quarrels connected with the use of the electrolytic patents had been incessant. There had been an agreement in 1901, when the industry was young everywhere. It ran out in 1905. A subsequent agreement ended with a quarrel in 1908. Last came an international price cartel in 1912. In all these affairs Britain took only a minor part, owing to the weakness of the home industry.[1]

The British electrical industry was also relatively weak. In it patent agreements were of the first importance as new developments came with the twentieth century. Lamps furnish the best, and the best-known, illustration.[2] For twenty-eight years (1878–1906) the 'Edi-Swan' carbon-filament lamp was unchallenged. In Britain, though in no other European country, patents had given the original makers a long monopoly. By the time that monopoly expired, in the 'nineties, there was no doubt that the German electrical industry was ahead of the British. The American industry always had been ahead, and others were at least abreast. In 1906 the first tungsten-filament lamps were brought out by a German and an Austrian firm. The tungsten was 'squirted' to make the filament. With some trouble the General Electric Company of London secured the rights for the British market in 1907. Two years later, the General Electric Company of New York introduced the drawn tungsten-filament lamp, and in 1913 the gas-filled lamp. So about that time there naturally appeared in England a Tungsten Lamp Association, "closely associated with patent rights"[3]—their acquisition, use, control and profitable exploitation. As a result of the patent-securing, and of other enterprise, the British industry turned out 25,000,000 lamps in 1913, and the country imported only 3,300,000 more. In the absence of a tariff, the result is creditable to the manufacturing and negotiating skill of British electricians.

These are only samples about which the facts are tolerably well known of the many "understandings, agreements and associations embodying arrangements for the regulation of prices... [and] the delimitation of markets..."[4] made between British and foreign manufacturers. Dreamers of business dreams hoped for far more decisive things. Here is an illustration. There was

[1] Plummer, *International Combinations*, p. 68, as above.
[2] *S.C. on...Prices*, p. 3.
[3] *Ibid.* p. 11.
[4] Hilton, in *Report on Trusts*, p. 26.

formed in 1904 the International Federation of Master Cotton Spinners and Manufacturers. It was designed as a statistical and informative organisation and never became anything else. But its most prominent man, Sir Charles Macara, was talking and writing about the elimination of cotton price fluctuations by concerted international buying and holding of the cotton crops. It is possible that his support of this policy before a Cotton Conference at Atlanta, Ga., in 1907 may not have attracted the men of the Cotton Belt.[1] His sincere industrial internationalism was shared by few except some like-minded dreamers in America, but it was significant. Ten or twenty years earlier it could hardly have been formulated by a man of practice.

Had the International Cotton Federation ever really tried to become sole buyer of the world's cotton, it would certainly have found itself compelled to apply coercive measures to sellers and outside buyers. Probably it would have fallen back on some variant of that system of deferred favours which was springing up at various points in the field of "agreements and associations". It can be pictured offering a deferred payment to cotton-growers or merchants who promised to sell to it alone; just as the shipping conferences—sellers not buyers—regularly gave deferred rebates to those shippers who pledged themselves to patronise no outside line.

Whatever the ultimate origins of the deferred rebate and associated systems, and obviously individual trading gives opportunities for promising favours to a client who gives you plenty of business and agrees to stand by you, their organised use by trading groups had been developed in ocean transport since the days of cables, compound engines, and the regular sailing of cargo-carrying liners—that is since the late 'seventies, when fierce competition on a falling market had led inevitably to rate-agreements, so-called conferences, among the lines.[2] The Calcutta Conference of August, 1875, was the first; and in September, 1877, the lines which were parties to it offered a deferred rebate to merchants who would agree to ship Man-

[1] Macara, *Getting the World to Work* (1922), pp. 16, 90, etc., and Plummer, *op. cit.* p. 65.

[2] The *Report of the R.C. on Shipping Rings* (1909, XLVII. XLVIII) is the great source of information. Cp. Owen, D., *Ocean Trade and Shipping* (1914), pp. 66 *sqq*.

chester piece-goods only in their vessels.[1] Before 1886, conferences with deferred rebates had been set up for the China trade (1879) and the Australian trade (1884). In 1886 came the West African Conference; the South African in 1895; that for Brazil and the River Plate in 1895–6; that for the West Coast of South America in 1904. By 1908, except in the North-Atlantic trade, the system applied "to practically all the cargo, except coal and special shipments, shipped outwards"[2] from Britain. Only a selected list of inward cargoes was affected. These were all 'choice cargoes' in the terminology of the conferences, because bulk imports like grain and timber came in tramp steamers at competitive rates. Tea from Calcutta was a 'choice' cargo, for tramps never took tea; but Calcutta jute, like Rangoon rice, was always an 'open' one.

The absence of cargo conferences and rebates in the North Atlantic trade was due to the dominance of passenger traffic there. Atlantic liners always had plenty of space for 'choice' cargo—little else could now get over North-American tariffs—which space they let at low regular rates. There was no object in offering shippers further inducement to hire it. The shipper, fairly certain of cheap space whenever he shipped, was not tempted to favour one line above another. Like a passenger, he used the sailing which suited him best.

In the twentieth century some of the conferences regulated the sailings, so that the shipper who accepted their terms was sure to find ships of one line or another at regular intervals. Some permitted random sailings. Any trade that required an organised service could not escape a conference or its equivalent.[3] All the conferences gave uniform rates, and reasonably stable rates, and the same rates for all shippers, great and small. Before the day of the conference big men could stand out for privileges. These were the weighty arguments put forward in defence of the system. It was also urged, though perhaps less conclusively, that without the deferred rebate or some equally effective tie on shippers the advantages could scarcely be had. But that a conference might sometimes abuse its position was obvious, especially if it were dominated by a single powerful line. It was generally thought in the first decade of the twentieth century that the South African Conference and the Union Castle Line thus abused their power. The South African trade,

[1] *R.C. on Shipping Rings*, p. 12. [2] *Ibid.* [3] *Ibid.* p. 76.

with its export of gold, diamonds, ostrich feathers, mohair and the like, and its import of manufactures, was in the unfortunate position for the shipper of being mainly 'choice' both ways; so that traders were conscious of the conference and its authority, as they said its tyranny, every day of their lives.

Just as a trade association usually dealt with a single commodity or group of closely associated commodities—so a conference dealt with a place and a direction, Calcutta Outward or Colombo Homeward. Consequently, in both classes of organisation, an important firm would belong to several at once, as the Peninsular and Oriental and Guest Keen and Nettlefolds did. Originally purely British, in those nineteenth-century days when there were few lines on the outer seas which were not British, the conferences had latterly admitted some of the continental lines, and so were governed by international treaties. The *Hamburg-Amerika* was not much concerned with conference routes; but the *Nord-Deutscher Lloyd*, which began regular Australian sailings in 1888, used several. So did the *Messageries Maritimes* and some other important continental companies.

The trade without an association of some kind was by 1914 rare. But most of the associations still only did labour business, as and when required, or watched over the legal and technical interests of their trade. The remarkable growth of activities in one way or another restrictive of competition should not obscure the very wide fields in which competition flourished as before. "What is notable among British consolidations and association", an official reporter wrote in 1919, "is not their rarity or weakness so much as their unobtrusiveness".[1] He had in mind the competition-restricting types. And though, thanks to this unobtrusiveness, there were more of these than could be accurately described, there were a great number of "industries, trades and services in which combination has made hardly any headway".[2] That was written after four years of war organisation had stimulated combination abnormally. It was no accident that of the five hundred or so associations of the competition-restricting type known to the Board of Trade in 1918 nearly a fifth were in the iron and steel trades.[3] In the building trades, as opposed to the building supply trades, they were rare, although groups of builders had often been suspected of collusive tendering, and

[1] Hilton, in *Report on Trusts*, p. 17. [2] *Ibid.* p. 20.
[3] *Papers.*

there were hundreds of local builders' associations for dealing with the men.[1] The furniture-making trade as a whole was highly competitive, in spite of the Bedstead Alliance. Rather strong in electrical engineering, in general engineering competition-restricting associations, and indeed associations of any kind outside the technical Institutes, were few and weak. In shipbuilding and marine engineering there were none, though the average business unit was huge.[2] In the whole field of mining and quarrying, down to 1914, associations had really done nothing but negotiate with labour and keep an eye on the law. In the textile trades the great consolidations worked against a strictly competitive background of spinners and manufacturers, whose rare associations only served to show up the stiff individualism of the mass.[3] The number even of public companies in the woollen industry was still negligible; and the Board of Trade list of associations in the wool country contained very little beyond the addresses of the local Chambers of Commerce. Now a Yorkshire Chamber of Commerce was not an anti-competitive organisation.

In the boot and shoe, the wholesale clothing, the knitting, and the allied industries, with their whole range of distributive trades, there had been concentration and consolidation but little deliberate control of competition. The boot factory with its own shops was well known. But it was in strict competition with other factories and other shops. The only monopolistic organisation in that group of trades which the official hunters after monopoly and combination of 1918–21 were able to track down was the very conspicuous Anglo-American United Shoe Machinery Company of 1900–1, whose excellent machines were leased on stringent and ingenious terms to nearly all the trade. "Eighty per cent. of the shoe factories" were "tied houses as regards their machinery";[4] but they competed briskly with one

[1] In 1914 the Labour Department of the Board of Trade knew of 1487 employers' associations "concerned with labour matters". Of these 468 were in the building trades; 161 in baking and confectionery; and 106 in printing. *Eighteenth Abstract of Labour Statistics* (1926, Cd. 270), p. 191. This is of course a list quite distinct from that quoted on p. 316.

[2] The fact is commented on in the *Report on Trusts*, p. 20.

[3] Cp. *Factors in Commercial and Industrial Efficiency*, 1927, p. 81; *Report on Trusts*, p. 39.

[4] *Report on Trusts*, p. 28. The Company is discussed in all the post-war reports on the basis of material in the *Papers of the Committee on Trusts*. Cp. p. 183 above.

another, and the argument most regularly used in defence of the Anglo-American was that by its leasing system expensive machines had come into small men's hands and so kept competition active.

There was approximately perfect competition also in agriculture, in the fisheries, and in the paper and printing trades; in such new industries as cycle and motor-car manufacture, or such newly revolutionised industries as that of the laundries. Master printers had their federation but printing tenders were competitive. Among the laundries the post-war committee of inquiry[1] could not find any price-controlling combination within their terms of reference. On the land, the National Farmers' Union and the Central Chamber of Agriculture were above suspicion. Nor was there combination in domestic service. More than three-quarters of the occupied people in the country were producing goods or selling services whose price or output had been affected in no appreciable way by association among those for whom they worked; and the influence of association over the trades of the remaining quarter was patchy. If attention had been confined to the goods alone, to things grown, taken, extracted or made, things of the classes which contain wheat, fish, coals and boots, it would probably have been found that far more were produced under conditions of approximately free and open competition than not.

The trade association proper, as distinct from the joint-stock amalgamation, could not register under the Companies Acts or the Partnership Acts; but as "the imposing of restrictive conditions on the conduct of any trade or business" and "the regulation of the relation...between masters and masters" had been among the possible statutory objects of a trade union ever since 1876,[2] it might register as a trade union; and very often it did. But though associations which so registered enjoyed the appropriate privileges and immunities—they might not, for example, be sued for damages—a registered trade union had little more hold over its members than a private club, which was what an unregistered association in effect was. A trade unionist may resign when he pleases, which means resume competitive activity at will, if his union happens to be a trade association. If

[1] I.e. the *S.C. on...Prices, under the Profiteering Acts.*

[2] They are always so stated in the laws, e.g. that of 1912–3, 2 and 3 Geo. V, c. 30. And see the *Report on Trusts*, p. 18.

he breaks the rules he can only be expelled, which is presumably what a rebel member of a trade association wants. All this made even the registered trade association at best a loosely knit and unsatisfactory affair. Further, under the Trades Union Act of 1913 the Registrar was not to register a union unless its "principal objects" were statutory objects; and from that time there was some doubt whether an association whose principal object was the regulation of prices could expect to secure registration.[1] However this was an obstacle which, if real, could be overcome by a little judicious reticence; and in fact registration as a trade union, in spite of its limited attractions, appears to have been as common after 1913 as before, although price regulation was the most usual activity of what might be called a positive trade association.

The secrecy of some of the trade associations and their fear of public opinion and the State, even at the opening of the twentieth century, recall the attitude of the trade unions a century earlier, when they also worked with considerable effect in the shade. Throughout the last quarter of the nineteenth century the unions, now well in the light, were watched and studied by the national government with a care and consecutive attention not at that time given to the associations; and their legal needs had been provided for—to the full, as was supposed—by those statutes of which the associations subsequently made somewhat unexpected use. In the middle 'eighties, when the consecutive attention began, there was much uncertainty about the number of trade unionists in the country; but it was then probably about a million.[2] In the course of a few years however the collection of statistics by the new Labour Department of the Board of Trade became reasonably complete; and in the early 'nineties the ascertained total remained steady at something above 1,500,000, falling a little from 1892 to 1895. It rose sharply with the turn of the price-curve and the trade revival of 1896–7; just as it had risen during the trade revival of the late 'eighties.

Not that trade-union growth was a mere function of the business cycle, although that aspect of it deserves more attention

[1] It is stated, e.g. in the *S.C. on...Prices*, p. 4, that the Electric Cables Association, being registered as a Trade Union, cannot regulate prices "under the Trades Union Act, 1913".

[2] Vol. II. 155. This includes Ireland. But trade unionism was very weak in Ireland.

than it has sometimes received. A well-established union can often be seen reacting directly to the course of trade and the growth of its own industry. Between 1885 and 1890 the Amalgamated Engineers grew from 51,700 to 67,900; that old strong society the London Compositors from 6400 to 8900, and its neighbour the Typographical Association from 6600 to 9000; even the Boilermakers and Iron Shipbuilders, desperately hard hit as they were in the middle 'eighties, from 28,200 to 32,900. But the main cause of general expansion was the Socialist-inspired propaganda of the new, the fighting, unionism of Tom Mann, John Burns, Ben Tillett and their sympathisers inside and outside the ranks of wage-earners.[1] They attacked what they reckoned the smug and stupid Friendly Society obsession of the leading unions. These, Burns wrote in 1887, were being crushed by "their reckless assumption of the duties and responsibilities that only the State or whole community can discharge, in the nature of sick and superannuation benefits".[2] Their real business, he held, was to fight for better wages and better working conditions until they could secure control of the State, which would then do the rest. It was not the working of a trade cycle which raised the membership of the Yorkshire Miners' Association, during the same five years 1885–90 from a reputed 8000 to a reputed 50,000; which more than doubled the membership of the Amalgamated Society of Railway Servants, though leaving it even then only at 23,500;[3] or which created out of nothing many societies among the relatively unskilled, headed by the Gas Workers and General Labourers Union of 1889, societies whose aggregate membership in 1890–2 was over 100,000.[4] The depression of 1886; the championship by Socialists of the cause of the London unemployed, well advertised by the government's interference with it, in 1886–7; the successful strike of match-girls in 1888, and the far greater strike

[1] Webb, S. and B., *History of Trade Unionism* (1902 ed.), p. 369 and *passim*.

[2] *Ibid.* p. 371. Cp. p. 482 below.

[3] Alcock, G. W., *Fifty Years of Railway Trade Unionism* (1922), p. 625.

[4] The formations of 1889 include, besides the Gas Workers and General Labourers, the Gas Workers Brickmakers and General Labourers, the Covent Garden Porters, the Knights of Labour Durham Branch, the Labour Protection League, the National Amalgamated Labourers, the National Amalgamated Union of Labour, the National Labourers' Union, the United Labourers of Dublin, and several unions of canal boatmen and lightermen. *Report...on Trade Unions*, 1902 (Cd. 1348), pp. 67, 112, with dates of foundations, as in all the *Reports* of this series, of which that of 1902 is the fourteenth.

of Thames dockers in 1889, showed what union, even if only temporary, could do for the economically weak in London, where permanent unionism had never been strong; and gave fuel and drive to the union movement throughout the country.

Yet in spite of the spread of membership among the unskilled, when the numerical rise of the late 'eighties had ceased and the slight reaction of the early 'nineties was spent—that is in 1895, the big battalions of the trade-union army were recruited very much where they had been ten years earlier; among the skilled men of the building trades, the coal-miners, the engineers iron-shipbuilders and metal workers generally, and the cotton operatives.[1] These four divisions included nearly two-thirds of the whole army; and 80 per cent. of all the women trade unionists in the country were members of cotton unions, mostly weavers. About half of the remaining few thousand women trade unionists were in the linen and jute and the hat and cap trades; the rest were scattered over the other textile and clothing trades, with a thin sprinkling elsewhere. Outside Lancashire, in short, the woman trade unionist was rather a curiosity.[2]

Eighteen years later in 1913, when the total number of trade unionists had much more than doubled (from 1,504,000 to 4,135,000) the four dominant groups together contained not quite half of it; but this decline in relative importance was then very recent.[3] In 1910 they still held their old position, with about two-thirds, and the coal-miners were as important as they had ever been, with upwards of a quarter of the total. This position of pre-eminence they had held since 1900, when their aggregate membership first passed 500,000. Their trade was expanding unwholesomely fast and an extraordinarily high proportion of the men now joined the unions. The average number of workers in and about the pits had been 732,000 for the decade 1893–1902: the actual number in 1913 was 1,128,000.[4] And in 1913 there were 890,000 enrolled union members. That, it is true, was an abnormal figure and meant the enrolment of nearly every man of age to join. Special circumstances had pushed it up from the 742,000 of the previous year; but even the lower figure implies a trade unionism of unusual width and power.

[1] Cp. vol. II. 155. [2] Figures in the *Report* of 1902.

[3] Figures from the various *Reports on Trade Unions*, summarised in the *Eighteenth Abstract of Labour Statistics* (1926).

[4] Including the lads, and a few thousand pit-brow lasses in Lancashire and Cumberland.

The decline in relative importance of the four leading divisions of the trade-union forces between 1910 and 1913 was chiefly due to the extraordinarily rapid recruitment during these years for the divisions of the transport workers and the general labourers. In 1910 there had been 257,000 transport workers in union, including the seamen.[1] The figure of 116,000 railwaymen forming part of this total was already a notable advance on the 23,500 of 1890 or the few thousands of the early 'eighties. But by 1913 there were 326,000 railwaymen trade unionists, and no less than 694,000 transport workers of every kind—railwaymen, seamen, port workers, busmen and tramwaymen and the fast growing body of goods transport workers on the roads. Already the enrolled transport workers were more numerous than either the metal or the textile workers; far more numerous than either the cotton operatives alone or the building craftsmen; and second only to the coal-miners. Five years later they would be ahead of the coal-miners; six years later ahead of all miners whatsoever. This was fitting in an age of extended and accelerated mobility; though extension and acceleration were not the efficient causes of the growth.

Recruitment for the division of general labour was even more successful during these last years of peace. The strength of the division rose from 81,000 to 358,000. This was an uncertain success, as recruitment in that area had proved more than once before. True, the ground gained by 1913 was never lost. But the figure was to rise so high as 1,261,000 in 1920 and to be down to 511,000 in 1924. No section of trade unionism is more sensitive to the swing of the trade cycle; and in 1912–13 that swing was strongly upward.

Two other groups of trade unionists which were growing abnormally fast in the twentieth century were those of the women and the public servants. They overlap one another and the women overlap other groups. Among the 433,000 women trade unionists in 1913 there were 88,000 teachers or other public servants and 260,000 textile workers, of whom 214,000 were cotton operatives. Indeed by this time the textile trade unions nearly had a female majority, and the cotton unions had a heavy female majority.[2]

[1] The earlier seamen's statistics are very uncertain.

[2] Total membership of textile unions, 1913, 523,000; of cotton unions, 372,000. Female membership of textile unions, 1913, 260,000; of cotton unions, 214,000. For women trade unionists in 1886, see vol. II. 167.

Among central or local government servants there had been unions before 1880; but except for the National Union of Teachers, they had not been strong. Even in 1901 their total membership, excluding the teachers, was only 45,000, of whom 25,000 belonged to the Postmen's Federation. Twelve years later there were 235,000 trade unionists in the public services not counting the 113,000 teachers. Together, the two groups were already almost as numerous as that of the cotton operatives (372,000) though not nearly so coherent. In this connection it is not to be forgotten that the public services themselves were expanding fast. Omitting the police, there were twice as many servants of the central government, and considerably more than twice as many servants of local governments, in 1911 as there had been in 1891.[1]

Among the main trade-union groups of 1913, the coal-miners, as has been seen, had recruited a very large proportion of their trade. There were non-unionist adult miners everywhere, or almost everywhere, but except in outlying places they were a minority, often a despised and rejected minority. In cotton also unionism had got somewhere near its possible maximum among the men; and this was no new thing. There were 236,000 male cotton operatives in Britain in 1911 and there were 145,000 male trade unionists.[2] As the normal male unionist spinner employed two piecers, and as nearly a third of the piecers were lads, with a few girls, not yet of trade-union age; as there were about 23,000 of these unionist spinners; and as there were plenty of lads' jobs in other sections of the trade, the maximum enlistment of adults must very nearly have been reached. A mule-spinner had to be a trade unionist; there was no question about that; and nearly all other adult male workers in fact were.[3]

In the building crafts the position was quite different, as it always had been. There were upwards of 200,000 carpenters and joiners in Britain in 1911 and only 73,000 members of the various carpenters' and joiners' unions. Not more than 36,000 bricklayers and masons were in union that year, out of the 180,000

[1] *Census of 1911: General Report* (1917, Cd. 8491), p. 268.

[2] The year 1911 is taken for the convenience of comparing trade union with Census figures.

[3] Cp. Webb, S. and B., *Industrial Democracy* (1897), p. 475. In 1910 there were 22,992 spinners in the union, with 29,621 male and 1862 female piecers. On the assumption of two piecers to every spinner, this leaves 14,500 piecers not yet in unions: *Report on Trade Unions in 1908–10* (1912, Cd. 6109), p. 27 for the figures. This *Report*, the seventeenth, is the last of the series issued before 1914.

masons and bricklayers of twenty years old and upwards in the country. Union membership in both groups increased rapidly during the next two years, partly because the Unemployment Insurance Act of 1911 made membership convenient for men who had hitherto been indifferent to it.[1] It is possible that 50 per cent. of the eligible carpenters and joiners were enrolled by 1913. But the percentage of bricklayers and masons enrolled was certainly much lower. No elaborate explanation is needed of this relatively poor enlistment. Masonry was declining: regular apprenticeship to it was about dead.[2] Building as a whole was slack in the early years of the twentieth century. Steel frames and concrete and machine-made joinery were disturbing the old technical framework of all its crafts; and such times of slackness and disturbance are always bad for trade unionism. The crafts were scattered of necessity over the whole face of the country; and the unions hardly could be. In the 'nineties the Amalgamated Society of Carpenters had branches in 400 separate towns or villages;[3] but there were carpenters, joiners and bricklayers in far more places than that. Bricklaying and carpentry are easily picked up; and although the bricklayers' unions, where strong enough, would not allow a man to lay bricks one day and be a bricklayer's labourer the next,[4] they were in fact recruited mainly from among these labourers, though apprenticeship was not extinct. Where there were no unions, men tumbled up to the trades anyhow or by way of some rough village apprenticeship; and such men might well take no interest in trade-union affairs. The position was much the same among painters, slaters, and tilers; but the main unions of the plasterers and plumbers were strong, if not everywhere dominant.

The main unions. Thanks to their history, the building trades suffered from a diversity, conservatism, and competition of unions which was, and in retrospect is, the despair of the trade-union idealist.[5] The new unionism of the 'eighties had passed them by. They competed with one another for members. They had a long series of demarcation squabbles, among themselves and with outsiders—bricklayers versus tilers; plumbers against

[1] Cp. Postgate, R. W., *The Builders' History*, p. 401.

[2] Postgate, p. 365. Cp. vol. II. 156.

[3] Webb, S. and B., *Industrial Democracy*, p. 53.

[4] Cp. Webb, *Industrial Democracy*, p. 489; Postgate, p. 355.

[5] See the building trades evidence before the *R.C. on Labour* (1892, XXXVI. Part 2), Q. 17,200–18,200; Postgate, pp. 331, 376; Cole, G. D. H., *The World of Labour* (1913), p. 265; vol. II. 158.

sanitary engineers. Clinging to their craft traditions, and to the belief that this was eternally a bricklayer's job, and that a plumber's, while the only proper jobs for a labourer were fetching and carrying, they made no sustained effort to organise their unskilled camp-followers; and yet it was from among these that most of their recruits came.

But although in no building craft was unionism nearly co-extensive with craft membership, and although the total membership of all the building unions declined from 1901 to 1910, and even in 1913 had not got back quite to the 1901 level, in most places of importance trade-union officials negotiated with master builders the working rules by which the daily life of the whole industry was controlled. Codifications and revisions of traditional practice, these rules dealt with wages, hours, holidays, apprenticeship, meal-times and a crowd of smaller matters rather mysterious to outsiders but of inherited importance in an ancient group of outdoor crafts.

That the general labourers who had joined unions were a small percentage of the whole body needs no statistical proof. In the metal-working trades, the proportion of unionism varied greatly from group to group. It was highest, "practically co-extensive with the industry", among the Boiler-makers and Iron-shipbuilders. Their secretary in 1892 had claimed a 95 per cent. recruitment;[1] and even if he exaggerated a little, there is no reason to think that the percentage, whatever it was, declined in later years.[2] It was high also among the little, exclusive, old-fashioned crafts of the cutlery trades, such as the Razor Hafters with their less than 100 members and their rule that "no boys be admitted to the trade except members' sons".[3] It was lower, very much lower, among the intricate and always changing light metal trades in the Birmingham area and elsewhere; although there were some thirty separate unions of brass and copper workers in the country, besides the Amalgamated Brass Workers whose membership fluctuated between 6000 and 11,000. Among the thirty unions of 1910 were the Birmingham Brass Lock Finishers, with 57 members, and the Aberdeen Brass Founders, with 36.

[1] Knight, R., before *R.C. on Labour* (1893, XXXII), Q. 20,725.

[2] Comparisons of trade-union and Census figures are not possible here because the Census classifications are somewhat artificial. The Census of 1911 (*Report*, p. 121) keeps Boiler-makers and Shipbuilders apart and seems to assume that all Boiler-makers were engaged in making boilers, discussing their numbers entirely in terms of high- and low-pressure.

[3] Webb, *Industrial Democracy*, p. 458.

The greatest of the metal-working unions, the Amalgamated Society of Engineers—which had 52,000 members in 1886, 91,000 in 1897, and 110,000 in 1910—was never nearly coextensive with the trade, for much the same reasons that the building unions were not. Boiler-making and iron-shipbuilding were concentrated, locally and industrially. There were engineers of one kind or another by this time everywhere, and there were a number of small unions which competed with the A.S.E., from the ancient Steam Engine Makers of 1824 to the Birmingham Hot Water and Steam Engineers of 1903. Yet the chief difficulty of the A.S.E. was not the competition of such rivals—the Steam Engine Makers, much the biggest, had never more than 13,000 members—but the ease, the growing ease, with which engineering could be picked up by the smart lad or labourer who started, perhaps as a minder of some straightforward machine in a large works, perhaps as a general utility hand in a little rural agricultural engineering shop, recently a blacksmith's forge. Whereas by the early 'nineties the Boiler-makers were in a position to negotiate a comprehensive and binding apprenticeship treaty with their few employers, under which no one who had not been regularly apprenticed had any chance either of membership in the union or of a job in the trade, among the Engineers apprenticeship regulation of the old sort had completely broken down.[1] For a whole generation, from the 'fifties to the 'eighties, the A.S.E. had tried without effect to exclude unapprenticed men. After that the attempt was abandoned, and before 1900 "any adult man who obtained employment at the standard rate of his particular town and grade was, in practice, welcomed as a recruit".[2]

The conquest of the railway service by trade unionism had been not only unusually rapid but also unusually complete at the last, as the figures show:[3]

	1881	1891	1901	1911	1913
Persons occupied on the railways	166,000	223,000	322,000	378,000	? 390,000
Membership of all railway unions	? 10,000	49,500	82,000	185,000	? 326,000

Down to 1910, when the aggregate membership was still only 116,000, the two principal societies, the Amalgamated Railway Servants and the Associated Engineers and Firemen had not

[1] See Webb, *Industrial Democracy*, p. 470 and *passim*. [2] Webb, p. 472.
[3] They come from the various *Reports on Trade Unions*.

pulled well together. The Amalgamated in its early days had been largely a friendly society, founded by a millionaire Member of Parliament and presided over into the 'nineties in succession by an LL.D., a Canon, and a second Member of Parliament. The Railway Companies had always refused to recognise its right to represent its constituents, and had tried to coerce its members with a rough hand. Indeed even in 1910 it was not numerically representative. The Associated, which in 1910 had 20,000 members, was more representative of its select group, and it had a different tradition. It was younger than the Amalgamated and perhaps it had been a little patronising. Certainly it had provoked bitterness. "I am amazed as I have gone through this history", a chronicler bred in the Amalgamated was writing twelve years later, "to see how little intelligence has ruled with them [the Associated], how self-centred they have been, how quick to twist facts and present warped statements, to aid a cause by cunning which could not be achieved by reason";[1] and so on. Down to 1907, the Companies as a whole were still refusing to allow men who wished to present grievances "to be accompanied by anyone outside the Company's own staff",[2] and in that year a great railway strike was only just averted. In 1911 it came, and 145,000 men stopped work. But it ended "with mysterious suddenness. Mutual concessions were made by masters and men after hearing a confidential statement from the Chancellor of the Exchequer";[3] for it was the month of the Agadir crisis. Returning from holidays abroad, Englishmen saw the long coal trains pounding South to refuel London: it was a new sight. The railwaymen went on with recruitment and organisation. The settlement of 1911 had involved that full recognition of unionism for which they had fought; and in 1913 the Amalgamated, absorbing various other societies, though not all, and abandoning the name of Servant, became the National Union of Railwaymen with a membership of 268,000.[4]

Once well started, unionism had run fast along the rails.

[1] Alcock, *Fifty Years of Railway Trade Unionism* (the principal source), p. 372. And cp. Thomas, J. H., *My Story* (1937), who does not mention that he began in the Associated but moved over to the Amalgamated, as Alcock records.

[2] Alcock, p. 377.

[3] Churchill, Winston S., *The World Crisis*, I. 64–5. Cp. Thomas, *op. cit.* p. 34; Alcock, pp. 427 *sqq.* Alcock does not refer to the confidential statement. Cp. p. 500 below.

[4] Besides Alcock, see, for these final absorptions, Cole, *The World of Labour*, p. 221.

Railwaymen had the advantage of constant intercourse with one another and a limited, if exceedingly powerful and semi-public, group of employers. Having become a majority unionists could persuade, or dominate, their neighbours, very much as colliers could in the pits, as unionists in the scattered trades could not. With tramwaymen and busmen serving great companies or municipalities it was much the same. By 1910 their chief union, the Amalgamated Tramway and Vehicle Workers,[1] had 17,000 members. But the London Cab-drivers, many of whom worked for small proprietors and whose trade was beginning to change over from the horse-cab to the taxi-cab, were perceptibly weaker in 1910 than they had been in 1897, three years after their foundation. However, in trades so mobile and inaccessible to trade-union organisation, it was to the credit of the organisers that more than 3000 cabmen and nearly 6000 carmen were in the London unions at the later date, even though they were only a small fraction of the potential membership. Before 1889 there had been no road transport unions worth mentioning, in the London area or out of it.[2]

Beyond the major groups of trade unionists old or new, the printers and lithographers, though strong in their two main unions as they had been for many years, suffered like the carpenters and the engineers from diffusion and also from the very strength of the two unions.[3] A little printing was done in every place that could call itself a town, and even in some villages. As the London Society of Compositors would not admit women, several London master printers in the 'nineties had subsidiary works somewhere in the Home Counties where the rule did not apply.[4] As the Typographical Association, with headquarters in Manchester and many branches, tried to enforce the curious rule that there should not be more than three compositors' apprentices in any shop however large, and none at all in shops employing less than six men, all small and some large firms preferred to be non-union houses if they could;[5] and in-

[1] Originally the Tramway, Hackney-carriage Employees, and Horsemen of 1889.
[2] Cp. vol. II. 170.

[3] See the evidence of H. Slatter (Typographical Association), and C. W. Bowerman (London Compositors) before the *R.C. on Labour*, Group C. Q. 22,770 *sqq.* and Q. 22,916 *sqq.* (1893–4, XXXIV). And cp. vol. II. 169.

[4] See Webb, *Industrial Democracy*, p. 500.

[5] Their witness before the *R.C. on Labour* admitted (Q. 22,799 *sqq.*) that it was troublesome to small masters. On it, see Webb, *Industrial Democracy*, p. 466.

numerable printers inevitably learnt their trade in a non-union atmosphere. On this point the London Compositors were more rational: they made no objection to the time-honoured ratio of one apprentice, whether regularly bound or not, to every three journeymen. But the apprenticeship rules, even when reasonable, combined with the exclusion of women and the high union wage-rates in cities to keep many large printing houses, besides the little shops, in quiet country places where unionism was weak. There was a good deal of printing done in Cambridge, but the Typographical Association had no branch there in the nineteenth century. For these various reasons, not 40 per cent. of the men and lads who described themselves as printers in 1911 were also trade unionists; and this in a highly skilled trade, and a trade only partially transformed by recent mechanical changes, and a trade in which union or club traditions were usually strong and old.

Among trades in which unionism was abnormally weak, pottery was conspicuous. Plenty of unions had been formed among potters since the first of 1824, but they had been small and local and usually short-lived. "There was a stamp of futility on everything the unfortunate potter touched" an old potter was writing in 1903.[1] A year earlier the Board of Trade had reported on seventeen pottery unions. Seven of these had recently been dissolved, and the aggregate membership of the rest in 1901 had been 5100.[2] By 1910 the number of unions had fallen by amalgamation and death, to four; the aggregate membership to 4700. There were some 70,000 people in the trade. Nearly 30,000 of these were women and girls; but the unions admitted women. If the figures reported are correct, as they seem to be, the women dropped in and out of membership oddly. In 1909 there were 1050 and 358 in 1910. In 1911 a recruiting campaign brought many of them, or some different women, in again.[3] The trade was technically old-fashioned.[4] There was a great deal of piece work. Working conditions had once been intolerably bad. They were not yet generally good; and it had become almost an axiom with trade-union organisers and students of society that bad working conditions and weak

[1] *When I was a Child*, by an Old Potter, quoted in Warburton, W. H., *The History of Trade Union Organisation in the North Staffordshire Potteries* (1931), p. 176.

[2] *Report on Trade Unions*, 1902, p. 89.

[3] Figures from the 1912 *Report on Trade Unions*, p. 58; and Warburton, p. 215, for the recruiting campaign.

[4] Above, p. 188.

unionism went together. Masters and men alike followed their private ways in the social isolation of the Five Towns. The masters were no better organised than the men, from whose ranks most of them had "very recently"[1] sprung; and many working potters had inherited the individualist and driving outlook of employer piece-workers. So they passed up easily into pure employers when they got the chance. Sometimes they came down again. A potters' union, that of the Hollow Ware Pressers, had a rule in the 'nineties which it would be hard to parallel at that date in any other organised trade, though the movement to which it referred may have been found in many trades: "members who become employers may be reinstated within three months after their return to the trade."[2]

Trade unionism almost as weak as that of the potteries could be found in industries not nearly so isolated or technically so late developed. Wool is a notable instance. True, in the final processes of dyeing and finishing, as in cotton dyeing and finishing and the cognate cotton processes of bleaching and printing, the unions were now exceedingly strong. These four interlocking trades—many fabrics which come to the dyer are mixtures of the two fibres—employed on cotton and on wool 84,000 people in 1911. They contained 45,000 trade unionists at the end of that year, and in 1913, when the numbers in the trades cannot have grown much, 66,000. The strong and efficient Bradford Dyers' Association had treaties latterly with its men—Dyers, Bleachers, Finishers and Labourers—which gave them almost everything that a trade unionist could wish: the right of the unions to be consulted when fresh men were taken on; the obligation on all adults who worked for the Association to belong to some union; a pledge that no wage changes should be made without the written consent of a union official; the establishment of a Reference Board, with secretaries from both sides, for the settlement of small differences; a plan for making displacements of labour as little distressing as might be; and many like provisions.[3] It is to be noted that the four trades affected were primarily men's trades, though about a sixth of the workpeople and some of the unionists were women.

[1] Warburton, p. 187. And cp. Arnold Bennett, *Clayhanger*.

[2] *Rules* of 1890: Warburton, p. 188, n. 1.

[3] Agreement of July 1, 1914, between the Bradford Dyers' Association and the Dyers' Unions and the Gasworkers and General Labourers Union, printed in Milne-Bailey, W., *Trade Union Documents* (1929), pp. 237–44.

The contrast between the labour organisation in these final processes and in the earlier ones, the woollen and worsted industries proper, is overwhelming: 223,000 people in the trades of combing, spinning and weaving, and of trade unionists only 23,000 in 1911 and 32,000 in 1913. Fifty-seven per cent. of the people were women and girls; but the cotton unions were full of women while the wool unions had only a few thousands. And of the 23,000 unionists of 1911 more than 3000 belonged to the societies of the directive overlookers who watched the women at their work. Deduct again some 6000 Machine Woolcombers in Bradford—recently enlisted: there were only 1800 in 1909—and spread the rest over the West Riding, parts of Lancashire, the Tweed towns, the Stroud valley and some other places, and the entire inadequacy of trade unionism in wool becomes apparent.[1]

It was little more adequate in the other textile industries, except among the flax and jute workers of Dundee, where the two chief unions had over 11,000 members by 1910, of whom 9000 were women—a remarkable contrast with the 5000 women in all the wool industries everywhere. Unionism was growing also at Dunfermline and Forfar. Elsewhere in linen it was weak but so was the industry, except about Belfast. In hosiery it was as feeble as in wool: 6000 members of 14 or 15 detached unions were scattered over a trade which found work for 68,000 people in 1911. In silk, a diminishing industry, it had been just as feeble down to 1906, when the Amalgamated Women Workers of Leek began to stir. By 1910 they alone had nearly 5000 members; and the other unions in a trade which employed about 32,000 people had 3000. That was good so far as it went. Much further it was not likely to go in a trade placed as silk was.

Unionism was strong in the ancient craft of the hatters, though machinery and shiftings of the centres of production had interfered with its growth and working;[2] strong among certain sections of the tailors; weak among workers in the clothing factories and the cappers; negligible among the hundreds of thousands of seamstresses, dress-makers, milliners and all the stitching trades, with their small business units, their upstairs gentility and their

[1] Figures from the *Reports on Trade Unions*; and cp. Clapham, J. H., *The Woollen and Worsted Industries* (1907), pp. 204–13.

[2] The main concentration was now at Denton, near Stockport, where most of the great 'London' firms had factories. As that was a trade-union area, this was no drawback.

echoes of the Song of the Shirt down all the lower corridors. Among the dispersed and declining hand boot-makers it was rather weak, though small numbers and real skill made their local groups good bargain drivers, whether the members were formally in union or not;[1] but in the rising, the risen, trade of factory boot-making it was unusually strong and efficient, and as a rule very politic. The great bootmakers' union, the National Boot and Shoe Operatives of 1874, had trebled its numbers between 1885 and 1891, when they reached 30,000. They grew further before a long and rather mistaken struggle in 1895 led in a period of numerical decline, which extended down to 1906.[2] But at its worst the union had 24,000 members; from 1907 to 1910 it averaged 30,400; and after that, like most other unions, it grew fast. All the while, before the struggle and after, when its management became more politic, it had an effective share in the general control of the machine boot trade and a most efficient administrative organisation.

At the close of 1910, when there were some 2,500,000 trade-union members in the country, they were spread among no less than 1153 distinct unions. A third of the unions had less than 100 members, many of them very much less. These small societies were common in the Sheffield, and in all the light metal, trades. The Razor Hafters with 66 members and the Birmingham Britannia Metal Workers with 62 were not the smallest. They were common also among old-fashioned crafts which retained the local club without any effective federation: of 30 unions of coopers, 18 were of this type, Alloa Coopers, Sheffield Coopers, Swansea Coopers. The Burton Coopers were naturally a large and powerful society, and so were the Liverpool Coopers who worked for the ships. Small unions were to be found too in all sorts of queer trades where no union could possibly be big—the Cigar Sorters and Bundlers and the Bone Brush Makers, both of London; the Cocoanut Fibre Weavers of Diss; the Birmingham Horse Collar Makers, and the Bradford and District Amalgamated Chimney Sweepers. In their trade and locality many of these were at least as efficient in self-defence and self-assertion, in pursuit of all the recognised methods of trade unionism, as some of the national unions, or as some of those wide

[1] Their main union, the Amalgamated Society of Boot and Shoe Makers, of 1862, had 3928 members in 1897 and 1448 in 1910.

[2] For the struggle see Webb, *History of Trade Unionism* (1902 ed.), pp. xvi, 393, 495, and *Industrial Democracy*, p. 187.

federations of unions so many of which had come into being since 1886.[1]

England, a friendly but impatient critic of trade unionism was writing in 1913, "has evolved a Trade Union structure which is the merest chaos".[2] He found the federations especially chaotic, not amenable to definition, not in harmony with the new thought of the day, and so slightly repulsive to the revolutionary academic mind. "It is never possible, without particular study of each case, to discover what the mere fact of Federation implies."[3] (And why indeed should it be?) "Some Federations are merely political, some in practice concern themselves almost solely with demarcation disputes; others are regarded by their promoters merely as steps to Amalgamation and yet others are the real centres of industrial action." The Miners' Federation of Great Britain, formed in the rush of union activity in 1888–9 and originally the organ of the left wing as opposed to the industrial conservatism of the leaders in Northumberland and Durham, had gradually become a central representative body for nearly the whole trade, after its older rival the National Union had been dissolved in 1898.[4] There were no demarcation problems as between Lanarkshire, Durham and South Wales. By its very origin the Federation had some difficulty in formulating programmes, industrial or politico-industrial, equally attractive to all its constituent states; for they were little less. But that is the normal position of all federal governments; and a certain restiveness of some of the states under federations into which perhaps they came late and rather unwillingly is also normal. This Miners' Federation, the greatest in the country by 1908–10, when unions with a membership of 600,000 were represented in it, was one of the federal types.

[1] The federations existing before 1886 were—Leicester and District Building Trades of 1874; Nottingham and District Building Trades Council of 1872; Northumberland Fed. of Miners, Deputies and Mechanics of 1882; Durham Mining Federation of 1878; Nat. Fed. of Colliery Enginemen and Boilermen of 1873; Nat. Fed. of Blastfurnacemen, etc. of 1882; United Journeyman Brass Founders, etc. of 1866; London Gold and Silver Trades Council of 1885; United Textile Factory Workers of 1883; Gen. Un. of Assoc. of Loom Overlookers of 1885; Amalgamated Weavers of 1884; Lancs. Amal. Tape Sizers of 1880; Mutual Assoc. of Journeyman Coopers of 1878. In all 13: in 1910 there were 114. *Report on Trade Unions*, 1912, pp. 116 *sqq.*

[2] Cole, *The World of Labour*, p. 211. [3] *Ibid.* p. 217.

[4] Webb, *History of Trade Unionism*, p. 380; Welbourne, E., *The Miners' Unions of Northumberland and Durham*; Jevons, H. S., *The British Coal Trade*, p. 480.

In the building trades there was a very different type. There a number of local Federations, or Building Trades Councils, representing the lodges of the various crafts, had been formed mainly during the 'nineties. There were not many of them; they had never shown great vitality; and their nominal members, that is to say the members of the lodges in which a majority had voted for federation, were in 1910–13 only a petty fraction of the building workers.[1] In one or two places affiliation had been transferred from a Building Federation to a general Trades Council. In very many the formation of a Trades Council—there were more than 250 of them now—had made sectional organisations rather superfluous, and in the eyes of some labour strategists undesirable. The action of the local Building Federations was not properly co-ordinated with that of the national unions of Carpenters, Bricklayers and Stonemasons. Whatever the causes, the Building Federations were not only few but dwindling.

It was Robert Knight's great Federation of Engineering and Shipbuilding Trades, founded like the very different Miners' Federation in 1889,[2] which critics had chiefly in mind when they spoke of federations which concerned themselves "almost solely with demarcation disputes". A humble duty perhaps, but in 1889–90 a most necessary one. Unhappily the Federation did not perform it with much success during its early years, largely because at that time the Amalgamated Engineers had refused to come in. Was this job an engineer's or a boiler-maker's or a plumber's? Was that a shipwright's or a carpenter's? Inter-union squabbles about these things led to "disorganisation and chaos"[3] on Tyneside between 1890 and 1893. In the twentieth century, when the Engineers had joined, the Federation included them and the Boiler-makers, the Shipwrights, Painters, Plumbers, Carpenters and many more. Demarcation disputes had become fewer, but the Federation had not changed its principal objective. It only took action when invited, either in an inter-union dispute or in one between unionists and employers. It had no coercive powers and inadequate funds. Membership was cheap and could be lightly undertaken. So reformers whose ideal federation was one powerful for economic war looked on it coldly. What might its nearly 400,000 members not have

[1] On them see Cole, *The World of Labour*, pp. 266–9. His discussion suggests that they were more important than they really were.

[2] See Webb, *Industrial Democracy*, p. 132.

[3] *Ibid.* p. 513.

achieved after 1910 had they been working together for common ends?

The most interesting of all the federations was the General Federation of Trade Unions set up by the Trade Union Congress in 1899. Its main object was the establishment of a central fund, raised by the contributions of its constituent societies, from which any one of them might be helped when engaged in a trade dispute. At the end of 1900, sixty-four societies with 387,000 members had joined; ten years later the numbers were a hundred and thirty-two and 710,000. But the hundred and thirty-two were not a tenth of the unions, though the 710,000 were more than a quarter of the unionists. The miners, the railwaymen and some other strong groups never joined. The Federation was no stronger financially than numerically: the maximum contribution was 4*d.* per quarter per member of the constituent society, in return for which it promised 5*s.* per member per week during a dispute of which it approved. In 1910–11 it paid out more than twice its incomings, mainly to the Boiler-makers; and it continued to overspend during the unrest of 1911–13, without increasing its contributing constituency so fast as trade-union membership in general grew. It never became that central body for co-ordinating industrial action by the unions—with expert official knowledge blessing and financing the wise strikes, damning and starving the foolish—which its founders and its Secretary, W. A. Appleton, had planned. When National Health Insurance came in 1911, the Secretary wished to make it the Approved Society for the whole body of trade unions, which would have added greatly to its strength. He failed, as might have been expected, seeing that only a minority of unionists had any link with his Federation. It did however become the Approved Society for a considerable group of the weaker unions.[1]

The "mere chaos" of British trade-union structure, so tiresome to systematic minds, was due like other chaotic things in the country to the spontaneity of industrial growth and the absence of central planning.[2] In Germany a Social Democratic

[1] *Report on Trade Unions*, 1912, pp. lviii–lix, 116 *sqq.*; Webb, *History* (1902 ed.), p. xiii; Cole, *op. cit.* pp. 243–4, 280; Milne-Bailey, *op. cit.* p. 27: it "soon degenerated into a mutual insurance organisation, and its strength and importance have continued to dwindle ever since". This is perhaps too severe for the first decade of its history.

[2] Citrine, W. M., *Report on Trade Union Organisation* (T.U.C. Annual Report, 1925) and *The Trade Union Movement of Great Britain* (1926), p. 27; extracts in Milne-Bailey, *op. cit.* pp. 86, 122.

Party had, so to speak, designed trade unionism: in England trade unionists, where they were strong enough, had sent their own representatives to Parliament. Latterly they had participated in a Labour Representation Committee and a Labour Party of which, at that time and later, they were both the strength and the weakness. The structure of the unions varied as much as their size and their resources, but retained that bias towards over-simplicity and confusion of powers which it inherited from its origin in the small self-governing local club, where all things can be decided by all, the committee can be re-elected annually, and the Secretary, well known to every member, is their factotum. This was the pattern of the little friendly society or the village cricket club. The many hundreds of small local unions were still of this type, and very properly. All the Razor-Hafters who were likely to turn out on any given night could easily meet and vote. But down to 1895 so great a society as that of the Boiler-makers was ostensibly governed in this way. The executive committee changed every year, and the handful of other paid officials serving for only a few years had to be re-elected by popular vote. They always were: the maxim that no public man was so secure in office as a trade-union official was establishing itself. Robert Knight was secretary and master of the Boiler-makers for more than a quarter of a century. Although in theory the mass meeting of the branches was supreme, the annually changing executive was supreme in fact, and the very able and upright permanent official naturally dominated the executive. From 1897 the executive became more stable: its seven members now served for three years, two or three of them retiring each year. Thus some continuity was established; and the secretary remained.[1]

It was noted as a politico-economic anomaly in the 'nineties that, "until the present generation",[2] no trade union had based its constitution on the parliamentary model of an elected assembly appointing and controlling a cabinet served by permanent officials. Crude democracy outside the small local unions had bred dictator secretaries, good and bad, or else

[1] Webb, *Industrial Democracy*, pp. 28–31. Any short account of trade-union organisation and functions for this period is necessarily based on that penetrating and almost exhaustive analysis. The editions used here are 1897 (the first) and 1902. The page references are to the first edition; but the text was unchanged in the third (1920).

[2] *Industrial Democracy*, p. 11.

indiscipline leading to inefficiency and to frequent breakdown. Even powerful unions with central executives often left so much authority to the local groups, the primitive cells, that there was constant danger of the circumference controlling the centre. So it was in the building trades, and very noticeably in the Amalgamated Society of Engineers, the model amalgamated of the second half of the nineteenth century.[1] There, in the 'nineties, strike pay of 5*s*. was voted at the centre, out-of-work pay of 10*s*. at the branch, but from the general funds. So a branch could, and did, go its own way and have its own quarrels and drag the centre after it; for when you strike you are out of work. Agreements with employers and with other unions were imperilled and a general distrust of the Engineers' policy fostered. But for this, the great strike in which they found themselves involved in 1897 might possibly have been averted, though considering the points at issue and the fighting spirit of employers and men that is perhaps unlikely.[2] At least it might have ended more favourably for the men.

It is not however to be forgotten that, whatever the constitution, thoroughly centralised control was much more difficult to establish, and from the national standpoint less certainly desirable, in scattered variegated industries such as engineering and building than in concentrated industries like cotton-spinning, dyeing, boiler-making or machine boot-making, industries whose unions were so constituted that treaty making and the application of treaties became relatively easy. The cotton spinners were the model parliamentary democrats of the' nineties and later.[3] They were governed by an assembly of about a hundred, elected by the "provinces and districts". From its decisions there was no appeal, either ostensible or dangerously real, to mass meetings and branch clubs, as in so many unions. This assembly chose the government, a small mixed body with

[1] Cp. vol. II, 159–61; *Industrial Democracy*, pp. 48, 49, 97.

[2] The employers "asserted, apparently with truth, that the then existing conditions of employment [by insisting on time-rates of pay and so obstructing the introduction of new processes] militated against efficiency"; Webb, *History of Trade Unionism*, ed. 1902, p. xvii. This made them hostile to collective bargaining. "The workmen...were at least equally shortsighted...they met the employers' expedient with no alternative proposal of their own" (p. xviii). "The London branches precipitated a rupture by a demand for the Eight Hours' Day" (p. xix). The men lost all along the line; but as their loss was recorded in a collective agreement, they made a certain gain in principle. Cp. p. 489 below.

[3] *Industrial Democracy*, p. 38.

a bare majority of working spinners and a minority of the permanent officials of the districts. The assembly also elected the secretary and fixed his salary. Like any member of Her Majesty's Civil Service, candidates for this high office had to pass a competitive examination. Once appointed, the secretary, in theory as well as in fact, served like a judge during good behaviour, "so long as he gives satisfaction" said the rule.

The Spinners' secretary had an adequate staff: it was he and they and the permanent officials of the districts who enforced treaties, smoothed over minor disputes in conjunction with the representatives of the employers, and carried on the day to day administration of union affairs and funds.

The railway unions, and the gasworkers', the dockers' and the other new unions of the late 'eighties, were governed with less, but still considerable, parliamentary form by annual assemblies of district delegates and executive committees elected by the districts. The local club of the local craft had small place in the traditions of the railwaymen. They thought naturally in terms of areas and long distances. Besides, they could move about easily.

Cotton spinning was an old revolutionised industry with a long tradition of unionism, although in its federal form the Amalgamated Spinners dated only from 1870. The National Union of Boot and Shoe Operatives had been registered only in 1874, when the real industrial revolution in boot-making had barely begun.[1] But the Midland boot-makers had always been politically minded and adventurous. Were not some of them represented in the 'eighties by Bradlaugh and Labouchère? At that time the union was still comparatively small and its organisation primitive. Between 1885 and 1890 its numbers more than doubled (from 10,000 to 23,000) and in 1890 it adopted a modern constitution, with equal electoral districts, a National Conference of district delegates to revise rules and give a general direction to policy, and an executive of representatives of the districts and elected permanent officials.[2] District mass meetings were permitted, but the executive got its real contact with its constituents through the National Conference. Its position was unusually strong, because the constitution had made it the final court of appeal when a member challenged a decision of his district branch.

[1] Vol. II. 93 *sqq.*, 168.

[2] Webb, *History*, p. 495; *Industrial Democracy*, p. 47.

The Miners also made great, if not quite universal, use of representative institutions.[1] Many of the county and area associations, or federations as some of them were called, did so before 1890. Others, such as the South Wales Miners' Federation finally established in 1898, adopted them later. There were representative assemblies, meetings of delegates they were usually called, which chose the executive and appointed the permanent officials. Northumberland and Durham however, with a few minor coalfields, clung to the old type of constitution right into the twentieth century. All power lay nominally with the lodge and the mass meeting and crucial decisions were carried by direct vote. In either case, effective power in ordinary times was with the executive and the secretaries, who were no more—if anything less—likely to be thrown over by crude democracies than by meetings of delegates. A representative system could not prevent the struggles which sprang from discontent at particular pits, though the old-fashioned constitutional theory of the Northern Coalfields made the appeasement of such struggles somewhat more difficult. The typical miner was little more amenable to the vote of a delegates' meeting than to a cumbrous mass vote of his fellows; so that peace depended everywhere, other things being equal, on the tact and authority of the officials.

The organisation of the Miners' Federation was necessarily representative. Its parliament was the Conference of Delegates from each county or district association—South Wales it might be or Cannock Chase. The Conference made the rules, drafted the policies, and could in theory at least levy unlimited contributions on the associations. There was no provision for appeal to mass meetings, no referendum by ballot; and the Conference itself chose the central executive and the permanent officials. The only check on it was the, not very great, risk of a secession. The risk was not great because, with all their varied local problems and customs, the miners' rank and file had acquired a very great uniformity of politico-economic aims. After holding out against the Federation for nearly twenty years, under the guidance of their elder statesmen, first Northumberland and then Durham (in 1906–7) applied for admission,[2] just because the principles for which it had fought—a 'living wage' instead of a wage governed by Sliding Scales; a universal law-based

[1] *Industrial Democracy*, p. 43.

[2] Welbourne, *The Miners' Unions of Northumberland and Durham*, pp. 308–9.

eight hours' day for miners; and a free use of the weapon of the strike to gain these major ends—had attracted the rank and file increasingly.

There were strikes so great, and so dourly fought, in the late 'eighties and the 'nineties, in 1907–8 and again from 1910 to 1913, and many of the best-known trade-union leaders were so resolute in their advocacy and use of the strike weapon on what they counted fitting occasions, that contemporaries were apt, and historians may be tempted, to overrate the place of the strike in the industrial life and organisation of late Victorian, Edwardian, and early Georgian England. Looking back from the comparative industrial peace of 1901 over what seemed the stormy 'nineties, and furnished by the Labour Department of the Board of Trade with precise figures of working days lost through industrial disputes, the historians of trade unionism pointed out that, as a statistical proposition, strikes and lock-outs combined accounted "for much less loss of working time in the year than our laudable custom of treating Good Friday and Christmas Day as Sundays".[1] Even in the stormier years 1910–13, the annual loss of working time, averaged in the same way over the whole wage-earning population, was still under the two days;[2] although in 1912—the worst year of all before 1921—it rose to about four.

Again, the dramatic appearance on the industrial scene of great public figures—Lord Rosebery, Bishop Westcott, Lord James of Hereford, Sir Courtenay Boyle—towards the end of some major struggles of the 'nineties must not be misinterpreted. True, Sir Courtenay Boyle, who was Permanent Secretary of the Board of Trade, actually drafted the agreement which settled the long strike of 1895 in the boot trade.[3] But he did not impose it. He was not exactly either arbitrator or umpire, though he was certainly very influential. And the function, the most important and honourable function, of the other public men was that of bridge builders between hostile shores, purveyors of reason, of sweetness and light, finders of the gestures and the forms of words which lower tempers and save faces; not that of devisers, still less that of dictators, of peace terms. Other great

[1] Webb, *History* (1902 ed.), p. xv.

[2] Assuming a wage-earning population of ten millions, it works out at 1·76 days. See the diagram, p. 499 below.

[3] *Industrial Democracy*, p. 241.

strikes of these years were settled by the parties in stubborn negotiation without such aids, as when cotton-spinners in both senses of the word, after a twenty weeks' struggle, sat all night at Brooklands in 1893 to arrive at an agreement which averted general war in cotton-spinning for over fifteen years. (There were of course frontier incidents.) The conference at Brooklands was a civilised one, to which the representatives of both sides travelled in the same train.[1]

The great engineering struggle of 1897–8 was also settled by the contending parties. But then one of them, ill-organised and ill-advised, was beat. "After dispersing the greater part of their accumulated funds, the Amalgamated Society of Engineers, with their smaller allies, had practically to accept the employers' terms."[2]

For one reason or another, most of the permanent or semi-permanent conciliation and arbitration machinery which had been erected in various trades since the 'sixties had broken down before 1890.[3] The Nottingham Hosiery and Glove Trades Board ceased to work in 1884; the Leicester Hosiery Board at about the same time; the Potteries Board in 1891–2. There was no general arbitration in Durham mining after 1882. When the Royal Commission on Labour was sitting in the early 'nineties, although some arbitration courts were working well in the building trade, and the North of England Iron and Steel Board was giving general satisfaction, there were complaints from the men's side of the failure of the Midland Iron and Steel Board to impose its findings on non-federated masters, and the bearings of the Conciliation Board in the Machine Boot Trade were getting hot.[4] Workpeople had rejected local decisions, sometimes even the findings of the central umpire.[5] Employers were equally dissatisfied. In 1894 they left the Board, refusing to accept arbitration on the issue of time versus piece-work.[6] The upshot was that strike of 1895 which was settled, most unusually,

[1] For the conference, see *Industrial Democracy*, p. 200. There was no serious trouble again in the cotton industry until 1910; Bailey, *op. cit.* p. 29; Cole, *The World of Labour*, p. 54. Cp. p. 498 below.

[2] Webb, *History* (1902), p. xix.

[3] Vol. II. 173 *sqq.*

[4] See generally the Memorandum on Arbitration drawn up for the *R.C. on Labour* (1892, xxxvi. Part 5) and Lord Amulree, *Industrial Arbitration in Great Britain* (1929).

[5] Webb, *Industrial Democracy*, p. 187.

[6] Webb, *History* (1902), p. xvi.

"by the half authoritative influence of the Board of Trade",[1] acting through Sir Courtenay Boyle. This initiated a long spell of relatively peaceful relations, which were greatly improved by the growing power and efficiency of the Machine Boot Makers Union under its new constitution.[2]

Efficient organisation on both sides was in fact more valuable than any formal machinery of arbitration in settling all minor and some major differences. One reason why the North of England Iron and Steel Board worked so well was that all the lesser and the local differences were handled by a standing joint committee.[3] Only the disputed shillings and pence of the wage went to arbitrators, or to an umpire; and there was no difference of principle about the economic basis of payment. Where there were such differences—time *versus* piece wages among bootmakers and engineers; the wage fluctuating with the selling price of coal *versus* a minimum standard at the mines—no ordinary arbitration machinery would work, and neither side was likely to give the conciliator a hearing until trial by battle had been attempted and found inconclusive or too costly. The tendency from 1893–5 onwards, in all the best organised trades, was for the experts of the two sides to smooth out minor differences until, as a rule only at long intervals, some great principle was at issue or some great passion stirred, when the expert had to stand aside until the smoke cleared. Recognition of the union, an eight-hour day, the principle of a living wage—these were things which must be accepted or refused: there was no room for friendly give and take. But it was the daily activity of the experts, playing on the ordinary human reluctance to lose a day's work or a day's pay, and on the decency of average employers and average workpeople, which kept the loss of time through disputes so low. "The mere extension of national agreements and factory legislation", it was put on record in 1897, "has already, in the most highly regulated trades...transformed the Trade Union Official from a local strike leader to an expert industrial negotiator, mainly occupied, with the cordial cooperation of the secretary of the Employers' Association and the Factory Inspector, in securing an exact observance of the Common Rules prescribed for the trade."[4]

Besides the ever widening Factory Code, a new Conciliation Act (59 and 60 Vict. c. 30) was put on the Statute Book in 1896.

[1] Webb, *History* (1902), p. xvii.
[2] Cp. p. 489 below.
[3] For it see vol. II. 175–6.
[4] *Industrial Democracy*, p. 825.

The opportunity was taken to repeal some well-intentioned dead letter laws, the Master and Workmen Arbitration Act of 1824, Lord St Leonard's Conciliation Act of 1867 and Mr Mundella's Arbitration Act of 1872. The Government in 1896, influenced apparently by the experience of the Board of Trade in connection with the boot-trade settlement of the previous year, had prepared a rather ambitious plan for an Arbitration Act.[1] But, in its final form, the Act only provided for the voluntary registration of Arbitration and Conciliation Boards; for optional inquiry by the Board of Trade into industrial disputes, either of the usual sort or those between unions; for the taking of steps by the Board to promote conciliation; and for the appointment by it of a conciliator or arbitrator, at the request of both parties to the dispute, but not otherwise.[2] There was not much registration of Boards, for they were breaking down. Still, the Act proved useful, though in a limited sphere. Twenty-eight cases were handled under it during the first year's working.[3]

But there were 926 officially recorded trade disputes in 1896. In the next ten years 5614 were recorded. Of these, 161 were settled by arbitration and 188 by conciliation and mediation. By no means all the conciliation settlements were made under the Act of 1896, though a considerable number were. Meanwhile 4004 of the quarrels were settled by negotiation between the parties or their representatives and 1182 by victories for employers—returns of the men to work on the employers' terms without negotiation, or replacement of strikers by blacklegs.[4] There was little change after 1906. In the stormy four years 1910–13 there were 3686 disputes, 64 per cent. more per year than in the decade 1897–1906. Of these 2741 were settled by negotiation between the parties, a slightly higher proportion than in the earlier decade; 92 by arbitration, a slightly lower proportion; 296 by conciliation, a much higher proportion; and only 538 (or 14·6 per cent. as opposed to 21 per cent. in 1897–1906) by employers' smashing victories.[5] The last figures suggest that, as might be expected in years of active trade, rising prices and growing trade-union strength, employers at this time either

[1] This Bill, "to confer additional powers on Boards of Conciliation and Arbitration", was not even printed.

[2] The Act (59 and 60 Vict. c. 30) is reproduced in Milne-Bailey, *Documents*, pp. 254–6.

[3] *Industrial Democracy*, p. 243, n. 1.

[4] *Eleventh Abstract of Labour Statistics* (1907, Cd. 3690), p. 94.

[5] *Eighteenth Abstract*, 1926, p. 150, reproducing earlier *Abstracts*.

did not care or were not able to press too hard on their work-people. The quiet growth of settlement by conciliation is interesting; but even so, for every dispute thus ended, either with or without the intervention of the Board of Trade, more than a dozen were ended by the disputants alone. There were Board of Trade conciliators whose names were known and honoured throughout the country; but thousands of little-known secretaries and delegates of trade unions and employers' associations, with easy knowledge of the technical and to an outside conciliator probably rather mysterious details of this or that industry, averted or finished off the ordinary trade disputes.

The work of the trade-union official, local or central, got no lighter with time. He inherited and embodied the confusion of powers of the primitive trade club. Unions seldom provided, or could afford, a complete office staff for their secretaries. New duties were piled on the old officials. They had to move about a great deal. The coming of health and unemployment insurance added to their burdens. Before insurance came, the creation of the parliamentary Labour Party had sent a number of general secretaries to Westminster, without relieving them of their secretarial duties. With the local official of an important union absorbed in the technical administration at which he was often most efficient, and the central official laden with miscellaneous and conflicting obligations, the well-informed and deliberate working out of general trade-union policy was in considerable danger of neglect.

A few of the unions realised this and had improved their headquarters machinery. The Amalgamated Railway Servants had started administrative devolution; and when they became the National Union of Railwaymen they gave their General Secretary four Assistants to deal with particular sections of the work.[1] But such systematic reorganisation was both late and rare, although the great growth of the major unions and of their activities made it most necessary.

The local Trades Councils could hardly be classed as part of the industrial organisation of the country even in 1913. Their numbers grew and so did the number of trade unionists who were affiliated to them through their unions. But after the early 'nineties the proportion of all the trade unionists of the country

[1] See Cole, *The World of Labour*, p. 283, where most of these comments are made.

so affiliated did not grow. In the twentieth century it fell. These are the figures.

	No. of Trades Councils	Members of Unions represented	Percentage of total Trade Union membership
1895	163	702,000	45
1905	239	902,000	45
1910	252	1,009,000	40
1913	329	1,495,000	36

The Councils, closely associated with local Labour Parties, were becoming more important in municipal politics, especially in centres where Labour was unusually strong such as Glasgow, Sheffield and Nottingham. They watched fair-wage clauses in municipal contracts; encouraged what in the years about 1900 was called municipal socialism; and generally served to amplify the voice of the wage-earning class. They passed a great many resolutions. But they had no definite industrial functions. They might give their blessing to one party in a trade dispute and lend their name and influence for the collection of funds if the dispute dragged. Now and then they made small grants out of their own funds, small because those funds were always scanty.[1] But, as the figures show, they had no right even to speak for the majority of trade unionists.[2] Many of the great unions, notably that of the miners, took no interest in them and never had. They had no sort of control, executive or financial, over any national union whose local branch was affiliated to them; and though they might give support in a trade dispute, or if so minded assist in a final conciliation, they were hampered at every point by this lack of real administrative power.[3]

Like the Councils, the Trades Union Congress was more a political than an industrial organism—"a deliberative body which meets only once a year and remains in session no more than a single week; it cannot execute its decisions."[4] Its constitution had changed little since it was first gathered together in 1868.[5] It was a voluntary assembly of representatives of affiliated

[1] They were derived mainly from contributions, usually of 2*d.* per member or less, from the unions represented on them. *Report on Trade Unions*, 1912, p. lx.

[2] Though they might have such a right, when well supported locally.

[3] See vol. II. 171; the note on Trades Councils in *R.C. on Labour* (1892, XXXVI. Part 5); the account of their weakness in the 'nineties in Webb, *History*, p. 467; the *Trade Unions* reports of 1902 and 1912; and the memory of any one over fifty at all interested in local economics and politics.

[4] Milne-Bailey, *op. cit.* p. 190.

[5] Vol. II. 172.

unions, just as the Councils were; but unlike them it usually secured the adhesion of unions containing about two-thirds of the total membership in the country. The representatives were able to cast as many votes as their unions had members. Originally called together by a Trades Council, it had decided in 1894 to exclude the Trades Councils from affiliation, on the ground that a man represented through his central union ought not to be represented a second time through his local branch.[1] Its critics said that the Congress Committee had found the leaders of the Councils too advanced; for there was a sharp struggle during the 'nineties in the Congress world—liberal versus socialist or semi-socialist. In 1890 Congress had been captured by the new unionists and had committed itself—by resolution—to an eight hours' day and even more revolutionary proposals.

Later a reaction came and then a rebound. In 1899 it did the most creative things of its life hitherto, when it set up the General Federation to co-ordinate the trade-union movement, and passed by votes which were held to represent 546,000 against 434,000 trade unionists, the resolution which laid the foundation of the modern political Labour Party.[2] The only permanent organ of Congress was its Parliamentary Committee, formed originally to keep touch with and influence labour legislation, not to organise labour representation. This Committee remained and, under the resolution of 1899, co-operated as time went on with the other societies and organisations which were interested in that representation. But, by handing over industrial organising work to the General Federation, the Congress, as scoffers have said, reserved to itself during the first decade of the twentieth century the functions of a debating society.[3] The outer world followed its resolutions to learn what the reputed majorities of organised labour were thinking; a public man could not afford to remain in ignorance of them. But they controlled no one and nothing. The General Federation, as has been seen, never acquired the controlling powers for which it was designed; and Congress remained a council of opinion not a council of action.

[1] Milne-Bailey, p. 27.

[2] See a hundred places, among them, Beer, M., *A History of British Socialism* (1920), II. 317 and Ensor, R. C. K., *England 1870–1914* (1936), p. 265. The vote led to the establishment of the L[abour] R[epresentative C[ommittee].

[3] Milne-Bailey, *op. cit.* p. 27. Milne-Bailey was Secretary of the Research and Economic Department of the Trades Union Congress when he published his book in 1929.

CHAPTER VI

COMMUNICATIONS

THE system of "iron veins" that traversed the frame of Britain was, as a system, all but complete in the 'eighties; although the metropolitan electric tube line system began only with the opening of the City and South London in 1890. Indeed the surface railway route-map even of 1912–13 was very little changed from that of 1872–3;[1] though the making of new routes stopped only with the century, after the Great Central had run its first train into Marylebone Station in March, 1899. This Great Central line to London was a belated, and almost certainly superfluous, product of the original era of fighting construction, driven through by a surviving pioneer, a man of the now extinct stock of the railway kings, Edward Watkin. He was managing the Manchester Sheffield and Lincolnshire Railway in 1854, a dozen years before the Midland got to London; and as Sir Edward Watkin, Bart., M.P., he was chairman of the same line when his plan for a London extension and terminus was finally sanctioned by Parliament in 1893.[2] Four years later the company took its new name.

It had been an enterprising, fighting, unprofitable concern from the first. Its old name went back to 1847, and was assumed after the Manchester and Sheffield (of 1836) had struggled, at huge labour and expense, through the Pennine Hills by the Woodhead Tunnel and had then united with the lines, made or planned, running eastward into Lincolnshire.[3] For the next fourteen years it paid no ordinary dividends worth mentioning. By 1865 the dividend was 2¼. In 1868 it was 1¼. In 1877, when the line was thought to be improving its position, it was 2⅞. But in the 'eighties the shareholders would have "thought themselves lucky if any one would guarantee them a return of 3 per cent."[4]

[1] As reproduced in vol. II. 184.

[2] For Watkin, see vol. II. 186, and especially Cleveland-Stevens, E., *English Railways, their Development and their Relation to the State* (1915), pp. 288 *sqq.* He is met in all the railway inquiries and histories. He resigned the chairmanship of the new G.C.R. in 1894, and died in 1901.

[3] For dates, etc., see Sherrington, C. E. R., *Economics of Rail Transport in Great Britain* (1928), I. 131 *sqq.*; Jackman, W. T., *Transportation in Modern England* (1916), II. 567, 601; vol. I. 394, 409; vol. II. 183, 186.

[4] Acworth, W. M., *The Railways of England* (1st ed. 1889), p. 254.

In 1902, now the Great Central with Marylebone Station three years open, it had £17,878,000 of ordinary and preferred capital receiving nothing, out of a total of £30,236,000. That was the worst; but the next ten years did little for the ordinary shareholder.[1]

Having never made railway traffic pay, the 'M.S. and L.' had tried many other things. It had been the first railway to own a steamer; it had put much money into docks and their equipment, to the great advantage of Grimsby; and had even—in the 'eighties—laid out an amusement park at Cleethorpes.[2] Of course it had hotels. As the Great Central, it had finished Immingham Docks just in time for war to lay them idle in 1914.[3]

When, as its chairman, he was planning the London extension, Watkin was chairman also of the Metropolitan and of the South Eastern railways. And they were not his only railway interests. One other was the project for a Channel Tunnel. He dreamt of linking up these four through London and of running 'his' traffic from the industrial North into France; but that he was too old to accomplish. Nor could he, or any one else, have put it through after the financial catastrophe of the Great Central. It is "very doubtful", an expert railwayman was saying in 1910, "whether any capital spent in the last twenty years in competitive schemes has realised an adequate return";[4] and so, for such schemes, it was hard to raise. The last new railway to succeed had been the Barry Dock coal line. It opened its first section in 1888 and its last in 1897. But its circumstances were exceptional in those great days of the South Wales coal export.[5] Another now forgotten new line of the 'nineties, the Lancashire Derbyshire and East Coast—it never got to the first or the last: its maximum extension was from Chesterfield to Lincoln—was absorbed by the still unprosperous Great Central in 1907, when Watkin's old company was, very wisely, strengthening its posi-

[1] It was considered an improving line in 1907; *Economist* Dec. 7 and 21, 1907. By the end of 1912 the preferred ordinary shares stood at 32, the deferred at 15.

[2] Acworth, *op. cit.* pp. 249, 254. I hope I am not biassed against the 'M.S. and L.' by memories of the foul air of its Woodhead Tunnel and of a railway accident on it near Penistone in the early 'eighties in which I might very easily have been killed.

[3] They were opened in 1912 but were not in full work by 1914.

[4] *Report of Dep. Com. on Railway Agreements and Amalgamations* (1911, XXIX. Part 2), Q. 12,316.

[5] Sherrington, *op. cit.* I. 75.

tion on the South Yorkshire, Derbyshire and Nottinghamshire coalfields.

There were of course extensions, coal-pit lines, branch lines and loop lines built by existing companies in the twentieth century; but the route mileage of British railways, which had been 16,904 in 1887, grew only from 18,680 in 1900 to 20,281 in 1913. Of these 1601 miles of new line, 395 ran over rather light soil in Scotland. Geographically, the British railway system was about finished.

In the 'eighties the organisation and working of the system had still been models for the world, as they had been in the 'seventies, when Frenchmen and Germans wrote laudatory accounts of them[1] and Edward Watkin took his great experience to the United States to reorganise the Erie Road. "It was the example of what England could do", England's leading railway economist wrote in 1899, "which stimulated American and foreign railways to the vast improvements which they have made in the last ten years." The "gap between us" was "fast closing up", he said. At several points it was negative. Foreign inquirers no longer came to England. They thought "there was nothing new in English railway matters to be studied";[2] so went to America instead. The English lines themselves began to put a value on American experience about the turn of the century, and to build locomotives called Atlantics after a type first used on the Atlantic Coast Line Road in 1895. It was about this time also, after compound locomotives had been much used in America, that a patent was taken out for the only system of compounding which was ever much adopted in England.[3]

British railways had not been idle in the 'nineties, though others were more active. There had been a great increase of four-track mileage all over the country. The services to Scotland and Ireland had been vastly improved. The Great Western had got rid of the last of its broad-gauge sections in 1892, and so had made its whole system accessible to standard rolling stock. It had been given a complete overhaul and its management was wideawake—but it did not put a luncheon car on to its Cornishman until 1899. The London and North Western lit its principal

[1] Malézieux, J., *Les chemins-de-fer anglais en 1873* (1874); Schwabe, H., *Ueber das Englische Eisenbahnwesen* (1871); and Gustav Cohn's great *Englische Eisenbahnpolitik* (1874–5).

[2] Acworth, *op. cit.* (5th ed.), pp. xiii, 470–1.

[3] Sherrington, *op. cit.* I. 175. See vol. II. 191 n., and cp. Acworth (5th ed.), p. 454.

trains with electricity in 1895; but it was only after 1900 that steam heating generally superseded the metal foot-warmers thrown on to the floor, which, with the oil-lamps pushed through the roof, had been universal up to the 'nineties. Locomotives and trains became steadily heavier; for, other things apart, the new dining, sleeping and corridor coaches were bulky. Goods trains and goods delivery became faster; the average consignment became smaller.[1] But to the increase in size of locomotive, coach or coal-waggon limits were set by bridges in congested towns, the short radius of curves, and the whole lay-out of stations, docks and staiths. These things could be altered only in time and at great expense. In this as in much else, Britain, the pioneer country, suffered. The suffering did not end with the century. When in 1908 the Great Western built a famous huge 'Pacific' type locomotive—once again an American nickname—its weight and its very long wheel-base were found to be unfit for many sections of the Great Western road.[2]

As prices rose after 1896, while the amenities which the railways offered in competition with one another became more elaborate, and the companies' power to charge more for them was checked both by the widespread possibility of a resort to water transport and by recent government activity,[3] the general ratio of working expenses to receipts for the British railway system deteriorated. In the 'seventies and 'eighties it had never been above 55 per cent. and in good years was so low as 52 or even 51. By 1900 it was 62: its average for the years 1900 to 1913 was between 62 and 63.[4] Naturally dividends fell, though not disastrously. London and North Western 'consols' were still normally worth more than 130 in 1912–13 and North Eastern 'consols' more than 120. But this seemed low to those who remembered North Westerns at 186 twenty years earlier.

Unable to raise their rates or fares, the companies pursued economy by way of increased co-operation. By this time, thanks to the working of various conferences, there was no real competition between them in the fares and rates. All lines used the same goods classification, and transit charges for Class V goods

[1] 'Became' is an assumption, for no regular statistics were published. For the small consignment see p. 358 below.

[2] Sherrington, *op. cit.* I. 178. The Pacific type was in fact first used in New Zealand.

[3] Below, p. 355. For water competition, vol. II. 193.

[4] Figures from the *Statistical Abstracts of the U.K.*

or first-class passengers from x to y were based on the shortest route which any company could offer between the two points.[1] Precluded from attracting business by offering a lower rate, zealous local agents had done it in a score of other ways—they weighed goods for nothing, warehoused them cheap, allowed traders to leave full trucks in sidings for days on end without extra charge, or were complaisant about the claims which customers might make for delay or damage to goods in transit. They tried to be prompter, more businesslike, more polite than their rivals. From 1900 onwards however fewer conveniences were given gratis and there was more agreement about the charges to be made for them. Above all, the companies had set up a Joint Claims Committee to promote uniform treatment of a very delicate matter about which traders were particularly sensitive.[2]

All this was not enough, and the railway strategist inclined more and more towards what had been known in the jargon of railway inquiries for more than thirty years as the policy of 'districting'.[3] A model railway of the early twentieth century was the North Eastern. Its general managers were men of vision who believed in education, the value of railway statistics, big coal waggons, and a discriminating study of American methods. Unlike some of their colleagues, they recognised the trade unions.[4] In 1904 the North Eastern had introduced automatic signalling, and it had electrified its suburban lines on Tyneside to compete with the municipal electric trams.[5] It had always controlled a district, a monopoly area like those of the French railways, and its management was publicly conscious of the advantages of this arrangement.[6] Other railways coveted it. The need for economy, and for the co-operation which might bring economy, was driven home to them by the growing strength of the Amalgamated Society of Railway Servants and the attitude of the new Liberal ministry of 1905–6. When, in 1907, the rail-

[1] See Acworth, *Elements of Railway Economics* (1905), p. 112, and the evidence before the *Dep. Com.* of 1911.

[2] *Dep. Com.* of 1911, Q. 488 (W. F. Marwood of the Board of Trade), Q. 14,253 (A. K. Butterworth of the N.E.R.).

[3] Vol. II. 184, 188.

[4] Tomlinson, W. W., *The North Eastern Railway* (1914), pp. 728, 748 *sqq.*, 750; Alcock, *Fifty Years of Railway Trade Unionism*, p. 382; Trevelyan, G. M., *Grey of Fallodon* (1937), p. 86. Before he went to the Foreign Office in 1905 Grey was chairman of the North Eastern. Cp. p. 491 below.

[5] Tomlinson, p. 729.

[6] *Dep. Com.* of 1911: evidence of A. K. Butterworth, Q. 14,162 *sqq.*

waymen put forward their national programme, with higher pay and shorter hours as its main items, and the mediation of Lloyd George from the Board of Trade had prevented a strike,[1] the companies realised that their acceptance at his hands of a complex system of conciliation and arbitration boards might not mean the carrying out of the whole national programme, but would certainly raise working expenses. And they had the impression that the Government wished them to co-operate and consolidate[2]—as it very probably did, so far as governments may be said to have wishes. There was a recent and what seemed a decisive precedent, so recent as 1899.[3] Most people had agreed for years before 1899 that an allowance of three separate railways for the South East corner of England—the London Chatham and Dover, the London Brighton and South Coast and the South Eastern—was excessive. Consolidation had often been discussed. There were standard Victorian jokes at the expense of these lines and the Chatham paid no dividend. While Sir Edward Watkin was in the South Eastern chair, a rather senseless and personal feud between his line and the Chatham kept these two lines apart. After his retirement in 1894, their officers turned to the very extensive powers of co-operation which were already conceded to them in their various Acts, and might well have been used earlier. Arrangements were completed in 1898 for a general consolidation of working and management. Shareholders and the public were kept fully informed. And when the companies went to Parliament in 1899 for a confirmatory Act no serious objection was made.[4] Theirs was not a large district and the Brighton line remained independent.

Elsewhere greater companies had all sorts of particular working arrangements with one another, running rights over one another's tracks, poolings of receipts at specified points, and leases of lines from neighbours some of whom no longer really existed—like the notorious Manchester and Milford, which was given on railway maps about 50 miles of line, all in the County of Cardigan. But full amalgamation required an Act of Parliament; and a general working union, if not clearly provided for in existing Acts, might be quashed by the Railway and Canal Commission.[5] It was a question, then, for companies seeking

[1] The best account is in Halévy, *Hist. du Peuple anglais, Epilogue*, II. 104 *sqq.*

[2] Guy Granet, of the M.R., stated their grievance in 1911, Q. 18,195 *sqq.*

[3] Cleveland-Stevens, *op. cit.* pp. 309–11.

[4] To the Act 62 and 63 Vic. c. 168.

[5] See vol. II. 195–6.

economy by way of co-operation, how far they could go with quiet poolings and agreements that could not be challenged, and beyond that what Parliament might be expected to allow. In spite of its acquiescence in 1899, Parliament was suspicious and easily roused by Chambers of Commerce and traders generally, who had an inherited feud with the companies and responded easily to cryings against 'railway monopoly'. Also railways which wanted to co-operate might have to face the interested opposition of other railways.

The Great Central, with no dividends, was naturally in the former group, and its recent bid for London traffic had driven some important companies into the latter. Late in 1907, to the "general satisfaction" of shareholders and "all others interested in railway economies",[1] a working agreement was announced between it and the Great Northern. There was to be a joint managing committee and a sharing of net receipts on the basis of the 1906 takings, with adjustments later.[2] The two companies relied on a railway Act nearly fifty years old (21 and 22 Vict. c. cxiii of 1858) which gave powers to the Manchester, Sheffield and Lincolnshire to make some such agreement with the Great Northern. There was at once a little flutter in their shares.[3] But the agreement was challenged, and the Railway Commissioners decided against it, partly on the very reasonable ground that the North and South running Great Central of 1907 was not the East and West running Manchester, Sheffield and Lincolnshire of 1858.[4] The Court of Appeal upheld the Commissioners (March, 1908) and Great Central 4 per cent. Preference dropped 20 points from a recent maximum.

The defeated companies then tried Parliament, but now in association with the Great Eastern, with which they proposed a Working Union in 1909. This was a proposal for genuine 'districting'. East of the Great Northern main line to Doncaster there was hardly anything which did not belong to one of the three. It was however unfortunate for the districting argument, and possibly for the success of the Bill, that the Great Central new main line ran West of the main lines of both the Midland and the London and North Western so far as Rugby, and North of that wriggled across and across Midland lines all the way to Sheffield.[5] It was not therefore surprising that the proceedings

[1] *Economist*, Dec. 7, 1907.
[2] *Economist*, Dec. 21, 1907.
[3] *Economist*, March 7, 1908.
[4] Sherrington, *op. cit.* I. 243.
[5] Cp. the map in vol. II. 184 with the existing course of the line to Marylebone.

of the Bill revealed a great divergence of opinion both in and out of Parliament.[1] Only just passed on the second reading, it was eventually withdrawn, although Bonar Law the Conservative Leader and Richard Bell, the M.P. of the railwaymen, had both voted for it.

One thing which no doubt influenced its promoters was the growing intimacy between the Midland, the London and North Western and the Lancashire and Yorkshire. Ever since the two latter had planned an amalgamation, and been refused it by Parliament, in 1872, their relations had been close and friendly. Nineteen years before 1872, there had been talk which was perhaps not utterly forgotten of an amalgamation between the North Western, the Midland—then a veritable Midland—and the North Staffordshire.[2] Since 1900, local pooling and other co-operative agreements had been arranged; and in 1908 a very comprehensive one was made between the Midland and the North Western.[3] It was so quietly done that nearly a year later its terms were not known to the public.[4] They included the pooling of receipts from all traffic that was reckoned competitive and from some that was not. Next year, just when the Great-Northern-Eastern-Central Bill was before Parliament, the Lancashire and Yorkshire came into the pool. Similar arrangements between the chief Scottish companies were made about the same time. The trading public, imperfectly informed of the terms but apprehensive about the consequences, and familiar with the terms of the much criticised and abandoned Bill for Eastern England, became restless. It was given the usual opiate—a Departmental Committee on Railway Agreements and Amalgamations, whose report did not appear until 1911. The General Manager of the North Western told this Committee in 1910 that his line, and he believed the public, owed a great deal to their pools; and that he looked forward to complete amalgamation with his two friendly neighbours. In a wider amalgamation he saw no advantage. He would leave the Great Northern group to do as they wished. That was his notion of 'districting'. "I would...district",[5] he said. The Committee in its *Report* was unanimously in favour of "more perfect understandings and

[1] See the notes on the course of the Bill in Parliament in *Economist*, March 27, April 10, April 17, 1909.

[2] Vol. II. 184.

[3] *Dep. Com.* 1911, Q. 155 *sqq.* (W. F. Marwood).

[4] *Economist*, June 19, 1909.

[5] *Dep. Com.* 1911, evidence F. Ree, Q. 15,621.

co-operation";[1] but said nothing precise about amalgamations or 'districting'. This mattered the less because no action was taken on its report: the Board of Trade had other railway pre-occupations in 1911, when 145,000 railwaymen struck.[2]

One welcome thing at least the strike brought to the companies. Government, which was on the whole friendly to the men, allowed that the cost of meeting some of their claims might fairly be passed on to the public; and by the Railway and Canal Traffic Act of 1913 (2 and 3 Geo. V, c. 29) empowered the companies to raise rates and fares where it could be proved, to the satisfaction of the Railway Commissioners, that expense had been incurred in consequence of improvements in the conditions of labour. Rates were in fact immediately raised by 4 per cent. This same year a Royal Commission, presided over by Lord Loreburn, was instructed to examine again the already endlessly examined question of the relationship of the railways to the State. But before this Commission, starting at the ordinary pace of Royal Commissions, had got into its stride, the railways, with remarkable efficiency and speed, were moving the units of the British mercenary army to Southampton. The sittings of the Commission were broken off and never resumed. It was by this time obvious that if only the governing powers of Britain could have certain of their inhibitions shaken, the railway system of the country might be rearranged without too much opposition from those who now controlled it.

That an Act of Parliament was required in 1913, in a country whose traders spoke much of freedom and the value of individual initiative, before any railway company could put up its charges by even 4 per cent. was one of the results of the great price-fall and of the depression of profits which accompanied it.[3] The Act which made that of 1913 necessary had come towards the end of the fall, in 1894.[4] Quite early in its course, when the fall still looked like only an ordinary reaction from the inflated prices of the early 'seventies, traders with a variety of particular grievances against the railways and a general, and most comprehensible, wish that when all other things were falling railway charges should fall too, had secured an inquiry into Railway Rates and

[1] *Report*, p. 18. [2] Above, p. 327. [3] Cp. vol. II. 196, 385.

[4] The best and most impartial narrative of the complicated events leading up to the Act is Mavor, J., "The English railway rate question", *Quart. Journ. of Economics* (Boston), April, 1894.

Fares. It was the first of the many railway inquiries to be so limited. That was in 1881.[1] When, in 1885, the associated companies had drafted Bills embodying the recommendations of this Committee as they read them, traders and industrialists asserted —prices were falling unusually fast just then—that the companies were only trying to raise goods rates and legalise preferential treatment of competing imports.[2] The companies certainly had no wish to see rates lowered. They had spent heavily during the boom years of the 'seventies. They wanted a return on their money, and their main item of current expenditure, wages, had not fallen. After 1885, several regulative railway bills were drafted and abandoned, by Joseph Chamberlain and other ministers, in the intervals of the fight over Irish Home Rule. By 1886 it was fairly certain that Parliament would act soon and that goods rates would not much longer be regulated only by the obsolete maximum tolls of the railway charters and a few score of specific decisions in the Courts.[3] More than forty years back the "parliamentary" 1*d.* a mile third class had become the standard to which all other passenger fares were adjusted. Parliament in fact dealt with the goods rates in 1888, by the Railway and Canal Traffic Act of that year (51 and 52 Vict. c. 25).

This was an ambitious and formidable piece of legislation; for the official regulation of goods rates is a very different matter from the fixing of a maximum mileage charge for third-class passengers. Parliament recognised this and so went to work with ponderous deliberation. Every railway company was to submit a revised classification of merchandise traffic—revised, that is, from the rude classification made for purposes of railway tolls in the original Acts[4]—and a revised schedule of maximum rates and charges, including the much discussed and much misunderstood 'terminals', charged for services rendered at either end of the haul, which were distinct from the rate charged for actual transport and from the underlying toll for the use of the road. More than twenty years before, the companies had tried to secure parliamentary approval of the principle of the 'terminals' and had been willing to accept classified maximum terminals in return.[5] They had failed. The terminals had continued unregulated as a perpetual source of friction, though their

[1] *S.C. on Railways (Rates and Fares)*, 1882, XIII.

[2] Cp. Acworth, *Railway Economics*, p. 133.

[3] Vol. II. 197.

[4] Vol. I. 413–14.

[5] Vol. II. 195.

levy had been sanctioned by the Courts.[1] Now the companies in their new schedules were to explain precisely the circumstances in which, and conditions on which, the various terminals were to be collected.

When the revised classifications and schedules were complete, which would not be soon for there were hundreds of millions of distinct experimentally fixed rates to be systematised, they were to be approved by Parliament. The classification was not too hard. The Railway Clearing House had used one for many years. It graded goods according to their value, fragility, ease of handling, and so on, from consignments of awkward statuary down to gravel. It was so satisfactory that the Royal Commission of 1865–7 had recommended its legal recognition.[2] Modified as it had been since then to meet changed conditions, it served as a basis for the new classification; though even so the railways found the new one tiresome and, as they alleged, unworkable.[3] The rates gave vastly more trouble. The companies and the Board of Trade could not agree. During 1889 and 1890 two special commissioners, Mr Courtenay Boyle of the Board and Lord Balfour of Burleigh, sat for eighty-five days to consider the companies' proposals, to which more than 4000 objections had been tabled.[4] After that the Board submitted to Parliament thirty-five Provisional Orders with schedules of maximum rates, one for each great railway company and one for each of several groups of small ones. These went to a Joint Committee of the two Houses in 1891–2, where the rates were again considered. A number of maxima which the companies had declared too low were raised at this stage, and the "expected loss to the companies" was thus "materially reduced".[5] The upshot was a series of Railway (Rates and Charges) Order Confirmation Acts. Originally fixed for August 1, 1892, the day on which the new rates were to come into force was postponed until January 1, 1893. The whole procedure so far had been thorough and deliberate to a fault and the inquiry by Commissioners, as was to be expected, most impartial.[6]

When the new rates were analysed it appeared that the old antiquated tolls for the use of the road had been absorbed into

[1] In Hall *v.* L.B. and S.C.R., 1885 (L.R., Q.B.D. XV. 505). See Mavor, *loc. cit.* p. 288.

[2] Vol. II. 194.

[3] Acworth, *Railway Economics*, p. 136.

[4] *S.C. on Railway Rates and Charges* (1893–4, XIV), p. iv.

[5] *Ibid.* p. v.

[6] So Mavor, an outside witness, p. 293.

conveyance rates which covered the toll, the haulage charge, and a charge for the use of the company's waggons.[1] Differential rates for distance—a lower charge per mile for a long mileage—and for large consignments were approved; but specially low rates for whole train-loads were not, and even special truck-load rates were not much encouraged, all, as it would seem, to meet the case of the typical British small average goods consignment and the natural, if economically unreasonable, grievance of the small man who could not send a truck-load and disliked favourable treatment for those who could. Terminals were finally recognised. They were subdivided in principle into station terminals, for the use of the place, and service terminals, for what was done in it. All the rates and their constituent parts were maxima. Outside critics thought that existing rates had been used as a basis, not on any reasoned theory, but "in a purely empirical fashion".[2] So they had; but no railway system, public or private, has ever been very successful in applying reasoned theory to its rates. The results of that "eminently British spirit of non-logical compromise"[3] by which these maxima were arrived at deserve no close study because what had been hammered out painfully, if not logically, over three years was interfered with after twenty months.

When the appointed day (January 1, 1893) arrived the companies were not all ready. They and their advocates said that they had not been given time enough to make up their minds about the many millions of distinct problems.[4] For the elaborately devised maxima were only maxima, not working rates. Some, a minority, were equal to or below what the railways had in fact been charging. These naturally became the new rates. But most were well above, and it had to be decided how near to them it was desirable or practicable to go. A great part of the traffic of the country had been carried at special rates, fixed to meet water competition for the most part, and more intricate and apparently irrational in Britain than in any other country because of the ubiquity of that competition. The companies had planned to raise some of these in order to recoup themselves for the legally imposed cuts. Even their parliamentary critics expected

[1] The problem has always been complicated in this country by the existence side by side of private and company's waggons.

[2] Mavor, p. 294.

[3] Acworth, *Railway Economics*, p. 143.

[4] "The time allowed was quite inadequate"; Acworth, as above, p. 151.

a few rises where the special rates had been exceptionally low.[1] No one however who was not in the confidence of the General Managers, least of all the Board of Trade, expected in the autumn of 1892 what the companies did in January 1893.[2] They inserted all the maxima in their rate books for the time being, until the new special rates should be worked out; and it was asserted, and not denied, that they never told their Station Masters that these new rates "were in a vast number of cases provisional only".[3]

If this was vice or guile, as their enemies implied, it was stupid vice or very foolish guile. "Traders, who had been accustomed to pay on certain traffic, say 12*s*. a ton, received invoices claiming 16*s*. or 18*s*. or 20*s*.",[4] and no explanation. (World prices were still falling and British unemployment was rising.) Angry correspondence passed between the Board of Trade and the Railway Association.[5] Members of Parliament had full mail bags of complaint; the President of the Board talked about "bringing the railways to their senses"; and by May a Select Committee of the Commons was holding yet another railway inquiry. It was this Committee which reported that the most that either Parliament or the Board had expected was the raising of a few abnormally low rates. It also argued, not too plausibly, that the maxima had not been made to be used, certainly not to be used at once, but were a kind of iron ration for emergencies in the future. The companies, it said, might have kept their old rates, except those which were above the new maxima, and made modest changes piecemeal.[6] That was certainly what discreet management should have done, though the railways maintained that as the law and their time allowance stood it was not possible. Before the end of the year they were admitting indiscretion, when they told the Commons' Committee that, so soon as their new rate schedules were complete, they would refund any overcharges made since January.[7]

[1] *Report of S.C.* 1893–4, p. v.

[2] *Report of S.C.* 1893–4, p. vi. The Board in the autumn "were not aware of the intention of the companies".

[3] *Report*, p. vii, introduced with an "apparently".

[4] Acworth, *Railway Economics*, p. 149. Acworth is quoted because he was in general on the side of the companies. See his book *The Railways and the Traders* (1891).

[5] *Report*, p. viii.

[6] *Report*, pp. vii, xii. The dominant consideration leaks out on p. xii: "in the opinion of your committee the raising of established rates...especially in times of depression, is a most serious matter." No doubt.

[7] *Report*, p. x.

This did not save them from an odd and very short Act of Parliament which received the Royal assent on August 25, 1894—57 and 58 Vict. c. 54. The main clause of this Act declared that, if anyone should plead that a railway company had, since December 31, 1892, "directly or indirectly increased any rate or charge", and that such increase was "unreasonable", the burden of proving the contrary before the Railway and Canal Commission should lie on the company. "It shall not", the remarkable clause went on to state, "be sufficient to show that the rate or charge is within any limit fixed...by any Provisional Order confirmed by Act of Parliament." Parliament with a great pother fixes maximum charges for railway services but at once enacts that no railway may take refuge behind the plea that such maxima are, in the real world, reasonable. Incidentally, the general right of a railway to change its rates provided they were kept within its maxima, and the changes did not involve "undue preference", was now for the first time curtailed by the law.

"English railway rates", it was being explained to American readers just before this Act was passed, "do not fluctuate nearly so much as rates in America, while sudden and considerable changes are almost unknown. The changes following upon the legislation of 1891–2 are the most violent that have taken place in England for many years."[1] The commentator's first sentence helps to explain the Act of 1894: "sudden and considerable changes" seemed shocking, and the clumsy suggestion that they had come to stay led to clamour and a reversing of the parliamentary engine. His second sentence the Act stultified, by making the unchanged rates of December 31, 1892, in effect the 'reasonable' rates, upward divergence from which had to be justified to the satisfaction of the Courts. The Act therefore tended to perpetuate the stability which had for so long distinguished English from American railway charges.[2]

The companies, always liable to challenge if they raised a rate—although their liability was reduced by the costliness of proceedings before the Railway and Canal Commission[3]—hesitated to do so unless they were very sure of their ground. The Commission in fact sanctioned various increased rates after 1894, the justification most often accepted by it being some permanent increase in the cost to the company or companies of

[1] Mavor, *loc. cit.* p. 314 n.

[2] Cp. Acworth, *Railway Economics*, p. 158.

[3] *Report of the S.C.* 1893–4, p. xii.

handling a particular class of traffic;[1] but the issue was always so uncertain that a company, or rather those conferences of companies which fixed all the more important through rates, not only hesitated to initiate a rise but also to initiate an experimental reduction. For if the experiment proved unsuccessful the proposal to restore the old higher rate might lead to litigation.

So British rates as a whole retained that stability which had marked them before the law-making of 1891–2; and the companies, when faced by the increased working costs which came with the price-rise after 1896, tried various methods of co-operation already familiar, and as much combination as the State would permit, to keep expenses down. Since all other prices were rising, a moderate general rise in railway charges might have seemed reasonable to a detached mind. But the railway managers had learnt the imprudence of suggesting it. So abstract a thing as a general price-rise was not likely as yet to be pleadable in Court, even though the Commissioners had allowed in various test cases that particular increases in working costs were a reasonable defence for the increase of particular rates. When defending their pooling arrangements in 1911, spokesmen for the railways were careful to point out that pooling had not raised a single rate, and had lowered some.[2] They knew well that in the public and parliamentary eye rate-raising was the original railway sin, and that any railway policy which led to it would stand, unreasonably, condemned.

There is no doubt that this reluctance of the companies to raise charges in a time of rising prices was an important, possibly the important, cause of stagnant railway wages and so of the labour troubles of 1910–11. But those troubles at least gave the railways a plea for a general rise which Parliament and the public could understand. And the Act of 1913, which authorised such a rise to cover wage concessions to the men, could be read as only an application of the ruling which, in particular cases and for particular rates, the Courts had already given. It is an obvious enough ruling to the detached mind. But the average consumer's mind, which took rises in coal or tobacco prices as natural if tiresome, and the trading or industrial mind, which in its own sphere always identified a rising with a bright market, did not yet take a detached view of a rising market for transport

[1] Acworth, *Railway Economics*, p. 155.

[2] F. Ree of the L.N.W. before the *D.C. on Railway Agreements and Amalgamation*, Q. 15,763.

facilities. It was unthinkable that a penny a mile 'parliamentary' should ever become a penny farthing; and a general rise in goods rates was almost as bad. The former outrage was not contemplated in 1913, and the small percentage rise in goods rates of 4 per cent. could be defended on comprehensible grounds of social policy.

Within a year the notion that any price could be a semi-permanent thing was being undermined. Within four years few economic irregularities or novelties would be entirely unthinkable.

Though motor-traction came rapidly into use after 1906, no long distance transport worth mentioning, either of passengers or goods, was done by road in 1913–14. "Motor omnibuses", it was noted in 1913, "now run as far out as to Windsor, Barnet, Epping";[1] but even that was very new. The coastwise shipping and the railways, in close and intricate competition, ruled the long haul almost unchallenged. Between 1904–6 and 1910–12 the average number of passengers carried annually on the railways increased by 9 per cent.; the tonnage of general merchandise by 10; the tonnage of minerals by 12.[2] Though the companies could not keep their ratio of working costs to gross receipts below 63 per cent., as compared with the maximum of 55 in the 'seventies and 'eighties, railway stock was still attractive to investors. There was the competition of canals and inland navigations as there always had been, but with one prominent exception—the new Manchester Ship Canal—these did very little more carriage in the early twentieth century than they had done in 1888.[3] Even including the Ship Canal, whose sea-borne traffic was not really comparable with that of an ordinary canal, the tonnage of merchandise moved inland by water in Britain in 1905 was certainly not one-tenth of that moved by rail. Deducting this sea-borne traffic to Manchester, but including the rest of the traffic on the Manchester system, it was not one-twelfth.

Critics of the railways, with those who believed that the relative stagnation of inland transport by water was due rather to

[1] Webb, S. and B., *The Story of the King's Highway*, p. 261.

[2] From the *Statistical Abstracts*.

[3] Statistics in *R.C. on Canals and Waterways*, vol. IV. (1908), 2, 80. The figures of canal transport are defective and probably exaggerate it. They "are swollen by the totals of all cargoes carried on to a second or third waterway", *Fourth and Final Report of the R.C. on Canals, etc.* (1910, XII), p. 48.

some combination of state neglect and railway iniquity than to geographical and economic causes, could point to a slight decline in the traffic on those waterways which the railways owned or controlled, compared with a respectable increase since 1888 on the independent canals, over and above the new Manchester traffic. It was also noted that traffic had increased on two waterway systems of considerable importance, the Leeds and Liverpool Canal and the River Dun Navigation, since the complete control of these systems by railway companies had ceased, of the former in 1874 and of the latter in 1895. The Leeds and Liverpool paid fair dividends, earned mainly on its plains section across the Lancashire coalfield. The Dun Navigation and its associated canals also had a coalfield behind them and lay, for the most part, below the 100-foot contour line. Since 1895 it was the property of a new company, the Sheffield and South Yorkshire Navigation, which had carried out new works in the Ouse flats in connection with its northern neighbour, the Aire and Calder Navigation.[1] This was a rare thing for an English canal in the twentieth century. But in 1905 the Sheffield and South Yorkshire paid no ordinary dividend—there had never been more than ½ per cent.—and the preference dividend stood at 3 per cent. The company was complaining of railway competition alleged to be unfair—steel firms bribed to use the rail by orders for railway metal and exporters tempted to do the same by offers of cheap freights on railway-owned steamers. However, the Navigation was alive; and the Great Central Railway, from which when still the Manchester, Sheffield and Lincolnshire it had bought its waterways, was in no better financial position.[2]

The argument from the comparative success of these freed systems was good as against railway ownership or control in those particular cases. But it was far from certain that freedom would have meant more water transport in every case; that, for example, a canal running more or less parallel to a railway and controlled by it—the Kennet and Avon or the Trent and Mersey—would have done more business in open competition with it. It was not usually to a railway's interest to neglect its canals. In fact the average density of traffic in 1905 was greater on railway-owned than on free canals.[3] This is not decisive, because the

[1] *R.C. on Canals, etc.* IV. which contains a summary history of every canal, p. 352. Cp. vol. II. 198, 200.

[2] Above, p. 348.

[3] Largely owing to the very dense traffic on the Birmingham Canals; *Final Report*, p. 51.

railways had wisely never tried to acquire control over several of the longest and quietest waterways in the Midlands and the South; and they had almost emptied those of the Fen District of their traffic without buying up one of them.[1] But it shows that railway control at least did not necessarily imply stagnation or decline where there really was work for a waterway to do.

Those canals or navigations which, owing to their situation, were strong and able to compete effectively with the railway or any other form of transport had never lost their independence, and continued to carry on the work for which they had been designed. The Weaver Navigation from the salt towns of the Cheshire plains to the Mersey is a case in point.[2] Its history began in 1721. It was a Trustee system not a company, and in 1895 the Trust had been made representative of all the interests concerned. The works had been much improved between 1866 and 1875, when an hydraulic lift was installed at Anderton near Northwich, by which barges could be transferred from the Weaver water to that of the railway-controlled Trent and Mersey Canal, on their way to the Potteries.[3] Below the salt towns, "the whole of the salt trade outwards" passed down the Weaver, and could "thus be carried far cheaper than by the railways".[4]

A second successful water system, the Aire and Calder Navigation, was even older. Its original Act was 10 and 11 Wm. IV, c. 19. It was the only system which had been reported to be spending "large sums on improvements" in 1872.[5] Deepened and with its locks lengthened during the 'sixties, it had ever since been able to carry boats up to 170 tons. Latterly it had developed a system by which strings of "compartment boats", floating metal tanks dragged by a small steamer, could move up to 900 tons of coal at once from the fields of the West Riding to the company's docks at Goole. What had once been a mere navigation of the two rivers had become a complex system of canals and stretches of river, which linked up with the now rather unimportant waterways crossing the Pennines, but did its main and always important work below the 100-foot contour

[1] Vol. II. 199.

[2] *R.C. on Canals*, IV. 385; and Leech, Sir Bosdin, *History of the Manchester Ship Canal* (1907), I. 27.

[3] *Final Report*, p. 36. The canal has a place in an early chapter of Arnold Bennett's *Clayhanger*.

[4] Leech, as above; and vol. II. 199.

[5] Vol. II. 198; and see vol. I. 76 and the *R.C. on Canals*, IV. 229.

line between Leeds and the sea. It was both a carrier and a levier of tolls on the boats of "the various by-traders"[1] who used its water; and in the first capacity it had to meet their competition besides that of the railways. But a fair part of the recent modest increase in free canal traffic had been on the Aire and Calder.[2] Though not a gold mine to its shareholders, it paid dividends more regularly than some considerable railway companies.

Manchester lies lower than Leeds and nearer to the sea. The flats of South Lancashire and North Cheshire had been the field for the first great successes of English canals—and of English railways. Before the railways had succeeded, there had been a plan, and a stillborn company, in that year of projects 1825, for a canal to carry ships of 400 tons from Manchester to the estuary of the Dee. They had sung about it in the Theatre Royal, Manchester, and lampooned it in verse from Liverpool.[3] For the next half century there was intermittent talk of a Ship Canal, always loudest when trade was worst. One of the Anti-Corn Law lecturers of 1845 issued a prospectus for a company with a capital of £3,000,000, whose canal was to run not to the Dee but to the Mersey. There were meetings but no subscribers.[4] Finally, in the depression of the late 'seventies, a plan began to take shape among a group of enthusiasts. By 1882 a Provisional Committee was at work, and after that for three years there was continuous war in the Private Bill Committees of both houses of Parliament, before the first of nearly a score of Manchester Ship Canal Acts got on to the Statute Book in 1885. Two previous Bills had been rejected.[5]

Manchester and her advocates had spoken, with the usual smack of forensic exaggeration, about high railway rates and an unholy conference between rail and waterways to maintain them; about excessive dock charges on ships at Liverpool and the iniquity of levying dock dues on all merchandise there; and about alleged apathy or incompetence in the Mersey Dock and Harbour Board.[6] Apart from specified grievances, they claimed

[1] *R.C. on Canals*, IV. 229. [2] *Final Report*, p. 51.

[3] Leech, *Manchester Ship Canal*, I. 59–60, with the music. [4] Leech, I. 71.

[5] Leech is the main source. See also the files of the now extinct *Manchester City News*, which was an eager advocate from the start. The *Manchester Guardian*, critical at first, came over later.

[6] For which see vol. II. 520 and the *R.C. on...the Port of London* (1902, XLIII), p. 93. Some Liverpool shipping men, e.g. Thomas Ismay, were equally critical of the Board at this time; Leech, I. 46–7.

the right of Manchester to improve her geographical position in any reasonable way. Liverpool and the interested railways argued alternatively, again following the precedent of the Courts, that the scheme was not practicable; and that if it were it would rob them of trade in confident anticipation of which they had incurred vast expense. Further that it would damage the estuary of the Mersey, which the Liverpool authorities had been accused by the other party to the suit of neglecting.

To meet this engineering criticism, in the scheme finally adopted the canal was made to run alongside the estuary for twelve miles, debouching into it at Eastham, instead of running down the middle nearly to Liverpool, shut in by great training walls, as originally designed.[1] Yet the estuary argument was brought on to the field in the last action. It met a volley of *tu quoques*: Liverpool had neglected to dredge away the Mersey bar and had pitched sewage and dock-dredgings into the water above it; while at Glasgow the Clyde Navigation Trustees by dredging enterprise had made the once shallow Clyde fit for great ships.[2]

The actions before the Private Bill Committees were terribly expensive and the raising of capital to make the canal was not easy. Daniel Adamson, the leader of the canal party in Manchester, sanguine but no financier, fancied "that the masses of the people would rush in and provide what was required",[3] somewhat as "domestic servants, costermongers, greengrocers and labourers"[4] had found money to finish the Great Eastern. There was genuine popular enthusiasm: co-operators and trade unionists worked hard; but £8,000,000 was wanted and the first public appeal brought in less than £1,000,000. The house of Rothschild was then approached and asked to raise £6,000,000 for the rather narrow commission of 1 per cent. They failed and the issue was withdrawn. Next came a fresh spell of propaganda and another appeal to the masses. The original subscribers agreed to the creation of preferred capital, £4,000,000 worth;[5] and this, issued jointly by Rothschilds and Barings, was successfully disposed of in London, the ordinary capital having been raised locally. In November 1887 the first sod was cut.

[1] The change was suggested by Lyster, the engineer of the Liverpool Docks; Leech, I. 251.

[2] Vol. II. 521 and see the *Harbours Return* (*...of works executed within the last twenty years*), 1903, LXIII. 189, under Glasgow.

[3] Leech, I. 317.

[4] Vol. II. 70.

[5] Leech, II. 1 *sqq.*

But the work was not finished for more than six years. When it was finished the share, loan and debenture capital of the Company stood at about £15,000,000, of which however £1,710,000 had been spent on the purchase of the Bridgewater Canal system as a going and prosperous concern.[1] The original estimate of the contractors for the bare cost of construction, excluding the cost of land, had been £5,750,000; but there had been more than the usual misfortune and miscalculation of a great engineering enterprise. It would never have been finished at all had not the Manchester City Council decided in 1891, when £10,000,000 had been spent and no more was in sight, to lend the Canal Company £3,000,000 if Parliament would permit. It did. But that was not enough.[2] In 1893 the City found another £2,000,000, in return for a majority representation on the Board of Directors. So that year the Canal was completed.

Fourteen years later, during the fierce and rather unwholesome trade activity of 1907, the company earned nearly enough to pay all the interest on these and its other borrowings; next year, with the slump, not so nearly. There was recovery in the good last years of peace; but even then the ordinary shares of the Manchester Ship Canal were seldom quoted, and the price of a £10 preference share fluctuated round about 30*s*. Manchester as a whole was satisfied that the local losses on the ordinary shares had been worth while. It was proud of the determination and of the broad back of its City Council; and it had seen industrial establishments of every kind growing up about the docks and along the canal. The opinions of the widely scattered preference shareholders, who had found more than a quarter of the swollen costs of construction, were not collected. They had taken an ordinary investor's risk and were not less fortunate than some lenders to foreign governments, or than some few preferred lenders to British railways; though even the holder of deferred ordinary stock in the contemporary, and probably superfluous, Great Central Railway had a property about as valuable as theirs.[3]

[1] Capital details in *R.C. on Canals, etc.*, IV. 32, and Leech, II. 15, 255.

[2] The inquiry committee of the City Council, in a report of 1891, attributed the huge error in estimated cost to (i) unforeseen cost of making Ellesmere Port; (ii) protective clauses imposed by Parliament; (iii) the death of the contractor and financial disputes with his executors; (iv) rise in costs of labour and materials; (v) disastrous floods in November, 1890. Leech, II. 89.

[3] Great Central deferred stood at about 14 in 1912–13.

"The remarkable and unquestionable benefit to the trade and prosperity of Manchester"[1] from the canal can certainly not be questioned. Liverpool had not suffered the horrible things that her advocates had prophesied. While she was fighting the Manchester Bills in 1882–5, the shipping cleared from her port annually averaged not quite 5,000,000 tons: in 1912–13 it was nearly 7,500,000 tons, as against a clearance of 1,100,000 which Manchester had built up in twenty years. If Manchester had not built up the 1,100,000 it is by no means certain that Liverpool would have got much beyond the 7,500,000. She might not have dredged away the Mersey bar, increasing the depth at low-water spring tides from 11 to 28 feet, or reduced her port charges, as in fact she did.[2] She also extended her docks and improved their equipment, especially by the construction of an overhead electric railway along their entire length.

Competition had been stimulating to her. This stimulation must be considered in any attempt to picture (to calculate is impossible) the national, not merely the Mancunian, benefits of this unprofitable-profitable undertaking. Some at least of the industrial establishments which grew up about the canal and its docks would presumably have grown up at Manchester in any event: the canal was planned in times of dull trade and finished just before the price-rise set in. Many more might have grown up elsewhere, maybe near Liverpool. Increases of population, rateable value, and the like, which Manchester controversialists set out in their balance sheets,[3] might have occurred somewhere else, somewhere nearer to tide-water. But the easy delivery and despatch of commodities—cotton, food, and cotton goods above all—to and from the wide and most populous area for which Manchester is the distributing centre, into which centre the economical ocean-going steamer could now penetrate, was a certain national asset. In the long, and perhaps even in the rather short, run it probably much more than offset the losses made in rendering that centre accessible. When to this is added the stimulus to effort and economy in Manchester, in Liverpool, and among the railways which linked them—to look no further

[1] *Final Report of R.C. on Canals*, p. 164.

[2] Leech, II. 258; vol. II. 521; and *Return of Works*, 1903, under Liverpool—"no serious attempt had been made to give increased depth of water over the bar until...1889". On a little coasting steamer crossing the bar at low tide in 1882 or 1883 (he forgets which) the lead was being heaved, to the great excitement of one small boy on board.

[3] As in Leech, II. 253.

afield—the picture of national gain on the balance from what its critics had used to call the 'Manchester ditch' becomes convincing, if still rather hazy in its outlines.

It was when the indirect gains from the 'ditch' were beginning to be generally realised, and when even its financial prospects brightened enough to produce quotations of 40*s*. for the £10 preference share, during the trade revival of 1905–6, that a Royal Commission was instructed to survey the Canals and Inland Navigations of the United Kingdom. The impetus came from the Chambers of Commerce, especially from those of the Manchester and the Birmingham areas. The former appreciated the advantages of water transport as proved on the Ship Canal, the Bridgewater system, the Weaver Navigation, and the Lancashire plains section of the Leeds and Liverpool Canal; the latter wanted to share in them and to prevent heavy industry from shifting out of the Midlands towards the sea. As always, slack trade in the years of comparative stagnation and rising unemployment from 1900 to 1904, had brought its crop of suggestions for reducing costs of carriage. A series of Canal and Waterway Bills had been laid before Parliament. In 1905 the Manchester Chamber had asked for the creation of a Public Trust, with a financial guarantee from Government, to superintend the remodelling of the whole system of inland navigation. This was the proposal on which the Commission, which sat for more than three years and issued eleven volumes of evidence and reports, was particularly expected to advise.[1]

All the theories and superstitions about water transport which had haunted Commissions and Committees for half a century were reconsidered. The railways were as usual put into the Dock; but it may be said that they were honourably acquitted. The Commissioners could not state that, as a class, railway owned or railway controlled canals were worse kept than others.[2] They allowed that the system of the Birmingham Canals, which carried on its 159 miles of inter-urban narrow ways more than a fifth of all the tonnage moved inland by water in the country, could hardly have been so well maintained had there not been behind it the mighty London and North Western Railway. "A quite independent witness said that the railway works this canal

[1] *Final Report of the R.C. on Canals*, p. 6, for the Bills and the proposal from Manchester.

[2] *Final Report*, p. 74.

'splendidly'."[1] That very important cross-country line, the Trent and Mersey, the property of the North Staffordshire Railway Company, was invaluable to the Potteries and compared "favourably...with any independent canal".[2] The free Regent's Canal, from Paddington to Limehouse, charged just as high rates as the Birmingham system, whose charges had been quoted as an instance of railway extortion.[3] It was true that the Birmingham rates were stiff but so, in that high-lying country of old coal workings and pumped up canal water, were the maintenance costs;[4] and to the charge that it failed to give special quotations for through business the Birmingham administration replied, firstly, that not much offered and, secondly, that its canals were already congested with the local traffic.[5]

Although they did not mention it in their main report, the Commissioners learnt that various railways kept various canals in order at a loss. They were bound to do so under their Acts, and being bound had no reason to discourage any traffic which might have reduced their losses. Only the traffic was not there. In this fashion the Great Western kept up the Kennet and Avon Canal, and the London and North Western the narrow Huddersfield Canal with its forty-two locks on the Yorkshire side and its summit tunnel which has not a tow-path. In 1905 no through traffic at all passed the summit.[6] Why should it, when the busiest and one of the best managed stretches of railway in the country took goods at the speed to which Lancashire and Yorkshire were accustomed through an adjacent tunnel? Even the now free Leeds and Liverpool, wide on its whole length and with a much easier terrain in the Aire Gap, did very little long haul business through the hills.[7]

The Commissioners, obsessed with the importance of developing through traffic by water, noted that most through routes had narrow links like the Huddersfield Canal. They did not draw the obvious conclusion from the fact that the Leeds and Liverpool, which with its efficient neighbour the Aire and Calder joined the Eastern to the Western sea, had not. They praised the Grand Junction, one of the few canals which had

[1] *Final Report*, p. 75.
[2] *Final Report*, p. 35 and, in the evidence, Q. 1461.
[3] *Final Report*, p. 72.
[4] See the details in vol. IV. 210, of the *R.C. Reports*.
[5] *Final Report*, p. 71.
[6] *R.C. Reports*, vol. IV. 194, 305; *Final Report*, p. 40; and cp. vol. I. 76, 81, 83.
[7] *Final Report*, p. 40.

"moved with the times";[1] but again overlooked the conclusion which might have been drawn from its dependence on short haul traffic in the metropolitan area.[2] Perhaps this was because they hoped that their main proposal would do away with that dependence.

The proposal was to create, as a beginning, under a new Waterways Authority and with government credit, a 'Cross' of improved canals, on which boats of 100 tons—or alternatively, and at much greater cost, of 300 tons—could pass from the Thames to the Mersey and from the Severn to the Humber.[3] The crossing was of course in the Birmingham area, which was expected to benefit much. Hopes were held out that a magnified Grand Junction Canal might bring 3,000,000 tons of coal yearly from Midland fields to Brentford and Paddington; though why public credit should be used to cheapen London coal—this was the assumption—by diverting traffic from railways, whose coal charges into London were limited by the competition of sea-borne coal, was not made clear. 'Paddington coal', as it used to be called, brought in by canal, had failed to compete, first with the sea-borne, and then with the rail-borne coal.[4] Even with the public credit behind it it might fail again.

Yet the Commissioners agreed that only goods of the coal class, the cheap bulk consignments, were likely to make much use even of greatly improved waterways. The problem of how collieries, quarries, and heavy industrial establishments not already served by canal cuts were to be linked with the 'Cross' was not properly faced; nor the ease with which railway sidings to such places are made appreciated. There was the further problem of narrow canals whose banks were "lined with manufactories",[5] as they were in the Birmingham area. To widen these would mean much house-breaking and presumably heavy compensation. To leave them narrow would mean unloading the 100, or 300, ton boats into smaller ones, at the junction with the 'Cross', and so sacrificing much of the undoubted economy of through haulage by water.

That an improved and technically unified canal system would be useful to trade—to some trades and some traders—was obvious. But would it be useful enough at the suggested price, which was high? Canals with natural advantages had been able to raise capital in the open market. No one proposed that the

[1] *Final Report*, p. 30. [2] *Final Report*, p. 53. [3] *Final Report*, pp. 93 *sqq.*
[4] Vol. I. 82; vol. II. 201. [5] *Final Report*, p. 32.

State should widen the tunnel above Huddersfield: that was too patently uneconomic. The analogy from Manchester was not convincing: the great advantage there was that sea-borne cargoes could be discharged or loaded 35 miles inland, right among their consumers and producers. Above all, the trade of the country was based more and more completely every year on small consignments and quick transit. That was true even of the coal trade to London, in which a single truck-load direct from a pit-siding was quite a common unit, the 100 or 300 ton consignment a rare one. Great consignments, for gasworks and the like, normally went by sea. Most of these arguments were put forward by dissenting members of the Commission, which like many Royal Commissions was far from unanimity.[1] Those who used them might well have quoted what a leading European authority on the economics of transport wrote just before they began to work. When people talked about the technical superiority of artificial waterways over railways, he said, he always got the impression that it was really a question of how "the public finances might be sacrificed to particular business or agricultural interests".[2] It is fair to state that the agricultural interest in Britain had shown no liking for canals, and had not asked for a penny to be spent on them.[3] A boat moving slowly with a cargo of 100 tons of grain was not attractive; still less so if the load were milk or poultry, fruit or vegetables. Covent Garden did not trade that way. Nor, in the sphere of another important interest, did Billingsgate.

The Commission was appointed just too early for its proposals to be influenced by the possibilities of a form of transport which would require neither canal cuts nor railway sidings. That form, when it came, would not much affect primary traffic in coal and such things. Still, technical imagination thrown forward along the lines of motor-buses which were thickening on the streets of London while the Commission sat might have anticipated the next turn of the wheel;[4] and might at least have suggested a pause before the last type of transport but one was artificially revived. There was a small steamboat then employed in carrying

[1] Sixteen signed; six signed with many reservations; three refused to sign. Russell Rea, the chairman, signed with heavy reservations (*Final Report*, p. 193).

[2] Cohn, Gustav, "Ueber Reaktion im Verkehrswesen", in *Zur Politik des... Verkehrs- und Verwaltungs-Wesens* (1905), p. 293.

[3] *Final Report*, p. 194: a note by one of the dissentients. [4] Above, p. 139.

timber from Grimsby into industrial Yorkshire, up that excellent free navigation the Aire and Calder. Not very many years later its work was being done by motor-lorries.[1] Possibly those in high administrative places had the necessary technical imagination. Or perhaps they had used the inquiry by Commission merely as a way of shelving a tiresome matter of no urgency: for this there were precedents. Or perhaps, and most likely of all, the effective imagination in high places was financial. There were many better supported claims on the exchequer between 1910 and 1914 than this rather half-hearted demand for millions to make a 'Cross' of waterways. Whatever the cause, no statesmen backed it.

The claims of the new rival form of transport they did however back, cautiously and experimentally, just when the Canal Commission was winding up its work; for the Development and Road Improvement Funds Act (9 Ed. VII, c. 47) had received the Royal Assent on December 3, 1909, and the new Road Board which it set up held its first meeting on May 10, 1910.[2] This favours the theory of technical, and not merely financial, imagination in high places. The Fund which the Board had to administer came from Motor-Car Licence Duties and the taxation of Motor Spirit. But although the existence of the Board gave Parliament a point of contact with the management of the King's Highways, no Minister of the Crown had direct responsibility for any of them; and, by an almost unbelievable bit of constitutional pedantry and inertia, down to 1914 "no questions as to the state of the roads was even allowed to be put to the Government in the House of Commons".[3] So persistent was the tradition that, whatever the Local Authorities might be, the roads—all the roads—were their business. From 1871 to 1895 a Standing Committee of the Commons had systematically refused to renew any of the Turnpike Trusts, which also were local things.[4] They were nearly all extinct when the Local Government Act of 1888 (51 and 52 Vict. c. 41) handed the care of the main roads to the new County Councils. It might have been supposed that the Local Government Board and its ministerial President would have had some responsibility for the

[1] Information from the former owner of the steamer.
[2] *Road Board: First Report*, 1911 (XL. 713).
[3] Webb, S. and B., *The History of the King's Highway*, p. 244.
[4] Vol. II. 207.

way in which this essential bit of local administration was conducted; but the parliamentary convention was that they had not.

In 1864 a witness had told a Committee of the Commons that in its usage the Great North Road was as local as any "ordinary parish highway".[1] During the next twenty years a little, a very little, non-local road traffic had been created by venturesome touring cyclists; but even in the late 'eighties the cyclists were neither very numerous nor taken very seriously. Governing people had hardly allowed them a claim to the roads at all. It was enough that the highways conformed to the standards of local horse users, and satisfied local needs. Meanwhile the last Turnpike Trusts had been dying, and no uniformity or general vigour of administration was to be expected from the jumble of Quarter Sessions, experimental Highway Districts, Boroughs, Rural Sanitary Districts and Highway Parishes which was responsible for the roads of Britain.[2] Even after the County Councils had been set up, there were for a time more than 5000 parishes, urban and rural, with supreme authority over their own particular roads. It was natural that the more vigorous county councils should be fully occupied at first in making up the arrears of road maintenance due to its neglect "for many years prior to... 1888",[3] in the era of divided and uncertain control. As a result, expenditure on roads from the county rates was heavy long before the growth of motor traction in the new century led to a cry for more. In fact, the annual increase of expenditure during the first decade of the motor age, 1903 to 1913, was not much greater than it had been in the previous fifteen years.[4]

Activity and expenditure had been stimulated by the final readjustment of the machinery of control under the Local Government Act of 1894 (56 and 57 Vict. c. 73) which abolished both Highway Districts and 'Highway Parishes' and entrusted what now became the District Roads to the Urban and Rural District Councils. By 1914, outside London and the County Boroughs, there were 27,879 miles of main roads under the County Councils, and 111,884 miles of district or secondary roads under the District Councils of England and Wales.[5] But

[1] Vol. II. 206, n. 3. [2] Vol. II. 206.

[3] *Road Board: Second Report*, 1912–13 (XLVI. 563), p. 8. [4] *Ibid.* p. 6.

[5] *Third Report*, 1914 (XLVII. 753), p. 6. And cp. the position early in the nineteenth century, vol. I. 93.

this in no way guaranteed any unity of control or uniform standard of maintenance, even for what in France would have been classed as national roads. There were twelve distinct managements on the first eighteen miles of the main West Road out of London and seventy-two on the 302¾ miles of the Great North Road from London to Carlisle.[1] But it is to be remembered that to an average late Victorian the words Great North Road had meant little or nothing; and that a town-bred Cambridge undergraduate of the 'nineties could wonder incuriously why a small neighbouring railway station should be called Old North Road.

There had been little progress in the art of road making since the time of Telford and Macadam, except in cities and great towns, where the squared granite sets, the newer wood blocks, or the Val de Travers asphalt laid by alien workmen in list slippers, had replaced the gravel, the cobble stones, or that broken granite 'macadam' which was still universal on the best country roads. Wood blocks and Val de Travers aliens were not often seen outside London; and there were cobble or other rough local stone pavings in many towns of the second rank, especially in the stony North and in Scotland.

Road transport by tramway in the late nineteenth century was confined almost entirely to the paved urban roads, and to the passenger and parcels services; although there were a few inter-urban steam-tram connections in the industrial North. The tramway system was not very progressive. There were 779 miles of tramway and light railway, to adopt the official description, in Britain by 1886. There had been only 136 miles ten years earlier. Fourteen years later, in 1900, the mileage had not got beyond 1040; although in the interval the electric tram had come into very general use outside Britain. The delay in its adoption had been due principally to lack of imagination among law-makers, when faced with the general problems of the age of electricity, and to the inertia which assumed that a tram was normally a thing drawn by horses, controlled by laws and by-laws appropriate to the horse.[2]

But when the twentieth century opened, this phase of delay was over. Municipalities, some of which already owned electric generating plants and were also the tramway authorities, with

[1] Webb, *The Story of the King's Highway*, p. 243.

[2] Vol. II. 203–4.

power to work or license, very naturally developed their own electric tramway systems when they felt financially strong enough.[1] At the same time the British Electric Traction Company was fostering subsidiary companies to serve urbanised areas and groups of smaller towns—the South Yorkshire Electric Traction, the Potteries Electric Traction, and the like—wherever they could secure the necessary licences from a series of adjacent Borough and District highway authorities.[2] The bulk of the work was done in the first seven years of the new century. From 1040 in 1900, the tramway mileage of the country had risen to 2232 by 1907. Much further it never got. Extensions of the existing systems, mainly those of strong municipalities, carried the mileage to 2530 by 1914. Ten years later less than another hundred miles had been added. After that the pulling up of tramlines set in.[3]

The check would certainly have come earlier had not so much municipal capital gone into tramways just before the motor-buses—the *motores bi* of the Oxford poet—came in hordes on to the London streets in 1905–6.[4] The London tramway authority was the County Council. Its policy, especially that pure and reformed part of it which had recently produced tramlines and electric standards along the Embankment, was not appreciated by everyone; it had only been applied on comparatively few routes. Although the Council published impressive traffic statistics for its trams, the Londoner's normal journey was still made by bus. The omnibus licensing authority in London was the Commissioner of Metropolitan Police. Provided they were safe, there was no reason why he should refuse to let motor-buses replace horse-buses. The County Council admitted that many London routes were quite unfit for tramway traffic; and it had no power to stop buses from running in competition with its trams. They always had run. But in the Midlands and the North, and indeed almost everywhere outside London, the Town or City Council was at once the tramway and the omnibus licensing authority, and if "jealous for its tramway receipts",[5] as it might

[1] There is some interesting early history of municipal tramway enterprise before electricity in *R.C. on Labour*, 1892, XXXVI. Part 2, Q. 15,746 *sqq*. For the later period, Webb, *The...King's Highway*, p. 261.

[2] The author held a few shares in the B.E.T.C. and the P.E.T.C. to keep in touch with what seemed at the time a development of first-rate importance.

[3] Tramway figures are in the *Statistical Abstracts*.

[4] Above, p. 139.

[5] Webb, *The...King's Highway*, p. 261, quoted because the authors have a minimum of anti-municipal bias.

be, was slow to issue omnibus licences. Besides, there were streets in Bradford or Halifax in which if you had trams it was not wise also to have buses.

That traffic considerations were hardly dominant was shown however in many places, some of whose streets were also difficult, but whose tram and omnibus licensing authorities did not own trams. As the motor-bus spread from London to the provinces a wail began to rise from the Electric Traction Companies against local authorities who, having imposed onerous licensing conditions on a tramway enterprise, shortly afterwards issued other licences to bus companies to compete with it.[1] A new form of transport had never trodden on the wheels of its predecessor so quickly, and some wailing was inevitable.

The Act of 1896 which freed the owner of an early Daimler or Panhard from the obligation to drive as if his car were a traction-engine had freed all other owners of what the law classed with the Daimler as light locomotives.[2] When motor-car legislation took shape under that name in 1903, there was a good deal of heavy iron-tired and mostly steam-driven traffic on the roads—faster than the old traction-engines, though not yet very fast—besides the 15–20,000 rubber-tired cars whose maximum speed was not to go beyond twenty miles an hour. The number of both groups grew amazingly fast. Within two or three years the general public was worrying about the roads. The bicyclists, more numerous and much more genteel since the middle 'nineties,[3] and the owners of cars, few at first but most respectable and audible, had been worrying for a decade or more: the former had started and the latter had patronised the typically English Roads Improvement Association, which so early as 1902 was experimenting at Farnborough with methods for controlling road dust.[4] The work of this Association was so successful that severe critics of the still unsystematic road management in Britain admitted, in 1913, that "a larger mileage of dustless roads" was to be found there "than in any other country".[5]

Dust was only a symptom of the wear and tear of relatively defective roads. It could be reduced, though not abolished, by general use of the best established methods of construction. The

[1] Shareholders heard this wail annually.

[2] *R.C. on Motor-Cars*, 1906 (XLVIII), p. 2, and p. 139 above.

[3] When, for a time, bicycling in Battersea Park was fashionable. See the files of *Punch*.

[4] Webb, *The...King's Highway*, pp. 243, 248.

[5] *Ibid.* p. 249.

Royal Commission of 1905–6 agreed with the Road Improvers that up and down the country there was a great deal of very bad road-making by the local authorities;[1] but it advised, and wisely advised, nothing revolutionary. Well-bottomed granite-finished macadam, its *Report* said, was still the best thing known. On the merits of the various systems of tar macadam, still in their experimental stage, it was not prepared to pass judgment.[2] But these systems, tested and encouraged by the Roads Improvement Association, gave the country in the next seven years its satisfactory quota of dustless, if black and unsightly, highways.

Motorists were now an organised interest, rich and uncommonly well represented in Parliament. They were apt to argue that taxes levied on their machines and motive fuel should be returned to them in better roads, a type of argument which had never been applied to the inhabited house duty or even the carriage tax. Yet it was reasonable that a fast-rising income from these sources should be used, at least in part, for road improvements which both were desirable in themselves and would make it rise faster. It was also reasonable to defend additions to the levies by a promise that the yields should be spent on the roads. Considerations of this sort lay behind the creation of the Road Board in 1909–10.[3] It was thought of from the first as a central co-ordinating body for inquiry and research, a kind of nationalised Roads Improvement Association, with a control of policy based on its partial control of the new Roads Improvement Fund.

From this Fund it was empowered to recommend advances, by way either of grant or of loan to County Councils and other Highway Authorities; also—and this was a great and novel function for a central body—to "construct and maintain any new roads which appear to the Board to be required for facilitating road traffic". However, it decided not to use, or even prepare to use, this second function at the start, but to concentrate on the problem of the road crusts; because the "existing waterbound surfaces"[4] were fast going to pieces, or rather to dust and mud, under the wheels of more than 100,000 motor vehicles. In its first two years it advised the spending of a little

[1] *Report*, p. 20.

[2] *Report*, p. 19. Experiments in 'tarmac' long preceded the motor-car. There was a road in a Manchester suburb from which free tar oozed in irresistible blobs in warm weather in 1882–3: perhaps there were others.

[3] The Act is 9 Ed. VII. c. 47, which received the Royal Assent on December 3, 1909.

[4] See its *First Report*, 1911 (XL. 713), pp. 3, 6.

money for road widening and diversion and bridge-building; but in the second year (1911–12) nearly 83 per cent. of the grants and loans went for betterment of the crust.[1]

So things remained down to March, 1914. The crust, the Board said in its 1914 Report, was still the most urgent matter. But it was now facing the problem of construction. There had been negotiations both with the London and the Middlesex County Councils about improvement of the western approach to London; and the Board was able to report in 1914 that arrangements with the Middlesex Council for building the Brentford Loop, from Kew Bridge to Hounslow, were complete and had received the sanction of the Treasury.[2] This was the first important scheme for a really new road which the Board had brought to a conclusion; but it was helping in various places to finance the necessarily expensive promotion of roads from the secondary to the main grade, as traffic on them became more dense. New construction had been deliberately held back. The Act under which it worked instructed the Board to adjust employment-making expenditure to the trade cycle, to have "regard...to the general state and prospects of employment" (§18)—another legislative novelty—and since 1910 business had been active and unemployment unbelievably low.[3]

With the help of the more enterprising local authorities the Board had been able to gauge roughly the growth of traffic in the London area and so the urgency of its work. For the year 1911–12 its best statistics came from Kent. The busiest stretch of Kentish road reported on was that between Eltham and Sidcup. The figure given was 772 vehicles passing daily, of which 318 were motor-cars or motor-cycles.[4] Thirteen every hour, day and night: a remarkable figure. Next year it had exactly doubled, while the horse-drawn traffic had fallen from nineteen per hour

[1] *Second Report*, 1912–13 (XLVI. 563), p. 5.

[2] *Fourth Report*, 1914 (XLVII. 753), p. 9.

[3] Road-making in bad times was an economic device well known to the French Intendants of the eighteenth century and had been practised—stupidly—during the great Irish Famine. But it was new to the English Law. Charles Booth had explained to a Select Committee in 1894 (*S.C. on Distress from Want of Employment, Third Report*, 1895, IX. Q. 10,534) how it was "conceivable that a large public undertaking at exactly the right moment might set the ball [of economic revival] rolling". That policy found its best-known advocates in Sidney and Beatrice Webb. By 1937 it has perhaps sometimes been forgotten that the adjustment of capital expenditure to the trade cycle has so old and respectable a history.

[4] *Second Report*, p. 45.

to sixteen. But Eltham to Sidcup was not the busiest measured flow of traffic in 1913. That was in Surrey, where eighty-two motor vehicles, including the cycles, honked down Kingston Vale every hour.[1] Besides the cars and the cycles, buses out of London had now appeared on these rather remote suburban highways.

During the difficult years of the middle 'eighties, when a Royal Commission was inquiring into the Depression of the national Trade and Industry and Manchester was planning to raise hers by becoming a seaport town, the dock at Tilbury, built by the East and West India Dock Company, was finished. At the opening ceremony, on April 17, 1886, a great shipowner, Sir Donald Currie, suggested that the Thames might take a lesson from the Mersey and consolidate its various and competing dock enterprises under a single Dock and Harbour Trust.[2] The suggestion was opportune, though it was not acted on for more than twenty years. The Tilbury Dock had been planned as a rival to the Albert Dock of the London and St Katharine Company; and now, after costly delays, reckless financing, engineering difficulties and quarrels with contractors, it was being opened at a moment when the trade of the Port of London, and indeed of the whole country, was stagnant.[3] The Thames lightermen said it was too far down river for them; so they and the wharfingers boycotted it.[4] Business was only attracted to Tilbury, or retained at the Victoria and Albert, by offering cut-throat terms to shipping lines. The first result was that for 1886–7 the London and St Katharine dividend fell to 1 per cent. By 1888—although trade took a turn for the better that year—the harder hit East and West India, unable to pay interest on some mortgages, was in the hands of receivers.

Distress made bedfellows of these two leading Thames companies; and they secured parliamentary sanction during 1888 for a working agreement under a Joint Committee, but without capital consolidation. The Committee started with heavy handicaps. The receivers were in at the East and West India Docks,

[1] *Third Report*, 1913 (XXIX. 665), pp. 57, 60.

[2] Broodbank, Sir J. G., *History of the Port of London* (1921), I. 238. Cp. vol. I. 5–6; vol. II. 520.

[3] Broodbank, I. 237–8.

[4] The wharfingers had been competing sharply with the Dock Companies during the depression. The great dock strike of 1889 brought them together. Broodbank, I. 243, 263–4.

and a final settlement with the creditors was not reached till 1898. By an ancient clause in all Dock Acts, the so-called "free water clause", a dock company might not levy tonnage dues on goods landed on its wharves to be carried away in lighters; and it was said that by the 'nineties three-quarters of the goods were so handled.[1] Besides that, much unloading was done by lighter from ships at their moorings, or direct from the ship to the endless riverside wharves. Again, the whole trade of London was only expanding slowly; and a technical inquiry made in 1894–6 suggested that further progress was doubtful, in view of the ever-growing size of ships, unless the Lower Thames channels could be deepened.[2] For that part of the existing trade which needed docking facilities the river was, if anything, over-docked; and there was always the competition of the wharfingers. In these circumstances dock company dividends were meagre and the raising of money for dock improvement difficult.

By 1901 the regime of the Joint Committee had been followed, as might have been foreseen, by that of complete amalgamation, under a private Act of the previous year (63 and 64 Vict. c. cxi). It had been succeeded too, before this Act came into force, by the appointment of a Royal Commission to inquire into all aspects of the problem of the Port of London, an inquiry for which the London County Council, hankering not unjustifiably after some kind of proprietary control of the Port, together with the London Chamber of Commerce, the repository of traders' grievances, with other interests, had for some years been pressing.

No inquiry was needed to show that the control of London's river was mixed and imperfect. The dock companies, established when open competition was in the ascendant, had ended with this amalgamation which controlled 80 per cent. of the docking facilities. The City Corporation had long lost its power over the shipping, though it was the Sanitary Authority of the port and was well represented on the Thames Conservancy. The Watermen's Company licensed lighters and lightermen: Trinity House licensed pilots. The Conservancy, which dated from 1857, had been revised in 1894, in order—among other things—to give the County Council adequate representation. It had not however been very active: the deepening of the Lower Thames recommended in 1896 had been imperfectly, critics said most

[1] *R.C. on the Administration of the Port of London* (1902, XLIII, XLIV); *Report*, pp. 79–80.

[2] *Report of Lower Thames Navigation Committee*, in App. 1 to the above *Report*.

inadequately, carried out.[1] There were the examples of a unified control on the Mersey, now generally allowed to be both active and efficient, and at various leading ports of the Continent to be set over against this disunion, partial monopoly, and reputed incompetence. The central point of the Commissioners' Report, unification of some kind, was easily anticipated.

They made it temperately. Acrid critics had said that London's trade was stagnant because of the shortcomings of its mixed management: this was not endorsed. After all, that trade, measured roughly by the entrances and clearances of shipping, had grown by nearly 50 per cent. in the fifteen years from 1886 to 1901—more than that of Liverpool, though not quite so much as that of Liverpool and Manchester taken together. More could not reasonably be expected of an old established port which was essentially a terminus for sea-borne traffic.[2] Special circumstances connected with the growth and course of liner sailings had, it is true, brought far swifter expansion at Southampton. But nothing that London might do or neglect would affect the size of ships, or the routes and British ports of call of the Hamburg-Amerika and the Norddeutscher-Lloyd. There was naturally, the Commissioners explained, much room for improvement—in the docks, for which the principal company could raise no money; in the river, where the Conservancy had been supine; and in general administration.[3] As improvement had been at least hindered by "the dispersion of powers among several authorities and companies",[4] the moral was that anticipated—concentrate.

Public opinion agreed, although the interested parties differed over the finance of the proposal; but the course of political affairs delayed concentration for six years.[5] Then the complex Port of London Act (8 Ed. VII. c. 68), negotiated by Lloyd George and seen through the Commons by Winston Churchill, received the Royal Assent on December 21, 1908. The Conservancy was pushed above Teddington Lock. The Eastern boundary of the

[1] The whole story is told in the *Report*, Part II, and in condensed form in Broodbank.

[2] The stagnation of the re-export trade was due mainly to causes beyond English control. See the evidence of D. Owen, Q. 5161 *sqq*., and the *Report*, pp. 21–2.

[3] *Report*, pp. 37, 75, etc.

[4] *Report*, p. 124.

[5] A Bill introduced by Gerald Balfour in 1903 failed; Broodbank, II. 322. And during the Tariff Reform controversy of 1903–5 London was forgotten.

port was drawn outside the Nore. Eighteen elected members, representing the various port-using interests, and ten members nominated by public powers composed the Authority. The Authority took over all the docks on the negotiated terms. It took over also the ancient licensing rights of the Watermen's Company. Trinity House was untouched and the City remained the Sanitary Authority. Port rates might be levied on all goods entering or leaving, and dock dues—with a common maximum —on all vessels using the docks. Port of London Stock, of various grades, was to be issued to buy out the dock companies and pay for new developments.

In the five years of peace allowed to it, the Authority dredged, repaired, improved and re-equipped as it was meant to do; and it planned, but was not able to finish, one new dock, South of the Royal Albert.[1] Under its charge the trade of the port grew, but not abnormally; not in fact quite so fast as during the last years of the old order. This proves nothing in particular, except that those critics of the old order who argued direct from slow growth to incompetence had argued loosely. If told this, they might have retorted that, had the old order not been changed, there would have been no growth at all; but the general course of British trade and of London's expansion suggest that such a retort would have been a weak one. What is certain is that, under the new control, the trade of the river was handled, after a time, with greater convenience and dispatch. Even a slight improvement here was of national importance, for a third or rather more than a third, by value, of all the imports of the United Kingdom came up the Thames, just as a third or rather more than a third of the exports went down the Mersey. Both figures had been remarkably constant for many years before 1914: that of the Thames was 34·5 per cent. in 1882, 33·8 in 1899, 33 in 1913; and that of the Mersey 1 or 2 per cent. higher.

The Mersey figure here given includes the traffic of the Manchester Canal. By 1912–13 Manchester actually did more sea-borne trade than Glasgow, although her trade was still not one-sixth of that of Liverpool. Her docks, not yet fully utilised, were of 120 acres to Liverpool's 420. Liverpool had been improving her docks "without cessation", as she proudly reported to the Board of Trade in 1903.[2] Another dock, to be bounded

[1] Broodbank, II. 345 *sqq.*

[2] *Harbours*; *Return of Works executed within the Last Twenty Years*, 1903; Liverpool.

by another 770 feet of her continuous "vast sea wall" of granite, had recently been put in hand. By 1914 the wall was eight miles long and the first part of her last dock system, the Gladstone, was open.[1] Across England, the Northern industrial estuary East, the Humber, with its three ports, one old and two new—Hull, Grimsby and Goole—was increasing its business faster than the Northern industrial estuary West, though still far behind it. The Mersey, out and in, carried more than a third of the overseas trade of the United Kingdom; the Thames rather less than a third, because London had not yet Lancashire's supply of high-priced outward cargoes; the Humber rather more than one-tenth. Helped by dock-owning railways, Hull easily held her place as the third port of the Kingdom. The Alexandra Dock, east of the town, which had been in full work since 1885, had to be enlarged in 1899; and in 1905 a beginning was made with what would be the greatest dock on the East Coast north of the Thames, and the first in Britain to be electrically operated throughout.[2] Like its neighbour, the Great Central Railway's dock at Immingham, north-west of Grimsby, it was finished just in time to be laid idle by war.

Immingham, a dock system of 45 acres, was the great enterprise of the twentieth century on the south side of the Humber. At Grimsby there had been no major construction since the 'eighties. But the existing docks, extended and improved in various ways, had allowed her trade to double in value between 1900–2 and 1912–13 without too much pressure. At the last she stood well ahead of Bristol, Newcastle and Leith; just ahead of Harwich, who did a valuable short distance trade in the narrow seas; and not very far behind Glasgow or Manchester.[3]

It was Southampton, among British ports, that dock reformers in London, and even confident organisers of docks at Liverpool, had feared most as a competitor. Her position in England and close by the sea route from North European waters to the Ocean; the special convenience of her four daily tides and the sheltered approach to her Water; the ease with which that Water could be

[1] For the dock position generally in 1914 see the *Shipping World Year Book*. And cp. vol. II. 521 *sqq*.

[2] *Return of Works*, Hull; Spender, J. A., *Weetman Pearson first Viscount Cowdray* (the contractor), p. 146. Pearson was at work at the same time on the Liverpool Docks and on the Royal Albert extension—later the King George V Dock on the Thames.

[3] *Return of Works*, Grimsby; the *Shipping World Year Book*, 1914, and the annual *Trade Returns*.

made navigable for the greatest ships; the enterprise of the South Western Railway, which had bought out the Dock Company in 1892, and of the Harbour Board—these had given her a place apart in the new era of very great ships. (Her Empress Dock was the only dock in Great Britain where the greatest ships could berth at any hour of the day or the night.) Her place might have been nearly as important had the *Aquitanias* and *Titanics* never been designed, but she certainly was in heavy debt to those who designed them. In 1901, it was claimed that Tilbury Docks could take the largest ship then afloat, the *Oceanic*.[1] In fact they did not. The *Oceanic's* 686 feet of length was soon passed; but however many the feet, the docks and Town Quays of Southampton made room for them. Extension and improvement never stopped.[2]

In the early 'eighties, although the chief South African, West Indian, and South American lines were based on Southampton, the tonnage cleared annually from the port was less than 1,000,000. Between 1899 and 1902 war traffic blew it up to a maximum of 1,808,000. But peace brought hardly any deflation. By 1906 the clearance figure was 1,955,000. Then came an apparent inflation which was half artificial: vessels calling off the port to land or take up passengers and mails began to be returned as entering or clearing Southampton. (They did usually enter and leave Southampton Water.) With this help, the clearance figures rose to 3,571,000 in 1907 and to 5,742,000 in 1913. Though deceptive in their fashion they evoke a true picture—a string of pictures—of the great ships calling and calling again, or genuinely clearing, undisturbed, until that day in August 1914 on which eighty special troop trains ran into Southampton Docks.[3]

Passenger traffic was of the first importance at Southampton, but the cargoes were unusually valuable. Their steady growth corrects the jerk in the tonnage statistics. Trade fluctuations made no serious dent in the mounting curve. The whole trade, in and out, had been worth £14,000,000 in 1887 and £26,000,000 in 1900. In 1913 it stood at £54,000,000—far below London and Liverpool; well below Hull; but in the same group as Manchester

[1] *R.C. on the Port of London*, p. 66.

[2] There is a short account of the growth of Southampton as connected with the railway in Sherrington, *Economics of Rail Transport*, I. 42. For 1903, *Return of Works*, Southampton. For 1914, the *Shipping World Year Book*.

[3] *Official History of the War*, I. 31.

and Glasgow, whose figures were swollen by heavy imports of food which Southampton and its rather rural hinterland did not require. Yet if the trade of Southampton had only grown as fast as that of the United Kingdom, between 1887 and 1913, it would have been worth not £54,000,000 in 1913 but only £30,500,000.

Bristol's trade in the same period had grown only a very little faster than that of the whole country. This was partly because, of all the greater ports, she did the most one-sided business. Glasgow and Grimsby, with the pure coal ports, normally exported more than they imported—Glasgow and the coal ports very much more. Liverpool exported rather less than she imported, if British produce alone is counted, but rather more if the re-exports of foreign and colonial produce are added. At Hull, exports, including re-exports, stood to the imports in the ratio of rather less than 3 to 4. At London, the heavy re-exports, particularly of wool, rubber, tea and the like, kept the ratio at 3 to 5. But for the re-exports, it would have been much lower, because of London's relative industrial weakness and huge consuming power. At Bristol the ratio was less than 1 to 4. For the whole country a considerable excess of imports was normal and wholesome. For a single port, so heavy an excess, if not necessarily unwholesome was at least cramping. Leith, Edinburgh's purveyor, came nearest to Bristol, with a trade slightly greater and a ratio of exports to imports of rather less than 1 to 2.

Whatever the ratio, any port whose trade had grown as fast as that of the country was busy and able to spend money on its works. There had been extensions of wharves in Bristol City and at Portishead. The Royal Edward Dock was new at Avonmouth; and in 1896 a considerable Avon improvement scheme had been put in hand.[1] Altogether the state of the port was creditable to the Corporation of Bristol, which alone among the Corporations of the major ports had retained that complete control of shipping and harbour which at one time had been normal. Leith had been perhaps more active. Dock and harbour works carried out in the late nineteenth century had been completed with the opening of the Imperial Dock in 1902. This brought the dock acreage up to 99 and allowed of the convenient handling of that increase of about 40 per cent. in the tonnage using the port which came in the next decade.

Glasgow had made her river harbour—half a mile above Glasgow bridge for small craft, and four miles below it for the

[1] *Return of Works*, Bristol, and *Shipping World Year Book*, as above.

rest—so efficient by the 'eighties that maintenance and ordinary betterment sufficed.[1] She had added one wet dock, the Prince's, with graving docks attached. There had been reconstructions of quays, dredgings, and the normal activities of the Navigation Trust. These had sufficed for the great and steady, but never unusually quick, increase in the tonnage moving up and down the Clyde. During the five years 1884–8 it had averaged 2,370,000 tons, exclusive of the local and the coasting traffic. By 1909–13 it stood at 5,410,000, traffic having grown at almost exactly the same rate as that of the whole United Kingdom.

The most rapid increase in tonnage, and so the greatest need for harbour development, had been at the coal ports; for the export of fuel, not counting the bunker coal and the shipments coastwise, had nearly trebled between 1884–8 and 1909–13. It had trebled, if the years 1886–7 and 1912–13 are compared. Many of the leading general ports, except London and those of the South Coast, shipped coal—Liverpool and Manchester a little; Goole, Glasgow, Grangemouth and Leith much more; Grimsby and Hull more still. These last two were becoming coal ports of the first rank, with the rapid eastward development of the Yorkshire coalfield, shipping between them 7,712,000 tons in 1913. But the bulk of the export was done through the coal ports proper—the Tyne, with Blyth, Sunderland and Hartlepool; Cardiff and the other outlets for the coal of Glamorgan and Monmouth; and the ports of the Kingdom of Fife. Whereas for more than half a century the new means of communication had worked to concentrate general trade more and more into the greater ports, turning the lesser into holiday places,[2] the coal trade had been a creator of ports.

The Barry Docks, nine miles south-west of Cardiff, though grouped with Cardiff in the national trade returns, really formed a new port, not just an extra Cardiff dock. Begun in 1884 and finished in 1889, the 114 acres of the three basins had been busy ever since. Their opening had in no way checked enterprise at Cardiff. To the old Bute Docks there the Roath Dock, the South Bute Dock, and later the Queen Alexandra Dock of 52 acres were added. In 1913 the composite port of Cardiff Barry and Penarth sent overseas 20,095,000 tons of coal, coke, and manufactured fuel. Newport, Monmouthshire, boasted in 1914 that it owned "the world's largest dock":[3] its whole system, named

[1] *Return of Works*, Glasgow; cp. vol. II. 521.

[2] Vol. II. 522.

[3] Advertisement in the *Shipping World Year Book*.

after Queen Alexandra, for dock-makers have always been loyal, covered 213¼ acres and loaded 4,842,000 tons of coal, with other bulky things. At Swansea, whose coal trade was rather less, Edward VII had cut the first sod of the King's Dock in 1904: it supplemented the Prince of Wales', his also, of 1881, which had required extension in 1898. Important works had also been undertaken at other points on the Glamorgan coast, such as Port Talbot, whose coal trade was growing fast.[1]

On the North-East Coast, Blyth—a difficult port to make, on a river mouth running south-east by south among rocks—had shipped only 150,000 tons of coal in 1883.[2] In 1885–6 it extended its East breakwater pier in solid concrete and built a West pier out eastwards towards its tip. Twelve years later 900 more feet were added to the East pier. The coal shipped rose to 1,041,000 tons in 1887; to 2,276,000 in 1897; and to 4,475,000 in 1913—more than from Swansea or Sunderland. But though Sunderland and the Wear were passed by Blyth, the Tyne held its coal position against all ports except Cardiff. Both were composite. As a general port the Tyne was more important and its coastwise coal trade was also more important; but its coal export proper reached a maximum of 13,619,000 tons—against Cardiff's 20,095,000 tons—in 1913. New wet docks the Tyne did not require: as at Glasgow the stream was the harbour.[3] But the two great breakwater piers at its mouth, begun in 1856 and not finished thirty years later, were never spared by the seas. The northern was damaged in 1893–4 and breached in 1897. Behind the 100 yard breach, as it might have been at Badajoz, a new line of defence had to be constructed.

Growing coal exports from Fife had been accompanied, indeed rendered possible, by important extensions of harbour accommodation on the northern shore of the Firth. In 1887 the North British Railway had opened a dock for coals at Methil, North-East of Kirkaldy. Coal was also shipped from Burntisland to the South-East. The three places were lumped together in the trade returns at that time under the port of Kirkaldy. In 1886 only 503,000 tons of shipping had cleared from the composite port, by no means all in coal. Trade grew so fast in the 'nineties

[1] *Return of Works* and *Shipping World Year Book*, as above.

[2] *Return of Works*, Blyth, and Baldwin, C. E., *The...Port of Blyth* (1929), an account of a type that might be multiplied. Good port histories are few.

[3] *Return of Works*, Glasgow. The chart of 1914 was almost identical with that given in Dorn, A., *Die Seehäfen des Weltverkehrs* of 1891.

that a second dock was opened at Methil in 1897. In the 'tens the Board of Trade recognised not one port but three ports; and in 1913 Burntisland shipped 1,952,000 tons of coal overseas and Methil 2,594,000 tons. Neither exported anything else worth mentioning. The small export trade of the mother port of Kirkaldy included only 106,000 tons of coal, and had for long required nothing more than upkeep and renovation work on her harbour.[1]

So it was with most general ports of the second and lower ranks, Scottish, English and Welsh. The more active among them, such as Aberdeen, Dundee, Barrow and the Channel ports, had always work on hand though little of the first importance, except that great Admiralty Harbour at Dover which was a product of the new phase in British naval policy. But railway policy and competition had improved a number of places on the West Coast, from Ardrossan southwards, with a view to the Irish trade, and had created the new harbour and dock on Fishguard Bay. Fast turbine steamers were running thence to Rosslare by 1913; and Cunard, Booth, and other lines were calling there.

Ports which had declined into holiday places did not revive commercially, although they were usually active in embellishment. The building of "iron promenade piers not made for trade"[2] had slackened. Bangor had finished "an open ironwork pier", made partly for trade, in 1896; and Minehead was proud of a new 700-foot structure which was not quite finished in 1903. "The deck houses", Minehead explained, "are not yet all erected, there being at present only" a lavatory and "a room to be used either as a left luggage office or a shop."[3] No other new piers of this class were reported for the whole twenty years 1883–1903; and after Minehead had decided on the use of the spare room little more was done. Most frequented places had got their open ironwork piers long ago; and the fashion for them was passing.

After 1909, the Development Commissioners, instructed to take special care of the fisheries, were touring the coasts for fishing harbours to be developed. Properly neglecting those where the business was really active—Lowestoft, Hull, Grimsby—by 1912 they had scheduled for treatment one harbour in England and Wales and eighteen in Scotland.[4] They were getting

[1] *Return of Works*, Kirkaldy; *Shipping World Year Book*, 1914.
[2] Vol. II. 518. [3] *Return of Works*, Bangor, Minehead.
[4] *Second Report of the Development Commissioners*, 1912–13 (XVII. 837).

to work on those of the Moray Firth. Neglected quays and river mouths in out-of-the-way places, on which public money may be spent, are easily found. It would have been as easy to find neglected lead-mines in the English hills or half derelict slate-quarries in Wales. These however the Commissioners were not instructed to revive, and no doubt their first spendings on the fisheries did someone good. The word uneconomic had begun to sound hard and old fashioned; but probably both it and the word unimportant were applicable to these harbour developments in and beyond the Highlands.

While the Post Office of the 'seventies was trying without success to make a profit on the recently nationalised telegraph system, W. H. Preece, electrician to the Office, had "brought over the first pair of practical telephones"—in 1877.[1] Asked in the House next year whether he proposed to introduce the telephone, the Postmaster-General said that he did not.[2] But he took the precaution of inserting in a telegraph bill a clause which included telephones in his monopoly. The House of Commons struck it out. Two years later however the High Court decided that Edison's telephone was a telegraph, and a telephone conversation a message within the meaning of previous Acts.[3] The defendants were the United Telephone Company, an amalgamation of the Bell and Edison interests. Consequently, during the experimental period of British telephone development in the early 'eighties, the various companies were operating under licence from the Postmaster-General. These and all subsequent licences were timed to expire on December 31, 1911. Changing its initial policy, the Post Office, presided over at that time by Henry Fawcett the blind economist, had opened in 1881 a few metropolitan telephone exchanges of its own. These were not a success: in 1888 Her Majesty's Government had only 1370 subscribers.[4]

The situation at that time was thus. The United Company held the two controlling patents; but these ran out in 1890 and 1891 respectively. It had reserved the London area to itself and

[1] *S.C. on Telephone Service*, 1895 (XIII. 21), Q. 2554. See vol. II. 208–9, for the telegraph.

[2] Hansard, Feb. 21, 1878.

[3] Baldwin, F. C. G., *The History of the Telephone in the U.K.* (1925), p. 45; *Economist*, Dec. 25, 1880; Holcombe, A. N., "The Telephone in Great Britain", *Quart. J. Econ.*, Nov. 1906.

[4] Holcombe, as above, p. 108.

had licensed provincial companies to use its patents. Two of these companies, the National of Glasgow and the Lancashire and Cheshire, had grown really strong; but like all others they had perpetual friction with local authorities over the wayleaves for their wires.[1] The Postmaster-General had eased the terms of his licences—in the early 'eighties five miles was the maximum radius allowed to any exchange—but he still used them in various ways to protect his telegraph system, on which, in spite of the attraction of the new sixpenny telegram, there was an "appalling deficiency".[2] All parties were looking to the expiry of the patents, when the Post Office would have an opportunity to acquire the whole telephone system. To strengthen their financial and bargaining power, the three main companies came together in 1888, selecting National rather than United as their joint label, not only, it appears, because it was "rather a better term"[3] but because the National shares "were nearer to par in market price".[4] At the time of amalgamation the capital was raised to £4,000,000: the *Economist* said that it was 50 per cent. water.[5]

Before the High Court decision of 1880, and since the Postmaster-General had become more open-handed with his licences in 1884, experiments had been made with inter-urban trunk lines; but London had only got its first trunk at the end of the latter year. The Post Office built it; the United Telephone Company worked it; and it ran to Brighton. From 1884, trunk lines were erected at a fair pace, especially in Scotland and the North—Edinburgh and Glasgow, 1884; Manchester and Liverpool, 1885; Manchester and Leeds, 1886; and so on. Most were the work of the companies, some the work of the Post Office.[6] A majority began with single earth circuit lines, but a few, including all those of the Post Office, had the better metallic circuits from the start. Meanwhile London was "still struggling along with grounded circuits",[7] a bewildering number of exchanges, and a tangle of overhead wires running in all directions.

[1] Baldwin, *History of the Telephone*, pp. 190–1; and see the *S.C. on Telephone and Telegraph Wires*, 1884–5 (XII. 101).

[2] Buxton, Sidney [Lord], *Finance and Politics* (1888), II. 52.

[3] J. Staats Forbes, Chairman of the United, to the *S.C. on Telephone Service* of 1895, Q. 4189.

[4] Baldwin, *op. cit.* p. 191.

[5] "Telephone Amalgamations and the P.O.", *Economist*, June 8, 1888.

[6] Baldwin, *op. cit.* pp. 471 *sqq.*

[7] Holcombe in *Quart. J. Econ.* p. 113.

"No city in civilised Europe was so behindhand", the Duke of Marlborough said in the Lords in July, 1889.[1] What hope was there of our getting to "something like the continental level", the *Economist* was asking in July, 1890.[2]

The National Company, steadily absorbing others, usually argued that its shortcomings were due to lack of statutory power to acquire wayleaves for its wires: each wayleave involved a separate and tiresome bargain.[3] Critics replied that statutory powers were for the State. Already in 1888, the Associated Chambers of Commerce were voting for a national telephone system and the *Economist*, true to the Bagehot tradition, was "vastly preferring" a state to a private monopoly.[4] Four years later the London Chamber of Commerce was complaining to Government of the London service. But by then the chance of nationalisation had slipped. The controlling patents had run out and the Postmaster-General had not stepped in. At the time of the complaint, he was considering a new compromise with private management.

The National was just disposing of a rival. The New Telephone Company, a London concern of 1885 in course of liquidation, had been revived when the Edison patent was expiring in 1891 by the Duke of Marlborough, who meant to give London a metallic circuit system in competition with that of the National. But the negotiators of the National brought the New to terms in July, 1892: it was agreed "to adopt as far as possible the better features of both systems":[5] "unhappily, the poor Duke disappeared suddenly"[6] from this world in November; and until its dissolution in 1898 the New was an appendage of the National.

That compromise which the Post Office now favoured was embodied in the Telegraph Act of 1892 (55 and 56 Vict. c. 59). Trunk lines were to be taken over gradually by the Office, which was to lease to the companies its powers of acquiring local wayleaves. By 1895 the Postmaster-General had 2651 miles of trunks—for whose use he charged only very modest royalties—and the companies, in effect the Company, had the local profits.

[1] Hansard, July 4, 1889.

[2] "The P.O. and the Telephone Companies", *Economist*, July 12, 1890.

[3] J. Staats Forbes, *S.C. on Telephone Service*, Q. 4312.

[4] The article of June 8, 1888, quoted above. Cp. vol. II. 189, for Bagehot and monopoly. For the Chambers of Commerce, Baldwin, *op. cit.* p. 574.

[5] From the 1893 Report of the National quoted in Baldwin, *op. cit.* p. 238.

[6] Forbes' evidence, as above, Q. 4513.

Telegraph losses due to long distance telephone competition fell on the Post Office. Technically, there had been considerable progress: the twin-wire metallic circuit was coming in fast, and James Staats Forbes, the fighting chairman of the National, was boasting that they had now done for London what "the poor Duke" had set out to do; but English experts held that the British telephone system was still "imperfect...as compared with other countries",[1] and American experts would no doubt have said more than that.

Before the century was out the problem had taken a new form. In several great cities—Liverpool, Manchester, Birmingham, Leeds—the local authorities had given facilities for putting wires underground, to help the installation of metallic circuits. But Glasgow, at war with the National Company, refused facilities and threatened to start a rival municipal system. A special commissioner reported against this scheme in 1897; but a more complete inquiry in the following year reversed the recommendation, with the result that in 1899 municipal telephone systems were approved by law.[2]

The Committee of 1898 really favoured State management. "Our trunk system which is in the hands of the Government... is the most extensive in Europe."[3] It was the exchange system, in private hands, which was defective. As things stood however, the Committee proposed not nationalisation but "general immediate and effective competition [in exchanges] either by the Post Office or the local authorities"[4] with the monopoly of the National Telephone Company. Hence the change of law in 1899, and a revival of Post Office metropolitan exchanges which followed it.[5]

Municipal telephones were not very successful. Only six places ever really tried them; though several others got leave to try. In 1905 the municipal subscribers were barely 5 per cent. of the total.[6] Tunbridge Wells had already surrendered to the Company. Swansea did the same later. In 1906, Glasgow, the pioneer, and Brighton sold out to the Postmaster-General. So

[1] Forbes, *S.C. on Telephone Service*, Q. 4515; Col. R. E. Crompton, Q. 3216.

[2] A. Jameson, Q.C., *Report on the Tel. Exchange service in Glasgow*, 1898, XLIX. 1; *S.C. on Telephones*, 1898, XII. 1; Holcombe, *loc. cit.* pp. 120 *sqq.*

[3] *S.C. on Telephones*, p. iv.

[4] *Ibid.* p. xiii.

[5] Baldwin, *History of the Telephone*, p. 354.

[6] *S.C. on Post Office (Telephone Agreement)*, 1905 (VII. 113), iv. and Q. 32 (Sir R. Hunter, Solicitor to the P.O.).

did Portsmouth in 1912. Hull alone kept its own system of exchanges over the Great War.[1]

The Postmaster, for his part, had been walking delicately. When he reverted to the policy of London exchanges, he did it in co-operation with the Company. (He was in a strong bargaining position just then; for on July 24, 1900, an injunction had been issued by the Court to stop the Company from opening up London streets to lay wires without his consent and that of the County Council.) By an agreement of November, 1901, his London subscribers were to have access to the Company's systems and vice versa. Much more important, the agreement provided for the purchase of the Company's metropolitan plant and assets by the State, at a valuation and without any payment for goodwill, on December 31, 1911—the date foreshadowed long before. This agreement served as a model for the national agreement of February 2, 1905, which settled in principle the long wrangle between public and private monopoly, and settled it for the same date, December 31, 1911. In 1905 the Postmaster owned 60,000 miles of double-wire trunk lines, and the Company 316,000 out of the 357,000 telephone installations; so the treaty was between contracting parties not too unequal, though the reserves of power were with the Postmaster.[2]

There remained a few years during which the Company was inert because under sentence of death, whilst the Postmaster's staff planned for their new functions, and the telephone habit in Britain slowly grew. Then the transfer and an arbitration over the price to be paid. The Company began with a claim for £20,900,000. It got only £12,500,000, an award with which its many critics were content.[3]

Financially, the position of the Postmaster as an owner of wires was not yet much better than it had been thirty years earlier.[4] His telegraph receipts were inelastic, and in the year that he took over the telephones the deficit on them was £1,287,000, even on a non-commercial basis, that is not allowing for interest on capital, depreciation, and so on. His telephone account, since it became important after 1899, had been more satisfactory. With the taking over of the National system it began

[1] See the *Annual Reports of the Postmaster-General*, e.g. 1902–3 (1903, XX. 181), p. 22; 1913–14 (1914, XLIV. 737), p. 22.

[2] Report and evidence of the *S.C. on Post Office* (*Telephone Agreement*), 1905; Holcombe, *loc. cit.* p. 131; Baldwin, *op. cit.* p. 593.

[3] See, e.g., the *Economist*, a consistent critic, Jan. 8, 1913.

[4] See vol. II. 210.

to show a profit, even on a commercial basis. But for the Great Interruption of 1914–18 his two accounts might soon have reached the balance not reached actually until 1923–4—and then only by excluding losses made in the Irish Free State—when telephone profits exceeded telegraph losses.[1]

From the time of Marconi's first visit to it in 1896 the Post Office had shown keen interest in wireless telegraphy. Naturally; for it owned, wholly or in part, most of the short sea telegraph cables and worked in close association with the great companies who owned the ocean cables. With the support of the Office, and of Sir William Preece its far-sighted engineer, Marconi began his experiments on the Bristol Channel. By 1900, wireless was being tried in naval manœuvres; and in December 1901 the first message, a single letter S, was sent from Poldhu to Newfoundland. Then all the world became excited, especially its fighting and its shipping quarters. *The Times* equipped the *Haiman* with wireless in 1904, to collect and despatch news of the Russo-Japanese war at sea. Governments got into touch with one another and the first International Radiotelegraph Convention was signed at Berlin in October 1906.[2] But the direct economic significance of wireless telegraphy, unlike the economic and political turmoil about the companies admiralties and war offices which occupied themselves with it, was still very limited. The most obvious application was to shipping. Now in March, 1908, only 72 British ships had wireless installations; in March, 1912, 450; in March, 1914, 879.[3] The 879 no doubt included all the great liners. A year earlier the *Carpathia* had raced through icy seas at the *Titanic's* wireless cry. But there were 21,000 ships, and nearly 13,000 steamships, on the British register in 1914. Money and reputations had been made and lost over dealings in Marconis; the electrical industries had been given a new province to occupy; but the wireless message itself had so far done little towards the filling of anyone's belly, the raising or lowering of anyone's wage or salary or profit-rate or rent; or towards the determining of any price. It had not even had effect on the prices of Marconis

[1] Figures in the *Statistical Abstracts*.

[2] The first Act of Parliament dealing with wireless was of 1904 (4 Ed. VII, c. 24: "to provide for the regulation of Wireless Telegraphy"). The main sources of information are the *Annual Reports of the P.M.G. The S.C. on Marconi's Wireless Telephone Co....Agreement* (1912–13, VIII) was mainly occupied with wringing dirty linen: see Ensor, *England*, 1870–1914, pp. 456–9.

[3] From the *Annual Reports*, e.g. 1913–14, p. 18.

and electric shares. You can telegraph or telephone a quotation within the day. If the nations were eager about it and anxious, that was chiefly because they were drawing nearer—some of them with averted eyes—to the bridge of war.

As for the air, it was even less a way of communication with economic significance than what men called the ether, that all pervasive medium in which, as they supposed, wireless waves were spread. The air, it is true, was invaded by heavy things. The internal combustion engine had helped man to do what he had dreamed of since first he watched the birds. Icarus had not fallen this time. Blériot had landed in Kent. But there were not yet any "pilots of the purple twilight dropping down with costly bales"—hardly even with profitable letters. What messages any of them dropped generally referred to the ranges of guns and the movements of marching columns or of ships. Experimentally, they were dropping bombs. Late in August, 1914, the Royal Flying Corps, taking the field for the first time, assembled 63 machines on the aerodrome at Maubeuge.[1]

[1] *Official History of the War*, I. 48. Blériot landed in Kent in July, 1909.

CHAPTER VII

THE ECONOMIC ACTIVITIES OF THE STATE

"COBDEN would hardly recognise the world", the journal which specially represented the Cobden tradition was writing sadly in 1894, in an article headed "The Advance towards State Socialism". Workmen, it said, had long since come to regard the State "as the biggest and, on the whole, most trustworthy trades-union attainable"; they had asked more and more of it. "And as at the same time, the directing classes happened to be full of pity, and the State itself rich", it "assumed the character of universal intervener". Now it fixes rents in Ireland and the Highlands and is being asked to fix them in Wales. It supervises all factories and all ships; keeps a tight hand on the management of all friendly societies; inspects all foods; and regulates all popular education even in its theological parts. Some people in authority want it to regulate the hours of labour[1] and to control immigration, which in practice would mean "the reintroduction of the abhorred passport system". Last and latest, that great new sub-state, the London County Council, covets fresh functions every year.[2]

The list of functions coveted or acquired by the State and the sub-states might have been drawn out much further, as Stanley Jevons had drawn it out, but not censoriously, a dozen years before.[3] An influential man whom the journal had very much in mind had in fact once quoted Jevons in the House to the effect that "the State is justified in passing any law, or even in doing any single act, which in its ulterior consequences adds to the sum of human happiness".[4] This was a view which Chamberlain, the Radical Unionist, shared with Randolph Churchill, the Tory Democrat; with Robert Blatchford the Socialist, and with a great number of plain men, labelled or unlabelled. When the

[1] Joseph Chamberlain did; Garvin, J. L., *Life of Joseph Chamberlain*, II. 544.

[2] *Economist*, April 7, 1894. See Dicey, A. V., *The Relations between Law and Public Opinion in England* (1905), a classical treatment, for the general trend of opinion and legislation.

[3] Vol. II. 388.

[4] Joseph Chamberlain; Garvin, *Life*, II. 534. It was in a discussion of a miners' eight-hours bill, Hansard, Fourth Series, II, March 23, 1891.

State acted on this view, confirmed individualists chanted 'State Socialism', a term imported recently from Germany.

Their mouthpiece, the Cobdenite journal, reverting to its point thirteen months later, described the way things had come about in a sentence of insight and some eloquence. "Little by little, and year by year, the fabric of State expenditure and State responsibility is built up like a coral island, cell on cell."[1] These things will pass, and that quickly, had been its earlier comment. Perhaps the comment had been made to keep up the editor's heart. Real coral islands, growing unconsciously and with no apparent design, are most durable.

Design there had been, but the coral-island simile was not fanciful. Just because it existed, with knowledge and some power, each efficient organ of the State, central or local, tended to acquire more power and more knowledge and to build up a solid mass of functions, building fastest in stormy weather. From what was little more than an organisation for collecting much needed agricultural statistics there had emerged in 1889, in a time of rural distress, the new Board of Agriculture—"a Ministry which was progressively to foster, and to direct, the farmer"; and to apply a land law which had changed the relations of lord and tenant from top to bottom.[2] The Board's mere existence was annoying to the *Economist* of the early 'nineties and has been deplored, or at least criticised, by respected agriculturists since.[3] Trade depression due to falling prices led to that railway legislation of 1888–94 which, for the first time, interfered with the right of a railway to change its rates provided it kept within its maxima, and greatly increased the responsibility and power of the railway department of the Board of Trade.[4] Logical necessity, and the application of Jevons' doctrine of adding to the ultimate sum of human happiness, had extended the principles of the factory law to the Labour of Children and Young Persons in Shops.[5] When this Shops Act of 1886 was found to be "generally unenforced and even to a great extent unknown",[6] the administration of shop law was transferred, in

[1] *Economist*, May 25, 1895, on "State Interference".

[2] Venn, J. A., *Presidential Address, Section M, British Association*, 1936, p. 208: and p. 115, above.

[3] E.g. Lord Ernle, *English Farming Past and Present* (1912), p. 400; and his article "An Agricultural Department", *Nineteenth Century*, April, 1889.

[4] Above, p. 356.

[5] See vol. II. 418.

[6] *S.C. on Shop Hours Regulation*, 1892, p. iii, quoted in Hutchins and Harrison, *A History of Factory Legislation*, p. 221.

1892, to the local authorities, as likely to be the more active, including that authority reputedly so covetous of power, the London County Council. The mere establishment of this and the other County Councils, in the late 'eighties, meant more, if *ex hypothesi* better, government; and was of course so intended, especially by its greatest advocate, then out of office, Joseph Chamberlain, who drawing on memories of his Birmingham mayoralty wanted to see the local authorities gradually become great owners of land, wanted "to municipalise it—a barbarous word, which however expresses my substitute for the absurd schemes of Land Nationalisation", as he once said.[1]

There were many sorts of Socialists in Britain. Everywhere they were a small minority, though in some places their numbers were growing fast. It has been said that "for ever convert made by *Das Kapital* there were a hundred made by *Merrie England*"[2] —issued from the offices of Blatchford's *Clarion*, which began to appear at Manchester in 1891.[3] As yet professed and thoroughgoing Socialists of any school had exceedingly little direct influence on government or legislation; but they believed that the wind was blowing their way. "You will see then", Blatchford wrote, after a reference to Building Acts, Factory Acts, Truck Acts, Free Education Acts, telegraph purchase and corporation gasworks, "that Socialism has begun, so that the question of where to begin is quite superfluous". Joseph Chamberlain had said much the same thing in 1885,[4] though with a different stress and intention. "You tell me that my programme is Socialism?" "Of course it is Socialism"—"The Poor Law is Socialism; the Education Act is Socialism; the greater part of municipal work is Socialism: and every kindly act of legislation is Socialism." That is as it may be, and in any case is mainly an affair of definition. However the definition ought to run, the municipal work and the kindly acts went forward, faster than some few wanted if not half so fast or so far as others desired; and a rather cynical Whiggish statesman remarked

[1] Lord Balfour, *Chapters of Autobiography* (1930), p. 220: this was in 1886.

[2] *The Manchester Guardian*, quoted in A. M. Thompson's Preface to Blatchford's *My Eighty Years* (1931), p. xiii.

[3] There is an account of Blatchford, which does not mention *Merrie England*, but explains that Blatchford understood class warfare "without ever having read a single line of Marx", in Beer, M., *A History of British Socialism* (1920), II. 307–9. After 20,000 copies of *Merrie England* had been sold at 1*s*., in 1894 it was issued at 1*d*. *My Eighty Years*, p. 196.

[4] In his Warrington speech, Garvin, *Life*, II. 78.

placidly, in a phrase worn smooth with much handling in late Victorian years, that we were all Socialists now. He meant to suggest that those who wished to make the world perfectly recognisable to Cobden were both a small and a dwindling minority.

It was he, Harcourt, who erected in 1894 what was to prove, during the next forty years, a most effective engine if not for the introduction of Socialism at least for that levelling of properties which Socialists of all tinges welcome—the reformed death duties. In 1887–8 the unreformed duties had brought in £8,284,000; in 1895–6, reformed, they brought £14,100,000. In 1913–14 the figure was £27,400,000 and in 1923–4 £57,800,000. When Harcourt planned the reform, the whole revenue of the State was considerably less than twice this last figure.[1]

As they stood in the middle 'eighties, the unreformed duties, the product of much controversy and compromise, were needlessly intricate. This Chancellors of every shade of Liberalism or Conservatism allowed. To the three old duties—probate, legacy and succession—there had been added in 1881 the so-called account duty, whose chief object was to check evasions of the probate duty. For his never-opened Budget of 1886 Randolph Churchill had planned a sweeping reform and an increase of duty which would have "prejudicially affected" the estate "of nearly every member of the house of Lords".[2] He meant to assimilate the duties on real to those on personal property, and to focus a system of modest graduation not on the size of the estate passing at death but on the amount which each beneficiary received—on "what the living man got, not what the dead man left".[3] Whether he knew it or not—no doubt his Treasury and Somerset House advisers did—he was following the lead of John Stuart Mill who, wishing ultimately to limit not what "anyone might bequeath, but what anyone should be permitted to acquire by bequest or inheritance", was anxious meanwhile to apply "the principle of graduation (as it is called)" to taxes to be levied on all such acquisitions.[4]

[1] All taxation figures of importance for this period are in Mallet, B., *British Budgets*, 1887–1913 (1913), designed as a partial continuation of Buxton's *Finance and Politics* (1888), which had carried the financial story to 1885–6.

[2] Churchill, Winston S., *Lord Randolph Churchill* (1906), II. 197.

[3] *Ibid.* II. 194.

[4] Mill, *Principles*, quoted in vol. II. 391–2. Mr Winston Churchill has kindly reported that he does not know whether Lord Randolph had or had not read Mill.

Lord Randolph Churchill's successor, the discreet financial Goschen, in six consecutive budgets never got beyond repeated statements that the death duties needed reform and the introduction, in 1889, of a new estate duty of 1 per cent. on all estates above £10,000, in which critics—some in fear and some in hope—thought that they could detect the principle of graduation. Harcourt went no further in his first budget; though when, during the discussions, the old controversy over the equal taxation of what had sometimes been called industrial and spontaneous, sometimes precarious and permanent, sometimes earned and unearned incomes arose, he pointed out that the alleged injustice might best be met by way of the taxation at death of the sources of unearned, or permanent, or spontaneous incomes.[1] This he took in hand in the budget of 1894, one of the significant budgets of the century. Like Randolph Churchill he assimilated the taxation of real to that of personal property—he was, as he used to explain, a younger son—and adopted "the principle of graduation (as it is called)"; but unlike Churchill he concentrated his fire, probably for the tactical reason that this would produce the maximum result, not on the size of the bequest or inheritance but on that of the dead man's estate.[2] And on this the drum-fire of the death duties has been concentrated ever since. Churchill, with characteristic daring, would have put kinship out of court. The amount of what you received was to him the essential, not any blood-tie between you and the deceased. Harcourt retained the traditional and defensible leniency towards direct heirs and near kinsmen. So he got two duties instead of the existing five or Churchill's projected one—the estate duty dependent on the size of the estate, irrespective of its composition or destination, and the legacy or succession duty which varied with the relationship of the beneficiary to the person from whose estate he benefited. Estate duty varied from 1 per cent. of estates greater than £100 to—as a financial writer of 1913 put it—"no less than 8 per cent."[3] of estates greater than £1,000,000.

During the next twenty years no change of principle was made in Harcourt's death duties. Some old-fashioned economists and average men of affairs denounced them as a form of national living upon capital.[4] Younger economists explained that this

[1] Cp. vol. II. 401. [2] See Mallet, *op. cit.* pp. 82–3.

[3] Mallet, p. 85.

[4] See e.g. Lord Courtney's arguments quoted in Mallet, p. 76.

was not exact. Conservative Chancellors found them much too useful to be abandoned; and when, after a whole decade, there were again Liberal Chancellors they could easily stiffen the percentages or steepen the graduation. The increase of yield in the Conservative decade (22·7 per cent.) was simply a function of increasing national wealth. The great increase between 1905–6 and 1913–14 (59·0 per cent.) was composite in origin. More wealth was passing at death and there was a heavier squeeze of it as it passed.

The fabric of the Income Tax was almost untouched while Gladstone lived and for eight years after his death. He always denounced the tax—in 1887 as "the most demoralising of all imposts", a "tangled network of man traps for conscience", and "an engine of public extravagance".[1] But it remained. In time of war, the Boer War, the standard rate was pushed up to 1*s*., to 1*s*. 2*d*., to 1*s*. 3*d*. in the pound. That it should stay at 11*d*. in time of peace, though only a year after war had ceased, was unprecedented and shocking to an economical retired Chancellor of the Exchequer in 1903.[2] Between Victoria's Jubilee and the outbreak of the Boer War it had varied between 6*d*. and 8*d*. There had always been in the House of Commons advocates of one fundamental reform—differentiation between 'earned' and 'unearned' incomes. For over thirty years their leader was J. G. Hubbard of the Bank of England. When Hubbard went to the Lords in 1887[3] his place was taken after a few years by Mr (later Sir) George Bartley. But no Chancellor was convinced, and Harcourt, as has been seen, maintained that his revised death duties met the case. Chancellors from both parties did however move steadily towards graduation at the lower end of the scale, by successive manipulations of that principle of abatement established in the earliest days of the tax. In the 'eighties incomes below £150 were exempt and those between £150 and £400 did not pay on the first £150. The injustice towards the income of £410 is obvious, but with the tax at about 6*d*. in the pound was tolerable. From Harcourt's 1894 Budget onwards, and particularly with the heavier taxation of the war and post-war years, abatements dwindling with each hundred of income were allowed, first to £500, then to £600, then to £700. The absolute exemption level was raised by Harcourt to £160, and

[1] Writing in *The Nineteenth Century*, June, 1887. Cp. vol. II. 399, 405.

[2] Sir Michael Hicks-Beach; Mallet, *op. cit.* p. 220.

[3] As Lord Addington. See the *D.N.B.* and cp. vol. II. 401 *sqq.*

there remained. Small injustices survived at the various margins, as was inevitable, but the burden on incomes measured in hundreds had been eased and a rough graduation for them secured. In 1905–6, with the standard tax at 1*s*. the man with £300 a year paid 5·6*d*. in the pound and the man with £600 a year 9·6*d*.[1]

There was naturally a growing desire, and that not only among reformers of the far left, to carry the principle higher up the scale. After all, graduated taxation had been part of Chamberlain's programme twenty years before, and of Tom Paine's more than a hundred; but the dominant Chancellors of those twenty years, Goschen, Harcourt and Hicks-Beach had no belief in it. They were told, on high economic and administrative authority, that it would weaken the chief pillar of the tax's yield, collection at the source.[2] Even when Chamberlain's son came to the Exchequer, in 1904, he did not put graduation into his first or even his second budget. There was a departmental committee at work on the Tax in 1905, but it was not instructed to consider general principles.[3] However, in response to Liberal and Labour importunity, the Chancellor did ascertain what other countries and what the colonies were doing with their Income Taxes, when they had any.[4] A great deal of very recent experiment in graduation and differentiation was disclosed, but nothing helpful. Most countries were satisfied with some variant of the British system of graduation by abatement. Many kept income taxes on earnings and income taxes on property in separate compartments. No German state taxed its greatest income at more than 5 per cent., which was what all British incomes over £700 were paying just then; and the highest rate reported on was 10·47 per cent. in the Grisons, paid only, one must assume, if paid at all, by a few rich hotel-keepers of the Engadine.

The Liberals, in power from the end of 1905, set up a Com-

[1] Besides the year-to-year history in Mallet, *op. cit.*, see Seligman, E. R. A., *The Income Tax* (1911), Bk. I. ch. 3: "The Modern [English] Income Tax, 1862–1911".

[2] Alfred Marshall used to tell his pupils this in the 'nineties and it was apparently the Treasury view.

[3] Its report (*D.C. on Income Tax*, 1905, XLIV. 219) deals with fraud, methods of computing profits, and so on. It is fully summarised in Seligman, as above.

[4] *Return, shewing Colonies which have established systems of graduated Income Tax* and *Reports...respecting Graduated Income Taxes in Foreign States* (1905, LIII. 183 and LXXXV. 33).

mittee in 1906 which reported that motion on both lines was desirable and practicable;[1] and in 1907 Asquith, who was still Gladstonian enough to hold that a tax of 1*s.* in the pound was unjustifiable "at a time of peace", got to work. He cut the tax to 9*d.*—but only for earned incomes under £200. The abatements up to £700 remained and, with the 25 per cent. reduction of the standard rate, they greatly eased the burden on the middle-class earner. This helps us, said Asquith with another Gladstonian inflection, to treat the Income Tax "as a permanent part of our fiscal machinery", "as I intend it should be treated".[2] A foreigner might have admired the swift English resolve to make permanent a tax which had existed continuously for sixty-five years. Asquith made up for his loss on the Income Tax by a first steepening and stiffening of the Estate Duty, but only on estates worth upwards of £150,000.

Differentiation up to the £2000 level worked well, though for two generations nearly all experts had said that it could not. At the lower rate, more earned income was disclosed; so, as Asquith said in 1908, the novelty "paid for itself". That year, having just become Prime Minister, although he opened the Budget he kept it, so to speak, neutral, leaving Lloyd George the new Chancellor to innovate further in the next year. The innovations were comprehensive in this and other fields of taxation. There was a second stiffening and steepening of death duties; a raising of the standard income-tax rate to 1*s.* 2*d.*, and of the rate on earned incomes between £2000 and £3000 to 1*s.*; and—far more significant—the adoption from the Select Committee's 1906 Report of a super-tax of 6*d.* in the pound on all incomes above £5000, to be levied on the amount by which they exceeded £3000.

This was the Budget which the House of Lords threw out. Its successor was a replica; and there were no further changes of importance in the last troubled years of peace. Income Tax and Super-Tax together yielded £44,800,000 in 1911–12 and £47,200,000 in 1913–14. Ten years later the yield, in less precious money it is true, was £330,000,000. It had been higher in the interval, when some people had been schooled into paying

[1] *S.C. on Income Tax*, 1906 (IX. 659). "Its members approached their deliberations with their minds made up, some in favour of graduation, some in favour of differentiation and some in favour of both", Mallet, who gave evidence before it, wrote: *op. cit.* p. 280.

[2] Quoted in Mallet, p. 275.

an income tax of 6*s*. and a super-tax also of 6*s*. There had seldom been such tax-paying, or more smoothly working machinery for the transfer of wealth from the purposes of peace to those of war, and, when war was over, from class to class.

In the last years of the Gladstonian financial era, the British tax system had been reduced to its simplest recorded form—a light if "demoralising" Income Tax; very light death duties; stamps on deeds, cheques, and a few other things; remnants of the land tax, and an inhabited house duty; customs duties on tobacco, wine, spirits, tea, coffee, cocoa, dried fruits and little else; excise duties on beer and spirits and their sale; and a mixed bundle of licence duties, on guns, dogs, pawnbroking, hawking and a few other objects or activities. The last remnant of the sugar duties, that on sugar used in brewing, had gone in 1881 with the customs duty on malt; and radical tax-reformers were looking forward to what in late-Victorian political slang was called "the free breakfast table". This Chancellors were reluctant to concede, for the imported breakfast table drinks brought in about £5,000,000 a year; although it was highly probable that, assuming an average consumption of these, plus an average consumption of beer and tobacco, the wage-earning household contributed more than its equitable share to the cost of government. The reply that no man need smoke or drink was not perfectly convincing; though there was force in Goschen's argument that the abolition of the tea-duty, this "poll tax on a very low scale",[1] would leave important sections of the community completely untaxed.

Cautious statesmen like Goschen and Salisbury, men conservative in every sense, thought that simplification had already gone too far, that the customs and excise revenues, and with them the whole revenue, were too absolutely dependent on the yield of two or three great taxes.[2] It is not surprising. In 1895–9, for example, when the total tax revenue of the country was £73,600,000, the net receipts from 'drink', imported or home-made, and from licences taken out by those who sold it, came to £29,100,000; from tobacco to £8,900,000; and from tea to £4,600,000; these three sources of revenue thus contributing

[1] Quoted in Mallet, *op. cit.* p. 31.

[2] Mallet, p. 59: "he was the first of modern Chancellors of the Exchequer to raise the cry that the basis of our taxation was dangerously narrow." And see Farrer, T. H., *Mr Goschen's Finance*, 1887–90 and Lady Gwendolen Cecil's *Salisbury*, IV. 181.

58 per cent. of the total flow. Yet neither Goschen nor any other Conservative Chancellor tried to widen the tax system while the country was at peace; and the Whiggish Harcourt did his work on the death duties.

Widening would have been approved by an important section of Conservative opinion at any time after the issue of the Fair Trade programme in the early 'eighties.[1] The retaliatory and Imperial sections of that programme attracted even the then Radical Joseph Chamberlain, who first began to doubt his inherited Free Trade creed, as he used to say, "when, as President of the Board of Trade I had to answer a motion of Ritchie's in favour of retaliatory tariffs".[2] Lord Salisbury in 1887 had snubbed off the National Union of Conservative Associations when they brought him a Fair Trade resolution;[3] but realising the handicap of British commercial diplomacy in a world of tariffs, and not convinced that Free Trade practised by a single nation was for its good, he would have liked at least some duties with which he could negotiate. He must have noted how in 1890, when Goschen reduced one of the few remaining customs duties, that on currants, he was able to associate the change with an offer of reduced duties on British manufactures from the appreciative Greeks.[4] But although, in the late 'nineties, Chamberlain's activity at the Colonial Office showed that he would never let a Free Trade upbringing stand in the way of what he believed good for the Empire, and that he had now no more love for *laisser faire* in imperial affairs than he had ever had for it in municipal and social affairs,[5] Conservative Chancellors continued to declaim in their budget speeches what one right-wing Conservative, an agricultural member who wanted taxes both on imported manufactures and imported corn, called "the stalest pamphlets of the Cobden Club".[6]

Even two and a half years of war (1899–1902) had curiously little effect on the tax system. Existing taxes were of course

[1] Vol. II. 250.

[2] Fitzroy, Sir Almeric, *Memoirs* (1925), I. 141. John Morley used to say later that Chamberlain's free trade was always "only skin-deep": "*au fond*, he looked at the problem from the manufacturer's point of view, which welcomes a tariff as an instrument of monopoly." This was said in 1912. *Ibid.* II. 501.

[3] *Salisbury*, IV. 177–8.

[4] "An interesting example of a tariff bargain...perhaps the last in our commercial history", Mallet, *op. cit.* p. 31.

[5] Cp. Spender, J. A., *The Life of Lord Oxford and Asquith* (1932), I. 150.

[6] Mr James Lowther, quoted in Mallet, p. 115.

raised; but it was not until 1901 that the sugar duty was revived —"I am bold enough to propose a duty on sugar", the Chancellor said—and with it that export duty on coal which Peel had used in the 'forties.[1] The Chancellor, Hicks-Beach, argued that the coal tax was not an ordinary indirect tax burdensome to British consumers because, thanks to Britain's semi-monopolistic position, the foreign consumer would pay it.[2] Many disagreed with him and the Miners' Federation threatened a strike. Next year, though the war was all but over, he revived that small 'registration duty' on imported corn which Robert Lowe had rather pedantically dropped in 1869. Sound Liberals had held not many years back that Lowe's action was unnecessary;[3] but now it was argued that 3*d*. a cwt. on imported wheat (the average price of a cwt. of imported wheat that year was 6*s*. 8¼*d*.) was an intolerable thing, "an infamous tax".[4] Intolerable and infamous, it is fair to add, mainly as a precedent and an opener out of possibilities.

It went in the following year and Joseph Chamberlain went from the ministry with it; but the coal export duty lived to be abolished by Asquith in 1906; when after nearly three years' argument the country had rejected—for that time— a Chamberlain policy of retaliatory tariffs and colonial preference, a policy which had developed, in the course of the argument, most of the features of a general system of protection.

So for eight years the simple schedule of things taxable was retained, though that last great Liberal Government never managed to free sugar;[5] and the extra revenue which the State

[1] Vol. I. 498.

[2] See Hansard, Fourth Series, XCII, April 18, 1901. In a letter to *The Times* of April 22, Alfred Marshall expressed a cautious half-approval of the export duty on coal: "it is not, as some have asserted, to be condemned on general economic grounds"; but "is it worth while?"; we are very vulnerable to retaliation; yet "I admire the courage of the Chancellor".

[3] Buxton, Sidney (Lord) had written in 1888 (*Finance and Politics*, II. 93) after setting out all the "strict free-trade" arguments against the registration duty—"it is pretty certain that if the duty were still in existence it would now be retained". For 1869, vol. II. 243.

[4] By Sir William Harcourt; Mallet, *op. cit.* p. 210.

[5] Nor did it reverse the policy embodied in the Brussels Sugar Convention of March 3, 1902, though it modified it. By that Convention the chief European beet-sugar producing countries agreed not to give bounties on sugar-exports, and Britain undertook to put a tax equal to the bounty on any sugar so subsidised. All producing countries had adopted the bounty policy in turn. This had damaged cane-sugar interests and helped British consumers and sugar-using

required—£33,000,000 more in 1913–14 than in 1904–6—came from automatic increase in the yields of all taxes during the last years of trade activity and rising prices, and from what seemed to the well-to-do the ruthless pressure of Income Tax and Death Duties.[1]

In at least one other matter of finance, besides his formal assumption that the Income Tax up to his day had been still on trial, Asquith showed himself a faithful Gladstonian; he was resolute to pay off the national debt, which during his Chancellorship and the peace years of his service as Prime Minister fell from £797,000,000 to £708,000,000.[2] Seeing that it had stood at £778,000,000 in 1879, a peak year, and that there had been a good deal of warlike and other exceptional expenditure in the intervening generation, it cannot be said that Chancellors of the Exchequer as a class had neglected their duty. In 1879 the weight of debt had been £22·7 per head of the population (of the United Kingdom). In 1914 it was £15·3; and they were decidedly richer heads. The burden might have been increased something like tenfold (as it was to be) without becoming more crushing than that which a much smaller and very much poorer population had carried after Waterloo.

From 1879 to 1899 debt reduction went on steadily by the working of Northcote's sinking fund of 1875[3] and the devotion

industries. As early as 1887 five of the chief producing countries had declared against the principle of export bounties; but it was not until Britain, the chief open market for all their surpluses, took a decided line under Chamberlain that a settlement was reached. Most free traders denounced the Convention because (*a*) it was the first breach in a policy of unrestricted imports, (*b*) it might injure sugar-using interests, (*c*) it smacked of Imperial Protectionism.

The Convention came into force on September 1, 1903. The average price of untaxed imported beet-sugar rose a little. The figures suggest, but do not prove, that the price after the Convention was on the average higher than it might have been had bounty-feeding continued unrestricted. Retail sugar-prices rose very little, although it was a time of general rise. The cheapest price for loaf-sugar before the Convention and Hicks-Beach's tax was 2*d*. a pound. In July, 1914, the rather inferior and lightly taxed granulated sugar could be bought for the same sum.

[1] It has not seemed necessary to go into the exceedingly complicated story of the Lloyd-George land value duties because, *first*, they had only begun to give trifling yields before 1914 and, *second*, they were subsequently abandoned and have not yet been revived. Their very great interest is therefore more political than economic.

[2] These are the aggregate gross liabilities, as given in the *Statistical Abstracts*.

[3] See II. 407.

of realised surpluses to repayment, though there was some intermission of both these processes in difficult or careless years. By 1899 the aggregate gross liabilities of the State were down to £635,000,000. The chief financial event of these years had been Goschen's conversion of the three per cent. consols in 1888.[1] A financier by training, he had noted the steady rise of the three per cents. before he came to the Exchequer. Their price had first stood at par for over a month in April, 1881. The lowest monthly average price since had been 96¼ in April, 1885. Since February, 1886, that price had never been below par and had once got above 103. The moment seemed propitious. The field was familiar and Goschen took it with confidence. Between April, 1888, and October, 1889, the holders of £565,500,000 of various sorts of 'threes' accepted his offer of 2¾ until 1903 and 2½ thereafter on a stock irredeemable till 1923. Holders of £19,250,000 stock were paid off at par. The new stock dropped a few points below par later in the year, and remained below until 1894. Then it mounted steadily until for 1897 it averaged over 112, and for July of that year 113½. All interest rates were low in the middle and later 'nineties, but the price was largely artificial. For many purposes consols were either obligatory, as for Savings Bank investments, or conventionally necessary; so that the amount coming on the market was limited. It was limited further by the steady paying off of the national debt.[2]

This phase in financial history ended with the Boer War. New debt was created and interest rates rose. By 1903 the gross liabilities of the State stood at £798,000,000, and in the latter part of the year the new consols, their interest rate having fallen to 2½ in April, stood at only a little above 88. After that, and more markedly after 1908, the price slipped away with trade revival and rising interest rates, in spite of the policy of vigorous debt reduction initiated by Asquith. For 1913 it averaged only 73 21/32 and for July, 1914, 74 13/16. So the country went into war with its credit at 3·3 per cent., just about where it had stood on the eve of the great French Wars in 1792–3. The moment chosen by Goschen for his conversion had proved better than he could possibly have known.

[1] See Elliot, Hon. A. D., *Life of Lord Goschen* (1911), II. 145 *sqq.*, with a long curious letter from Lord Randolph Churchill warning Goschen against conversion: "it is not and cannot be popular": "the great houses do not consider the circumstances propitious"; and so on.

[2] Giffen, Sir R., "Consols in a Great War", *E.J.* Sept. 1899.

The public expenditure of the early 'eighties, when total payments out of the Exchequer averaged £87,600,000 a year, had seemed disastrously high to men bred in the careful Gladstonian tradition.[1] By 1912–14 every one was talking of that portentous thing the £200,000,000 Budget; and in fact the payments out for 1913–14 came to £197,500,000. Down to 1904–8, when the figure remained almost steady at just under £151,000,000, the rise had not been unduly disproportionate to the rise in the national capacity to pay. Estimates of the national income suggest that an expenditure of about £120,000,000 in 1904–8 could have been borne as easily as one of £87,600,000 in 1881–6.[2] The new onerous payments were an Income Tax 50 per cent. higher than it had been in 1886; Death Duties bringing in £11,000,000 more; and the revived duty on sugar. War and its sequelae were responsible for the first and third, the unrepudiated and most convenient legacy from Harcourt to his Conservative successors for the second.

No important new form of spending by the central government had been devised down to 1904–8. The figure entered under Education, Science and Art in summaries of the nation's accounts had become steadily greater since the introduction—all by Conservative or Unionist governments—of compulsory elementary education in 1876, of free elementary education in 1891, and of an expanded secondary educational system since 1902. This had meant more and more grants in aid of the heavy educational expenditure of the Local Authorities. By 1905–6 the Education-Science-Art entry stood at over £16,000,000. But as it was already approaching £6,000,000 in the late 'eighties, and grew semi-automatically with a population still growing fast, not more than £7–8,000,000 can be debited to policies new since 1886; though by Gladstonian standards that is an exceedingly large sum.

Apart from a substantial grant in aid of Poor Law medical expenditure and of the maintenance costs of pauper lunatics, some few thousands for teachers in Poor Law Schools, and, after 1905, a contribution towards an experimental and sporadic form of unemployment relief,[3] the central government paid out

[1] Cp. vol. II. 397.

[2] An estimate for 1883 is £1,289,000,000: one for 1907 is £1,800,000,000. Stamp, Sir J. C., *British Incomes and Property*, p. 427.

[3] For the general policy of grants-in-aid, see Hasluck, E. L., *Local Government in England* (1936), pp. 237 *sqq.*; and for some special applications, Aschrott, P. F., and Preston Thomas, H., *The English Poor Law System* (1902), p. 276.

nothing to prevent or relieve destitution until the passing in 1908 of 8 Ed. VII, c. 40: *An Act to Provide for Old Age Pensions*. In the financial year 1886–7 local authorities, English, Welsh and Scottish, had spent £9,100,000 on poor relief—considerably less than 1 per cent. of the estimated national income; not an extravagant act of corporate charity. Twenty years later they spent £16,100,000, which was nearly 1 per cent. of a revised estimate. Employment conditions were worse, and the proportion of people relieved to the whole population appreciably greater, at the earlier than at the later date. Retail prices were much the same, though wages in 1906 were decidedly higher. But wages were not an important item in the expenditure of the Guardians of the Poor. In short, as "the directing classes happened to be full of pity, and the State itself...rich",[1] the Guardians had become more liberal, or lax, according to the standpoint of their judge. The directing classes had been widened, and their pity increased, since the political reforms of the earlier 'eighties and the reorganisation of local government accompanied by a stirring of social conscience in the later. To win a seat and influence on a Board of Guardians was a seemly ambition for a social reformer from any class; and in 1894 the property qualification for membership of the Guardians was abolished.

In the middle 'eighties the normal policy of the Boards, and the universal policy of the inspectorate of the Local Government Board, had been strict.[2] "The House" should still be "deterrent", and outdoor relief to able-bodied adults must go. It nearly went. After rising a little in the bad trade of 1885–7, but never beyond 80,000—it had been 129,000 for a much smaller population in 1867—the mean figure of outdoor relief to the able-bodied was down to 59,000 by 1900; abnormally low, it is true, but the average for the 'nineties was less than 68,000. In the 'tens, special investigators working for a Royal Commission found "that there existed practically no systematic Outdoor Relief to men who could properly be classed as able-bodied

[1] Above, p. 397.

[2] Vol. II. 396, 432, 439; for cross-currents in the late 'eighties and 'nineties see *Report of the R.C. on the Aged Poor*, 1895 (XIV, XV); Webb, S. and B., *English Poor Law History, The Last Hundred Years* (1929), ch. IV; Aschrott and Preston Thomas, *op. cit.* pp. 99 *sqq.*; [Nicholls and] Mackay, T., *A History of the English Poor Law* (1899), vol. III, ch. 23.

and not mentally defective".[1] Occasional relief to such people in exceptional cases, or in times of unusual distress, there always was; and at the close, from 1911, while the category of able-bodied outdoor relief was officially abandoned, this most proper emergency relief to people who in fact were able-bodied was tacitly sanctioned.[2]

Meanwhile the ratio of total pauperism—the ill-sounding and hated word was still in regular official use[3]—to population, which had been lower than at any time during the previous half century in 1884–6 (2·8 per cent.), fell lower still, several times during the 'nineties being so low as 2·5. In the early twentieth century it seldom got higher, and in 1912–13 was at 2·15 for England and Wales and 2·3 for Scotland.[4]

This fall in the proportion of the population relieved went hand in hand, as the expenditure shows, with a more generous, if not yet a conspicuously generous, treatment of those whose claims the Guardians and the watch-dogs of the inspectorate allowed. Inspectors of the 'tens, bred in the older tradition, usually held that Guardians had become deplorably open-handed and the Board itself, urged on by a pitiful Parliament, too easy-going since about 1890.[5] There had been continuous official and public discussion of Old Age Pensions, which—pending a decision by Parliament—had led to a steady bettering of conditions for aged folk in the Guardians' care. Concessions intended for them were apt to be allowed to all. There might be tobacco and snuff now in all workhouses; dry tea also, with milk and sugar, for women to serve to their own taste; and books. Nurses, trained ones, were obligatory in place of fellow inmates, though they were not always easily got.[6] In 1900 a circular of the Board definitely advised adequate outdoor relief instead of the House for aged people of good character. This had always been a possibility and a common practice, but the traditional advice from headquarters had been against it.[7]

[1] Webb, *op. cit.* p. 500. Mrs Webb was a member of the Commission.

[2] Webb, pp. 778–9.

[3] E.g. in the *Forty-second...Report of the Local Government Board*, 1913 (XXXI).

[4] The figures are in the *Statistical Abstracts*.

[5] This point of view is reflected in Mackay, *op. cit.*

[6] *R.C. on the Aged Poor, Report*, p. xxxiv; Aschrott, *op. cit.* p. 272; Webb, *op. cit.* pp. 332, 359, 483.

[7] For the circular, Webb, p. 353: it was reported in 1895 that the "deserving" aged poor in workhouses were "few in number", not counting the sick and infirm, and that the decision of policy with regard to them was left entirely to the Guardians, *R.C. on...Aged Poor*, pp. ix, xvi.

The suggestion of workhouse books, made by the Board in 1891, was linked with a suggestion for workhouse toys. A little army of infants and children below school age had been permanently resident in the general mixed workhouses or their infirmaries. The army shrank; but there were still several thousands in 1913–14, on the eve of the date (March, 1915) as from which their removal became compulsory under an order of the Board.[1] In 1906 they were still too often in charge of aged women inmates, occasionally even of certified imbeciles. At a higher level of organisation, the babies were found in one House "under the charge of the laundress, who also looks after the female tramps". At the highest, "in the great palatial establishments of London and other large towns...the infants in the nursery seldom or never got into the open air".[2] All this was at a late stage in the story. But even the laundress cost more than her predecessor the aged inmate, and the palatial establishment more still.

Since the bad early days of the reformed Poor Law, when there was no child policy at all, ways of dealing with growing children always more costly had been tried.[3] The special workhouse school had a long and rather squalid history, running back to the time when there was no national system of education. It still survived in 80 (out of about 600) Unions to the end of the nineteenth century.[4] Most Unions now made use of the Board Schools, which from 1891 were free. There remained however the problem of the Poor Law children's home life. The traditional Scottish method of boarding them out, both before and during their school days, had been studied by English experts so far back as 1869, but had been coldly viewed by higher and lower powers in England.[5] A few Boards of Guardians had experimented with it, both about that time and later; but the Local Government Board of the 'eighties "continued to watch the spread of the system with suspicion".[6] It was only after the new breath began to blow in 1889–90 that the spread was encouraged. By 1900, about half the Unions in the country used the system to some extent, and some 8000 orphaned or deserted

[1] *Report of the L.G.B.*, 1913, p. xlvii; Webb, *op. cit.* p. 753.

[2] *R.C. on the Poor Laws*, 1909 (Cd. 4499), quoted in Webb, pp. 307–9, where the reprinted octavo, not the original folio, edition (Cd. 4499) is used. See below, p. 422, n. 1.

[3] See especially Aschrott, *op. cit.* pp. 253–65; Webb, *op. cit.* pp. 246–306.

[4] Webb, p. 271.

[5] Vol. II. 436–7.

[6] Webb, p. 274.

children benefited under it. The main criticism was that the sum allowed for the Poor Law child was more than the village labourer, with whom he was usually boarded, could afford to spend on a child of his own—another cause of rising Poor Law expenditure.[1]

More expensive still, yet adopted by several metropolitan Unions and important provincial towns, was the so-called Cottage System, in which cottages—often associated with schoolhouse, chapel, workshop and infirmary—were erected to house the children and their foster-parents. The Scattered Home or Sheffield System, in which children were placed under a foster-mother in houses hired not built for the purpose, was less expensive yet, as compared with the old Poor Law methods, not cheap. Started at Sheffield in 1893, it was imitated in a dozen or more large towns during the next seven years; so that when the new century opened more than 10,000 children, from seventy-four urban Unions, were being brought up either in these Scattered Homes or in the specially built Cottages. By 1912–13, some 33,000 English and Welsh children were housed in places of one sort or another apart from the Workhouses; and in Scotland, out of 8449 Poor Law children, 7437 were boarded out.[2] It was in outlying English rural districts that arrangements were most backward, and in the counties of the South-West that most children remained to be ordered out of the mixed Workhouses in 1914–15.[3]

Outside the London area, where ever since the late 'sixties the Metropolitan Common Poor Fund had been used for the development of all kinds of specialised institutions,[4] expenditure on the sick poor had grown slowly before 1886–90; although the Poor Law Board, and its successor the Local Government Board, had tried hard to impress on Guardians that they had a new duty to the sick, whose conditions were no longer to be made deterrent.[5] In London, Poor Law Dispensaries had been established, and the special small-pox or fever hospitals had come to be used by 1886—most properly—first for urgent and then for non-urgent cases where there was no question of pauperism. From the 'eighties, the pace outside London quickened. Dispensaries and

[1] Aschrott, *op. cit.* p. 260.

[2] *Report of the L.G.B.*, 1913, p. xii; of the *L.G.B. for Scotland*, 1913 (XXXIII), p. xvii. The earlier facts are in Aschrott and Webb, as above.

[3] Webb, p. 753.

[4] Vol. II. 431.

[5] For the sick, see Webb, *op. cit.* pp. 314 *sqq.*

specialised hospitals became more common. In all great towns the Workhouse Infirmary, though it might be part of the Workhouse pile not a separate institution as in some of the London Unions, was equipped and staffed as a proper hospital.[1] By 1895 plenty of evidence as to its general excellence was being laid before a Royal Commission;[2] and soon the competition between these State hospitals, as they were sometimes called, and the great voluntary hospitals of London and the provinces began to be a matter of common discussion.

But, right down to 1914, Separate Infirmaries "in no way inferior to the best general hospitals"[3] were to be found in less than 10 per cent. of the Poor Law Unions. This was natural. The single rural Union or the small country town was economically minded and not financially strong; and co-operation among Unions, which might have led to the building of first-rate infirmaries, had always been exceedingly difficult to negotiate. For one thing the rural poor, ever since the days of the East Anglian Incorporations, had hated being moved far by compulsion.[4] The Union Workhouse itself might be far enough from Helion Bumpstead or Huish Episcopi: an infirmary of grouped Unions would be further still. Sometimes there was a good voluntary hospital within reach, at least as near as the infirmary of a group of Unions could possibly be placed.[5] Often, no doubt, the deciding factors were not the wishes of the poor but the lack of sympathetic imagination and the dislike of higher Poor Rates among rural Guardians and their electors. Something was done in single Unions where some dominant group showed enterprise. In the two years 1898–9 five new infirmaries were built in Devon and Cornwall, counties which were not leaders in Poor Law administration.[6] But some form of improved sick-ward was all that the rural Workhouse usually provided, so inefficient and so uninteresting and unpromising in its work, from the professional point of view, that "even when trained nurses were obtainable, they did not remain long".[7] That opinion was expressed in 1914.

[1] Though often lightly staffed and not equipped as a quite first-rate hospital.

[2] *R.C. on the Aged Poor*, p. xxxii.

[3] Webb, p. 762, quoting the *Forty-third Report of the L.G.B.*

[4] See vol. I. 353, 359, for the East Anglian Incorporations.

[5] As, for instance, Addenbrooke's Hospital, Cambridge. Dislike of the voluntary hospital may explain the slurring over of this possibility in Webb, *op. cit.*

[6] Aschrott, *op. cit.* p. 271, n. 2, quoting the *Twenty-ninth Report of the L.G.B.*

[7] Webb, p. 762, quoting the *Forty-third Report of the L.G.B.*

The duty of the State to undertake, or at least to organise, an honourable rather than a pauper maintenance for the aged had been part of the English radical tradition since Tom Paine's *Rights of Man*, and more faintly of the philanthropic tradition since the proposals for a National Friendly Society of his contemporary the Rev. John Acland.[1] It was one of the real victories of the spirit of *laisser faire* that these traditions were so completely obscured, at least in governing minds, during the mid-nineteenth century. Mill had thought that the whole subject of Poor Laws "would be of very minor importance if the habits of all classes of the people were temperate and prudent, and the diffusion of property satisfactory". As things were, however, he conceived it "to be highly desirable, that the certainty of subsistence should be held out by law to the destitute able-bodied",[2] and no doubt *a fortiori* to the aged; but he undertook no special inquiry into ways and means, and his whole discussion of the Poor Laws had a smack of 'deterrence'. His hope for the future was a better diffusion of property by way of co-operation, and ultimately "a qualified Socialism".[3]

Magnificent work done throughout the century by the Friendly Societies had strengthened the hope that in the end growing temperance and prudence might suffice to meet all risks both of sickness and of old age, even among ill-paid wage-earners. "Some of our best courts", a representative of the Foresters told a Royal Commission in 1895, "are in the agricultural districts where wages are lowest."[4] "I regard all this problem of poverty", Mill's successor in the leadership of English economists said to these same Commissioners, "as a mere passing evil in the progress of man upwards; and I should not like any institution started which did not contain in itself the causes which would make it shrivel up, as the causes of poverty itself shrivelled up."[5] It was a faith of his time, and still more of his place. Were the Chinese "man"; and was the poverty of China—where "whole provinces, as large as European states, may properly be described as congested districts"[6]—a "mere passing evil"? However he added—"I would far rather have

[1] Vol. I. 295, 313; vol. II. 434–5.

[2] Mill, *Principles*, Bk. V, ch. XI, §13.

[3] See vol. II. 483.

[4] *R.C. on the Aged Poor*, Q. 12,489, Mr Stead of the Foresters.

[5] Alfred Marshall, Q. 10,356.

[6] Tawney, R. H., *Land and Labour in China* (1932), p. 103.

Mr Booth's scheme or Mr Moore Ede's scheme than things as they are"; for the shrivelling up of the causes of poverty even in England was not going on fast enough.

The schemes of which he spoke were variant proposals for Old Age Pensions, very familiar to social reformers at the time. During the 'eighties, the one best known had been that of Canon Blackley, devised during the depression of the late 'seventies.[1] It suggested a provision for all wage-earners of 8*s*. a week in sickness and of 4*s*. a week on reaching the age of seventy. It was based on the handling and investment by the State of sums provided mainly by the wage-earners themselves—in youth, before their liabilities thickened. While it held the field, and while the problem of the aged was engrossing many philanthropic minds, Bismarck followed up his Sickness and Accident Insurance Laws of 1883–5 with his Invalidity and Old Age Insurance Law of 1889. The basis was to become familiar in Britain more than twenty years later: employers, workpeople and the State all contributed. The provisions were intricate, arranged to produce different results for differing groups, but holding out prospects of an average pension of about 3*s*. 6*d*. a week in old age. German wages were not high: those earning 2000 marks a year (say 38*s*. a week) were considered too well off to need insurance; so the proposal about corresponds in value to that of the Blackley scheme. But it was not universal in its application: "the great army of casual labourers and unemployed will receive no benefit", an English admirer of Bismarck wrote.[2]

Joseph Chamberlain's biographer has described his pronouncement in favour of Old Age Pensions two years after Bismarck's Old Age Insurance Law as daring.[3] In the personal and political circumstances of 1891 perhaps it was. But for a Radical from the left to advocate something like, though not too like, what Tom Paine had proposed or Otto von Bismarck had executed may not seem daring to posterity. After that came the battle of the schemes and ten years of almost uninterrupted Commission and Committee; the Royal Commission on the

[1] Vol. II. 435.

[2] Dawson, W. H., *Bismarck and State Socialism* (1891), p. 127. The details of the original schemes are in Pfafferoth, E., *Führer durch die gesammte Arbeiterversicherung* (1889).

[3] Garvin, *Joseph Chamberlain*, II. 508. The proposal was for a government grant in aid of voluntary contributions, and its critics asked whether improvident people would make them. See the *Economist*, May 16, 1891. Chamberlain advocated a different scheme later.

Aged Poor with a remarkable body of Commissioners, ranging from the Prince of Wales through Joseph Chamberlain to Joseph Arch; a Committee; a Select Committee; a Departmental Committee; in 1903 a Bill; a Select Committee on the Bill; then more Bills. There were contributory schemes of many kinds and non-contributory schemes; schemes which favoured 'voluntary assisted insurance' and schemes based on compulsion; schemes to give pensions to wage-earners only, and schemes to give them to all people below a certain level of income; and a famous scheme which, to ensure and perpetuate the honourable character of the provision, would have given a 5*s*. pension at 65 to every one, literally every one, at a cost of £24,500,000.[1]

Nothing happened except—an important exception—a growing consideration for old people in the care of the Guardians. From 1899 war diverted public attention and national resources. When war was over, Joseph Chamberlain's influence had also been diverted; though when he launched his Tariff Reform campaign in 1903 he held out hopes that, if the country followed him, some of the money raised by tariffs might be spent on Pensions.[2] The work was left to those who overwhelmed him politically in 1905–6.

Financial reasons prevented them from undertaking it at once. They might even have been expected to wait a little longer than they did—for a Report from the Royal Commission on the Poor Law and the Relief of Distress, which had been accumulating information since 1905.[3] But the divergent Reports of the Commissioners were not ready until 1909, and Pensions were announced in the Budget of 1908. All the finer drawn schemes were rejected and the pension made simple, prompt, and non-contributory; mainly because, after such long discussion and wealth of promises, any scheme whose full benefits, as Asquith said, could not "come into operation until after the lapse of twenty or more years"[4] would have rung rather hollow. Every British subject who was not a criminal, not a person who had habitually

[1] The whole history and the schemes are summarised in a Memorandum accompanying *Tables which have been prepared in connection with the Question of Old Age Pensions*, 1907 (LXVIII, 385). And see Ensor, *England* 1870–1914, pp. 237–8. The 'famous scheme' is that of Charles Booth, whose paper on "State pensions for the aged", *S.J.* 1891, may be regarded as the start of the final movement.

[2] Recalled in the obituary notice in the *Annual Register*, 1914.

[3] Eventually embodied in 37 folio volumes of 57 parts.

[4] Quoted in Mallet, *British Budgets*, p. 292.

failed to work 'according to his ability, opportunity, and need', or not a person in actual receipt of poor relief other than medical relief, was to receive 5*s*. a week at the age of 70 if his income from all sources was not above £21 a year, and an allowance graded down to 1*s*. if his income was between £21 and £31.[1] After that nothing. Asquith, with considerable diffidence for there were many unknown quantities in his calculation, put the initial cost to the Exchequer at about £6,000,000. It was already a good deal more than that in 1909–10; and in the Appropriation Act of 1913 (3 and 4 Geo. V, c. 35) the sum set aside for the Old Age Pensions was £12,600,000.

The Act of 1908 was the first solid instalment of that social reform to which Liberals, and the small associated parliamentary power of Labour, were committed. It was also, though perhaps not with design, a step towards that break-up of the Poor Law which became a fighting catchword after the Reports of the Royal Commission had been issued in the following year. Most certainly the Commission had not been appointed to plan break-up. Why it had been appointed is not yet clear; but it was probably because the President of the Local Government Board in 1905, a thinker, was conscious of the cross-currents of thought on social policies then flowing, and wanted to see them charted.[2] He had himself been officially responsible for an Act swept up by one of the currents, the Unemployed Workmen Act of 1905 (5 Ed. VII, c. 18), which those committed to the other—with many people committed to neither—thought was only a bit of dangerous wreckage.

Since the early 'eighties, Socialist propaganda and philanthropic solicitude had fastened on that unemployment cause of poverty and destitution which Henry Fawcett in his *Pauperism and its Causes* of 1871 had ignored.[3] (Indeed when he wrote, the words 'unemployment' and 'the unemployed' were not coined.[4]) In descending curves of trade activity, charitable groups and well-meaning municipalities had got to work now and then—but in London always—with relief funds and relief

[1] *An Act to provide for Old Age Pensions*, 8 Ed. VII, c. 40.

[2] Webb, *op. cit.* p. 471. Mrs Webb, a Commissioner and well-placed for acquiring information, suggests this probability. The President was Mr Gerald (now Earl) Balfour.

[3] Vol. II. 433 n. 4.

[4] 'Unemployment' is first recorded in the *N.E.D.* from 1888, 'unemployed' as a noun from 1882. This is also pointed out by Webb, p. 633 n. and by Ensor, *England*, 1870–1914, p. 112.

works which attracted undesirables as often as they helped the honourable unemployed. The Act of 1905—experimental; enacted for three years; but prolonged regularly—in fact sprang out of efforts made in London, during 1903–4, to improve the administration of such haphazard and often unwholesome relief. Unhappily, the system set up by the Act proved to be not very much better. Provision was made for the creation of a Distress Committee in every borough above a certain size which demanded one, and in London—through all its history the Act was mainly a Londoner's Act[1]—for a Central Committee to coordinate the work of the Metropolitan Borough Committees. Committees might provide "temporary work or other assistance" for an unemployed man whose case was "more suitable for treatment under this Act than under the poor law". That was splendidly vague. A man so relieved was not to lose his electoral rights as the 'pauper' always had. It was its vagueness and, as they held, misplaced political generosity which made Poor Law administrators of the old strict school hate the Act.[2]

While the Royal Commission was sitting and sending out its inquiries East and West and South and North, the Poor Law, both English and Scottish, was being administered with increasing kindliness—it was never very kind—and applications to the Distress Committees under the Act of 1905 rose to a maximum of 197,000, for England and Wales only, during the slack trade which followed the international crisis of 1907.[3] Nothing revolutionary had happened in Scottish Poor Law administration during the previous twenty years. Scotland's 'combination poorhouses'—the combination was of the great Scottish parishes—having been built late, lacked "the repulsive features of those English workhouses that were built immediately after the passing of the Poor Law" of 1834.[4] They needed less adaptation to the needs of a kindlier time. In any case they were not important in the social life of the country. Only 1 sane

[1] E.g. in 1913–14 11 English or Welsh Distress Committees 'outside London' received help from the L.G.B.: but the 11 included Barking, East Ham, Edmonton, Leyton, Tottenham, Walthamstow and West Ham, and only four non-metropolitan boroughs—Bradford, Hull, Norwich and Swansea. *Forty-third Report of the L.G.B.*, 1914, p. lxxi. There had been more committees, but they had ceased to function with the improvement of trade: Webb, *op. cit.* p. 651.

[2] The official title of the Act is notably vague—"An Act to establish organisation with a view to the provision of Employment or Assistance for Unemployed Workmen in proper cases."

[3] By 1913–14 they were down to 24,000: *Forty-third Report*, as above.

[4] Vol. II. 437.

Scot in every 448 was a poorhouse inmate in 1888. Twenty years later, in the bad year 1908, the ratio had risen, but not beyond 1 in 312. Children had nearly all been boarded out for many years. The process of offering indoor relief or nothing had apparently been slightly more successful in bringing adults into the poorhouses, and retaining them there, since 1886–8 than in earlier years, when the governor of the Dalkeith house had explained how "they just come in at the tae door and...gang out at the tither".[1] Its effect in keeping down out-relief had been continuous. The number of sane Scots and their dependants relieved 'out' was almost identical in 1888, 1898 and 1912, in a population which had grown some 15 per cent. between the first and third dates.[2]

"The Royal Commission of 1905–9", one of its members wrote twenty years after, was "from a constructive point of view, as big a failure as the Royal Commission of 1832–4 was a success." "It ranged those who were interested in social reconstruction into two opposing camps...and even the changes which the Majority and Minority alike advocated long failed to pass into law." Therefore they need not be set out here. "What it achieved", the reminiscent member continued, "was a couple of discoveries."[3] These reputed discoveries deserve record; for the claim seems on the whole just. To the majority of the governing world they apparently were discoveries. The first was "that the 'Principles of 1834' had been, almost unawares, gradually abandoned in practice by...governments, whether Conservative or Liberal"; and the second, "that there had grown up, during the preceding half century, an array of competing public services which were aiming, not at the prevention of pauperism, but at the prevention of the various types of destitution out of which pauperism arose". When the now abandoned Principles of 1834 were formulated—or were believed to have been formulated—there was no Public Health Service, no National Education System, no representative local self-government, no proper apprehension of unemployment as "a problem of industry",[4] no Old Age Pensions, and none of

[1] Vol. II. 437.

[2] Statistics from the 1913 *Report of the L.G.B. for Scotland*, pp. xiii–xvii. The number relieved had been only 3–4000 (5 per cent.) more in the slump of 1908.

[3] Webb, *op. cit.* p. 470. And cp. Hasluck, *Local Government in England*, pp. 270–1; Ensor, *op. cit.* pp. 516–18.

[4] The sub-title of Sir William Beveridge's decisive book *Unemployment* (1909).

those projects for various kinds of destitution-preventing Insurance which were ripening for use in 1909. *Ad hoc* representative bodies, the Guardians, had been created to relieve, house, keep healthy, educate, discipline—whether they merited discipline or not—and maintain until the parish buried them, a mass of people who had only one thing in common, their destitution. Society, through its various organs, was now trying to do for all citizens, and was often doing well, many of the things which the Guardians had done for the destitute, and because grudgingly often ill. The School Boards, a later series of *ad hoc* authorities, had gone—at least in England. There were few good reasons for perpetuating special elected bodies to deal with the maintenance, health, and education of the destitute, when the general elective local governing bodies were dealing with so many of these things normally for all, and the central government had just provided honourable, if only partial, maintenance for the aged with the declared object of keeping them out of the range of these special elected bodies.

But though no one knew it, the Guardians had still more than twenty years' expectation of life in 1909. The Government of the day, partly justified no doubt in its neglect of the Commission's findings by the polemics which broke out between the opposing camps of the Commissioners, and handicapped by the stubborn conservatism of the ex-socialist President of the Local Government Board, John Burns,[1] proceeded with its policy, its very wise policy, of cutting at some of the roots of destitution; and may be pictured—though the picture simplifies and rationalises over-much the way in which Cabinets make plans and arrive at decisions—as planning to reduce destitution and the cost of its relief to a minimum, and then decide the fate of the Guardians. There seemed reason to think in 1912–13, when for the first time in very many years expenditure "on the relief of the poor and matters connected therewith" fell appreciably, that the Old Age Pensions were really doing one of the things for which they had

[1] See Ensor, as above. The Commissioner who later lamented the "ranging" of "those who were interested in social reconstruction into two opposing camps" had something to do with that unhappy result; for the Minority, of whom she was one, took steps to give their views a start with public opinion which many disinterested people regarded as too clever, and which the Prime Minister is believed to have resented. They published their Report in handy octavo form while the Majority was still lumbering in official folio. This made a Majority octavo necessary—and led to the modern policy of publishing most government literature in the handier form.

been designed. But expenditure rose again next year; and after that the setting of the problem was brutally shaken. The destitution of whole nations became a sinister possibility, and the nineteenth-century vision of a smooth "progress of man upwards" was blurred; lost, some people said.

It is at least possible that, had Bismarck not fallen from office in 1890, a great industrial nation might have experimented in unemployment insurance during the nineteenth century. He thought it the form of social insurance which wage-earners would value most, as the importance of unemployment pay in the voluntary working of British Trade Unions suggested. But he and his advisers had realised its difficulties and had made their start on other ground. In Britain there was a great and well-grounded reluctance to do anything which might weaken the voluntary activity either of the Trade Unions or of the Friendly Societies. This meant circumspection and delay. But as Bismarck's sickness and invalidity insurance had been reasonably successful in a state which could not be called democratic; as social insurance of all kinds had attracted democratic statesmen more and more, particularly in some of the British Dominions, since Germany showed the way; as trade unionists were only a small minority among wage-earners, and their systems of unemployment and sick pay by no means always actuarially perfect; and as the undoubted success of the Friendly Societies among ill-paid wage-earners had not yet built up a barrier which could be counted on to protect the poor against the destitution risks that sickness may bring with it; for these reasons imaginative British statesmen, now having the power, were eager to experiment in all forms of national insurance without damaging the structure and effectiveness of the Societies or the Unions, if that were possible; but anyhow to experiment.[1]

Their piecemeal, empirical methods were what their nationality and their political environment dictated. Old age had been dealt with in 1909, in a plain way that all could understand. The arguments of expediency in favour of that way were overwhelming, but it is probable that, for the future social health of the

[1] But note that "the nation owes its present system of...national insurance against involuntary Unemployment mainly to the elaborate studies (and consequent inventiveness) of two of the ablest of our Civil Servants, Sir Hubert Llewellyn Smith and Sir W. H. Beveridge...who found in Mr Winston Churchill...a Minister sufficiently appreciative and courageous to adopt so novel and adventurous a scheme..."; Webb, *op. cit.* p. 669.

nation, some element of contribution by beneficiaries would have improved the pensions system. However that may be, the system was a first barrier against destitution, strong if low. There is no absolute reason why one's old age should be insured against gratis, one's sickness or lack of work by a complex system of compulsory contributions. But that was what happened. Nor is there any pure reason why a general and thoroughly worked-out system of contributory health insurance, for all people below a prescribed level of wealth, should be set up by the same Act as establishes a tentative system, also contributory, of unemployment insurance applicable only to certain selected trades. Yet this was what political convenience required.[1] The National Insurance Act of 1911 (1 and 2 Geo. V, c. 55), a code of 116 pages, preserved in this its short title the two words with which, thirty-three years earlier, Canon Blackley had headed the article whose publication led in the final phase of the movement for what he had also called compulsory providence.[2] His scheme had dealt, rather crudely, with old age and sickness, but had not touched the unemployment of healthy men. In the Act of 1911 unemployment clauses were the most novel and significant section.

The health clauses had required long and dexterous handling of the British Medical Association and the great Friendly Societies by Lloyd George. These last now appeared, by a typical British incorporation of the voluntary with the statutory, as societies approved for the administration of those sickness, disablement, or maternity benefits which the Act offered in cash. Medical benefit, the cost of the services of the medical men who became panel doctors, and sanatorium benefit, were paid direct to the doctors and the sanatorium authorities by Insurance Committees created for the purpose in each area of Local Government. Since membership of an approved society was not compulsory, though providence now was, arrangements were made for what was called deposit insurance through the Post Office; but when the system got to work in 1912–14 it fell almost entirely into the hands of the approved societies, as was in fact designed and desired. The cost was met by a contribution from the Exchequer and a joint contribution from employer and employed made through the stamped insurance card which was

[1] But the two Parts of the Act have since been dealt with in separate series of amending Acts as if they were the separate laws which in reality they are.

[2] Vol. II. 434.

to become so familiar. In 1911 the card was an important administrative innovation—made in Germany and imitated here.[1] So Britain, and even Ireland, acquired the habit of licking stamps; although in the heat of the fight—passions ran hot wherever Lloyd George's Welsh plume waved—associations of ladies his enemies were formed, and pledged not to lick.

Comprehensive in its health sections, the Act was designedly selective and experimental in the section that dealt with unemployment. Groups of industries were picked out which were well known to suffer more than others, either from necessary seasonal unemployment, or from that cyclical unemployment connected with the making of durable capital goods which seemed, and still seems, almost equally necessary. The selected groups were the Building Trades proper; Construction of Works, that is of roads, railways, docks, harbours and the like; Shipbuilding; Mechanical Engineering; Ironfounding; the Construction of Vehicles; and Sawmilling when carried on in connection with any other insured trade. These groups contained about two million British men and youths: they were essentially men's trades. By 1913–14, when the system was in full work, the total number of persons insured against unemployment in the United Kingdom was 2,326,000—over 800,000 in each of the two biggest groups, Building and Engineering; more than 250,000 in Shipbuilding; more than 200,000 in Vehicle-building; and the balance in the other trades.[2]

Unemployment Insurance had an easy start; for trade-union unemployment, which in 1909 had stood at 13 per cent. in the Engineering Shipbuilding and Metal-working group, and at 11·7 per cent. for the Carpenters and Joiners, was down by 1913 to 2·2 per cent. for the first group and to 3·3 for the second. The strain was first felt, in a very different world, in 1921.

Before the Insurance Bill was read a first time, steps had been taken to minimise involuntary and needless unemployment by the creation of a network of public Employment Exchanges, or Labour Exchanges as they were called in both popular and official language, with a half reminiscence of the very different institution of the same name which Robert Owen had started

[1] Clapham, J. H., *The Economic Development of France and Germany*, 1815–1914, p. 337.

[2] See Cohen, J. L., *Insurance against Unemployment* (1921) for a general narrative and discussion.

under King William IV.[1] The idea of a public house of call for men seeking work and employers seeking workers was obvious and not new. Other countries had experimented with it long before; there had been voluntary experiments in England and plenty of discussion;[2] but the first statutory recognition was in an Act of 1902 (2 Ed. VII, c. 13) which authorised, but did not enjoin, the setting up of Labour Bureaus in the new London Metropolitan Boroughs. The Unemployed Workmen Act of 1905 was intended to generalise this system in all Counties and County Boroughs.[3] In fact it did not. The Act was mandatory not permissive; but as both the local authorities and the then President of the Local Government Board were apathetic, it was not carried out—except in London, where a start had already been made, and in Lanarkshire. By a blunder in legislative design, the Bureaus or Exchanges were too closely associated with the Distress Committees provided for by the Act. This suggested that the Exchange was an emergency device not a bit of permanent machinery like, for example, a domestic servants' registry office. Yet the consequences of this blunder could be circumvented.

They were circumvented by the Central Unemployed Body for London. Conceiving of the Exchanges as permanent, it separated the administration of distress relief from their normal work. "After some careful experimenting...the whole of the metropolis was gradually covered by a network [of Exchanges] ...telephonically inter-connected and reporting to a common centre."[4] By the end of 1908, thirty-two London Trade Union branches, recognising the utility of the Exchanges, had put their 'vacant books' into the hands of the exchange officials.

Differing in many things, the Poor Law Commissioners of 1905–9 were unanimously in favour of a national system of Exchanges which should have nothing to do with the Poor Law and no distress emergency character. Partly in consequence of this unanimity, the system which had been planned as comprehensive in the year of their appointment was made effectively comprehensive in the year of their report, by 9 Ed. VII, c. 7: *An Act for the establishment of Labour Exchanges*. Administered by the very able Labour Department of the Board of Trade, the

[1] Podmore, F., *Robert Owen* (1906), ch. XVII, "Labour Exchanges".

[2] See Joseph Chamberlain's letter to Salisbury of 1894; Garvin's *Chamberlain*, II. 615.

[3] Webb, *op. cit.* p. 660.

[4] Webb, p. 661.

Act became a working reality at once. The London Exchanges were taken over; during the years 1910–11 others were organised throughout the Kingdom; and in the trade activity of 1913–14 more than a million employment vacancies a year were being filled through them.

Such a sensible and belated national convenience as the Labour Exchange invited little criticism even from the most hardened individualist, and the thin ranks of the hardened individualists had thinned again since the 'nineties. Once designed and erected, the Labour Exchange was almost as obvious a public institution as the Post Office. Another Act of the year 1909 marked a more pregnant innovation, or rather reversion, in national policy. This was 9 Ed. VII, c. 22: *An Act for the establishment of Trade Boards for certain Trades.* Boards of Trade to fix their wages had been demanded by some of the distressed Hand-loom Weavers in the days of Owen's Labour Exchanges, when memory of the wage clauses of the Elizabethan labour code and of the Spitalfields Acts was still green. The Committee of 1834, which considered the Weavers' Petitions, had not "felt warranted in giving a decided opinion" "as to the practicability and efficiency" of this plan, or of several others.[1] Then came more than a whole generation of legislators to whom public, or semi-public, fixing of wages was not only patently impracticable but also rather shocking. But before 1890, that is before hand-loom weaving was quite extinct even in the cotton industry,[2] those in authority had become solicitous about 'sweating' in other industries, and a House of Lords Committee had issued five Reports on the Sweating System.[3] If 'sweating', that Committee suggested, meant the paying of wages unfit for an adult, there was plenty of it: its evils could "hardly be exaggerated".[4] In 1897 two linked evolutionary socialists were arguing in favour of a National Minimum of wages—"a definite

[1] *Committee on the Hand-loom Weavers' Petitions*, 1834 (x), *Report*, p. 2.

[2] Vol. II. 81.

[3] 'Lord Dunraven's Committee'; *S.C. of the H. of L. on the Sweating System*, 1888 (XX. XXI); 1889 (XIII. XIV); 1890–1 (XVII). Much familiar information was collected about tailoring, shirt-making, cabinet, chain and nail making, and so on. The report is that of surprised, simple-minded, honest men. There was a *Report on Nail Makers and Small Chain Makers*, independent of the Lords' inquiry, in 1888 (XCI. 459) made to the Board of Trade by John Burnett.

[4] "We have endeavoured to extract...a clear idea of what they understood by the term 'sweating'. The replies received were neither clear nor consistent", *Report* (1890–1), p. xliii. So to the conclusion quoted above.

sum of earnings per week below which no employer should be allowed to hire any worker".[1] Eleven years after that (in 1908) a Select Committee on Home Work—of all workers the woman home-worker is most easily and most often sweated—was asking almost in fear whether or not Wages Boards for the cure of sweating were practicable, and suggesting that they might be tried experimentally in selected trades.[2]

As those now in authority were experimentally minded, the Act with its "certain trades" was put through. Next year the first three Boards were established; one in an old home of sweating in every sense, the domestic 'hammered and dollied or tommied' chain-making industry of the Black Country; one for the paper-box trade, mainly of the London East End; and one for the widespread trade in 'ready made and wholesale bespoke male garments'. Shirt-making, with some others, only got its Board in 1914.[3] The work of establishing and operating a Board was necessarily slow, and all the early boards, under a common official and impartial chairman, "displayed care and prudence".[4] So it is neither surprising nor discreditable that the first schedules of 'minimum time rates for male and female workers' only came into operation, in the tailoring trade, in 1912, and were finally made obligatory by a Board of Trade Order under the Act, dated February 20, 1913.[5] The avowedly experimental system was thus in a very early phase of its application in 1914. Only a few hundred thousand workers were even scheduled as within its range, and the effects of the wage-rates approved for some of them had yet to be tested. They might help the workers or they might kill the trades. Each alternative would have its merits: but the merits would be of different sorts. There was however the established novelty of a wage, outside government employment, sanctioned by an official order. It was not quite ninety years since the Justices of the City and the Tower Hamlets had been forbidden by law to do this any longer for the silk-weavers of Spitalfields.[6] Now it was done for the weakest and the most oppressed among the people.

[1] Webb, *Industrial Democracy*, p. 774.

[2] *S.C. on Home Work*, 1908 (VIII), pp. xiii–xv. The literature of the subject, mostly dealing with later developments, is in Webb, *Poor Law History*, p. 559 n.

[3] For early Boards and their dates see *Forty-third Report of the L.G.B.*, 1914 (XXXVIII), p. lxvi, and *Report of the Com. on Trade Boards*, 1922 (X).

[4] *Report* of 1922, p. 7.

[5] *L.G.B. Report*, as above.

[6] Clapham, J. H., "The Spitalfields Acts", *E.J.* Dec. 1916.

If the strongest body of organised wage-earners, the coal-miners, had had their way, there would have been not merely an officially sanctioned but a statutory minimum wage for them by 1914. Regulation of mines and miners was nothing new. Except the textiles, theirs was the oldest regulated industry.[1] And the first wage-earners to sit in Parliament were miners. In 1887 the Coal Mines Acts, which ran back to 1850 and 1842, had been consolidated and amended.[2] The new Act made that watch-dog of the miners' interests, the checkweigh-man, thoroughly independent, as the miners had always wished. It dealt with every kind of safety precaution, from the use of the lamp to the prevention of the rope slipping on the winding drum. Naturally it maintained the prohibition of women's work underground. But on the side of wages it did no more than repeat the old clause of 1842 which forbade their payment in public houses. For twenty-one years there was a lull in which only short amending Acts were passed, and then, with more miners in Parliament, came the Act of 1908 (8 Ed. VII, c. 57) 'for the purpose of limiting hours of work below ground', which the public knew as the miners' eight-hours' day Act. No coal worker was to remain below ground "for the purpose of his work and of going to and from his work" for more than eight hours in the twenty-four. In 1911 the Coal Mines Acts were again consolidated, into a code of 70 pages.[3] Lastly, in a time of anxiety and storm, came the Act of 1912: *To provide a Minimum Wage...in Coal-Mines*, 2 and 3 Geo. V, c. 2.[4] There would probably have been a wage figure in its text—the miners fought for this—had Asquith not been Prime Minister. Foreseeing and fearing party wage-bids at elections, he would sanction the minimum policy to end strife, and would set up machinery to determine the level, but he would not tolerate a statutory wage figure.[5] District conferences were to determine district minima. A government representative was to attend each conference, and failing agreement he was to decide the wage. It was a sort of arbitration, in principle very near to the method of the Wage Boards. And that was the last peace-time law for miners.

Like the safety sections of the Coal Mines legislation, the Factory and Workshop Acts were already so well developed by

[1] Vol. I. 575–6; vol. II. 100, 420.
[2] In 50–1 Vict. c. 58.
[3] 1 and 2 Geo. V, c. 50.
[4] See below, p. 501.
[5] Spender, J. A. and Asquith, C., *The Life of Lord Oxford and Asquith*, I. 352.

1886–7 that interest concentrates principally on extensions and administrative novelties, above all on the special attention given to sanitation and to dangerous trades.[1] Factory Law and Sanitary Law had separate origins, and it is curious to note how long they had kept apart.[2] Down to the 'sixties, the Factory Inspectors had legally nothing to do with cleanliness, ventilation, or disease in factories; and even the great Factory and Workshop Act of 1878, though it paid more attention to questions of safety than any previous law, and made the administration of safety provisions more elastic, contained no section dealing with specially dangerous or unwholesome occupations.[3] Its elasticity did however help inspectors to deal more effectively with a trade whose insanitary and dangerous nature had been known for centuries—the making and handling of white lead.[4] And in the title of the next Factory Act, which came after the unprecedentedly long gap of five years, White Lead Factories are mentioned by name with Bakehouses and other 'certain Factories and Workshops'. It was an Act meant to close known, and now labelled, gaps in the old law.[5] Like it, an Act of 1889 (52 and 53 Vict. c. 62) was only of particular application, dealing with the special problem of unhealthy humidity in cotton-cloth factories.

But the great amending Factory and Workshops Act of 1891 (54 and 55 Vict. c. 75) gave administrative enterprise wide scope. Besides revising many details of the existing law, it empowered the Home Secretary to issue and enforce special rules in any industry—not being a domestic industry; a significant exception —which he had himself certified to be dangerous or injurious to health, or dangerous to life or limb. For three years, from August 1892 to June 1895, this law was administered with great energy by Asquith; and towards the close of his stay at the Home Office—in 1895—a brief amending Act extended widely that sanitary control of industrial life which thirty years before had been outside the scope of the inspectors.[6] Not less than sixteen

[1] See vol. II. 417 *sqq.*

[2] The main source of information is Oliver, T. (editor), *Dangerous Trades*, 1902. Dr Oliver was the medical expert of the Home Office Dangerous Trades Committee.

[3] Cp. *Dangerous Trades*, p. 36.

[4] *Factory Inspectors' Report for* 1879 (1880, XIV. 93), p. 87.

[5] It is 46 and 47 Vict. c. 53.

[6] *Dangerous Trades*, p. 41; Hutchins and Harrison, *A History of Factory Legislation*, p. 325.

trades—from arsenic extraction and lucifer-match-making to flax-spinning and quarrying—had been certified, and supplied with their special safety codes, under the Act of 1891; the medical knowledge of the whole country had been linked to the Home Office by an order instructing all practitioners to report to the chief inspector their cases of industrial poisoning; and women had been appointed to the inspectorate for the first time in 1893.

It was a woman inspector who wrote of the next Factory Act, the consolidating Act of 1901, when in the making, that the Grand Committee on Trade was "practically unanimous" in giving the Home Office "power to prohibit, limit, or control use of any material or process in industry", and to regulate every detail "in matters of health by means of departmental orders".[1] This was the last great Factory and Workshop Act of the era; and its fine-meshed, wide-cast, 'bureaucratic' net was what the men of that day were learning to use or tolerate, if not always approve. The only addition to the series in the next thirteen years was an Act of 1907 (7 Ed. VII, c. 39) which brought laundries, now become factories by the oldest definition for most of them used power, well within the cast of the net. No new general law was needed. The code of 1901 was comprehensive and, where it failed, the departmental order came into play.[2]

Meanwhile another code, much less comprehensive, far harder to administer, and so incomparably less efficient was being elaborated for the protection and control of workers in shops. A prime obstacle to efficiency was that some of the least controllable and longest-houred shops were among those which served classes who, when working in factories, were themselves protected and controlled. Wage-earners wanted to shop late on Saturdays; perhaps on Sundays; often at odd hours and in obscure places. The case for laxity in their interest was sometimes overworked, but it was solid.

The Commissioners of 1875–7, whose inquiry prepared the way for the Factory Act of 1878, had taken some evidence about

[1] Miss A. M. Anderson in *Dangerous Trades*, p. 43. The Act is 1 Ed. VII, c. 22.

[2] How thoroughly Factory or Mine Law was administered is a difficult problem. To this day the Inspectorate is hardly large enough to guarantee compliance with all its requirements, especially in new, small, and out-of-the-way factories and industries.

shops and had discussed shop-labour in their Report, but had decided to make no recommendation.[1] Ten years passed, and then a Bill was drafted in commenting on which a Select Committee pointed out that some shop assistants worked eighty-four or eighty-five hours a week.[2] The Bill which became law as 49 and 50 Vict. c. 55, was modelled with ridiculous precision on the early Factory Acts. It was "to regulate the Labour of Children and Young Persons in Shops". Children did not need much regulation; for now they had to be at school and there had never been a great deal of use for them in the shops. The central clause was therefore one that fixed a seventy-four hours limit to the work of 'Young Persons'. Central but ineffective; for early Factory Act history was repeated, and the law "remained generally unenforced and even to a great extent unknown".[3] It was re-enacted with improvements in 1892 and improved again in 1893 and 1895, under the Asquith administration at the Home Office. Entrusted now to the County and County Borough Councils, who were given power to appoint their own inspectors, it became more of a reality—where the Councils were active—but remained a law for children and young persons only. And although an Act of 1899 was intended "to provide for seats being supplied for the Use of Shop Assistants",[4] the shop girl resting on a seat was still uncommon when Queen Victoria died.

There was legislation about early closing and early closing days for shops in 1904; but it was only in 1911 that the law's primary solicitude was transferred from the Young Person to the Shop Assistant, defined in the Act of that year as "any person wholly or mainly employed in a shop".[5] Hours, meal-time breaks, free half-days and early-closing rules were imposed—with certain special exemptions—in the interests of shop assistants as a class; and it became the duty of local authorities to see that these rules were properly enforced. Hitherto this had not been their duty but only their right. After a quarter of a century of intermittent experiment, a net appropriate to the conditions of workers in shops had been designed and cast.

[1] Vol. II. 418.

[2] *S.C. on Shop Hours Regulation*, 1886 (XII); and see Hutchins and Harrison, *op. cit.* p. 221. There had been several Bills in the interval.

[3] *S.C. on Shop Hours Bill*, 1892 (XVII), p. iii. The chief Factory Inspector had pointed out in 1886 that the law as drafted would probably not work, *S.C.* of 1886, Q. 5 (A. Redgrave).

[4] 62 and 63 Vict. c. 21.

[5] The Act of 1904 is 4 Ed. VII, c. 31; that of 1911, 1 and 2 Geo. V, c. 54.

Closely associated with the problems of the shop, the factory and the mine, those of the employer's liability for accidents and of compensation for workmen injured in the exercise of their calling had been handled, though at first reluctantly. A beginning had been made in 1880 in assimilating the legal position of a servant injured when at work to that of a member of the public injured by his or his employer's negligence.[1] At common law the two positions had been quite different, to the injured servant's disadvantage. The imperfect Act of 1880 was passed for seven years only. After 1887 it was renewed from year to year. In 1893–4 a more comprehensive scheme of Asquith's was spoiled in the Lords by the insertion of a contracting-out clause. But in 1897, at Chamberlain's inspiration and insistence, a still wider scheme was passed into law as the Workmen's Compensation Act (60 and 61 Vict. c. 37). Abandoning the difficult doctrine of negligence imbedded in the common law, the new law took the plain ground that compensation for injury or death at his work is due from the industry which he serves to the workman or his heirs. The financial liability was one against which the industry could conveniently insure—and promptly did, as a rule on very reasonable terms. This law of 1897 did not include seamen, oddly enough; nor agricultural labourers, nor domestic servants. The agricultural labourers were brought in in 1900 and the seamen in 1906. In 1906 also industrial diseases were grouped with industrial accidents, so that sufferers from them acquired compensation rights; but the last gaps in the law were not stopped until the passing of the Workmen's Compensation Act of 1925.[2] It is curious to note how often a whole generation slides by while some part of British social legislation is being made as nearly as possible watertight.

No doubt one reason for the omission of seamen in 1897 was that they had long been treated as a class apart and already had a body of law of their own. Their welfare and the safety of passengers on the seas had been watched over by parliament, not adequately it may be but most sincerely, since early in the century. The great Merchant Shipping Act of 1854, passed in the high noon of *laisser faire*, and its many successors, especially that of 1876, constituted a regular code of maritime safety and justice.[3] But as conditions at sea were always changing, and

[1] Vol. II. 419. [2] 15 and 16 Geo. V, c. 84.
[3] Vol. II. 409–11.

standards of safety and comfort at home rising, the code needed constant rectification and expansion. Samuel Plimsoll, the seaman's friend, left the House of Commons in 1880. Five years earlier, to secure the Act of 1876, he had made himself notorious—and set a bad example—by improvising a scene on the floor of the House for the sake of his scattered and inarticulate clients.[1] Chamberlain took up their cause when at the Board of Trade in the early 'eighties, but left no important mark on the law.[2] Between 1887 and 1894 however, far later than Plimsoll would have wished,[3] the manning, paying and certification of masters' clauses in the general shipping law were applied more strictly than heretofore to trawlers; an important Act (of 1888) improved the law regulating life saving appliances; the load-line which had come to bear Plimsoll's name was more finely drawn in the interests of safety; and the whole existing mass of Merchant Shipping law was consolidated into a 300-page code (57 and 58 Vict. c. 60 of 1894).

This served for twelve years; although at the end of ten the Cunard Agreement Act, pledging the credit of the State to a shipping company for what were held to be objects of national utility, marked the start of a different, and for Britain a very new, class of relations between government and the mercantile marine.[4] There were important novelties also in Lloyd George's Act of 1906 (6 Ed. VII, c. 48), which amended the general law as laid down in the code of 1894. Many of the clauses merely carried further and brought up to date rules for the food, accommodation, health and payment of seamen which had been part of the law for half a century. But some contained protective innovations, in the main very simple and reasonable, but watched with an exaggerated suspicion by certain members of a parliamentary majority which owed part of its size to advocacy of the strictest doctrine of Free Trade. There were restrictions on the granting of pilots' licences to aliens and on the employment of seamen "with insufficient knowledge of English". British rules about the load-line, the loading of grain and timber cargoes, and the treatment of steerage passengers were to be applied to all foreign ships frequenting British ports; when such ships came from a country whose level of safety equipment was

[1] Ensor, *England*, 1870–1914, p. 37.

[2] Garvin, *Chamberlain*, II. 412.

[3] See his evidence before the *R.C. on Labour*, 1892 (XXXVI. Pt. II), Q. 11,244 *sqq*.

[4] Above, p. 277.

"in His Majesty's opinion" inferior to the British they might be required to conform; and if they showed signs of sailing with defective equipment they might be detained. British law had set a high standard of shipping decency: Lloyd George and his advisers were determined that no foreign ship should gain in competition with a native by undercutting it. "Just what we want in the field of tariffs", the followers of Joseph Chamberlain said.

To Lloyd George, opportunist and realist, it all seemed plain good sense, as did another Act of his, of the following year, which raised similar doubts and hopes among the doctrinaires of the two tariff camps. It was a Patents Act (7 Ed. VII, c. 29) depriving foreign patentees of the right which they had hitherto possessed to take out a British patent but not work it—to get the monopoly of production in Britain and to produce elsewhere. That the law had remained like that so long proves the almost superstitious reverence for competition in the work rooms of the Board of Trade. An inventive Englishman might block another Englishman's production: that was a denial of free competition, but was what the patent law was for. Foreigners—so the inaction implied—should enjoy, together with the free run of the English market for their goods, the Englishman's production-blocking rights. The new law however required a foreign patentee to work his patent within three years in the United Kingdom or lose it. Plain good sense, Lloyd George and most Englishmen said. But there was sense also in the fears and hopes of the doctrinaires. It is a short step from a law which compels new and important acts of production to be carried on in the United Kingdom rather than somewhere else to a law which encourages the carrying on of selected acts of production there by means of a tariff. No such step was taken by a Liberal statesman until war had thrown its glare on some pivotal acts of production imperfectly provided for in Britain—key industries, not pivot industries, they came to be called. But there was already economic nationalism, a sensible dose of it, in the policies of Asquith's President of the Board of Trade; and in its interest the state was occupying bits of economic territory which the mid and late Victorian British state had been almost alone in leaving unoccupied.

The whole of the semi-economic territory of Public Health had been lightly occupied since the passing of the consolidating and amending Act of 1875.[1] But the various occupying forces were, and remained, ill-co-ordinated.[2] Headquarters at the new Local Government Board were unimaginative and often inert. Gladstone, it has been rightly said, had no "adequate sense of the importance of local government", and no interest in sanitation.[3] No great parliamentary sanitarian arose to correct his omissions. Chamberlain had the root of the matter in him but was generally busy with other things; and the Liberal President of the Board from 1905 to 1914 proved an unexpectedly good Gladstonian. So the principle of the great Sanitary Commission of 1869–71, that "all powers requisite for the health of towns and country should in every place be possessed by one responsible local authority",[4] was never enforced; a recently appointed chief medical officer of the Local Government Board was telling the Poor Law Commission in 1908 that "a very large proportion of the smaller sanitary authorities" were "unworthy of their powers";[5] and twenty years later many of the small rural or urban councils were described as "so unwilling or unable to fulfil their duties" that their constituents were living under what a critic, with the usual touch of critical overstatement, called "medieval sanitary conditions".[6] There was a fairly steady flow of health legislation. But there was no systematic overhauling of the administrative machinery; and, under fear of the principle of *ultra vires*, no specialised local extension of health-preserving work could be undertaken without precise parliamentary sanction.[7] The title of one law passed in the year of Victoria's second jubilee is instructive. Posterity may find it incredible; but there it is, 60 and 61 Vict. c. 31: *An Act to permit Local Authorities to provide Cleansing and Disinfection for Persons infected with Vermin.* A reader turns the page for an *Act to permit Local Authorities to empty Privies.* This however he does not find; for they already enjoyed that right.

[1] Vol. II. 424.

[2] "The members of a single working-class family may [still] be tended within a short space of time by half a dozen separate health authorities"; Robson, W. A., *The Development of Local Government* (1931), p. 296.

[3] Ensor, *op. cit.* p. 23; and see p. 125. An unpublished story of Gladstone perhaps deserves insertion here. He told Augustine Birrell how his father would sometimes come back from the hustings "all covered withs pittle". To Birrell's expressions of disgust he replied: "Oh! Do you think so? These old customs! These old customs!" Birrell is the authority: he may have polished the story.

[4] Vol. II. 423–4.

[5] Quoted in Robson, *op. cit.* p. 302.

[6] Robson, *op. cit.* p. 302.

[7] See vol. II. 421 for *ultra vires*.

Enterprising authorities in the great cities got the necessary sanctions by their local Acts. Much pioneering work had always been done in that way. A Liverpool Act of 1847 has been claimed as "the first real sanitary Act passed by Parliament".[1] Certainly it was a year ahead of the first general Act. Since that time, experiments made in the cities had often been embodied in statute law; and perhaps this was the best method of procedure in a difficult legal field, as it was certainly the true British. But the acquiescence of the centre in pressure from points on the circumference did not always make good law. It was mainly because of such pressure that another Act hard to believe in got on to the Statute Book in 1898, the Act by which a parent might be allowed not to have a child vaccinated if he "conscientiously believes that vaccination would be prejudicial to health".[2] And what if some verminous person had the conscientious belief of certain medieval saints that vermin should be cherished?

It was not until after 1908, with a change in the supreme medical control at the Local Government Board, that much inspiration radiated from the centre; though a few years earlier the more inspired headquarters of the Board of Education had begun to organise, on German models, the medical inspection and medical care of the schools, and had instigated that provision of free or cheap meals for school-children which was sanctioned by an Act of 1906.[3] The most important health campaign of the late nineteenth and early twentieth century, the fight for the reduction of infantile mortality, was entirely personal and local in origin—started by people of goodwill and enterprising medical officers of health. Here one important model was French, the *Gouttes de lait* of Dr Budin, begun in Paris in 1892; another was Belgian, the infant welfare centre opened in Ghent by Dr Miele in 1903.[4] Liverpool had added women to its sanitary inspectorate in 1897, with an eye to the health of the children. Manchester had semi-official women health visitors about the same time. The first English milk dispensary was opened at St Helens in 1899; and in 1901 the Liverpool Corporation established milk depots to supply appropriate grades of milk for infants whom

[1] Hope, E. W., *Health at the Gateway* (1931), p. 51.

[2] 61 and 62 Vict. c. 49.

[3] This section is much indebted to Ensor, *op. cit.* pp. 518 *sqq.* And see Hasluck, *Local Government in England*, p. 295.

[4] Hope, *op. cit.* pp. 103–4.

their mothers could not suckle. It had to construct its own plant, as no known firm made anything of the kind.[1] In 1907 the first School for Mothers on Dr Miele's lines was opened in St Pancras; and after that the associated movements of education and milk supply spread slowly, and more often than not only semi-officially, from the great unwholesome cities where they were most needed to towns of the second rank.[2]

Work in the cities was rewarded uncommonly soon. Between 1895 and 1900 infant mortality at Liverpool several times exceeded 200 per 1000, and was never so low as 175. It fell steadily, with fluctuations due to epidemics, to a maximum of 155 and a minimum of 125 in the five years immediately preceding 1914. By 1927 it was 94, while that of all England and Wales was 70, of Scotland 89, and of Norway—the best record in Europe—51. This last figure shows how the Liverpool of the 'nineties contrasted with something approaching an ideal.[3]

One cause of infantile mortality in the slums was the drunkenness of mothers: the child was overlain in a drunken sleep. In the Children's Act of 1908 (8 Ed. VII, c. 67), whose passing coincided with the start of a more imaginative health policy at the Local Government Board, there were clauses intended to safeguard infants and young children against the risks which they ran when their parents were habitual drunkards. Whether the law was or was not in any direct way responsible for that saving of infant life which followed, it is a landmark in the history of the legal protection of children. Many of its sections were taken from earlier Acts now consolidated and improved. Their variety and range illustrate the obligations which the State had by this time undertaken and the inhibitions which it imposed. 'Baby farming' and the insurance of babies with a view to profiting by their anticipated and perhaps hastened death; cruelty to children and the sins of the drunken parent; juvenile smoking and juvenile drinking; the use of child witnesses in cases of unnatural or abominable crime; the safety of children in places of entertainment, and the treatment of vermin on their bodies; the prohibition of imprisonment for those under fourteen, its strict limitation for those between fourteen and sixteen, and the regulation of the reformatory and industrial schools to

[1] Hope, p. 104.

[2] McCleary, G. F., *The Early History of the Infant Welfare Movement* (1933).

[3] Liverpool figures in Hope, *op. cit.* p. 110; others from the *Stat. Year Book of the League of Nations.*

which they might be sent—these are principal items in the subject matter of this notable codifying Act.

An Act of a newer sort, which might have proved even more notable if its design had been as satisfactory as its professions, was that for Housing and Town Planning of the following year (9 Ed. VII, c. 44). The new era in transport was beginning. Imagination and freedom in planning had not been needed so urgently since the early railway age—when few had thought about them. Now many were thinking, and there were abundant continental examples, with some English. No limit can be set to the good which might have been done by a law generously designed and universally adopted. But the law was neither. It provided far too many facilities for the obstruction of planning: it was not pressed vigorously by headquarters on the local authorities or adopted at all widely by them. Its results were negligible. Not ten thousand acres of future town-land were planned under it in ten years; and when war was over the rush of new building began substantially under the old haphazard conditions. So the Act remains only a signpost pointing to ground which the law, and with the law beauty and common sense, might have occupied but did not.[1]

This was the more unfortunate because many of the municipalities and the new County Councils had shown themselves enterprising and enlightened during the previous twenty years, and might have been trusted. Their activity had led to a rather barren dispute about what its critics called municipal trading and some of its advocates municipal socialism. The main stimulant of controversy was the rise in rates which had been continuous—from an average of 3*s.* 6*d.* in the pound of English rateable value in 1895 to 6*s.* in 1905, with a corresponding rise in Scotland.[2] This covered a growing mass of sanitary, poor relief, police and educational expenditure which could not possibly be classed under trading, and hardly under Socialism. But it was easy for a critic of some new economic enterprise of doubtful profit, such as an electric-tramway system, to make play with the burden of the rates. Except for the electric trams, there was very little that was strictly new in municipal economic

[1] Cp. Ensor, *op. cit.* p. 518.

[2] Cp. *Memoranda on Public Health and Social Conditions*, 1909 (Cd. 4671), pp. 74 *sqq.* and Hasluck, *Local Government in England*, p. 214. By 1914 the figure was 6*s.* 11*d.*

activities about the turn of the century; and the novelty was exaggerated in metropolitan discussion because, before its County Council was made, greater London had no municipality to act. There had been as much, or more, municipal socialism in oligarchic Tory Liverpool before 1834 as ever there was in Progressive London,[1] in Radical or Unionist Birmingham, or in those Northern towns where Labour parties were growing strong. The Corporation of Liverpool was a great landowner. It had built docks and markets and bath-houses and "large blocks of dwellings out of its own corporate estate",[2] and had owned waterworks, long ago. By 1855 it was the proprietor of more than 400 tenements, and by 1909 of more than 2000. Manchester had owned gasworks before it had any legal right to do so, before it so much as had a Mayor and Corporation.[3] From gas it moved naturally to electricity, and from electric supply to electric trams, during the short period in which they seemed to be without doubt the best means of urban transport.

Here, incidentally, cropped out a valid argument against municipal trading. Some monopolies a municipality must permit and must keep in its own hands, or at least apportion and control. The grotesque early history of competition among the London water companies in Queen Anne's reign, when "two or even more companies would lay mains in the same street", is sufficient proof.[4] But the monopoly of so unstable a utility as a particular means of transport may lead to obstruction of newer and perhaps better means. The reluctance of Corporations who owned electric tramways to license the early motor-buses, and the readiness to do so of the Corporations through whose territory the trams were run by private companies, may have been exaggerated but were real—and most natural.[5]

A society in which local authorities had to receive special legal permission to cleanse verminous persons was not likely to suffer much by their ill-considered trading or administrative experiments. It was much more likely to suffer from their inertia and dull routine administration. Fear of the penalties of *ultra vires* prevented any one of them from doing the sort of thing that the

[1] Webb, S. and B., *The Manor and the Borough* (1908), pp. 481 *sqq.*

[2] Vol. II. 492; and cp. Hope, *op. cit.* pp. 167, 172.

[3] Vol. I. 191 n.

[4] Scott, W. R., *The Constitution and Finance of...Joint-Stock Companies to 1720* (1911), III. 27. The mains were mostly hollowed elm logs.

[5] Cp. p. 137 above.

Manchester Commissioners of Police had done some eighty years earlier when they built their unauthorised gasworks. If an experiment was not licensed by statute law, or explicitly provided for in one of the town's own Local Acts, there was no chance of its being made. And a clause in a Local Bill authorising experiment might very easily be struck out in Private Bill Committee.[1] A town strongly governed—as Birmingham had been during Joseph Chamberlain's mayoralty and since—would take full advantage of its statutory liberties and stand out for a maximum of special permits. Birmingham was the first, and up to 1914 the only, city in Britain to run a municipal savings bank; though many North Country towns took money on deposit from their citizens—a municipal equivalent of the central government's floating debt. That was statutable, or at least not assailable at law. But even Birmingham would probably not have dared, had it desired, to insert in a Local Bill a clause authorising Chamberlain's roughly sketched scheme for the municipal buying up of the whole local liquor interest.[2]

The amount of new municipal trading was after all not important, if viewed nationally; and of trading in the popular sense of competitive selling there was singularly little. London grew warm for and against County Council trams, which were said not to pay, and County Council steamboats which certainly did not pay. But London gas and water and electricity all remained in the hands of companies until 1903–5, when the water companies were consolidated and ownership vested (by 2 Ed. VII, c. 41), not in the Corporation of the City nor in the County Council, but in the newly devised Metropolitan Water Board—neither exactly a company nor yet a local authority, but perhaps rather more of the former. Water and gas companies often had perpetual concessions and could not be dealt with summarily. There was a clause in the Public Health Act of 1875 which contemplated the transfer of water supply from a company to a local authority; but it was not much used, and most of the transfers, like the creation of the Metropolitan Water Board, were effected by special Acts. Of such Acts there were about 100 between 1876 and 1913.[3] Not all were made use of, but the great majority were; and as many towns had controlled their own water supplies long before 1875, by 1899 out of 265 municipal

[1] Cp. Robson, *op. cit.* p. 204.

[2] Garvin, *Chamberlain*, II. 476.

[3] *Return of Waterworks and Water Companies*, 1913 (LXXIX. 543), p. xxiii.

boroughs in England and Wales 173 owned waterworks.[1] By 1913, only 26 out of the 97 towns which at the Census of 1911 had returned more than 50,000 inhabitants were supplied with water even in part by a company. The most considerable places so supplied entirely were Bristol, Grimsby, Newcastle, Portsmouth, Shields, Sunderland, West Hartlepool and York.[2]

There had been transfers of gas undertakings also, but on a much smaller scale. While the total area supplied with gas grew fast, the division between municipal and company supply did not greatly change, mainly because London remained a company area. Between 1890 and 1913 the number of municipal gas enterprises in England and Wales grew by 80 per cent. and of company enterprises by only 28 per cent.; but in the same period, while the number of municipal gas consumers grew by nearly 160 per cent., that of company gas consumers grew by 273 per cent.; and at the close the gross takings of the companies were nearly twice those of the municipalities.[3] In Scotland all was different. There were hardly any companies and everything was municipal, as it had been from the start.

In electricity also there was very little transfer. There had indeed hardly been time for any. When the first electricity companies were founded the possibility of transfer had very properly been contemplated by Parliament. And at first—from the law of 1882 to that of 1888—the concessions were made for 21 years only, a period which, combined with the rather harsh method of valuation contemplated at its close, was too short to be attractive. Its fixing had most unfortunate results in checking private enterprise in the 'eighties, and since 1888 it had been doubled.[4] But it had helped to keep the field clear for adventurous Corporations in places where municipal water and gas were already matters of course. Towns of the second and lower ranks, where company gas was general and company water not uncommon, usually looked to companies for their electricity. Hence the chief novelty was the establishment of electricity works and electric trams in places which, like Manchester, were very familiar with municipal enterprise on the grand scale, from the tapping and urbanising of a Thirlmere to the financing of a Ship Canal.

1 *Return of Waterworks and Water Companies*, 1913 (LXXIX. 543), p. xviii.
2 *Ibid.* p. xxiii.
3 *Gas and Water Return of* 1890 (LXVII); *of* 1913 (1914–16, LXI).
4 Above, p. 132; cp. Darwin, L., *Municipal Ownership* (1907), p. 18.

Such complaints as there were of competitive municipal selling were as a rule ludicrously petty—that the municipal gas office sold gas fittings, or something of that kind.[1] For in fact municipal ownership was "almost entirely confined to industries tending to become monopolies",[2] as it still is. When, in 1909, elaborate returns of what were called their reproductive undertakings were called for from forty to fifty British cities and boroughs, as material for the discussion of municipal trading, most of them reported on water, gas and electricity; many on tramways, markets, baths and working-class dwellings; waterside places often on harbours, docks or ferries; a considerable number of places on cemeteries; few on anything else. Three or four now had depots for the sale of sterilised milk. Three still had their own telephones. The London County Council had its steamboats, but there was no competition there: it was the very case for them that no one would run such things to get profit. Brighton had its aquarium and an abattoir. Blackpool sold sea-water. Wolverhampton sold ice. Oldham made its own flagstones for paving, and Bradford ran its wool-conditioning house to the great advantage of the trade on which its whole life was based. Beyond that nothing, or almost nothing.[3]

In effect then the trading controversy, when not petty, was over the control, administration and ownership of monopolies. As a matter of pure profit and loss, the most careful and detached contemporary student, whose bias was if anything slightly against municipal ownership, concluded provisionally "that England, if she is not losing, is gaining nothing whatever"[4] by it. If that was the worst, it was very easy, not only for those who saw in the municipal monopoly a preparing of the way for national ownership of many things, but for followers of Bagehot and Mill, who did not believe in private monopolies, and for a crowd of plain men who followed only instinct, to side with what individualist partisans called the grasping and ambitious municipalities.

The growth of their 'reproductive' enterprises, and the growth of their responsibilities for the health, relief, education and housing of the people and for all kinds of public works, had

[1] *S.C. of Lords and Commons on Municipal Trading*, 1900 (VII. 183); 1903, Its *Report* (VII. 1).

[2] Darwin, *op. cit.* p. 89.

[3] *Return...of Reproductive Municipal Undertakings*, 1909 (XC).

[4] Darwin, p. 48.

placed on the local authorities a burden of debt which accounted for a good part of the rise in rates, and from time to time made public men anxious. In 1874–5 the local debt of England and Wales had been £92,000,000. In 1887–8, on the eve of the reorganisation of county government, it was £192,000,000. After ten years of County Council and municipal activity, in 1898–9 it stood at £275,000,000. By 1913–14 the comparable figure was £485,000,000. Of this £232,000,000 was assigned in official returns to the 'reproductive' undertakings. In Scotland the rate of growth had been much the same—from about £28,000,000 in 1887–8 to £44,500,000 in 1898–9 and £67,000,000 in 1913–14.[1] But in the aggregate local debts, which in the 'seventies had been not one-sixth of the national debt, were by 1913–14 comparable with it. The growth was not mainly due to special lavishness in borrowing for reproductive work in the new century. Owing to great water enterprises and the like, this part of the English debt stood already at £124,000,000 in 1898–9—that is before the principal electrical and tramway developments. While reproductive debt had thus grown by £108,000,000, other debt, starting it is true from a higher level, had grown by £102,000,000. This was the measure of the extra capital cost of fresh duties laid on local governing bodies and of their greater zeal in carrying out duties which had always been theirs.[2]

Those local enterprises which were strictly economic were also, as has been seen, far less novel in principle than some contemporary critics implied. They were less novel too than much of the legislation which flowed from the acceptance, the only half conscious acceptance, by all political parties of the doctrine that the State is justified "in doing any single act, which in its ulterior consequences adds to the sum of human happiness".[3] Titles and preambles of minor Acts of Parliament, even in the 'eighties, illustrate this acceptance, whatever became of the Acts in application: "Whereas it is expedient to provide for the Fencing of Quarries": "For the better Prevention of the

[1] Exact figure for Scotland in 1887–8 cannot be given (*Stat. Abstracts*); for 1892–3 it was £29,000,000.

[2] The figures are in the *Statistical Abstracts*. As given here they do not include the debts of the Port of London Authority and the Metropolitan Water Board, because neither of these is a municipality though both are public authorities.

[3] Above, p. 397.

Fraudulent Sale of Margarine": "To regulate the Sale of Horseflesh for Human Food"; and such like.[1]

At the end of the 'nineties, just halfway through the period now under review, came that minor Act which gauged perhaps better than any other the strength of the current which had set in against *laisser faire* and old style utilitarianism, the Money-lenders Act of 1900 (63 and 64 Vict. c. 51). Waggish people called it an Act for the suppression of Isaac Gordon, a money-lender of the time who had made himself obnoxious to society. It was more than that. In effect it revived the Law of Usury, the last remnants of which had been swept away, as was fancied for ever, in 1854.[2] Behind it lay not the strict superstitious medieval view that there can never be a just price for the loan of money, but the kindred more refined view that prices arrived at in any bargain may be inequitable, unjust, and therefore to be set aside. Soon slightly puzzled judges were working out, as the Act bade them, a case law of the 'excessive' and the 'harsh and unconscionable', in short the just price, in monetary transactions. They were applying without knowing it the early fifteenth century teaching of St Antonino of Florence, that whereas there is no serious risk of injustice or the unconscionable when two equals in business make a free contract, there may well be injustice when one of the parties consents through prodigality or necessity.[3] The law was used to reopen and revise contracts made by spendthrift drunkards, the feeble-minded, and people in dire need. Remaining a working reality, it was buttressed by an Act of 1911 which forbade any mere money-lending business to register itself as a bank so as to catch such conies.[4]

The period closes with this usury law which would have worried Jeremy Bentham; a system of old age pensions which would have disturbed John Bright and cheered its protagonist Tom Paine; a "national friendly society" and experiments in insurance against unemployment which might have commended themselves, one cannot but think, to the Rev. John Acland but hardly to Gladstone; an attitude towards the poor law that Henry Fawcett would have regarded with disgust; and, among many other legislative novelties or reversions, some semi-official

[1] The Acts quoted are 50 and 51 Vict. c. 19 and 50 and 51 Vict. c. 29 of 1887; and 52 Vict. c. 11, of 1889.

[2] Vol. II. 407–8.

[3] See Robertson, H. M., *The Rise of Economic Individualism* (1933), p. 57.

[4] 1 and 2 Geo. V, c. 38.

wage-fixing that recalls the Elizabethan Labour Code, and a system of Death Duties and Income Tax which might well, as critics of Pitt's first Income Tax had feared, lead to "a plan for equalising fortunes", Parliament having already accepted the shocking inference which they found implicit in his law "that because a man possesses much therefore more shall be taken from him than is proportionably taken from others".[1] With a whole powerful party in the State committed to tariff protection; a young rising party committed to economic changes far more radical; and with a ministry of Liberals the best informed of whom lived and worked on two planes—the public plane of social reform and the hidden plane of a possible war[2]—the world of 1914 might have been even less recognisable to Cobden than the world of 1894.[3]

[1] Lord Auckland's speech of Jan. 8, 1799, quoted in Seligman, *The Income Tax*, p. 77.

[2] Winston Churchill, *The World Crisis*, I. 24; Trevelyan, G. M., *Grey of Fallodon*, p. 211.

[3] Above, p. 397.

CHAPTER VIII

LIFE AND LABOUR IN INDUSTRIAL BRITAIN

BEFORE the end of the nineteenth century there were clear signs that the historically very abnormal growth in the population of Britain, which had been going on for over a hundred years, was slackening and might be about to cease. That growth itself would cease there was at that time no convincing reason to suppose.[1] The lowest birth-rate among Western peoples, that of France, had only just fallen below 22 per 1000 in 1900; and it did not seem likely that the British rate, which had only recently come below 30, would go so far as that. Even if it did, Britain was now countering death more efficiently than France, or indeed than any other great country. With a death-rate which, since the influenza epidemic of 1895, had kept below 18 per 1000, and for the whole decade of the 'nineties had been barely 18, a fall in the birth-rate even towards 22 would not mean that stagnation with which it had by this time become customary to reproach the French.[2]

But after 1900 the birth-rate slipped down with a steady persistence that began to look inevitable. "There is as yet no indication of any check in the decline", the census commissioners for 1911 wrote, at a time when the figure stood round about 24, "while it is obvious that the death-rate cannot continue to decline indefinitely."[3] This glimpse into the obvious was offered because, down to 1911, the countering of

[1] But Cannan, E., "The Probability of a Cessation of the Growth of Population in England and Wales during the Next Century", *E.J.* 1895, had drawn a hypothetical diagram which showed cessation in 1991; had said that he himself expected it earlier; and had mentioned "the possibility of a decline". Later discussions are Newsholme, A. and Stevenson, T. H. C., "The decline of human fertility in the U.K. and other countries as shown by corrected birth-rates", *S.J.* 1906; Yule, G. U., "Changes in the Marriage- and Birth-Rates in England and Wales during the past Half-Century", *S.J.* 1906; and Baines, Sir J. A., "The Recent Trend of Population in England and Wales", *S.J.* 1916.

[2] For statistics, see *Memoranda and Charts on Public Health and Social Conditions*, 1909 (Cd. 4671); and for a general survey, Carr-Saunders, A. M., *World Population*, 1936; Kuczynski, R. R., *The Balance of Births and Deaths* (1928, 1931) and *The Measurement of Population Growth* (1935), contain the most important recent work.

[3] *Census of England and Wales, General Report*, 1917 (Cd. 8491), p. 22.

death had about balanced the check to generation. From 1909 to 1914 the death-rate was only a little above 15. The countering had been so successful that the natural increase—the percentage gain by excess of births over deaths—for 1901–11 in England and Wales had been a shade higher than in the previous decade, and decently comparable with that of any decade since 1861.

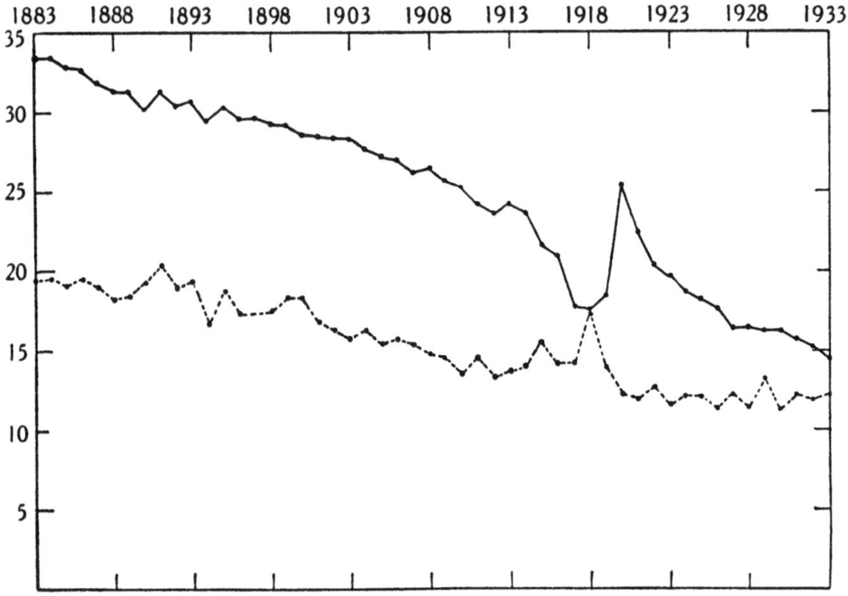

Birth- and death-rates.

Birth-rate (crude) per 1000, England and Wales, ——.

Death-rate (crude) per 1000, England and Wales (civilian rate only, 1914–18), ----.

The Scottish birth-rate kept close to the English until 1895: after 1895 it was normally 1–3 points higher. The Scottish death-rate after 1900 was normally 1–2 points higher than the English.

There was still work to do in life-saving at all stages, particularly in infancy, but that did not invalidate the proposition that lives must end.

The actual percentage growth of population from 1901 to 1911 was the lowest of any decade on the census list for England and Wales, and the lowest but one for Scotland, because some of the natural increase had been provided for elsewhere by a revival of emigration in the new century. For Scotland "elsewhere" includes England: by migration and emigration she had lost 254,000 people.[1] Emigration from all Britain had been heavy during the 'eighties.[2] So for that matter had immigration. In England and Wales there were living 80,000 more people of foreign birth and descent at the census of 1891 than at that of 1881; and in Scotland a few thousands more. The majority of them were Jews from Russian Poland. They replaced some of the emigrant English and a very few of the emigrant Scots. Others were replaced by Irishmen, for whose movements into Britain there are no figures—only the fact that the Irish population, in spite of a favourable relation of birth to death, fell during the 'eighties, partly in this though mainly in other ways, by nearly half a million. The net result for the decade in England and Wales was a population 601,000 less than it would have been if the only force at work had been the natural increase. There was a corresponding net loss in Scotland which has not however been so exactly calculated.[3]

During the 'nineties emigration fell off greatly, with the crises and depressions in the new countries of both hemispheres.[4] The great increase in the number of British subjects born abroad but resident in Britain returned at the census of 1901, when compared with that of 1891, suggests a considerable reflux of emigrants.[5] At the end of the decade the net loss by excess of emigration over immigration was only 68,000 for England and Wales and a few thousands for Scotland. The Scottish population showed a growth in that decade nearly 50 per cent. greater than in 1881–91, and over 70 per cent. greater than in 1901–11.[6] Irishmen were coming in and Scots were not finding their way into England and the world quite on the accustomed scale.

The revival of emigration in the twentieth century started slowly, but was well under way by 1904. Almost stopped in 1908 by the economic collapse of 1907, which was particularly complete in America, outward movement was resumed in 1909; quickened in 1910; and reached a maximum in 1911–12. Already by April 1911, when the census returns were sent in,

[1] *Census of Scotland*, 1911, *General Report* (1913, LXX), p. vi.

[2] Vol. II. 441.

[3] The facts and figures are in the 1911 *Census Reports, passim*.

[4] Above, pp. 27 *sqq*.

[5] Born abroad but resident in England and Wales, 1891, 35,000; 1901, 92,000. In 1881 the figure was 56,000, which also suggests a reflux after the trade depression of the 'seventies: *Census Report*, 1911, p. 217.

[6] This is the percentage growth.

the net loss by emigration from England and Wales since April 1901 had been 502,000;[1] and the maximum had still to come.

Britain reared her population from her own various stocks with very little foreign admixture; although some people in the island felt that the immigrant Irish, especially the concentrated Irish of Merseyside and Clydeside, were at least a semi-foreign element. Interchange between England and Scotland and England and Wales went on as before. That between England and Scotland can be followed in outline because Scotland keeps her own census. The road South was still wide open. In 1911 there were nearly twice as many people born in Scotland and domiciled in England as *vice versa*; and it is not unlikely that many of the English-born in Scotland were of Scottish descent. There was one person of Scottish birth in England for every 14·7 in Scotland. Of real foreigners Scotland had, as always, very few; though her share, trifling down to 1891, had more than doubled since, mainly owing to a curious migration of Polish miners into Lanarkshire.[2] Relatively to population, the foreign-born in England and Wales were now not much more numerous than in Scotland; if London were excluded not so numerous. There were only 231 Italians and 271 Americans in all the Ridings of Yorkshire; though there were more than 5000 Russians, that is to say Polish Jews, in Leeds.

Of 285,000 foreigners in England and Wales, 153,000 were in London; and of the London foreigners 53,000 were in the Metropolitan borough of Stepney. London as a whole had 63,000 'Russians'; and no doubt a number of other Jews were to be found among her 27,000 'Germans' and her 8000 'Austrians'. Outside London and Leeds the only important Jewish concentrations were in Manchester and Liverpool. In the whole country the foreign-born Jews, most of whom had arrived since 1881, must have numbered something between 75,000 and 100,000 out of a British Jewry—largely composed of their children—which may have been three times that size.

[1] *Census Report*, p. 22.

[2] Strictly, they were mostly Lithuanian. A few went into ironworks as furnace-fillers. The first English words they are said to have learnt were "hurry up". "In the 'nineties they were in such large numbers that the Miners' Rules posted up at the collieries were, in some cases, in Polish, and there were Lithuanian Co-operative Stores in Lanarkshire": extract from a letter from Sir George Mitchell to my informant, Mr A. M. Stephen. The information about the furnaces comes through the same channel from Mr G. Pate, Manager at Carron. The numbers of foreign-born persons enumerated in Scotland were: 1891, 16,000; 1901, 30,000; 1911, 36,000.

The old Jewish families, when still identifiable as such, made up a very small if important group in the population.[1]

The rest of the foreigners, except the 12,000 London Italians, were individuals rather than groups; and many of them, including many Italians, were birds of passage—artists, musicians, writers, seafaring men, long-stay travellers from America, men of business from all over the world. Permanently domiciled individuals were easily assimilated; but the major Jewish groups lived localised and apart. Manchester, Leeds and Liverpool,[2] as well as London, had their distinct Jewish quarters, with notices in Hebrew and Kosher meat shops, quarters in which an old Nonconformist chapel might well become a synagogue of the orthodox Ashkenazim;[3] for the Gentile did not stay.

Just before he died, in 1885, Lord Shaftesbury had spoken of the "enormous" improvement in sanitation and housing which he had seen since the 'forties.[4] In London that improvement, coupled with the progress of medicine and surgery which had preceded and accompanied it, had led to a fall in the death-rate of nearly 3 per 1000 between 1851–3 and 1881–3. Some other ways of stating the figures would give less favourable results; for although there had certainly been progress, the territory conquered from death since the middle of the century had hardly been consolidated by the early 'eighties. Marked improvement without serious set-backs came later. In 1888 the London death-rate for the first time fell below 20 per thousand. After 1899 it never again reached 20. For 1903–7 it averaged 15·8, only a fraction above the very satisfactory corresponding average for the whole of England and Wales.[5] During the next six years it always kept below 16; and the national rate, including Scotland whose rate was normally rather higher than England's, twice stood below 14. In 1854 William Farr had thought that an urban death-rate of 20 should be "practicable".[6] A rate of 15 had been far outside his hopes.

London was fortunate. Berlin had been about equally healthy since 1890—not before—but Paris and other great capitals were

[1] For the difficulty of measuring the British Jewry, see Ruppin, A., *The Jews in the Modern World* (1934), p. 26.

[2] Of Manchester and Leeds I write from personal knowledge. For Liverpool, see *Social Survey of Merseyside* (1934), I. 73.

[3] I have known at least one such—in Manchester.

[4] Quoted, vol. II. 442.

[5] *Memoranda...on Public Health, etc.* § II.

[6] Quoted, vol. II. 440, n. 2.

worse. London was fortunate too among British towns, because of her large acreage of comfortable houses filled with well-nourished and well-doctored people. But for that—and some contributory causes[1]—her death-rate would not have been so near the national average. Liverpool was normally at least three points worse than London; and the average industrial town, both in England and Scotland, was also worse.

Until the twentieth century however there had been no real improvement, in London, England or Scotland, in town or country, in the most dominant of all the various death-rates—that among infants during their first year of life.[2] To this more than to any single cause was due the slow and delayed fall in the general death-rate. In 1850, a healthy year, the infants' death-rate for England and Wales had been 146 per thousand births, and for London 140—or about one infant lost in seven. In 1865, an unhealthy year, the same two rates had been 160 and 171. In 1898, the healthiest year of the late 'nineties, they were 148 and 162. In unhappy years and places, one infant in five might die in the first year. In London, for 1898 and again for 1899, the figure was exactly one in six—167 to the 1000. Then the change came. For 1908 the English figure had fallen to 120, the London figure to 113. By 1913 the English figure was down to 108, less than one child lost in nine. Ten years later the average loss would be below one in thirteen.[3] It is no doubt "practicable", in Farr's wording, to reduce the figure to one in twenty-five, or less. Among the comfortable classes and in the British climate the loss of a child in its first year has now become exceedingly rare. But in all the world's history up to 1900, especially in its urban history, nothing had been more common. Nor had there ever been a great society so thoroughly urbanised as the British. The historian sees a swift and mighty triumph over death in the achievement of the few years between 1899 and 1913.

By the middle 'eighties bare essentials for a healthy urban life had already been provided in all the greater communities. Water was abundant and pure—often more abundant and usually

[1] She has a high proportion of immigrants of the healthiest ages, who have survived the risks of infancy and not met those of old age.

[2] Nearly all the relevant facts are in [Sir] Arthur Newsholme's *Report...on Infant and Child Mortality* to the L.G.B. in 1910 [Cd. 5263]. See also the *Annual Reports of the Registrar-General.*

[3] Recent figures for all countries are conveniently summarised in the *Stat. Year Book of the L. of Nations.*

purer in towns than in the country—though every town had tenements and courts and streets where the supply was inadequate. Scavenging, paving, lighting and sewerage were reasonably good. Even the much abused London vestries, when their day ended with the London Government Act of 1899, were allowed to have done these things well of recent years.[1] The "disgrace to the metropolis and to civilisation" of a Thames at Woolwich "for its whole width black, putrid, sewage",[2] as reported in 1884, had been taken in hand. Infectious disease was usually kept within bounds; though epidemics of one kind or another were recurrent, and the spread of new or changing diseases needed constant vigilance. So did the administrative machinery designed to give protection against diseases which were well known. In the early 'nineties the country was again threatened with an invasion of Asiatic cholera, to which its world-wide and dense maritime connections made it specially liable. Again, as in 1884, gaps were found in the defences.[3] One-third of the sixty Port Sanitary Districts were in excellent order; one-third in fair order; one-third inefficient. All the great ports but one were in the first class. The exception being Liverpool, and "most inefficient", was serious.[4] With it were grouped, of important places, Falmouth, Harwich and Newhaven. Liverpool quickly put her house in order; and some of the other "defaulting authorities" —as severe inspectors called them—were awake to their responsibilities before the inspector's report went in. Wakeful enough at least to beat off the cholera that time; and neither cholera, nor plague, nor any of the other tropical and subtropical scourges against which their defence line had been designed broke through again.

When first visited in 1892 the backward Port Sanitary Districts were found to be actually behind the average inland district, instead of ahead of it as their posts of danger required. There was a deficiency in regular medical officers of health, in sanitary inspectors, and infectious diseases hospitals; besides the resulting neglect of that inspection of ships which was their particular duty. Inland sanitation was far from perfect. Every great town had its filthy black patches of disease and death; and

[1] Jephson, H., *The Sanitary Evolution of London* (1907), p. 396.

[2] Quoted, vol. II. 444.

[3] Vol. II. 425.

[4] *Report...on the Port and Riparian Sanitary Survey of* 1893–4 (1895, LII), p. 38. Cp. Jephson, *op. cit.* p. 361.

some of the lesser towns and industrial villages, mining villages nearly all, were one great patch of what, so late as 1910, was called "insanitary barbarism". "A large part", it was then written, "of the densely populated parts of the counties of Durham and Glamorgan and certain parts of Lancashire, Staffordshire, and Yorkshire, are in a profoundly lower condition as regards elementary sanitation than other parts of England."[1] The Glamorgan mining village with its ill-drained, unmade streets, liable to flooding and subsidence, was at the bottom of the scale; though some Durham villages ran it close. Immigrants from the country who had peopled these pit villages of Glamorgan were "not accustomed to have water laid on, to use water closets or drains, or to dispose of their house refuse except by burying it in the garden". They and their children were apt to throw the refuse into the back streets. Occasionally "liquid manure from stables" escaped to join this refuse; and in "some parts of the district" the back street was "resorted to for purposes of defaecation". The area referred to was the Maesteg Urban District; the year 1908; and it was noted that "few persons alight from Maesteg Station without being provided with leggings or jack-boots, and these are very necessary".[2] Similar details of filth, if seldom quite so bad, could be multiplied from the five black areas noted, and from some others.

These reports were sent in during the struggle for saving infant life; when it was truly said that "infant mortality is the most sensitive index...of social welfare and of sanitary administration".[3] By 1908 there had been improvement everywhere: the English infantile death-rate was down to 120 per 1000. But for Glamorgan it was 154 and for Durham 151. South of the Tees, in the mainly rural North Riding, it fell to 115. In still rustic Oxfordshire, England's healthiest county for infants, it was 73. How much greater the chances of surviving one's first year now were in a great city than in a third-rate industrial town or urban district of mining villages is illustrated by the London figure of 113, and more fully if important towns in selected counties are set over against small towns or urban districts with bad records in the same county. The bad records are nearly all black with coal dust.

[1] Newsholme's *Report...on Infant...Mortality*, p. 63. Great sanitary reformers seem seldom to write elegant English: it is hardly to be expected of them.

[2] Dr S. W. Wheaton's 1908 *Report on Maesteg U.D.* to the L.G.B., quoted by Newsholme, p. 87.

[3] Newsholme, p. 74.

Infant Mortality per 1000 Births 1908

England and Wales	120·4		
Average of Cardiff and Swansea	134·7	Aberdare U.D.	213
		Maesteg U.D.	173
Sunderland	144	Houghton-le-Spring U.D.	191
Liverpool	142	Burnley	202
Manchester	152	Ince U.D.	183
		Ashton-under-Lyne U.D.	183
Huddersfield	112	Featherstone	208
Leeds	138	Wombwell	185
Wolverhampton	132	Tunstall U.D.	211
Burton-on-Trent	112	Burslem U.D.	184
Newport, Mon.	135	Abertillery	178

In Scotland the position was similar. Glasgow, in spite of the antiquated and insanitary lay-out of its older parts, was as good as Leeds; Edinburgh was not much worse than London.[1]

British sanitary barbarism must not be too harshly judged. The decade average of infant mortality in efficient Prussia never got below 200 during the nineteenth century. In 1908 it equalled that of the Maesteg Urban District, where the back streets were so misused. The twentieth-century record for the whole of France was about the same as that for Liverpool, with its crowds of "smoky dwarf houses".

That the discrepancies were due primarily to sanitary rather than to narrowly economic causes was demonstrable. Evidently more infants die in poor than in comfortable quarters, and in the extremes of poverty and wretchedness their deaths were terribly frequent. But there was no exact relation between income and loss of infant life. Ireland was poor enough, but the Irish infantile death-rate was well below the English. Oxfordshire was not rich. Nor did bigger families necessarily mean more danger to the infant: Irish families were bigger than English. Miners were not ill-paid compared with other wage-earners. Their wives rarely went out to work leaving children to the care of others. In textile towns this was more common; but if the figure was high in textile Burnley it was admirably low in textile Huddersfield; as low as in the beery but seemingly wholesome air of Burton-on-Trent.[2]

[1] Facts and figures are all selected from Newsholme, App. II and III (Tables).

[2] Pioneering infant welfare work was done at Huddersfield; not, to my knowledge, at Burton.

Some remodelling of notorious insanitary areas in the great cities had certainly made them healthier. Shaftesbury Avenue was cut through Seven Dials in the 'eighties.[1] In the 'nineties the London County Council, adopting a policy of pulling down and rebuilding, cleared out Clare Market, in parts of which there had been 800 people to the acre and a death-rate of 41·32 to the thousand. The Council also remodelled some fifteen acres of the Boundary Street area. Perhaps more important, for in London and everywhere else areas remodelled were only tiny parts of the whole, was the London building law of 1894 which for the first time prescribed that the open space in rear of a building should be proportionate to its height. Meanwhile medical and sanitary opinion became more critical of the blocks of model dwellings which the Peabody Trust and other well-intentioned reformers had put up.[2] An ill-regulated 'model' might no doubt be as unwholesome as a great house that had tumbled down to tenements; but, as the Peabody trustees were able to prove fifteen years later that both the general and the infantile death-rates on their property were well below the London averages, it was evident that no charge of ill-regulation lay against them.[3] However, only a very small percentage of Londoners were housed in the 5000 or so Peabody tenements of the twentieth century, or in any structures of the same sort.[4] And although other cities and towns, following Joseph Chamberlain's Birmingham and an earlier Liverpool, had both cleared sites and done a little tentative building, either under local or statute law, so that in the municipal trading inquiries of 1909 a certain amount of expenditure on working-class housing was reported by many of them, the people were in fact being housed as they always had been by private enterprise.[5] The important function of the municipal authority was not building but the regulation of buildings. This it did by its building by-laws, which might be wooden and woodenly or imperfectly administered, yet were designed to promote health. But the by-laws had little real control over dwelling houses already standing. In London particularly the degradation of large houses into tenements, that ancient decay in cities, was most imperfectly checked or regulated into the twentieth century.[6]

[1] Cp. vol. II. 489. [2] Jephson, *op. cit.* pp. 363–4, 367, 368.

[3] The evidence is in Newsholme, *op. cit.* p. 61.

[4] Cp. vol. II. 492. The Peabody Trust in 1909 owned 5687 "separate dwellings": of these 300 were cottages, the rest flats in 'models'. [5] Cp. p. 443 above.

[6] Jephson (*op. cit.* p. 430) was complaining of the lack of control in 1907.

Control of new building was the more important because there was so much of it, though less than there might and should have been.[1] In London the new tubes, the electrification of the old underground system, the electric trams and the motor-buses were hastening that dispersal of population into ring suburbs and dormitory towns which had been begun by the radial railways. In other towns the new style trams and buses were working with the railways to the same end.[2] That emptying at night which was now almost complete in the City of London had spread, first to the inner ring of parishes, and so outwards, until by 1911 only nine out of the twenty-eight new Metropolitan Boroughs, and they the outermost, showed any increase of population for the decade; only the two outermost of all—Wandsworth and Lewisham—any great increase; and the whole of Administrative London, the territory of the County Council, for the first time a decrease, though a small one. But for the filling up of Wandsworth and Lewisham it would not have been small.[3]

West Ham was nearly full by 1901. It had grown by 30 per cent. during the 'nineties, but by only 8 per cent. since. Beyond it, East Ham, having already grown by 194 per cent. during the 'nineties, had added 39 per cent. to its 96,000 of 1901. Ilford, Southend-on-Sea (which might "almost be regarded as one of London's eastern suburbs"),[4] Walthamstow, Enfield, Edmonton, Tottenham, Willesden, Ealing, Acton, Wimbledon, Croydon, Gillingham had all grown by more than 30 per cent. in the decade—most of them by between 30 and 40 per cent., but Ealing by 85, Ilford by 89, and Southend by 117. Outside the metropolitan radius the only records of growth among large places comparable with these were Smethwick in Birmingham's orbit (30 per cent.), Bournemouth (32), the Urban District of Rhondda (34), the Urban District of King's Norton and Northfield, a Birmingham overspill (42), Wallasey, an overspill of Birkenhead and Liverpool (46·5), and Coventry, the home of the cycles and the cars (52). Although the textile and boot-making towns had not grown much in the decade—Halifax had even declined—and had not thrown off considerable satellite places in recent decades, there was plenty of building towards their circumference and on the edges of the Urban or Rural Districts into which their new electric trams ran.

[1] Cp. p. 30 and p. 62 above.
[2] Cp. Ensor, R. C. K., *England*, 1870–1914 (1936), pp. 280, 509.
[3] *Census Report*, 1911, p. 42.
[4] *Census Report*, 1911, p. 41.

Urban growth near or beyond the often arbitrarily fixed municipal boundaries helped to satisfy the deeply-rooted English desire, Lord Shaftesbury's ideal, "that every man should have his own house".[1] At the crowded core of London, but very little in any other town, regular blocks of tenements newly erected in the 'eighties had filled quickly. In the outer parts of London they filled slowly.[2] In the satellite towns they were hardly attempted. At the census of 1911 the population dwelling in flats was separately set out for the first time.[3] The flat was defined as a "structurally distinct dwelling within the same building",[4] and included both dwellings in the regular blocks and those in that type of small house built to hold two families which is common on the North-East coast and known in some parts of the London area. Some confusion no doubt arose in the enumeration between flats so defined and tenements in ordinary large old houses, and between the two-tenement house designed as such and the merely overcrowded house; but the broad results were probably not much affected. They are as follows for England and Wales:

Proportion per cent. of total population enumerated in 1911 *in*

	Ordinary dwelling houses	Flats	Shops, hotels, institutions, ships, etc.
All Urban Districts (inclusive of London and the County Boroughs)	85·2	3·7	11·1
London	75·6	10·4	14·0
All Rural Districts	91·4	0·3	8·3

The London flats include those of the well-to-do, of which by 1911 there were many. Outside London this kind of dwelling was still very rare, as subtraction of the London flat-dwellers from the urban flat-dwellers including the Londoners shows. The residue is barely 600,000 and includes the dwellers in houses of two flats on the North-East coast and elsewhere.

A statistical effect of London flat building, and of the continuous degeneration of old houses into tenements, was to increase slightly the number of "persons per inhabited house", in many metropolitan boroughs and in one or two satellite towns, between 1901 and 1911. In other towns and counties, with only one or two exceptions, there had been a fall—certainly connected with the fall in the birth-rate; for it was most marked in those

[1] Quoted, vol. II. 489.
[2] Vol. II. 496.
[3] *Report*, Table LXXXIX, p. 199.
[4] *Ibid.* p. 194.

textile, or part textile, towns where that fall had begun. In them there was little risk of confusion about the meaning of an inhabited house. It was a wage-earner's separate dwelling, normally one of a continuous row; a small villa, semi-detached or detached; or a rare business man's house of some size, which might contain ten or more people. For purposes of averaging the first class swamped all the rest. Here are some samples covering twenty years.[1]

Number of Persons per Inhabited House

	1891	1901	1911
Blackburn	4·91	4·66	4·39
Bradford	4·72	4·36	4·08
Halifax	4·45	4·21	3·97
Huddersfield	4·55	4·25	4·17
Leeds	4·71	4·53	4·37
Nottingham	4·65	4·57	4·38
Rochdale	4·35	4·12	4·00

In 1891 the towns of this class, with other representative industrial towns such as Manchester, Sheffield, Leicester and Birmingham, all had an average house population between the 4·65 of Nottingham and the 5·04 of Manchester.[2] Now all were under 4·50 and several very near 4·0. Halifax and Rochdale were the two lowest figures in the whole country.

Down to 1891, in spite of their small house populations, the Yorkshire textile towns had stood high on the black list of urban overcrowding, because they contained so many stone-built, durable, two and three-room cottages. About 20 per cent. of the people of Bradford and Huddersfield, and more than 21 per cent. of those of Halifax, had been overcrowded according to the census test—living more than two persons to a room. By 1911 the Bradford figure was down to 9·3, the Huddersfield to 12·8, and the Halifax to 12·0. There was great need of improvement, and the census standard for the not overcrowded—man and wife in a bed-sitting room; man, wife and two children in living room and bedroom—was low; but the progress is undeniable.

Thanks to their relatively late industrial development, the towns of the central and eastern Midlands retained that honourable lead in housing conditions which they had held in 1891.[3]

[1] *Census Report*, 1891 (1893–4, CVI); *Census Report*, 1901 (1904, CVIII); *Census Report*, 1911, as above—inhabited house statistics.

[2] Cp. vol. II. 493.

[3] Cp. vol. II. 494.

Only 1·1 per cent. of the population in Leicester and Northampton, 1·9 per cent. in Derby, 2·9 in Lincoln, and 4·3 in Nottingham was 'overcrowded'. Northampton and Leicester were better than Bournemouth, and all five were better than Brighton. Leicester had halved its already low figure in the twenty years. There had been some progress almost everywhere, but in many important towns there was no ground for complacency. The progress was however slightly greater than the figures in the table here given show; for in 1891 calculations were only made of overcrowding in tenements of four rooms or less, and the census of 1911 showed that there was some overcrowding in five and even six-room tenements. The London figure for 1911 on the 1891 basis would be not 16·7 but 16·05.[1]

Percentage of the Population living more than two to a Room; 1911, in all tenements; 1891, in those of less than five rooms

	1891	1911		1891	1911
England and Wales	11·2	8·6	Liverpool	10·9	10·1
London	19·7	16·7	Manchester	8·2	7·2
West Ham	9·3	15·3	Oldham	10·1	7·2
Plymouth	26·2	17·5	Preston	4·1	5·6
Bristol	8·0	4·8	St Helens[2]	—	17·0
Birmingham	14·3	10·1	Bradford	20·1	9·3
Coventry[2]	—	5·3	Halifax	21·3	12·0
Derby	2·7	1·9	Huddersfield	19·9	12·8
Dudley[2]	—	15·0	Hull	7·9	8·2
Leicester	2·2	1·1	Leeds	16·5	11·0
Lincoln[2]	—	2·9	Sheffield	11·6	8·4
Northampton[2]	—	1·1	Newcastle	35·1	31·6
Nottingham	3·62	4·3	Sunderland	32·1	32·6

Behind the tolerable 1911 figure for London were hidden whole Municipal Boroughs, the boroughs of the poor, with figures as bad as any in the country—Bermondsey 23·4; Bethnal Green 33·2; Stepney 35·0; Shoreditch 36·6; Finsbury 39·8. "When I grow rich, said the bells of Shoreditch. When will that be? said the bells of Step-ney. I'm sure I don't know, said the great bell of Bow." It is the ring of old London outside the City, not so full of people as it was once, but its rooms much too full. West Ham, though not legally part of London, is unhappily moving towards a London standard of overcrowding.

[1] *Census Report*, 1911, pp. 180, 185; *Census Report*, 1891, p. 22; further details in the County Reports of the two censuses.

[2] These towns are not included in the table of overcrowding in "32 of the largest municipal boroughs" given in the 1891 *Census* (1893–4, CVI).

In the South-West, Plymouth, always overcrowded, had made progress, and Bristol, for a seaport, had done excellently. In the Midlands Birmingham made a poor showing. There was "never any serious overcrowding", Chamberlain had said in 1884,[1] when no statistical test had been applied. The census of 1891 showed an amount which was rather serious; and the Birmingham of 1911 should have been able to do better than Liverpool, with its intractable waterside and Irish populations. Apart from Dudley and West Bromwich, whose figure lies between those of Dudley and Birmingham, and some Urban Districts in the old Black Country, there is no very dark spot in the Midlands and many obvious bright patches. Coventry had grown by over 50 per cent. in ten years, and private building enterprise had housed its 36,000 new citizens, imperfectly no doubt, but without grave inconvenience.

Of Yorkshire and Lancashire there is further to be said—that Liverpool's position is on the whole creditable and Hull's slight relapse hardly discreditable, for in a great seaport either figure is low; that some special local or statistical explanation is wanting for Preston's reputed regression; that the other figures on the whole speak well for both counties, except those of St Helens which suggest the comment that perhaps only those who would endure such a measure of overcrowding would also bear with its unusually defiled atmosphere.[2]

Twenty years—any twenty years—could not be expected to break down that one or two-room habit of living which, with its resultant overcrowding, began somewhere not very far North of Teesdale and stretched all over Scotland.[3] But it was discreditable to overcrowded Sunderland that, whereas overcrowded Newcastle showed improvement, she showed none.

In Scotland itself, where the one room or the "but and ben" house was common in the country, about the coal-mines, and on the skirts of the towns, and where the old way of living in "houses" which an Englishman called tenements or flats was so persistent that "recent examples" of these buildings could be seen in 1911–14, in "small country burghs immediately surrounded by fields", and so uniform that the tall buildings, with their common staircases opening on to a court or a close

[1] Quoted, vol. II. 492.

[2] Perhaps the same sort of argument applies to Dewsbury, where the rags are. Its 1911 figure, 16·6, was nearly as bad as that of St Helens.

[3] Cp. vol. II. 494.

"only a few feet wide", were "to be found from Dumfries in the South to Lerwick in the far North"—in Scotland there had been little change.[1] The urban "house" seldom had three rooms. So 47·9 per cent. of the people of Scotland lived in 1911 in one or two-room dwellings.[2] The corresponding figure for England and Wales was 7·5. The Scottish, and its cousin the Northumbrian, room was "generally much larger"[3] than the English or Welsh. Some men with experiences of both thought it was 20, some as much as 50 per cent. larger.[4] The facts have never been ascertained. On the other hand, far more English than Scottish houses had a fair-sized scullery, which the census enumerators of 1911 were carefully told never to count as a room.[5]

One-room houses were still being built in twentieth-century Scotland, rather freely in Lanarkshire. They were in great demand, especially by young married couples. "For every two persons wanting a room and kitchen house, there will be ten wanting single-room houses", a Glasgow building contractor said in 1914.[6] The result on overcrowding statistics was to be expected.

Percentage of the Total Population of Scotland living more than

	Two in a room	Three in a room	Four in a room
1891	48·2	25·3	11·3
1901	45·7	22·9	9·6
1911	45·1	21·9	8·6

There was the same percentage of Scots living more than four to a room in 1911 as of Englishmen living more than two. If the Scottish figure of 'more than two' had fallen in twenty years as the English fell, it would have been not 45·1 but 37·0—and even so would have been higher than that of Shoreditch.

Scots were not worse paid than Englishmen. They were at least as intelligent, industrious, and physically capable. Food

[1] *R.C. on the Housing of the Industrial Population of Scotland*, 1917 (Cd. 8731), pp. 41, 42.

[2] *Ibid.* p. 44, quoting the *Census Report* of 1911.

[3] *Report on the Cost of Living of the Working Classes*, 1908 (Cd. 3864), p. xx. And see vol. II. 507.

[4] *R.C. on Housing*, as above, p. 44.

[5] Their instruction was: "Count the kitchen as a room, but do not count scullery, landing, lobby, closet, bathroom, nor warehouse, office, shop": *Census Report*, 1911, p. 169.

[6] *R.C. on Housing in Scotland*, Q. 27,745 (Mr Nichol).

and clothes cost them no more. The State did no less for them. Their housing was determined not so much by economic necessity as by tradition—a tradition in stone, traditional domestic habits—of astonishing persistence. By acquiescing, or while acquiescing, in this tradition, Scotland acquiesced also in a general death-rate which, since about 1895, had been normally a point or two higher than the English; acquiesced in its main cause, an infantile death-rate considerably higher; and in a demoralising mass of one-room family life. Reformers had started a campaign against that life long before—to attack the two-room home in Scotland would have been quixotic—yet in 1911, out of Glasgow's population of 784,000, there were still 105,000, more than all the people of Halifax, Northampton or Reading, packed in one-room dwellings. In thirty years the figure had fallen by only 21,000.

An obstacle to the campaign, and to housing improvement in England, had been a contraction of house-building in the new century, marked after 1907. Capital which, had conditions been attractive, might have gone into building was being exported in unprecedented quantities.[1] Political controversialists said that the check was due to Lloyd George's land taxation of 1909: land-handling people were worried with complex valuations, and builders who had counted on rising site values were discouraged.[2] No doubt Lloyd George was a contributory cause. Apart from his direct action he charged the future with uncertainty. (There was uncertainty abroad also: that was overlooked by investors in American rails or the tramways of Kieff.) But there were causes deeper and older than the People's Budget. Speculative building was done everywhere on borrowed money. The price of that rose in 1906–7, and again after 1909; it was dearer on the average from 1900 onwards than it had been in the 'nineties.[3] After 1909 building wages began to rise, and labour costs had risen earlier.

Some Glasgow statistics show an early check to building there, which helps to explain the failure to reduce overcrowding. In the years 1901–4, 13,080 houses with an estimated 34,500 rooms had been built in the city. Only 3488 with 9460 rooms were built in

[1] Above, pp. 30, 62 and diagram on p. 25.

[2] See, for example, the discussion in the *R.C. on Housing in Scotland*, pp. 365 *sq*. Cp. Ensor, *England*, 1870–1914, pp. 509–10.

[3] *R.C. on Housing in Scotland*, pp. 298, 359. The facts were of course the same for England, but the Scottish evidence only was collected at a date needed for the argument.

1907–10, and in 1910–13, when all the adverse forces were at work together, a mere 945 with 2751 rooms.[1] It will be noted that even at the last a new Glasgow house had barely three rooms.

The marked slackening in the reduction of overcrowding during the decade 1901–11 which the Scottish figures show is found also in the English figures. The census overcrowding returns of 1901, like those of 1891, are not strictly comparable with those for total overcrowding given in 1911; but when allowance has been made for this, stagnation, or even a slight worsening, is seen in many towns, decided improvement in few. The County of London overcrowding figure for 1901 was 16·01. The corresponding figure for 1911 was 16·05.[2] Stepney in 1911 was a little better than in 1901, Bethnal Green a little worse; and so on. As might have been feared, things were getting worse in London's ring and dormitory towns, which, like West Ham before them, were being brought within range of the intense central urban pressures; though in none of them except Willesden was the total overcrowding figure for 1911 alarming.[3]

Housing conditions are not a complete test of a civilisation, nor is the amount of overcrowding according to any official definition an absolute gauge of housing conditions; but the conditions have more than a purely economic meaning, are perhaps most important in spheres of value higher than the economic; and other gauges—of dirt, crime, disease—are apt to give readings which agree rather closely with those of the overcrowding gauge.

Supply and demand were working together as usual to determine the stock of houses and the amount of overcrowding. The chief obstacles on the supply side have been noted. The demand for more or better wage-earning men's houses was kept down by a general stagnation of wages, nominal and real, which marked the early twentieth century. In the late 'eighties there had been a sharp and satisfactory rise. Money wages in the mass, that is the national wage bill calculated so as to allow for the constant shifting of individuals from worse to better paid work, and averaged over all wage-earners, had fallen, it has been estimated,

[1] *R.C. on Housing in Scotland*, p. 358.

[2] The figure given on p. 460 above includes overcrowding in those large houses or tenements which were not examined in 1901 and 1891.

[3] The main source is the section 'Tenements' in the *Census Report* for 1911 (pp. 170–96) and the appended diagrams. There are similar, but less complete sections, in the *Reports* of 1901 and 1891.

only in the ratio of 156 to 148 in the twelve years from 1874 to 1886. But real wages in the mass had not fallen, even in those difficult years, and even when allowance is made for the heavy unemployment of 1886. They had in fact risen a little; for retail prices had fallen more than money wages. The real wage ratios, so calculated, for 1874 and 1886 are 131 and 136. (The base line in these calculations is the position in 1880, which is taken as 100.) Wage-earners of unchanged grade, the average human units who entered a trade young and stayed in it, had naturally been less fortunate than labour in the mass.[1] For some grades there had been sharp falls in money wages, for which the fall in the cost of living had not brought compensation, quite apart from any extra loss due to abnormal unemployment. The natural man thinks more of his money income than of other people's calculations of what it will buy; and if he is a blast-furnace man with a fallen wage, he probably does not give thanks because he is still better off than he would have been as the agricultural labourer that he once was. So the world of labour was very restless in 1886.

But from 1886 to 1890–1 everything went better. The average money wage in the mass moved from 148 to 163; real wages, allowing for unemployment, from 136 to 162 in 1890, when there was next to no unemployment, or 159 in 1891 when unemployment was rather worse. The money wage of the average wage-earner of unchanged grade when in full work moved up in the ratio of 130 to 141; or allowing for unemployment, heavy in 1886 and so light in 1890, of 116 to 138. And retail prices in 1890–1 were just about what they had been in 1886.

Retail prices went on falling until 1896, when they were some nine points below 1886. And as money wages, however viewed, remained approximately stable, the condition of the average wage-earner improved quietly but steadily. It was best of all during the brisk trade of 1898–9, and with the strain of a war, which otherwise interfered with no economic activity, upon the labour market in 1900–1. True, retail prices were rising at last, but they were still a point or two lower than they had been in 1886; and both money wages in the mass, and the wages for any

[1] See Wood, G. H., "Real Wages and the Standard of Comfort since 1850", *S.J.* 1909; as used in vol. II. 450–2. As a study on exactly the same lines does not exist for 1908–14 it has not been possible to construct a complete diagram in succession to that in vol. II. 452. For readers' convenience, there is some repetition in the text from vol. II of the principles on which the statistical conclusions are based.

given grade of work, were higher in 1900–1 than they had ever yet been. The rise in money wages was not however so great as to make average wage-earners thankfully conscious of it. Often it had been fought for as a right withheld. Still, for work of a given grade and allowing for more regular employment, the wage index had moved from the 116 of 1886 and the 138 of 1890 to 147 in 1900. Of the rise in real wages which had come, as it were, while they slept, and of late had hardly been perceptible—since prices were no longer falling—wage-earners were naturally even less conscious. Grandfather might talk of the hungry 'forties, and you thanked God that you had not been young with grandfather. For that fall in the price of bread and some other things which had come since the 'seventies there was not much thanksgiving; the less because since 1896 it had stopped, and even shown signs of reversal.[1]

Yet a man's real wage in 1900 was in fact about 50 per cent. more than that of someone doing similar work had been in 1850; and the average wage, the mass wage, much more than that, because of the huge transfer in half a century from ill-paid to well-paid work. Real wages, so regarded, had risen not by about 50 but by about 75 per cent.[2] But of this individuals were rarely conscious. Not very many had changed their line of work as men. The transfer had usually been made by lads going into better-paid work than their fathers; and the policeman or railwayman might wonder, with half-pitying and natural admiration, how mother had managed to rear us on father's agricultural wage.

The year 1900 was a peak year for wages however they are regarded—in the mass or for a particular grade of work, in money or in what money will buy. Eleven years later, in the census year, the average of the chief industrial wage-rates was to a decimal point the same as it had been in 1900. The peak had proved to be the escarpment edge of an uneven plateau.[3] Inclusion of agricultural wages, which had moved a little to earners' advantage, would give the general level of the plateau the faintest upward tilt—but miners were not in the habit of getting comfort by averaging their pay with that of agricultural labourers, and were angrily conscious of the undulations in their line across the

[1] Bread in London was at its very cheapest in 1901 (see the diagram above, p. 12). But it had been relatively dear in 1897–8. The Board of Trade weighted Index Number for 23 articles of food in London shows a minimum (91·7) in 1896. The base line (100) is the price-level of 1900.

[2] Wood's estimate in *S.J.* as above.

[3] Diagram, p. 468 below.

plateau. For the building trades the line had been almost a dead level.[1] For engineering and the textiles, first a dead level and then an undulating upward tilt. It is the miners' route which gives the averaged route its shape.[2] They had topped the plateau edge at its highest point; dropped into a deep trough; crossed a low ridge in 1907; and in 1911 were still 11 per cent. below their level of 1900. This illuminates much of the social history of the decade. Miners had barely got back to their 1900 level in 1913, whereas by that time the textile people were nearly 12 per cent. above it.

The figures of which this is a parable are those of wage-rates only. They neglect the regularity of work. Employment had been excellent in 1900. It was not so good again until 1913, and there had been some bad years between, especially 1908 and 1909.[3] This made things worse for the miners, and discounts both the stability of builders' wage-rates and the slight rise in those of engineers and textile workers. Further, on any showing, the cost of living had gone up. The course of rents is not accurately known; but they are believed to have remained fairly constant down to 1912—one reason why, with rising costs, building was not active. Coal was throughout cheaper, sometimes 20 per cent. cheaper, than it had been in 1900—the consumers' gain from the miners' discontents. Clothes were getting a little dearer, especially after 1907 when textile wages were going up. And food was dearer. The official estimate was a rise in London food prices of 9·4 per cent. between 1900 and 1911. The estimated rise for clothing was rather more—12·4 per cent. That for the whole cost of living, including coal and rent, was naturally rather less; for clothing is not an important item in an average wage-earner's budget and coal was relatively cheap.[4]

Other estimates give slightly different results; yet it would

[1] Wages did not fall at all, and did not rise more than 0·5 per cent. until 1912.

[2] The textile line is shown in the diagram. It is based on the "recognised percentage changes in the piece rates...in cotton spinning and weaving and linen and jute manufacture"; but there is no reason to think the wages in wool moved very differently. The engineering figures are based on minimum weekly time rates in seven large towns: the highest point between 1900 and 1911 is only 102·2 in 1908. The mining figures are based on the tonnage or shift rates for hewers on all the chief coalfields. They are in the *Abstracts of Labour Statistics*.

[3] Above, p. 58, and the diagram of trade-union unemployment on p. 29.

[4] These are the Board of Trade estimates in the *Abstracts of Labour Statistics*. The *Report on the Cost of Living of the Working Classes* of 1908 (Cd. 3864) is a main source of information.

be safe to assume an average rise in the cost of living of between 7 and 9 per cent. by 1911, and of more by 1913; but after 1911 all wages were rising.

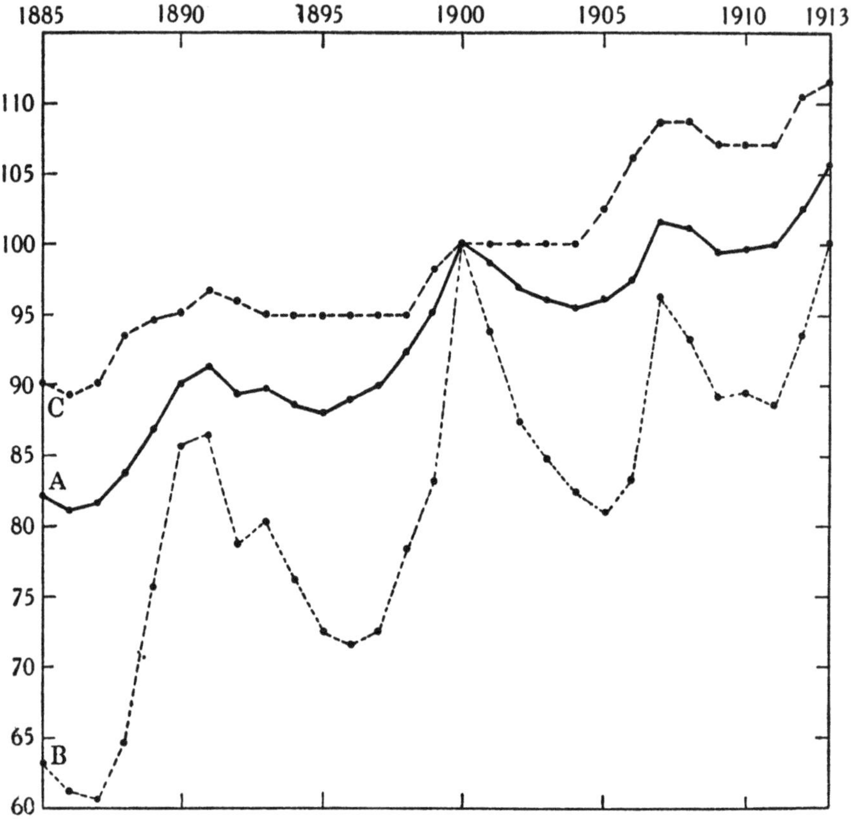

Industrial wage-rates.

Course of industrial wage-rates: building, mining, engineering, textile, —— A;
mining only, ---- B;
textile only, ---- C.

(Wages in 1900 = 100.)

The inclusion of agriculture would raise the figure for 1911 to 101·1.

An enquiry into London wages made in 1913 suggested that, taking everything into account—money wages, the amount of unemployment, and the cost of living—real wages had not even by the end of 1912 got quite to the level of 1900, though they were very near it.[1] London figures, having a wide range and not

[1] Wood, Frances, "The Course of Real Wages in London, 1900–12", *S.J.* 1914. Cp. the estimates of the course of prices and real wages in Layton, Sir Walter, *An Introduction to the Study of Prices*, and the discussions in Pigou, A. C., *Industrial Fluctuations*.

being affected by the special vicissitudes of coal-mining and the heavy trades, are fairly representative for the general wage-earning population outside those trades and the localised textiles. The addition of coal-mining and heavy industry would make the average national industrial real wage worse than the London wage. If agriculture and the textiles were also brought in, the national real wage might be as high as the London wage.

In short—the average true lie of that plateau was not quite level. When account is taken of how much work there was to do and of what money would buy, it appears as tilted slightly to the disadvantage of the wage-earner. It is not even certain that the wage-rises of 1912–13 corrected the tilt; though probably they did, because that of 1913, at any rate, was not accompanied by a rise in the cost of living.

Women's wages had continued to move roughly parallel to those of men.[1] There were fewer vicissitudes, as there always had been, because there were no women in heavy industry. It seems that the—very imperfectly known—wages of domestic workers, who included more than a third of the occupied women in 1911, had risen a trifle faster than those of other women down to 1903–7.[2] But there was said to have been no appreciable advance for ordinary young general servants between about 1898–9 and 1914; though there had been some rises in the upper ranks, as might have been expected. When in 1916 a war-time enquiry was made by a body keen to search out abuses, "little complaint as to money wages" was found.[3] The complaints were about quite different things.

The average wage-earner, man or woman, had long been free of encroachment on wages by means of truck. The law was revised in 1887 and again in 1896; but the problem was small and by this time less one of truck proper—payment in doubtful goods or goods of undoubted price—than of fines, deductions from wages, and charges, which might be excessive, for tools, light, or power. When the matter was enquired into in 1905–6 some remnants of truck proper were found in Cornish and

[1] The textile wage figure used above includes a mass of women's wages.

[2] Layton, [Sir] W. T., "Changes in the wages of domestic servants during fifty years", *S.J.* 1908. Cp. Wood, G. H., Appendix on Women's Wages in Hutchins and Harrison, *A History of Factory Legislation.*

[3] *Report...on Women in Industry*, 1919 (XXXI. 241).

Shetland knitting, Bristol corset-making, Somerset glove-making and in Harris of the tweed.[1] There were still plenty of fines. Working girls might be fined for wearing hair-curlers or "cheeking the foreman". Some penalising of minor irregularities there had to be, though there was no need to call curlers irregular; and some Trade Union leaders preferred the fine to its alternatives, suspension or dismissal for trifles.[2] In Sheffield, where strong remnants of independent craftsmanship survived and men were still "not favourable to the ordinary factory system as it exists elsewhere",[3] payments for room or light or power were still common and not generally unpopular; and the miner, when he had to do it, was craftsman enough not to mind finding his own pick.

There was a little payment in drink—agricultural labourers' cider in the West, and a traditional allowance of beer in a few Black Country coal mines, where the "pit water" was "warm and unpalatable".[4] Both groups wished to go on drinking; but the Black Country men were half inclined to demand the price of beer. Their employers would only offer the cost of that beer, a delicate and interesting distinction.

These are curiosities. More attention was rightly paid to the truck-like abuses which might arise when shop assistants lived in.[5] But the practice was not normal. Almost unknown in Scotland, it was general in Wales, sporadic in England. It was certainly declining at the time of the enquiry, though grievances arising from it were far from extinct.[6] By girls in decent establishments it was often liked. Here, as in other spheres of truck, the law had prevented most real abuses, and good sense or convenience were cutting down the practices liable to abuse.

Although until 1913 employment both of men and women was not again so good as it had been in 1900, these were not years of unusual unemployment. Nor had the 'nineties or the late 'eighties been. The average annual amount of trade-union unemployment for the years 1901–13 inclusive was only 4·5, and for

[1] *Dep. Com. on the Truck Acts*, 1908 (LIX). Cp. vol. II. 458.

[2] *Ibid.* p. 23, quoting R. Bell and others.

[3] *Ibid.* p. 45.

[4] *Ibid.* p. 64.

[5] *Ibid.* pp. 68 *sqq.* Special report by Miss Deans, who visited some places complained of and was "bound to say" that she did not find the Shop Assistants' Trade Union "complaints substantiated".

[6] For which see Paine, W., *Shop Slavery and Emancipation* (1912), with an Introduction by H. G. Wells—who understood the thing.

1887–1900 just 5·0. The peaks of 7·5 in 1893 and 7·8 in 1908 were well below the disastrous 10·2 of 1886; and a spell of rather high unemployment only once lasted for two years.[1] There was no drawn-out under-employment, no slow death of a great trade like that of the hand-loom weavers. What might have become by later definition the special area of Cornwall had been relieved by emigration to the Rand, Malaya, any and every place where precious and half-precious metals are mined. When the motor-bus came the busman shaved and took to machinery; though later some hansom cabmen were left stranded. Other adjustments were made, not entirely without friction and distress, but mainly by the diversion of young people from declining to expanding trades. There were fewer coachmen, grooms and horse cabmen in 1911 than there had once been, but more than two strong divisions of professional motor drivers raised since 1901;[2] and also since 1901 nearly 28,000 more tramwaymen. The electrical industries had grown eightfold since 1891, and now employed more than 100,000 men. If employment in agriculture had declined, the railway service, to which the transition from agriculture was so easy, had nearly doubled. Coal-mining too had increased fast—by 60 per cent. since 1891, and by more than 100 per cent. since 1881. It had been easy of access for the able-bodied. As a group, the textile industries were still expanding, if not so quickly as the population; and the slight contraction in wool, flax and silk had been slow and had caused only local discomfort.

For women new careers had opened, while there had been very little slackening of demand for them in the old, except in those where any slackening was wholesome. There were fewer washerwomen and seamstresses, more charwomen, workers in hospitals and institutions, and clothing-factory hands. If there were fewer indoor domestic servants in 1911 than in 1891, nearly a million and a half maids were still serving, and the demand for the better of them was certainly not satiated. The decline, though only a small percentage of that great army, did however mark the beginning of a new age.[3] Some of the 40,000 more nurses and the 45,000 more women teachers might have "gone into service" in an older world of fewer women's careers.

Between 1861 and 1881 the number of women metal-workers

[1] Diagram, p. 29 above.
[2] At the 1911 Census, 47,000: in 1901 there had been 703.
[3] The decline was most conspicuous in Scotland.

had fallen, with the fall in domestic nail and chain-making. There had been 10,000 women nailers, a wretched host, in 1851: only 1700 were left by 1911. There were still 2100 hand chain-makers—about to get a Trade Board—in the Cradley Heath district. Yet in spite of decline in the bad old crafts, the number of women metal-workers had doubled between 1891 and 1901. There were 7000 in cycle and motor works, where there had been almost none, and where there was now "no clear demarcation between men's and women's work".[1] Instead of hammering out nails and tacks, women were feeding nail, tack and screw machines—set for them by men. In the brass trades they made light cores; they mounted, polished and packed. At Sheffield they did appropriate jobs in the file, cutlery, hacksaw, and electro-plate trades, with much work in the warehouses. And in some specialised Midland factories they did small capstan lathe work, also pressing, stamping, milling, enamelling and assembling. Besides the true metal trades, instrument-making, toy and games material making, and the rising electrical industries made factory work for women. Only a few hundred women were in the electrical industries in 1891. By 1911 there were considerably more than 9000.[2] And that was only a beginning.

The greatest change of all was in commerce. At the census of 1851 nineteen women had been returned as commercial clerks.[3] Who and where were they? It is said that women first entered the drapery trade—there were no young ladies in John Gilpin's shop—during the Crimean War.[4] Dickens, who died in 1870, had not known the woman clerk. We should have met her if he had. David Copperfield's Dora could only hold the pens and Caddy Jellyby was an inky amateur. There were, it is true, a few more women in clerical work by 1871 than there had been in 1851; but there were only 7000 in 1881 and 22,000 in 1891. Then the change came. By 1911 there were 146,000 female "commercial or business clerks", and of other women in commercial occupations, substantially the same class, 11,000. The girl book-keeper, secretary, and shorthand-typist had arrived.[5]

[1] *D.C. on Women in Industry*, 1908, p. 11. [2] *Ibid.* plus the census returns.

[3] Vol. II. 24. [4] *D.C. on Women in Industry*, p. 9.

[5] In a volume of Charles Booth's *Life and Labour of the People in London* published in 1896 (VII. 275) it is said that "as typewriters, copyists and telephone operators they are said to excel". When in 1889 Rudyard Kipling met an educated girl doing type-writing in California he wrote about "a young Lady who in England would be a Young Person": *From Sea to Sea*. But the Bank of England began employing women in 1893. Acres, *The B. of E. from Within*, II. 560.

The figures are strictly clerical and include none of the shop-girls, in drapery or any other trade. A generation earlier the alternatives for most of these young commercial women would have been this shop work—wide open by 1880—or the better sorts of stitching, or high-grade service—shop-girl, dressmaker, lady's-maid. There was a further possibility open to the best educated and most refined, to become "Only the Governess".[1]

For the group was recruited, or so memory and untested observation suggest, mainly from the families of clerks, shop-workers, small tradesmen and poor professional men. Recruitment from families of skilled manual workers was just beginning. A Lancashire spinner's daughter might be doing clerical work in the Co-op. instead of going into the mill. But these careers were still beyond the reach of girls from average rank-and-file wage-earning homes. It is probable therefore that their emergence did not much affect the prospects of family earnings in such households. These depended as before mainly on the outlets into factory work, all other kinds of manual work, and domestic service. Such outlets had certainly widened. The chocolate factories, the jam factories, the biscuit factories, the tobacco factories, the corset factories, and a score of other sorts, all the places in which the minor luxuries of a richening people were made, were expanding—when some older staple trades were not; and, like the new style light metal and electrical works, they were staffed by women under male authority.

It is probable therefore that in many wage-earning families there were greater opportunities for increasing the total family income than there had been in the 'eighties. The decline in domestic service and in heavy work for women itself suggests, though it does not prove, this. But just how great and how widespread these opportunities were at successive points in time statisticians have not yet been able to determine. Perhaps they never will. Some studies were made by contemporaries of particular places at given dates; but any statement about the movement of family earnings, even in a limited area, would be speculative and insecure.[2] With this qualified agnosticism the historian must as yet rest content.

[1] The title of one of the novels of Rosa Nouchette Cary.

[2] After Charles Booth's *Life and Labour*, in which some pioneering work on family earnings was done (IX. 279–82) in 1897, came, in 1902, Rowntree, B. S., *Poverty, a Study of Town Life*, which contains a careful study of family earnings in York.

At first sight it is surprising that in this diversified, active, rather regularly employed economic society of the early twentieth century there should have been those eleven years of stagnation in wage-rates, and almost certainly some, although perhaps only a very little, decline in the real wages of the average earner. Surprise is lessened, if not dissipated, by closer consideration of the circumstances in 1900 and of the course of wages in different trades. On the industrial wage-rate curve the peak of 1900 shows unusually high. A line drawn through the three other peaks—1891, 1907, 1913—ascends in an almost perfectly straight line. So does a line drawn through the bottom points of the troughs—1886, 1895, 1904, 1909. Above the line drawn through the peaks 1900 stands lonely, abnormal.[1] Why?

Improving trade, declining unemployment and some brisk fights for wages during 1897–9 were followed by still more active trade in 1899—and then war. During war came 1900; a year in which it has been estimated that 22 per cent. more was paid out in wages than had been paid out in 1895;[2] a year of export coal values, and of general coal prices, such as had never been known.[3] Before 1899 the highest coal export year had been 1890, with £19,000,000. In 1896 the figure had slipped to £15,000,000. By 1899 it had climbed to £23,000,000. In 1900 it stood at £38,600,000. These prices left their mark on miners' wages and miners' wages left their mark on the general curve. In the history of textile—and building, and engineering—wage-rates 1900 is not an abnormal year. A small rise had come with good trade: the rise stopped. That was usual. In textiles the rise was resumed quite soon, sooner than it had been in the 'nineties. In engineering it came a trifle later and was less marked. In building it did not begin until the eleven years were over, for reasons that have already been discussed. To the slow, very slow but real, rise of agricultural wages there was no check in 1900 at all.[4]

Some lag in real wages during times of rising prices there has always been. Well-organised collective industrial bargaining

[1] Diagram, p. 468 above.

[2] Pigou, A. C., *Industrial Fluctuations*, p. 356, quoting an estimate of Bowley, A. L.

[3] Taking the retail price of coal in 1900 as 100, it was 68·2 in 1896, 79·3 in 1899, 89 in 1901 and 83·8 in 1910. B. of T. Index No. in *Abstracts of Labour Statistics*.

[4] Cp. p. 97 above and especially n. 1. There was an almost imperceptible check to agricultural wages in 1902, but otherwise the rise was steady 90 (per cent. of the 1900 level) in 1887 to 95·1 in 1897, 102·5 in 1905, 111·1 in 1913 and 114·2 in July, 1914. See p. 98 above.

tends, and is intended, to minimise it. But before 1914 not all industrial bargaining was well organised, there was no general familiarity with cost-of-living figures, and no regularised adjustment of any wage-rates to them. So a lag of a few years, if the rise were slight and intermittent, was to be expected. And this rise was both. Retail prices, and living costs generally, were falling until 1896. From 1896 to 1900 there was a rise of some 9 per cent., but this only brought the estimated cost of living 1 per cent. above what it had been in 1892. True, it washed out the advantages of the wage-rise of the late 'nineties—except for the miners, whose rise had been greater than any, and who did not pay 1900 prices for their coal. But it was not pronounced enough to create real discontent.

For the next seven years there was a very slight, undulating, and almost imperceptible upward movement in the cost of living, the maximum estimate for which is some 3 per cent.[1] Few people are actively conscious of a rise in their household expenses which averages less than 0·5 per cent. per annum. From 1907 the rise steepened, but even so—it is estimated—averaged only 1 per cent. per annum. Still, by 1912 food prices were 14 per cent. above the level of 1900; and a rise of 1*s*. in 7*s*. on food bills, over a period easily remembered, is not a thing to be ignored. The average miner's wage, as has been seen, was not yet back at the 1900 level. No other important group of wage-earners had pushed their full-time money wage so much as 14 per cent. above 1900. It is not a mere accident that 1912 was a year of industrial strife, or that the miners were both storm troops and rearguard in action. More days' work were lost in fighting that year than in the six years before it.[2] The lag in real wages was beginning to hurt—and seemed to be drawing towards an end; for in 1913 money wages rose sharply, while food and clothing prices did not.

This rise of 1912–13 in money wages and in real wages coincided with the hugest recorded exports of British capital.[3] Since 1905 those exports had been unusually heavy. Checked in 1908–9 they became heavier still from 1910. These facts are

[1] See Wood, Frances, "The course of Real Wages in London", *S.J.* 1914, as above, and some estimates of Bowley, A. L., in a letter to the *Daily News*, Oct. 9, 1911.

[2] See the diagram of days lost, p. 499 below.

[3] See the diagram, p. 25 above.

relevant here because it has been argued that a stagnant phase of real wages in Britain, and of real incomes generally,[1] was connected with the abnormal capital exports of the decade 1903–13. Instead of bringing home in useful, consumable, things—so the argument runs—all that was owed her from abroad on old investments, for shipping services, and for her other invisible exports, Britain was reinvesting much of this fund in enterprises and public securities overseas which at best would only pay in the future and at worst would not pay at all. In connection with this investment she was sending abroad great masses of capital goods. By 1910 the actual quantity of things sent abroad in return for any given quantity of things imported was much greater than it had been in 1900. Britain was denying herself unconsciously for foreign investments' sake, just as, twenty years later, Soviet Russia denied herself consciously for the sake of home investments, during her first five-year plan. The results, the argument suggests, were similar: resources frozen for the time in capital goods at home or abroad, or in loans bearing foreign promises to pay, could not at the same time be used to improve standards of income and of living. Britain was like the thrusting, self-making, nineteenth-century manufacturer who lived hard and let his wife do housework while he put every shilling into the mill. Only Britain's mill was overseas.[2]

The argument seems to run true, but even those who designed it are uncertain of its weight and range. They cannot deduce from it amounts, if any, of real wages so to speak withheld. When particular years or small groups of years are taken, it may fit them badly. Real wages were just about as low in 1904, when capital exports were insignificant, as in 1910 when they were very high.[3] After 1911 real wages improved while the capital exports went still higher. There is reason to think that the national home money income, that is to say wages and all else except the income from foreign investments, grew rather faster than the

[1] Cp. Bowley, A. L., *The Changes in the Distribution of the National Income, 1880–1913*, p. 26, for the general stagnation: "average (real) incomes were quite one-third greater in 1913 than in 1880; the increase was gained principally before 1900...."

[2] A paraphrase of the technical argument in Taussig, F. W., "Great Britain's Foreign Trade Terms after 1900", *E.J.* 1925, and *International Trade* (1927), ch. 21. The reference to Soviet Russia is not in Taussig, nor is that to the thrusting manufacturer. For the Trade Terms, cp. p. 68 above.

[3] The Layton estimate in his *Introduction to the Study of Prices* makes them identical; Mrs Wood's London estimate puts 1904 at 100 and 1910 at 98·2.

cost of living during the years 1911–14.[1] It remains possible, even probable, that there might have been earlier improvement, and more improvement, in real wages had there been less export of capital. What the amount of this potential improvement might have been there is no means of ascertaining; so the matter remains one of curious speculation only.

The wage, whatever its level and its real purchasing power, was given in return for a day's work, which had shortened perceptibly in a number of occupations since the 'eighties, though on the average not conspicuously. That 54 or 54½-hour working week, exclusive of overtime, to which most important trades had settled down in the 'seventies remained unchanged in some trades and places forty years later.[2] Engineers in Scotland, for example, who for a few years had managed to hold a 51-hour week, but had been forced back to 54 in 1879, were still at 54 in July 1914. By that time, however, in the leading English and Welsh engineering centres, the standard week was of 53 hours, and in London, Sheffield and Manchester a few firms, some of them famous, had deliberately adopted the 48-hour week as the more satisfactory.[3] In the associated trades of electrical installation and shipbuilding the normal week ranged also from 48 to 53 hours, though a 54-hour week was the rule on the Clyde.

Coal-miners had all enjoyed their maximum 8-hour day underground since the Act of 1908.[4] In some important districts the Act merely registered a *fait accompli*; indeed one of the difficulties which had to be overcome by its promoters was the fact that the Northumberland men had already secured an even shorter working day for hewers by private arrangement with the coal-owners.[5] But, taking the industry as a whole, the Act brought about a shortening as against 1907, and registered a more perceptible shortening since 1887; though nothing revolutionary.

Working away persistently at local bargains with associated master-builders, the organised building trades, which had secured something like an average all-the-year-round week of 54 hours during the 'seventies—longer in summer, but shorter in winter—had almost everywhere forced even their summer hours below that level by 1914, in which year a summer working

[1] Bowley, A. L., *The Division of the Product of Industry*, pp. 14, 21.

[2] Cp. vol. II. 449.

[3] For example, Mather and Platt of Manchester.

[4] Above, p. 429.

[5] Shorter for hewers only: hence the complications.

week of more than 54 hours was hardly to be found, except in one or two places among the painters. Seven years earlier it was found locally in all the trades, although 54 or less was already normal, and the Aberdeen plumbers, in isolated glory, had attained the 48-hour week. By 1914 this had been bettered in a few places: Liverpool had a 46½-hour week for bricklayers, carpenters and painters, though one of 49½ hours for plumbers and plasterers. For the country as a whole, the 50-hour summer-time rate for the main building trades, which was common to London, Hull, Newcastle and Edinburgh, may be reckoned approximately representative.[1]

The printing trades, or at least their most prominent and best known sections, had won a 54-hour week in the 'seventies, like so many others. (In the early nineteenth century the week had been 63 hours and had only fallen to 60 in 1866.)[2] Some twenty years later there was a general, but not quite universal, fall to 52; but the 54-hour week survived in outlying places down to 1907 and later. In that year, of forty-one places reported on, seven retained the 54-hour week;[3] eight had weeks of between 54 and 52 hours, usually only 52½; twelve had 52 hours; the rest were already lower, though nowhere below 50. These are the hours for ordinary jobbing compositors' work. The men who by night printed the morning papers had already in a number of important places secured the 8-hour 'day' which they deserved. Seven years later it had just begun to appear in ordinary printing, and the normal week in large towns was of 50 or 51 hours. Roughly speaking, the printer's day had been shortened by half an hour in forty years.

The textile day and the factory day generally had been less curtailed. Set by the standard laid down for women in the Factory Acts,[4] it had fallen with that standard only from the 56½-hour textile week of 1874 to the 55½ hours of the Factory Act of 1901 (1 Ed. VII, c. 22). Non-textile factories and workshops in 1901 retained the 60-hour week, whether children and young persons were employed in them or not, the law thus hanging some considerable way behind what had been agreed on in the greater self-determining trades. Shops, still un-

[1] Figures were regularly collected from 1886 by the Labour Department of the Board of Trade and are in the *Abstracts of Labour Statistics*.

[2] Vol. II. 448.

[3] Barrow, Brighton, Ipswich, Norwich, Plymouth, Portsmouth, Southampton.

[4] Set, but not limited; some men stayed on to clean machinery, etc. Cp. vol. II. 448.

regulated in the 'seventies and 'eighties, now had a maximum working week of 74 hours, including meal times, provided they had "young persons" on their staff. And so to the domestic factories and workshops, in which "prohibition of employment on Sunday was the only restriction on the employment of women";[1] and to those domestic shops and working places where no one outside the family was employed, and you could put in as long a working day as you pleased. But these were relatively much less numerous than they had once been; and although ways of overworking children, outside their school hours or when their school time was over, were always being devised, this was a limited evil which does not invalidate the general conclusion that the working week in British industry had been shortened by a maximum of about 10 per cent. in the most favoured trades, and by an average which probably lay somewhere between 2½ and 5 per cent.

The 8-hour day had been one of the British wage-earners' dreams since someone in Chartist times had coined the jingling lines:

> Eight hours' work, eight hours' play,
> Eight hours' sleep and eight shillings a day.

From the 'eighties, it recurred again and again in resolutions of congresses and the fighting programmes of trade unions. Among the miners, who were so often in the fighting line, the demand for an 8-hour day had been associated with a struggle against the principle of basing wages on the selling-price of coal—the sliding-scale—which, when formally adopted, perpetuated that violent fluctuation of wages that had accompanied all the commercial vicissitudes of the coal industry throughout the century.[2] The miners' argument was that the extremes of fluctuation were due to reckless competition of coal-owners on a falling market, and their snatching at maximum profits when markets rose. To the owners, who took competition for granted, the principle of the sliding-scale was obviously just: "when we do well, they do well; and when we do badly they share our burden." They had often acted on it roughly and informally, and had managed to get it adopted formally on a great many coalfields during the

[1] Abraham, M. E. and Davies, A. L., *The Law relating to Factories and Workshops* (4th ed. 1902), p. 34.
[2] See vol. II. 165; Webb, *History of Trade Unionism*, App. II. Sliding Scales; Ashley, W. J., *The Adjustment of Wages* (1903), pp. 54 *sqq.*

price-fall of the late 'seventies and early 'eighties, beginning with South Staffordshire in 1874. Formal adoption was still spreading in 1887, when the scale appeared for the first time in Scotland, on the Lanarkshire field. But by that time the miners' campaign against it was well under way, and the Lanarkshire men terminated their agreement two years later.

The conflicting principle of the "living wage", a first charge on industry to be made as high as possible and levied in the deepest of cyclic troughs, had many implications which its advocates did not always pursue. If it is to be applied generously it seems to require some growing efficiency of labour; and the crude productive efficiency of mining labour was at this very time ceasing to grow.[1] If it is to be applied with a prospect of general success, it suggests a control of the market which coal-fields specially interested in the export and bunkering trades—Northumberland, Durham and South Wales—did not always enjoy. This no doubt helps to explain the conversion of the Northcountrymen to the doctrine of the sliding-scale, and their adhesion to it for a number of years. The main support for the opposite doctrine came at first from inland fields with pre-dominantly home markets. Yorkshire and Lancashire unions joined with others in September 1888 to form the Miners' Federation, which adopted an aggressive policy and what have been called "the semi-Socialistic principles of a minimum wage and a legal [eight hours] day".[2] The Federation grew astonishingly fast and by 1893 had more than 200,000 members. As it and its influence grew, surviving sliding-scale agreements were steadily terminated, though the minimum wage was not always insisted on.[3] By 1894, sliding-scales were formally recognised only in South Wales, a weighty exception, in part of Staffordshire and in the Forest of Dean.[4] South Wales struck against the principle four years later, but without success; and it was not until 1903 that the alternative principle, in the form in which it was by that time approved by the Miners' Federation, of a minimum wage *x* per cent. above some datum level (in South Wales that of December 1879) and a maximum *y* per cent. above it, was entered in a South Wales agreement.[5]

[1] Above, p. 63.
[2] Webb, *History*, p. 380.
[3] Ashley, *op. cit.* pp. 43, 55.
[4] Webb, *History*, p. 485.
[5] The 1903 agreement is printed in Ashley, *op. cit.* p. 219: the basis for most of the agreements was the rate of 1888. Cp. Jevons, H. S., *The British Coal Trade*, p. 492.

It is worth noting that the acceptance of this minimum and maximum policy, in what came to be known as the Federated Districts and in Scotland, had prevented miners' wages generally from going so high in the 1900 boom as they would have gone under a pure sliding-scale system. The subsequent fall it did not prevent, nor did the miners' leaders expect that it would. "The moment the market comes down, the wages must come down—we know that",[1] they said. Their accurate contention was that the peak of 1900 would have been higher, the trough of 1905 deeper, under a system which tied wages strictly to prices.

The steadily rising line of the bottom points of the miners' wage-rates troughs, from 1887 to 1911,[2] may be taken as evidence of the general success of their minimum-wage policy; but this policy did not guarantee work. It was always open to employers in slack times to pay the standard rates for only four days' work a week, instead of the usual five or five and a half. And, as has been seen, the miners themselves recognised that—as the world stood—those fluctuations both in their actual and their standard earnings which were great enough to leave a deep mark upon the whole course of wages in the country were not to be avoided.

The semi-socialistic policies to which the Miners' Federation committed itself in 1888 were conceived in the years of ferment of the early 'eighties, during which Karl Marx died in the England that Henry George visited; when Fabian Societies and Democratic Federations and Socialist Leagues were being formed; when Comrade William Morris was saying that "he did not know what Marx's theory of value was, and was damned if he wanted to know", but did know that "the rich were rich because they robbed the poor", which was political economy enough for him; while prices fell plumb from 1883 to 1887 and unemployment rose, until at the turn of 1886–7 the Northumberland miners embarked on a seventeen weeks' strike, which they lost, to save themselves from a reduction in the basis wage of their sliding-scale, which they had to endure.[3] (Though it may not be called a minimum wage, there must be some basis from which a sliding-scale can slide.) During this strike orators from the South, preaching State ownership of the mines, were well

[1] Quoted in Ashley, *op. cit.* p. 54 n. [2] See the diagram, p. 468 above.

[3] The quotation is from Philip, Viscount Snowden, *An Autobiography* (1934), p. 62; for the strike see Welbourne, E., *The Miners' Unions of Northumberland and Durham*, pp. 236–41; for the early 'eighties generally, vol. II. 477–87.

received in some places: their visit helped to prepare the way for the policies of the Miners' Federation.[1] And in many parts of the Trade Union world there was now minority tilting against the old, liberal, no-strike, friendly society type of official leader.[2]

With the trade revival of 1887–8 all wage-rates turned upward, those of the miners very sharply, rising to a short-period peak in 1891. Trade-union employment was wonderfully good in 1889 and 1890, good in both 1888 and 1891. There was the offset of a rise in a number of retail prices, including that of bread—though even so bread was cheaper in 1891–2 than it had been ten years earlier. But trade-union employment and the purchasing power of decent wages had little to do with the two most striking, and perhaps most important, events in the world of wage-earning during 1888–9; for both fell out below the existing bottom level of regular trade-union activity, and in regions where neither wages nor working conditions were decent. They were the strike of the London "match-girls" in 1888 and that of the London dockers in 1889. Victory for the six or seven hundred women workers who came out from the lucifer-match factories was a trifling thing to the statistical eye; but it seemed to be a symbol, a symbol of the weak things of the world confounding the things that were strong; although in fact one very strong thing, public opinion skilfully roused and directed, was on the match-girls' side.[3] Also they were London match-girls: their well-deserved victory might not have been won, or if won might not have become so notorious, if they had made matches in Coatbridge or Sunderland.

Much more important, though much less talked about, was the winning of an 8-hour instead of a 12-hour day by some of the gas stokers, without a strike. The 12-hour day had survived, through inertia and the administrative difficulties of a three-shift system, in a few continuous process industries, of which gas was the most important. Gas-workers, disorganised, could not insist on that system. Now, outside Socialists and one most able insider, William Thorne, rapidly built up the Gasworkers' and General Labourers' Union. By June, the South Metropolitan Gas Company had conceded the 8-hour day: they and the other companies held that the carbonising shift meant only 6 hours' work, if 12 hours' duty; but allowed that the 12-hour shift at the

[1] Welbourne, *op. cit.* p. 241.

[2] Above, p. 320, and vol. II. 159–60.

[3] Webb, *History of Trade Unionism*, pp. 388–9.

retorts was severe.[1] Early in August the other principal companies came into line; and as trade was good, the market rising, and some at least of the directors not unsympathetic, the shortened day was actually accompanied by an increased wage.[2] Though the South Metropolitan reverted to the 12-hour shift—there was a fight over this—at the end of the year, the new plan was widely adopted in the gas industry and was bound in time to become universal.

The outside public, little interested in peaceful industrial evolution, hardly noted this decisive rearrangement in the principal continuous process industry—the less so perhaps because it was completed in a holiday month.[3] But within a few days holidays were disturbed by news of a strike at the London Docks. It seemed a paltry affair at first, but it became general; for the well-paid and organised stevedores and lightermen came out in sympathy with the ill-paid and disorganised dockers proper. The conjuncture was unusual. Dock-companies had not been doing well for years. They had felt the competition of the wharves and were seeking the economies of co-operation.[4] It was their instinct to economise on labour. Some kinds of labour were not cheap. Skilled stevedores, who packed export cargoes, made up to 36*s*. a week. The close corporation of the apprenticed watermen and lightermen—England's surviving guild—could take care of itself. The Surrey-side timber porters, carrying great weights up springy planks to the summits of growing piles of deals, were powerful fellows who commanded consideration. So did the less skilful but sturdy grain porters. Every dock and wharf had some decently paid permanent men. But below all these came the casuals, the mere dockers, graded at the docks though not at the wharves into 'preferables' and 'generals', taken on by foremen or contractors for the job and paid, formerly 4*d*., now generally 5*d*., in a few cases 6*d*. an hour, with a 'plus'—a bonus arbitrarily divided—for some classes of cargo. It was a quarrel about a 'plus' on August 13 which started the strike.

[1] "The South Metropolitan Gas Co. and the Gasworkers' Union", *Economist*, Dec. 7, 1889.

[2] The account in Webb, *History of Trade Unionism*, p. 389, makes the affair rather more condensed and dramatic in August than apparently it was.

[3] I could find no reference in *The Times*. The more industrially minded *Manchester Guardian* had a useful note from its London correspondent on Aug. 20.

[4] Above, pp. 380–1.

With business on the river stagnant or dwindling, dockers' employment had become even more irregular. As the last resort of London's failures it was always heavily overcrowded. But at the moment, in the trade revival of 1888–9, it was fairly brisk. Wages generally were going up and even well-paid river-side workers were ready for a wage-fight in a good joint cause. Their attitude towards the casuals who struggled at dock gates for the chance of earning 5*d*. an hour was undoubtedly generous; but they had their own sectional objectives, reasonably enough. Better pay with more regular work for competent dockers, though as cool economists pointed out it might well mean less work for the more wretched casuals, would improve every efficient man's takings.

The dockers' demands, put into shape by a committee which contained several experienced trade-unionist stevedores, were: "the tanner", 6*d*. an hour and 8*d*. for overtime; no contracting or piece-work; and no hiring for less than four hours' pay. These were Middlesex terms. The tanner did not greatly interest the more specialised and better paid Surrey men. Many of them handled timber by the piece—the quicker up the plank the more pay—and meant to go on doing this. In the end they had their own committee and their own settlement.[1]

For five weeks London river was paralysed. The Socialists from outside, led by Burns, Mann and Tillett, who had stirred and tried to organise the dockers before the strike, now worked hard for victory. The public was sympathetic. Trade unions and middle class sympathisers subscribed; but the bulk of the subscription—£30,800 out of £48,000[2]—came, amazingly enough, from Australia. Without Australia the men could hardly have held out or won. At the last it was the conciliatory diplomacy of Cardinal Manning which smoothed the way to settlement, in September. Substantially the men got their terms: as from November 4, the 6*d*. and 8*d*.; contract work to be reformed and the plus equally divided; and no man to be taken on except for special afternoon jobs for less than a 2*s*. job. A Union with a reputed membership of 30,000 had been built up; but even sympathetic watchers noted, what the less sympathetic had

[1] These paragraphs are based almost entirely on Smith, H. Llewellyn and Nash, Vaughan, *The Story of the Dockers' Strike*, 1889. This is the only account of a nineteenth-century strike by observers who were at once well-informed, sympathetic, and critical. It is so good that perhaps I, and previous writers, have given more space to the strike than its historical importance merits.

[2] *The Annual Register*, 1889.

foreseen, that the lowest class casuals would be worse off than ever, squeezed out by the better organised, better paid, more really preferable body of workers which any process of what came to be known later as decasualisation of labour tends to build up.[1]

"For almost, if not quite, the first time", a detached contemporary wrote, "the representatives of the skilled workmen showed a readiness to throw in their lot with...unskilled labour...and for quite the first time the sympathies of the middle classes at home, and even in the colonies, were with the men and against the masters."[2] But when, a year later, the Southampton dockers tried to consolidate the trade-union position by striking to get rid of non-union labour there was no such sympathy, and they lost decisively.[3] Their case lacked the pathetic London appeal, and they seemed to be fighting not for bread but for privilege.

Besides, the peak of industrial and commercial activity was passing. Wage-rates in general were still going up in 1891, but so was unemployment. With 1892 the rates began to fall, the unemployment to increase. The so-called New Unionism—more pugnacious, less respectable, more interested in the victory of principles than in insurance benefits, more socialistic—was in the ascendant in the trade-union sky. The president of the Trade Union Congress of 1890, a bourgeois chronicler had noted, was "more Socialistic in his leanings than any of his predecessors in the chair":[4] he wanted to nationalise land, mines and railways, and to have more labour representation in Parliament. He was a symbolic figure. The first recorded strike of civil servants, London post-office clerks, in 1891, though it lasted only a week before they "made their submission, was significant". There would have been some strikes on the falling market in any event; but the new influences made them much more likely, likeliest of all among the miners with their tradition of very elastic wage-rates.

Strikes began, on a large scale, on March 12, 1892, when all work ceased in Durham—after a sharp fall in the price of coal.[5] Wages, which in 1891 had been some 40 per cent. above the level of 1888, must come down, said the coal-owners. The miners would neither negotiate nor accept arbitration; they even withdrew the engine men, and water began to rise in the pits. Their

[1] Smith and Nash, *op. cit.* p. 164; anticipated by the less sympathetic *Economist* of Aug. 31.

[2] *The Annual Register*, as above.

[3] *Ibid.* 1890.

[4] *Ibid.* 1890.

[5] Welbourne, *The Miners' Unions*, p. 272.

apparent object was to keep wages at their 1891 peak, and as the world lay this was unattainable. They fought on week after week. "They had drawn their dividends from the stores. They had sold their shares. Their children were dependent on charity...."[1] By May they were ready to accept a $7\frac{1}{2}$ per cent. reduction of wages; then one of 10 per cent. which had been the original figure of the owners. It was the owners who stiffened this time. Prices had fallen further and they wanted $13\frac{1}{2}$. When the men, obviously beaten, asked for arbitration, which they themselves had refused at the start, it was refused to them. Now both sides had shown their unreason, and now it was that Bishop Westcott called both sides to consider peace. He induced the owners on June 1 to be satisfied with their original 10 per cent.—"solely on the grounds of the...prevailing distress", they said.[2] Early in the following year the revived Joint Committee of owners and men, for which he had worked, gave them another 5 per cent.

In Northumberland, steered by Thomas Burt the first British miner to become a Right Honourable, the men accepted a moderate wage reduction without fighting. A slight rise early in 1893 stirred Burt's hopes and those of John Wilson, the sobered leader of the Durham men, who became if not a Right Honourable yet the Chairman of a County Council, and of the Bishop who was thinking always and only of social peace. Half-way through 1893 the price and wage-fall was resumed; but these men kept the sullen and weakened North Country quiet.

War was transferred that year to the Federated Area, in which the Miners' Federation pledged to the 8-hour day and the living wage was dominant. It now included every important field up to the Tees, except South Wales, and had its fighting headquarters in Lancashire and Yorkshire.[3] The point directly in dispute was the same as elsewhere—the owners' demand, delayed because they served inland markets, for a sharp wage reduction such as the North had been forced to accept;[4] but, as might have been expected in the Federated Area, the fight was really for that thing so desirable and so hard to determine, the living wage. Was the wage of 1888, to which no one proposed to return, not live-on-able? Was a living wage necessarily the same thing as the best figure yet reached? The men inclined to

[1] Welbourne, *op. cit.* p. 281.

[2] *Ibid.* p. 284.

[3] Cp. p. 339 above.

[4] The account in *The Annual Register* for 1893 is full and good: there is also some account in the *Economist*, *Comm. Hist.* 1893.

the latter view. They wished to retain the wage of 1891. Their financial position was weak but they were stubborn. Through the late summer and the autumn they held out, four months in all. There was unaccustomed tension over a great part of industrial England; miners wandering into suburban places where they had not often been seen;[1] fears of violence usually quite groundless; a solitary clash with the troops at Featherstone—two men killed and, among a people little used to killing, never forgotten.[2]

When winter fuel began to be needed, in November, the Government decided to promote a settlement. Settlement was bound to come soon in any case, and the main business of the accomplished aristocratic conciliator, Lord Rosebery, was to bring it about with a minimum of bitterness. The men were to go back to work at the old rate until February 1, 1894. (With the winter demand and the depleted stocks, prices to permit of this for the cold weeks from November 17, the date of the settlement, were reasonably secure.) Machinery for conciliation and collective bargaining was to be re-established.[3] This did not prevent the further drop of coal prices and wages that the slackened industrial demand and the still falling level of general prices carried with them; but the bottom of the miners' wage-rate trough for the country as a whole, reached in 1896, was a full 16 per cent. above the 1887 bottom of the last trough, and the cost of living had fallen perceptibly in the interval. From 1896, first slowly then precipitately, miners' wages mounted to the peak of 1900; and there were no more widespread strikes either in the Federated Area or in the North. It was during an early stage of the rise, in September 1898, that, after long and not unfriendly industrial diplomacy, arrangements for high minimum and restrained maximum rates were entered into in the various subdivisions of the Federated Area.[4]

The South Welshmen, eager and ill-organised, had been out for four months that year, and only went back to work in September. It was a mystery to the outside observer that they could endure so long. They had a feeling, on the whole justifiable,

[1] In one of which my home was at that time. The miners worked only a few miles away but were foreigners in the suburb which, so far as it had an industry, was textile.

[2] For Sir George Elliot's plan for a national coal-mine amalgamation, published while the strike was in progress, in September, see p. 220 above.

[3] Cp. Webb, S. and B., *Industrial Democracy*, p. 225.

[4] The date was Sept. 29: *The Annual Register*, 1898. And cp. p. 480 above.

that they did not do so well out of their trade as other miners. They had learnt to distrust the sliding-scale arrangement under which they worked. Wages, they felt, might well slide upwards with prices indefinitely; but they should never go below a "living" basis for the hewer: the basis put forward was 1*s.* a ton. If prices would not permit of this, then, it was suggested, outputs should be cut down until they could—a reliance on the monopoly position of Welsh steam-coal in world markets which may at that time have been justified. But all was vain. Endurance had its limits. The terms of settlement were the owners' terms. The old sliding-scale agreement, modified by a "very slight and imperfect"[1] concession to the principle of the minimum wage, was revived and extended to January 1, 1903. This yielded a 5 per cent. rise at once, which was some compensation, but would have come without the strike. And it was accompanied by the apparently vindictive, and certainly unwise, abolition of the prized monthly holiday—"Mabon's day".[2] A dictated peace big with future wars. But until 1900 the scale slid up easily.

The falling prices, the tendency to a fall in wages, and the rising unemployment of 1892–3 had brought not only two coal strikes but that rare and formidable thing a long strike of the highly organised and resistant unions of the Lancashire cotton spinners and card-room operatives. Mill-owners asked for a 5 per cent. reduction in wages. The unions refused, and some 15,000,000 spindles stopped on November 7, 1892.[3] They did not turn again for twenty weeks, until the conclusion of that all-night sitting in an inn at Brooklands, at the very end of March 1893, which became one of the most familiar, and is one of the best documented, events in the Labour history of the late nineteenth century.[4] The Brooklands Agreement gave textile wage-rates—in which those of cotton were dominant—that smooth stability which marked them during the next twenty years. In spite of the great strike, it will be noted that there was after all a decline in 1892–3, although not of 5 per cent.[5]

Strikes usually vain when strong forces were at work to drive wages down, and strikes, often successful, to secure the wage-earner's share of swiftly rising markets had become familiar,

[1] *The Annual Register*, which gives a full and impartial account of this strike.

[2] The name is from William Abraham (known as 'Mabon') the leader under whom this concession had been won.

[3] *Economist, Comm. Hist.* 1892.

[4] Webb, *Industrial Democracy*, p. 200; above, p. 341.

[5] Diagram, p. 468 above.

and might almost be counted on. But important strikes in a wage trough, or at a time of slowly improving wage-rates and employment, were less likely. When they occurred they could usually be traced to some defect in industrial organisation. The great strike of 1895 in the machine-made-boot industry for example, affecting "practically the entire industry from one end of the Kingdom to the other"[1] arose out of the defective working of a new, most elaborate and apparently hopeful system of local conciliation boards, with a national conference, local umpires to be called in when the boards could not agree and a national umpire, Lord James of Hereford. The industry was young. Points at issue were incredibly technical. Umpires who could understand them were likely to be connected with the trade and so open to suspicion of bias. There were frictions, long irritating delays, refusals to abide by decisions, complaints—from the employers' side—that issues and principles which they supposed the boards and conferences were not meant to handle were in fact being handled. The publicity of the proceedings was all against compromise and the healthy working of secret diplomacy. After two years, in 1894, the federated manufacturers seceded; the strike followed; and in the agreement brought about by the mediation of the Board of Trade on April 19, 1895, the national conference was dropped and certain important matters were excluded from the jurisdiction of the boards. Reduced to the function of local technical adjustment, these worked well from that time forward; and soon wages began to rise.[2]

The Engineers and Plumbers of Tyneside had produced idleness and want for three months in 1892 because they could not agree "as to which of them should fit up two-and-a-half inch iron piping";[3] and it was defects in the organisation of the Amalgamated Society of Engineers—though not such a childish blunder as that of 1892—which gave the great engineers' contest of 1897–8 its form and scope and disastrous issue.[4] Employers felt trade reviving and wanted to make the most of it. Wages were already rising. The Union would do nothing to revise practices and agreements which the employers said interfered with the introduction of new machinery and the maximisation

[1] Webb, *Industrial Democracy*, p. 187: above, pp. 341–2.

[2] This whole account is based mainly on *Industrial Democracy*: cp. pp. 341–2 above; and see the *Labour Gazette*, April–May, 1895.

[3] *Industrial Democracy*, p. 95.

[4] See above, p. 337 n. 2 and p. 341.

of efficiency. Friends of the unions have admitted that this contention was just.[1] The employers on their part came to think, if they had not always thought, that collective agreements were merely so many bars to progress. The almost complete absence of adequate central control in the A.S.E. allowed a group of relatively subordinate sections, the London branches, to bring on a fight by an ill-timed, though not unreasonable, demand for an 8-hour day. In July the lock-out or strike began: like so many industrial disputes it is described in both ways, and it partook of both characters. Employers wanted change—towards individual bargaining: working engineers wanted the unreformed *status quo*, plus, in so far as they really agreed with London, the 8-hour day.

The wide-scattered and only half-organised employers, with their often divergent interests, held together unexpectedly well. They put pressure on one another to come in or to stand fast, not by picketing or outward violence, but quietly over dinner-tables and in hotels, as employers can.[2] The men "put themselves fatally wrong with public opinion by not recognising the need for maximising productivity and by not proposing their own way of attaining this end".[3] The A.S.E. and the smaller unions which supported it spent most of their reserve funds to no purpose and then surrendered almost unconditionally; but to effect the settlement "the employers found themselves driven to a system of Collective Bargaining even more systematic and national than before prevailed",[4] the bargain by which their terms were accepted.

And as wages went on rising until 1902, with employment either "good" or "very good" all the time,[5] the A.S.E. soon filled up its fighting chest; and it enlisted more recruits than ever—but it did not modify its organisation or set up an efficient headquarters staff, such as the cotton-spinners had.

It was in those years of maximum employment that the South Wales miners indicated by a strike their feeling that they were not getting a fair proportion of prosperity. The feeling was shared by railwaymen, in South Wales and beyond. Railway work was regular and much sought after. Therefore wages tended

[1] Webb, *History of Trade Unionism* (1902 ed.), pp. xvii, xix.

[2] An employer who had been subjected to pressure in this way once explained the method to me. If my memory is correct, it was his own dinner table. I have no doubt that his was not an isolated case.

[3] Webb, *History of Trade Unionism*, p. xix.

[4] *Ibid.*

[5] The classifications of the Labour Department of the Board of Trade.

to be low; and as the companies were ponderous and cautious, wage changes were delayed and few.[1] Hitherto most of the companies had treated the not very powerful trade-union movement among the rank and file with suspicion or contempt. An active trade unionist might find himself removed—"transported" his sympathisers called it[2]—to some remote station: general managers normally refused to negotiate with anyone but their own employees. Recently however, in 1897, the North-Eastern officials—following earlier precedents in the history of their line—had concluded a settlement with representatives of the A.S.R.S. who were not in their employ. The settlement followed an unimportant strike and an important award by that great arbitrator of the 'nineties, Lord James of Hereford.[3] In 1900 the Great Eastern men threatened a strike, and gained something by the threat; but the only accomplished strike that year was one of ten days, undertaken against the advice of Richard Bell, the active secretary of the A.S.R.S., by the men of the Taff Vale Railway on the coalfield of Glamorgan. In itself quite unimportant, the strike had unusually heavy consequences for the life of railwaymen, trade unionists, and the nation.[4]

For the Company sued the Union for damages; and after the decision granting damages had been reversed on appeal, it was reaffirmed by the House of Lords in July 1901. Damages had been awarded against trade unionists but never before against a trade union. The prevalent legal view had been that, since the legislation of the 'seventies, a trade union, "neither a corporation nor an individual",[5] although it could own property and act by agents, could not sue or be sued in a court of law. The Lords Justices of Appeal now reversed this presumption and the anomalous position resulting from it. "If the Legislature has created a thing which can own property, which can employ servants and which can inflict injury, it must be taken to have impliedly given the power to make it liable in a court", Lord Halsbury declared;[6] and Lord Macnaghten "saw nothing

[1] Cp. p. 351 above.

[2] Alcock, *Fifty Years of Railway Trade Unionism*, p. 275.

[3] Tomlinson, *History of the North Eastern Railway*, pp. 748–50 gives the history and the precedents. Cp. Alcock, *op. cit.* p. 292.

[4] *The Annual Register*, 1900. The strike has, quite properly, been buried under the weight of legal and political literature bearing on the decisions.

[5] Farwell, L.J., in the *Taff Vale Case*: Schloesser, H. H., and Clark, W. S., *The Legal Position of Trade Unions* (1912), p. 17.

[6] *Ibid.* p. 19. See *R.C. on Trade Disputes and Trade Combination* (1906), Q. 19, 27.

contrary to principle or contrary to the provisions of the Trade Union Acts in holding that a trade union may be sued by its registered name".[1]

Three years earlier another decision which became notorious (the final decision in Allen *v.* Flood) had seemed to endanger that right of the trade unionist most prized, most difficult of definition, and most easily overstepped, to "picket peacefully" the places at which a strike has been declared.[2] Judged in complete political detachment, the right to picket, of Brown to argue with Jones to induce him not to work for Robinson, appears stronger than the right of a now fairly powerful—if once weak—property-owning body to inflict through its agents injuries, which when inflicted by an individual would be tortious, and yet not be liable for damages. The chance therefore that Allen *v.* Flood would lead to an unjust limitation of trade-union rights was less than the chance that the Taff Vale case would bring with it a limitation of what for a quarter of a century had certainly been held to be justifiable trade-union privileges. But both decisions were calculated to strengthen the determination of trade unionists and their friends to secure more influence on law-making. They swung, as they had more than once swung before, from "the method of collective bargaining" to the "method of legal enactment".[3]

As far back as 1893 had occurred what a participant has called "the most important political event of the nineteenth century",[4] the formation of the Independent Labour Party. In 1899 the Trade Union Congress had agreed to join with this party and other Socialist organisations to secure a more adequate representation of Labour interests in Parliament. The result was the Labour Representation Committee, at first a poor weak thing: "in February 1901", Snowden wrote, "I well remember the feeling of despondency which prevailed. It looked as if this new effort was going to share the fate of previous attempts to secure the direct representation of Labour."[5] But later, as the possible consequences of the Taff Vale decision came home to trade unionists—though damages were sought and awarded only in

[1] Quoted in Milne-Bailey, *Trade Union Documents*, p. 452. All the decisions applied only to registered trade unions.

[2] See Schloesser and Smith, *op. cit.* pp. vii, 72, for the various decisions and the law of picketing.

[3] Terms coined by Mr and Mrs Webb.

[4] Viscount Snowden, *An Autobiography*, I. 53.

[5] *Ibid.* p. 94.

South Wales[1]—the representation movement slowly acquired momentum. It was helped by the unpopularity of Joseph Chamberlain's tariff proposals of 1903 among politically-minded wage-earners brought up to associate tariffs with "the little loaf": they had been called upon to resist them "as they would a malignant disease", and not to forget the days when "their fathers and mothers were almost starved".[2] To the end of 1905, the result in Parliament was only four avowed Labour members; but after the general election of 1906 there were twenty-nine.[3] Of these twenty-three were nominees of the Trade Unions.

In the years between the Taff Vale decision and the election of 1906 wage-rates remained all but stationary except in coal-mining, where their fall was sharp enough to pull down the national average by several points. Employment slackened up to 1904, but never became really bad. The rise in the cost of living since 1900 was as yet very slight. The shadows of Taff Vale fell across the way of the trade-union leader. His following did not grow. Trade-union membership for the whole country, after rising from 1,500,000 to just over 2,000,000 in 1900, got no higher until 1906. None of the labour disputes was of magnitude; none raised great issues or riveted public attention.[4] But below the surface currents were beginning to run, not strongly but just perceptibly, towards revolutionary methods and contempt for that parliamentary action to forward which the Labour Representation Committee existed. Their principal sources were abroad—in the American Socialist Labour Party, led at that time by a man of "flint-like orthodoxy", who "believed literally in every word Marx had written";[5] and in the Syndicalist move-

[1] An important point emphasised by Beer, M., *A History of British Socialism*, II. 322.

[2] From a Manifesto quoted in Alcock, *op. cit.* p. 349.

[3] Snowden, *op. cit.* II. 119. The larger figure (53) given in Ensor, *England 1870–1914*, p. 437, is due to the inclusion of a group whom Snowden the Puritan rejected, known at the time as the Lib.-Labs.

[4] There was a rather important strike in the Grimsby trawling fleet, in 1901, which lasted many weeks: *The Annual Register*, 1901. But see the diagram, p. 499 below.

[5] Beer, *op. cit.* II. 355 n. The man was Daniel De Leon, an academic Socialist, whom Beer describes as "one of the straightest Marxists I had ever come across". The word 'straightest' (? 'straitist') is a little ambiguous. Ensor, *op. cit.* p. 438, also discusses this foreign influence. For France and the French literature see Levine, L., *The Labour Movement in France, a Study in Revolutionary Syndicalism* (New York, 1912).

ment of France which, in exalting the economic factor above the political, sneered at parliaments and preached the coming revolutionary rule of trade unions—syndicates. All this was very remote from the spirit of the new British parliamentary Labour group, whose most pungent and convincing speaker, a man who had never handled hammer or sickle, found his trade-union colleagues "a very commonsense lot"; and who wrote towards the end of his career "I have never read Karl Marx".[1]

Early in the life of the new Parliament, a great Liberal majority, with support from a Labour group whose weight in a division was important for the first time, passed the short Trade Disputes Act of 1906 (6 Ed. VII, c. 47). Clause 2 empowered any person or persons "to attend at or near a house or place where a person resides or works or carries on business or happens to be", in order to persuade peacefully "any person to work or abstain from working". So, in cases of picketing, only the simple word "peacefully" was open to judicial interpretation. Clause 4 declared that "an action against a trade union, whether of workmen or masters...in respect of any tortious act alleged to have been committed on behalf of the trade union, shall not be entertained by any court". Nothing could be more precise; and masters are left on a level with men. Neither the Amalgamated Society of Engineers nor the Licensed Victuallers Association, nor any of the shyer masters' associations which took the trouble to register as trade unions,[2] could from now on be convicted of tort, whatever they did; for evidence would not be heard. The historian knows and appreciates those social and political forces which produced this result—the sincere conviction that the unions had been unfairly attacked; the belief that, if they were to function properly, they must retain the position which had in practice been theirs from 1876 to 1901; the weight of the trade-union vote—but the result must seem to him the more anomalous, he need not say unjust, with each stage in the growing strength of "trade unions whether of workmen or masters".

The Amalgamated Railway Servants, secured now against blows such as they had suffered from the Taff Vale Company, growing fast since 1905, and very conscious of the inferiority of status which the refusal of most of the Companies to recognise

[1] Viscount Snowden, *Autobiography*, I. 62, 90.

[2] Above, pp. 302 *sqq.*

them carried with it, set out at the opening of the busy—the over-busy—year 1907 to secure by a national movement improved hours and wages, but above all recognition. Discussion went on for months, mainly through manifestoes in the press and pronouncements by Railway Chairmen. Among these, Lord Claud Hamilton of the Great Eastern reiterated opinions already familiar about the proper position of servants, and Alfred Baldwin of the Great Western "objected to the Amalgamated Society being allowed to interfere between the directors and their employés";[1] only the North-Eastern board held to the view which Edward Grey had stated shortly before he left its chair for the Foreign Office, at the end of 1905, that the other lines made a mistake in not letting "the men be represented by the man or men of their choice".[2] By the autumn, something like a general railway strike seemed imminent. But railways were under the Board of Trade where a supple, daring, negotiating mind was now in authority. Lloyd George stepped in and dominated his first Peace Congress. Late at night on November 6, by that last-minute agreement which the saving of the faces of negotiators in industrial disputes has made traditional—to the inconvenience of the public—both sides accepted the principle of boards of conciliation and arbitration. "The settlement", Richard Bell the railwaymen's leader explained to his constituents, "is not what we asked for, viz. recognition of our officials to negotiate on behalf of our members, but it is a tremendous advance";[3] for the method hitherto had been hierarchical—claims and grievances had to go up through heads of departments and so to the directors in an Olympian board-room, far above the praying hands.

A few days after this settlement, the Bank of England announced 7 per cent. for the first time since 1873 as a precautionary measure.[4] The American crisis had come. Trade was slackening, wholesale prices falling, unemployment increasing throughout the winter. Soon the more elastic wage-rates, with some of the less elastic, showed signs of contraction. At the very beginning of 1908, proposals for wage-cuts brought out the shipwrights and engineers of the North-East coast. In May there was trouble again there, which extended to the shipbuilding

[1] Alcock, *op. cit.* p. 376.

[2] Trevelyan, *Grey of Fallodon*, p. 86; cp. the narrative in *The Annual Register*, 1907.

[3] Alcock, *op. cit.* p. 388.

[4] See diagram, p. 17, and p. 57 above.

industries of the Clyde, Barrow and the Mersey. In the autumn came that now rare thing a strike of Lancashire cotton-spinners and card-room operatives against a threatened reduction. They were out for more than a month, but failed to prevent an equally rare thing—a fall in textile wage-rates, though a very slight one, that left them in 1909–11 still 7·1 per cent. above the level of 1900. But miners' rates even in 1907 had not got back to the abnormal 1900 level, and by 1909 were nearly 12 per cent. below it. For trade unions 1908 was a year of resistance, with losses of work through strike or lock-out which were relatively serious; 1909 a year of temporary acquiescence in not very serious defeat, and a year in which a minimum of work was so lost. In both years, if the trade-union world be taken as a whole, more time was lost through ordinary unemployment than in any year since 1886.[1]

Late in 1909 came what to fighting trade unionists, though by no means to all, was the provocative decision of the House of Lords in the long drawn-out and complex case of Osborne and the Amalgamated Society of Railway Servants.[2] In 1907 Osborne and the Walthamstow branch of the Society, of which he was secretary, had objected to levies for political purposes, that is for labour representation, imposed by the Society as a whole. They went to the courts to settle the principle. By the Court of Appeal and by the Lords their objection was upheld, mainly on the ground that the powers of a trade union or other statutory corporation "must be expressly conferred by or derived by reasonable implication from"[3] the Act or Acts under which it is constituted; and that in this case the relevant Acts neither conferred nor implied any right to levy political contributions.[4]

Trade had been quickening some time before the Osborne judgment. Employment was improving steadily. So trade-union leaders entered 1910 and those years of high economic activity which reached to 1914 with a legal grievance, a following all of

[1] See the diagram, p. 29 above. By this time strikes of any size were regularly reported in *The Annual Register*: before the Dock Strike of 1889 they were not. It is an interesting reflection of the changed attitude and interests of the *Register's* public.

[2] For which see Schloesser and Smith, *The Legal Position of Trade Unions*. For railway trade-union opinion on it, and on Osborne, see Alcock, *op. cit.* p. 336.

[3] *Ibid.* p. 20.

[4] A decision reversed by an Act of 1912–13 (2 and 3 Geo. V, c. 30) on the *Objects and Power of Trade Unions*. In 1912 the 100 principal Trade Unions paid £469 from their Political Funds; in 1914, £20,000; in 1924, £240,000.

whom had suffered less or more from wage-cuts and unemployment, a group of men of their own sort in Parliament, a conjuncture which would justify and facilitate struggles to regain what had been lost, and behind all that ancient source of rational discontent and every form of Socialism—the still conspicuously unequal distribution of British wealth. Eighty or ninety years back early Socialists, just beginning to be so described, had made use of Patrick Colquhoun's estimate that only a quarter of the national income went to the wage-earners.[1] Now those who did not go beyond the diagrammatic frontispiece of a book which ran through three editions in its first six months during 1905–6, Money's *Riches and Poverty*, were told that 38,000,000 of "the poor" got a little more than a half of that income; 3,750,000 of "the comfortable" one-seventh; and 1,250,000 of "the rich" just over one-third.[2] Had Colquhoun not been forgotten, the improvement in the estimate from the point of view of "the poor" might have been welcomed; but the balance remained unequal enough to give driving force to any claims made on their behalf, and to the author's demands, far from original but for that very reason all the more easily received, for more progressive taxation and for the nationalisation of industries whose continuance in private hands encouraged the existing unequal distribution. Six years later, old age pensions having been established and every sort of device for bettering the condition and share of "the poor" discussed, a professed economist was for the first time analysing in a series of chapters the problems of "Direct Transferences of Resources from the Relatively Rich to the Relatively Poor".[3]

Throughout 1910 and 1911 employment improved but wage-rates lagged. Their upward movement was barely perceptible: in some trades there was no movement at all, and in mining there was even a slight fall during 1911. On the railways, the natural sluggishness of the great companies in wage matters was increased by their extreme reluctance to sanction wage concessions which might force them to go to the Railway and Canal Commissioners for leave to make any consequential increase in railway rates.[4] The land lying thus; the Taff being a Welsh

[1] Vol. II. 477.

[2] Money's figures were: poor, £880,000,000; comfortable, £245,000,000; rich, £585,000,000.

[3] Pigou, A. C., *Wealth and Welfare* (1912), Part III, chs. 8–12.

[4] Cp. p. 361 above.

Vale, and Welsh colliers as well as Welsh railwaymen having been cast in damages under the decision named from it; the Welsh miner and the mixed immigrants who worked with him being of inflammable temper, their organisation new and defective; doctrines of direct action, the 'lightning strike' and fighting for its own destructive sake being preached by the revolutionary minority; the Welsh mining village being what it was and is—industrial warfare was more probable than industrial peace on the South Welsh coalfield, and might break out almost anywhere.

Early in 1910 a Welsh strike over the application of the Miners' Eight-Hour Day was rather narrowly averted. There were local troubles at Welsh collieries in the course of the summer; and in November 30,000 men were out and the troops were called in.[1] The last was one of those ugly conflicts which had—and have—been specially common in Glamorgan. In other districts and trades—the North-East coast and the North-Eastern Railway, the Clyde, the Lancashire cotton industry even—there were partial, angry, inconsequent strikes up and down the year, but mainly in its later months. Only one of them—the lock-out of the North-East coast boiler-makers, resulting from a breach of agreement by the men—led to a long stoppage; so that the numbers concerned in strikes and lock-outs and the amount of working time lost in consequence that year were, from the national point of view, still inconsiderable. This was partly because the judicious trade-union leader does not declare war lightly, nor until he is sure both of the pressure from below and of an upward swing of trade and employment which will make his strategical position strong. But one of the troubles of these years was the spirit of revolt against such judicious leadership, a spirit against which Arthur Henderson protested to no great purpose at the Trade Union Congress in the autumn.[2]

Even in 1911, when clashes became more frequent and angrier, the main cause for anxiety was the spirit shown, not the amount of time wasted in fighting. On a rising market—there was no doubt about the rise in 1911—much time is not often lost. Employers want to get on with their work and are usually quick to make terms. When the market is falling they are often ready

[1] When the name of Tonypandy became as notorious as that of Featherstone had been in 1893: *The Annual Register*, 1910; Ensor, *England* 1870–1914, pp. 439–40.

[2] Ensor, *op. cit.* p. 439.

to save, even for prolonged spells, that circulating wage capital which they are determined not to pay out at the old rate if they can help it. A further reason why relatively little time was lost on fighting in 1911 was that the first part of the year was quiet. It was suggested at the time, has been repeated since, and is in itself probable, that an element of ill-temper and unreasonableness in the world of industry after the equinox was due to the abnormal heat of the summer of 1911.[1] Men working and sweating in August cities lacked self-control. But there was

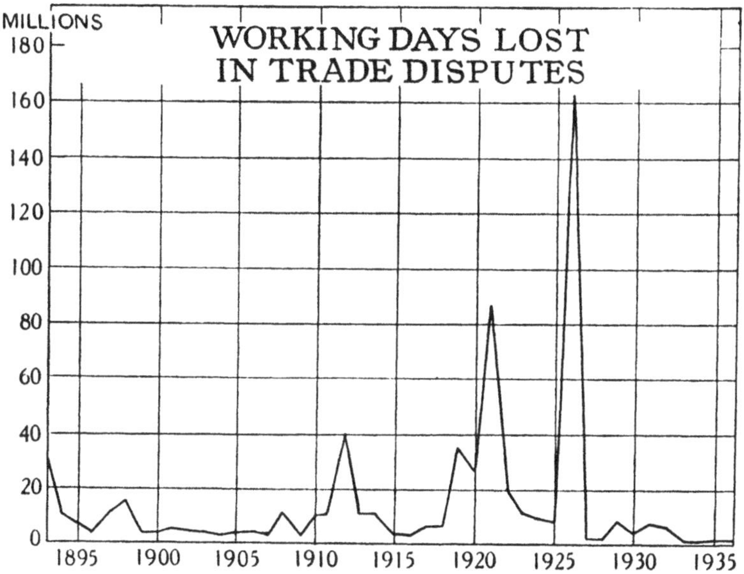

reason as well as unreason in it all. Apart from any wider grievances, the wage-lag persisted; and, as 1912 and 1913 showed, the state of trade and prices justified rising wages.

The strikes that fired the heather ended just after the equinox. Patient seamen and firemen at the chief ports struck on June 14 for better wages and the higher overtime pay usual in industry. They got what they wanted within a fortnight. A month later the London dockers very naturally tried to improve the basic "tanner" that they had won twenty-two years before. When they got their 7*d*., on July 27, from the Port of London Authority, the better-paid 7*d*. men of the shipping companies demanded 8*d*., struck for ten days and got it, in the heat-wave of early August.

[1] *The Annual Register*, 1911, based on the press of the year: Ensor, *op. cit.* p. 442, where some temperatures are given.

The London carmen were out; Glasgow tramwaymen; London taximen; Manchester carters; and a group of negro workmen at Cardiff. In London there was even a short schoolboys' strike against homework,[1] forerunner of 'student' movements in other lands twenty years later. At Liverpool and Manchester the docks were not pacified so easily as in London. The Liverpool waterside people have never been gentle: there are many Irish among them. Now the troops had to be called in and blood was shed.

That day (August 15) the unions of the railwaymen decided to risk a national strike—"our first", as their historian writes with a touch of militant pride.[2] "Liverpool being the storm centre, the Executives of the four railway unions met at Liverpool",[3] and heard all the local atmospherics. Railwaymen had been dismissed there for improper striking. Judgment might have been cooler at York. There was the wage-lag and a good deal of past history to justify firm policies; but the reasons assigned—the dismissals and the alleged dishonest action of the companies in connection with the agreement of 1907—half suggest the August temper. The twenty-four hours' ultimatum suggests it more clearly. So does the rhetoric of the manifesto to the men—"to-day the railwaymen are worse than slaves".[4]

Two days later the leaders saw the Prime Minister. He was preoccupied with international politics and very stiff. He felt and said that the Government could not allow the transport of the country to be paralysed. So the strike began—not quite universally; it was weak in the South-West; but almost universally in the industrial Midlands and the North. Then Lloyd George was called in—it was less than a month since his Agadir speech—and having, as is believed, discussed with both parties things political and economic, he arranged a settlement at a typical settlement hour, Saturday, August 19, 11 p.m.[5] The men went back; the strikers were reinstated; no one was to be penalised for breach of contract; the machinery of the 1907 settlement was to be speeded up, and a special commission of enquiry was to be appointed by the Government. Nothing was put in writing about recognition; but the negotiations formed a precedent. The companies had of necessity been moving towards recognition since 1907; now they were in effect there. But the

[1] Duly reported in *The Annual Register*.

[2] Alcock, *op. cit.* p. 428.

[3] *Ibid.* p. 424.

[4] Given in full in Alcock, *op. cit.* p. 428.

[5] Cp. p. 327 above.

prompt and moderate settlement hardly fits the slave talk of the manifesto. "Consider it, as it was for the moment, as a drawn battle", the men's historian writes.[1]

It was in 1912 that loss of work through industrial warfare became abnormal. The miners took the field and, battle once joined, it had never been the miners' way to break off action quickly. They took a grim pride in their staying power. Late in 1911 arrangements had been made by which the Miners' Federation could declare a strike that would be national. In January 1912—when a truce had just been arranged after a short winter lock-out in the Lancashire cotton industry—they held a ballot on the issue of minimum wage or strike. Only in Durham was there a really important no-strike minority;[2] and the strike was announced for February 29. Government suggested a way out. The English coal-owners accepted. The Welsh, the Scots, and the Miners' Federation refused. So on March 1 the strike began; and by March 11 over 800,000 miners and perhaps a million and a quarter of men in other industries were idle. It was in these circumstances that the Government introduced that Miners' Minimum Wage Act into which Asquith stubbornly refused to put a precise figure: he would not go beyond district conferences and, if necessary, an official decision, or arbitration, of the local minimum.[3] Even before the Bill was passed, on March 28, there had been sporadic attempts of minority miners to resume work. When the whole body were balloted on acceptance of the Act there was only a small majority for refusal on a 75 per cent. poll;[4] and on Easter Eve (6 April) the Federation Executive decided to call the strike off. Some of the fighting men in Lancashire and Yorkshire resented their decision; and the resumption of work was not smooth but was soon general. Very little coal had been raised in Britain for five weeks.

It was a year of national, or would-be national, movements. There was now a Transport Workers' Federation of nearly thirty societies.[5] Late in May it called a London strike, on such

[1] Alcock, *op. cit.* p. 433.

[2] The figures were: for the strike, 446,000; against, 116,000. In Durham: for, 57,000; against, 29,000. They are in *The Annual Register*, 1912, which again gives a full story; and cp. Jevons, H. S., *The British Coal Trade*, pp. 520–65.

[3] Cp. p. 429 above.

[4] For refusal, 244,000: for acceptance, 201,000. The leaders assumed that the numerous abstainers from the poll were willing to accept but not to say so. See Robertson, D. H., "A Narrative of the Coal Strike", *E.J.* 1912.

[5] Dockers, lightermen, carmen, and the like, from a number of ports, with the Seamen's and Firemen's Union.

inadequate grounds that many members of these societies themselves resented it. Besides, transport workers—dockers, carmen, and the like—are rather easily replaced, and the Port of London Authority had a stiff-necked chairman, Kearley the Great Grocer, now Lord Devonport. He resisted all attempts at any settlement but that of surrender. An effort to bring out the men in other ports made on June 10 succeeded only in part: Liverpool refused absolutely, and work was not much interfered with in the other Northern, or in the Scottish and Irish, ports. Distress in London became grievous, though gifts to relieve it came from so high as the King and Queen.[1] The Government saw no way to intervene; and at the end of July, after prayer for the striking of Lord Devonport dead had been offered by Ben Tillett on Tower Hill, the strike was called off.[2] Union transport workers returned to scuffle with the free labourers who had helped to their defeat. Most of them had the satisfaction of getting back their jobs, for they were the better men.

Mass strike movements were over for the time; but neither 1913 nor 1914 was a quiet year. About as much time was lost on fighting in each of them as in 1910 or 1911, though far less than in 1912.[3] In June–July 1913 came that rare thing a strike of agricultural labourers, of a fortnight's duration—not in East Anglia but in Lancashire. A rather long strike of Birmingham light-metal workers was ended at the same time by the concession of a minimum wage—of 23*s*. a week. In August, London painters and decorators, groups of wage-earners in government offices, London bakers, and the china-clay workers of Cornwall were out; their most serious grievance being in each case the wage-lag, though there were others. These overlapped a long drawn out and more revolutionary struggle—centring about the Irish Transport Workers Union—that went on in Dublin through the summer and autumn. It interested the British world of labour profoundly, but the only British strikes of any importance connected with it were unauthorised refusals of Welsh railwaymen to handle "tainted" Irish traffic.

[1] The London County Council, which had fed necessitous school-children in term time, refused to go on feeding them in the holidays.

[2] It was said, in *The Annual Register* for 1912, p. 194, that the crowd "did not take the prayer seriously; but Cunninghame Graham, who followed, approved of the prayer, remarking that he thought 'the Great Power was on strike too'".

[3] The statement of Ensor, *op. cit.* p. 444, that the transport workers' failure in 1912 "put an end for the time being to the strike-ferment in England" is perhaps too strong.

As Christmas drew near postal workers were threatening—but postponing over the Christmas rush—a strike for a wage-rise greater than one recently granted; while at Leeds volunteers were living in the gas and electricity works, stoking the furnaces, to break a strike of municipal employees. These episodes were fateful if of themselves rather small.

When 1914 opened the wage-lag had been nearly made up; and wages continued to rise until July, though more slowly than they had risen in 1912–13. But as the wage-lag was by no means the sole cause of industrial unrest and industrial war, so this comparatively satisfactory balance was not sufficient to end them. A good deal of time was lost in fighting on one industrial front and another before fighting of the other sort put a stop to it; and the enemies of Britain could suppose that economic discord would combine with Irish Civil War and an hysterical women's movement to keep her out of the mêlée, or to weaken her arm if she dared to enter it.

During these pugnacious years 1911–14 John Burnett's forecast of 1886, that although strikes had not yet been entirely superseded yet there was a general tendency in that direction, seemed unusually mistaken and remote.[1] In the year of maximum strife, 1912, 36·1 per cent. of the total expenditure of a hundred principal unions was on strike pay. But this was quite abnormal as was the whole amount expended that year.[2] In the decade 1892–1901, in spite of the New Unionism of the 'eighties with its fighting creed and of the many notable strikes, the percentage was only 19·4; and in the pacific decade 1901–10 it fell to 10·7.[3] The rest of the money paid out, averaging nearly £2,000,000 a year in the latter decade, went on unemployment pay (27·2 per cent.), sickness and accident pay (18·1), superannuation pay (13·5), funeral allowances (9·7) and administrative and general expenses. Payments of the friendly society type, with the vital unemployment pay, remained the basic financial liabilities of a union. Just as, on the average, not a great deal of time was spent in fighting, so not too much money was devoted to its support. But for the miners' tenacity in defence and the elasticity of miners' wages, both the abnormal figure of 1912 and the decade average figures would have been far smaller.

[1] Vol. II. 160.

[2] £4,350,000 as against £3,000,000 in 1911 and an average of £2,200,000 for 1901–10.

[3] *Report on Trade Unions*, 1902, p. xxv; *Ibid.* 1912, p. xliii.

Meanwhile the Friendly Societies proper had grown much quicker than the population, registering an increase of saving capacity and of the willingness to save. In 1885–7 the 'branchless' societies of the old fashioned type that had sprung from village clubs had reported more than 2,000,000 members; the great Orders—Oddfellows, Foresters, Shepherds and the rest—about 1,750,000; and the more commercial collecting societies, which specialised in provision for death, more than 3,000,000.[1] By 1910, the last year of the period for which statistics of all these classes are available and the year before National Insurance began to affect their activities, the figures stood at 3,854,000 for the 'branchless' societies; 2,783,000 for the Orders; and no less than 7,159,000 for the collecting societies. Every year hundreds of new societies, or new branches of the Orders, came into being.[2] There was also constant death. During 1912, when miners were not able to save, "in the manufacturing counties of the North nearly one-sixth of the total number of [branchless] Societies went out of existence".[3] But new societies or fresh recruitment, especially in the South, more than filled the gap; and even at the end of 1912 the total membership was well above that of 1910.

Since the consolidating Act of 1875 (38 and 39 Vict. c. 60) the legal, one might almost say the constitutional, position of the societies had been perfectly secure; and the administrative oversight of the Registrar under the law had done much to improve and standardise their practice. Four more Friendly Societies Acts, passed between 1886 and 1896, preceded the consolidating Act of that year (59 and 60 Vict. c. 25) which repealed them.[4] It was linked to a new law regulating the Collecting Societies and Industrial Assurance Companies, the former being now for the first time legally recognised as not of true friendly society type.[5] They differed in size and in spirit, in management and in finance.[6] When they were thus legally separated from the Friendly Societies, their average membership was over 90,000: in 1911 the two greatest among them, the Royal Liver and the Liverpool Victoria, contained more than two-thirds of the whole huge membership of over 7,000,000.[7] In spirit and management they

[1] Vol. II. 476.

[2] *Report of the Chief Registrar of Friendly Societies* for 1908, p. 149 (1909, LXXIX), for example, gives 299 new branches for the year.

[3] *Report* for 1912, p. 15 (1914, LXXVI).

[4] *Report* for 1896, p. 2 (1897, LXXXII).

[5] The Act is 59 and 60 Vict. c. 26.

[6] Cp. vol. II. 473 and p. 300 above.

[7] *Report* for 1911, pp. 92 *sqq.* (1912–13, LXXXI).

were akin to such profit-making Industrial Assurance Companies as the Prudential, with which they were now legally associated, and had not much in common with the Oddfellows, still less with the Philanthropic Order of True Ivorites, St David's Unity, of Wales, or the Achei Brith Brethren of the Covenant among the North London Jews. Of the 8*s*. 5*d*. which was the average member's annual payment to a Collecting Society in 1911, not less than 3*s*. 8*d*. went in collecting and management expenses.[1] In return the member got his burial money or whatever it might be. Apparently in his ignorance he thought the trouble-saving bargain worth his while; although, as at all times in the history of collecting and industrial insurance, his society's financial success depended far too much on his possible lapse—he began to subscribe; could not keep it up; and forfeited his claim.[2]

When the two types of society were legally distinguished in 1896 the average Friendly Society or branch of an Order (and in the Orders branches had a great, perhaps a too great, measure of autonomy) contained only 181 members: friendliness was a real possibility. The funds averaged £5 4*s*. 9*d*. per member: there had been substantial acts of saving. In the Collecting Societies the corresponding average was only 14*s*.[3] In spite of the acts of saving and of the devoted work of a succession of Registrars—John Tidd Pratt, J. M. Ludlow and E. W. Brabrook—Friendly Society finance was not yet satisfactory to actuaries, even in the greater Orders. In 1897 the Foresters had 933 courts—a branch is a court among the Foresters—with an estimated surplus, and no less than 3038 with an estimated deficiency.[4] That is to say, on various hypotheses as to the interest which their funds would earn, in more than three-quarters of the courts subscriptions were not high enough to meet the outgoings on sickness, death, disablement and so forth which the court might reasonably anticipate. By advice and insistence on proper valuations of the funds Registrars toiled to improve the position. It improved, but only in part. In 1908, of the valuations received from societies without branches two-thirds showed deficiencies.[5] The returns were far from ex-

[1] *Ibid.* p. 16.

[2] Cp. vol. II. 474. The attack on the system in Wilson, Sir A. and Levy, H., *Industrial Assurance* (1937), only appeared when this chapter was completed.

[3] *Report* for 1896, p. 2.

[4] *Report* for 1897, p. 144 (1898, LXXXVII).

[5] *Report* for 1908, Part A, App. O, p. 40 (1909, LXXIX).

haustive and no doubt the many obscure societies that failed to make them contained at least as high a proportion of deficiency. The Orders were more accessible to the Registrars; but in spite of their growing centralisation, a branch of the Manchester Unity of Oddfellows or a court of the Foresters—the two greatest and most representative Orders—retained its financial independence and so its right to work to a deficiency.[1] They might be forced to impose friendly levies to meet their accruing liabilities, or else to curtail promised benefits. When National Insurance was introduced experimentally in 1911, there were still a great number of societies or branches thus actuarially unsound; other societies in which deficits in the management fund were met improperly from the benefit fund. But this last abuse was only serious among Collecting Societies, for they alone spent much money on management.[2]

On December 31, 1910, the Orders and their branches had funds valued at £28,000,000; the ordinary class of benefit-paying Friendly Societies, £13,000,000; Deposit Societies, Death and Burial Societies and a few other 'branchless' types about £6,000,000. Their 6–7,000,000 members—more than twice as many as the trade unionists in 1910, with whom however they overlapped—were not all wage-earners; but their very numbers show that they and those other millions who subscribed to the Collecting Societies and the Industrial Insurance Companies were predominantly wage-earners or belonged to wage-earning families.[3] It was perfectly clear that the wage-lag, bitterly as it had been resented at times, had not impaired the financial strength of the wage-earning classes or interfered with the resolve of the most prudent and comfortable among them to make all possible provision for the risks of life and the certainty of death; or with the resolve of nearly all of them to provide at least for the cost of a decent funeral. Thinkers and dreamers might well be discontented with the order of society or with the rate at which that order was being changed; but no honest man with a

[1] See the evidence of the Chief Registrar (Sir E. W. Brabrook) before the *R.C. on Labour* (1893–4, XXXIX). Q. 1261 *sqq.*

[2] *Report* for 1911, p. 17.

[3] The much richer Building Societies, whose story it has been impossible to include, for reasons given in vol. II. 476, n. 6, included many wage-earners but probably a majority of people slightly higher on the income scale. Their total membership in 1911 was 639,000; their funds no less than £77,000,000. The relatively high average of funds per member (£120) suggests the dominant social type.

reasonably long and accurate memory, and some appropriate knowledge, could deny that it was a better order, if better only by a little, than at any time in the modern industrial age. Whether that age was itself in any profound sense good some doubted, as many have doubted since. "Lo, this only have I found", they were disposed to quote, "that God hath made man upright; but they have sought out many inventions." Those who so quoted were disposed to argue that with all their inventions men were no wiser, no happier, no clearer eyed than those of other ages, and possibly less upright. Of uprightness, wisdom and the clearness of the eye the economic historian as such may not profess to speak. He moves on the lower plane, the plane of commodities and comforts. Moving there, he does not hesitate to compare that time to its advantage—not only with other times in the industrial age, but with any time certainly known to him. And to those who lean towards quotation from the Book of Ecclesiastes he replies from that same discerning Book: "Say not thou, 'What is the cause that the former days were better than these?' for thou dost not enquire wisely concerning this."

EPILOGUE

And downward from an hille, under a bente,
Ther stood the temple of Mars armipotente,
Wroght al of burned steel, of which thentree
Was long and streit, and gastly for to see.

GEOFFREY CHAUCER, *The Knightes Tale.*

The necessity of a public defence, has given rise to many departments of state, and the intellectual talents of men have found their busiest scene in wielding their national forces.

ADAM FERGUSON, *An Essay on the History of Civil Society*, 1766.

EPILOGUE

On the British industrial society with its subordinate agriculture there fell—to the intense surprise of by far the greater part of its members—war. Though surprised, the majority accepted or hotly approved the conduct of its political leaders; and a critical people recently disunited went into unexpected and unknown war with a singularly common consent. Kitchener, their new War Minister, told them to prepare for years of fighting; but few in any station of life took his warning to heart at the first. Soldiers in all European armies had apparently expected the next war to be a short if bitter struggle and had made their preparations accordingly—partly because all were planning swift decisions in the field; partly, it would seem, because Treasuries and their experts had been convinced that no country could stand for very long the economic strain of modern warfare, and had advised their fighting departments in that sense. This was the dominant opinion among British economic practitioners, thinkers, and writers, great and small. Those who believed that the stronger combatants, and Britain in particular, could at need bear a prolonged strain fancied that economic pressures must bring a rift somewhere in the weaker parts of the opposed alliances within a year, or two at most, whatever happened in the field. They underrated the staying power of agrarian and the adaptability of industrial, or semi-industrial, civilisations when fighting for their lives. Those who looked out through war-hating, liberal, City eyes were convinced that more than a year's war was out of the question. Five days after the battle of the Marne, when Britain's daily expenditure was perhaps a quarter of what it ultimately became, the *Economist* wrote about "the economic and financial impossibility of carrying on hostilities many months on the present scale". To which at least one economic thinker, accustomed to looking through the film of money and finance to the underlying realities, replied: "Nonsense, the thing" (he may have said "the bloody thing") "can go on so long as there is something to eat and something to shoot off." And one of the great combatants fell out, after two and a half years, mainly because of a standing lack of things to shoot off. Two others, the two most industrial, tried in their different ways to deprive one another of things to eat; and few military considerations were more decisive in the last year than the relative measures of their success. A Belgian scholar, interned in the heart of Germany, noted how courage sank when that wheat from the Ukraine, which was to have been the contribution of a beaten Russia to German victory, never came. When hungry German troops overran British lines in Picardy in March 1918, they were surprised and delighted, but in the end discouraged, by the plenty of good food and soldiers' luxuries found in the canteens; for they had been told that it was Britain who was short of things to eat—as indeed she was, though her armies were not; but short only to discomfort, not to despondency or death.

The military and the diplomatic historians must settle whether the war of 1914–18 need have become a test of national economic endurance: the economist notes that it did. In a world noisy with glib economic explanations, an economic historian of modern Britain is naturally inclined to ask—at the risk of providing obvious comments on simple-minded questions—whether that industrial and capitalistic civilisation which he has been studying was more prone to war than other civilisations; whether the private control of the means of production *per se* made war more likely; and whether the entry of his own country into war in 1914 was determined, directly or indirectly, by economic factors or calculations.

His answers to the two first queries, or perhaps rather his speculations about their themes, will be affected by his estimate of the connection between modern industrial civilisation and the unprecedented growth of the world's population during the nineteenth century. If, with a living student of population, he holds that this growth was not mysterious but "merely the response to increase in skill"[1] he will debit to that civilisation, with its many inventions, those overcrowdings, overflowings, lamentations about *Völker ohne Raum*, demands for places in the sun and silent resolves to hold places already secured there, which although they did not directly bring about the war of 1914 at least prepared nations to stand up and take it. But even if he accepts without qualification the doctrine of response to increase in skill, he will bear in mind how the skill increased so fast that the growing populations of all the great combatant

[1] Carr-Saunders, quoted in vol. I. 57 n. 1.

nations were beyond a doubt becoming more not less prosperous, though at varying speeds and with occasional setbacks. There was no economic compulsion to raid one another for food or comforts, such as there may well be among growing primitive tribes in barren lands.

Whether increasing skill is the single simply-working cause of the growth in population, or only one cause among a bundle, it has at best an indirect connection with the private ownership of the means of production. The critics of private property and private capital regularly argue that skill may progress without at least the second; and defenders of private capital will not deny that skill increased in the socialistic empire of the Incas, or is increasing in the Russia of to-day. If skill produced a superfluity of people, and the superfluity tended to produce frictions between their governments, the frictions need not be debited to capitalism; the less so seeing that, of all European countries to-day, population is growing fastest in that where capitalism is a term of contempt.

When growing nations have arrived at the point of dependence on export trade, either for their existence of for the maintenance of that standard of life to which they have become accustomed, competition for markets leads to clashes of interest and jealousies that may foster warlike emotions among those sections of the population—sections varying in size and influence from century to century and from country to country—which think instinctively in fighting terms. Hence the superstition once current in Germany that England meant to attack her, and in 1914 did attack her, out of commercial envy; or the corresponding belief in England, perhaps equally superstitious but not so easily proved so, that Germany would challenge her one day out of economico-political ambition and a belief in the rights of the strong man armed over the markets of the world. Some Germans had certainly talked and written in this strain. The stubborn dogma that there is a given amount of trade, so that if you have it I cannot have it too, the dogma of the older Mercantilism, has great vitality; and unhappily there are groups of circumstances, short-period situations, particular branches of trade, in which it is not superstitious. Lancashire and Japan cannot both have the major part of the trade in winding-sheets for the Chinese. Whether predominance in that trade is worth a great war is most doubtful, and probably at no time has Lancashire even fancied that it was; but the prospect of the loss of it stirs up unpleasant emotions which may take a warlike tincture.

These things have no essential connection with capitalism as a form of industrial and commercial organisation. No doubt those who before 1914 procured for Britain from overseas her luxuries, her raw materials, and much of her necessary food, and those who conducted the export trade which paid for them, were private controllers of capital working for gain. Historically, luxuries and gain came first, necessary food and raw materials later. But it was exactly in the nineteenth century that the provision of food and materials became the main function of the importer, and so indirectly of the exporter. Given the population and its level of wealth and desires, their work was essential; although in a collectivist or a managed economy exports connected with certain classes of foreign investments, or otherwise held to be undesirable, might have been regulated or curtailed—whether in the ultimate interests of the country or not would have depended on the wisdom of the responsible officials. The search for markets and the desire to retain them, with all the frictions which they may set up in a world of expanding national economies, were not vicious products of capitalist greed. Russia to-day shows no less interest in her export trade of timber, oil, wheat and latterly gold than capitalist England did in hers of cotton, coal, or machinery. And if Russia should become sufficiently industrialised to desire widening markets for her manufactures it is not likely that she will deny herself the appropriate methods of securing, exploiting, and retaining them. The process has begun already in Sinkiang and other parts of inland Asia.

Export by private capitalists has often been reproached with producing friction between peoples, decay of primitive civilisations, and minor wars, by indiscreetly and perhaps immorally pushing its wares into unwilling markets, or among tribes which they demoralise, and then demanding support from its government. There are notorious cases—in the nineteenth and other centuries—in which the charge can easily be sustained. But governments are at least free to repudiate unprincipled merchants. They cannot well repudiate themselves. Except on the rather naive assumption that governments are normally more discreet and more moral than individuals ("If we did for ourselves what we are doing for Italy", Cavour said, "we should be great knaves") it is unlikely that government control or management of foreign trade would have tended to reduce international friction. The great amount of such control in the world of to-day does not appear to increase international harmony. If Smith, Grant and Jones put up the prices of British coals the foreign buyer will grumble and go elsewhere if he can; but if the British Government puts up the prices, that is likely to be treated as an unfriendly act. It is sure at least to be frictional. Italy was estranged from England by the high prices demanded for British coals while the government still controlled the mines in 1919–20. France, so far as is known, bore no malice because of the equally high prices charged at that time by individual Yorkshiremen for their cloth.

Merchants and manufacturers of the nineteenth century thought of themselves as lovers of Peace, which they certainly were, and of their work as a fosterer of Peace, which has not yet been proved false in spite of secondary trade wars. The charge most often brought against them then was that they loved Peace too well, for their pockets' sake, Peace without Honour. High-spirited writers were glad when, against the wishes of the Manchester people, Britain fought Russia needlessly in the Crimea.

> No more shall commerce be all in all, and Peace
> Pipe on her pastoral hillock a languid note.

At least, during the generations when these economic men had most power, the world for ninety-nine years was free from that 'general war' with which the statesmen of the eighteenth century had been thoroughly familiar. After 1918 someone wrote a book called *The First World War*, and many people shuddered at his 'First'; but those older wars which reached from the Ohio to Manila, or from the Malay Archipelago by way of Egypt and the Cape of Good Hope to New Orleans and Buenos Ayres, were about as wide as the then known world would permit; and some European peoples were involved in them who in 1914–18 managed to stand aside.

Industrialists—and men of science and government arsenals—made terrible engines of war, while statesmen trained whole nations to fight. In most countries a limited group of industrialists, with attached shareholders and wage-earners, were interested directly, not so much in an outbreak of war on a great scale—as business men they had to weigh the risks of that—as in expensive preparations for it. But neither history nor the present state of the world suggests that the making of all the armaments in the arsenals would have done much to ensure peace. Philip of Spain and Louis XIV of France, the Venetian Republic in its fighting days and the First French Republic, all had fairly complete control, if not actual monopoly, of their national armaments industries. It was when England was most pugnacious that all the great ships were built in royal yards. Armaments industries in contemporary Italy, Germany and Japan, as in re-arming Britain, are semi-public in character. The reputedly efficient and very great armaments industry of Russia is inevitably a State monopoly. There may be good reasons of various sorts for a more complete nationalisation of armaments industries to-day; it can hardly be proved that the private, as opposed to the public, manufacture of arms and instruments of war in Britain had anything to do directly, or even remotely, with its outbreak in 1914.

That 'capitalists' in general worked for, or even favoured, war because it would bring high interest rates and handsome profits is a clumsy generalisation, hardly worth notice were it not to some extent current, from the observed fact that it did bring the rates to all and the profits to many. Very properly, no one has ever suggested that wage-earners accepted the war of 1914 because of the extraordinarily high pay eventually received by munition-workers and others, or because war and the social policies arising from it, or stimulated by it, would bring to them certain substantial and permanent gains, as in fact they did. The reasonable expectation of the 'capitalist' in 1914 was loss of trade, high taxes and, in his family, death; of the wage-earner, death, taxes and unemployment. Neither had second sight and neither must be judged as if he had.

Industrialists as a class were everywhere pacific, merchants and money-handlers even more so. The average German industrialist may have been a shade less peace-minded than others. Germans had a well-grounded confidence in their army. The two wars which made the second Reich had been short and were held to have been economically profitable. When, after 1914, he thought that his country was winning, or when in Russia and Roumania for a time she had won, the German industrialist's mouth was wide open for iron-fields, oilfields, colonies and economic concessions of every kind. But greed for other people's good things, when it seems that they may legally be had for the taking, is not peculiarly German. That German industrialist who slightly disgusted a Prussian general by coveting a hundred years of peace in which to knock England out was fairly representative of his class all the world over. It was for the sake of the interests of men like him that Wilhelm II desired, with perhaps two-thirds of his will, to be remembered as The Peaceful. British industrialists had for years been worried over German competition. A great group of them now wanted to abate it by tariffs; but the notion that it would be expedient to abate it by war was remote from their ways of thinking.

As for the pure capitalists of the City and the Stock Exchange, the men who handled the abstract values, not the things, who knew, or in imagination multiplied, the havoc which war must make among foreign investments and credits given to foreigners—they were in an agony of anxiety in early August 1914. The policy of "strict neutrality" and the ultimate chance of mediating effectively "between exhausted combatants" was what a journal which represented them tolerably well was writing about on August 1. "Old women" the sturdy Asquith called them. Few of them, it may be surmised, had any great fear of losing a possible war; but they were shaken by the prospect of war losses.

It is hard to associate any thought of an economic calculation with the memory of the man who led Britain into a war that he hated. True, Edward Grey had been Chairman of the North Eastern Railway, and he went back to its chair from Whitehall. Behind those considerations of obligation and honour which would probably have led him to take sides for war in any event lay his conviction that a German hegemony in Europe, won by force, would be too dangerous for Britain to be allowed—and among the things endangered were Britain's economic interests; what she held, not anything she coveted; but she held much. Nothing suggests that this, rather than her freedom to develop as she desired, was in the forefront of his mind; yet, if to have it somewhere in the mind is to make an economic calculation, he made one. But in 1912 he had wondered whether, if he were God, he would not say "this boasted civilisation...is so abominable that I will sweep it away". "If God does think that," he added, "then the great industrial countries will perish in catastrophe." And again in January, 1918: "I feel deep in me that the civilisation of the Victorian epoch ought to disappear."[1] Perhaps one day an ingenious man of letters, armed with these revelations of his mind, will set out to prove that he contrived a war to hasten its end.

Here it is suggested that this civilisation which Grey of Fallodon thought abominable was less warlike in spirit than most which had preceded it, although the crowding that it caused, or permitted, suggested violent solutions to violent minds—as it still does; that the individual selfishness to which it gave scope, in the ownership of property and other ways, was not more threatening to the peace of the world than that centralised, impersonal, property-controlling or property-owing state selfishness which shows signs of succeeding it for a time; and that the chief director of British foreign policy at the close, though bound by his position to defend the abominable civilisation with other British interests in his care, had no more thought of material gain for his country than for himself.

As the testing of economic endurance began to hurt a little, and that was not before well down 1916, the staying power and the adaptability of Britain's industrial civilisation proved unexpectedly great. It was as well. There has never been a country and an Empire which stood to lose so much by defeat in war. Agrarian civilisations can recover in a few harvests. What the chaos might be, and how long it might continue, in a defeated, thoroughly industrialised, modern country can only be imagined with the aid of what happened in Germany after 1918—and German civilisation was far less industrial than British. Staying power was not however inherent in the system, even if adaptability was. It depended utterly upon the control of the sea. That was why after the first phase of clearing the seas of enemy surface craft was completed, the economics of war for a time appeared deceptively straightforward. Campaigns wasteful of shipping were initiated at half a dozen points. Supplies of all sorts, both for Britain and her allies, came in abundantly. Special expenses incurred in America and elsewhere were easily met by exchanging for War Loans some of those overseas investments which for 1913 are estimated to have brought in £210,000,000 of income, and so had a capital value of about £4000,000,000.

After the first jerk from peace to war conditions, the antici-

[1] Trevelyan, G. M., *Grey of Fallodon*, pp. 177, 341.

pated unemployment faded away to nothing; and the department which a provident Board of Trade had sketched out in advance for such an emergency, when everyone expected war and unemployment to go hand in hand, was reporting not how many people were out of work, but in what industries too many people were working who might be turned into soldiers or munition makers, and preparing propaganda literature intended to encourage women to enter all kinds of unlikely careers and to wear breeches for work on the land.

As pressures increased in 1916–17, and with the unrestricted submarine attack on shipping of 1917 became painful, industry and commerce which had been reasonably free so far—it is surprising how little the export trade of 1916 differed from that of 1913—had to accept more and more government supervision, or self-regulation under instructions from Whitehall. The thing had begun gradually with the prior claims of the fighting department on the stocks and services of industry; it grew with the Ministry of Munitions; and ended with a complex system of controls, controllers, and 'priorities' which so covered the industries of the country that a man could not put steel into corsets—the corset of 1917 was full of steel—without a certificate from the Minister of Munitions that it was necessary to support the tired backs of his women workers; and hairpins might only be made out of wire that the Admiralty did not want, 'fallen' wire which was not springy. When peace came, common bricks appeared to be under two or three separate controls and had to be rather arbitrarily "decontrolled"—a new past-participle for a novel process.

Control had begun, and was nearest to actual ownership by the State, with railways, munition works and mines. For munitions there were controlled works and works which, in principle though often not in location, were extensions of the existing dockyards and arsenals. It was with the shipping crisis of 1917 that control spread to industries less directly connected with the fighting line, mainly because of the need to economise shipping itself. There was tonnage control, British and inter-allied, and in the end a Ministry of Shipping. A Committee had looked for that bulk import which could be cut off with least inconvenience and had selected timber, which in 1913 had made up about one-fifth of the British imports by weight. A timber controller, a home timber campaign, and Canadian lumbermen in English amenity woods were the result. The rationing of import space according to the fighting value of the industries which asked for it brought on a crisis in the cotton industry and a Cotton Control Board. Cotton was far the hardest hit of all the greater industries, for only a small part of its output got on to any ship or into any trench; and aeroplane fabric was of linen. Wool and linen were in the very opposite position—wool from the start, and linen as the needs of the air became pressing. For wool, whole national clips had been bought in the Dominions; and there was a continuous struggle to buy or to grow more flax, the old Belgian and Russian supplies being cut by the line of war. Nearly all the metal industries, except hairpins and lead soldiers and such like, were linked up with Munitions, which also needed plenty of coal. In Agriculture, for which there was no need to create a Ministry, the State was now all but omnipresent, with women's labour campaigns, ploughing-up campaigns for bread corn, potato campaigns and much else. "The fabric of State expenditure and State responsibility...built up like a coral island cell on cell"[1] had for a generation and a half been built up fastest in stormy weather. Now in a great storm, it grew with terrific speed; and although, when the storm was over, large parts of the fabric of responsibility were knocked away, they had been seen by all; by not a few admired; and, with the experience gained, could easily be set up again.

As for the fabric of expenditure—in the financial year 1913–14 the central government spent £197,000,000; in the year 1917–18 it spent £2,696,000,000, though of pounds already less valuable. Nearly £3,000,000,000 was budgeted for 1918–19, but as peace came it was not all needed. Expenditure on this scale, and the way in which money was borrowed for it through the banks, had entailed an inflation, slight at first and neither recognised nor admitted, but in the end considerable, though never disastrous. About £123,000,000 of gold coin had gone out of circulation, but by December, 1918, Bank of England notes issues were £40,000,000 above the figure of June, 1914; and there were more than £300,000,000 of Government currency notes circulating with them. This was the amount of circulating money that the new price-level required. Not until 1923–5 had the expenditure got below £800,000,000: to £700,000,000 it never got. At this level it came to about one-

[1] Quoted p. 398 above.

fifth of the statisticians' estimate of the aggregate national income; and there were county and municipal budgets to be added. The expenditure of £796,000,000 for 1924–5 included £357,000,000 for the service of the national debt (against £24,500,000 in 1913–14)—mainly a national pocket to pocket payment this, most of which went into the better lined pockets. Their owners had however acquired a settled high-tax-paying habit which eleven years earlier, when some of them had already been grumbling for a long time about confiscatory taxation, would have been quite unthinkable. And, with them, the whole nation was paying taxes on a new scale. There was a great deal to show for these taxes: the pocket to pocket element entered into very many of them. The points of immediate interest are, the size of this storm-time fabric of State expenditure, and the social adjustments to it already made which would permit of its continuance.

Its continuance, but hardly its conspicuous increase; for within ten years of the end of the war a thing vastly more important than any change in tax-paying habits or government controls, a thing which a few observers had foreseen before 1900, had become certain—that during the twentieth century, and much earlier than could have been anticipated in the nineteenth, the population of Britain would cease to grow, would in fact begin to fall. In 1911 it had been 40,887,000. In spite of war it was 42,769,000 by 1921. An old, but not very old, nineteenth-century estimate had anticipated 56,620,000 for 1951. By 1931 it was certain that 50,000,000 would never be reached and that no amount of activity in the saving of life could prevent decline from setting in within a decade. For by 1926 what statisticians have since called the 'gross reproduction rate' in England and Wales was, in their terminology, already just below unity; that is to say each 100 women of child-bearing age (married or unmarried) were not leaving behind them quite 100 girls who might become mothers. The 'net reproduction rate', the reasonable expectation for the next generation, was lower still, because when probable mortality is taken into account the number in the second generation who are likely to become mothers is reduced.[1] In 1921 even this net rate had been just above unity. Had 1921 conditions

[1] A very condensed and necessarily not quite exact summary of the statisticians' conclusions. See the books quoted on p. 447, n. 2 above.

of marriage and the average size of families been stabilised, there would have been some further growth of the population owing to saving of life, and then very nearly a dead level.

The 1921 conditions were not stabilised. The birth-rate continued to fall and with it the supply of potential mothers. By 1931 the net rate was well below unity. It was reckoned to be 0·81; that is to say, the reasonable expectation from the facts as shown by vital statistics was that each 100 women of marriageable age would be replaced by 81 women grown to that age. And already there were fewer children living, girls and boys, in the group below 5 years old than in the group from 5–10. If 1931 conditions were stabilised a slight fall in the near future was certain—no population in which the bottom group is not the largest can be a genuinely growing one, though the fact may be masked for a time by life saving in all groups—and an appreciable fall was also certain, far before the end of the century. For the working of a sustained net reproduction rate below unity is cumulative with the generations.

There was a contemporary tendency to connect the falling birth-rate of the 'twenties, the only fact about population universally known, with legacies of the war, with fears of fresh wars, or with the acute industrial depression of 1921–3. No doubt these had their influence, especially the last; a connection between good times, marriage and birth is demonstrable. But the connection between marriage and the amount of birth needed to maintain a population—three or four bearings—is less close than it once was; and in the curve of the birth-rate over fifty years from 1883 to 1933—years of prosperity and adversity, of peace, war, and again peace—the sharp and easily explicable irregularities of war time and of the first two or three years of peace stand out against a downward sweep which looks almost as inevitable as that of the rivers flowing to the sea.[1] Moreover the death-rate of the 'twenties seemed a great deal more favourable than it really was. Owing to increased longevity and the fall of the birth-rate, the population was for the time being ill-balanced. Young children and old people are death's commonest prey: he was striking the aged later and of the infants he had fewer among whom to strike. But the time would come when the aged, and all the very numerous middle-aged, would have to go.

[1] See the diagram on p. 448 above.

In this England did not stand alone; she was a part of West European civilisation. The prospect for Scotland was much the same. Irish population had long been falling and the fall had not yet ceased. For France, Germany and Belgium; for Denmark, Sweden and Austria, calculations made in the years about 1930 and based on the facts of the 'twenties gave results similar to the English—an inevitable fall, variously estimated, in the next thirty or forty years. A German statistician made his voice heard in the streets with a cry of *Volk ohne Jugend*. Had Germans studied the Jewish statistics carefully, they might have saved their own honour a few years later; for their Jews were dying out. In Prussia in 1929 the Jewish birth-rate was 9.1 and in Bavaria 9.8:[1] those are extinction rates.

Outside Europe the United States population was no more than replacing itself by 1931. A fall seemed probable before the year 2000, unless it were prevented by immigration; and the United States had ceased to welcome immigrants from the still populous European East and South, or from Asia. British Canada was in much the same position, only the position was masked by the sustained birth-rate of the Catholic French Canadians. Australia and New Zealand had been anxious for years about the course of their populations; "the children, nine and ten" of whom Rudyard Kipling wrote had never been so common as he fancied; and now the average woman of child-bearing age was barely leaving one other such woman after her to carry on the race.

For almost every country the figures, where they existed and could be read with tolerable certainty, pointed towards a declining birth-rate—in Spain, Portugal, Italy, Poland, Bulgaria, the Ukraine; the Argentine, Japan; possibly in Russia proper, although there the rate still appeared to be extraordinarily high; but not in India. Of China no one could speak with any confidence; but probably among its population of anything from 400,000,000 to 500,000,000 people the birth-rate was still very high as the death-rate certainly was. In spite of the declines, in none of these South and East European and Asiatic countries was the stationary or falling population level yet in sight. But the speed with which the birth-rate had fallen in the North-West (it had barely begun in Germany before 1900, yet was

[1] Ruppin, A., *The Jews in the Modern World* (1934), p. 73.

conspicuous by 1914) suggested that vital changes might come among educated peoples within half a generation. Any change where the rate was relatively high was now certain to be downward.

Stabilisation at some point in the twentieth century, followed perhaps by a small decline, both in Britain and North-Western Europe as a whole, might reasonably have been anticipated during the decade that ended in 1914. During the next half-generation they were assured. It was possible that serious decline might be averted; but the changes in social habits necessary to avert it seemed most unlikely in Britain and in nearly every country of the North-West. The late marriage and the small family had set in first among comfortable folk. As comfort spread so did they. So far as population went, at least that "stationary state" which John Stuart Mill had discussed and hoped for in the middle of the nineteenth century, when to most of his contemporaries it seemed of all things most unlikely, was at hand. Its coming would change, was changing, the whole economic and social climate. Clouds lay heavy and obscuring on the further horizon. Germans, more than usually given to pessimistic speculation at this time, had been discussing in semi-philosophic, 'world-historical', terms *The Downfall of the West*. Now, as the precise figures of death and birth were ticked out, they were preparing to ask *Are the White Races dying*?[1]

From the side of national resources at least Britain might face a stationary or falling population with some complacency. The fewer the people, the further an improved, encouraged and reorganised agriculture would go towards feeding and supplying them; and war left behind it a resolve, vague and hesitant but real, to reorganise, encourage and improve. Guaranteed prices for wheat and oats were tried, abandoned, and in the end, although not until the 'thirties, restored. Subsidised sugar growing, another outcome of war conditions although not established until six years after the war ended, was introduced and retained in the face of most pertinent criticism. Neither policy could have been so much as discussed twenty years earlier; both were valuable to important groups

[1] Spengler, O., *Der Untergang des Abendlandes*; Burgdörfer, F., *Sterben die weissen Völker*? (1934). Burgdörfer is also the author of *Volk ohne Jugend* referred to on p. 523 above.

of farmers and landworkers. Their survival, whatever their exact merits, with the relieving of agricultural land from rates at the public expense in 1923–5, indicates the new fumbling resolve to make the best of the land somehow, without too much attention to precedent.

This same fumbling resolve was shown in forest policy. Commission after Commission had reported that nineteenth-century Britain was almost incredibly short of common, cheap, available timber. War-time timber needs and policies had underlined reports which no one had believed to the point of vigorous action. If war had continued for another year—and in September or October 1918 nearly all responsible people thought that it would—the timber situation might have become critical. Hence the vacillating policies of reafforestation so hard to carry out on a crowded island, where this area hopes to be left untouched because of its beauty, that for the sake of the grouse, a third for the preservation of its curious fauna and unique desolation; where it is nearly always someone else's countryside which can best, in the national interest, be covered with the predominant regimented conifers that industry and good forestry require and most Englishmen, with Wordsworth and other sages, dislike. There were therefore those to whom the prospect of fewer people and a less demand for conifers might appeal.

The slower the population grew the less anxious would be that problem of coal supplies which Stanley Jevons had raised sixty years back. It had ceased to be really anxious before 1914; but it was still possible to argue in 1915 that, from the 287,000,000 tons of 1913, the British output might rise to 472,000,000 by 1941. This was on the sanguine assumption of a revived growth of the export trade and of a 1941 population of 52,700,000.[1] Oil-fuel, coal economy, hydro-electric developments, strife in the industry, national sufficiency policies abroad and a stagnation or shrinkage of world trade kept coal exports down; and population prospects had changed. As 1941 came near an output of not more than 250,000,000 tons seemed much more likely, and the date of possible trouble from coal-exhaustion withdrew almost indefinitely. Even in 1926 a Royal Commission talked of five centuries, of seven—or more.

[1] Jevons, H. S., *The British Coal Trade*, p. 752. There may have been a dash of piety in H. S. Jevons' argument: he anticipated trouble within 200 years.

A possible slackening of national demand for iron-ore might also be welcomed—though few either welcomed or discussed it. For years Britain had been greatly dependent on imports. The normal figure in 1910–14 had been from 6,000,000 to 7,000,000 tons, against a home production rather more than twice as great—but on the average much poorer in iron. With huge effort, these essential 6–7,000,000 tons had been got into port from 1914 to 1918: there must be many bones of seamen and cargoes of ore on the bottom along the sea roads from Bilbao and Narvik. While the industry remained active after the peace, in 1920, the tonnage of ore raised at home was 12,700,000, the import 6,500,000. British coal-measure iron-stones were pretty well worked out. The expectation of life for the Cumberland hematite and the Cleveland ores was certainly not long. Seventeen years later it was being said that there was low-grade ore enough, in Lincolnshire and the Midlands, to yield 10,000,000 tons of steel a year (the 1920 figure was 9,000,000) for a century. Perhaps there was more. The earth's crust contains an astonishing amount of iron, and fresh ways of extracting it will no doubt be found out. Even so, seeing that a century is a little thing in the life of a nation, a prospect of more economical use was much to be desired, on the assumption that the age of steel would endure; though whether a declining population in a steel age would use much less steel is a problem that depends for its solution on a great many technical—and social and military—unknown quantities.

At least it was not probable that, as a result of this defect in resources, Britain would lose her iron and steel industries, in whole or in part, as she actually had been and was losing sections of her jute and cotton industries, to the countries which supplied the raw materials; for those from which the iron-ore chiefly came, and seemed likely to come, were all poor in coal.

Statesmen who in the years 1919–25 were steering a rather shaken Britain back towards more familiar economic channels than those of the war map, with a hankering after the oldest and most familiar—free-trade, gold standards—had little time to think much about the longer future of population and resources. The resources they saw surprisingly intact; the mechanical equipment at many points improved; economic adaptability apparently increased, and some obstructive conservatisms forgotten. (But they were tired men dealing with tired men.) Even the foreign investments remained very valuable and productive, though some had been sacrificed to pay debts in America, others lost in Russia or Roumania. They were added to somewhat recklessly in the early years when a battered Europe was looking for supplies and re-equipment, and Britain, helpful if sometimes rather condescending, was ready to supply both. Her people lent to Austria, Greece, Estonia, Germany, France—to states new and old: in one year, before the devastated French textile regions had been restored, they sent enough wool fabrics to France to give every man, woman and child in the country a yard.

But in helpfulness she was surpassed by the entirely unshaken United States, always rich, and now, as it seemed, rich beyond all European standards. If for a time Britain clothed much of Europe, America fed much more. Britain's lending power for re-equipment was smaller than she realised; her loans, old and new, were less secure than she supposed—as she was to learn after 1930. The resources of America were nearly as great as they appeared to be. The country from which so recently as 1901 "financiers for the first time came to the aid of European governments",[1] and which on balance had been a debtor later than that, lent abroad—it has been estimated—during ten *post-bellum* years a sum comparable with what Britain, the great nineteenth-century lender, had lent during that whole century. For a time Britain was completely overshadowed. People talked of the final transference of the money power from London to New York, of that completed westward movement of the world's centre of economic gravity which Richard Cobden and Adam Smith had foreseen.

But America was unaccustomed to her new creditor position. She continued, like a good and punctilious debtor, to aim at selling much, buying little, and retaining that delusive 'favourable' balance of trade. She was reluctant to allow foreigners to dress her, or carry for her at sea, or do any fresh useful thing in return for her sustained sellings and new lendings. She was paid the balances, so far as they were paid at all, mainly in gold, of which she acquired a vast sterile heap. Then troubles of her own set in; and finally she withdrew (it could only be for a time) with huge losses to herself and severe hardships to others, from that business of large-scale lending which she had so

[1] Quoted on p. 35 above.

recently begun. Consequently, by the early 'thirties, Britain—though in grave economic discomfort—would find herself less completely overshadowed than she had been in the 'twenties. But though transient, the complete overshadowing did mark a permanent shift of the economic balance of power. It had been long anticipated, but had been hastened by the brutal circumstance of war.

To both America and Britain, the Europe of the 'twenties soon proved a poor seller and a sluggish buyer, though a very willing borrower. Britain had difficult internal readjustments to make. The depression came sooner and sharper than the world of business expected. By 1922 there was a general trade-union unemployment figure of 15·2 per cent., in the engineering, shipbuilding and metal trades of 27·0 per cent.—levels hitherto unheard of. After that there was recovery; but the world had been too thoroughly dislocated for recovery to be rapid or complete. For years Russia was in cloudy isolation. Then slowly—from 1924 onwards—she began to sell again her timber, her oil, her grain when she had any to spare, and to buy with difficulty in Britain some of her indispensable capital equipment. But even in 1929 she and all the small states cut out of her, with Poland, cut in part out of Austria and Germany, did not take nearly so large a share of United Kingdom exports as the old Russian Empire took in 1913. The share had never been large: a sluggish and reluctant buyer Russia had always been.

Germany, defeated, revolutionised, curtailed, her foreign trade connections broken, saddled with impossible reparations liabilities, her main industrial region occupied for a time to force her to pay them and her currency ruined to frustrate the plans of the occupying power, was yet in a fair state of economic activity by the end of the first *post-bellum* decade. Her old trade relations with Britain had revived. In 1913 she was the best foreign buyer of United Kingdom produce and manufactures. By 1929 she was second only to the United States—above France, above the Argentine. As seller to the United Kingdom in 1913, she was behind the United States only, though far behind. By 1929, she had nearly regained that position, though the Argentine with its food and raw materials had got a little above her. Neither imports from nor exports to Germany had their former absolute importance; it was a poorer Germany in trade with a doubtfully richer Britain; but this restoration, in circumstances of maximum difficulty, of something very like the old trading relationship pointed to the persistent working of simple economic forces—when they are left free to work.

Satisfactory commercial intercourse with the scattered fragments of the old Austrian Empire was not much easier to foster than intercourse between them; but it was natural that something like the former relations with European nations which had been allied or neutral should set in, once the first dislocating rush of restocking and re-equipment was over. Neutrals and allies fell approximately into their old places as purchasers and purveyors, purchasers of British coal and manufactures, purveyors, the Scandinavians mainly of timber and ore, the Danes of dairy produce and bacon, France of her long list of fine manufactures and good things to eat and drink; but in nearly every case their purchases from Britain were on a somewhat reduced scale, if quantities are taken, or the prices of 1913 translated into those of 1928–9.

There had been fighting in Africa, heavy fighting in nearer Asia; but the regions heavily fought over had been neither great producers nor great buyers, and the immediate effect of the fighting and of the developments of transport that had been needed to sustain it—in Palestine and in Irak—was to improve producing and purchasing power rapidly. Most of Asia and Africa, with the whole of Australasia and America, had suffered only from those delays and temporary disorganisations which war, and especially the later conditions of warfare at sea, had brought about; and their British parts from those direct sacrifices which they had freely made.

It might perhaps have been expected that Britain would soon gain in trade with the outer continents, and most easily in imperial trade, anything lost for a time in Europe. Important recoveries and gains there were; but during the first decade the imperial trade grew very leisurely. For many years, in the later nineteenth century, the percentage of British exports sold under the flag had fluctuated about 30; by 1913 it had risen above 37; by 1929 it was rather more than 41; and the total exports of 1929, when allowance has been made for the changed level of prices, were certainly no greater than those of 1913. The slow growth, and the decline in foreign markets which it implied, were connected as everyone realised with the strong position in both groups of markets gained by the United States and

Japan in the years when the United States were neutral and Japan, though an ally both generous and loyal, was, from her very geographical position, involved only in a limited liability warfare which left much of her economic energy free.

The trade of the United States had naturally made most progress in the Americas, though the fitness of American manufactures for young wide countries gave them advantages also in Africa and Australasia. In 1913 the Argentine had taken 31 per cent., Chile 30 per cent. and Brazil 24 per cent. of her imports from the United Kingdom. By 1929 the corresponding percentages were 19·6, 17·7 and 19·2. Most of the balances had gone to the United States. Japan had made progress everywhere, but chiefly in Asia and with textiles. At first the threat to Lancashire—not only from Japan—was imperfectly realised. She was busy. In the restocking boom of 1919–21 the cotton towns saw company promotion, amalgamation, value inflation enough to satisfy the greediest buyer of stocks and seller of shares. When the excitement and the appropriate dejection after it were over, that is in 1924, exports of cotton yarns and fabrics still formed a quarter of the export values of the country, as they had in 1909–13 when the industry was in vigorous health.[1] But signs of ill health might have been noted in 1920 by people not too busy to look. Though prices were about three times those of 1913, the pounds and yards of cotton manufactures shipped, even during that year in which the export of wool fabrics was vastly greater than it had ever been before, were less in each important group but one than they had been in 1913; in the rougher groups markedly less. The world at its nakedest seemed to need Lancashire less than Yorkshire. The sole exceptional group was that of the 'finished threads': J. and P. Coats and their fellows were holding the markets. Nearest to them came, as it was right that they should, those who supplied the finer cotton goods—things dyed in the yarn or in the piece.

By 1929, a year of reasonably good trade and no intolerable unemployment, the value of cotton goods exported had shrunk much more than that of the total exports. All prices were falling (the wholesale Index Number of 1924 was 166; of 1929, 136) but cotton no longer formed a quarter of the whole, or as in the mid-nineteenth century 30–40 per cent., but 18·5 per cent. only. (There was worse to come—the trade shrinkage and shattering unemployment of the early 'thirties.) What was

[1] See p. 66 above.

happening down to 1929–30 was what any careful student in the years before 1914 would have anticipated—some day. The pace of its happening and the industry's unpreparedness were the unanticipated things. It had been reasonable to expect losses at the lower end of the trade, particularly in Asia; more British concentration on finer work, including the new artificial silk; and probably some contraction of the whole industry, all spread over a generation or more. Unhappily, as things fell out, just before 1914 there had not only been no contraction but considerable expansion. The wool industries had employed no more people in 1911 than in 1881: cotton employed nearly 20 per cent. more, and that was 100,000. The first slight shrinkage was recorded in 1921. So the blows were falling, and were to fall, on a relatively overcrowded industry.

There were other important industries during the 'twenties similarly overcrowded in relation to their prospects, immediate or distant. It was gradually becoming apparent, as has been seen, that any chance of a regular coal output so great as the average of 273,000,000 tons during the last years of the peace (1911–13) was remote. For 1920–9 the average—excluding 1921 and 1926, years of seriously interrupted output—was 251,000,000. And yet in 1921 there were nearly 16 per cent. more people describing themselves to Census officers as miners than there had been in 1911, and even in 1931 still 3 per cent. more; although since 1924 the numbers reported as actually engaged at the pits had fallen much further. Here was the raw material of trouble. There was no systematic concerted action among employers. Mining areas and enterprises were often isolated, each with its own group of miners' families—and mechanical coal-cutting was at last making serious progress. In 1901 only 1½ per cent. of the total output had been cut by machinery; by 1924 the proportion was nearly 19, and it would be 38 by 1932.

For the railway service, contraction of employment was planned as part of the reorganisation undertaken when the railways were handed back by the State to the Companies, the new amalgamated Companies. The territorial policy adopted was what railwaymen of the nineteenth century had called 'districting'; only the districts were huger than they had ever contemplated, or would have been allowed by Parliament to contemplate. When the districting was complete only one name survived from the early railway age—that of the Great Western.

Staffing economies were proceeded with cautiously; but they brought inevitable disappointment of hopes for promotion, and recurrent suggestions of unfairness and hardship connected with the introduction of labour-saving devices, or with the imposing of heavier responsibilities upon individuals. Between 1921 and 1931 the total employment figure of the British railways fell by 120,000 or over 16 per cent. In the same decade however the number of those who in official language were "gainfully occupied" as "drivers of self-propelled vehicles" had grown by 224,000, or over 126 per cent. For the benefit of the 401,000 "gainfully occupied" motor drivers (there were in 1931 only 616,000 railwaymen) and of the hundreds of thousands driving themselves not directly for gain, the face of the country was being changed, as it had not been since the railways were themselves new.

An expansion between 1911 and 1921 of some 40 per cent. in the numbers employed in iron and steel manufacture, engineering and shipbuilding was what the busy years 1911–14, and the war of steel, had required. Some considerable expansion would probably have come in ten years of peace. Even the peace of the twentieth century is steely and mechanical. But the replacement activity of 1919–21 in the shipyards was abnormal—there had never been so much mercantile tonnage built as in 1920—and could not continue, the more certainly because Britain had rashly taken part of her reparation from Germany in great ships. In relation to immediate prospects therefore this central group of industries was also overcrowded. For many firms and workers the outlook after 1921 was bleak. But ships wear out. The maximum launching of 1920 was not much above the previous maximum of 1913. Steel-using and mechanism were on the increase. In relation to ultimate prospects and employing capacity the group was not much overcrowded. The greatest economy of labour, the highest degree of automatism, had been encouraged to meet the needs of war. Economy and automatism would certainly extend; but there was no reason to expect any sudden disturbing jerk of extension.

Conspicuous expansion of employment in the chemical, electrical, gas and electric supply, and motor car industries; and in transport, communication and distribution generally, as reported at the Census of 1921, was healthy and for the future promising. Expansion in the service of the Government

—central and local—and in the service of sport and entertainment was significant. A slight contraction in the great building industries group had no special significance: the group was subject to decade fluctuations, and in fact expanded again before 1931. A continued contraction in agriculture was what anyone would have expected and everyone deplored. And a sharp contraction in the great industry of private domestic service was to be welcomed or deplored according as the observer set more value on the levelling of incomes, love of personal independence and burdening of the greater incomes with taxes, which were among its prime causes, or on the growing need, in a civilisation run by machinery, for people to spend their lives—as the sports and entertainment servers did—not in making things but in doing services for one another.

With the exception of the decline of the export trade in coal, connected with world-wide politico-economic circumstances which in their turn were connected with war, all the chief commercial and industrial expansions or contractions were predictable and most of them would probably have occurred—though some more slowly—had there never been a war. It was not because of war, but because of intelligence and economy, that in 1929 gasworks, railways, domestic consumers and general industries used no more coal than they had used in 1913; though the fall in the coal consumption of the iron and steel industries had points of contact with *post-bellum* circumstance. The fall in employment on the land had no important connection with war. The general sluggishness of international trade, like the particular British losses in that trade already noted, had a direct connection. But, all things considered, it is the predictable, the continuous, in the broad outer movements of British economic life during the decade after the great upheaval—and longer—which will probably most impress historians of the future. That attempts were made to preserve some continuities which were to prove incapable of preservation may not greatly alter the conclusion.

With this high degree of continuity, conspicuous changes in the internal organisation of the British economy were naturally rare. Most of the changes were rather accelerations than innovations, including even the planned recasting of the railway system. Had the railway companies been left free from 1850 to 1914, something like it would almost certainly have emerged.

There was however at least one major breach of continuity which in any other country would have been a matter for the widest discussion. Perhaps it was because it occurred in the field of rural economy that it received, and still receives, curiously little attention in Britain. The Board of Agriculture inquired about it intermittently, and rather languidly, in England. The Scottish Department of Agriculture collected figures but did not discuss them in its Reports. And yet there had been within half a generation a sharp reversal of a secular trend in land-ownership. For two centuries at least before 1914 the proportion of the farm-land of England cultivated by its owners had been falling. Until towards the end of the second century the statistical evidence is defective, but there is not much doubt about the fact. For the later nineteenth century the proportion in England and Wales was round about 12·0 per cent. In 1913 the figure for England and Wales was 10·7—in 1919 it was 12·3 and in 1921 over 20. By 1927 it was more than 36; for Scotland about 28. It is possible that at no time in English history had there been so much cultivating ownership.[1]

The general course of events is clear, but the relative importance of the forces at work on the buying and the selling sides has not yet been properly elucidated. In the year 1920 the farmer, who for six years had been doing well—so far as prices went, was receiving a wholesale price for most things that he produced about three times what he had received in 1911–13, when by general consent he was not in misery. Then came sharp falls all along the line, and from 1923 to 1927 the prices were only between 50 and 60 per cent. above the 1913 level. But that was approximately true of all prices. Agriculture had not yet fallen out of step, as it fell later. There were large undissipated balances in many farmers' banking accounts. An ambitious man could easily buy, and ex-service men of means not bred to farming were also buying. At the same time land was being put on the market by the needs of owners pressed by war taxes and death duties, or by the cool intelligence of owners—single or corporate—who saw that their chances were good. The sitting tenant often became an owner, borrowing to buy most likely, for fear of having the farm bought, and his fate determined, over his head. He might not wish to buy in the least. Later, when agriculture again fell into the trough, it

[1] The figures include a great many very small holdings which were not really 'cultivated'; but that is equally true of the rented holdings.

was of these forced purchases and the tax-forced sales that most was heard. But there were many of the other sorts, how many is not known and perhaps never will be.

During the difficulties and agricultural experiments of the decade that followed 1927 the fact that more than one farmer in three, instead of only one in nine, had no shock-absorbing landlord above him was a new thing of the first importance.

In industry there had been no corresponding breach of continuity. Where there was change it was due, as a rule, only to the acceleration of forces already at work before 1914. And even such accelerations were often delayed until far down the 'twenties by the industrial discord of the difficult early years; by the inability of tired and sometimes angry men to do more than cope with that discord; and by their inevitable and rather prolonged absorption in the day to day problems of transfer from a war to a peace footing. Armament firms were thinking how they should make ploughshares; only as they had energy to spare, how they might combine in making them, or for any other purpose. And yet public and still more official opinion was far more friendly towards combination of all sorts, now seen to have some of the merits of co-operation—a blessed word, than it had been before 1914. Co-operation had been urged on the great group of industries which came within the scope of the Ministry of Munitions as a patriotic duty. Employers' organisations which had practised secrecy because they were conscious that the public, and perhaps the Government, were suspicious of them could come into the open, though some of them did so still rather shyly.

Price regulation had lost much of its unpopularity for a society in which prices, and so much economic functioning that lies behind them, had been regulated from Whitehall, or by some local industrial authority affiliated to Whitehall, like the Cotton Control Board. Public opinion now approved of association of firms and would hardly balk at the greatest amalgamations, provided all was open and above board. Organised wage-earners had always preferred to deal with well-organised employers; and dogmatic socialists saw in great amalgamations the fulfilling of a Marxian forecast, the facilitation of an ultimate and predestined transfer of industrial control from private to public hands. The greatest of the new amalgamations, Imperial Chemical Industries, already had a half-public character, built up as it was with the good wishes and, so far as its inherited function of making the country independent of fine imported dyestuffs went the help, of the State. But it was only the size, and the atmosphere more kindly to growth, that were new. The chemical industries had been the field for some of the earliest British amalgamations, and trade associations of one kind or another were older still.

Where there was no quickened movement towards industrial co-operation and larger units, official or semi-official opinion was now likely to be critical, as the Royal Commission on the Coal Industry of 1925–6 was of the 1400 British colliery undertakings with their 2500 mines: "the experience of recent years has not been encouraging. The process of fusion appears to have come almost to a standstill." The Commission had reached the definite conclusion that the size of the average British undertaking was not economically the best, and cited the larger average unit in Westphalia or in the reconstructed coalfield of the Pas de Calais. Nothing was more old England, more continuous, more nineteenth-century, than the individualistic and pugnacious coal industry. Handed back from war control by the State somewhat run down in equipment and nerves by its admirably successful effort to give the nation coal enough in time of war; subject to repeated inquiries into the state of its health; rushing into a wasteful civil war which reduced its output for 1921 by a third; artificially busied late in the year by making up the loss and by a coal strike in the United States; busied again in 1923–4 by the cessation of German coal production in the Ruhr, at the time of the French punitive occupation; securing by these windfalls high profits and increased wages when other industries were in distress; subsidised by the State in 1925–6, when its delayed troubles came—it plunged into the greatest of its civil wars, all but dragging the whole country with it, in 1926, when the British trade balance was upset by the cessation of coal exports and foreigners sent coals to Newcastle. After that for long years it struggled on in shallows and in miseries, demand and output stagnant or declining, numbers painfully and slowly contracting. It furnishes the extreme instance of delayed acceleration, almost of a reversal of forces. Not that the forces making for that fusion which the Commissioners of 1925–6 desired had been very strong before 1914. Their figure of undertakings shows this. But they were working, if intermittently and quietly: in the 'nineties there had been 2000 undertakings of some importance. That the working had "come almost to a standstill" is hardly surprising in the light of the vicissitudes of 1918–26. You cannot well repair your house in the hurricane season, as the statesman said of parliamentary reform and the French Revolution.

But in industry and commerce generally, fusions of one kind and another and the growth of great new industrial units—for the making of motor-cars, or the making and retailing of clothes, or a score of other things—were going on as fast as any group of progressively minded Commissioners could have wished. (But Commissions of Inquiry into rapid and presumably healthy growth are seldom set up, so the facts were not officially sifted.) The holding company was being utilised more and more; and the complexity and fluidity of structure, particularly in the heavy, the ex-munitions industries, were so great that cross-cuts of the organisations taken every five years, or even less, would have shown marked differences in the sections. There had been large, and again often shifting, amalgamations in shipping; others in cotton; a consolidation of Cable and Wireless interests into a massive concern; and an extraordinary national and international growth of the associated enterprises—business one can hardly call it—which carried the name, and the imprint of the daring and expansive personality of W. H. Lever, first Lord Leverhulme, the soap-maker who before he died could have claimed many other descriptions.

Fusion and concentration among the banks, thorough already in 1914, had been carried so far by 1929–31 that anything further seemed almost unthinkable—unless it were that nationalisation which political events in 1931 made men discuss. At the head of the banking system, the Bank of England stood in more intimate association with Government and with greater control over the whole body of money-handlers than ever before. Fourteen years of anxious co-operation with the Treasury, in war and after war, had preceded the relaxation in 1928 of the antiquated rules of Peel's Act which had controlled its note issue. Government had abandoned the war-time currency note and—as Peel had designed, but after more than eighty years—only Bank of England notes now circulated in England. That was a small thing compared with the fact that, even in democratic countries like Britain, as an economist wrote in 1937: "the power of Governments over Central Banks, and the influence of Central Banks over their financial communities had grown beyond all knowledge." The completion of banking concentration was easily predictable in 1914. These growths were not. They were new things begotten of war and its derangement of currencies, "inconceivable thirty years ago", as the economist said.[1]

For a time in the late 'twenties they were less obvious than they afterwards became because, resolute to maintain continuity, Britain had returned to the gold standard and with it to something like nineteenth-century Bank of England semi-automatic policy and working—a Bank Rate varying with the reserves of gold and intended to control them. Britain had gone back to gold after the Napoleonic Wars: she would go back again. The Committee on the Currency of 1925, which in effect said this, discussed—in print—neither the devalued sovereign nor the managed currency, possibly on a gold basis, which had been suggested as ways of avoiding discomforts that might spring from a straightforward return to the gold standard at a time when sterling prices and gold prices were out of step; as they were in 1925. Some discomforts everyone knew there must be. Critics of the policy which Government took over from the Committee anticipated many. When, six years later, extreme gold and currency discomforts let to the abandonment of the policy, the critics' whole case seemed proven; but it is far from certain that the ultimate distress was inherent in the original decision. However that may be, it was the severing of the link between sterling and gold that necessitated and revealed the growth of the power of Government and of the influence of the Central Bank.

Growth of the business unit in industry or in commerce was nothing new. It continued quietly; but for the preoccupied and fluctuating business world of the 'twenties the growth is not easily measured, and there is some danger of exaggerating the importance of the great obvious new concentrations and units, Imperial Chemical Industries or the Cowley Works. The growth in general industry, and the steadily spreading mechanisation which accompanied and in part caused it, were registered by the factory inspectors; but it was not inspectors' business to report fusions, or the extent to which separate factories were under a single financial control. In the sluggish years after the *post-bellum* collapse, when for a time factory building and com-

[1] Robertson, D. H., in *Lloyds Bank Review*, Sept. 1937.

pany promotion stopped almost dead, not to revive until 1926–9, the actual number of factories grew very slowly; but the number of registered workshops steadily declined. Between 1907 and 1927 however factories had increased by almost 40 per cent., workshops had fallen by 26 per cent.—"the fall having taken place in the dress-making, laundry and baking industries", where the factory had still most ground to conquer. Motor transport, more elastic and pervasive than the railway, everywhere bringing the countryman into town, was undermining "the small country establishments, the saddler, blacksmith, village tailor, dressmaker and milliner, all steadily going out of business. This decline", the Chief Inspector reported in 1928, "is most apparent in East Anglia and the rural areas of Wales." The last of the old rural industry was dying in its most secluded homes. And in London, where little manufacturing businesses had always shown unexpected powers of survival, "the small employer is finding great difficulty in competing with larger establishments and a number of men who formerly employed others have reverted to the position of employees".

Here and there the workshop or home-work maintained, or even tightened, its grip on various jobs done 'out', in the clothing and boot-making trades for example. Sheffield still had its "little mesters" working in tenement factories; now and then for some special reason they even gained ground, a grade of work that had been done in the big establishments being passed to the tenements; but the only field in which the small concern could be said to be really making headway between 1921 and 1931—and that by no means all along the line—was in retail trade. In spite of the great stores and the multiple shops, in a dozen widespread sample towns, there were more grocers', bakers' and butchers' shops; more chemists', tobacconists' and newsagents'; and many more confectioners', fried-fish dealers' and opticians'—per 1000 families or per 1000 of the population —in 1931 than in 1921. But of drapers' shops and china-shops and pawnbrokers' shops there were fewer, of the last two far fewer.[1] In towns all of which were being fast decentralised, the nine types of shop supplying daily necessaries or minor luxuries in daily request (opticians handle 'radio') were wanted in almost every street or small housing group. But you may even take a bus to buy a set of teacups; and happily there was not so

[1] Ford, P., in *E.J.* 1936, p. 359.

great a demand for the 'broker of pawns' as there had been in good Victoria's day.

In the higher and general organisation of industry, two developments of the years 1918–21 hardly fulfilled the expectations of these first sanguine years. It seemed likely then that the whole, or very nearly the whole, body of wage-earners would soon be enrolled in the Trade Unions; and it was hoped that in the Joint Industrial Councils, the 'Whitley' Councils which were being set up before war had stopped, and very rapidly after the Armistice, the collective wisdom and good sense of all parties in industry would be pooled for the maintenance of industrial peace; the encouragement of education, invention and research; and the promotion of laws advantageous to each trade and to the country. The membership of Trade Unions in Britain and Northern Ireland was reported to be nearly 8,000,000 in 1919 and 8,346,000 in 1920. The potential maximum—excluding agriculture and domestic service—was probably not 50 per cent. more than that. The figure for 1913, far the highest recorded to that date, had been 4,135,000. But the impressive figures of 1919–20 melted away, until the average for 1928–30 stood at only 4,830,000. By 1933, with the coming of the second *post-bellum* depression, it would be only 4,389,000 —appreciably less, as a percentage of potential membership, than it had been in 1913.

The 1919–20 figures in part represented a wave of passing emotion. Besides, coal-mining, cotton-working and railway work—which between them had supplied about two-fifths of the 1913 membership—were employing fewer people every year. Trade depression had always brought falls in trade union membership; and there was depression enough, especially in the heavy trades. The growing industry of the roads, the industries of entertainment and sport, and all the new light manufacturing industries so characteristic of the age, with their large numbers of female workers, were refractory material for the trade union organiser. And, as everyone could see, there was a shifting of industrial activity from the North, where unionism had always been strong, to the Midlands, the South, and especially the London area where it had usually been much weaker. Between 1923 and 1933, the number of those insured under the Unemployment Insurance Acts grew in the Midland area by 16·8 per cent.; in the South-Western by 22·9 per cent., in London by 23·2 and in the South-East by 38. (London was much more important numerically than South-East and South-West put together.) Meanwhile in the North-East, the North-West, in Scotland and Wales, the increases varied from 4·1 in Wales to 9·4 in the North-East. And the total of the four faster growing areas was, by 1933, just about the same as that of the four slower.

Perhaps even more than the high trade union figures, the long list of Joint Industrial Councils and of the less formal Interim Industrial Reconstruction Committees which came into existence during 1918–21, represented a passing phase of opinion. To some extent they also represented a need that was passing, the need for reconstruction after war. They did their most useful work in industries hitherto imperfectly organised, by widening the area and improving the methods of collective bargaining—for it was the familiar wages, hours and conditions of work problems that took up most of their time in practice. Industries already well organised for this work often felt no need of a Council: there was one for wool but not one for cotton; for pottery but not for dyeing; for china-clay but not for coal. Many of the Councils were short-lived. There were 73 in existence at the end of 1921, and 14 of the Reconstruction Committees were subsequently organised as Councils. But by June 1925 only 50 Councils survived. The troubles of 1926, the year of the general strike, were not favourable to growth or even survival; and by the end of the decade, though a number were still at work, and one or two more had been formed, they were hardly taking that part in the economic life of the country which had been anticipated. Just a few had done all that had ever been hoped—not only settling difficult matters of wages and working conditions and hours, but organising education and promoting industrial research. Many had become rather formal and ineffective.

The Trade Unions had on the whole strengthened their position, in spite of falling numbers and the events of 1926, when a special Trades Union Congress gave its General Council power to call a national strike to support the wage claims of the miners. Responsibility for that nine days' paralysis of British economic life is not to be discussed here. It was followed by a sharp fall of Trade Union membership—from the 5,500,000 of 1925 to the 4,800,000 of 1928; for though men came out most loyally when called, many came with reluctance; the faith of some in Trade Union policy had been shaken; and the long-drawn-out and nationally disastrous strike of the miners did nothing to revive it. But the rise of the Labour Party to power gave the Unions a contact with, and an intermittent control over, Government such as they had never before possessed; important amalgamations of Unions were proceeding, parallel to the capitalistic industrial amalgamations of the day, which increased their weight and at need their fighting strength; the Industrial Councils movement, though only partially successful, had improved what might be called their constitutional position; and the growing importance of the General Council of the Congress, now a permanent body with an efficient secretariat, gave them a central organ—not exactly a government, but something rather like a government. Whether due more to the wisdom of that government, or to the emergent good sense of both sides in industry, to exhaustion after the fighting of 1926, or to dull resignation in the long bad times from 1930 to 1934—the decade following the national strike was almost free from losses of working time through industrial disputes. For the whole mass of wage-earners and the whole period, it averaged not a third of a day a year.[1]

While semi-voluntary unemployment sank to that negligible level, the unemployment that no one wanted, except a handful of idlers and incompetents, varied from a minimum of 8·6 per cent. of the insured population of Great Britain in May 1927 to a maximum of 28·8 per cent. in August, 1932. Before the troubles of 1926 it had varied from the 7·8 of December, 1920 to the 23·0 of May, 1921, when sudden general depression and the voluntary unemployment of fighting coal-miners hit the rest of industry together. The average of 15·8 for the last six months of 1921, or of 14·1 for the whole of 1922, is therefore more fairly representative of bad times in the early 'twenties.

These exact figures were a by-product of the rapid extension of unemployment insurance immediately after the war. Perhaps the experimental insurance of more than 2,000,000 workers in selected trades, under the Act of 1911, might have been widened so as to include all strictly industrial wage-earners by 1920, war or no war; but widening would probably have been gradual. There was no possibility of systematic widening during

[1] Cp. the diagram of p. 499 above.

the war; but by the Munition Workers' Insurance Act of 1916 more than a million people whose ultimate unemployment, at least for a time, seemed certain were brought within the scheme. By 1920 the total of insured persons in the still United Kingdom was 4,197,000. Thus universal insurance came with a jerk, very opportunely as it turned out, in view of the pending collapse; and by July, 1921—when the collapse had come—11,081,000 people were insured against unemployment, and not far short of 2,000,000 were unemployed, in Great Britain alone. In the late 'twenties the insured population was approximately 12,000,000, the percentage unemployed never for any month below 8·6, or the number below 1,000,000; so that foreign critics fell to talking of the irreducible million. For the decade 1921–30, which includes the whole of the first depression, the dislocation of 1926, and some dark early months of the second depression in the latter part of 1930, the average percentage of insured persons unemployed was 12·2.

Exactly how this compared with any similar long-period average of unemployment before the war is not easy even to estimate. For the troubled decade of the 'eighties, the limited group of Trade Union unemployment figures then available give an average of 5·3; for the much less troubled years 1900–13 the average, for a larger group, is 4·5. It is certain that if unemployment insurance had been as widespread and comprehensive in 1900–13 as it was in 1921–30 the figure would have been higher: all kinds of unskilled and casual workers, particularly liable to unemployment, who had been outside the Unions were now insured. On the other hand, some of the worst unemployment of the 'twenties was in trades where unionism had always been strong—coal, shipbuilding, engineering—and from which therefore unemployment had always been reported. The engineering, shipbuilding and metal-working group of Unions reported precisely as much unemployment in 1925 (13·5 per cent.), when by the standard of the 'twenties trade was good, as they had reported in that dark year of the 'eighties, 1886. In 1922 they had reported just twice as much. For the three fairly comfortable years 1923–5, the figure for all the Unions averaged 9·9 per cent., that of the new system 10.9.[1] It seems unlikely therefore that, had the new system existed since 1880, the average for the 'eighties would have been above

[1] Since 1926 the publication of the old series of Trade Union figures has been discontinued.

7·0 or that for 1900–13 above 6·0. Perhaps 6·5 and 5·5 would be more likely figures. On these assumptions, something like 6·0 per cent.—or a half—of the aggregate unemployment of the 'twenties might be traced to the special circumstances of the *post-bellum* time. This fits in with the unhappy experience of the engineering and shipbuilding group, whose worst year between 1920 and 1930 was twice as bad as their previous recorded worst.

When at work, the average wage-earner of the middle and late 'twenties was probably better off than he had been in July, 1914. Great numbers were demonstrably better off; for other great numbers the decision is delicate; certain important groups were undoubtedly worse off—and among these three sections the word 'average' can have no very exact meaning. Almost perfectly stable wage-rate conditions, and fairly stable price conditions, set in after the sharp price-fall at the end of the *post-bellum* trade boom, in 1921–2. The cost of living as officially calculated settled down for the next seven years at about 70 per cent. above July, 1914, being above 70 for the first four years and below it for the last three. It is a somewhat arbitrary estimate, this cost of living figure. It takes no account of the cost, disproportionately increased by taxation, of the 'necessary' luxuries, tobacco and beer. Nor does it include the new compulsory insurance contributions—at once a form of saving and a necessary expense. And there are other considerations which help to support the conclusion that a wage-earner whose pay had gone up in exact correspondence with this official cost of living figure would feel—unemployment apart—slightly worse off than before. It is what men feel that matters; so it is fair to assume that those whose wages in the middle 'twenties were not some 80 to 90 per cent. above what they had been in July, 1914, were reasonably dissatisfied with the recent course of events.

Fortunately large and important groups had not this cause for dissatisfaction. At the bottom of the earnings scale, labourers—in building, at the docks, in gas and electricity work, in engineering, in agriculture—together with the less skilled among the railwaymen were being paid, in the years 1925–9, at rates varying from about 80 per cent. above those of July, 1914—for agricultural and engineering labourers—to 100 per cent. and upwards for building, gaswork, dockside, carting and many other types of labour. If an average rate for, say, 1909–13 were taken as base instead of July, 1914, the improvement would show greater. The railwaymen had done best of all; some of them had secured rises approaching 150 per cent. It was only in shipbuilding and mining that some groups of unskilled or semi-skilled men could show a rise no greater, or little greater, than that of the official cost of living.

These trades, with the associated engineering and metal-working industries, provided the core of trouble among the skilled men. The building operatives, the skilled railway workers, printers, bootmakers and other important groups, had secured, like most of the labourers, an 80 per cent. rise at least; some of them upwards of 100 per cent. Textile wages—of which it is harder to write in few words with approximate accuracy than of almost any others—suggest a fairly satisfactory 80–90 per cent. rise in wool, but a less satisfactory 65–70 per cent. in cotton. Miners in 1926 were fighting to retain a wage which in 1925, for the whole of Great Britain, had averaged 62 per cent. 'per man shift' above the level of June, 1914. This, the most significant figure available, suggests that they were already a little worse off when at work than in July, 1914—though the problem is complicated by their abundance of cheap domestic coal and by some other considerations. They lost the fight; and in 1928–9, with a man-shift wage only 43 per cent. (and a cost of living index 65 per cent.) above 1914, they were certainly worse off. So were the whole mass of the engineers of all sorts, the shipwrights and the ship-joiners: in no case, from 1923 to 1930, was their average recognised rate of pay more than 50 per cent. above July, 1914, and in some it was barely 43.

It was thus in contracting and over-staffed industries, whose contraction was connected—as in cotton, coal, much engineering, and shipbuilding—with the state of world markets, that the wage situation was least satisfactory. The demand for railway work was contracting also; but railway service is not marketed abroad. It was, in the phrase of the day, a sheltered occupation, as were many of the others that were best paid. Wool was relatively happier than cotton, because less dependent on markets overseas. Cotton was so dependent that its worst was yet to be. The long prospects of engineering, shipbuilding and coal were far better. In the early 'thirties all engineering wages would rise: cotton wages would fall again.

The lowest industrial grades had not merely secured the greatest rise in earnings; they also gained most from contributory unemployment insurance, its non-contributory extensions, the rapid spread of wage regulation by Trade Boards in trades where there was risk of sweating, and the great freedom with which relief under the still surviving Poor Law was given after the war. They had been most liable to spells of unemployment and least able to make provision against it by membership of a Trade Union. The allowances of different kinds which they and their families might now expect during these spells were nearer to their normal earnings than they were to those of skilled men. The acceptance of Poor Relief was not the humiliation to rank and file London dockers or Irish labourers on Merseyside—they received a great deal—that it would have been to spinners in Bolton or fitters in Glasgow, had they been forced to claim it. The consequence was a real betterment in the social depths and just above them, specially marked in London, but not confined to it.

In London these depths had been widest, if not deepest. But London trades were not those which were now suffering most in work and wages; they were fairly sheltered. In 1927–9, good years, the percentage of unemployment there was about the same as it had been in 1913–14, also good years. For the whole country it was between two and three times as great. With this shelter for nearly all, satisfactory wage-rises for most, and the certainty of relief in old age and time of trouble, the position of those lowest social grades whom Charles Booth in 1892 had classed as "the poor" and "the very poor" had greatly changed. The main changes had begun with the pensions and sporadic insurance of 1908–11; greater had followed 1918. "The most dreaded features" of life below the 'poverty line' "have been largely removed", the *New Survey of London Life and Labour* recorded in 1930. It was no longer necessary to think of "the poor" and "the very poor" as "hanging on the brink of a gulf of destitution". And although, in those places where unemployment was far worse than in London, "the poor" and "the very poor" suffered with their neighbours, their relatively good pay when at work, and their expectations when work failed or working days were over, set a fence for them about the brink of the gulf.

Public opinion was most concerned, and rightly, with those districts and industries in which, even during the relative prosperity of the late 'twenties, skilled men by scores of thousands could not exercise their skill and young men were acquiring none. In 1925, when the Trade Union unemployment percentage for the representative building Union of the Carpenters and Joiners was so low as 2·2—no more than the inevitable minimum due to individual misfortune and short intervals between jobs—the aggregate figure for engineering, shipbuilding and the metal trades was, as has been seen, 13·5; and things were much worse in particular sections and places. In June, 1927, when the British figure for the whole mass of insured workers was at 8·8, almost the absolute minimum for the decade, the London figure at 5·1 and the South-Eastern at 5·7, the North-Eastern was 12·3 and the Welsh 18·0—and even that was a better record than Wales would show again for ten years. The gaunt problem of the utterly unemployed pit-village, or of the town given up to coal and heavy metal industries where a majority were unemployed, was taking shape.

It was made more difficult by the admirable growth in recent decades of social services of every kind, of schools and hospitals and public institutions—and of social insurance itself. There were pit-villages, and some others, which a wise and kindly dictator might have been well advised to blow up. There were even towns whose continued existence was a doubtful advantage, if viewed in the light of eternity. But the problem was one of years not of eternity; and few could bring themselves to contemplate even the evacuation of the gloomiest pit-village lying on coal-seams inferior, no longer wanted, or nearly worked out. Deliberately to connive at the decay of an ill-placed or apparently superfluous town would have meant a sacrifice that could not be justified of social values to a necessarily uncertain economic forecast. People began to think—beginning too often rather late—of how in such a town old industries could be revived or new ones started which might at least ease its declining years.

Thinking began late because, during the greater part of the 'twenties, the nature of the problem was hardly realised. Nor was it then so urgent as it ultimately became. The old British safety valve of emigration was still working, at first quite efficiently. During 1920–1 there was a balance of migration outwards from Britain to countries beyond Europe of 292,000. (But in the single year 1913 it had been 242,000.) After that, there was an average annual balance of 108,000 and in 1929 itself 93,000. This, though not comparable with the great migration immediately before the war, was fairly comparable with longer period averages—and many of those who might have become emigrants had fallen in battle. Not till the collapse of 1929–30 in America did British emigration first sink away to almost nothing and then—an unheard-of phase—become negative. In 1932, 49,000 more British subjects came in than went out. The safety valve no longer worked.

The consequences were for the 'thirties. The 'twenties, with their universal social insurance and the belief among the miners, subconscious, not clearly formulated, but easy to understand, and widespread down to 1926, that somehow, by organisation or by threats, a decent prosperity for them all could be twisted out of the community—the 'twenties were preparing the way. It was inevitable that the certainty of a living, mean though it was, from 'the dole' should check enterprise among the more inert, encouraging them to hang on in the place where they were born in the dull conviction that the trade which they—or their fathers—had practised must revive again there some day. Why migrate? Still more decidedly, why emigrate? No questions could be more natural. The type of conviction that inspired them is not confined to unemployed wage-earners. And sometimes, although it might be after many years, the revival blindly trusted in would come.

There was migration and emigration, from villages where there was no work to do and towns that had become ill-placed for industry, but the flow of migrants was viscous and it had the unavoidable result of taking away the enterprising and leaving the inert and those made unadaptable by age. Although there was still a growth of population in Wales by excess of births over deaths, the whole insured Welsh population—employed or unemployed—declined by nearly 2·5 per cent. between 1923 and July, 1929. In Scotland, never quite so hard hit as Wales but suffering acutely from the troubles of the coal and metal industries, the insured population grew in the same period by only 1·6 per cent.; whereas for the whole of Britain and Northern Ireland the growth was 8 per cent. and in London 13·6. With the dead stoppage of emigration from 1930, even though slow migration continued, the numbers grew a little everywhere; and down to January, 1933 unemployment grew with them, an unemployment of which this reversal of the century-old emigration process was however only one cause among many.

With all this, when the eye turned away from such places as West Durham and some of the valleys of Glamorgan, from Clydeside and darkened patches of the North-East and North-West English coasts, it could hardly overlook the improvement in the well-being of British wage-earners which had come since the inauguration of the new social policies in 1908, and especially since the war. Those unskilled and less skilled workers who had gained most were the majority. The feeling that there was something vaguely unjust in the good fortune of the sheltered trades could not obscure the fact that they were an exceedingly important part of the community. With all the less skilled, they had both their satisfactorily risen wages and the new and real, if modest, security of the insurances and the pensions.

True, the almost complete interruption of house-building during the war years and the shiftings of population which set in as soon as war was over led, for a time and for many, to unconscionable rents and overcrowdings that built up a heavy debit against the wages and insurances. But after the inevitable dislocations and particular overcrowdings of the very first years, when building schemes—public, semi-public or private—had made no real headway, it was not often even suggested that the people were worse housed than they used to be; though it was maintained, and with justifiable passion, that they were not nearly so well housed as they ought to be. Through a tangle of policies and political recriminations, house-building went forward in jerks. Even in 1922 about 119,000 new houses were built in Britain. By 1924, private unsubsidised building had come as an effective supplement to the work of the local authorities and that building with a State subsidy which had been started in 1919–21, when costs were impossibly high. From 1926 the annual average of new houses exceeded 215,000. By the end of 1929 the aggregate for ten years was 1,382,000. Of these exactly a third had been built without any public assistance. None as yet had had time to fall down.

For the country as a whole various statistical tests, with many that are not statistical, point to an increase of average well-being, in spite of the sharp depression of 1920–2 and the long-drawn-out troubles of particular trades and areas. Some of the older statistical tests have ceased to be of much value. A heavy figure of what was now coming to be called public assistance—the poor relief of the nineteenth century—may, does, imply only a greater readiness to award and a lessened reluctance to accept it. The figures naturally rose in bad times, but can no longer be used in the old crude way as tests of social health. The simple, useful, old fashioned tests of popular 'luxury' consumption—sugar, tea, tobacco—are partly vitiated for comparative purposes because the 1913 figures include all Ireland with its separate standards. Yet that will not explain away a rise of nearly 50 per cent. per head in the consumption of tea, and of more than 50 per cent. in that of tobacco between 1913 and 1929; though partial explanations may be found in the marked fall in the consumption of beer and a familiar change in the habits of women. (The woman wage-earner however was not yet a great smoker.)

More direct tests are more certain. That of Trade Union funds is particularly interesting. Helped by the high wages and good employment of 1919–20, and in spite of exceedingly heavy outgoings on dispute benefit in connection with the strikes of 1921, the aggregate funds of the British Unions had risen to £12,556,000 at the end of 1925. (They had been £6,471,000 at the end of 1913.) During 1926 no less than £11,993,000 was spent on dispute and unemployment benefit. For the next three years dispute benefit was kept low; but, as the Unions were very strongly represented in the industries hardest hit, unemployment benefit remained high—just over £3,000,000 a year as compared with £500,000 in 1913. And yet by the end of 1929, with a membership 350,000 less than it had been at the end of 1926, the aggregate funds stood at £11,361,000. The resilience and sustained power of contribution indicate great strength under difficulties among the membership of the Unions.

The Co-operative Movement, having none of the wastes of militancy—for trade union dispute benefit is first cousin to national expenditure on war—had no setbacks to record. Its history furnishes decisive evidence of the growing comfort of those wage-earners who formed the great majority of the co-operators. The number of retail societies declined a little further: like joint-stock and other competitive firms they were subject to the law of concentration. But their membership more than doubled between 1913 and 1929, when it stood at 6,129,000; their sales far more than doubled and, even allowing for a two-thirds rise in the prices of what they sold, which is somewhere near the true figure, increased by over 50 per cent.; their dividends on purchases doubled, so that the members took away £20,110,000 in dividends alone in 1929; and their surplus on the year's working doubled also. Besides their dividends on purchases, the members received £4,500,000 of interest on share capital, more than three times the sum paid sixteen years earlier. And the whole expansion showed that smooth wholesome continuity which had distinguished the movement for two generations.

Friendly Society history had become less significant than co-operative history, and much less significant than it had once been, since the Societies were approved by the State as agents for its own system of health insurance. Membership of a society of some kind had become almost automatic for all insured people, and was no longer proof of foresight, saving-power, friendliness or thrift. The alternative of becoming a deposit contributor through the Post Office was taken by only a small minority. The true Friendly Societies, both those without branches and the many-branched Orders, already approved in 1913, grew in membership rather faster than the population—from some 6,500,000 in 1913 to about 7,500,000 in 1929. Their payments out for sickness benefit grew rather faster again—but then the cost of sickness had gone up—and this at least indicates the will and the power to carry two insurances; for nearly all their members now contributed to the national scheme. The remarkable growth of the collecting societies, which considerably more than doubled the number of their assurances during the same period (from 7,500,000 to 17,500,000) is less satisfactory. In 1929 their income was £12,740,000 and their outgoings on commission to their collectors and management expenses no less than £4,056,000—as against a total of only £5,247,000 for all the insurance claims met, cash bonuses paid, and policies surrendered. Whether the maintenance and growth of so wasteful a system is evidence of increased well-being or not is hard to say. Clearly there would have been greater well-being with less waste; but the situation at least suggests a certain lordly neglect of the pence usually associated with comfort, though perhaps due mainly to ignorance.

How far the statistics of savings banks and of the new savings certificates—a war-time device carried on into the peace—can be used as a test of well-being among wage-earners is again uncertain. They do at least in the main reflect savings by those in no sense well-to-do; although there had always been some savings-bank accounts in comfortable bourgeois families, and many families in all ranks had taken their permitted maximum, or some fair sized block, of the attractive and patriotic certificates. But the very number of savings-bank depositors (10,541,000 in 1913 and 12,032,000 in 1929, with an average deposit of about £30) show that most of the accounts came from wage-earning families, though probably most of the money did not. It is certain that the certificates were largely held from the start in such families, though just how largely is not known. It was in the year when pressure on wage-earners' savings first became acute—1926, the year of strife—that the sum remaining invested in the certificates, which had risen continuously since 1916 to the great figure of £376,000,000 in March of 1926, began to fall a little. It seems likely that wage-earners, no doubt with some others, were cashing out.

"The Commons of the...Realm, as well Men as Women", the preamble to a statute of 1463 had stated, "have worn and daily do wear excessive and inordinate Array, to the great displeasure of God", the harm of the Realm, and the breach of existing laws to the contrary. When the law said Commons it was sincere; for it forbade Knights to wear cloth of gold, besides forbidding all those who had less than 40*s*. a year—the national rank and file—to wear "any Fustian, Bustian, nor Fustian of Naples, Scarlet Cloth in Grain, nor no Furr but black or white Lamb". Had medieval views of the health of the realm and of God's pleasure in relation to clothes persisted, some similar law might well have been laid before Parliament in 1929–30. For any one who could compare in memory the "Array" of British workers, "as well men as women", over the previous twenty-five or thirty years knew that there had been a growing comfort, a growing obliteration of the class distinctions of dress, and a growing gaiety which the fifteenth century would have reckoned inordinate. What might have been forbidden, what are the modern equivalents of the Fustians and Bustians and Furr other than black or white Lamb, let everyone determine. There were things which many might have wished to forbid, on aesthetic or even moral grounds, had they been sure that their displeasure was also God's. Some were sure; but they lacked legislative power.

Few historians doubt that, although there may have been something conventional, and was a strong flavour of crude protectionism, in the prohibitions of 1463 (note the Fustians of Naples), the "excessive and inordinate Array" at which they were aimed was a product of increasing national weli-being. There is no need to interpret the changes of the twentieth century in any other way; although the skill of merchant tailors in dressing people as they wished to be dressed at reasonable cost must be taken into account; although there was no doubt some sacrifice of better things to strictly luxurious "Array"; and although it would have been easy to go about the country collecting individuals, places, and economic groups who were not tempted to sin in their Array because their margin for expenditure on it was no greater than it had ever been—or even appreciably less. But the bare feet and the clothes "worn to threads and loops", through which "the skin shows here and there", of late Victorian poverty were gone, or nearly gone. In 1931, in a textile valley where for two years and more a reputed 80 per cent. of the population had been out of work, a surveyor reporting on an extensive mortgage on industrial house property, and explaining that "the interest upon your clients' mortgage comes out of the Dole," noted with great satisfaction "the way that the houses were kept, and the extremely tidy habits of the women". Even in those desperate conditions, at least tidiness was now possible, though this was one of the places that were spared the temptations of Array—and probably one of those where savings, in certificates or at the Co-op., were being drawn on to the point of exhaustion.

Such drawings in times of distress checked the real, but still exceedingly slow, spread of property ownership downward through society. Not the spread but the curiously unequal distribution was what was still most obvious, in spite of Death Duties, a War Income Tax, and various devices for what economists called "Transferences of Resources from the Relatively Rich to the Relatively Poor". One of these devices was the Old Age Pension; in connection with which it has to be remembered that a legal claim to even 5*s*. a week at 65 is the equivalent to the ownership of approximately £150; for property is claims, not things, as is specially apparent in the 'joint-stock' society of the twentieth century.

Putting aside the capital value of this and other claims of "the Relatively Poor" upon the aggregate resources of the country, it has been estimated that, in the years 1924–30, of the people of Britain aged 25 years and over, between 76 and 79 per cent. each owned £100 worth of property or less, collectively from 3 to 6 per cent. of the national capital; that 15 to

17 per cent., each owning property worth from £100 to £1000, held collectively 10 to 11 per cent. of the national capital; and that the tiny groups of people each of whom was worth £100,000 or more owned not less than 23 per cent. of the whole. These and the group below them, owners of from £25,000 to £100,000, together came to not more than 0·35 of the people and owned about 42 per cent. of its property. So the estimate runs.[1] Its decimals—not given here—and even its units, may be questioned; but the approximate accuracy of its general conclusions probably no one would dispute.

The old and most wise desire for policies favouring a more equal distribution of property was not often, at this time, expressed in exactly the old words. But those reformers who had become unreasonably suspicious of the notion of individual property desired, to a man, policies favouring a more equal distribution of claims upon the national resources. The two desires are only aspects of a single desire which, in one or other of its forms, all men of good will and good sense were bound to share. The justifiable points of difference among such men were those of method, of pace, and of degree. How much sacrifice of other values is involved with any suggested device for attaining the admitted good of greater equality? Is a particular experiment desirable in some given set of national and international circumstances? Most fundamental of all; what degree of economic equality is, even in the longest run, to be wished? Hanging behind all thought and discussion of such matters were—or should have been—the reflections that almost the least propertied of their countrymen was already a privileged member of the human race; that the talk of a world of plenty which needed only to be organised, a way of speech then coming into fashion among social experimentalists, was not yet relevant to a world some two-thirds of whose inhabitants had not, by Western standards, decent clothing for their backs or plain food enough to eat; and that the privileged position of Britain, and indeed of the white races, though much less insecure than some pessimists maintained, was not quite certainly a part of the permanent divine order of things.

[1] That of Daniels, G. W. and Campion, H., in *The Distribution of the National Capital* (1936). The estimates, being based largely on probate figures, are naturally least certain for the lowest group.

INDEX

For EU product safety concerns, contact us at Calle de José Abascal, 56–1°, 28003 Madrid, Spain or eugpsr@cambridge.org.

www.ingramcontent.com/pod-product-compliance
Ingram Content Group UK Ltd.
Pitfield, Milton Keynes, MK11 3LW, UK
UKHW010855060825
461487UK00012B/1142

* 9 7 8 0 5 2 1 1 0 1 0 8 0 *